Camp: Queer Aesthetics and the Performing Subject

CAMP: QUEER AESTHETICS AND THE PERFORMING SUBJECT

A READER

Edited by
Fabio Cleto

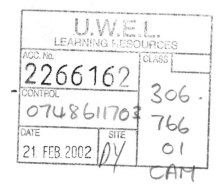
EDINBURGH UNIVERSITY PRESS

© Selection and editorial material,
Fabio Cleto, 1999

Edinburgh University Press
22 George Square, Edinburgh

Typeset in Sabon and Gill Sans
by Bibliocraft Ltd, Dundee, and
printed and bound in Great Britain
by The Cromwell Press, Trowbridge

A CIP record for this book is available
from the British Library

ISBN 0 7486 1170 3 (hardback)
ISBN 0 7486 1171 1 (paperback)

The right of the contributors to be
identified as authors of this work has
been asserted in accordance with the
Copyright, Designs and Patents Act
1988

CONTENTS

ACKNOWLEDGEMENTS

The necessity for this book was first conceived in early 1994, when Franco Marenco asked me to contribute a chapter on camp to his monumental *Storia della civiltà letteraria inglese* (1996). A year later I presented a paper at the 'Moving the Borders' conference in Varenna (Italy), where I had the pleasure of meeting Alan Sinfield, whom I thank – along with Remo Ceserani, Maria Teresa Chialant, Vita Fortunati, Paula Graham, Don Spalding, Paola Splendore, Gregory Woods – for the challenging comments, suggestions and critiques they moved in the seminar (and out of it) to my paper. I would also like to thank Gian Piero Piretto, who in December 1995 invited me to deliver a lecture at the University of Milan on the aesthetics of Kitsch and camp; Daniele Borgogni, Giovanni Cianci, Silvana Colella and Giuseppe Sertoli, whose friendship and intellectual reward made my doctoral experience definitely worthwhile; my colleagues at the University of Bergamo, Giuliano Bernini, Rossana Bonadei, Giovanni Bottiroli, Alberto Castoldi, Mario Corona, Erminio Corti, Richard Dury, Alessandra Marzola; and Stefano Rosso who hosted my Bergamo seminar on camp in spring 1996; and my students (especially Raul Calzoni and Stefania Consonni) whose lively response has given, in these years, a (however illusory) meaningfulness to my work.

I would also like to express my gratitude to those who have made this volume possible: Seán Burke, who first perorated its publication; James Dale, Carol Duncan, Dilys Hartland and Jackie Jones at Edinburgh University Press; the anonymous referees for their invaluable encouragement and suggestions; Chris Nealon and Carole-Anne Tyler for commenting on the project and an early draft of the Introduction, and all the contributors for creating indeed, with their writings, the necessity for a Reader.

My gratitude also goes to Victor Banis, Mirko Baruscotti (that old friend and brilliant scientist whom I have had the honor of pushing, from his favourite molecule 'cAMP' – cyclic Adenosine Mono Phosphate – of cell biology, towards the inverted roads of 'Camp' in the New York Public Library rooms), David Bergman, William L. Clark, Daniela Daniele, Massimo Fusillo, Joshua Glenn, Daniel Harris, Alan Hollinghurst, Donatella Izzo, Robert F. Kiernan, Patrick Mauriès, Gary Morris, Umberto Pasti, Sandy Paul, Marco Pustianaz, Silvia Scotti and Angelo Signorelli for pointing out or tracing secondary sources, thus helping me a great deal in compiling the 'Digging the Scene' bibliography which follows. But this book wouldn't have been possible if I hadn't benefited from a

State Grant in 1997-98, for which I am grateful, and if I hadn't had the precious chance to pursue my research as a visiting scholar at the University of California, Berkeley and Riverside. For that opportunity, I would like to thank Zhenya Bershtein, Emory Elliott, John Ganim, Chris Nealon, and the bunch of friends (Fulvio Bernardinis & Gioia Re, Nasreddin Budraa, Danette Diomedes, Pekka Kuusisto, Antonio Rauti, Jamaila Stevens, and all from the 'Wednesday Group') I was so lucky to meet there, making California a more homely place for a somewhat old-fashioned European.

A final thanks goes to a few friends – Trevor Joscelyne, Gianni Melendez, Luisa Villa – who have helped me in many ways, and to Alessandra and Sara, my mentors in love and affection. This book is dedicated to my priceless 'without-whoms', Francesca and Graziella; and to Giuseppina and Ines, who took me by the hand in my first days and who may not see this book published, but whose presence will nevertheless take me, as far as I will be able to reach, into the new century.

COPYRIGHT ACKNOWLEDGEMENTS

13. Eve Kosofsky Sedgwick, From 'Wilde, Nietzsche, and the Sentimental Relations of the Male Body', extracted from *Epistemology of the Closet*, Berkeley: University of California Press, 1990. Copyright © University of California Press. Reprinted by permission of Eve Kosofsky Sedgwick and The University of California Press.

14. Linda Mizejewski, 'Camp Among the Swastikas: Isherwood, Sally Bowles, and "Good Heter Stuff"', excerpted from *Divine Decadence: Fascism, Female Spectacle, and the Makings of Sally Bowles*, Princeton: Princeton University Press, 1992. Copyright © Princeton University Press. Reprinted by permission.

15. Jonathan Dollimore, 'Post/modern: On the Gay Sensibility, or the Pervert's Revenge on Authenticity', in *Sexual Dissidence: Augustine to Wilde, Freud to Foucault*, Oxford: Clarendon, 1991. Copyright © Oxford University Press. Reprinted by permission.

16. Pamela Robertson, Excerpt from 'What Makes the Feminist Camp?', in *Guilty Pleasures: Feminist Camp from Mae West to Madonna*, Durham: Duke University Press, 1996. Copyright © Duke University Press. Reprinted by permission.

17. George Piggford, '"Who's That Girl?" Annie Lennox, Woolf's *Orlando,* and Female Camp Androgyny', *Mosaic*, 30:3, September 1997. Copyright © The University of Manitoba. Reprinted by permission.

18. June L. Reich, 'Genderfuck: The Law of the Dildo', *Discourse*, 15:1, Fall 1992. Copyright © Wayne State University Press. Reprinted by permission.

19. Andrew Ross, 'Uses of Camp', *Yale Journal of Criticism*, 2:1, Fall 1988. Copyright © Johns Hopkins University Press. Reprinted by permission.

20. Sasha Torres, 'The Caped Crusader of Camp: Pop, Camp, and the *Batman* Television Series', in Jennifer Doyle et al. (eds.), *Pop Out: Queer Warhol*, Durham: Duke University Press, 1996. Copyright © Duke University Press. Reprinted by permission.

21. Matthew Tinkcom, 'Warhol's Camp', in Colin MacCabe, Mark Francis and Peter Wollen (eds.), *Who Is Andy Warhol?* London: British Film Institute, 1997. Copyright © British Film Institute. Reprinted by permission.

22. Judith Butler, 'From Interiority to Gender Performatives', in *Gender Trouble: Feminism and the Subversion of Identity*, New York: Routledge, 1990. Copyright © Routledge. Reprinted by permission.

23. Carole-Anne Tyler, 'Boys Will Be Girls: Gay Drag and Transvestic Fetishism', based on 'Boys Will Be Girls: The Politics of Gay Drag', in Diana Fuss (ed.), *Inside/Out: Lesbian Theories, Gay Theories*, New York: Routledge, 1991. Copyright © Routledge. Reprinted by permission.

24. Pamela Robertson, 'Mae West's Maids: Race, "Authenticity", and the Discourse of Camp,' forthcoming in Henry Jenkins, Jane Shattuc, Tara McPherson (eds.), *Hop on Pop: The Pleasures and Politics of Cultural Studies*, Durham: Duke University Press. Copyright © Duke University Press. Included by permission.

25. Johannes von Moltke, 'Camping in the Art Closet: The Politics of Camp and Nation in German Film', *New German Critique*, 63, Fall 1994. Copyright © Telos Press. Reprinted by permission.

26. Caryl Flinn, 'The Deaths of Camp', *Camera Obscura*, 35, May 1995. Copyright © Indiana University Press. Reprinted by permission.

POSOLOGY
(OR, HOW TO READ A READER)

When I took charge of compiling a Reader on camp, I accepted the both gratifying and challenging task of selecting 26 essays from the by now abundant bulk of critical writings (exceeding 1000 items) on camp; and the arbitrariness of all selection, the provisionality and partial character of all forms of canonicity is made even more poignant when related to an issue, camp, which combines its recent and still precarious institutionalisation (of which a Reader is in itself a sign) with its enacting a restless questioning of the very process of canonisation. I have thus tried to select not just those that seemed to be 'the best essays', with a valutative choice that inevitably reflects my own particular critical interests and may not be shared by all readers, but rather to select the best *and/as* most significant essays, that is to say the essays that have marked the critical apprehensions of the camp issue, each of them representing a whole nexus, or paradigm, of 'performance of camp' on the epistemic stage. Of course, this strategy hasn't prevented some very painful exclusions, and I have tried in the introductory sections to account, as far as possible, for many appreciable interventions that haven't been included here.

This Reader, being structured in a volume-bound cognitive order, can't exploit the illusory 'freedom' of hypertextual reading, and it retains a linear organisation that has to be briefly explained here. While the Introduction addresses the broader scope of the definitional enterprise by way of a metaphorical suggestion, the volume is divided into five sections, which are in part chronologically, in part thematically, arranged, but which – as the definitional assumption I formulate in the Introduction suggests – constitute a whole, however twisted and processual, building, with various epistemic and historical (the two being inextricable) 'wings' representing that queer discursive architecture which I claim camp may be taken for. Needless to say, when you visit the Louvre in Paris you are not required to visit the whole of it, and at once, nor to appreciate with the same intensity and pleasure all the rooms and exhibitions hosted there. But I trust many readers will find it worthwhile to stop here, and for more than one day.

I made an effort to reprint all the essays without deletions, just as they were first published, and when that was unavoidable, I asked the authors (namely, Linda Mizejewski and Carole-Anne Tyler) to make the cuts personally, or (in

Pamela Robertson's case) to approve the extract. And I have not modified the original (US or British) spelling, for the localising effect that spelling may produce should be taken as a denaturalization, if there needs be one, of the specific framework in which the writings came into being. The one and only intervention I made on the essays is in the reference system, which all the essays now share. As the 'Digging the Scene' chronological bibliography closing this volume hosts virtually the totality of critical writings on camp, and the vast majority of works quoted in the included essays, it seemed advisable to combine an economic organisation of bibliographic space with the usefulness of a bibliography as a single, and exhaustive, overview of the critical corpus on the issue. All the items on camp are therefore referred to with the author–date system, and should be traced in that final bibliography, whereas the full reference to the items cited with the author, or author–title system, can be found in the 'References' section closing the single essays.

Un peu trop, pour moi c'est assez.
—Jean Cocteau

If primates have a sense of humor, there is no reason why intellectuals may not share in it.
—William Plank, 'Ape and *écriture*: The Chimpanzee as Post-Structuralist' (1989)

INTRODUCTION: QUEERING THE CAMP

Fabio Cleto

DIAMONDS (ARE A GIRL'S BEST FRIEND)

'Camp is a great *jewel*, 22 carats', British comedian Kenneth Williams once stated in an interview to the London magazine *Gay News*, acknowledging that his performances in films, revues and plays, radio comedy shows and television cabaret, and notably in the popular *Round the Horne* radio and *Carry On* screen series of the 1960s and 1970s,[1] revealed 'only a *facet*' of its complexity (Howes 1983). In Williams's image resides a metaphorical definition, offered by means of appropriate nonchalance and an allusive falsetto voice, of the enigmatic charm camp has retained for critics and camp-followers of sorts, providing the justification for its practice, that is, its fun and intellectual *pointe*. Just like a diamond, camp – that signpost of contemporary popular culture and of pre-Stonewall queerdom – is inscribed within the signifying system of preciousness and luxury, and draws its significance *when*, and *as*, culturally constructed. No diamond sheds its light independently from the culture producing, refining and forging it, cutting the stone into a prism whose intensity of refraction equals its currency value as a seductive sign of a peculiar kind of power, the power inscribed in the domain of the 'aesthetic', the 'ephemeral', and the 'superfluous'. As an indication of privilege, though, it presupposes the materiality of labour, social hierarchy and technology, in scanning and mining the landscape in order to trace the *in nuce* gem among the plethora of materials that geological processes have layered over the ages, and in turning an opaque carbon mineral into the most exquisite and translucent cultural product, that only the select can afford to wear or offer, flaunting its – along with their – exclusiveness. Besides, no gem can be detached from the social contract that values it, and as such both camp and diamonds imply their *sine qua non* of potential neglect. The camp gem requires a discerning eye or, in critical jargon, a certain deployment of (cultural) capital, not only to ratify the refined stone as a desirable ornament, but also to distinguish it from its cheap counterpart – a banal, and rather vulgar, zircon – which virtually anybody can have access to, and which brings with itself the seamless, dreadful realm of anonymity.

Williams's metaphor, obscuring and non-definitive as much as it reveals and describes, is quite eloquent about the discursive management of the issue both in popular representations and on the academic scene. Camp studies, solicited and developed within theoretico-historical frameworks (cultural materialism, lesbian/gay/queer studies, sociology, feminist, gender and media studies, etc.) which can be gathered under the umbrella concept of 'cultural studies', have in fact by now legitimated the inclusion within the range of appropriate objects of cultural analyses of an issue for many years confined to subcultural argot, a handful of novels, and fashionable periodicals, that is, an issue gaining access to the sanctioned institutional spaces of Arnoldian 'Culture' only as a socio-logical test-case on subcultural deviance (see Section I), or as a derogatory, dismissive term illustrating the degeneration of contemporary or 'postmodern' culture (see Rubin 1974; Edel 1979: 18; Calinescu 1977, rpt. 1984: 312; Jameson 1984). The emergence of camp as a worthy academic issue, in fact, takes part in a restructuring of disciplines and a reassessment of 'Culture' itself: when David Bergman edited the first collection of essay on gay camp in 1993, he pointed out the AIDS equalling of silence and death on one side, and poststructuralism (camp being, in virtue of its paradoxical deployment on the inside/outside, expressive/secretive axes, 'the poststructuralist mode *par excellence*', 1991, rpt. 1993: 94) on the other side, as discursive conditions 'to make camp intellectually and politically respectable' (1993b: 9).[2] In short, an age was required in which sexual and epistemological borders, cultural hier-archies and the very idea of 'respectability' were under siege, and in which queer issues gained intellectual and market value, with some queer theorists becoming 'academic stars' (1993b: 9), in order to distinguish the camp diamond from the zircon it had been taken for – to make it, out of metaphor, one of the most salient issues on the critical stage of this queer end-of-the-millennium, of our possibly lower-key 'naughty nineties'.

And still, despite the remarkable profusion of research in the last ten years (witness 'Digging the Scene', the bibliographic essay closing this volume), the slipperiness of camp has constantly eluded critical definitions and has pro-ceeded in concert with the discursive existence of camp itself. Tentatively approached as *sensibility*, *taste*, or *style*, reconceptualised as *aesthetic* or *cultural economy*, and later asserted/reclaimed as *(queer) discourse*, camp hasn't lost its relentless power to frustrate all efforts to pinpoint it down to stability, and all the 'old' questions remain to some extent unsettled: about how camp might be defined and historicised, about its relation – be it ontological or happenstantial – to homosexuality (is it an exclusively gay cultural mode of representation, or what? if so, how subversive is it and how much does it comply, or has it historically complied, with the compulsory heterosexual, and both gyno- and homophobic, dominant structures of interpellation?), where and in what forms it can be traced, and about its relation to postmodern epistemology and theories of textuality/subjectivity.

Nearly half a century now after intellectuals started producing it as critical issue, camp may thus still remain, in an early and acute commentator's words, *'un object de discourse impossible [. . .] un mot – et, sous cela, une éthique, une esthétique, un savoir-vivre – qui transit la description, qui renvoie à une certaine violence'* ('an impossible object of discourse, a word – and, by that, an ethic, an aesthetic, a *savoir-vivre* – that exceeds description, and refers to a certain violence'; Mauriès 1979: 9, my translation).[3] A discursive resistance, a semiotic excess, which indeed translates directly into the exuberant, virtually inexhaustible camp corpus of reference. Examples spring from any age and place, its 'camp sites' ranging from High Art to pop culture, from high life and showbiz to the outlandish rhetorics of politicians, gathering on the very same 'queer' campground Oscar Wilde with Charles De Gaulle and, yes, with Benito Mussolini (oh, dear), John Waters's favourite Divine with the lower-case (and 'nonetheless' more sublime) divinity of Greta Garbo, Caravaggio with Andy Warhol, Art Nouveau with the so-called 'Fleamarket School', Mozart with David Bowie, Diaghilev's *Ballets Russes* with the 'orgasmic dance' of Michael Clark, rococo churches with Philip Johnson's Postmodern, etc. The suspensive, indefinitive *'et cetera'*, in fact, can be taken for the definitive mark of camp, signalling as it does its 'necessary inconclusiveness and mobility' (Merlino 1983: 123; my translation). Which in fact explains the first critical approaches by way of *exempla* (see Isherwood 1954, Sontag 1964b, Dyer 1976, Babuscio 1977, and Booth 1983, all reprinted in this volume), the production of camp encyclopaedic dictionaries (see for example Core 1984, and more recently Roen 1994, 1997; Murray 1994; Finnegan 1996)[4] and the constitution of a 'new camp' when a new list of artifacts was added to the camp pantheon (cf. Godfrey 1992, and Musto 1993).

Representational excess, heterogeneity, and *gratuitousness* of reference, in constituting a major *raison d'être* of camp's fun and exclusiveness, both signal and contribute to an overall resistance to definition, drawing the contours of an *aesthetic of (critical) failure*: the longing, in fact, for a common, constant trait (or for an intrinsic, essential, stabilising 'core') in all that has been historically ascribed to camp, or the identification of its precise origins and developments, sooner or later ends up being frustrating, challenging the critic *as such*, as it challenges the cultural imperatives that rely on the manageability of *discrete* (distinct and docile) historical and aesthetic categories. In Patrick Mauriès' phrasing, *'l'incohérence violente de ses diverses références [. . .] constitue une agression culturelle, qui peut disqualifier les meilleurs intelligences d'autant plus, peut-on ajouter, que cet aspect ne se justifie pas d'un projet délibéré qui lui donnerait son unité'* ('the violent incoherence of its many references constitute a cultural aggression, disqualifying the best brains, and even more so because this feature can't be justified by inscribing it within a deliberate project that gives it some unity'; 1979: 108–9, my translation). In other words, camp's being 'neither a consistent theoretical perspective, nor a certain group of artifacts' (Finch 1986: 36; reprinted here), it follows that '[t]rying to define Camp is like attempting to sit in the corner of a circular room. It can't be done, which only adds to the quixotic appeal of the attempt' (Medhurst 1991a: 154). Examples and their theoretical grid, theory and practice, twine, whirl and wind around each other in a perpetual theatricalisation of camp's instability. And camp *must be* an 'objet de discourse impossible', working as it does through a radical semiotic destabilisation, in which object and subject of discourse *collapse onto each other*. The definition of a corpus of reference, of the theoretical perspective and of the cultural authority of the critic, thus fail at once and by the very same gesture, and such failure moves in concert with 'the quixotic appeal', the sphinx- or diamond-like attraction to endless questioning (including, oh yes, the questioning of the critic's legitimacy as the *arbiter* of the right, true and worthy).

The feature of excess – being the engine, beginning and end of critical reflection – has a twofold outcome. On the one side, it characterises the whole critical scene, which can be best described as babel-like, disagreement reigning. Consider the 'weak', non-dogmatic approach of David Bergman, delineating the very few spots of critical agreement:

> First, everyone agrees that camp is a style (whether of objects or of the way objects are perceived is debated) that favors 'exaggeration', 'artifice', and 'extremity'. Second, camp exists in tension with popular culture, commercial culture, or consumerist culture. Third, the person who can recognize camp, who sees things as campy, or who can camp is a person outside the cultural mainstream. Fourth, camp is affiliated with homo-sexual culture, or at least with a self-conscious eroticism that throws into question the naturalization of desire. (1993b: 4–5)

Bergman's aside, in the first paragraph ('whether of objects or of the way objects are perceived is debated') points out a site of *debate*, rather than of consensus. The objectification of camp into a *style*, in fact, has been pointed out as a major strategy of domestification that bourgeois epistemology might have posited, a strategy effacing the gay subjectivity and thus making camp available to bourgeois consumption in the 1960s. And camp's affiliation with 'homosexual culture, or at least with a self-conscious eroticism that throws into question the naturalisation of desire', along with the marginality of camp as one of its definitional features, is both a claim many critics (including myself) would subscribe to, a claim that can be traced in Susan Sontag's ground-breaking 'Notes on "Camp"' (reprinted here), and a claim that has elicited an angry, polemical response within the gay community since its first appearance in 1964, giving vent to a self-alleged *reclaiming* enterprise which hasn't concluded its theory yet (see further for a wider argument on this). Being *affiliated* (the term coming from the late Latin *affiliatus*, 'adoptive son') with homosexual culture, camp is not the direct and legitimate offspring of a homosexual selfhood active with the *properties* of 'biological paternity'. The origins of camp are elsewhere – where, we can't say – and only through a cultural process, so to speak, of *adoption*, camp has been brought to its supposed or reclaimed 'homosexual paternity'. (My use of *paternity* instead of *parenthood* is not due to a lapse of reactionary ignorance: by and large, in fact, those who have spoken on behalf of camp as a gay property and offspring, as we shall see, assume *male* homosexuality as the real 'parent' and 'owner'). This is therefore an area of 'agreement' that excludes a most significant tradition of criticism.

Which brings us to the second outcome of the feature of excess being the engine of critical reflection. Camp's resistance to critical discourse has elicited a process of critical management relying on the systematic reduction of that evanescence and mobility which are inscribed in the very existence, aesthetical and phenomenological, of camp as an issue. Critical 'failures' in drawing the contours of such an elusive category thus proceed at one and the same time with a process of 'betrayal' of its irreducible complexity as a necessary condition of critical discourse – in Sontag's words, '[t]o talk about Camp is [...] to betray it' (1964b: 275). Sontag's pioneering essay ascribes such betrayal to a metaphysical condition of camp as *sensibility* ('A sensibility [...] is one of the hardest things to talk about', 275); and yet, even without relying on this esoteric dimension, that is, if we choose to approach the issue through the later, and more materialistic, categories that have been deployed in order to frame it, both *failure* and *betrayal* can be traced as features of all camp effects, as part indeed of its own activation and horizon of possibility, as the essays included in this Reader constantly reveal and enact.[5]

Rather than justifying the failure in definition and account of camp by charging the critical interventions with 'inadequacy', the essays here clustered as the best and most significant pieces of criticism should be seen as *adequate*, appropriate responses to a conundrum issue which in itself works through failures, excess and betrayal. The refusal of any stabilising strategy denying its own betrayal seems to indicate the way that must be followed in order to give camp a *dimension of possibility* as an object of discourse, and by the same gesture to best value its multifaceted charm, reconstructing and reconstruing 'camp' as the sum of its historical and discursive complexity – which has *critical discourse* among the significant elements of that accretion into complexity. When Jonathan Dollimore touched on camp in his *Sexual Dissidence* (see 'Post/modern' reprinted here), he asserted that its definition is 'as elusive as the sensibility itself, one reason being simply that there are different kinds of camp' (1991: 310). My suggestion is that we rethink the manifold variety of *kinds* of camp as a variety of re/presentations and historical rearticulations of the camp discourse, grounded in the varying modes of circulation of the elements (aristocratic detachment, theatricality, ironical distance, parodical self-commitment, sexual deviance etc.) which have been over the years ascribed to 'camp'. And the *variety* (with all the implications of divergence such a word carries in itself) of criticism takes part in this epistemic condition of being, for its representations are inscribed in a cultural paradigm, and they significantly contribute to crystallise, or 'cut', one facet of camp. The definition of camp may thus well reside, I think, in its modes and reasons of resistance to definition,[6] or in a *metaphor* of such indefinability as materially constituted.

Let's then turn again to diamonds. Pursuing the metaphorical path, the camp diamond-like appeal can be pointed out as inherent to its complexity and lack of a substantial, stabilising core, in concert with its operativeness on the spectres of appearance and frivolity. The beams of light are produced in a diamond precisely by the refraction of an outer source on and through its multifaceted surface. The more numerous the facets, the more precious and exclusive the jewel (and camp is a '22 carats' jewel – not bad, really). And the facets, the effects of human labour, offer themselves in fact as metaphors of *critical* labour, of various critical paradigms; as metaphors of those paradigms which haven't produced the domestification of the 'camp issue' into a stable object of discourse, but rather its opposite – the refining of a prism whose degree of diversity and heterogeneity, of disagreement and discursive contest, equals the intellectual and political *refraction* value of the camp gem as site of ('perverted', deviated) critical *reflection*. This is not said, of course, in order to promote a reckless critical relativism (given the lack of an intrinsic principle of stability, and the parallel critical utility, the necessity indeed, of dissent, all 'cuts', all positions have the same worth). The camp diamond, as we know it, hasn't been produced by neat and definitive cuts, but rather through a refinement into facets, all critical writings participating in the struggle (in the refraction as distorted reflection) *between* and *within* paradigms – with some better, so to speak, jewellers at work. But we shouldn't allow ourselves to forget that the 'jewellers' are those culturally ratified as the authors of – and thus credited for – the cut, which is nonetheless the result of a much wider process, involving more than just the one who's authorised the 'last touch' or signature: involving, that is, other more obscure workers, starting with the miners, and the whole cultural apparatus of material (tools, infrastructures, etc.) and symbolic production referred to above, and which in its turn produces the many jewellers and, *through* rather than *by* them, the many facets of the camp jewel.

In their 'state of the art' value, this Introduction and Reader do not therefore aim at unknotting the conspicuous *complexity* of the camp jewel, which is, I am persuaded, possibly its ultimate *pointe*, but rather to follow such diamond-like premises. Consistently with the culturalist approach exemplarily articulated by Andrew Ross in his brilliant 'Uses of Camp' (1988, reprinted here), much contemporary criticism avoids the pitfalls of essentialising or deterministic definitions, taking into account the performative (theatrical and non-referential) existence of camp as both theory and field of reference, by analysing it in terms of its circulation within culture and its production through 'camp effects', that is to say by unfolding the multilayered and contradictory *uses* of camp diachronically, and synchronically by different communities. Diamonds in fact are not only prismatic but also a means to very different ends. You can adorn yourself, in a self-fashioning destined to that most theatrical of settings – seduction – in which the seducer's role can be played by the person wearing it, by the one giving it as a gift, or by the culture ratifying diamonds as seductive signs, specters of appearance. Diamonds can also be used for pragmatic ends in many working tools, or in order to play – in the camp nostalgic mode – old vinyl records requiring the 'reading' of a gramophone needle along their tracks; but they can also be used, à la James Bond, to stylishly cut window panes and, so to say, to break into a culture – which is what we can achieve by using camp as an operative key to issues of sexual politics, the subjecting process of subjectivation, the confrontations of art and the marketplace, high and mass culture, canon/taste and power, transgressive reinscriptions and their containment.

In 1954, long before camp gained access to public discussion and entered the gateways of academia, Christopher Isherwood wrote that, after grasping it, you would want to use the word *camp* 'whenever you discuss aesthetics or philosophy or almost anything', wondering 'how critics manage to do without it' (1954: 126). The resistance of institutions to the queer challenge of camp may keep such 'doing without' very much alive; but the same effect may well be produced by any reductionist and deterministic deployment of the issue, prescribing one camp facet, or use, while it proscribes all other facets. The undisposability of camp as a critical term, the one advocated by Isherwood, can be supported if we acknowledge it as a systemic interpretative tool, a tool that best works by postulating its systemic (on the diachronic and synchronic axes), relational existence within culture, and within itself. The camp gem's facets are critically enlightening not so much in their single, specific reflection, but as *refracting* the outer, cultural light through their *systemic*, inter-relational complexity. Which is to say that the essays included here, and many of those that could not be included, are inextricably interrelated for reasons far beyond their all being devoted to the very *same* – however unstable, problematic, different and intrinsically *diverse* – word, or beyond their codified articulation which relies on other critics' work, drawing authoritativeness from or disputing it in order to credit the essay's author as 'laureate critic'. The essays are inextricably intertwined because, by epistemologically constituting the facets through which camp has been construed, they build up camp as an object of (relatively) 'possible discourse', and as a powerful diamond-like *refractor*, however enigmatic that may be. Singularly taken, all essays 'betray' camp with the fascinating violence of the incisive instrument that forges the gem; and that betrayal, if framed with other critical betrayals, is both the necessary step to refine the camp gem, and the appropriate approach, the one that produces the precious jewel out of the raw stone. And what, we may well ask, is the balance of camp-as-diamond, what is the balance of an evanescent issue that, in resisting attempts to set it down to a stable object of discourse, unsettles the equilibrium of critical and cultural categories, along with its own? Again, drawing on the metaphor, the camp gem requires a frame to support and value it. This Reader means to provide such a frame: if it succeeds, that is, if it turns out to be a quality frame, it won't be in offering an easy way, a reductionist understanding, but in making it possible to appreciate the complexity of the prismatic jewel *as such*.

There are limits to Kenneth Williams's metaphor as a path to definition, though (no *straight* paths are available, in camp). Once cut, the diamond draws its worth from its advertised 'eternity', the features of its marketing as a symbol of eternal love, conjoined with the domain of the ephemeral and frivolous. The paradoxical investment of a deep value of bonding in that which is valuable precisely because entirely deployed on surfaces and mobile appearances works through a connotation of the eternal, the permanent solidity of the stone, onto the endless flux and mutability of the refraction of a definitionally mobile external source of light. And yet, the stone is supposedly there *once and for all*, a crystallised prism whose complex system of facets cannot be changed – you can cut a diamond only into smaller, and much less precious, gems, and that can only take place as a recycling of a damaged (or stolen) stone. But camp is a prism constantly rearranging its equilibrium of facets, a prism that has so far resisted all attempts to critically, discursively *crystallise* it. It is not only the camp refraction that's unstable and mobile, but the camp diamond itself. And my deployment of a 'systemic' order and cognitive value does not subscribe to any *static* implication of the metaphor – on the contrary, it is an attempt to emphasise the relational existence of camp as both subject and object of discourse, as field and theory of reference, as a clandestine key to break into a culture by queering historico-aesthetical categories, by camping them up. Last, but not least, the camp-as-diamond, opposed to camp-as-zircon, may account for the critical neglect that camp has suffered (and still suffers, to some extent), or for the recognition it requires on the decoding eye's part (camp being, in a popular phrasing, 'in the eye of the beholder'), but is extremely risky for its opposition of an authentic to a 'fake', second-rate, cheap version, something which has been claimed by critics within a most common 'betrayal', a reductionist move meant to tame its instability, as we shall see, but which is nonetheless a move delegitimated by camp in its queer deconstruction of the opposition between 'original' and 'copy', 'true' and 'false', 'primary' and 'secondary'. And however suitable to the aristocraticism of camp in its historical derivation and 'queenly' semiotics, the social hierarchy inscribed in diamonds betrays not only many uses of camp in working-class settings – such as the butch-femme formation (see Case 1988, reprinted here), or the 'feminist camp' traced by Pamela Robertson (1996, excerpted here) – but also the broader, complex relation of camp with power and its social devices, its hierarchy of dominant and deviant, which made it a survivalist strategy (working through a reinscription of stigma) for the subordinated, the excluded, the unnatural, the fake or, in Andrew Ross's phrase, 'history's waste'.

In moving strategically to another image which presides over this attempt at re(de)fining it, we'll look for a *spatial* metaphor allowing us, in Andy Medhurst's quoted words, to 'sit in the corner of a circular room' – a metaphor, that is to say, *closer* to camp in its vagrant etymological derivations, as we shall see. And camp will be described, in the next paragraphs, as *a queer, twisted discursive building*, the site of an improvised and stylised performance, a proper-groundless, mobile building without deep and anchoring foundations, a building devoid of the *stasis* potentially implicated by the diamond metaphor: a provisional building erected, so to say, on 'discursive sands', making the ephemeral not part of a cultural connotation (such as the diamond's), but ingrained in its ontological horizon of possibility, which – *literally* – can't be *settled down*. This suggestion will be a tentative one, not one that is explored in all its implications (that would take a whole volume in itself). Despite the possibly 'excessive' ambitions of such a suggestion, this is nevertheless the space to indicate the queer path to follow, and the critical *necessity*, in defining camp, to let ourselves be tempted by the quixotic appeal (if a Reader doesn't address, however tentatively, the definition of its object, it leaves out a not so disregardable question – *what* are you expected to be reading *about?*), by giving a framework that justifies how, and why, the *state* of the art is, and appropriately so, in *exuberance*.

PROCESSING 'THE QUEER'

The lofty (and modestly camp) level that brought us here can be made to converge on a much more direct question: what is camp, after all? Again, in asking the question, theory and practice mingle – *what* practices can be, and have been, called camp, and what constitutes *it* as a label applicable to some (indefinite) field of reference? Let's start by looking at the sign itself, *camp*. It first entered the sanctioned space of 'the language' in a dictionary of late-Victorian slang, meaning 'actions and gestures of exaggerated emphasis', '[u]sed chiefly by persons of exceptional want of character' (Ware 1909: 61), gaining currency in the slang of theatricals, high society, the fashion world, showbiz, and the underground city life. Indeed, the word could also find some clandestine circulation in high culture, as it has been used since the 1920s to describe a literary style with, say, the writings of Oscar Wilde, Max Beerbohm, Ronald Firbank and Carl Van Vechten as literary enactments of precisely those strategies – aestheticism, aristocratic detachment, irony, theatrical frivolity, parody, effeminacy and sexual transgression – traced in the drag urban scene which is evoked in Isherwood's *The World in the Evening*, and finds its seminal study in Esther Newton's *Mother Camp* (1972). It is usually thought that in the first half of the twentieth century camp was a homosexual lingo (mapped in Rodgers 1972), a way to communicate among those 'in the know', while (for survival reasons, both legal and psychological) excluding those whose 'normality' couldn't be let into this outlaw, and yet proximate community. Camp theatricality would indeed be induced by a consciousness of the role-playing activity grounded in the necessity of passing for straight (see, especially, Babuscio 1977), camp-coded signs and innuendoes by the necessity for clandestine recognition and communication among 'peer queers', and such indirectness might be abandoned in favour of outrageous bitchiness only when camp was deployed on the 'safer grounds' of the drag underworld.

When in late 1964 Sontag published the landmark 'Notes on 'Camp''', *camp* had rearticulated itself and its field of reference was even more composite: it included, for instance, the popular taste for forgotten cultural forms which characterised young countercultures such as Teds and Mods (witness the Mods' relish for Victoriana and the Union Jack), or as in the fleamarket fashion of the time. It also might refer to pop music (with performers deploying its androgynous and transgressive representational strategy, as in the case of the Kinks, the Rolling Stones, the New York Dolls, Dusty Springfield and David Bowie); to Andy Warhol's Pop Art and his Superstars; and to the appreciation of low culture – snobbish precisely because practised by 'cultured' people – such as television and trashy cinema. As Sontag's essay disseminated camp as the cipher for contemporary culture, as a refined – and, most infamously, apolitical – aesthetic taste for the vulgar and the appreciation of kitschy middle-class pretensions, the issue even captured the mass media indeed and became a popular fad. Sontag has been thus charged by gay critics with turning a basically homosexual mode of self-performance into a degayified taste, a simple matter of ironically relishing an indulgence in what is 'so-bad-it's-good'. As we'll see shortly, Sontag's (non-)definition of camp as an elusive sensibility is charged with consenting its appropriation and reorientation by dominant culture (cf. Miller 1989), indulging in a nostalgia paradoxically eliding the historical existence of the object of nostalgic desire itself, just as it elides camp's alleged origins within the homosexual subculture.

And yet the sign *camp* is of *unknown origins*, and slippery in itself, being an adjective (*camp*, *campy* or *campish*), also in nominal use (*camp*), an abstract or adjectival noun (*campness*, *campiness*), an adverb (*campily*), a verb both transitive and intransitive (*to camp*, *to camp it up*), and an indifferently lowercase or capitalised lexical entry. A theorisation passing through the functioning of the sign rather than its meaning (that foolish ambition) ascertains the failure in offering a sign at least stable in its lexical functions, for *camp* is 'like the nominalists' *flatus vocus* [sic], an empty, universal term', functioning 'as all parts of speech, all parts of a sentence: verb, noun, adjective, adverb; subject, object, modifier' (Bredbeck 1993: 276), and referring to a quality of the object *not existing prior to its nomination* (see the discussion in Beaver 1981, reprinted here).

The only limit to its existence as a sign, on the other hand, does not offer itself as a simplification. The limit is posited by the fact that the word *camp* can*not* be adequately translated from English – and it circulates in fact not only in the United States and Great Britain, but also in Australia and New Zealand, where it can be found as *kamp* (cf. Baker 1941; Johnston 1976; Laurie 1985) –

into other languages.[7] There are only partial correspondences with terms that have in fact been claimed as camp's etymological 'ancestors' – such as the Italian *campeggiare*, or the French *se camper* – or with terms emerging from the gay and drag subcultures raging outside the English-speaking world (in Italian and French, again, with words such as *diva* and *folle*, or in *campanero*, Spanish slang for an effeminate man used in Guatemala); but there is no single term accounting for the many deployments of *camp*.[8] The lack of a specific, single term does not however deny the existence, outside the English-speaking world, of the many practices that *camp* refers to. The European and Latino gay subcultures, for instance, have many similar (although culture-specific) traits to the camp underworld; and in the arts one runs into twentieth-century figures such as, among the many, Luchino Visconti and Alberto Arbasino, Jean Cocteau, Philippe Jullian and Jean Genet, Pedro Almódovar and Louis Antonio de Villena, Werner Schroeter and Rainer Werner Fassbinder, Vaslav Nijinsky, Anna Pavlova, Serge Diaghilev, Alla Nazimova and Erté (Romain de Tirtoff), Yukio Mishima or the 'baroque' Latin American writings of Severo Sarduy, Manuel Puig, Lezama Lima and Carlos Fuentes.[9]

And yet, these figures have been inscribed in an anglophone framework, for they have either explicitly been using the English term,[10] or they have interacted with the framework of intelligibility that 'constructs' camp as a cultural phenomenon, that is to say, they have been decoded as camp within – and through – a semiotic system belonging to an English-speaking culture, however complex and non-unitary that may be in itself. The limitation of *camp* not existing in other languages (while there are indeed many 'camp sites', many phenomenological similarities, within other cultures), in short, does not contribute to any definition; on the contrary, it raises another question, opens another space of instability, for it is hard to determine how far such framework may have intervened in perceiving a campiness in what may not be traced to the same semiotic in its culture of 'original' production. The problem we are facing is nothing other than the issue enacted by camp at large, that is to say the unavoidable overlapping of subject and object of perception, of read object and reading subject, with the overstructure of preconceptions and pre-understandings that the subject brings to the object, 'perverting' all 'originary' intention, deviating it toward unpredicted – and often undesired – ends: in short, demystifying the 'myth' of authentic origins (see below for a wider argument). This is a question (mark) that won't let its line be straightened up into an exclamation (mark), but from its sinuous and persistent presence we can infer that the lack of our four-letter-word hinders the linking of the manifold camp phenomenology into the system of intelligibility (into a tradition, a history, theory and practice) activated by the camp *flatus vocis*, and that its deployment on cultures that haven't produced it as a term betrays the complex configuration, the specific relational activation, of camp itself.

And what relation does camp have, we may ask, with that other queer term – *queer* – which has already made its insistent appearance in the former paragraphs, and 'camps' in the very title of this Introduction? *Queer* and *camp* in fact share the contemporary critical stage, the latter being a central issue for 'queer theory', one of its partially definitional objects of analysis (cf. Sedgwick 1995; 1996; Walters 1996), and maybe even its 'ancestor', for – according to Gregory Woods – contemporary queer culture has 'inherited the structures and stratagems of Camp'.[11] But the two terms have in fact shared the critical stage, we might say, since their very coming into (discursive) being. On one side, Isherwood opposed in 1954 the 'utterly debased form' of 'Low Camp', the one used 'in queer circles' (exemplified by 'a swishy little boy with peroxided hair, dressed in a picture hat and a feather boa, pretending to be Marlene Dietrich'), to the much higher complexity of 'High Camp' which is 'something much more fundamental', the critical term he advocated (1954: 124). These words apparently draw a line from the world of drag queens and the one of 'camp', which relies on a more esoteric philosophy: in Esther Newton's words, 'the drag queen is concerned with masculine-feminine transformation, while the camp is concerned with what might be called a philosophy of transformations and incongruity' (1972: 104–5; reprinted here). And yet, rather than demarcating alternatives, such opposition works by juxtaposition of the two roles – which are 'strongly associated', 'intimately related', for '[b]oth the drag queen and the camp are expressive performing roles, and both specialize in transformation' (100, 105, 104) – within Isherwood's 'queer circles'. And in fact, as camp was entering the 'proper language' pages of Webster's Dictionary in 1966, Vivian Gornick claimed in the *Village Voice* columns that 'it's a queer hand stoking the campfire'.

Possibly because of such intertwined existence of camp and queer, the definitional promise had to be given up for camp until *queer* was addressed by cultural theory. The lexical entry *queer* is in its turn an indefinable issue and a vagrant entry, rich in implications and historico-theoretical nuances that are worth considering, though briefly, here. Just like camp, it works as all parts of speech, and has no static grammatical functioning, for it is at once an adjective, a noun and a verb. This polivalence, this move across grammatical boundaries, enacts at the level of the signifier its queer (unstable and vagrant) signifying process, its 'continuing moment, movement, motive – recurrent, eddying, *troublant*', for *queer* 'means *across* – it comes from the Indo-European root – *twerkw*, which also yields the German *quer* (transverse), Latin *torquere* (to twist), English *athwart*' (Sedgwick, *Tendencies*, xii). As such, *queer* seems to have entered English language, through the queer gates of the Elizabethan underworld (see the occurrences in Barisone, 56, 82–3, 207–8), in the eighteenth century with the value of *oblique, bent, twisted, crooked*. All these semantic nuances, along with the more recent, and derogatory, meaning of 'homosexual', are in fact recorded within that most helpful of resources on these issues, the Oxford English Dictionary, which for the noun and adjectival forms gives the following: '1. Strange, odd, peculiar, eccentric, in appearance or character. Also, of questionable character, suspicious, dubious. [...] 2. Not in a normal condition. [...] 3. Queer Street: An imaginary street where people in difficulties are supposed to reside; hence, any difficulty, fix, or trouble, bad circumstances, debt, illness etc.' (OED, 1933, 41). And for the verb: '1. trans. a. To quiz or ridicule; to puzzle. b. To impose on, swindle, cheat. [...]. 2. To spoil, put out of order. [...] 3. To put (one) out; to make (one) feel queer' (42).

The estranging, alienating effect of eccentricity, anticonventionality, or perversion of doxastic prescription links *queer* with its 'troubling inauthenticity' – witness the occurrences of *queer money*, 'counterfeit money', at least since 1740 (cf. OED Supplement, 1982, 972). And 'queer' would thus be the inauthentic subject, living in conditions of forgery, unstable precisely because devoid of a stabilising core of 'true being', that clandestinely breaks into the structures of Capital and into the economy of social contract, and that – given *on the queer* as 'not quite honest or straight' (OED Supplement, 1961, 151), 'engaged in the forging of currency' (OED, 1933, 42) – unsettles the rectitude, or straightness, of orthodoxy (*orthodoxy* coming from Greek *orthodoxía*, a compound of *dóxa*, 'opinion', and *orthós*, 'right', 'correct', 'proper', 'straight'). 'Queer' works by means of a spatial metaphor, twisting and bending straight principles of common sense, and the idea itself of normality, which emerges as a normative order (a *norm*-ality), a sanctioned – in Michel Foucault's terms (cf. 'The Subject and Power') – regime of *comportamentalité* in which the subject is *conduit à se conduire*. A linear order deviating which you enact a provisional, subversive strategy, for *to queer* means, 'with a person as object, to spoil the reputation of, to put (a person) in bad odour (with someone); to spoil (a person's) undertaking, chances, etc.' (OED Suppl., 1982, 972).

Until the end of the nineteenth century, *queer* meant its own *undecidability*, unsettling in itself for the fact that one couldn't settle the sign's meaning, or its *queer(ing) direction* or *sense*: in Wayne Koestenbaum's words, '[t]he uncertainty of the word's meaning helps it designate incomplete knowledge: 'queer' signifies an illogical stab of doubt, the sensation of wavering between two interpretations – a hesitation that marks [...] the horror that comes from not being able to explain away an uncanny doubleness' (147). *Queer* was the ambiguous, the satanic 'deuce', the fundamentally unmanageable semantic instability, a pure semiotic uncertainty, an hermeneutical wavering on surfaces doomed to failure – inauthenticity and vacuity, in fact, was all that interpretation led to. It was only after the turn of the century that *queer* began signalling, along with its 'strangeness', the violence of stigma for 'homosexuality', and its first referent in this sense was the effeminate male upper middle-class model, the mode of existence based on Oscar Wilde's 'social body' – the effect, through his 1895 trials, of an exemplary punishment which turned Oscar Wilde into a public property, a common system of intelligibility, and his effeminate, aristocratic, 'aesthetic' *posing* into a sure sign of inner 'degeneracy'.

The stabilisation of the sign thus seems to move in concert with the birth of the homosexual as type, that creature brought forth by the nineteenth-century convergence of legal and medical discourses in order to bring queer sexualities within the realm of the knowable, by inscribing the mischievous crime of sodomy in the body queer, by turning an unidentifying practice into an identity (the word 'homosexual' itself being a mid-nineteenth-century creature). In Foucault's words, 'the homosexual became a personage, a past, a case history, and a childhood, in addition to being a type of life, a life form, and a morphology, with an indiscreet anatomy and possibly a mysterious physiology [...]. The sodomite had been a temporary aberration, the homosexual was now a species' (*History of Sexuality*, 43). Such discursive formation was in fact definitely processed in the English-speaking world through, appropriately we might say, the 'processing' of Oscar Wilde, as the readings of popular representation of the 1895 trials in Ed Cohen's *Talk on the Wilde Side*, and the analysis of the semiotics of 'effeminacy' in *The Wilde Century* (Sinfield 1994) have shown. What before the trials was *queer* – 'strange', slippery and undecidable, 'troubling' because failing ontological and hermeneutical categories, and condemnable for being so – was made into a *queer* stabilized into a sign denoting the 'love that dare not speak its name', and an inverted subjectivity, *anima muliebris in corpore virili inclusa*. Queer became, in short, a sign eventually *decidable* as meaning *homosexual*, with the Wildean model of subjectivity as its imposed referent.

It is in the wake of this bundling of senses and directions that queer finds its currency value within post-'gay and lesbian' activism, which implement in it a political tool of aggressive, confrontationist 'deviation' of sense, making it into a paradoxically and polemically cohesive reorientation of the stigma of heteronomination (opposed to the self-nomination of *gay* in the 1970s).[12] In contrast to the binary system of 'gay and lesbian', grown out of feminist theorizations on sexual difference in the 1970s, queer enacts a constructivist model of identity, framing both sex and gender, against essentializing approaches, as results of ideological interpellation (as both subjection and subjectivation) into s/ubjects.[13] The 'gay and lesbian' binarism, with its essentialist endorsement, is dismissed for enacting an assimilationist strategy that appropriates the modes of construction of dominant, bourgeois subjectivity fostering unity, unicity, stability, permanence and depth, in favour of the subordinate lesbian and gay subject.

As opposed to such strategy, 'queer' enacts confrontationist tactics, in which the subordinate, the deviant, voids the categories of the dominant, replacing them with their opposites (multiplicity, diversity, instability, change and surface), and in doing so it demystifies them as self-ratifying devices, as cultural constructs deployed to subordinate otherness.[14] The constructionist model of identity queer promotes is based on 'performativity', the model developed by Judith Butler – and, significantly, drawing on Newton's 1972 study of drag queens, *Mother Camp* – in which that most central of identity-defining sites in contemporary culture (as the exemplary case of Wilde reveals), gender, is the result, the effect rather than the cause, of repeated and stylised acts of performance, of 'corporeal signs and other discursive means'. Identity is thus reconfigured as a theatrical act, not an expression of an inner core of sorts, for 'interiority is an effect and function of a decidedly public and social discourse, the public regulation of fantasy through the surface politics of the body, the gender border control that differentiates inner from outer, and so institutes the "integrity" of the subject' (1990a: 136, reprinted here).[15] The very idea that sexual practices are grounded in personal identity, that sex constitutes the space of 'essence' and the typological categorisation of individuals, is a discursive effect, that can be deconstructed as such by queer performative identities.

Consistently with such ontological premises, queer theory has taken charge, within cultural studies, of investigating the *spectres* of genders and sexualities, and their relationship with signifying processes, with ideological apparatuses, and with the culture whose domination works through a hierarchised binarism of discrete (and as such untroubling, canny) categories. Queer theory sidesteps lesbian and gay studies by inscribing the homo/hetero binary within a wider design of (semiotic, and pragmatic) subordination on the axes of ethnicity, class and gender.[16] Queer thinking thus promotes a sabotage – or, in an appropriate British English phrasing, a stonewalling – of the manifold binarisms (masculine/feminine, original/copy, identity/difference, natural/artificial, private/public, etc.) on which bourgeois epistemic and ontological order arranges and perpetuates itself.[17] The demystification of cultural constructions can thus find a powerful weapon in the twisting of straightness (rectitude, correctness, normality), be that grounded in marriage-sanctioned, reproductive-oriented 'natural' sexuality, or in other semiotic devices deployed to the maintainance of an ordered social order. The inclusive gesture of 'queer' therefore claims to inscribe all subordinations (of class, gender and ethnicity) into a common design while apparently respecting each subordination (as deviation from the straight line of *comportamentalité*) in its historical and cultural specificity.[18]

Just as we have seen with *camp*, the inclusiveness of *queer* does not preclude disagreement; on the contrary, it fosters it. The facets of the queer diamond – in concert with those of our first diamond-like term – refer at least partly to different historical paradigms (which explains why, for instance, in early twentieth-century Britain the term *queer*, modelled on the Oscar Wilde, upper middle-class and dandified icon, excluded the lower-class same-sex sexual practitioner),[19] so that queer should be taken as a term operative with different ends at different times and for different groups, not all of them having the same access to that nexus of strategy and label. On the contemporary critical stage, in fact, lesbians are apparently represented by it as much as gays are, but not so other deviant sexualities, let alone ethnicities, or cross-class formations. *Queer* seems a more flexible term than *gay*, when it was first used in the 1970s to describe both male and female homosexuality; and yet *queer* seems (possibly because of its exemplary instance in Oscar Wilde's martyrdom) continually to risk falling into the very same erasure of lesbians that *gay* brought forth.[20] This is what Kate Davy laments when she observes that '[q]ueer's inclusive, universalizing move vis-à-vis fellow-traveling outsiders tends to, once again, ensure that lesbian sexuality will remain *locked out of the visible*' (1993: 78), and – in the words of another critic, Paula Graham, equally suspicious of queer's inclusive move – to apply terms such as camp or queer to lesbian cultural practices 'is more likely to obscure both the diversity and the specificity of the practices themselves, as well as the power-relations which structure them, than to facilitate a productive diversity of cultural reading and aesthetic practices' (1995: 180).[21]

And yet, resisting the inside alterity of queer (its difference within itself) by means of a prescriptive (and proscriptive) use, simply won't work. Queer won't let us forget its being a *tricky* word and strategy, and the proscribed alterity won't cease turning its silencing into a clamour – you cannot straighten an *across* movement. And this legitimates the deployment of queer as an alliance platform among subordinates by implicitly activating its etymologically 'perverted' sense, as suggested by Alexander Doty when he disclaims gay and lesbian exclusive property over queerness by taking queer as synonymous with 'non-, anti-, or contra-straight' (1993: 3). And it is in such extended 'meaning' that queer has its *pointe* as concerns camp, and not only because it encompasses the whole parodic apparatus that has been ascribed to female and same-sex mimicry (cf. Section III), for *queer*, when assumed as an 'explanatory term connoting a discourse or position at odds with the dominant symbolic order' (Robertson 1996: 10), enables 'not only gay men, but also heterosexual and lesbian women, and perhaps heterosexual men, to express their discomfort with and alienation from the normative gender and sex roles assigned to them by straight culture' (9–10). Camp and queer, in fact, share in their clandestine, substantial inauthenticity, and in their unstable and elusive status, a common investment in 'hetero-doxía' and 'para-doxía' as puzzling, questioning deviations from (and of) the straightness of orthodoxy, and through that the constitution of an aristocracy of 'queer peers' by way of a counter-initiation *devoiding* the subject of its fullness, and permanence – in other words, of its transcendent immanence.

Queer in fact holds a definitional promise for camp, and after years of virtual lack of confrontation with that frustrating enterprise, 1994 saw the publication of *The Politics and Poetics of Camp*, edited by Moe Meyer, the first volume which – under the aegis of queer – claims to 'attempt the sacrilegious' definitional enterprise (Meyer 1994b: 9).[22] As it might sound at least strange that a Reader pointing to queer as the twisted definitional route to camp doesn't include this work, I will need to address its worth (although a close reading can't be taken charge of here), and the reasons for its double failure, its double betrayal – of *both* camp and queer. And I think an appraisal of such a deployment of queer will show, through a negative signpost, a much queerer path to follow.

In the introductory essay Meyer postulates a binary opposition between *Camp* – whose capitalisation had not been charged with any specific significance in former years, and which is 'reclaimed' as the *original/originary*, *fundamental, political* and *intentional* parodic practice born out under the sign of Oscar Wilde's posing as 'the total body of performative practices and strategies used to enact a queer identity, with enactment defined as the production of social visibility' (1994b: 5) – and the lowercase *camp*, or *Pop camp*, finding its origins in that precise moment (Fall 1964) when Susan Sontag published her 'Notes on "Camp"', codifying the issue as an 'apolitical' taste, inoffensive to the bourgeois (ontological) order and therefore co-opted as an acceptable part of the 'pop' dominant system of ideological interpellation. As such, Sontag would be responsible for 'perverting' an originally perverse system of s/ubjectivation by turning it into a straight taste, a mass cultural phenomenon devoid of any 'queer visibility' intent, and an ironic mode which stabilises the ontological, epistemological, and political challenge of camp enacted as queer parody.[23]

'Pop camp', in other words, is described as a *trace* of the original, of 'Camp', a 'residual' copy, a trace thus sharing little with theories of the simulacrum that, following the claims of Jean Baudrillard and Paul Virilio, has been described as the copy of an absent original and the condition of existence within 'hyperreality',[24] and it works more like what remains from a brutal appropriation to popular, mass use, of a subordinate strategy. It is by means of this appropriation, with Sontag acting as the hero of dominant culture, that camp (or, we should say, Camp) has been dispersed into a complex, manifold and contradictory issue. It should not only be possible, but politically urgent, to *process* Sontag's 'Notes' (Meyer 1994b: 7–11), inscribing it as agent within the very same expropriation practice, and to give up the tradition of criticism – gay or heterosexual – claiming that camp is elusive, and to define it in a *unitary* key: 'there are not different kinds of camp [as suggested by Dollimore 1991: 310]. There is only one. And it is queer' (5).

Unity and identity are grounded in difference, and in a binary system of *one* vs. *other(s)*. And Meyer's binarism therefore opposes 'Camp' to 'Pop camp' as *pure* to *spurious* version, and relies, *while inverting it*, on the same hierarchy that Sontag suggested – the one between 'pure Camp', which is 'always naïve' (unintentional, the result of the perception of a 'failed seriousness', responsible for the turning of middle-class Kitsch into camp), and her second-rate 'deliberate Camp', for 'Camp which knows itself to be Camp ("camping")' is usually less satisfying' (1964b: 282).[25] This inversion of priority, meant to reclaim camp as property of queer visibility, would show how the depoliticisation and disengagement inscribed in Sontag's camp necessitates the elision of that subjectivity producing (itself through) Camp.

In order to restore camp to its original, and *true*, mode of existence, one would need to restore its critical and political value, and its foundational element, the one corresponding to its intimate essence – the *queer* – without which we have the fundamentally 'else' of Pop camp. The definition of 'Camp', in short, coincides with the definition of the element distinguishing original from copy. And that element is the queer, which in its social constructionist endorsement signals 'an ontological challenge that displaces bourgeois notions of the Self as unique, abiding and continuous while substituting instead a concept of the Self as performative, improvisational, discontinuous, and processually constituted by repetitive and stylized acts' (Meyer 1994b: 2–3).

In pointing out 'queer' as the key to the camp discourse, *The Politics and Poetics of Camp* seems to show us the appropriately convolute path to definition. And yet, there's something *queer* about such 'queer'. Some commentators, including reviewers (cf. the Meyer 1994a entry), have resisted its normative dogmatism, while others – like Caryl Flinn (1995; reprinted here) – have acutely sniffed a degree of essentialism (envisioned in the *oneness* of Camp) lurking in the texture of his proclaimed queer constructionism, and the volume would thus be continuing 'from a queer perspective what gay critics were arguing about camp in the 1970s and early 1980s' (1995: 80). As opposed to the culturalist approach advanced by Andrew Ross, oriented to the recovery of the social semiotic of camp in postwar culture through an analysis of its *different* uses, Meyer's queer 'stresses a relationship of likeness, in that the queer subject – frustratingly singular, ungendered, and unraced in Meyer's account – reactivates repressed queer readings of texts and icons' (60–1). In reclaiming camp through the recovery of its erased agent, the queer subjectivity, Meyer's will to ascertain a unified definitional ground would thus devoid that very subjectivity of a specific positioning within culture.

The problem in such 'queer', on the contrary, is not so much its being 'ungendered and unraced' but rather the very opposite: it is all too gendered, all too raced, all too specific, *while claiming* to include that otherness which nevertheless excludes. With *queer*, in fact, Meyer exclusively enacts the circulation (in itself, non-exhaustive) of the term in the first half of the twentieth century, that is to say the derogatory meaning of the effeminate upper middle-class male homosexual (in the Oscar Wilde fashion) that resulted out of the stabilising process of the 1895 trials, with Wilde posited as at once constituting the image of the male homosexual 'species', and the origin of 'Camp' (cf. Meyer 1994c). The oppositional element of 'Camp' – the element making it a political tool and distinguishing it from 'Pop camp' – would thus be the male homosexual subject, as its original producer and 'owner'.[26] That such matching implies a stabilization of both queer and camp, and one that excludes even lesbian formations (whose constitution can't be traced to the Wilde trials and stereotypical image), is therefore not surprising. In its declaration of intent, *The Politics and Poetics of Camp* reclaims in fact a 'queer signified' as the one and only legitimate signified of Camp's semiotic system, and 'the Homosexual' as its one and only *referent*. According to Meyer, Sontag 'complicated the interpretations by detaching the signifying codes from their queer signified', and '[b]y removing, or at least minimizing, the connotations of homosexuality, Sontag killed off the binding referent of Camp – the Homosexual – and the discourse began to unravel as Camp became confused and conflated with rhetorical and performative strategies such as irony, satire, burlesque, and travesty; and with cultural movements such as Pop' (1994b: 5, 7). But 'queer' in its potentially queering value does not invest just gender, but semiotic structures at large, the signs of domination moving in concert with sexual and non-sexual hierarchies, and the constitution of self-alleged naturality and univocity of the sign, in its relations of signifier, signified and referent. If we postulate, in a fundamental(ist) key, a *queer* (that is to say, here, *gay*) *signified* and a *Homosexual referent* as only rightful (correct, *straight*) semiotic counter-parts of the signifier *Camp*, we are doing nothing else than stabilising in a universally consensual (and 'natural') code a sign that works on the crisis of codes and signs, and through these, of the cultural hierarchies that are inscribed in all 'naturality of signs'.

The parody of 'Camp' refers to the notion of unstable, postmodern parody as manipulation of intertextual codes of instrinsically political value which is advocated, among others, by Linda Hutcheon (1989). And what we are urged to is an inversion on the axis of the power of representation, meant to restore the 'aura' of originality to Camp as specifically gay discourse (for 'Pop camp' is 'a strategy of un-queer appropriation of queer praxis whose purpose [. . .] is the enfusement of the un-queer with the queer aura'; 1994b: 5). But the reclaiming of a gay exclusiveness thus means reasserting, although with a shift between the two terms, one replacing the other, the logic of the original/originary – gay 'Camp' being the primary, original formation, and heterosexual 'Pop camp' being the secondary, the rough copy, the fake of reproduction organic to Capital and to bourgeois ideology – inscribed in that very (bourgeois) order that queer (money, subjectivity, epistemology) *queers*. In doing so, 'Camp' encompasses a deviation from the postmodern manipulation of intertextual codes that Hutcheon in fact advocates, the one sanctioning the death – through the defamiliarisation of productive processes, of the very romantic 'Benjaminian "aura" with its notions of originality, authenticity, and uniqueness, and with these go all the taboos against strategies that rely on the parody and reappropriation of already existing representations' (Hutcheon 1989: 35).

In excluding the complex relation of camp to the phenomenology of pop and Kitsch, for that relation partakes of the Sontagian expropriation of a specifi-cally gay formation, Meyer's straightened 'queer' excludes one of the radical implications of the queer unsettling strategies. Camp and the postmodern in fact overlap on the issue of pop culture, which is juxtaposed in a queer canonical position to High Culture; and in such juxtaposition one can envision a problematisation, a puzzling, of the whole social hierarchy inscribed in the very idea of 'High Culture'. When Hutcheon explores the politics of post-modern art, she points out its problematisation, by way of pastiche and parodic interplay of codes, of the principles of cultural authority that sanction the privileges of High Culture, and that artfully create an *aura effect* – inherent to the unique, original object which embodies the producer's (or, within the romantic ideology, the Artist's) authentic interiority, feelings, and intentions, and as such should be regarded as his/her property – as peculiarly inherent to

True Art. Kitsch, on the other hand, is the secondary, derivative, *fake* product, the (rough) copy of an *existing* original art-piece – not a simulacrum, therefore. The transgressiveness of camp relies in its privilege of the secondary and derivative, among which Kitsch and pop, of serial reproduction over the original, showing that the secondary is always already copy of a copy. An investment in seriality undermines in fact the original/secondary binarism that bourgeois epistemology posits within sexuality, and that camp, at least potentially, *queers* and *crosses*. In dealing with gay drag, in fact, Judith Butler envisions precisely such queer subversiveness:

> The replication of heterosexual constructs in non-heterosexual frames brings into relief the utterly constructed status of the so-called hetero-sexual original. Thus, gay is to straight *not* as copy is to original, but, rather, as copy is to copy. The parodic repetition of 'the original' [...], reveals the original to be nothing other than a parody of the *idea* of the natural and the original. (1990a: 31)

It is such queer framework that accounts, we might say, for the *historical* (that is to say, undeterministic) overlapping of 'homosexuality' and pop culture. And a most significant case is in fact Andy Warhol and his Pop Art, in which sexual and epistemological 'deviance', seriality and pop are inextricably intertwined with the sign of camp (see Section IV), that is to say, with camp as queer *money* on the cultural exchange market, and which we wouldn't know where to situate, either in 'Camp' or 'Pop camp'.[27] As the 'queer' epistemological frame of 'Camp' is not so different from – I am using Meyer's words, albeit against themselves – 'the entire concept of an identity based upon sexual orientation or sexual desire', from 'the bourgeois epistemological frames that stabilize' performative subjectivity into a 'homo/hetero binary' (1994b: 5), the deconstruction of that very binary (in concert with the one of primary/secondary, and original/copy) that *queer* brings to the bourgeois epistemic and ontological order is *aborted* rather than practised by a 'straigh-tened queer' funding the opposition between 'Camp' and 'camp trace'.

The problem with such a 'unified theory' of camp is thus not so much its continuing in a queer framework what was started in the 1970s by gay activists and critics, as Caryl Flinn generously concedes, for at the time the reclaiming of camp by the gay community by and large didn't have any 'exclusive will', not even in Richard Dyer's 'It's Being So Camp as Keeps us Going' or in Jack Babuscio's 'Camp and the Gay Sensibility' which – while anticipating in a jargon-free language many of the propositions of *The Politics and Poetics of Camp* – allow the existence of an otherness, though acknowledged as such, of what they call 'straight [read: heterosexual] camp' (Dyer 1976; Babuscio 1977, rpt. 1978: 431; both reprinted here). And in the 1970s the definition of camp as an eminently gay (or pre-gay) cultural formation had a cohesive, self-defini-tional and political value that doesn't apply to the 1990s scene, especially in those settings that have made 'queer' their strategy (see Section II). The problem is, in other words, selling essentialism (a position that is not devoid in itself, of course, of political relevance, and that can be even more valuable and subversive, *hic et nunc*, than queer's instability, as constructionists like Jonathan Dollimore and Alan Sinfield point out)[28] by repackaging it with a now more 'expendable-on-the-intellectual-market' term.

My claiming a failure of property by the gay community, or the absence of a gay core in determining camp, doesn't mean to state, of course, that camp hasn't been one of the most significant features of gay culture – nobody can deny that. Even 'Notes on 'Camp'", allegedly editing gays out of camp, acknowledges that 'homosexuals, by and large, constitute the vanguard – and the most articulate audience – of Camp', and those who have 'more or less invented' it (1964b, rpt. 1966: 290, 291). Whatever the origins of camp, one can't in fact fail to see a convergence between the use of camp within the pre-Stonewall gay community and the occurrence of the word in Ware's dictionary published in 1909. Given the stereotypical merging of theatricality, male homosexuality, and the aesthetic sense whose discursive origins can be traced in Oscar Wilde's martyrdom, we can draw an hypothesis in which the origins of camp and those, by way of the Wilde trials of 1895, of the homosexual as 'type', identifiable because articulated on the effeminate Wildean theatricality, are inextricable.[29]

On such bases – even though homosexuality can't be pointed out as the *raison d'être* and deep origin of camp, the inextricable birth of camp and 'the homosexual type' produce a discursive, rather than biological, *male* property – we might try and recover the reclaiming enterprise from the charge of applying the bourgeois epistemological framework it means to subvert, for that might be pointed out as the necessary historical framework to a cultural phenomenon which was constituted as an effect of that very same epistemological framework. And yet, the lexical origins of camp are once again queerer than many readings acknowledge, for there is at least *one*, and most significant, occurrence prior to the 1909 dictionary. We find it in an exchange of letters, in 1869, between two famous transvestite figures, Lord Arthur Clinton and Frederick Park (aka 'Fanny'): 'My campish undertakings are not at present meeting with the success they deserve. Whatever I do seems to get me into hot water somewhere' (quoted in Bartlett 1988: 168).[30] While this earlier occurrence inscribes camp in a queer setting indeed, Park's identity cannot be seen as part of the homosexual-as-type processed through the Wilde trials. Fanny's case is in fact usually referred to because it is significant of the absence of that stereotype in mid-century Britain: when he and Ernest Boulton were charged, in 1871, with sodomy, they were *released* for lack of *evidence*, although his and Boulton's appearance was much more 'explicit', we would say today, than Wilde's. Park's accusations, his supposed same-sex practices, may have had some reality, of course we will concede that (and with some enthusiasm); and he definitely was queer, in a historical sense ('Whatever I do seems to get me into hot water somewhere' strongly recalls the pre-homosexual definitions above); at the same time, the practices and the very act of dressing up in women's clothes didn't make him *a homosexual* in the normative (medical and legal) human-typological sense, nor was he a queer in the post-Wildean sense that will dominate the first half of the twentieth century, and that Meyer's reclaiming invests in the definition of 'Camp'.[31]

I said that resisting the alterity *within* queer (and within camp as queer) is doomed to failure, for that resistance will be always haunted by its proscribed ghosts. Queer *can't* exclude, in fact, precisely because it doesn't envision an horizon of property and propriety of itself, and of its 'own' discourse, which *in itself* exists as secondary, as copy of an *absent* original, and as challenging normative definitions. It is therefore not surprising that, even in a volume self-defined by a normative enterprise such as *The Politics and Poetics of Camp*, the queerness of camp emerges despite its editor's definitory intentions, for the essays included to support and articulate the definitional project don't in fact converge on an agreement – they, in some sense, 'betray' the enterprise. While for instance Margaret Thompson Drewal's essay on Liberace (the notorious arch-camp performer whose homosexuality was made public only after his death in 1987) unambiguously states the *gay* (however 'transvested') roots of the definitional 'queer',[32] Kate Davy challenges the claims of gay camp's intrinsic subversiveness by assigning it a reassuring value for bourgeois episte-mology, and by ascribing a much greater challenge to lesbian camp.[33] And Gregory Bredbeck opens his essay on 'textual cathexis' and the intersections with the sexological concept of narcissism in Wilde as an 'ur-form of con-temporary gay male political Camp', by stating that he is therefore not 'proposing a "universalized" Camp, some type of framework that will explain every form of Camp to every person' (1994: 52). Although Bredbeck's field restriction betrays the definitional intention of 'Camp', he may be offering something closer to a queer definition when he states that in asking questions like 'what *is* Camp?; *is* Camp gay?; *is* Wilde Camp?; *is* Camp political?' we are asking 'questions that overtly desire a determinism and degree of definition that betray Camp itself'; and that the only definitive answer to such nevertheless urgent questions is a camp one: '*only her hairdresser knows for sure*' (52).

QUEER INTENTIONS

Given the interaction of camp theory and practice, its ontological challenge to the constitutional processes of bourgeois subjectivity should also be seen as an ontological challenge *at the level of subject-matter*, that is in its being a subject which resists processes of categorisation, and of appropriation by a *single* critical perspective. The principle of incongruity, which was emphasised from the very critical 'beginnings', most notably in the writings, here reprinted, by Esther Newton (1972) and Jack Babuscio (1977), as a recurrent feature in camp phenomenology, should be fully recognised as inscribed in the camp 'theoretical perspective', in camp as an issue and as an historico-theoretical construction, delegitimising the will to identification of an *organic unity* postulated as producing the fundamental dis-organicity, the exuberance, the ec-centricity, the mobility and evanescence, of 'the issue'. A very first consequence of understanding camp as queer (discursive architecture) invests the dychotomic sets that have recurrently been deployed in order to frame it.

The state of the art, and the whole tradition of critical writings, can in fact be summarised in a series of oppositions, enacting the binary logic that is at once *challenged* and *invoked* by camp as a queer, transversal, 'across' issue. On the one hand, we find categories meant to organise the camp phenomenological plethora by emphasising a primary from a derivative camp. The opposition of 'Camp' vs. 'Pop camp' is just the most recent within a series starting with Isherwood's 'High' vs. 'Low Camp' (1954), and moving to Sontag's 'naïve' vs. 'deliberate Camp' (1964), Charles Jencks's 'camp' vs. 'non-camp' (1973), Dyer's and Babuscio's 'camp' vs. 'straight camp' (1976; 1977), Mark Booth's 'camp' vs. 'camp fads and fancies' (1983), and Rudnick and Anderson's 'true camp' vs. 'camp lite' (1989). On the other hand, we find a series of oppositions whose finality is the description of camp in its operative modes, and of its representational effects within culture: camp as sensibility vs. camp style and taste; camp as fully cultural and inauthentic vs. camp as their opposite, nature and expressive authenticity; camp as fully modern vs. camp as metahistorical; camp as a sign of homosexuality vs. camp as an aesthetical dimension; camp as a secret, closeted code vs. camp as flaunting, flamboyant, histrionic; camp vs. private, seclusive vs. camp as community experience; camp as index of visibility and homosexual self-expression vs. camp as invisibility strategy (the acting required in order to pass for straight) and homosexual (self)-reticence; camp as strategy of homosexual integration into heterosexist culture vs. camp as subversive of that culture's very assumptions; camp as aristocratic vs. camp as democratic; camp as ironic mode vs. camp as parody; camp as apolitical and conservative vs. camp as political, and progressive. The series, comprising and organizing a bunch of intertwined traits, could be long extended. But framing camp as queer suggests to deconstruct, to question, puzzle and *cross* these binary oppositions. And camp won't be traceable on one of these polarities, the one that should be taken as the originary and real deployment of camp: it will be in the *movement* across, in the mobile and transversal relation of the two polarities.

Out of this series, we may single out a most significant opposition, investing issues of agency, intention, and politics, which have haunted camp as a condition of its discourse at least since Sontag's 'Notes on "Camp"': the ones of naïve vs. deliberate camp.[34] Sontag's distinction between naïve and deliberate camp has been criticised indeed (see especially Booth 1983, reprinted here), but in different formulations has nevertheless been usually adopted as a first step to unravel the inextricable knot of camp, by renaming it, say, as an opposition between 'active and passive camp' (Melly 1969), or between a reading practice and a performance (cf. Bergman, who as late as 1995 describes camp as 'either a style of performance or a mode of perception', 131). What describes camp, according to Sontag, is its love of the unnatural, its standard of appreciation being not beauty, but artifice, paradox and exaggeration. What follows is that it is not necessary, in order to produce a camp effect, that artifice be deliberately proposed: in fact, '[t]he pure examples of Camp are unintentional; they are dead serious' (Sontag 1964b, rpt 1966: 282). In naïve camp, all that one needs is the *perception* – active whenever camp(ing up) eyes start looking at the world – of artificiality, especially in things that try and seem 'natural': in short, one needs to perceive a *failed seriousness*. Think of Marilyn Monroe's excessive 'femininity', or of Steve Reeves's 'masculinity'; or again, of what the Union Jack and the whole Hollywood mystique were in the 1960s, when their power and fascination-strength were going to the dogs (as discussed in Ross 1988). Yet, camp doesn't judge these things negatively as when we refer to Kitsch.[35] Camp recognises they are 'bad', but this is precisely the reason why camp adores them, by saying '[i]t's good *because* it's awful' (1964b, rpt. 1966: 292). As to 'deliberate camp', the focus is not in the perverted decoding, but in the very act of performance, intentionally, and paradoxically so, producing a failure of seriousness, acknowledging its 'essence' in the unnatural, in the *inessential* and the contingent, and privileging form and style over message or content in self-(re)presentation.

This opposition, along with its various reformulations, has proved most useful as it allows us to bring some cognitive order to the plethora of potential camp 'objects', offering a reason for the paradoxical camp canon – hosting in the very same list, for instance, the 'cold' soft-porn of Russ Meyer, with its deliberate theatricalisation and send-up of erotic conventions, and the less intentional (so I *must* guess), but definitely more outrageous, outfits and demeanour of the Queen Mother, that becomes camp through a subversive kind of 'reading'; or Noël Coward (Sontag's example) with, say, Wolfgang Amadeus Mozart (Isherwood's and Booth's example), whose campiness might be well the result of a retrospective identification between the camp subject and an idealised past Eden of theatricality. It is useful because, as all categorisation by means of a binarism, it classifies, and through 'the most basic theoretical strategy derived from Aristotle, division and classification' (Bredbeck 1993: 275), it *tames*, domesticates, brings to intelligibility and makes 'homely', the strange, uncanny, queerness of camp. But it is in fact a shaky opposition, and not only because Sontag herself gives the primacy of 'purity' to *unintentional* camp while claiming that, in order to determine camp, '[o]ne doesn't need to know the artist's private intentions' (282).[36] It vacillates because the two poles are inextricably intertwined under the aegis of *performance*. Both modes are indeed presided over by the artificial character of all social interaction, and by the theatricality of being, with doing as *acting*. The two modes see their common cipher in transvestism (sartorial and psychological), for camp is 'the love of [. . .] of things-being-what-they-are-not', and 'the triumph of the epicene style', of the 'convertibility of "man" and "woman", "person" and "thing"' (279, 280) and in the role that both decoding/perception *and* performance assume in the camp *transvestite order of knowledge*, the systematic belief – so to speak – in the fabulous, the unreal, and the *incredible*, feigning an interpretive collaboration with the performance that subverts its reality effect (naïve camp, a 'mode of perception'), or co-operating with the performance by pretending, as if being on a stage, to believe in it (deliberate camp, a 'style of performance').

In a famous paragraph, Sontag states the citational, ironic and theatrical character of camp: 'Camp sees everything in quotation marks. [...] To perceive Camp in objects and personas is to understand Being-as-Playing-a-Role. It is the farthest extension, in sensibility, of the metaphor of life as theater' (280).[37] Depth-anchored subjectivity is dissolved and replaced by the mask as paradoxical essence, or depthless foundation of subjectivity as actor (in itself, nonexistent without an audience) on the world as stage. And as an object of a camp decoding, the actor exists only through its in(de)finite performing roles, the ideal sum of which correspond to his own performative 'identity', personality being equal to a co-existence of *personae* on the stage of Being. Camp thus presupposes a *collective, ritual and performative existence*, in which it is the object itself to be set on a stage, being, in the process of campification, *subjected* (by the theatricalisation of its ruinous modes of production) and transvested. The subject is, in that very same process, objectified into a prop, a piece of theatrical furniture, a pure mask, dressing up with *other* intentions, or with an irreducible ambiguity of intentions, than its own declared ones. And both camp object and subject are made into a *situation*, a theatrical setting and scene, by taking part in the same role play in which the actors constantly refer to an extemporised 'script', and to an audience (however present *in absentia* – witness the case of the arch-queen Norma Desmond in *Sunset Boulevard* – that may well be the subject which acknowledges *it*self as a *plural* subject, and inhabited by social codes) in front of which both camp object and subject perform.

If naïve camp works by emphasising or demystifying the artificiality that passes for natural, queering straightness, and as such necessitates an external perception that travesties the object of perception and debunks its seriousness, deliberate camp is produced by a self-consciousness in the camp(ing) subject, extending the theatrical constitutive principle of that very subject to the other, and self-representing itself though the same debunking process that produces naïve camp. The deliberately camping subject fashions itself through *self-parody*, setting up a pantomime stage in which s/he is fully, and centrally, as at once actor and spectator, part of it. This is why, in the *two* 'types', we can subscribe Sontag's claim that camp wavers 'between parody and self-parody' (282), although the narcissistic frameworks makes it so that '[s]uccessful Camp [...] even when it reveals self-parody, reeks of self-love' (283), for camp, however sharp a blade it can be, 'is a *tender* feeling' as it 'identifies with what it is enjoying' (274). The polarities of seriousness and play, cynicism and affection, (self)mockery and (self)celebration, thus combine in a perpetual cross-dressing movement, in which the naïvely camp object can only be seen as an outcome of the intervention of a camp(ing up) subject.

Camp is a mode of perception, in other words, that cannot in its enactment leave out an element of performance on the part of the (naïvely camped up) object, the decoding of which emphasise its failure in performance, nor on the part of the subject, whose perception is in itself an act of performance, with its necessary audience and its allusive, winking narcissism. Vice versa, camp as a 'style' of performance doesn't exclude – quite the reverse: it presupposes – an element of perception, an encoding and decoding of the self and the world as stage, and of failure of intentions. And as such, the failure of the naïve/perception vs. deliberate/performance camp opposition is not limited to the fact that, against its sense and will to classify and divide, it doesn't actually oppose two kinds of camp but rather two intertwined aspects, or facets. The opposition – rooted as it is in the very intentionality that Sontag tries to keep at bay when she claims that 'the work tells all', and when she points out the camp devoiding of 'content' (content and authorial presence/intention having traditionally been linked in humanist interpretation) – fails because it doesn't account for so many instances that, although intuitively categorisable as camp, can't be brought to a belonging into neither one nor the other 'kind'.

The referral to authorial intention, even if we accept it in spite of its contradictoriness in the production of a camp effect, offers at the most an *illusion* of clarification, and an illusion that is opacified within 'Notes on 'Camp'' itself. In order to exemplify naïve camp, Sontag refers to the Art Nouveau artist who unwillingly 'creates' a camp artifact by producing the stereotypical elsewhere of orientalism while aiming, with naïve and failing seriousness, to re-present and bring back without distorting mediation, the very object of representation ('He is saying, in all earnestness: Voilà! the Orient!', 282). But the case of Art Nouveau is particularly ambiguous and can't be reduced to a mere failure of intentions, as emerges in the ironic, 'perverted', narcissic Art Nouveau travesties of Aubrey Beardsley's drawings, which Sontag herself assigns to the 'canon of camp' (277). And Art Nouveau, 'the most typical and fully developed Camp style' (279), reveals in Sontag's notes a perfect exemplification of the camp transvestic aesthetics ('Art Nouveau objects, typically, convert one thing into something else: the lighting fixtures in the form of flowering plants, the living room which is really a grotto', 279), and not of a passive exercise in perverted decoding of an alleged 'naturality'. The 'most typical and fully developed camp style' is thus not an example proper of 'pure camp', naïve variety, while some other Art Nouveau examples (say, the Royal Pavilion in Brighton, camping on the dust jacket of Kiernan 1990) can't persuade us that its exorbitant features are entirely an effect of its aesthetic programs, with that mannered orientalism and that 'grotesque sublimity', far from objectively inscribed, that for instance Reginald Hill could appreciate in St. Mark's Square in Venice, 'absurd, impossible, and beautiful beyond comprehension, as if Michelangelo, Christopher Wren, Walt Disney, and God had sat in committee to build it' (cited in Kiernan

1990: 149). And Sontag is not so inadvertent as to refer to Art Nouveau without recognising its problematic status, of course, by saying that '[a] full analysis of Art Nouveau [...] would scarcely equate it with Camp', given the 'political-moral' content of that 'revolutionary moment' and 'utopian vision [...] of an organic politics and taste', whilst 'such an analysis cannot ignore what in Art Nouveau allows it to be experienced as Camp', i.e. its occasional 'disengaged, unserious, "aesthete's" vision' (281).

Pointing out the clarifying element in authorial intention (be it in its absence or presence), translates in fact in a mere deferral of the question of what constitutes the foundation of camp's propriety. We can't in fact peacefully rely for stabilisation on a most problematic issue, the one of intentionality, that has been so central to bourgeois epistemology and that has suffered a relentless attack in critical theory, most notably in poststructuralist theories, during the entire twentieth century (on this debate, central to theories of subjectivity and of textuality, see Newton-De Molina, and Burke). And we can't do that even more so when dealing with camp, that as an issue problematises precisely the alleged stability of authorial intention. Where should we place the 'gallery' of camp icons such as Mae West, Greta Garbo, Rudolph Valentino, Gloria Swanson, Marlene Dietrich, Victor Mature, James Dean, Jayne Mansfield, Maria Montez, Joan Crawford, Bette Davis, Barbara Stanwyck, Judy Garland, Joan Collins, Marilyn Monroe, Tallulah Bankhead, to name just a few, that possibly constitute the nave of the camp architectural building? Will those figures belong to unintentional or intentional camp? Only the gallery hair-dressers would know, I guess.[38]

The figures in such gallery depend at least partly in their camp iconic status on a principle of ambiguity, not only sexual but of *intentions*: we can't really settle whether each of them made a conscious deployment of the camp fascination strategy (moving from the grotesque to the androgynous, from a self-parodic emphasis of the stereotypes of femininity and masculinity to aristocratic detachment and prima donna snobbery), or if they were articulating that strategy in spite of themselves, be that through an exercise in camp decoding (either retrospective or contemporary), or through the assignment of 'stage directions' that promote the star as camp icon, without her/his being conscious of that, as when Sontag refers to 'the way Fellini got Anita Ekberg to parody herself in *La Dolce Vita*' (283). This example, still, reinvests intentionality on the film-maker; I would suggest, following the Marxian *lignee* of Walter Benjamin, Pierre Macherey and Louis Althusser on the 'author' as culturally determined, that the director's 'choices' should be inscribed within the cultural horizon in which her/his subjectivity, and the personality of the star, is produced along with the artifact – that is to say, choices are made but not within conditions of one's choice. The intentionality opposition differentiates, in fact, among those who – deliberately camping – fully master the modes of their intervention, and the interpretive scene at large, and those who (paradoxically, as unwilling, 'responsible' for unintentional camp) are entirely determined as camp by the onlooker's perception. And it is precisely such clear-cut opposition between 'masters' and 'servants', between self-aware (active) and naïve (passive) participants, on the interpretive stage, that may be dismissed within a costructionist epistemic framework that is in many ways endorsed by camp, in which the elements of determination are distributed on both subject and object of perception. One can simply remark, with Alan Sinfield, that the whole nexus of implications of 'deliberate camp' is not necessarily available to the very consciousness of individual bearing, or performing, its indexes ('younger users today need not be aware of all this. They are camp because other gay boys are camp'; 1994: 156). As subjectivity is processually constituted within a field of *given* possibilities, relying on ideas of 'choice' and full 'self-awareness', however implicitly, means immediately giving vent to a critical 'failure'.[39]

The failure of an opposition based on intentionality lies in the link between intention and seriousness, the very principle of responsibility and accountability in acting on the world's stage, and in the queer relationship between camp and the serious. Camp certainly debunks seriousness, along with the 'original' intentionality of the camped up object of perception. This is not to say, though, that camp can't envision a horizon of seriousness, or that it simply works through a conversion of the serious into the frivolous (as naïve camp seems to suggest); on the contrary, seriousness always takes part in the production of a camp effect, and it does so through the self-undermining, queer strategy of its 'tranvestic thinking'. Christopher Isherwood stated that '[y]ou can't camp about something you don't take seriously', for camp requires that '[y]ou're expressing what's basically serious to you in terms of fun and artifice and elegance' (1954: 124). And Jack Babuscio devoted an important role, within his 'Camp and the Gay Sensibility', to the seriousness of camp as the theatre of a gay drama, the one of 'passing for straight'. And the camp voiding of the self in favour of the surfaces of theatrical, social roles, which might be exemplified in the camp following for the too-muchness of many cinematic stars, can't exclude its very opposite, the seriousness of self-representation: Judy Garland's popularity as a camp icon, in fact, 'owes much to the fact that she is always, and most intensely, herself', for 'Garland took on roles so disconcertingly close to her real-life situation and personality that the autobiographical connections actually appeared to take their toll on her physical appearance from one scene to the next', and solidified the impression 'of an integrity arising directly from out of her personal misfortunes' (Babuscio 1977: 46–7) – because, in short, she *confirms* in her film performances her existential being, and her extra-fictitious *self*.

Two ontological modes of existence which are seen as reciprocally exclusive – integrity and theatricality of selves – can thus be brought to co-exist and to fundate each other. And dealing with the very same gay cult for Garland, Richard Dyer writes that camp 'holds together qualities that are elsewhere felt as antithetical: theatricality and authenticity [. . .] intensity and irony, a fierce assertion of extreme feeling with a deprecating sense of its absurdity' (1986:

154). It is precisely this (unrestful) holding together of antitheses that makes camp irreducible to a set of features, for it works by *contra*diction, by *crossing* statements and their possibility of being. Intentions, seriousness and their correlates (politics and agency) are there, and yet they are only present in a queer articulation: not one that will concede itself as classifying tool, but rather as a puzzled, questioned issue.

CODA: 'BUILT UPON THE SAND'[40]

The instability of camp's phenomenological origins parallels the uncertainty of the etymological origin of *camp*, once again enacting camp's precarious foundations. The most credited sources are the French *se camper*, 'to posture boldly', that might have penetrated English through an upper-class usage, and the Italian *campeggiare*, in its theatrical/visual sense of 'standing out'.[41] While little research has been produced on this specific subject (see White 1966; Cawqua 1982; Booth 1983; Meyer 1993), which in fact holds the potential for an extraordinary ratification of camp's propriety, property, definition and history, the suggestions have become with the passing of time more and more confused and contradictory, representing, that is to say, the confusion and babel-like character of the 'state of the art' that I have touched upon earlier.

From this point of view, at least, contemporary critical scene isn't *too* different from the popular scene of the 1960s fad in newspapers and the mass-media for a 'new', and fashionable, word. The confusion was already all there when, in the 'Letters' section in the *New Statesman* of June 1967, readers produced an improvised 'seminar' with a range of imaginative hypotheses: a derivation from '[a] more than usually flamboyant and precious eighteenth-century English actor' named Josiah Camp, accountable for an indelible (and unlikely) legacy on the language, or an equally suspect 'KAMP' acronym for 'Known As Male Prostitute' – which was written 'on certain files in the Los Angeles Police Department at one time'. But we also find the more complex derivations suggested by Michael Allen – '[i]n the days when actors wandered from village to village they often lived rough in tents. This was camping. When one actor moved in to share the tent of another he was said to be camping with him' – and Pat Raymond:

> The original derivation must be from either fight or field, the two concurrent in the field of battle – Latin *campus* [...], Greek *kepos* – garden. An Army would pitch on this site, the fight itself being on a *campania*, plain, which gave us campaign. Camp in Middle English was battle, *kampf* in German. *Champagne* as an area is named from the Italian for plain and we get everything from champagne itself to champion to champing at the bit. And quaint and akimbo – crooked. So *camp*: a bubbly, emotive word for something quaint and (still legally) crooked.[42]

The theatrical/visual and geographical/martial proposals, which are intuitively related to *se camper* or *campeggiare*, converge on the virtually unregistered existence – of which we learn from Marcel Detienne and Jean-Pierre Vernant in their astounding *Les Ruses de l'intelligence* – of the Indo-European root *kamp*, applying to 'ce qui est courbe, pliable, articulé' ('what is curved, flexible, articulated'; 55, my translation), and as such inscribing in that apparatus of irreducible ambiguity which is the Greek *mètis* (the 'intelligence of the ruse'):

> *Les traits essentiels de la mètis [,] souplesse et polymorphie, duplicité et équivoque, inversion et retournement, impliquent certaines valeurs attribuées au courbe, au souple, au tortueux, à l'oblique et à l'ambigu, par opposition au droit, au direct, au rigide et à l'univoque.* (The essential traits of *mètis*, flexibility and polymorphousness, duplicity and ambiguity, inversion and deviation, imply values assigned to the curvilinear, the flexible, the tortuous, the oblique and ambiguous, as opposed to the straight, the direct, the rigid and univocal; 55, my translation)

'Quaint', 'akimbo', 'se camper', 'campeggiare', 'campanero' – and we can add the Italian *campire*, 'to paint (in) the background'. Even without improvising an etymological inference that would require a much longer analysis that can be exhibited here, we can register a constant presence in Romance and Germanic languages, of a lexical nexus that can be traced to the Indo-European root *kamp*, and finding its common trait in the ambiguous, bent, twisted, deviated, eccentrical and inverted. In other words, *camp* and *queer* are cognate terms: camp is queer as a mode of being, as posturing a body, as a modality of distribution within social spaces and within the economy of the social contract, and as a mode of communication – indirect, oblique and secondary, unstable and improvised according to its specific, *hic et nunc*, relation to the other.

Among the reasons for the reading of camp as a peculiarly gay cultural formation, of camp as 'passing art' or as code of recognition among homosexuals, is the convergence between camp and 'Polari', the lingo in use during the nineteenth century among itinerant theatrical companies, crooks and tramps, that survived in the twentieth-century slang of the gay underworld.[43] The theatrical, and wandering, existence of camp, as its very etymological 'origin' refers to, and as the gateway by which it surreptitiously entered the language, points towards a rethinking of the 'passing' thesis within an appropriately twisted key, one that gives up sexual determination. Camp emerges from such framework as an exercise in passing, oriented to the *mise en scène* of a performative and transient identity, investing mendaciousness not so much through the 'successful lie' of passing for straight, but rather as its very condition, as the constitutive principle of all 'identity'. Such notion of 'passing', in short, inscribes the gay (and African-American, too) notions in the *movement* across sexualities, classes and ethnicities clearly emerging in the Latin origin of the term, the one emphasised by the Oxford English Dictionary, according to which 'the primary signification was [...] "to step, pace, walk", but already in IIth c. [...] it had come to denote progression or moving on from place to place' (1933, 521).[44] Camp as passing art will thus postulate a subjectivity, and the discourse within which it both articulates and is articulated, as *nomadic* subject and discourse, according to the figuration that Rosi Braidotti, drawing on Deleuze and Guattari's 'nomadology' and theories of the 'rhizome', traces as peculiar of contemporary, or 'postmodern', culture.

In the wake of such 'queer origin' we can frame the camp mobile semiotics. The nomadism implied by the etymology and theoretical framework of camp as ephemeral architecture justifies its linguistic nomadism, producing a language articulated – similarly to the geographic displacements of nomadic populations – in cyclic itineraries, made up of the 'illegal', improper and temporary, occupation and reorientation, of the culture's common places (the *doxastic* sites) through an incessant movement on the discursive layers of the 'dominant' – what in his queer autobiography Roland Barthes envisioned as an exercise of *bathmology* (the science of ironic layers of language), and that Renaud Camus brought to its extremes in *Buena Vista Park* (1980), his camp *jeux d'esprit*. As shown by the bulk of criticism that has alleged camp as the site of a radical demystification of gender (see Section III), the semiotics of camp are inscribed with a politics of deterritorialisation, recontextualisation, and stratification (as implied by Judith Butler's 'performativity' and by a non-normative 'queer') through irony, mimicry and parody, invading not only the subject matter of camp representation but the mode of representation itself.

The camp obsession with images of power – its 'fascinating fascism', as Sontag (1975) called it, or the seductive power of camp cinematic divas, or comic pornography, or again its phallocentric representations) can be framed as a parodic form of 'mythology', producing a structure of *negative* and *deviant* knowledge, a counter-initiation (devoiding the subject and its reality of sense), a queer, heterodoxical elite producing a transvestite knowledge under the sign of paradoxicality and *paraphilia*. Indeed, the camp irony works as a way to assimilate and to exclude, within the same gesture. It is elitist because it creates a community, an aristocracy of taste which, dissenting from what is God-given or naturally 'true', imposes its own para/doxical standards of plausibility in terms of beauty (the culturally ratified as 'awful'), priority (the secondary) and meaningfulness (the nonsensical). In this sense, the elite is inextricably linked with its marginality, and its humour is based on the exclusion of those who represent the principle of *norm*ality. With a typically camp inversion, those who are 'normally' excluded become the subjects and objects of a cult, of a different variety of *religion* – in its etymological sense, as a tying up of relationships, recognitions, belongings – whereas those who are otherwise dominant are, for once, excluded. Excluded from understanding and from the in-group plausibility, deprived of hermeneutical power and, as far as the two are to some extent correlated, delegitimated in their pragmatic power.[45] The politics of camp in a way reveals itself to be a politics of radical dissidence. It is a dissidence of desire, at the level of sexual and/or aesthetical preference and hermeneutics, that is, a dissidence evacuating the knowledge/power order at it very roots – but at the one and same time, this very dissidence may not have been always progressive, and quite often it has actually played in the hands of the dominant.

We have seen that the conditions which produce a camp effect are by and large the impermanent building of an interpretative theatrical stage, and that these conditions also constitute the *status* of camp itself, which shares the same provisional, performative and processual premises, and ends up being a queer (unstable, twisted, disorganic), nomadic, *in(sub)stantial* or *ephemeral* discursive architecture: in short, an effect of performativity itself. And yet, one can claim that – performativity being a condition of existence of *all* subjectivity – what is missing is the specific *raison d'être* of camp; in Carole-Anne Tyler's still urgent question, '[i]f all gender is an act and not the direct expression of a biological essence, what counts as camp and why?' (1991: 31). The performativity of camp draws its significance as *camp* if framed, in Eve Kosofsky Sedgwick's words, as a 'queer performativity', through which a subjectivity is enacted that takes not the heterosexist imperatives of sexually and ideologically self-reproductive, marriage-sanctioned, sexuality as its exemplary performative act (as in what we might label 'orthodox', or 'straight' performativity), but rather the queer deviation, and demystification, of those very imperatives – the reason why Sedgwick also calls queer performative acts 'perversions' or 'deformatives' (1995: 109).[46]

It has in fact been possible (see Bergman 1991: 111–14; Mizejewski 1992: 63; Ivanov 1994a&b; Flinn 1995: 69–71; Healy 1995) to trace a convergence between the camp scene and the Bakhtinian carnivalesque, for the two share hierarchy inversion, mocking paradoxicality, sexual punning and innuendos, and – most significantly – a complex and multilayered power relationship between the dominant and the subordinate (or deviant), and finally the whole problem of how far a 'licensed' release can effectively be transgressive or subversive). Just like the carnivalesque scene, while inverting the principle of normality, camp invokes it, for camp presupposes the 'straight' sense that has to be crossed, twisted, queered. The difference between intentional and unintentional camp can be thus described as a different subject positioning, and a different arrangement of the exclusion/assimilation logic of camp: while the interpretive 'violence' of what has been labelled unintentional camp enacts a 'standing up', a superiority of the decoding subject, based on a deliberate misunderstanding (or, in Wayne Booth's terms, an *overstanding*), 'intentional' camp enacts the self-recognition of *understanding*. But this is an odd ('queer') sort of understanding, for it relies on puns and innuendos, and on deliberate misunderstanding, contractually agreed between the parts. The perfect example of a camp exchange, in this sense, might be the one between Ada Leverson and Somerset Maugham, as when he excused himself early from a party by saying 'I must keep my youth', she replied 'Oh, but you should have brought him' (reported in Core 1984: 122). I would in fact suggest that camp thus exists only insofar as there is a doxastic space in which to surreptitiously improvise the theatricalisation, the *mise en scène*, of a 'dressing-up party space' – and by describing it as *a party*, we activate indeed its complex system of inclusion/ exclusion, its grouping into *a camp* (in the very metaphor of both its vagrant movement, political alliance, and martial display, that the queer origins of the term itself promotes).

The camping up into a party thus operates by an 'improper' theatricalisation of space by means of the erection (all meanings intended) of *ephemeral apparatuses* – the term coming from the Renaissance and Baroque tradition of celebrations (which made a wide use of provisional apparatuses such as stage effects, fireworks, triumphal arches, false façades), and its retrieval within 'postmodern' urban architecture of the 1970s and 1980s, implying the constitution of recreational or cultural, highly spectacular and short-lived, exhibitions, besides and against more institutional and 'permanent' activities (thus linking two 'crowded camp sites', Baroque and the postmodern).[47] In such a framework, the oxymoronic 'straight (read: orthodox) camp' is a seeming impossibility that we should, still, acknowledge as revealing a bourgeois co-optation, which has not so much been perpetrated by Sontag (1964), but through the late 1960s and 1970s popularisation and mass-marketing of camp with icons such as, yes, Andy Warhol and David Bowie, or in artifacts such as *The Rocky Horror Picture Show*, bringing a party of the select and 'chosen' to a mass, *indistinct* fruition. In this postmodern, or 'democratised' camp (Booth 1983: 175) there may well be even the appearance of an irritating practice such as the one advocated in the 1993 *Esquire* 'Viva Straight Camp' piece, celebrating via the explicit removal of the queer challenge to sexual boundaries – 'Straight Camp is *not* about the blurred distinctions between gay and straight' (Anon. 1993b: 92) – the heterosexual party articulated on the icons of North American neoliberism, from Ross Perot to business class. In betraying the challenge to sexual identity, such piece and practice may in fact be easily charged with *denegation*, a denial which queerly affirms that very challenge – which is to say, if you haven't been invited to it, why not *spoil* the party, and organise a more exciting one?

And at the same time, the 'appropriate' queerness of camp can't be tamed into a homosexual property – on the contrary, such property should be refused as an effect of the bourgeois cognitive ordering and stabilising of a code of resistance to definition into a code of recognition of the 'unspeakable of the Oscar Wilde sort' (E. M. Forster's phrase in *Maurice*) – and that has among its potential enactments the co-optation into an instrument of maintenance of bourgeois epistemic and social order. Both camp and queer (and camp as queer) should in fact be assumed as *discursive processes*, and issues whose challenge has been administered by a twofold, and apparently contradictory, strategy: firstly, at the turn of the century, it was largely (though not exhaustively) made into a self-speaking *evidence*, a knowable semiotic system through

the imposition of a homosexual meaning and referent, thus making the performative gesture of camp a referential discourse. Secondly, in the 1960s and
1970s, it entered an even more complex phase, whose borders encompass the
precise moment in which this Reader itself appears, in which homosexuality
began coming out, and in which the refinement, or cultural 'surplus' signalled
by the camp 'aristocratic' effeminacy, was made available to a mass consumption – with an effacement, or repression, of its gay implications which nonetheless come back as *revenants* – not only through its normalisation into the
straight camp celebrated by *Esquire*, but also by a growing appeal of queerness
to the 'postmodern' subject. These contradictory rearticulations can thus be
taken as two major wings of camp as an epistemic building; but camp being a
queer architecture, built upon the sand of discursive and epistemic intersections, the two wings – while being the effect of an institutionalising enterprise,
the one against which the 'ephemeral architecture' of the 1970s was deployed –
are themselves devoid of the ontological foundation that would give them
stability, and shouldn't be assumed to have a totalising consistency not only
with the 'whole building', but even *within* themselves. If the early references
listed in the 'Digging the Scene' bibliography offer many non-univocal occurrences, the circulation of the camp discourse in the years 1960–80 can't be
reduced, thank goodness, to a mere depoliticised and unchallenging, nor
degayfied, phenomenon.

The 'state of the art' can't thus be reconstrued as a series of discrete epistemic
'plates', synchronically homogeneous – according to that Foucauldian archaeology which falls into what, within British cultural materialism, is referred to
as 'faultlines', the overlapping and self-contradictory status of epistemic
layers.[48] It should be reconstrued as a paradigm of exuberance. If camp 'is'
something, it is the crisis of identity, of depth, and of *gravity*. Not a stable code,
therefore, but rather a discourse produced by the friction with and among
other discourses; not a stable building, but a twisted, necessarily 'bent' architecture, an issue which is devoid of foundation not because it is a 'false
problem' (a construction lacking justification and critical interest), but because
it is a problem inscribed in and activating falsity and forgery, as produced by
the a-hierarchical bundling of an indefinitive series of ephemeral apparatuses,
the apparatuses of the incessant rearticulation, both as field of reference and as
theoretical perspective, of a nomadic discourse. Which is to say, eventually,
that camp might have become indeed inoffensive to contemporary ideological
structures, finding it helpful within a broader strategy aimed at political
'uncommitment' (in the blurring of distinctions, in the hyperreal abolishing
of both 'history' and 'meaning': how can camp be transgressive in a world in
which 'transgression' is made the norm?). Otherwise, camp might have become
the more significant because it offers a poignant instance of a culture arousing/
requiring the consciousness of the complex process of constant renegotiation
involving cultural and sexual borders, the strain of redefining norms in order to
contain dissidence, and the dissidence that these very redefinitions produce.

It is in the wake of such a contorted key to this convoluted framework, that we should give up the totalising reclaims of camp as political, or as a depoliticised, frivolous game. If there is an inalienable premise to the 'textualist', poststructuralist rethinking of history and of representation, whose refusal of depth was dismissed by Fredric Jameson with the epithet of 'camp or "hysterical" sublime' (1984: 77), this is certainly the recognition of the always already *political* character of the very representational process, and of the contest that it presupposes. Which means remarking the ingenuity of the definition of camp as a political 'original' as opposed to its aestheticised, and 'therefore' uncommitted, replica. That is to say, of a definition which precisely falls into the ingenuity which Sontag dispensed with in 1975, when she recognised the potential subversiveness of the camp send-up of femininity (see Boyers & Bernstein 1975).[49] Nothing, *pace* Matthew Arnold, can be legitimately charged with 'disinterestedness' and 'apoliticality', which – although 'politically disengaged' – is nonetheless implicated in a political praxis and in a ideological project; in other words, disengagement ends up being conservative, if not *reactionary* (which is nonetheless a form of political commitment, however distasteful). And at the same time, we should be aware too that – as Dollimore forcefully stated – 'nothing can be intrinsically or essentially subversive in the sense that prior to the event subversiveness can be more than potential; in other words it cannot be guaranteed *a priori*, independent of articulation, context and reception' ('Shakespeare, Cultural Materialism, and the New Historicism', 13). We should in fact never lose sight of Andrew Britton's invitation (1978; reprinted here) to reconsider the material politics of camp, rather that its abstract 'transgression', however that critique of camp might spoil our fun. The political, along with ontological, complexity of camp depends on its historical stratification, on how 'camp effects' have been articulated, and even on how we *now* read its articulations: even a politically reactionary use of camp (and there are and have been many such uses, actually, in both heterosexual and homosexual settings), can be queered, reoriented, and transformed into a powerful progressive tool, once we point out its reactionary implications.

Suggesting a framework of camp as queer discursive architecture gives an answer to the question which moves the definitional enterprise, drawing the contours of that space where it is possible to sit 'in the corner of a circular room' – in order to do that (twisting and bending Isherwood's words to our purpose) you just need a *queer circle* and a *stage*, a theatricalised space, with the provisional 'corners' of cognitive ephemeral apparatuses. And still, such an 'answer' is a good one, I think, precisely because it is in itself a queer answer, one that opens in its turn a swarm of questions. In approaching a nomadic category, it is necessary to localise its configuration, to identify the communities making a divergent use of it. In short, we need to ascertain where was the camp 'party', and who had access (and through which entrance) to it – who had been 'invited'? With what 'fancy dress'? Who participated as 'excluded', as embodying the very orthodoxy which camp para-doxicality presupposes? And how was that principle of norm-ality evoked, with what parodic mask was it present, although *in absentia*? What was the relationship between the nomadic party and the dominant, institutional, 'permanent' culture? With what degree of complicity and/or subversiveness? What elements of the nomadic party have been co-opted by the dominant culture, and how was the latter transformed in such process? What are the responsibilities, through compromise, of the party toward the reassessment of institutional culture?

In such programmatic 'failure', in such relentless questioning, lies, I guess, the possible value of the framework. *And* the justification for this Reader. For camp is a discourse enacting a 'sham', provisional, performative existence, and translating its definitional 'fakeness' onto critical constructions which cannot but be based on categories provisional and partial – from a position, on behalf of a position. We should thus posit all critical constructions within the history of discursive contest, of (re)presentation and (re)negotiation which has produced camp as discursive 'queer architecture', framing the critical readings not so much as readings of a common, stable (however theatrical) object, but rather as themselves *performances* of 'camp' – of a mobile knowledge – *on the critical, political and epistemic stage*, or as provisional 'wings' and 'chambers' of a queer building whose walls are erected, dismantled and moved elsewhere, as soon as their performing ends are accomplished. And in order to avoid the pitfalls of an objectifying history, the one precluding queer historiography, we should treasure the famous Wildean invitation – in 'The Critic as Artist' – to *rewrite* history; that is to say, we should acknowledge our necessary overlapping, as reading subjects, with the readings of camp as critical object here included. The result will thus be a multiple performance, gathering on the very same stage camp as critical 'object', camp as performed by the included essays, and as performed by the reader of this Reader. If that's not a ball, name one.

NOTES

1. See Medhurst 1992; Howes 1993: 105, 697–8, 928; Healy 1995.
2. The first condition, AIDS, while often pointed out as a sign of crisis for camp (AIDS urging the abandon of its indirection, its 'eloquent' silence), should be taken here as in itself one of the gay visibility factors that has among its side-effects the unprecedented critical relevance of camp as a gay cultural formation.
3. Patrick Mauriès's *Second manifeste camp* (1979), the very first volume entirely devoted to camp worldwide, and still a very fascinating piece of criticism, represents possibly the most painful exclusion from this Reader, which was decided on a complex basis. Firstly, Mauriès's work does not really offer itself to excerption, being articulated through a 'notational' (and explicitly Sontag-derived) organisation which might be taken as an unfragmentable whole of fragments. Secondly, it entirely belongs to a radically different scene – the Parisian intellectual scene of the 1970s, the one centred upon the *leçon* and queen image of Roland Barthes – from the North American and British context which (being *the* context of camp studies) constitutes the focus of this Reader, and it would require an entire set of considerations to frame it that couldn't be taken up here. Just like Renaud Camus's *Buena Vista Park* (1980), which only indirectly deals with camp but offers an invaluable insight into the camp ironic mode, while referring to the very same French scene, Mauriès first published

volume is nonetheless a must-read, its inaccessibility for those who can't read French just adding, so to say, to its camp 'exclusive value'.

4. Camp 'encyclopaedic dictionaries' provide a wide compendium of iconographic display too as part of the same exemplary approach. Booth 1983 and Kratzert 1987 – along with more Kitsch-oriented works such as Dorfles 1968, Sternberg 1971, and Brown 1975 – though not strictly speaking 'encyclopaedias', nonetheless offer a rich visual exemplification, and to some degree rely on the same sort of encyclopaedic approach.

5. Critical 'betrayals' as practices necessitated by the camp horizon of possibility are discussed at length in Cleto 1997.

6. On the indefinability of camp, acknowledged ever since the very earliest comments, see also Mauriès 1979: 65; Degen 1987: 87; Goodwin 1989: 38; Bergman 1993b: 4–5; Bredbeck 1993: 276; Doty 1995: 335. Such consensus is not totalising, though, due to the gay criticism reclaiming camp as *defined by* and *defining* gayness, that will be dealt with in the next paragraph.

7. At least in Italian, French, German, Spanish and Polish, that is to say, in the languages I have been able to check. On the complexity of translating camp see Harvey 1998.

8. For *campanero* see Murray & Arboleda, 175. Accordingly, writings in non-English invariably use *camp*: see for instance Arbasino 1968, 1971, 1978, 1980; Dorfles 1968; Sternberg 1971; Segura 1971; Buttafava 1976; Milani 1978; Mauriès 1979; Camus 1980; Daube 1982; Merlino 1983; Belluso & Merkel 1983; Polce 1983; Eco 1984; Del Sapio 1988; Ortoleva 1988, 1995; Piré 1988; Pasti 1989, 1990; Landi 1991; Martini 1991; Ceserani 1992, 1997a, 1997b; Ottonieri 1992; Cleto 1992, 1993a, 1996a, 1996c, 1997; Tee 1992; Daniele 1993; Makris 1993; Brousse 1994; Labranca 1994; Povert 1994; Yarza 1994a; 1994b; Ciment 1995; Razzini 1995; Brandhorst 1995; Zholkovsky 1990 (1994 version); Boym 1995; Hess-Luttich 1996; Pustianaz 1996; Santos 1996; Fusillo 1997.

9. On these figures, framed in their camp value, see Farber & Patterson 1975; Greenspun 1975; Baker 1978; Dyer 1979; Mauriès 1979: 26; Core 1984: 52–54, 90–91; Schwartz 1980; Marson 1981; Rentschler 1981, 1984; Yudice 1981; Corrigan 1984; Pally 1988, 1990; Elsaesser 1989; Garafola 1989; Moon 1989; Bacarisse 1990; Dollimore 1991: 313–19, 351–5; Smith 1992; Travers 1993; Shattuc 1993; Gemünden 1994b; Yarza 1994a, 1994b; Moltke 1994 (rpt. here); Ellis 1995; Gaitet 1995; Watson 1996.

10. Such is the case of Almodóvar and Arbasino (cf. the interview with the Spanish filmmaker in Pally 1988; and Arbasino 1968, 1971, 1978).

11. Woods 1992, rpt. 1994: 92. Woods's article makes such 'derivative' relation clear in its very title – 'Notes on Queer' – and in its paratactical, numbered order, which both echo Sontag's 'Notes on Camp'.

12. On the self-nominational *gay* cf. White 1980a; Sinfield 1991; Chauncey 1994; Dyer; Jacobs.

13. The 'ideological interpellation' key of constructionism makes clear its Althusserian and Foucauldian matrix, which exploits the ambiguity of the Latin *subjectus* as both subject *of* and subjected *to* self-identity.

14. Dollimore exemplifies the dialectic between the dominant and deviant on the meeting between André Gide's essentialism and Wilde's constructionism in 'Different Desires'. See also Dollimore 1986.

15. On the constructionism vs. essentialism debate see Fuss; and Stein; on performativity, besides Judith Butler's work, see Sedgwick 1995, and Parker & Sedgwick.

16. In *Between Men*, Eve Kosofsky Sedgwick writes that 'the placement of the boundaries in a particular society affects not merely the definitions of those terms themselves – sexual/nonsexual, masculine/feminine – but also the apportionment of forms of power that are not obviously sexual. These include control over the means of production and reproduction of goods, persons, and meanings' (1985: 22). On

homophobia as an effect of the system of binary oppositions affecting other discriminations see also Sedgwick 1990: 67–90; and Dollimore 1991: 233–75.

17. The critical production under the label of 'queer theory' is by now hard to circumscribe. Most significant instances are in any case Sedgwick 1991; Sedgwick, *Tendencies*; Butler 1990a; Butler's *Bodies that Matter* and *Excitable Speech*; de Lauretis; Schor & Weed.

18. On 'queer' as a strategy of alliance among equally subordinated (sexual, ethnical, class-related) groups, cf. Sinfield 1994: vii–xi.

19. Sinfield (1994: 145) notes that in early twentieth-century Britain, '[t]he lower-class boy might have same sex experiences with others of his own class, but need not regard them as involving a queer identity – because, after all, it was leisure-class men that had that'.

20. As early as 1975, Jill Johnston found it urgent to ask, in a *Ms.* issue, whether lesbians were spoken of as 'gay'.

21. Similar critiques are advanced in Jeffreys 1994; and Walters 1996.

22. The volume gathers contributions by Thomas King, Gregory Bredbeck, Moe Meyer, Cynthia Morrill, Kate Davy, Margaret Thompson Drewal, and Chuck Kleinhans.

23. On the stabilising effect of irony (which is only assumed in its stable version, the one that even a conservative critic such Wayne Booth juxtaposed to an *unstable* variant, available especially in twentieth century literature) see especially Morrill's contribution.

24. See especially Baudrillard, Virilio, Perniola.

25. Sontag, in fact, also uses the capitalised version, but of course without the 'discerning' value deployed in *The Politics and Poetics of Camp*.

26. Significantly, Meyer's essay is taken from his doctoral dissertation, in which however the definitional element of 'Camp' is ascribed not so much to queer parody but rather to '*gay* parody', and to the 'total body of performative practices and strategies used to enact a *gay* identity' (cf. Meyer 1993; my emphases).

27. We may ask, in fact: where should we place Andy Warhol in Meyer's dichotomy of 'Camp' vs. 'Pop camp'? Will he be Camp, because of his homosexual practices, and despite his compromise with Pop? Fortunately, the bulk of criticism on Warhol and other pop camps such as *Batman* give less reductionist and deterministic answers. On the broader convergence of lesbian, gay, queer and popular culture see the essays collected in Doyle, Flatley & Muñoz 1996; Hamer & Budge 1994; Burston & Richardson 1995; and Wilton 1995.

28. In contrasting André Gide's essentialism with Wildean anti-essentialism, Dollimore makes clear that the latter was subversive to the point of being *erased*; but that the latter's kinder fate (in 1946 he was awarded the Nobel prize for literature) shouldn't let us forget that 'six years later, the year after his death, his entire works were entered in the Roman Catholic Index of Forbidden Books' (1991: 18). And Alan Sinfield, in a chapter on 'Subcultural Strategies' within *The Wilde Century*, concedes that, under certain circumstances, essentialism may offer itself as a more suitable political strategy (1994: 176–212).

29. Ware's *Passing English of the Victorian Era* updated *Slang and Its Analogues*, the seven-volume dictionary compiled by John S. Farmer and W. H. Henley between 1890 and 1904, with the jargon of the new decade. This very first occurrence allows the inference that '[b]ecause the term "Camp" is not found in Farmer's dictionary, a conclusion is that it was a new word that entered the English language only during the first decade of the century' (Meyer 1994c: 75).

30. An even earlier occurrence would be found, according to A. St. John Grahame, in a pamphlet by 'the little-known Nonconformist radical Jacob Cadley' – *The Feet of Men*, 1849, hosting the word 'in its present context' (see Shaw et al. 1967: 833) – which can't be traced within the major British and US libraries catalogues. As the

'present context' of camp in 1967 was fairly blurred, it is hard to infer what that mid-nineteenth-century 'camp' refers to.

31. I am profoundly indebted to Alan Sinfield's *The Wilde Century* (1994), which in a post-Foucauldian framework refers to the 'Fanny and Stella' trial as a significant case of pre-Wilde homosexual non-evidence, in its recognition of the circulation of sexualities, identity constructs, and the evolving semiotics of 'effeminacy'.

32. What emerges surreptitiously in Meyer's account is in fact declared – and, if you like, unintentionally 'queered' – in Drewal's essay: 'what happens when Camp performance is detached from its gay identity and that identity is displaced or put under erasure? Or, from another angle, if gay signifying practices serve to critique dominant heterosexist and patriarchal ideology through inversion, parody, travesty, and the displacement of binary gender codes, then what happens when those practices are severed from their gay signifier and put into the service of the very patriarchal and heterosexist ideology of capitalism that Camp politics seeks to disrupt and contest? [...] When corporate capitalism appropriates Camp in its own interests and then poses as its signifier, then the representation bears only the residue of Camp politics. Detached in this way from a gay subject position, Liberace's performances constituted what Moe Meyer calls residual camp or "the camp trace"' (Drewal 1994: 149–50).

33. According to Davy, 'the wink of Camp (re)assures its audience of the ultimate harmlessness of its play, its palatability for bourgeois sensibilities. When the butch-femme subject winks, phallocratic culture is not reassured. Camp is neither good nor bad, it is just more or less effectively deployed. In the context of gay male theatre and its venues, Camp is indeed a means of signaling through the flames, while in lesbian performance it tends to fuel and fan the fire' (1992, rpt. 1994: 145).

34. The deep identity of Meyer's 'queer' subject, the oneness of 'Camp', corresponds for instance with the issue of *intentionality* and *agency* that are reclaimed along with the political significance of 'Camp'. The deletion of the 'gay agent' effaces the political value of camp, its intentionality and subversiveness, and, along with these correlates, the original and originary character of 'Camp'. See especially Meyer 1993.

35. On the relations of camp to Kitsch see Dorfles 1968; Sternberg 1971, Brown 1975; Suares 1975; Babuscio 1977; Calinescu 1977; Ross 1988; Long 1989; Sedgwick 1990; Labranca 1994; Kleinhans 1994.

36. The passage reads: '[i]t seems unlikely that much of the traditional opera repertoire could be such satisfying Camp if the melodramatic absurdities of most opera plots had not been taken seriously by their composers. One doesn't need to know the artist's private intentions. The work tells all' (282). In the logical fracture between the first and second period resides the tension, the problematicity of referring to intentions or to entirely give them up, albeit as institutions to be camped up: the problematic character enacted by the 'unintentional vs. intentional camp' opposition.

37. The metaphor of life as theatre can be traced at least from the medieval *theatrum mundi*. What makes contemporary (and camp) theatricality radically different, though, is the absence of a Divine Providence as 'director', as superior will orienting the actor's acts. On the medieval *theatrum mundi* in its distance from the contemporary social theatricality see Burns, 8–22.

38. The precariousness of the intentional vs. unintentional opposition of these figures finds, in fact, an echo in the research produced in recent years (most notably on Mae West and Madonna), showing that these different hypotheses refuse to stabilise in a definit(iv)e framework, valid for good (and for them all). See especially Ross 1993; Andermahr 1994; Ivanov 1994; Kellner 1994; Hamilton 1996; Robertson 1996.

39. The narcissistic camp self-awareness I refer to elsewhere, that is to say, enacts the constructionist modes of subjection/subjectivation, and the failure of our

'intentions', of ourselves, of those selves that are no longer 'our' selves. The constructionist crisis of intentionality is paralleled, in fact, within psychoanalysis and Derridean deconstruction, which represent two intellectual cornerstones in the development of a queer theory, and which both devoid the subject of its self-mastery and property. See Carole-Anne Tyler and Johannes von Moltke in this volume.

40. 'Built upon the Sand' is the title of one of the stories John Mosher set in Cherry Grove, Fire Island, the site of an Oscar Wilde visit in his 1882 North American tour, a traditional gay sea resort since the 1930s and a most significant case within the history of gay, and camp, communities. Mosher's title, appropriately, names the first chapter (pp. 15–35) of possibly the best study available on the Grove (Newton 1993).

41. *Se camper* was first suggested as an etymological origin in Brien 1967, and *campeggiare* in Hyde 1970: 22.

42. Shaw et al. 1967: 796. The improvised 'seminar' was concluded with a more articulated communication by Alan Brien, who – drawing on his reading of the *Random House Dictionary of the English Language*, concluded that '[t]he origin is said to be from the dialectal "camp – an impetuous, uncouth person, see Kemp". "Kemp" is described on another page as "Brit. dial." for "an impetuous or roguish young man" which seems not impossible (though I wonder whether there might not be an alternative descent from Old Icelandic "kanpr" meaning "cat's whiskers", modern "kemp" meaning "a coarse fibre in carpets"). Unless the word can be traced back long before the turn of the century, I prefer a modern derivation that roots Camp in the theatre and originally describes a style of performance, than an antique one which stems from Northern dialect and originally describes moral character' (1967: 874).

43. Polari, also spelt *palari* or *parlari*, is itself derived from *Parlyaree* (on which see Partridge), and survives through words such as *bona* ('good', 'attractive'), *varda* ('look'), *omee* ('man') and *polonee* ('woman'), and in a more daily, less esoteric circulation, thorugh the inverted use of the feminine such as in *Maryanne*, *Nancy*, *auntie* and *queen*. See Weeks 1977: 42; Hancock 1984; Burton; Lucas; Cox & Fay 1994.

44. For an excellent essay on 'passing' see Tyler.

45. Pragmatic and interpretive powers are inextricably intertwined, which is not to say that a lack of knowledge can't be transformed into a form of power, as is acutely shown by Eve Kosofsky Sedgwick, 'Privilege of Unknowing', in *Tendencies*. The whole history of liberal–humanist criticism, indeed, can be seen as an example of neglected knowledge going along with interpretive power.

46. The prescriptive character of orthodox performativity is traced by Sedgwick in J. L. Austin's exemplary case of marriage. On 'queer performativity' see also Sedgwick, 'Socratic Raptures, Socratic Ruptures'.

47. On such deployment in Italian architecture of the 1970s and 1980s see Podrini. On the Baroque tradition it draws from, see Fagiolo dell'Arco & Carandini, and Fagiolo & Madonna.

48. On 'faultlines' see Sinfield.

49. It is even more significant, in this sense, of an acknowledgement of its political value, the inclusion of 'Notes on "Camp"' – the only authorised reprint so far, apart from Sontag's own collections and this Reader – within *A Partisan Century*, a collection of 'political writings' from the *Partisan Review* (Kurzweil 1996a).

REFERENCES

Althusser, Louis, 'Idéologie et appareils idéologiques d'Etat', *La pensée* 151, 1970; 'Ideology and Ideological State Apparatuses: Notes on an Investigation', in *Essays on Ideology*, London: Verso, 1984, 1–60.

Austin, J. L. *How to Do Things with Words*, ed. J. O. Urmson, Oxford-New York: Oxford UP, 1970.

Barisone, Ermanno, *Il gergo dell'underworld elisabettiano*, Genoa: Il Melangolo, 1989.

Barthes, Roland, *Roland Barthes*, Paris: Seuil, 1975; trans. Richard Howard, New York: Hill and Wang, 1977.

Baudrillard, Jean, *Simulacres et simulation*, Paris: Galilée, 1981.

Benjamin, Walter, 'The Author as Producer' (1934), in *Reflections, Essays, Aphorisms, Autobiographical Writings*, New York: Schocken, 1986, 220–38.

Booth, Wayne, *Literary Understanding: The Power and Limits of Pluralism*, Chicago-London: Chicago UP, 1979.

——, *A Rhetoric of Irony*, Chicago-London: Chicago UP, 1974.

Braidotti, Rosi, *Nomadic Subjects*, New York: Columbia UP, 1994.

——, 'Toward a New Nomadism: Feminist Deleuzina Tracks: Or, Metaphysics and Metabolism', in Constantin V. Boundas & Dorothea Olkowski (eds.), *Gilles Deleuze and the Theater of Philosophy*, New York: Routledge, 1994, 159–86.

Burke, Seán (ed.), *Authorship from Plato to the Postmodern: A Reader*, Edinburgh: Edinburgh UP, 1995.

Burns, Elizabeth, *Theatricality: A Study of Convention in the Theatre and in Social Life*, London: Longman, 1972.

Burton, Peter, 'The Gentle Art of Confounding Naffs: Some Notes on Polari', *Gay News* 120, 1979, 23.

Butler, Judith, *Bodies that Matter: On the Discursive Limits of 'Sex'*, London-New York: Routledge, 1994.

——, *Excitable Speech: A Politics of the Performative*, London-New York: Routledge, 1997.

Cohen, Ed, *Talk on the Wilde Side*, New York-London: Routledge, 1993.

de Lauretis, Teresa (ed.), 'Queer Theory: Lesbian and Gay Sexualities', special issue of *differences* 3:2, Summer 1991.

Deleuze, Gilles & Félix Guattari, *Mille Plateaux: Capitalisme et schizophrénie II*, Paris: Minuit, 1980. *A Thousand Plateaus: Capitalism and Schizophrenia*, trans. Brian Massumi, Minneapolis-London: U of Minnesota P, 1987.

Detienne, Marcel & Jean-Pierre Vernant, *Les Ruses de l'intelligence. La mètis des Grecs*, Paris: Flammarion, 1974.

Dollimore, Jonathan, 'Different Desires: Subjectivity and Transgression in Wilde and Gide', *Textual Practice* 1:1, Spring 1987, 48–67.

——, 'Shakespeare, Cultural Materialism, and the New Historicism', in Jonathan Dollimore & Alan Sinfield (eds.), *Political Shakespeare: New Essays in Cultural Materialism*, Manchester: Manchester UP, 1985.

Dyer, Richard, 'In a Word', in *The Matter of Images: Essays on Representation*, London-New York: Routledge, 1993, 6–10.

Fagiolo, Marcello & Maria Luisa Madonna (eds.), *Barocco romano e barocco italiano. Il teatro, l'effimero, l'allegoria*, Rome: Gangemi, 1985.

Fagiolo dell'Arco, Maurizio & Silvia Carandini (eds.), *L'effimero barocco*, Rome: Bulzoni, 1978.

Farmer, John S. & W. E. Henley, *Slang and Its Analogues, Past and Present: A Dictionary, Historical and Comparative, of the Heterodox Speech of All Classes of Society for More than 300 Years*. 7 vols., London: Routledge, 1890–1905.

Foucault, Michel, *La Volonté de savoir*, Paris: Gallimard, 1976. *The History of Sexuality. Volume One: An Introduction*, trans. Robert Hurley, New York: Vintage, 1978.

——, 'The Subject and Power', in Hubert L. Dreyfus & Paul Rabinow, *Michel Foucault: Beyond Structuralism and Hermeneutics*, Chicago: U of Chicago P, 1982, 214–32.

Fuss, Diana, *Essentially Speaking: Feminism, Nature and Difference*, New York-London: Routledge, 1989.

Jacobs, Greg, '"Homosexual", "Gay", or "Queer": The Struggle over Naming and Its Real-World Effects', in Donna L. Lillian (ed.), *Papers from the Nineteenth Annual Meeting of the Atlantic Provinces Linguistic Association*, Charlottetown, Prince Edward Island, November 10–11, 1995, 93–114.

Koestenbaum, Wayne, *Double Talk: The Erotics of Male Literary Collaboration*, London-New York: Routledge, 1991.

Lucas, Ian, 'The Color of His Eyes: Polari and the Sisters of Perpetual Indulgence' in Anna Livia & Kira Hall (eds.), *Queerly Phrased: Language, Gender, and Sexuality*, New York: Oxford UP, 1997, 85–94.

Macherey, Pierre, *Pour une théorie de la production littéraire*, Paris: François Maspero, 1966; *A Theory of Literary Production*, trans. Geoffrey Wall, London: Routledge & Kegan Paul, 1978.

Mosher, John, 'Built upon the Sand', in *Celibate at Twilight*, New York: Random House, 1940, 122–28.

Murray, Stephen O. & Manuel Arboleda G., 'Stigma Transformation and Relexification: "Gay" in Latin America', in Stephen O. Murray (ed.), *Male Homosexuality in Central and South America*, San Francisco: Instituto Obregón; New York: GAU-NY, 1987, 129–91.

Newton-De Molina, David (ed.), *On Literary Intention: Critical Essays*, Edinburgh: Edinburgh UP, 1976.

The Oxford English Dictionary, vol. 8, Oxford: Clarendon, 1933. *Supplement*, ibidem, 1961.

A Supplement to the Oxford English Dictionary, vol. 3, Oxford: Clarendon, 1982.

Parker, Andrew & Eve Kosofsky Sedgwick (eds.), *Performativity and Performance*, New York-London: Routledge, 1995.

Partridge, Eric, 'Parlyaree: Cinderella among Languages', in *Here, There and Everywhere*, London: Hamish Hamilton, 1948, 116–25.

Perniola, Mario, *La società dei simulacri*, Bologna: Cappelli, 1983.

Podrini, Leone, *Materiale e immateriale. L'effimero nell'architettura contemporanea*, Rome: Maggioli, 1995.

Schor, Naomi & Elizabeth Weed (eds.), *Feminism Meets Queer Theory*, Bloomington: Indiana UP, 1997.

Sedgwick, Eve Kosofsky, 'Socratic Raptures, Socratic Ruptures: Notes Toward Queer Performativity', in Susan Gubar & Jonathan Kamholtz (eds.), *English Inside and Out: The Places of Literary Criticism*, New York-London: Routledge, 1993, 122–36.

——, *Tendencies*, London-New York: Routledge, 1994.

Sinfield, Alan, *Faultlines: Cultural Materialism and the Politics of Dissident Reading*, Oxford: Oxford UP, 1992.

Stein, Edward (ed.), *Forms of Desire: Sexual Orientation and the Social Constructionist Controversy*, New York: Garland, 1990.

Tyler, Carole-Anne, 'Passing: Narcissism, Identity, and Difference', *differences* 6: 2–3, Summer-Fall 1994, 212–48.

Virilio, Paul, *L'horizon négatif. Essai de dromoscopie*, Paris: Galilée, 1984.

SECTION I
TASTING IT

INTRODUCTION

The questioning urged by camp, along with the struggle to bring it to an articulable definition, converges on the major question mark of its phenomenological and historical origins. Lacking any evidence of its actual appearance in English, and of its nineteenth-century – and possibly earlier – circulation, a historical outline of camp as we know it may look at one and the same time at the early twentieth-century urban setting – in which camp referred to the slang of the underworld, of the demi-monde (theatricals, the fashion world and the show business), and of post-Wildean queerness – and its diffusion within the postwar pop 'euphoria' that established camp as part of the public discursive domain. As a *trivial*, street-linked and subcultural term, *camp* could break into print in the first half of the century only in those spaces whose location on the borders of culture made them 'appropriate' discursive spaces: i.e., in dictionaries of urban slang, and in a handful of creative works that either represented that very scene and its people, or were their representational outcome.

In order to have the first discussion of camp at some length we have in fact to skip to the mid-1950s and Isherwood's novel *The World in the Evening*; and this appearance marks indeed the beginning of the concurrent petition and unsettling (the *quest*-ioning) of binaries that the articulation of camp into a discursive 'possible' has fostered. But the antithesis of 'High Camp' and 'Low Camp' doesn't discriminate between two kinds of camp as deeply, intrinsically distinct, nor does Isherwood's sketch aim at a taxonomic understanding of the issue at stake. Rather, it enacts and exemplifies the seductive tactics that camp has retained, as a queer(ing) semiotic, for at least 100 years starting around 1860, and that the mainstreaming of the 1960s has not radically affected (it did affect the participants in the seduction role-play, not the dynamic itself). In his visit to Stephen, the Isherwoodian 'camera-like' narrator, Charles does not bring him to a knowledge of camp by explaining what it may mean, or by offering a definition. He *seduces* Stephen by bringing him, through a subtle courtship, into *another country* – a country which can't be reached by logical argument and description, or through a straight, rational path, but rather by way of an 'intuitive feeling' of its esoteric ('like Lao-tze's *Tao*') dimension.

The camp landscape Stephen is brought to is in fact outlined through the disposal of a plethora of incongruous 'objects', items borrowed from the galleries of High Culture and rearranged in an arabesque order, whose baroque dramatisation of 'elegance' draws the imaginary limits of an exclusive fancy-dress party in which the seriousness of High Culture is itself dressed (camped) up. The aristocraticism of the party to which Stephen, under a friend's presentation, makes his début when he starts performing camp (that is to say, when he starts deploying the inclusive/exclusive logic of the camp 'dressing-up') is signalled precisely by the snobbish abundance of the references, as in a collector's very private, 'hushed' showroom. And while this passage may well read as allusive to the post-Wildean, upper-class stereotype of homosexuality, it also severs itself from a deterministic linking of camp to the same-sex practices evoked within the limits of 'Low Camp', or rather gives the gender play of gay drag a 'philosophical' dimension. And it is precisely as a non-linear *movement* into an elitist space that camp finds its value as a critical term.

Within the short span of ten years, the showroom was no longer that hushed – it was on its way, in fact, to everybody's lips. By the time Sontag published 'Notes on 'Camp'', the word *camp* had already made its appearance within highly visible public spaces: in the pages of popular magazines such as *Life*, the *Spectator*, the *New Statesman*, and in literary magazines such as *Encounter*, the *Realist*, the *Second Coming* and the *Nation* (in two articles written by Sontag herself); and it 'camped' in the very title of a short story (a send-up of the James Bond spy fiction) by the British literary mandarin Cyril Connolly, published in a 1963 issue of *London Magazine*. And yet, Sontag was first in explicitly addressing the issue as a worthy intellectual object, one deserving the attention of cultural analysis; using what was still very much an esoteric term, what she introduced as a 'cult name', a 'private code' and a 'badge of identity', that could only be approached tentatively as that most elusive, inarticulable category, a 'sensibility or taste'. Isherwood emphasised camp as a twisted notion of elegance, thus giving an intellectual value to its queer expression of seriousness through artifice and exaggeration. Sontag's essay stated why critics, to evoke Isherwood's words, could *no longer* do without it.

While the passage from *The World in the Evening* seems to promote camp as a metahistorical aesthetical and psychological category (consistent with its enactment of camp as a mode of representation, irrespective of contexts and 'original' intentions), 'Notes on "Camp"' suggests a contextual specificity of the issue. It offers in fact a historical synopsis of the sensibility, tracing its origins to the eighteenth-century relish of artifice, and frames it as an 'unmistakably modern' taste, one speaking for the peculiar condition of postwar culture. Linking camp to the 'psychopathology of affluence', and to a diffusion within a wider social spectrum of the aristocratic pleasure of over-refinement, theatricalisation of experience and Being, and establishing it in syntony with the postwar crisis of the institutions of criticism, Sontag's piece aimed – through the notion of camp – at capturing the contemporary *Zeitgeist*. The very Sontagian conceptualisation as 'sensibility or taste' thus justifies its tentativeness as rooted at once in the unfathomable depths of (ineffable) 'human sensibility', and in the complex rendering of a whole epoch (the 'sensibility of an era'), according to the principles that Sontag calls forth by mentioning 'Huizinga on the late Middle Ages and Febvre on sixteenth-century France'.

The 'revolutionary' impact of the 1960s on the spheres of 'new' sexual and social plausibility was being echoed, in fact, by the challenge brought to the intellectual establishment by the pop phenomenology, and Sontag could well point out the camp emphasis on artifice and surfaces, on the appreciation of failed seriousness, of 'things-being-what-they-are-not' and of middle-class Kitsch, as a sign of the time (this clearly emerges in *Against Interpretation*, her 1966 collection of essays which are all, explicitly or indirectly, related to camp). Sontag construed camp, in fact, through a paradoxical combination of 'aristocratic' detachment and 'democratic' levelling of social (and cultural) hierarchies, with the dandification of the (wildely over-educated, we might say) masses producing 'the equivalence of all objects', and the transcending of the romantic disgust for the replica, be that the parodic repetition or the infinite technological reproducibility of an original which no longer holds its epistemic privileges. In other words, Sontag was depicting the new cultural scene of postwar culture as a camp landscape of *wild(e) indifference*: an indifference of original from derivative, of high from low culture, of subject from object; and an indifference to moral and political commitment, for camp required a detached vision making the degree of theatricality its only value parameter. And as such, the camp scenography of the 1960s looked very much like a queer stage, one that made its cipher out of what used to be eighteenth-century aristocratic refinement, nineteenth-century dandiacal self-dissipation in the textures of sartorial existence, and early twentieth-century upper-class effeminacy with its connotations of sexual exuberance from God-and Nature-sanctioned modes of existence.

Within weeks camp literally exploded as a mass media keyword, precisely because of its relevance to the contemporary cultural order, given the fashionable transgression, excitement and 'in' value of camp. And for such immediate adoption as a mass-marketable phenomenon, the issue withered within cultural criticism as swiftly as it had flowered – not the least because 'cultural theory' hadn't been articulating itself much, and understandably so, within those very institutions that it challenged. As early as 1974 Louis Rubin Jr. could easily affirm the sterility of Sontag's claims for anti-hermeneutic (surface-oriented) criticism in *Against Interpretation* by ironising on the virtual disappearance of her 'camp followers'. With the exception of gay criticism (cf. the next section), in order to find some other significant study we need to skip two more decades, when Mark Booth and Philip Core published their profusely illustrated monographs (in 1983 and 1984, respectively), which are in many ways – even beyond their acknowledging it – linked to Isherwood's and Sontag's writings.

If Philip Core adopted the encyclopaedic ordering of 'camp sites', in accordance with the collector's fascination for Isherwood's 'introduction', and of Sontag's canon of indifference, Mark Booth's volume attempts to bring some cognitive order to that landscape of debris not with the aid of an alphabetical device, but addressing that major question posited by 'Notes on "Camp"' – implicitly asking how useful a 'sensibility or taste' can be, as a *critical* term ('criticism', from the Greek *kríno*, being the faculty of judgement through distinctions) – that does not seem to differentiate among its possible referents. And yet, Booth offers an opposition paralleling in many respects Sontag's: he suggests the opposition between 'camp' and 'camp fads and fancies', which mitigates the intentionalist principle of naïve vs. deliberate by investing an apparently more coherent corpus of camp 'proper' (that is, the field of 'objects made by and for camp people') with the responsibility of activating an unknowingly, passive camp, one of those objects that 'although not intrinsically camp, appeal to camp people'. This would allow a tighter definition, for 'to be camp is to present oneself as being committed to the marginal with a commitment greater than the marginal merits'.

It comes as no surprise that both such opposition and definition are shaky enough, for they neither entirely get rid of the active/passive binarism, nor really discriminate among the close aesthetic and historical categories that Booth himself points out as areas of confusion that need to be clarified (witness the one between camp and Kitsch, which presupposes a 'Kitsch-man' whose taste goes for the unworthy, second-rate copy of an existing original art-experience, and thus falls into the field of such so 'defined' camp). And yet, they bring to the fore the odd relationship between camp and its close cousins Kitsch, pop and 'homosexuality', and especially with its historical 'antecedents'. In order to confer intelligibility to camp Sontag felt the urge to sketch a pocket historical account of its development, but in doing so she pointed out a series of figures as, at one and the same time, precursors and fully part of the camp aesthetic (from the Pre-Raphaelites to the French *précieux*), but which can't be traced to the naïve or deliberate camps – while Booth himself often wavers between labelling the antecedents as 'camp' and 'camp fads and fancies'. Sontag's sketch, along with the ones offered by Booth's volume and Core's introduction, thus solicits the question of how to historicise (to outline the development of) a phenomenon that works through the unsettling of allegedly stable historical categories (what Core points out by stating that camp is 'a form of historicism viewed histrionically'), just as it makes historical (or spatial) distance a defamiliarising, denaturalising condition for the necessary and paradoxical 'nostalgic' detachment inscribed in its activation.

The origins both Sontag and Booth identify in the remote past of seventeenth-and eighteenth-century theatricality can, in fact, be seen as in itself a retroactive effect of their performing camp as a theatricalised 'sensibility', 'taste', 'aesthetic' or 'mode of self-presentation', thus following the *à rebours*, 'against nature' path of self-recognition in the history of *paraître*, from the courtship ceremonial to the aristocratic and dandiacal ostentation of the *se campant* self. This very Section, and its positioning within the Reader, assumes in fact that camp theatricalises this very gesture of self-recognition; and that the discursive origins of camp *as we know it* may therefore be claimed to be, so to speak, *pop* ones, enacted precisely by the cultures producing the discursive conditions for the essays themselves. Any present conceptualisation of camp can't in fact dispense with its postwar popularisation, just as it can't dispense with its first stage of 'popularisation', that is to say, the early twentieth-century effect within popular consciousness of the Wilde trials, which through a mass media representation turned the posing, effeminate posturing of Oscar Wilde's queer body into a body of evidence, one that had in its very physiology the principle of its own degenerate sexual conduct. Which is like reminding us that, as the two decades intervening between Sontag's essay and Booth's and Core's volumes added their enterprise of historical reconstruction to this 'final chapter' devoted to the mingling with 'pop taste' announcing the crisis of camp's exclusiveness, these two mid-1980s volumes, with their 'coffee table', chic & cheap 'gift books' confection (Finch 1986) and mass-marketing appeal, were taking part in the very same process they were to some degree lamenting. These volumes were in fact offering themselves as handbooks which – in bringing the Isherwoodian seduction to the indistinct reading masses – could not, by enacting a 'pop performance', but *betray* the esoteric, elitist camp. And yet Sontag's, Booth and Core's writing, despite their problematic (because intentionality-bound and pop-oriented) *tasting* of the issue, present all the contradictions and issues that have haunted the critical enterprise in later years. Our possible criticism of that 'pop' betrayal can only be through (even if *against*) the very discursive categories of its failure.

I

FROM *THE WORLD IN THE EVENING*

Christopher Isherwood

When Charles Kennedy looked in to see me, which he did two or three times a week, it would usually be around six o'clock in the evening. The day after Bob's visit, he appeared, bringing with him a contraption which he called a monkey-bar. It was a kind of miniature trapeze hanging from a metal arm which was made to screw on to a bedstead. I could take hold of it and pull myself up in bed, whenever I'd slipped down too far.

'You know Bob was in to see me yesterday?' I asked, while he was installing it.

'Yes. He told me.' Charles spoke in his briefest staccato. He was standing at the back of the bed where I couldn't see his face, but I knew at once that something was wrong.

'As a matter of fact', I went on, 'I was expecting him to come again this morning. He promised to.'

Charles was silent.

'Is there any special reason', I persisted, 'why he didn't?'

Charles didn't answer at once. He shook the metal arm to make sure that it was firmly attached. Then he came around the bed and sat down on the end of it, facing me.

'It was probably my fault', he said. 'Bob and I had a big argument, last night. One of the biggest we ever had since we've been together.'

'What about?'

Reprinted from *The World in the Evening*, London: Methuen; New York: Random House, 1954.

'Well, it started about you.' Charles grinned at me painfully. He was obviously embarrassed. 'In fact, I suppose it was a rather ordinary kind of domestic jealousy scene. As far as I was concerned.'

'Jealousy? You surely don't mean that Bob——?'

'No – it wasn't quite as ordinary as that. But he came home and raved about you. How wonderful and sympathetic and understanding you were. Meaning that I wasn't.'

'But, Charles, that's ridiculous! If Bob does feel that about me, it's only because I'm a complete stranger. Strangers always seem to understand everything – until you get to know them.'

'That's exactly what I told him.' Charles smiled in a more relaxed manner. 'No offence to you, Stephen! I think you *are* an understanding person. And I think you might be very good for Bob. It was idiotic of me to get mad about it. Ordinarily, I wouldn't have. Only I happen to be under quite a bit of pressure, myself, right now.'

'Well, yes, I can imagine. With all your work.'

'It isn't the work that I mind. That's good for me. It keeps me from thinking. You see, the trouble is, Stephen, I don't really enjoy being a doctor. I'm not a bad one. As a matter of fact, I'm a lot better than average. I've got the talent for it, but no vocation. This isn't what I wanted to do in life.'

'What did you want?'

'I wanted to be a writer. Isn't that a laugh?'

'Why is it a laugh?'

'Because I can't write. Vocation but no talent.'

'Are you sure?'

'Absolutely sure. I found that out years ago. Oh, don't worry, I'm not about to ask you to read my stuff. There isn't any. It's all burned.'

'That's too bad.'

'Look, I'm not telling you this to get sympathy. I just want you to understand the situation. That's my personal problem, and ordinarily I can handle it. It's only when Bob needs help that I find I'm not on such firm ground myself. So then we're both in trouble. And when I can't help him and he turns to someone else, I get silly and jealous ... Bob's been going through a bad time lately. He told you all that, didn't he?'

'About being a conscientious objector?'

'That's only part of it. There's this whole thing of having been brought up as a Quaker. You see, Bob adored his Father and Mother. They do seem to have been pretty wonderful people, in their own way. When he was a kid, he believed everything they believed, on trust. Then they died, and he was put into a Friends' school, where the teachers weren't quite as wonderful as his parents; so he despised them for not being, the way teenagers do sometimes, and it all went sour on him.'

'He didn't tell me any of that.'

'No. I suppose he wouldn't. He hardly ever mentions his parents, because they're at the root of everything ... Anyhow, he decided that Quakerdom stank. And he's been trying to kid himself, ever since, that it never really meant anything to him. It's been working inside him all these years and now it's starting to act up. Just like with a lapsed Catholic ... The difficulty is, we get into a violent fight whenever we discuss this because he resents what he thinks is my attitude towards the Quakes. Actually, he'd resent *any* attitude I took toward them. He doesn't think I've got the right to have one.'

'You don't like them, do you, Charles?'

'That's what Bob thinks. He accuses me of sneering at them. But he's quite wrong. I respect them. And I admire them in a lot of ways. They don't sit nursing guilty consciences; they go right out and work their guilt off, helping people. They've got the courage of their convictions, and they mean exactly what they say, and they've found their own answers to everything without resorting to any trick theology. What I do hate about the Quakes, though, is their lack of style. They don't know how to do things with an air. They're hopelessly tacky. They've no notion of elegance.'

'But that's their great point, surely? They believe in plainness.'

'Plainness doesn't exclude elegance; it only makes it all the more necessary. Anyhow, "elegance" isn't quite what I mean ... In any of your voyages au bout de la nuit, did you ever run across the word "camp"?'

'I've heard people use it in bars. But I thought——'

'You thought it meant a swishy little boy with peroxided hair, dressed in a picture hat and a feather boa, pretending to be Marlene Dietrich? Yes, in queer circles, they call *that* camping. It's all very well in its place, but it's an utterly debased form——' Charles' eyes shone delightedly. He seemed to be in the best of spirits, now, and thoroughly enjoying this exposition. 'What I mean by camp is something much more fundamental. You can call the other Low Camp, if you like; then what I'm talking about is High Camp. High Camp is the whole emotional basis of the Ballet, for example, and of course of Baroque art. You see, true High Camp always has an underlying seriousness. You can't camp about something you don't take seriously. You're not making fun of it; you're making fun out of it. You're expressing what's basically serious to you in terms of fun and artifice and elegance. Baroque art is largely camp about religion. The Ballet is camp about love ... Do you see at all what I'm getting at?'

'I'm not sure. Give me some instances. What about Mozart?'

'Mozart's definitely a camp. Beethoven, on the other hand, isn't.'

'Is Flaubert?'

'God, no!'

'And neither is Rembrandt?'

'No. Definitely not.'

'But El Greco is?'

'Certainly.'

'And so is Dostoevsky?'

'Of course he is! In fact, he's the founder of the whole school of modern

Psycho-Camp which was later developed by Freud.' Charles had a sudden spasm of laughter. 'Splendid, Stephen! You've really gotten the idea.'

'I don't know if I have or not. It seems such an elastic expression.'

'Actually, it isn't at all. But I admit it's terribly hard to define. You have to meditate on it and feel it intuitively, like Lao-tze's *Tao*. Once you've done that, you'll find yourself wanting to use the word whenever you discuss aesthetics or philosophy or almost anything. I never can understand how critics manage to do without it.'

'I must say, I can hardly see how the Friends would apply it.' 'Naturally you can't. Neither can I. That's because Quaker Camp doesn't exist, yet. Some tremendous genius will have to arise and create it. Until that happens, it's as unimaginable as Rimbaud's prose poems would have been to Keats.'

2

NOTES ON 'CAMP'

Susan Sontag

Many things in the world have not been named; and many things, even if they have been named, have never been described. One of these is the sensibility – unmistakably modern, a variant of sophistication but hardly identical with it – that goes by the cult name of 'Camp'.

A sensibility (as distinct from an idea) is one of the hardest things to talk about; but there are special reasons why Camp, in particular, has never been discussed. It is not a natural mode of sensibility, if there be any such. Indeed, the essence of Camp is its love of the unnatural: of artifice and exaggeration. And Camp is esoteric – something of a private code, a badge of identity even, among small urban cliques. Apart from a lazy two-page sketch in Christopher Isherwood's novel *The World in the Evening* (1954), it has hardly broken into print. To talk about Camp is therefore to betray it. If the betrayal can be defended, it will be for the edification it provides, or the dignity of the conflict it resolves. For myself, I plead the goal of self-edification, and the goad of a sharp conflict in my own sensibility. I am strongly drawn to Camp, and almost as strongly offended by it. That is why I want to talk about it, and why I can. For no one who wholeheartedly shares in a given sensibility can analyze it; he can only, whatever his intention, exhibit it. To name a sensibility, to draw its contours and to recount its history, requires a deep sympathy modified by revulsion.

Though I am speaking about sensibility only – and about a sensibility that,

First published in *Partisan Review*, 31:4, Fall 1964, pp. 515–30.

among other things, converts the serious into the frivolous – these are grave matters. Most people think of sensibility or taste as the realm of purely subjective preferences, those mysterious attractions, mainly sensual, that have not been brought under the sovereignty of reason. They *allow* that considerations of taste play a part in their reactions to people and to works of art. But this attitude is naïve. And even worse. To patronize the faculty of taste is to patronize oneself. For taste governs every free – as opposed to rote – human response. Nothing is more decisive. There is taste in people, visual taste, taste in emotion – and there is taste in acts, taste in morality. Intelligence, as well, is really a kind of taste: taste in ideas. (One of the facts to be reckoned with is that taste tends to develop very unevenly. It's rare that the same person has good visual taste *and* good taste in people *and* taste in ideas.)

Taste has no system and no proofs. But there is something like a logic of taste: the consistent sensibility which underlies and gives rise to a certain taste. A sensibility is almost, but not quite, ineffable. Any sensibility which can be crammed into the mold of a system, or handled with the rough tools of proof, is no longer a sensibility at all. It has hardened into an idea ...

To snare a sensibility in words, especially one that is alive and powerful,[1] one must be tentative and nimble. The form of jottings, rather than an essay (with its claim to a linear, consecutive argument), seemed more appropriate for getting down something of this particular fugitive sensibility. It's embarrassing to be solemn and treatise-like about Camp. One runs the risk of having, oneself, produced a very inferior piece of Camp.

These notes are for Oscar Wilde.

> One should either be a work of art, or wear a work of art.
> – *Phrases and Philosophies for the Use of the Young*

1. To start very generally: Camp is a certain mode of aestheticism. It is one way of seeing the world as an aesthetic phenomenon. That way, the way of Camp, is not in terms of beauty but in terms of the degree of artifice, of stylization.
2. To emphasize style is to slight content, or to introduce an attitude which is neutral with respect to content. It goes without saying that the Camp sensibility is disengaged, depoliticized – or at least apolitical.
3. Not only is there a Camp vision, a Camp way of looking at things. Camp is as well a quality discoverable in objects and the behavior of persons. There are 'campy' movies, clothes, furniture, popular songs, novels, people, buildings ... This distinction is important. True, the Camp eye has the power to transform experience. But not everything can be seen as Camp. It's not *all* in the eye of the beholder.
4. Random examples of items which are part of the canon of Camp:
   Zuleika Dobson
   Tiffany lamps
   Scopitone films

The Brown Derby restaurant on Sunset Boulevard in L.A.
The Enquirer, headlines and stories
Aubrey Beardsley drawings
Swan Lake
Bellini's operas
Visconti's direction of *Salome* and *'Tis Pity She's a Whore*
certain turn-of-the-century picture postcards
Schoedsack's *King Kong*
the Cuban pop singer La Lupe
Lynn Ward's novel in woodcuts, *God's Man*
the old Flash Gordon comics
women's clothes of the 1920s (feather boas, fringed and beaded dresses,
   etc.)
the novels of Ronald Firbank and Ivy Compton-Burnett
stag movies seen without lust

5. Camp taste has an affinity for certain arts rather than others. Clothes, furniture, all the elements of visual decor, for instance, make up a large part of Camp. For Camp art is often decorative art, emphasizing texture, sensuous surface, and style at the expense of content. Concert music, though, because it is contentless, is rarely Camp. It offers no opportunity, say, for a contrast between silly or extravagant content and rich form ... Sometimes whole art forms become saturated with Camp. Classical ballet, opera, movies have seemed so for a long time. In the last two years, popular music (post rock-'n'-roll, what the French call yé-yé) has been annexed. And movie criticism (like lists of 'The 10 Best Bad Movies I Have Seen') is probably the greatest popularizer of Camp taste today, because most people still go to the movies in a high-spirited and unpretentious way.

6. There is a sense in which it is correct to say 'It's too good to be Camp'. Or 'too important', not marginal enough. (More on this later.) Thus, the personality and many of the works of Jean Cocteau are Camp, but not those of André Gide; the operas of Richard Strauss, but not those of Wagner; concoctions of Tin Pan Alley and Liverpool, but not jazz. Many examples of Camp are things which, from a 'serious' point of view, are either bad art or kitsch. Not all, though. Not only is Camp not necessarily bad art, but some art which can be approached as Camp (example: the major films of Louis Feuillade) merits the most serious admiration and study.

> The more we study Art, the less we care for Nature.
> – *The Decay of Lying*

7. All Camp objects, and persons, contain a large element of artifice. Nothing in nature can be campy ... Rural Camp is still man-made, and most campy objects are urban. (Yet they offen have a serenity – or a naïveté – which is the equivalent of pastoral. A great deal of Camp suggests Empson's phrase, 'urban pastoral'.)

8. Camp is a vision of the world in terms of style – but a particular kind of style. It is the love of the exaggerated, the 'off', of things-being-what-they-are-not. The best example is in Art Nouveau, the most typical and fully developed Camp style. Art Nouveau objects, typically, convert one thing into something else: the lighting fixtures in the form of flowering plants, the living room which is really a grotto. A remarkable example: the Paris Metro entrances designed by Hector Guimard in the late 1890s in the shape of cast-iron orchid stalks.

9. As a taste in persons, Camp responds particularly to the markedly attenuated and to the strongly exaggerated. The androgyne is certainly one of the great images of Camp sensibility. Examples: the swooning, slim, sinuous figures of pre-Raphaelite painting and poetry; the thin, flowing, sexless bodies in Art Nouveau prints and posters, presented in relief on lamps and ashtrays; the haunting androgynous vacancy behind the perfect beauty of Greta Garbo. Here Camp taste draws on a mostly unacknowledged truth of taste: the most refined form of sexual attractiveness (as well as the most refined form of sexual pleasure) consists in going against the grain of one's sex. What is most beautiful in virile men is something feminine; what is most beautiful in feminine women is something masculine ... Allied to the Camp taste for the androgynous is something that seems quite different but isn't: a relish for the exaggeration of sexual characteristics and personality mannerisms. For obvious reasons, the best examples that can be cited are movie stars. The corny flamboyant femaleness of Jayne Mansfield, Gina Lollobrigida, Jane Russell, Virginia Mayo; the exaggerated he-manness of Steve Reeves, Victor Mature. The great stylists of temperament and mannerism, like Bette Davis, Barbara Stanwyck, Tallulah Bankhead, Edwige Feuillère.

10. Camp sees everything in quotation marks. It's not a lamp, but a 'lamp'; not a woman, but a 'woman'. To perceive Camp in objects and persons is to understand Being-as-Playing-a-Role. It is the farthest extension, in sensibility, of the metaphor of life as theater.

11. Camp is the triumph of the epicene style. (The convertibility of 'man' and 'woman', 'person' and 'thing'.) But all style, that is, artifice, is, ultimately, epicene. Life is not stylish. Neither is nature.

12. The question isn't 'Why travesty, impersonation, theatricality?' The question is, rather, 'When does travesty, impersonation, theatricality acquire the special flavor of Camp?' Why is the atmosphere of Shakespeare's comedies (*As You Like It,* etc.) not epicene, while that of *Der Rosenkavalier* is?

13. The dividing line seems to fall in the eighteenth century; there the origins of Camp taste are to be found (Gothic novels, Chinoiserie, caricature, artificial ruins, and so forth). But the relation to nature was quite different then. In the eighteenth century, people of taste either patronized nature (Strawberry Hill) or attempted to remake it into something artificial

(Versailles). They also indefatigably patronized the past. Today's Camp taste effaces nature, or else contradicts it outright. And the relation of Camp taste to the past is extremely sentimental.

14. A pocket history of Camp might, of course, begin farther back – with the mannerist artists like Pontormo, Rosso, and Caravaggio, or the extraordinarily theatrical painting of Georges de La Tour, or euphuism (Lyly, etc.) in literature. Still, the soundest starting point seems to be the late seventeenth and early eighteenth century, because of that period's extraordinary feeling for artifice, for surface, for symmetry; its taste for the picturesque and the thrilling, its elegant conventions for representing instant feeling and the total presence of character – the epigram and the rhymed couplet (in words), the flourish (in gesture and in music). The late seventeenth and early eighteenth century is the great period of Camp: Pope, Congreve, Walpole, but not Swift; *les précieux* in France; the rococo churches of Munich; Pergolesi. Somewhat later: much of Mozart. But in the nineteenth century, what had been distributed throughout all of high culture now becomes a special taste; it takes on overtones of the acute, the esoteric, the perverse. Confining the story to England alone, we see Camp continuing wanly through nineteenth-century aestheticism (Burne-Jones, Pater, Ruskin, Tennyson), emerging full-blown with the Art Nouveau movement in the visual and decorative arts, and finding its conscious ideologists in such 'wits' as Wilde and Firbank.

15. Of course, to say all these things are Camp is not to argue they are simply that. A full analysis of Art Nouveau, for instance, would scarcely equate it with Camp. But such an analysis cannot ignore what in Art Nouveau allows it to be experienced as Camp. Art Nouveau is full of 'content', even of a political-moral sort; it was a revolutionary movement in the arts, spurred on by a utopian vision (somewhere between William Morris and the Bauhaus group) of an organic politics and taste. Yet there is also a feature of the Art Nouveau objects which suggests a disengaged, unserious, 'aesthete's' vision. This tells us something important about Art Nouveau – and about what the lens of Camp, which blocks out content, is.

16. Thus, the Camp sensibility is one that is alive to a double sense in which some things can be taken. But this is not the familiar split-level construction of a literal meaning, on the one hand, and a symbolic meaning, on the other. It is the difference, rather, between the thing as meaning something, anything, and the thing as pure artifice.

17. This comes out clearly in the vulgar use of the word Camp as a verb, 'to camp', something that people do. To camp is a mode of seduction – one which employs flamboyant mannerisms susceptible of a double interpretation; gestures full of duplicity, with a witty meaning for cognoscenti and another, more impersonal, for outsiders. Equally and by extension, when the word becomes a noun, when a person or a thing is 'a camp', a

duplicity is involved. Behind the 'straight' public sense in which something can be taken, one has found a private zany experience of the thing.

> To be natural is such a very difficult pose to keep up.
> – *An Ideal Husband*

18. One must distinguish between naïve and deliberate Camp. Pure Camp is always naïve. Camp which knows itself to be Camp ('camping') is usually less satisfying.

19. The pure examples of Camp are unintentional; they are dead serious. The Art Nouveau craftsman who makes a lamp with a snake coiled around it is not kidding, nor is he trying to be charming. He is saying, in all earnestness: Voilà! the Orient! Genuine Camp – for instance, the numbers devised for the Warner Brothers musicals of the early 1930s (*42nd Street*; *The Golddiggers of 1933*; . . . *of 1935*; . . . *of 1937*; etc.) by Busby Berkeley – does not *mean* to be funny. Camping – say, the plays of Noël Coward – does. It seems unlikely that much of the traditional opera repertoire could be such satisfying Camp if the melodramatic absurdities of most opera plots had not been taken seriously by their composers. One doesn't need to know the artist's private intentions. The work tells all. (Compare a typical nineteenth-century opera with Samuel Barber's *Vanessa*, a piece of manufactured, calculated Camp, and the difference is clear.)

20. Probably, intending to be campy is always harmful. The perfection of *Trouble in Paradise* and *The Maltese Falcon,* among the greatest Camp movies ever made, comes from the effortless smooth way in which tone is maintained. This is not so with such famous would-be Camp films of the 1950s as *All About Eve* and *Beat the Devil*. These more recent movies have their fine moments, but the first is so slick and the second so hysterical; they want so badly to be campy that they're continually losing the beat . . . Perhaps, though, it is not so much a question of the unintended effect versus the conscious intention, as of the delicate relation between parody and self-parody in Camp. The films of Hitchcock are a showcase for this problem. When self-parody lacks ebullience but instead reveals (even sporadically) a contempt for one's themes and one's materials – as in *To Catch a Thief, Rear Window, North by Northwest* – the results are forced and heavy-handed, rarely Camp. Successful Camp – a movie like Carné's *Drôle de Drame*; the film performances of Mae West and Edward Everett Horton; portions of the Goon Show – even when it reveals self-parody, reeks of self-love.

21. So, again, Camp rests on innocence. That means Camp discloses innocence, but also, when it can, corrupts it. Objects, being objects, don't change when they are singled out by the Camp vision. Persons, however, respond to their audiences. Persons begin 'camping': Mae West, Bea Lillie, La Lupe, Tallulah Bankhead in *Lifeboat*, Bette Davis in *All About Eve*. (Persons can even be induced to camp without their knowing it. Consider the way Fellini got Anita Ekberg to parody herself in *La Dolce Vita*.)

22. Considered a little less strictly, Camp is either completely naïve or else wholly conscious (when one plays at being campy). An example of the latter: Wilde's epigrams themselves.

> It's absurd to divide people into good and bad. People are either charming or tedious.
> – *Lady Windermere's Fan*

23. In naïve, or pure, Camp, the essential element is seriousness, a seriousness that fails. Of course, not all seriousness that fails can be redeemed as Camp. Only that which has the proper mixture of the exaggerated, the fantastic, the passionate, and the naïve.

24. When something is just bad (rather than Camp), it's often because it is too mediocre in its ambition. The artist hasn't attempted to do anything really outlandish. ('It's too much', 'It's too fantastic', 'It's not to be believed', are standard phrases of Camp enthusiasm.)

25. The hallmark of Camp is the spirit of extravagance. Camp is a woman walking around in a dress made of three million feathers. Camp is the paintings of Carlo Crivelli, with their real jewels and *trompe-l'oeil* insects and cracks in the masonry. Camp is the outrageous aestheticism of Sternberg's six American movies with Dietrich, all six, but especially the last, *The Devil Is a Woman* . . . In Camp there is often something *démesuré* in the quality of the ambition, not only in the style of the work itself. Gaudí's lurid and beautiful buildings in Barcelona are Camp not only because of their style but because they reveal – most notably in the Cathedral of the Sagrada Familia – the ambition on the part of one man to do what it takes a generation, a whole culture to accomplish.

26. Camp is art that proposes itself seriously, but cannot be taken altogether seriously because it is 'too much'. *Titus Andronicus* and *Strange Interlude* are almost Camp, or could be played as Camp. The public manner and rhetoric of de Gaulle, often, are pure Camp.

27. A work can come close to Camp but not make it because it succeeds. Eisenstein's films are seldom Camp because, despite all exaggeration, they do succeed (dramatically) without surplus. If they were a little more 'off', they could be great Camp – particularly *Ivan the Terrible I* and *II*. The same for Blake's drawings and paintings, weird and mannered as they are. They aren't Camp; though Art Nouveau, influenced by Blake, is.

What is extravagant in an inconsistent or an unpassionate way is not Camp. Neither can anything be Camp that does not seem to spring from an irrepressible, a virtually uncontrolled sensibility. Without passion, one gets pseudo-Camp – what is merely decorative, safe, in a word, chic. On the barren edge of Camp lie a number of attractive things: the sleek fantasies of Dali, the haute-couture preciosity of Albicocco's *The Girl with the Golden Eyes*. But the two things – Camp and preciosity – must not be confused.

28. Again, Camp is the attempt to do something extraordinary. But extra-ordinary in the sense, often, of being special, glamorous. (The curved line, the extravagant gesture.) Not extraordinary merely in the sense of effort. Ripley's Believe-It-Or-Not items are rarely campy. These items, either natural oddities (the two-headed rooster, the eggplant in the shape of a cross) or else the products of immense labor (the man who walked from here to China on his hands, the woman who engraved the New Testament on the head of a pin), lack the visual reward – the glamor, the theatricality – that marks off certain extravagances as Camp.

29. The reason a movie like *On the Beach,* books like *Winesburg, Ohio* and *For Whom the Bell Tolls* are bad to the point of being laughable, but not bad to the point of being enjoyable, is that they are too dogged and pretentious. They lack fantasy. There is Camp in such bad movies as *The Prodigal* and *Samson and Delilah,* the series of Italian color spectacles featuring the super-hero Maciste, numerous Japanese science-fiction films (*Rodan, The Mysterians, The H-Man*), because, in their relative unpretentiousness and vulgarity, they are more extreme and irresponsible in their fantasy – and therefore touching and quite enjoyable.

30. Of course, the canon of Camp can change. Time has a great deal to do with it. Time may enhance what seems simply dogged or lacking in fantasy now because we are too close to it, because it resembles too closely our own everyday fantasies, the fantastic nature of which we don't perceive. We are better able to enjoy a fantasy as fantasy when it is not our own.

31. This is why so many of the objects prized by Camp taste are old-fashioned, out-of-date, *démodé*. It's not a love of the old as such. It's simply that the process of aging or deterioration provides the necessary detachment – or arouses a necessary sympathy. When the theme is important, and con-temporary, the failure of a work of art may make us indignant. Time can change that. Time liberates the work of art from moral relevance, delivering it over to the Camp sensibility ... Another effect: time contracts the sphere of banality. (Banality is, strictly speaking, always a category of the con-temporary.) What was banal can, with the passage of time, become fan-tastic. Many people who listen with delight to the style of Rudy Vallee revived by the English pop group The Temperance Seven would have been driven up the wall by Rudy Vallee in his heyday.

Thus, things are campy, not when they become old – but when we become less involved in them, and can enjoy, instead of be frustrated by, the failure of the attempt. But the effect of time is unpredictable. Maybe Method Acting (James Dean, Rod Steiger, Warren Beatty) will seem as Camp someday as Ruby Keeler's does now – or as Sarah Bernhardt's does, in the films she made at the end of her career. And maybe not.

32. Camp is the glorification of 'character'. The statement is of no importance – except, of course, to the person (Loie Fuller, Gaudí, Cecil B. De Mille, Crivelli, de Gaulle, etc.) who makes it. What the Camp eye appreciates is

the unity, the force of the person. In every move the aging Martha Graham makes she's being Martha Graham, etc., etc. . . . This is clear in the case of the great serious idol of Camp taste, Greta Garbo. Garbo's incompetence (at the least, lack of depth) as an *actress* enhances her beauty. She's always herself.

33. What Camp taste responds to is 'instant character' (this is, of course, very eighteenth century); and, conversely, what it is not stirred by is the sense of the development of character. Character is understood as a state of continual incandescence – a person being one, very intense thing. This attitude toward character is a key element of the theatricalization of experience embodied in the Camp sensibility. And it helps account for the fact that opera and ballet are experienced as such rich treasures of Camp, for neither of these forms can easily do justice to the complexity of human nature. Wherever there is development of character, Camp is reduced. Among operas, for example, *La Traviata* (which has some small development of character) is less campy than *Il Trovatore* (which has none).

> Life is too important a thing ever to talk seriously about it.
> – *Vera, or The Nihilists*

34. Camp taste turns its back on the good–bad axis of ordinary aesthetic judgment. Camp doesn't reverse things. It doesn't argue that the good is bad, or the bad is good. What it does is to offer for art (and life) a different – a supplementary – set of standards.

35. Ordinarily we value a work of art because of the seriousness and dignity of what it achieves. We value it because it succeeds – in being what it is and, presumably, in fulfilling the intention that lies behind it. We assume a proper, that is to say, straightforward relation between intention and performance. By such standards, we appraise *The Iliad*, Aristophanes's plays, The Art of the Fugue, *Middlemarch*, the paintings of Rembrandt, Chartres, the poetry of Donne, *The Divine Comedy*, Beethoven's quartets, and – among people – Socrates, Jesus, St. Francis, Napoleon, Savonarola. In short, the pantheon of high culture: truth, beauty, and seriousness.

36. But there are other creative sensibilities besides the seriousness (both tragic and comic) of high culture and of the high style of evaluating people. And one cheats oneself as a human being, if one has *respect* only for the style of high culture, whatever else one may do or feel on the sly.

For instance, there is the kind of seriousness whose trademark is anguish, cruelty, derangement. Here we do accept a disparity between intention and result. I am speaking, obviously, of style of personal existence as well as of a style in art; but the examples had best come from art. Think of Bosch, Sade, Rimbaud, Jarry, Kafka, Artaud, think of most of the important works of art of the twentieth century, that is, art whose goal is not that of creating harmonies but of overstraining the medium and introducing more and more violent, and unresolvable, subject matter.

This sensibility also insists on the principle that an *oeuvre* in the old sense (again, in art, but also in life) is not possible. Only 'fragments' are possible ... Clearly, different standards apply here than to traditional high culture. Something is good not because it is achieved but because another kind of truth about the human situation, another experience of what it is to be human – in short, another valid sensibility – is being revealed.

And third among the great creative sensibilities is Camp: the sensibility of failed seriousness, of the theatricalization of experience. Camp refuses both the harmonies of traditional seriousness and the risks of fully identifying with extreme states of feeling.

37. The first sensibility, that of high culture, is basically moralistic. The second sensibility, that of extreme states of feeling, represented in much contemporary 'avant-garde' art, gains power by a tension between moral and aesthetic passion. The third, Camp, is wholly aesthetic.

38. Camp is the consistently aesthetic experience of the world. It incarnates a victory of 'style' over 'content', 'aesthetics' over 'morality', of irony over tragedy.

39. Camp and tragedy are antitheses. There is seriousness in Camp (seriousness in the degree of the artist's involvement) and, often, pathos. The excruciating is also one of the tonalities of Camp; it is the quality of excruciation in much of Henry James (for instance, *The Europeans*, *The Awkward Age*, *The Wings of the Dove*) that is responsible for the large element of Camp in his writings. But there is never, never tragedy.

40. Style is everything. Genet's ideas, for instance, are very Camp. Genet's statement that 'the only criterion of an act is its elegance'[2] is virtually interchangeable, as a statement, with Wilde's 'in matters of great importance, the vital element is not sincerity, but style'. But what counts, finally, is the style in which ideas are held. The ideas about morality and politics in, say, *Lady Windermere's Fan* and *Major Barbara* are Camp, but not just because of the nature of the ideas themselves. It is those ideas, held in a special playful way. The Camp ideas in *Our Lady of the Flowers* are maintained too grimly, and the writing itself is too successfully elevated and serious, for Genet's books to be Camp.

41. The whole point of Camp is to dethrone the serious. Camp is playful, anti-serious. More precisely, Camp involves a new, more complex relation to 'the serious'. One can be serious about the frivolous, frivolous about the serious.

42. One is drawn to Camp when one realizes that 'sincerity' is not enough. Sincerity can be simple philistinism, intellectual narrowness.

43. The traditional means for going beyond straight seriousness – irony, satire – seem feeble today, inadequate to the culturally oversaturated medium in which contemporary sensibility is schooled. Camp introduces a new standard: artifice as an ideal, theatricality.

44. Camp proposes a comic vision of the world. But not a bitter or polemical comedy. If tragedy is an experience of hyper-involvement, comedy is an experience of under-involvement, of detachment.

> I adore simple pleasures, they are the last refuge of the complex.
> – *A Woman of No Importance*

45. Detachment is the prerogative of an elite; and as the dandy is the nineteenth century's surrogate for the aristocrat in matters of culture, so Camp is the modern dandyism. Camp is the answer to the problem: how to be a dandy in the age of mass culture.

46. The dandy was overbred. His posture was disdain, or else ennui. He sought rare sensations, undefiled by mass appreciation. (Models: Des Esseintes in Huysmans's *A Rebours, Marius the Epicurean*, Valéry's *Monsieur Teste*.) He was dedicated to 'good taste'.

    The connoisseur of Camp has found more ingenious pleasures. Not in Latin poetry and rare wines and velvet jackets, but in the coarsest, commonest pleasures, in the arts of the masses. Mere use does not defile the objects of his pleasure, since he learns to possess them in a rare way. Camp – Dandyism in the age of mass culture – makes no distinction between the unique object and the mass-produced object. Camp taste transcends the nausea of the replica.

47. Wilde himself is a transitional figure. The man who, when he first came to London, sported a velvet beret, lace shirts, velveteen knee breeches and black silk-stockings could never depart too far in his life from the pleasures of the old-style dandy; this conservatism is reflected in *The Picture of Dorian Gray*. But many of his attitudes suggest something more modern. It was Wilde who formulated an important element of the Camp sensibility – the equivalence of all objects – when he announced his intention of 'living up' to his blue-and-white china, or declared that a doorknob could be as admirable as a painting. When he proclaimed the importance of the necktie, the boutonniere, the chair, Wilde was anticipating the democratic *esprit* of Camp.

48. The old-style dandy hated vulgarity. The new-style dandy, the lover of Camp, appreciates vulgarity. Where the dandy would be continually offended or bored, the connoisseur of Camp is continually amused, delighted. The dandy held a perfumed handkerchief to his nostrils and was liable to swoon; the connoisseur of Camp sniffs the stink and prides himself on his strong nerves.

49. It is a feat, of course. A feat goaded on, in the last analysis, by the threat of boredom. The relation between boredom and Camp taste cannot be overestimated. Camp taste is by its nature possible only in affluent societies, in societies or circles capable of experiencing the psychopathology of affluence.

> What is abnormal in Life stands in normal relations to Art. It is the only
> thing in Life that stands in normal relations to Art.
> – *A Few Maxims for the Instruction of the Over-Educated*

50. Aristocracy is a position vis-à-vis culture (as well as vis-à-vis power), and
the history of Camp taste is part of the history of snob taste. But since no
authentic aristocrats in the old sense exist today to sponsor special tastes,
who is the bearer of this taste? Answer: an improvised self-elected class,
mainly homosexuals, who constitute themselves as aristocrats of taste.

51. The peculiar relation between Camp taste and homosexuality has to be
explained. While it's not true that Camp taste *is* homosexual taste, there is
no doubt a peculiar affinity and overlap. Not all liberals are Jews, but Jews
have shown a peculiar affinity for liberal and reformist causes. So, not all
homosexuals have Camp taste. But homosexuals, by and large, constitute
the vanguard – and the most articulate audience – of Camp. (The analogy
is not frivolously chosen. Jews and homosexuals are the outstanding
creative minorities in contemporary urban culture. Creative, that is, in
the truest sense: they are creators of sensibilities. The two pioneering
forces of modern sensibility are Jewish moral seriousness and homosexual
aestheticism and irony.)

52. The reason for the flourishing of the aristocratic posture among homosexuals also seems to parallel the Jewish case. For every sensibility is self-
serving to the group that promotes it. Jewish liberalism is a gesture of self-
legitimization. So is Camp taste, which definitely has something propagandistic about it. Needless to say, the propaganda operates in exactly the
opposite direction. The Jews pinned their hopes for integrating into
modern society on promoting the moral sense. Homosexuals have pinned
their integration into society on promoting the aesthetic sense. Camp is a
solvent of morality. It neutralizes moral indignation, sponsors playfulness.

53. Nevertheless, even though homosexuals have been its vanguard, Camp
taste is much more than homosexual taste. Obviously, its metaphor of life
as theater is peculiarly suited as a justification and projection of a certain
aspect of the situation of homosexuals. (The Camp insistence on not being
'serious', on playing, also connects with the homosexual's desire to remain
youthful.) Yet one feels that if homosexuals hadn't more or less invented
Camp, someone else would. For the aristocratic posture with relation to
culture cannot die, though it may persist only in increasingly arbitrary and
ingenious ways. Camp is (to repeat) the relation to style in a time in which
the adoption of style – as such – has become altogether questionable. (In
the modern era, each new style, unless frankly anachronistic, has come on
the scene as an anti-style.)

> One must have a heart of stone to read the death of Little Nell without
> laughing.
> – *(In conversation)*

54. The experiences of Camp are based on the great discovery that the sensibility of high culture has no monopoly upon refinement. Camp asserts that good taste is not simply good taste; that there exists, indeed, a good taste of bad taste. (Genet talks about this in *Our Lady of the Flowers*.) The discovery of the good taste of bad taste can be very liberating. The man who insists on high and serious pleasures is depriving himself of pleasure; he continually restricts what he can enjoy; in the constant exercise of his good taste he will eventually price himself out of the market, so to speak. Here Camp taste supervenes upon good taste as a daring and witty hedonism. It makes the man of good taste cheerful, where before he ran the risk of being chronically frustrated. It is good for the digestion.

55. Camp taste is, above all, a mode of enjoyment, of appreciation – not judgment. Camp is generous. It wants to enjoy. It only seems like malice, cynicism. (Or, if it is cynicism, it's not a ruthless but a sweet cynicism.) Camp taste doesn't propose that it is in bad taste to be serious; it doesn't sneer at someone who succeeds in being seriously dramatic. What it does is to find the success in certain passionate failures.

56. Camp taste is a kind of love, love for human nature. It relishes, rather than judges, the little triumphs and awkward intensities of 'character' . . . Camp taste identifies with what it is enjoying. People who share this sensibility are not laughing at the thing they label as 'a camp', they're enjoying it. Camp is a tender feeling.

    (Here one may compare Camp with much of Pop Art, which – when it is not just Camp – embodies an attitude that is related, but still very different. Pop Art is more flat and more dry, more serious, more detached, ultimately nihilistic.)

57. Camp taste nourishes itself on the love that has gone into certain objects and personal styles. The absence of this love is the reason why such kitsch items as *Peyton Place* (the book) and the Tishman Building aren't Camp.

58. The ultimate Camp statement: it's good because it's awful . . . Of course, one can't always say that. Only under certain conditions, those which I've tried to sketch in these notes.

NOTES

1. The sensibility of an era is not only its most decisive but also its most perishable aspect. One may capture the ideas (intellectual history) and the behavior (social history) of an epoch without ever touching upon the sensibility or taste which informed those ideas, that behavior. Rare are those historical studies – like Huizinga on the late Middle Ages, Febvre on sixteenth-century France – which do tell us something about the sensibility of the period.

2. Sartre's gloss on this in *Saint Genet* is: 'Elegance is the quality of conduct which transforms the greatest amount of being into appearing'.

3

CAMPE-TOI!
ON THE ORIGINS AND
DEFINITIONS OF CAMP

Mark Booth

PREVIOUS VIEWS AND DEFINITIONS

The key to defining camp lies in reconciling its essential marginality with its evident ubiquity, in acknowledging its diversity while still making sense of it.

Recent attempts to define it were sparked off by Christopher Isherwood's discussion of the subject in his novel, *The World in the Evening* (1954). The story concerns the soul-searchings and sexual self-discoveries of a young Englishman in various glamorous locales. One of his self-discoveries is his awakening homosexuality; Isherwood obliquely refers us to the image of a butterfly breaking out of a chrysalis. Tied to this awakening is his realisation of the importance of elegance, or rather, not quite elegance, but camp, which is defined as a matter of 'expressing what's basically serious to you in terms of fun and artifice and elegance' of 'making fun out of' what you take seriously as opposed to making fun of it. Clearly, this is not a definition in the strict sense of the word, its function being suggestive rather than limiting. We may contrive to make our married lives or our office lives fun and/or elegant, but to do this might well be wholesome and even sensible – qualities that are inimical to camp.

His examples may also make us uneasy. To call Mozart camp smacks of impertinence; the Baroque, another candidate, was the militantly optimistic art of the Counter Reformation, designed to overwhelm the spectator with awe for the Catholic Church; it was a mainstream movement of great seriousness even

Reprinted from *Camp*, London-New York: Quartet, 1983.

though bits of it may look silly to (some) modern eyes. Perhaps we should pay Isherwood the compliment of believing that when he says that Mozart and the Baroque are camp, he does not mean what he says. What he may mean is that they may be enjoyed (by some people) in a camp way.

The World in the Evening never quite puts its finger on camp. Isherwood is pursued over page after page by the ghost of a good idea, but such is his facility that he manages to evade it.

The next significant examination of the topic, an essay called 'Notes on Camp' (1964) by Susan Sontag, suffers from the same kind of confusion. Like Isherwood, Sontag does not hazard a strict definition, but she does go further by positing a series of criteria. Thus camp, according to Sontag, is a way of seeing things as good because they are bad, particularly when: 1) they are marginal; 2) they are artificial or exaggerated; 3) they are *démodé*; 4) they emphasise style at the expense of content; 5) they are objects of the kind prized by daring and witty hedonists, and by 'the Dandies of Mass Culture'.

Sontag is feeling her way around largely unknown territory and, undoubtedly, she bumps up against some interesting points. However, looked at as a whole, the essay presents several difficulties.

It would, perhaps, be churlish to expect anything with a title as modest and downbeat as 'Notes on Camp' to be systematic; clearly the vast amount of research Sontag has done on camp has taught her its characteristic technique of forestalling criticisms (*Qui s'accuse, s'excuse*). Nevertheless, she should at least be consistent. Camp is 'unserious', but the rhetoric of General de Gaulle is camp. Wagner and Gide are not camp because they are 'not marginal enough', yet Pope, Congreve, poor old Mozart, Ruskin, Tennyson, Wilde, Burne-Jones and Sarah Bernhardt are all camp. What is 'extravagant in an inconsistent or unpassionate way' is not camp, yet les *précieux* in France, and Wilde, are mentioned as having been so. 'Who wants to be consistent?' said Wilde 'The dullard and the doctrinaire, the tedious people who carry out their principles to the bitter end of action, the *reductio ad absurdum*. Not I'. Nor Sontag.

The attempt to make sense of 'Notes on Camp', to find its unifying principle, is hindered by its style, and, more particularly, by Sontag's little epigrams, some of which are of an almost oriental inscrutability: 'To name a sensibility, to draw the contours of it, to recount its history, requires a deep sympathy modified by revulsion'.

Her choice of examples needs close attention too. She mentions Des Esseintes in Huysmans's *Là-Bas*. Unfortunately Des Esseintes figures in *À Rebours*, not *Là-Bas*. The dandy-like character in Pater's *Marius the Epicurean* is not Marius himself, but Flavius. [These and other inaccuracies occur in the original 1964 publication of Sontag's essay, but were corrected in the 1966 reprint within the *Against Interpretation* collection – *Editor's note*.] 'The ideas about morality and politics in *Major Barbara* are camp' she adds impressively. How extraordinary to find Shaw dubbed camp – Shaw, who was a sort of sanitised Nietzsche, a Nietzsche-for-all-the-family.

However, the seriously worrying thing about the examples in 'Notes on Camp' is not their intermittent inappropriateness or factual inaccuracy, but their sheer number. A definition of camp that includes Tennyson, the Goon Show, Dali, de Gaulle and children's cartoons is obviously casting the net too wide. In fact, Sontag has difficulty in finding examples of things that, according to her criteria, are not camp; she very properly mentions Jesus, then Napoleon, and Aristophanes's plays (a borderline case perhaps) and Beethoven's quartets (but not apparently the orchestral music?).

The difficulty in this definition is the same as that in Isherwood's; it might be more helpful to say of Tennyson and of children's cartoons not that they are camp, but that they have qualities that invite the patronage of camp people. This would help us to avoid talking as if camp somehow blended into Tennyson or whatever, when camp people began to appreciate them. Camp people and camp objects (that is to say objects made by and for camp people) might then usefully be distinguished from people and objects, which, although not intrinsically camp, appeal to camp people – we might call them camp fads and fancies. This distinction allows a much tighter definition of camp.

Taking examples first from 'Notes on Camp', and then our own, we might illustrate this distinction with two small charts:

A

Camp	Camp fads and fancies
Oscar Wilde, Ronald Firbank	Alfred, Lord Tennyson, Jean Genet
Aubrey Beardsley, some pop art, e.g. Andy Warhol	Edward Burne-Jones, Carlo Crivelli
Mae West, Tallulah Bankhead	Victor Mature, Jane Russell
All About Eve, *Beat The Devil*	*King Kong*, *Casablanca*, *Tom and Jerry*
The Temperance Seven	Wolfgang Amadeus Mozart, *Il Trovatore*

B

Camp	Camp fads and fancies
Dirk Bogarde, Sarah Bernhardt	Judy Garland, Joan Crawford
Interview and *Ritz* magazines	Fanzines
Lindsay Kemp	Nijinsky
P.J. Proby, Soft Cell	Shirley Bassey, Dollar
Fiorucci clothes and accessories	Granny specs, collarless shirts
Solid gold safety pin, real boa constrictor	Real safety pin, feather boa
Rocky Horror Show, *Valmouth*	*42nd Street*, *Babes in Arms*
Andy Warhol's *Marilyn*	Kitchener poster: Your Country Needs You
Anglo-Catholicism	Catholicism

Even with so few entries, it should immediately be apparent that there is tremendous variety in the right-hand column. The names have very little in common, except that they display qualities likely to endear them to the sort of people in the left-hand column: artificiality, stylisation, theatricality, naïvety, sexual ambiguity, tackiness, poor taste, stylishness, the portrayal of camp people (which brings in the novels of Genet). The entries in the left-hand column, by contrast, are relatively unified. To put it on a wildly fanciful level, you can imagine Wilde, Warhol and Bette Davis getting on famously, but not Tennyson, Genet and Jane Russell. In trying to make sense of both columns together, Isherwood and Sontag were setting themselves an impossible task.

There is one more distinction to be made before we attempt to define camp. It was F.R. Leavis who said of the poets Edith, Osbert and Sacheverell Sitwell that they belonged to the history of publicity rather than of poetry – Oscar Wilde, Andy Warhol and the rest in the 'camp' column have all been successful self-publicists.

Camp is primarily a matter of self-presentation rather than of sensibility. If you are alone and bored at home, and in desperation you try to amuse yourself by watching an awful old film, you are not being camp. You only become so if you subsequently proclaim to others that you thought Victor Mature was divine in *Samson and Delilah*. China ducks on the wall are a serious matter to 'straights', but the individual who displays them in a house of otherwise modernist and modish furniture is being camp.

Building on the work of Isherwood and Sontag, and incorporating the above distinctions, we are now in a position to define camp thus: *To be camp is to present oneself as being committed to the marginal with a commitment greater than the marginal merits.* Everything we should wish to discuss with regard to camp unfolds from this definition.

The primary type of the marginal in society is the traditionally feminine, which camp parodies in an exhibition of stylised effeminacy. In the extent of its commitment, such parody informs the camp person's whole personality, throwing an ironical light not only on the abstract concept of the sexual stereotype, but also on the parodist him or herself. For instance, a non-camp cabaret impressionist may impersonate many film stars, but only so fleetingly and superficially that there is no suggestion that he actually sees himself in terms of these stars. A camp female impersonator, on the other hand, may well continue to use the mannerisms of Bette Davis or Joan Crawford off-stage in a way which says as much about himself as it does about the stars.

Camp self-parody presents the self as being wilfully irresponsible and immature, the artificial nature of the self-presentation making it a sort of off-stage theatricality, the shameless insincerity of which may be provocative, but also forestalls criticism by its ambivalence. Non-camp people are occasionally frivolous as a holiday from moral seriousness; camp people are only occasionally not frivolous.

Other types of the marginal are the trivial, the trashy, the kitsch and the not-terribly-good. Thus, in the cultural sphere, to be camp is to be perversely committed to the trash aesthetic or to a sort of 'cultural slumming' (a phrase of Richard Hoggart's in *The Uses of Literacy*), which, being in theory incomprehensible to non-camp people, becomes fashionably exclusive.

Camp art is art that sympathetically, stylishly and attractively represents camp behaviour, or represents a non-camp subject in a camp way. In the case of decorative art, camp objects are those made by camp people to decorate the camp life-style. A work of art may be verified as camp if we catch in it a reflection of a camp ambiguity in the mind of its creator.

This neater, tidier definition maintains the distinction between camp and camp's fads and fancies, and it also helps to distinguish camp from various related phenomena with which it is often confused. It is worth taking a look at some of these confusions.

CONFUSIONS

Troglodytes sometimes confuse camp with homosexual. The unhelpful idea that camp originated in homosexual cliques in the 1930s was aired by Isherwood, popularised by Sontag, and has remained unquestioned in subsequent discussion. However, as we shall see, camp's origins are far from being so humble. Undoubtedly, the effeminate strain in leading camp personalities such as Beau Brummell and Andy Warhol has caused many to think of them as homosexuals, but, although some may have been squeamish about women, this hardly constitutes homosexual behaviour. Camp people tend to be asexual rather than homosexual. Brummell *et al.* were perhaps honorary homosexuals, or homosexuals in spirit rather than in practice. In camp culture, the popular image of the homosexual, like the popular image of the feminine woman, is mimicked as a type of the marginal. So, while it may be true that many homosexuals are camp, only a small proportion of people who exhibit symptoms of camp behaviour are homosexual.

Another common confusion is between camp and kitsch, which, as Roland Barthes has written, 'implies a recognition of high aesthetic values': it represents an unwitting failure on a massive scale. French Symbolist paintings are kitsch, and so are the apocalyptic fantasies of John Martin; the marble stadium that Mussolini built outside Rome is kitsch, as is his railway station in Milan, where even the concrete cherubs have the bald head and bull-neck of *il Duce*; the American Declaration of Independence is kitsch, as is most Sword-and-Sorcery science fiction and most Heavy Rock music; many people find Wagner's operas kitsch. 'The worst art is always done with the best intentions', said Oscar Wilde, perhaps providing the key to the distinction between kitsch and camp. Unlike kitsch, camp does not even have honourable intentions. Yet, although kitsch is never intrinsically camp, it has a certain toe-curling quality that appeals to the camp sense of humour. Kitsch is one of camp's favourite fads and fancies.

Off-stage theatricality, though not synonymous with camp, is certainly a common manifestation of it: camp people use the exaggerated gestures of the theatre to draw attention to themselves, a technique epitomised by Sarah Bernhardt. In her day, she was seen as taking off-stage theatricality as far as it would go. Nicknamed Sarah Barnum because of her tireless publicity-seeking, she drew attention to herself by wearing drag, sleeping in a quilted coffin and surrounding herself with exotic pets – a cheetah, six chameleons, a parrot called Bizibouzon and a monkey called Darwin. Her public persona was so outlandish that it seemed to vindicate even the most bizarre rumour. At one time, she was said to play croquet with skulls that she had dressed up in Louis XIV wigs. On stage, theatricality can be camp when the play itself is camp (e.g. *The Importance of Being Earnest*), when a camp person is being portrayed (e.g. *The Staircase*) or when actors send a play up by deliberately over-acting.

The phenomenon that best accommodates itself to comparison with camp is dandyism. At this point, the Victorian moralist, Thomas Carlyle should make his entrance, with his portly little figures of speech trotting after him, for he it was, in *Sartor Resartus* (1834), who set about defining dandyism. 'A Dandy is a Clothes-wearing Man' he wrote, 'a Man whose trade, office and existence consists in the wearing of Clothes. Every faculty of his soul, spirit, purse and person is heroically consecrated to this one object, the wearing of clothes wisely and well: so that as others dress to live, he lives to dress'.

Carlyle then goes on to highlight the hollowness of dandyism (as he understands it) by suggesting in a *recherché* simile that it bears 'a not inconsiderable resemblance to that superstition of the Athos Monks who, by fasting from all nourishment and looking intensely for a length of time into their own navels, came to discern therein the true Apocalypse of Nature and Heaven Unveiled'.

Carlyle's jokes will always be greeted with the reverence they deserve. Fervidly anti-dandy, he was concerned to discredit them, and duly did. But a closer examination reveals various aspects of the dandy that refuse to submit to Carlyle's authority. For instance, to see the original dandy, Beau Brummell, as simply a 'Clothes-wearing Man' is to diminish him to such an extent that he ceases to be recognisable. When Brummell's friend Byron said that there were three great men in the nineteenth century, Brummell, Napoleon and himself, he was evidently not anticipating Carlyle's view of Brummell merely as the man who invented trousers.

In his own lifetime, Brummell's reputation was principally as a wit. He is supposed to have said of the Prince Regent (later George IV), 'I made him what he is, and I can unmake him'. He also uttered the maxim: 'A well-tied tie is a men's first serious step in life', and 'I like to have the morning well-aired before I get up'. In fact, Brummell was the originator of that exclusive wit and provocative frivolity which we tend to think of today as inimitably Wildean, but which was really (all too imitably) Brummellian. He was also a collector of snuff-boxes, china plate and bibelots, and he wrote society verses including the famous *Butterfly Funeral*.

Brummell's spirit (and, after Brummell's, the dandy's) was consecrated not, as Carlyle supposed, simply to clothes, but to trivia, of which clothing was one example, along with pretty witticisms, snuff-boxes, verse and all the rest. Carlyle mistook an instance for the principle.

Nowhere does dandyism's campness come across better than in the Silver Fork novels; it was these novels of dialogue and decor that Oscar Wilde was avowedly trying to revive with *The Picture of Dorian Gray*. Written by followers of the Beau, and usually containing fictionalised portraits of him, they purported to depict the beau monde accurately. The first Silver Fork novel, written in 1825, was Plumer Ward's *Tremaine*, and Benjamin Disraeli wrote *Vivian Grey* in 1826. The two outstanding examples, however, were Thomas Lister's *Granby* (1826) and George Bulwer-Lytton's *Pelham: the Adventures of a Gentleman* (1828).

Granby contains an extended portrait of Brummell in the guise of Trebeck, 'the most powerful poseur of his year'. We follow him in his intrigues through the world of Dandy clubs, balls, the ballet and the opera. The tone is best conveyed by snatches of dialogue:

> 'I solemnly assure you', said Trebeck, 'that nothing was further from my intention than a compliment. Compliments are *mauvais ton* – are they not Lady Elizabeth? They are quite obsolete – went out with hoops and hair powder. Pray do not accuse me of wishing to revive them'.

> ... Lord Chesterton – a man deeply impressed with his own consequence, but not at all skilled in the art of impressing others with it.

The eponymous dandy hero of *Pelham* moves in similarly flippant circles. The book begins:

> The end of the season was unusually dull, and my mother, having looked over her list of engagements, and ascertained that she had none worth staying for, agreed to elope with her new lover.

Confusion between camp and aestheticism perhaps arose out of Oscar Wilde's early aesthetic pose. In fact, Wilde was never a true aesthete. Aesthetes want to see; camp people such as Wilde prefer to be seen. Where the aesthete makes his life a work of art, the camp person tries to do the same with his personality. The sociable sometimes socialite literature of camp should not be confused with the sad, solitary pleasures of the aesthete and his grubby cultivation of his mental garden. Camp literature is easily accessible and light-hearted; aesthetic literature is troubled by a Poe-faced symbolism. Serious aesthetes tend to be priggish, whilst camp people gaily publicise themselves as immoral.

Wilde's aestheticism was primarily a means of shocking others. He was relatively uninterested in nurturing inner-directed experiences, but espoused a sort of comic aestheticism. In his essay *Pen, Pencil and Poison*, he relates with obvious approval the story of the flamboyant dandy Thomas Griffiths Waine-wright, who murdered a girl called Helen Abercrombie, and, when reproached by a friend, shrugged his shoulders and said, 'Yes, it was a dreadful thing to do, but she had very thick ankles'. Wainewright's quip was evidently a springboard for much of Wilde's humour.

Another confusing term is preciosity, or indeed, *préciosité*. Our understanding of the *précieux* has been much coloured by Molière's comedy *Les Précieuses Ridicules*, which guys the pretensions to *préciosité* of two young country girls:

> 'Come and hold for us the counsellor of the graces', says one of the girls to a servant.
> 'Gracious me!' replies the servant, 'I don't know what creature that is: you must talk like a Christian if you want me to understand you'.
> 'Bring us the looking-glass, you ignoramus, and take care not to contaminate its surface with the reflection of your image'.

Understanding *préciosité* in terms of a comedy, we are perhaps apt to forget that it was partly a serious-minded movement concerned to refine and to clarify the French language. Some of its more extreme refinements and 'clarifications' may now seem silly and affected, but we should be wary of calling them camp on that account.

French critics make a useful distinction between mainstream *préciosité* and *coquetterie*, the latter being the fun-loving and irreverent aspect of *préciosité* that required poets to exercise their ingenuity in writing elegant banter to amuse salon guests – for example, verses to accompany the gift of a bouquet of flowers or to commemorate the death of a parrot. This sort of good-humoured commitment to the marginal might justifiably be called camp.

To be precious, then, is not the same as to be camp – humourless preciousness is not camp – but there is a vein of camp behaviour that is precious and is characterised by a humorous fastidiousness and mock-feminine hypochondria. A camp character in Ronald Firbank's *The Flower beneath the Foot*, complains that he has 'a hundred headaches'.

In *Revolt into Style* (1970), George Melly pointed out that in the 1960s, pop was more or less synonymous with camp. And if we look at Richard Hamilton's famous list of the attributes of pop, we can draw up a very similar list of attributes of camp, at least the camp of television entertainment and media advertising.

Pop	*Camp*
Popular (designed for mass audiences)	Easily accessible
Transient (short-term solutions)	Determinedly facile
Expendable	Trashy
Low cost	Mock luxurious

Mass produced	Mass-produced
Young	Youth worshipping
Witty	Witty
Sexy	Mock sexy
Gimmicky	Wilfully hackneyed
Glamorous	Mock glamorous
Big business	BIG BUSINESS

Some twenty years later, it is much easier to avoid confusing pop with camp. Although camp has been an important factor in determining the style of pop, it has become mixed with other styles – negro, folk, country, music hall and Hollywood razzmatazz. And although pop has served to jazz up and help popularise camp, it did no more than that, for camp is a much older (by some 300 years) and bigger phenomenon, taking in aspects of High Culture as well as popular performance.

Nowadays, if camp is liable to be confused with any one word, it is not with pop but with chic. Lucinda and Piers may seem very camp as they trip lightly from the social columns of *Vogue* to *The Tatler* and back again, but one need only remind oneself of the 1950s when doughty debs, charms all too palpable, were herded up from the country to be decked out in ropes of pearls and chiffons, to realise that this connection between camp and chic is, like the one between camp and pop, a matter of historical accident rather than conceptual necessity. Chic is, of course, the quality which the French regard themselves as having to a superlative degree, but it carries with it no implication that they regard themselves as being in any way marginal; on the contrary, they take it more as a mark of their racial superiority. Similarly, Shirley Temple may be very chic as an American ambassador, but she does not intend thereby to be camp. True chic is an expression through extreme elegance of superior power, as opposed to camp which is a self-mocking abdication of any pretensions to power.

ORIGINS AND ETYMOLOGY

An examination of the origins and etymology of camp provides historical support for my definition.

The far-fetched, the bogus and the patently ludicrous will always cluster round camp. There have been many extraordinary explanations of its origin. As Philip Howard (1997) recorded in *New Words for Old*, it has been located in the police files of New York City as KAMP (Known As Male Prostitute), as the name of homosexual brothels in the Australian outback of the nineteenth century, and as a slang word used by dandies to describe their assignations with soldiers spending the summer under canvas in London's Hyde Park. Colourful as these etymologies are, they must regrettably be discarded as retrojections of today's Isherwoodian and Sontagesque misconceptions.

Sontag asserts that before her essay, camp had only broken into print in Isherwood's *The World in the Evening* (published in 1954, not as she claims in

1948). But the word appears in at least one essay by the popular American journalist, Tom Wolfe, *The Girl of the Year* (published 1963 [1964, in fact. *Editor's note*]); and in the same year, the English literary mandarin Cyril Connolly wrote a spoof on spy fiction called *Bond Strikes Camp* (in which the beautiful Russian spy turns out to be 'M' in drag). Sontag could also have mentioned Angus Wilson's 1952 novel, *Hemlock and After* which refers, among other usages, to 'the blond malice of Sherman's camp chatter'. Even earlier Constant Lambert wrote in *Music Ho! A Study of Music in Decline* (1934): 'The change in style observable between the pre-war and post-war Diaghilev ballets reflects the purely fashionable change in the tastes of the concentration camp of intellectuals to whom Diaghilev played up'. And, 'With the minor Parisian figures, the camp followers of Diaghilev, it is fairly safe to assume that lack of individuality and desire for chic were at the back of their changes of style'. That the word 'camp' is used twice in the context of the camp people who gathered around Diaghilev is surely not a coincidence.

Ware's dictionary of *Passing English of the Victorian Era*, published in 1909, says this of camp: 'actions and gestures of an exaggerated emphasis. Probably from the French. Used chiefly of persons of exceptional want of character, e.g. "How very camp he is"'.

Following Ware, we find *se camper* in Théophile Gautier's *Capitaine Fracasse* (1863) – an elaborate and witty spoof on the Romantic novel, written in a lush, decadent style that he created as a pastiche of *préciosité*. It concerns an impoverished young baron who sets out to make his fortune, joining up with a wandering troupe of actors on their way to Paris. Matamore, a stock character among the comedians of the troupe, makes a fool of himself by falling in love with a lady, Isabelle, whose affections lie elsewhere. This vainglorious poseur defiantly presents the gift of his body to Isabelle: '*Matamore se campait dans une pose extravagemment anguleuse dont sa maigreur excessive faisait encore ressortir le ridicule*'. (Matamore camped it up in an extravagantly angular pose which his great thinness served to make even more ridiculous.)

Gautier is apparently using *se camper* here with the associations of an army camp. *Se camper* is to present oneself in an expansive but flimsy manner (like a tent), with overtones here of theatricality, vanity, dressiness, and provocation.

Tracing the origin of this sense of *se camper* provides a valuable signpost to the origin of the whole phenomenon. It is interesting that *Capitaine Fracasse* is set in the seventeenth century, of which it presents a nostalgic portrait, for camp people have always idealised seventeenth-century France, above all because of Louis XIV and Versailles.

Prinnie, the Prince Regent, and 'mad' Ludwig II of Bavaria justified their camp architectural follies by reference to Louis XIV: Versailles was the place where Robert de Montesquiou-Fezensac (who was the model for Marcel Proust's Baron de Charlus) held some of his legendary parties. In the novel *Venus and Tannhäuser*, Venusberg is Aubrey Beardsley's pornographic vision of Versailles, while the fearsome eyes of Vathek in William Beckford's Gothick novel, capable of knocking people backwards with just a glance, are the fabled eyes of Louis XIV.

Camp people look back on Louis XIV's Versailles as a sort of camp Eden, a self-enclosed world devoted to divertissements, to dressing-up, showing off, and scandal – in fact the world captured in Madame de la Fayette's *La Princesse de Clèves* (1678). 'There is only one thing worse than going to a party with one's beloved', she wrote, 'and that is not going with her'. How evocative that proto-Wildean sentiment is of a camp ambiance! The world Madame de la Fayette describes is one of an indefinitely prolonged adolescence, an interplay of appearance, pretence and deceit in the midst of which the greatest joy was 'to note the effect of one's beauty on others', where the greatest worry was keeping up with the latest fashion, and where love was always mixed with cynicism, and cynicism with love, auspicious circumstances for the ascendancy of camp.

Louis XIV's well-known policy of diverting the nobility from politics by means of fêtes and other such Versailles entertainments (Walpole called Versailles 'a toy' and 'a garden for a great child') – in effect, the policy of manoeuvring the nobles into the margins of French life made Versailles a paradigm of high camp society.

All camp people are to be found in the margins of society, and the richest vein of camp is generally to be found in the margins of the margins. Marginal to the king's own set at Versailles was that of his brother, 'the king of mischief makers', known simply as 'Monsieur'. Modelling his personal style on that of the effeminate Henri III, Monsieur surrounded himself with exquisites. He had been educated to be totally ignorant of all political and practical matters (so as not to be a threat to the king), possibly spending part of his childhood in girls' clothes: he grew up to wear rings, bracelets, ribbons, women's jewellery, perfume and sometimes even rouge. He was notorious for his underworld connections, for his irreverence (it was believed he used to take a large missal every day to mass, until someone found he was reading Rabelais), for his sodomy and for many things much too disgusting to include here. Monsieur's fêtes, without the ballast of power-affirming symbolism that the king's presence imposed, floated off into camp fantasy. He liked to throw parties to which everyone went as shepherds and shepherdesses – a pastime which, because of her peasant village at the Petit Trianon, we tend to associate more with Marie-Antoinette. Anne Marie d'Orléans describes how she and Monsieur (who had by now totally abandoned himself to absurdity with his minute cherry mouth and the record of his gluttony stretching out in front of him) dressed in silver fabric bordered with red piping and wore aprons of black velvet covered with red, white and black plumes, with their hair dressed in the style of the peasants of Bresse; they also carried shepherds' crooks of red lacquer decorated with silver. 'Bodily toil frees us from mental trouble', said the *précieux* philosopher, the Duc de la Rochefoucauld, 'and that is what makes the poor so happy'.

There is another first-hand account of Monsieur's set in a passage in the bizarre *Transvestite Memoirs of the Abbé de Choisy*, who was a well-known chronicler of court and church affairs. These memoirs provide a fascinating record of his and Monsieur's secret eccentricities.

> I opened five or six buttonholes at the bottom of my gown, in order to reveal a robe of speckled black satin, the train of which was not as long as the gown. I also wore a white damask underskirt, which could be seen only when the train was carried. I ceased to wear trunk hose; to me it was hardly becoming to a woman, and I had no fear of being cold because it was full summer. I had a muslin cravat, whose tassels dropped on a huge knot of black ribbon which was attached to the top of my *robe de chambre*. The gown revealed my shoulders which always remained quite white through the great care I had taken of them all my life; every morning, I lathered my neck with veal water and sheep's foot grease, which made the skin soft and white.

He tries to come to terms with his tastes:

> The attribute of God is to be loved, adored. Man, as far as the weakness of his nature allows, wishes for the same, but, as it is beauty that kindles love and since that is usually the lot of women, when it happens that men have, or believe themselves to have, certain traits of beauty, they try to enhance them by the same methods that women use, which are most becoming. They feel the inexpressible pleasure of being loved. I have felt this more than once during a delightful affair. When I was at a ball or the theatre, wearing my beautiful *robe de chambre*, diamonds and patches, and heard people murmur near me, 'There is a lovely woman', I experienced an inward glow of pleasure which is incomparable, it is so strong. Ambition, riches, even love do not equal it, because we always love ourselves more deeply than we do others.

But his happiest hours were spent in the company of Monsieur – 'I went to the Palais-Royal whenever Monsieur was in Paris. He was almost effusively friendly to me, because we had the same inclinations. He longed to dress as a woman himself, but did not dare, because of his position (princes are prisoners of their rank). In the evenings he would put on cornets, ear pendants and patches, and gaze at his reflection in a mirror'.

> Fulsomely flattered by his admirers, he gave a great ball every year on Shrove Monday. He ordered me to attend in a loose robe, my face unmasked and instructed the Chevalier de Fradine to lead me in the *courante*.
>
> It was a splendid assembly; there were at least thirty-four women decked with pearls and diamonds. I was admired, I danced to perfection, and it seemed the ball was made for me.

Monsieur opened it with Mademoiselle de Brancas, who was very pretty (she later became the Princesse d'Harcourt) and a moment later he went to dress up as a woman and returned to the ball masked. Everyone recognised him, just as he intended, and the Chevalier de Lorraine tendered him his hand. He danced the minuet and then went to sit amongst all the ladies. He had to be persuaded a little before he would remove his mask, although secretly this was all he wished to do, as he longed to be seen by everyone. It is impossible to describe the extent of his coquetry in admiring himself, putting on patches and then changing their positions. But perhaps I would have been worse. Men, once they think they are beautiful, are far more besotted with their appearance than women are.

In view of all this camping at Versailles, it is appropriate that what may have been the earliest mention of *se camper* in our sense is to be found in *Les Fourberies de Scapin*, a play by Louis XIV's beneficiary, Molière, first performed in 1671. It appears in a passage that Gautier may, consciously or unconsciously, have been echoing – a suggestion reinforced by the fact that Matamore's valet in *Capitaine Fracasse* is called Scapin.

In *Les Fourberies de Scapin*, the rascally valet Scapin persuades Octavio to bluff his way out of trouble with his father by dressing up as a stage villain and prancing around in front of him in a provocative manner:

'Wait, stop a minute', says Scapin to Octavio, as the idea dawns on him, and he begins to see the possibilities, 'Stick your hat on at an angle and look disreputable. Camp about on one leg (*'campe-toi sur un pied'*). Put your hand on your hip. Strut like a comedy-king!'

To understand the peculiar connotations of *se camper*, it is helpful to know a bit about army camps in France at this time. The idea of tents did not then call to mind the small khaki, utilitarian apologies of today, but great billowy creations of shining fabrics – satins and silks studded with jewels, tapestries and gold banners.

When Louis XIV went on manoeuvres, the courtiers who had been camping out in the apartments, rooms and corridors of Versailles, de-camped to follow the king. If they did not fight, they at least moved to a respectful distance from the fighting, to watch. In fact, as Saint Simon recorded, the spectacle and the display of court life was transferred to camp, which differed only in its lightness and its impermanence. The camp was an insubstantial pageant, a byword for transient magnificence where men were encouraged to wear their finest costumes, to preen themselves – indeed, to advertise themselves.

Camp behaviour was not thought incompatible with good soldiering – if anything, the reverse. Monsieur himself loved battles, not only for the exercise (part of the ever-futile fight to keep himself trim) but also because of the opportunity for swanking. The De Villiers Journal recounts a young French officer's complaints about camp life's drain on his purse: the expensive items were not, it seems, irrelevancies like weapons, but clothes, carriages and silver plate.

Again, the element of off-stage theatricality in Molière's use of *se camper* is significant. Puritans, both religious and secular, have always worried about the effect of theatre on moral seriousness; theatre falsifies the self, encourages insincerity and promotes frivolity. Versailles in its more camp aspects might have embodied their worst fears. Anthony Blunt (an account of whose own very camp schooldays is to be found in Louis MacNeice's autobiography) has noted that in the courts of this time the borderlines between stage and off-stage, between fête and daily life, were very vague. Often a masque or a play such as *Le Bourgeois Gentilhomme* would culminate in a ball, an invitation to which was extended to the whole audience.

In 1661, Mademoiselle de Sévigné recorded in her letters how the king would sometimes appear in costume on stage – sometimes even in ballets – and how, at other times, when carnivals spread through the streets surrounding the palace, he would mask himself and slip off into the crowd incognito, to who knows what assignations. Some people detected an air of pasteboard about the whole institution of the monarchy; the Prince de Conti referred to Louis XIV in a letter as '*le Roi de théâtre*' and was banished – the barb seems to have hit home. Amorality succeeded morality, and stylishness replaced graciousness: the courtiers in the pictures of contemporary artists such as Callot are consummate stylists, behaving almost as if they are on-stage, walking with a swaggering, dance-like action which in their day (if Moliere's usage was not unique) would have been called *se campant*, and which we should call 'camping it up'. If we translate their hyperbolic gestures into twentieth-century terms, we see queens lolloping about underneath the streetlights of Berlin or Mae West shakin' the shimmy.

Of course, Louis XIV did not build Versailles with the intention of making it camp, but, like peasants after a revolution, camp people have camped out in the palace. They have overrun the legend of Versailles and converted it to camp. Versailles stands in camp memory, not, as it was intended, as a symbol of Decorative Absolutism, but as a symbol of Absolute Decorativism.

4

FROM CAMP:
THE LIE THAT TELLS THE TRUTH

Philip Core

CAMP RULES

CAMP depends on where you pitch it.

CAMP is character limited to context.

CAMP is in the eyes of the beholder, especially if the beholder is camp.

CAMP is a form of historicism viewed histrionically.

CAMP is not necessarily homosexual. Anyone or anything can be camp. But it takes one to know one.

CAMP was a prison for an illegal minority, now it is a holiday for consenting adults.

CAMP is first of all a second childhood.

CAMP is essential to military discipline.

CAMP is a biography written by the subject as if it were about another person.

CAMP is a disguise that fails.

CAMP is free association; free-thinking is not camp.

CAMP is a lifeboat for men at sea.

CAMP is Royalism, Diabolism and British Socialism.

Reprinted from *Camp: The Lie That Tells the Truth*, London: Plexus; New York: Delilah, 1984.

CAMP is moral anarchy which makes room for the self without altering the attitudes of society.

CAMP is an ephemeral fundamental.

CAMP is cross-dressing in a Freudian slip.

CAMP is a verb and a gerundive.

CAMP is laughing at *The Importance of Being Earnest* without knowing why.

CAMP is laughing at *The Importance of Being Earnest and* knowing why.

CAMP is an art without artists.

CAMP is anti-art in the same way physical desire is anti-creative.

CAMP is a lie which tells the truth.

CAMP is behaving illegally with impunity; Hemingway defined it perfectly as 'grace under pressure'.

CAMP is embarrassment without cowardice.

CAMP is gender without genitals.

Ronald Firbank, the frivolous English author from the world of literary camp, once wrote, 'I must admit that somewhere deep down inside of me there is a field with cows browsing'. From a fop who kept pet goldfish and fed them real pearls (artificial ones, he claimed, 'they spat out'), such a confidence, set in a context of grand hotels and Edwardian society, is just one brilliant example of the stance of concealed normalcy essential to the camp psyche. Throughout history there has always been a significant minority whose unacceptable characteristics – talent, poverty, physical unconventionality, sexual anomaly – render them vulnerable to the world's brutal laughter. Hiding their mortification behind behaviour which is often as deviant as that which is concealed is the mainspring of camp.

A working definition is essential before we can pinpoint camp retrospectively and contemporarily. Camouflage, bravura, moral anarchy, the hysteria of despair, a celebration of frustration, skittishness, revenge ... the possible descriptions are countless. I would opt for one basic prerequisite however: camp is a lie that tells the truth.

First used by Jean Cocteau in a set of his aphorisms published by *Vanity Fair* in 1922, this phrase encompasses not only specific homosexuals who behaved exaggeratedly because of social displacement, but also those figures whose solecisms were not necessarily sexual but whose desire to conceal something and to reveal it at the same time made their behaviour bizarre to our way of thinking. I do not posit homosexuality as requisite for camp: quite the contrary. Camp is most obvious to me in a homosexual context, but I perceive it in heterosexuals as well, and in the sexless professionalism of many careers.

There are only two things essential to camp: a secret within the personality which one ironically wishes to conceal and to exploit; and a peculiar way of seeing things, affected by spiritual isolation, but strong enough to impose itself on others through acts or creations.

Camp depends on where as well as how you pitch it. In some senses it is in the eye of the beholder. While their motives may be clear to the camp, their resultant actions remain marked but mysterious to the observer. While camp is now often a joke or pose among gays, it is not without serious value because it originated as a Masonic gesture by which homosexuals could make themselves known to each other during periods when homosexuality was not avowable. Besides being a signal, camp was and remains the way in which homosexuals and other groups of people with double lives can find a *lingua franca*. After all, even a housewife has to learn the language of housewifery; for her such a language already exists. For the outsider, society prescribes no such learnable code; for his own sanity and merely to communicate with his fellows it must be devised. The duplicity of camp lies in the use of self as language; an instrument at once revealing and defensive. Compensation for a possible imbalance of these extremes leads to the ingratiating warmth of the camp personality, often as repellent as its strident and intentionally offensive *blague*.

These concepts were more consistently homosexual before such historical climaxes as the 1969 Stonewall battle between New York City police and harassed gays. The general loosening of bourgeois strictures in the 1960s produced a less repressive atmosphere and altered the language of camp. But now that these crises are fading and eccentricities once hailed as alternative lifestyles have become mere traits of the new bourgeoisie; now that the repressive (if distinct) manias of Margaret Thatcher, Ronald Reagan, Mrs Mary Whitehouse, Enoch Powell or the Yorkshire Ripper have opposed human freedom and the joyous nature of human sexuality, it is well to look again at the talented sufferings of men and women who were camp because they could not be anything else. Sensing our own camp in theirs, we may ask the eternally pertinent question: why do we hate someone because he or she appears to be different?

In the circumstances, it is better to allow the camp to define themselves. We offer here an alphabet of camp personalities and their artifacts – some surprising, some predictable – who preached with ceaseless conviction and some style the lie that tells the truth. They help to explain those oddities of taste which we cannot classify as either 'kitsch' or 'affectation'. Much Mannerist painting is obvious homosexual camp; its decorative nature allows great scope for externalising perversity. Louis XV's secret agent, the Chevalier d'Eon is High Camp. Condemned to the female attire he wore for undercover work, he profited cheerfully from this laughable ambiguity. Beau Brummell, despite his reputation as the first soberly dressed gentleman, is also High Camp; no other sensibility makes such a performance out of tying a cravat, or claims, 'I had heard of a farthing, but I could not believe such a coin actually existed'.

Johannes Winkelmann, the eighteenth century German apologist for Neo-Classical art, in a rhapsody more erotic than aesthetic, wrote about his revealing passion for the Belvedere torso. During the repressive second half of the nineteenth century, camp blossomed in the Decadent universe. Gabriele d'Annunzio, Italian symbolist and future Poet Laureate of Fascism, typified Straight Camp when he adorned his study with plaster casts of Michelangelo's slaves dressed by Poiret and hung with Lalique jewellery. Robert de Montesquiou, model for Proust's Baron de Charlus, maintained a pious horror of homosexuals, calling Wilde 'l'Antinouos de l'Horrible'; but he was definitely camp when he refused to visit the hyper-refined poet Hérédia before changing into a synchronised grey outfit to suit the poet's melancholy verses. Aubrey Beardsley's sexual passions seem to have been transvestite (with overtones of incest): only in our own time have the French transvestite mime troupe, La Grande Eugène, shown us how close his pen and ink fantasies were to the realities of camp. The Russian Ballet can be regarded *in toto* as impresario Serge Diaghilev's personal camp, though his own behaviour was aristocratically low-keyed. Certainly the designs of the Ballet – inspired by Poiret, Bakst, and most of all the arch-camp Erté – are the templates of much modern camp taste. In Somerset Maugham, Cecil Beaton, the dilettante actor Ivor Novello, and Noël Coward, we can pinpoint the sort of camp the English upper classes adore: an outrageous but unprosecutable *arbiter elegantiarum* who bullies the world of married society into accepting a homosexual's view of how it should dress, act, entertain and sometimes think.

Let us not forget the ladies. Outside New York, 'dyke' and 'fag hag' have not entered journalistic vocabulary as unpejoratively as 'gay' or 'camp'. 'Fag hag' is a patently male-devised phrase which resounds hideously in a way that 'drag queen', for instance, cannot balance. Yet its strident syllables perfectly equate the type of woman whose behaviour is exaggerated to appeal, not to lovers, but to male homosexuals. She does not want to be possessed, only desired, and is willing to accept the platonic accolades of men who love her style but hate her body. She may well hate her body as well, or adore it in a manner which denies its sexuality. The 'fag hag' is a rare type, in a world where vanity is a woman's privilege. As the Female Narcissist she is, in fact, perhaps the more ancient persona which Germaine Greer has rechristened the Female Eunuch. The Freudian pastime of naming types after legends does not really apply to her, however, because the Female Narcissist is no mere Echo of her former self. She ought more aptly to be named after whatever stream Narcissus gazed into so raptly.

The 'fag hags' parallel the 'dykes' however, and often their friends, or alternate selves. From the Empress Josephine through to the scandalous English saloniste Lady Blessington, Sarah Bernhardt or the bizarre Edwardian Marchesa Casati, those women who adore and prefer to be adored by homosexual men, together with those women who adore each other, have behaved with particular consistency. Their excesses exaggerated the gap between the genders and set the stage for the required enormities of *femmes fatales* and Hollywood stars. American authoress and lesbian hostess Natalie Barney photographed naked in a spring wood, her art nouveau hair trailing behind her, fulfils a fantasy more reminiscent of Proust's *Sodome et Gomorrhe* than his *Young Girls in Flower*. In the d'Annunzio/Debussy *Martyrdom of Saint Sebastian*, tied naked to a tree with coils of rope, the wealthy amateur ballerina Ida Rubinstein was a *fin-de-siècle* pin up for gay aesthetes and lesbians alike. The music hall male impersonator Vesta Tilley actually influenced fashions in haberdashery, twirling her monocle, strutting her spats and singing 'Burlington Bertie'. The women Beverly Nichols called 'the Boys of Radclyffe Hall' (referring to the female Oscar Wilde, author of the pioneering lesbian novel *The Well of Loneliness*) wore tweeds and crew cuts and created a conspicuous vogue for 'mannishness'. Elsa Maxwell (behemothly fat in Patou suits, and an obscure Californian snob) became the female Harlequin of Café Society, all of whose members she knew to kiss cheeks with, and most of whose parties she stage managed. Natalie Barney's lover Romaine Brooks (American disciple of Whistler whose painting did not quite, but whose tailoring greatly resembled the master's); Vita Sackville-West (as 'Julian', a wounded doughboy, she went on camping trips through London's West End with her lover Violet Trefusis) – all affected their own cars, tailormade suits, neckties, and what should be called the 'Girton' rather than the 'Eton' crop. That their attitudes are now common to middle class ladies of all nations indicates a peculiar kind of camp as an impetus in female fashion. Concurrently, the efforts of couturiers from Leroy (who 'did' Napoleon's Coronation) to Dior (whose New Look is said to have been modelled by a boy among the mannequins), the Kings of Fashion have made fortunes and changed the look of the world by means of male camp sensibility. There are *two* third sexes.

It is just such an imperceptible influence to which the Marquess of Queensberry referred in inexplicable outrage, when he wrote of his son's association with Oscar Wilde – 'I do not say you *are* it, but you look it, which is just as bad'. Camp is very annoying because it is a seduction which denies its intentions.

So, looking at men and women, and the fields of visual art, literature, fashion and entertainment, camp will still appear more general than we tend to think. To paraphrase: the past was a different country; they camped differently there; camp can be clearly seen to have grown, like some fantastic tumbleweed in the arid wastes of vanished snobberies and social prejudices just as in the well of loneliness sunk by sexual discrimination. In a world ruled by kings, snobbery was a force to the extent that frustrating concealments were often necessary to sustain an image out of keeping with lowly birth, while intellectual grovelling was often more extreme than would be acceptable today in exchange for patronage or merely tolerance. Society in general was smaller, and, like Hollywood, it offered a tempting but perilously conspicuous field for the talents of camp personalities. Extremes of riches and poverty gave rise to social divides between people with similar tastes but diverse class origin which remained unbridgeable; camp then, as now, may have pontooned this gap between the working man and educated or merely upper class homosexuals. The 'normal' man remains comfortable with camp because it amuses him.

Camp, itself evanescent and protean, inevitably has suffered in our exploitative era, from myriad misinterpretations and mutations at the hands of business interests. Mick Jagger, in the vanguard of pop stylistics, has emphasised his peculiar sexuality, now with a Nazi uniform, now with a dress. On to a skeleton with a toupee, Andy Warhol has, every five years or so, hung one trend setting garment which later pops up in a universal retake: silver sunglasses, a leather jacket, the Brooks Brothers button-down collar shirt, the Polaroid. The desire to appear to belong to Warhol, to resemble him or to know him is as strong as the lust elicited by Gary Cooper's beauty. Royalty, however plain, are by nature (or Divine Right?) very expensively dressed indeed; Prince Charles' face will always be tanned by the reflected light of that golden circlet. I mention all these alternate forms of dandyism in one breath because they all assume one essential of extrovert camp behaviour: people want to be entertained.

The essence of dandyism consists of being obsessed with and knowledgeable about the limits of 'how far one can go too far', as Cocteau said. Very far indeed is, of course, the answer to that in some worlds – pop music, fashion – but not so far in others – monied society, politics, the world of business. Where Alice Cooper could wear dead rats and sequins on stage, Princess Margaret's boyfriends had to keep a low, if trendy, profile; the fact that both were obliged carefully to consider this form of definition and adhere to it, at least as far as the press is concerned, defines a kind of contemporary camp.

1950s memorabilia, first collected by Duggie Fields in London, has flooded advertising and generated a whole range of imitations through shops like Christopher Strangeways. Straight undergraduates wore make-up in the 1970s. The suburbs collect Clarice Cliff porcelain and mirrored coffee tables. Drag queens meet royalty. Beaton photographs reach record prices in the salerooms. Beresford Eagan has an exhibition at the National Theatre in London. An effeminate gay looks at a leather-clad *antiquaire* and says 'Isn't he camp?' The same *antiquaire*, in a business suit, spends thousands on a painting by Tamara de Lempicka because 'It's so camp'. Barrowboys in street markets sport green and pink hair; their girlfriends wear motorcycle clothes. The phrases 'former male model' and 'Hello, sailor' are linked with British politics by the man on the street and not in a whisper. A monologue by Crispin Thomas about Ronald Firbank is a sellout. Hockney paints a picture of Divine. Sotheby's sells hats ... and macho dressing-up is seriously represented in a trash-smash hit film called *Cruising*, while skinheads – dressed with a phallic ostentation only found otherwise in gay pornography – react against the ambiguities of Punk.

Finally, also reacting against the mass vulgarity of Punk, many of the same teenagers turned themselves into the New Romantics; the buccaneers looked camper than anything since Tiny Tim, that guitar-plucking camp hero of the 1960s who sang 1920s songs in a high falsetto. Whether such a style will last or replace blue jeans is irrelevant; camp has taunted the media to concentrate on excesses, any excesses, and the New Romantics fitted the bill. The world of more commercial entertainment has followed suit; the bizarre tastes and enthusiasms of homosexuals have pervaded public taste, ever athirst for diversion even if it takes perversion to provide it, even if it means listening to Boy George or a revival of TV's *Avengers* star Honor Blackman's old single, *Kinky Boots*.

Clubs like New York's Mine Shaft or Toilet, where all forms of man-to-man sexual enterprise are allowed on the spot, have attracted spectators as notable as Jackie Kennedy and Andy Warhol; response to these has blended the snob appeal of Studio 54 (the New York disco you could only get into if they liked the look of you) with this debauch to produce such bisexual action spots as Plato's Retreat, where everybody – men, women, gays, straights – is all over everybody in an all-out orgy to disco music. Camp becomes very obscure in this brilliant light of trendiness, reduced to a commercial phenomenon easily recognised and easily accepted by the entire public: teacups with Prince Charles' ear on them to commemorate the Royal Wedding in London in 1981; a major TV serialisation of Waugh's *Brideshead Revisited*; Bette Midler, a former entertainer in New York's gay saunas, now a leading concert artist, a Piaf for a camp accepting world; a stage show for Quentin Crisp; the hats and hutsva of George Melly acclaimed as a major jazz entertainer in London; remakes of *The Big Sleep*, *King Kong* or practically any other old movie you care to name . . . the nostalgic bash is enormous and endless and in many ways purely and simply a money-making, public scale apotheosis of camp.

What is reassuring is that camp will re-emerge. Indefinable, unshakeable, it is the heroism of people not called upon to be heroes. It will find new ways to react both with and against public tastes, it will selfishly and selflessly shriek on, entertaining the self and the spectator in one mad gesture, oblivious of what it is required to do. Camp is always in the future; that is why the present needs it so badly.

SECTION II
FLAUNTING THE CLOSET

INTRODUCTION

When she celebrated the camp appreciation of intentional failures, and the reorientation of sense it entails, Sontag was possibly envisioning the unforecastable redirection of her critical endeavour itself. In the wake of 'Notes on "Camp"', the circulation of camp as an (object of) critical discourse up to the 1980s can be arranged into three different areas, or 'camps', as concurrent and contradictory refractions of that essay. Firstly, within the mentioned media fad, accompanied by the 'pop criticism' of Leslie Fiedler, the film criticism of Andrew Sarris, Richard Schickel, John Simon and Parker Tyler, and some 'unacademic' pieces of architectural and art history (most notably by Charles Jencks, C. Ray Smith, and Hilton Kramer). Secondly, although in a marginal position, within the legitimate spaces of academic writing with some rather automatic applications of Sontag's insights that did not add saliency either to their critical objects or to 'camp' as a critical term, simply renaming an already existing bulk of knowledge. Finally, and most significantly, within early gay activism and gay studies *avant la lettre*, an area which in the definition of camp as a gay issue was enacting, as we shall see, an equally self-definitional performance. Despite its likely (or declared) intentions, in fact, the very publication of Sontag's piece, and the pop, 'aestheticised' 1960s onwards circulation of camp, provoked resentment among gay practitioners for the betrayal inscribed in the so broadened accessibility to the camp discursive building. And yet, this very process of appropriation by the intellectual upper-middle classes may be claimed to have unwittingly acted as a spur, within the gay community, to face the issue and to give rise to a counter-process, one in which the reclaiming of camp and the constitution of a confrontationist identity went in concert.

While the number of occurrences from gay periodicals in the years 1965–80 is as conspicuous as they are unanalytic, the first study to assess the high significance of camp within the homosexual subculture was conducted, within a sociological framework, by Esther Newton in the late 1960s. Her excellent *Mother Camp*, first published in 1972, maps the world of stage and street female impersonation, in which camp and drag are distinct but equally central figures. In following the popular assumption that camp only exists 'in the eye of the beholder', Newton emphasises a radical dereferentialisation of camp (still labelled 'sensibility' or 'taste'), which she points out as 'not a thing' but 'a *relationship between* things, people, and activities or qualities, and homosexuality'. In doing so, though, Newton adds to the *vulgata* a stable referent, 'the camp', the individual practitioner: the sensibility/taste described by Newton is no longer the Sontagian sign and expression of an era, but rather an exercise in homosexual taste and a mode of existence. This double gesture, of radical dereferentialisation going in concert with a stable referent, is in fact a unitary definitional gesture, for in order to have a camp relationship one needs *a camp*, a homosexual subject activating it ('camp is in the eye of the homosexual beholder'). And it is precisely in the wake of this suggestion of the beholder's *eye* as a *gay I*, that a few years later – in an essay largely indebted to Newton's work – Jack Babuscio equalled camp with 'the gay sensibility', that catch-phrase of early identity politics, and charged the mainstreaming of camp with the effacement of the gay subjectivity inscribed in camp (by making it into a mere effect of an *unspecified* 'eye/I', a 'badge of identity' – in Sontag's words – that did not define that very identity).

That this very first study, Newton's, emerges from a sociological framework is just appropriate, given the 'sociological imagination' (Escoffier 1997) within which the homosexual discourse has developed in postwar culture. In restoring its appropriate setting, the drag subculture, Newton was in fact restoring camp to its alleged original existence, as a feature of 'genuine homosexual culture' (Altman 1971: 141) and as a specific 'strategy for a situation' (Newton's words), that is to say a peculiarly 'gay' way to handle the burden of stigma, reorienting it into 'a means of dealing with a hostile environment and, in the process, of defining a positive identity' (Babuscio 1977). In short, a survivalist strategy of making the homosexual experience within a homophobic cultural order 'so camp as keeps us going' (Dyer 1976). By construing camp as a set of representational strategies 'naturally' the outcome of a gay sensibility, and as a system of humour through which an oppressed social group transvalues negativity into a element of cohesion, Newton, Babuscio and the vast majority of early gay commentators were deploying an 'ethnicity model' (cf. Sinfield 1996), so that camp may be said to operate for (and to *belong* to) gay people just as soul did for the African-American community.[1] Defining camp as properly gay thus meant, at that stage, defining a gay collective identity, its history and cultural tradition, just as it posited the bases for the development into an academic discipline of a gay reading strategy and historiography, at work in the 'between the lines', 'secondary' camp decoding.

Both the demands of sociological research, and the urgency of self-definition that was posited within the 'popular' – i.e. 'unacademic' – editorial spaces of this early gay criticism, even those as articulated to be collected here (Babuscio's essay was based on his *Gay News* writings; Richard Dyer's was first published in the surely unscientific columns of *Playguy*; Andrew Britton's appeared in *Gay Left*), justified the attempt to define camp by isolating the unthinkable: a set of constant, constitutional, inherent features. And that essential, stabilising set is identified by Newton, and reprised by Babuscio with particular relevance to the cinematic experience, in the recurring presence, in *all* camp effects, of humour, irony, aestheticism, theatricality, and incongruity – all features that are peculiarly relevant to the homosexual situation, as they go at some length to explain, from the 'incongruity' of same-sex desire, to the theatricality of passing for straight.

This grid of recognisability enacts the most powerful attempt so far to stabilise camp, and as such, of course, it fails. Not so much because of the contradiction between the 'flaunting it' effect of camp and its being inscribed in the secretive logic of the closet, the one producing the experience of passing for straight (which works if one succeeds in *effacing*, not flaunting it). That contradiction can in fact be transvalued under the aegis of the queer reorientation of stigma: by taking camp not as a synonym of 'homosexuality', but rather of the community-building survivalist dealing with the *signs* of a stigmatised (homosexual) identity, gay camp can be construed as precisely that contradiction, *flaunting the closet*. The grid fails not only because the very alterity of these categories – the serious – can be, is indeed part, of the camp effect, as Babuscio exemplifies in Werner Rainer Fassbinder's *The Bitter Tears of Petra von Kant*. It fails because it relies on a set of categories that are, once again, not *discrete*, that it to say, categories which can't in fact be separate within the production of a camp effect, and which at the same time don't discriminate camp from other ironic, theatrical, humorous, and incongruous artifacts that 'the camp' wouldn't possibly establish his relationship with. The very notion of a 'gay sensibility' is highly problematic, and the chapter from Dollimore's *Sexual Dissidence* reprinted here (cf. Section III) is opened precisely by its precarious (and oxymoronic) status, one that doesn't face the question, among others, of its being 'transcultural, or historically rooted in the (varying) histories of the representation of homosexuality'.

Neither Newton nor Babuscio, in fact, fully subscribe to an equalling of camp and gay, the latter stating that 'not [. . .] all gays respond in equal measure to camp', the former delineating, in a later essay, the 'camp/theatrical sensibility' and the 'egalitarian/authentic sensibility', as the 'two major gay sensibilities' (1993: 85). But while this field limitation does not entirely get rid of the essentialism lurking in the 'gay sensibility', it surely highlights that camp does not extenuate the existential possibility of gay subjectivity, and it opens the possibility that camp, in its turn, may not be entirely encompassed by a gay transhistorical sensibility, determining its only legitimate mode of existence. Camp could be claimed – as Richard Dyer wrote in 1986 – as 'a defining feature of the male gay subculture' (178), with camp as *historical* factor of definition for that culture which can't nonetheless be defined by it (see also Tripp 1975; Cohen & Dyer 1980; Bristow 1989). But as Mark Finch made clear in an essay also published in 1986 (reprinted here), the very category of 'gay culture' is in itself a *partial* category, one 'more specific than it pretends', electing 'a discursive system developed out of a metropolitan, white, middle-class and male gay community' as representative of *all* gay experience.

The claims for gay camp can be best valued if historicised, that is, if inscribed as I suggested above, in that heady moment in the mid-1970s, when the urgency to articulate a gay discourse, and its plausibility of and within a 'gay culture', had political priority over the legitimacy of categories that we have been discussing here. But that heady moment, with its euphoric, discursive 'coming out' which produced the apologetic reclaimings of Babuscio and Dyer, should also be framed within the major phase of crisis of camp as a gay discourse, one posited – at least as much as by the mainstreaming of camp – by the effort, parallel to the self-definitional enterprise that camp entailed, to assess the politics of camp as a gay self-representational strategy within 'first wave' gay activism. As early as 1970, a few months after the riots at the Stonewall Inn in Christopher Street, New York, that inaugurated the confrontationist phase of gay rights movements such as the Gay Liberation Front and the Campaign for Homosexual Equality, Allen Young, Brian Chavez and Mike Silverstein shared the first three issues of *Gay Sunshine* in discussing how useful camp might still be, and if its survivalist strategy shouldn't be abandoned in favour of a more openly political strategy. A few years later, Andrew Britton published 'For Interpretation – Notes Against Camp' (reprinted here), the best example of that crisis, challenging the progressive assumptions that guided the camp followers' enthusiasm.

At stake here was how much a cultural formation born out of stigma wasn't constantly reasserting that very oppression; how much the send-up of the 'whole cosmology of restrictive sex roles and sexual identifications' (Babuscio) oper-ated as a parodic demystification of the power relations inscribed in gender roles, and how much on the contrary that very send-up was reinforcing those stereotypes whose camp demystification was claimed by apologists. This issue problematises, in fact, the complex relationship between camp and homosexual integration, one emphasised by the majority of commentators, starting with Sontag's claiming the 'propagandistic' nature in camp as 'a solvent of morality', one that helped gay people to pin 'their integration into society on promoting the aesthetic sense'.[2] And that acceptance as the court jester (or fashion designer, if you prefer), much in contradiction with the radicality of camp, is precisely what movements like GLF and CHE invited gay people to abandon in favour of an integration as *equal* subjects within the social contract. The claims of the gay left, best exemplified by Britton's piece, thus converge on the strategies of 'the gay liberal discourse', (Mark Finch's words) and of the 'egalitarian/authentic sensibility' (Esther Newton's formula): the sensibility, that is to say, springing 'directly from middle-class democratic and bourgeois ideology' (1993: 185), pointing to essentialism and naturality as the main, and *authentically radical*, route to improve the situation itself, rather than relishing the camp 'strategy for an [irremediably negative] situation'.

Dyer's 'It's Being So Camp as Keeps Us Going', and to a lesser extent Babuscio's 'Camp and the Gay Sensibility', are not so ingenuous as Britton suggests, though, acknowledging as they do the ambiguous political implications of camp, the very ambiguity that Esther Newton inferred from the practice of drag – potentially asserting the naturality of sex roles, and the rightfulness of stigma, while potentially demystifying the constructedness and artificiality of the gender system. And still, two decades after that debate, now that the reactionary implications of camp and drag all too often seem to have disappeared from the critical scene, and that the stigmatised 'queer' label (with groups like Queer Nation, Radical Faeries, OutRage, Act Up) has offered itself as a powerful platform for radical activism, Britton's invitation to localise the 'transgressive' practice of camp in its historical context, is worth bearing in (a critical) mind.[3] That is a lesson that can indeed be learnt from camp itself: Mark Finch's 'Sex and Address in *Dynasty*', in fact, is devoted to the localisation of spectatorship in a mainstream text such as the US serial (on which see also Feuer 1986), and charges the gay liberal discourse precisely with the effacement of its own historicity, queered as it is by its repressed alterity – the 'otherness' of camp, which in its pre-Stonewall existence as a gay cultural formation lies as a monument to the tough *material* route that brought gays to claims of 'equality' and 'naturality'.

Along with Finch's essay, Harold Beaver's 'Homosexual Signs', a homage to the Barthesian 'persona' and critical lesson first published in 1981, opens the second phase of gay readings clustered in this section, related to the full development of gay studies in the 1980s both within and outside academia, and of a more 'scientific' articulation of the camp discourse. Beaver exploits, develops and contrasts at the same time the thesis framing camp as a homosexual language, popularised by the whole tradition of lexological and sociological mapping of the subcultural and deviant, and attested even in 'pop' texts such as Core (1984), according to which camp 'originated as a Masonic gesture by which homosexuals could make themselves known to each other'. As a *lingua franca* or 'gay argot' based on a 'shared and secret knowledge' (Goodwin 1989: 29), camp intersects with Polari (cf. 'Queering the Camp') as a survivalist tool for self-recognition, and with the experience of passing. Beaver's essay, on the other hand, inscribes camp as a gay Masonic 'anti-expression' within a Barthesian reading of homosexuality as itself a semiotic issue and a semiotic construction. Beaver thus articulates the homosexual prodigious *consumption* of signs ('of hidden meanings, hidden systems, hidden potentiality') as the necessary condition to articulate its exclusion from the common code and social contract, by means of a 'parasitical', 'cannibalistic', secondary existence on that very common code (common sense, doxastic space) it *wastes*.

In such critical reading Beaver inaugurates in fact what, ten years or so later, would become a most common gesture within queer theory. Significantly enough, much earlier than Michel Foucault's genealogy became a major route for Anglo-American queer historiography, Beaver points to Oscar Wilde's downfall as *the* epistemic watershed in the constitutive process of the homosexual-as-type, that process which stabilised the queer sign, and that intervened in the erection of the early twentieth-century epistemic 'nave' of homosexual camp. As such, Beaver's essay converges on one of the very best gay biographies of Wilde to date, Neil Bartlett's *Who Was That Man?: A Present for Mr. Oscar Wilde* (1988, excerpted here), in which the codes of (auto)biographical writing and literary criticism merge to produce a major contribution to the rethinking of camp's origins. If Beaver shows the intertwining of sexual and aesthetic transgression in camp (on which see also Bronski 1984, and Dollimore 1991), the Bartlett chapter excerpted here, 'Forgery', beyond offering the 1869 occurrence of *camp* I have relied upon in the Introduction, highlights the linking of Wilde's guilt as an ontological as well as aesthetical threat – his linking with 'anyone who had signed no contract with truth' going in concert with his refusal of the social contract in favour of queer, *counterfeit money* (he was 'a creator of copies, borrowing and reprocessing fragments of his own and other people's works').

In showing how the queerness of camp and of its 'queen of queens' resides in the enactment of a personality and an issue entirely deployed on the authentic/ inauthentic axis, and on the instability of the Wild(e) *posing* sign, *processed* into a sign of homosexuality, Bartlett's reading enforces the problematicity of camp's origins. As the reappropriation of camp within gay studies implied a different epistemic framework, the origins have been identified not so much in seventeenth-and eighteenth-century France, with the camp Eden of Versailles, but rather in some proto-case of 'inverted' subjectivity and metropolitan space such as the eighteenth-century molly houses and masquerades, which cut across the social hierarchy of the time not only in terms of sexual behaviour but also in terms of class and gender (women and lower-class people being juxtaposed to the privileged ones) that had access to a space of 'exhuberant', carnivalesque social order (see Bergman 1991: 104–5). While such a retrospective search for origins always risks falling into the pitfalls of essentialist historiography, the most significant 1980s gay criticism on camp promotes the acknowledgement of the *partiality*, of the locally-bound character of the categories that are deployed on camp (be that 'gay culture' or whatever). And in the same year as the appearance of Bartlett's book, Sue-Ellen Case published 'Toward a Butch-Femme Aesthetic', the most influential essay on camp from a lesbian perspective, which marks a very *queer* appearance in the closet flaunted by camp.

In delineating camp as a possibility of a new heterogeneous, heteronomous position for women outside their traditional subject position of heterosexual context, Case links the butch-femme camp 'dynamic duo' (performing to excess and reinscribing the sterotypes of heterosexual coupling) to the 'second-wave' feminist refusal of biological determinism and the cleavage of sexual difference which camp has possibly endorsed (cf. next section). But what Case's essay *does*, within the specific history of camp, is bring what up to the late 1980s was 'a very rare bird, a lesbian camp' (Newton 1972), virtually absent from camp theory, to an unprecedented visibility and significance.[4] While according to Case lesbian camp – 'the style, the discourse, the *mise en scène* of butch-femme roles' – is the outcome of the closet, it cannot be taken simply as a duplication of its male counterpart. The setting of the butch-femme dynamic duo, its history, its class relations, are *different*. Lesbian criticism, which has reasons to regard with suspicion the inclusive gesture of camp and queer (cf. Davy, Graham, Walters, Jeffreys quoted in the main Introduction), has not so far produced its own historical account of lesbian camp's origins, and its relations with the male gay closet.[5] And yet, its 'secondary' status within camp theory, by replicating and reinscribing the male closet, produces a typical and *double* queering effect – this time, not only on the heterosexual 'original', but also on the ontological 'priority' of its male counterpart.[6]

NOTES

1. Newton invites us, in fact, to compare 'camp humor with the humor system of other oppressed people (Eastern European Jewish, Negro, etc.)'; and this suggestion is partly carried out in Murray 1983. Besides the writings of Newton, Babuscio, Dyer and Britton, reprinted here, for this phase of early gay criticism see especially Cory 1951; Cory & LeRoy 1963; Silverstein 1970; Altman 1971; Conley 1972; Humphreys 1972; Rodgers 1972; Escoffier 1973; Evans 1973; Russo 1976; Bronski 1977; Weeks 1977; White 1977.
2. Newton states that the camp 'builds a bridge to the straight people by getting them to laugh with him'; according to Babuscio, while 'camp advocates the dissolution of hard and inflexible moral rules, it pleads, too, for a moral of sympathy'; and to Dyer, the camp '[m]astery of style and wit has been a way of declaiming that gays have something distinctive to offer society'.
3. See Dollimore's words quoted in the final section of the main Introduction. Alan Sinfield also invites us to address camp and drag 'not in the abstract but as social practices' (1994: 200).
4. This doesn't mean that camp had never been mentioned in relation to lesbian cultures before 1988 (witness Simon & Gagnon 1967; Morgan 1973; Johnston 1975; Stanley & Robbins 1976; Zimmerman 1980; Hayes 1981; Ashley 1982; Laurie 1985); rather, that these items hadn't 'gained access' to the theoretical and definitional studies of camp.
5. Since 1988 quite a few essays have appeared on lesbian camp, although not so many as those produced from a gay perspective (which is reflected in the very composition of this Reader), and most often directly indebted to Sue-Ellen Case's essay. See especially Jeffreys 1990; 1993, 1994; Clark 1991; Davy 1992; Dolan 1992; Kennedy & Davis 1992, 1993; Reich 1992 (reprinted here); Weiss 1992; Crowder 1993; Gever, Greyson & Parmar 1993; Hart & Phelan 1993; Smith 1993; de Lauretis 1994; Doan 1994; Hamer & Budge 1994; Morrill 1994; Nataf 1995; Wilton 1995a;

Beemyn & Eliason 1996; Horne & Lewis 1996a; Humberstone 1996; Newton 1996; Walters 1996; Boyd 1997; Bruzzi 1997; Halberstam 1997; Foster 1997; Kennedy 1997; Wolf 1997.
6. A similar point can be made for *bisexual* camp, on which see Garber 1995; Loftus 1996; Michel 1996; Bryant 1997.

5

ROLE MODELS

Esther Newton

THE ACTRESS

Female impersonators, particularly the stage impersonators (see Newton 1972: 1–19), identify strongly with professional performers. Their special, but not exclusive, idols are female entertainers. Street impersonators usually try to model themselves on movie stars rather than on stage actresses and nightclub performers. Stage impersonators are quite conversant with the language of the theaters and nightclubs, while the street impersonators are not. In Kansas City, the stage impersonators frequently talked with avid interest about stage and nightclub 'personalities'. The street impersonators could not join in these discussions for lack of knowledge.

Stage impersonators very often told me that they considered themselves to be nightclub performers or to be in the nightclub business, 'just like other [straight] performers'.

When impersonators criticized each other's on- or off-stage conduct as 'unprofessional', this was a direct appeal to norms of show business. Certain show business phrases such as 'break a leg' (for good luck) were used routinely, and I was admonished not to whistle backstage. The following response of a stage impersonator shows this emphasis, in answer to my question, 'What's the difference between professionals and street fairies?' This impersonator was a 'headliner' (had top billing) at a club in New York:

Reprinted from *Mother Camp: Female Impersonators in America*, Englewood Cliffs: Prentice Hall, 1972.

Well [laughs], simply saying … well, I can leave that up to you. You have seen the show. You see the difference between me and some of these other people [his voice makes it sound as if this point is utterly self-evident] who are working in this left field of show business, and I'm quite sure that you see a *distinct* difference. I am more conscious of being a performer, and I think generally speaking, most, or a lot, of other people who are appearing in the same show are just doing it, not as a lark – we won't say that it's a lark – but they're doing it because it's something they can drop in and out of. They have fun, they laugh, have drinks, and play around, and just have a good time. But to me, now, playing around and having a good time is [sic] important to me also; but primarily my interest from the time I arrive at the club till the end of the evening – I am there as a performer, as an entertainer, and this to me is the most important thing. And I dare say that if needs be, I probably could do it, and be just as good an entertainer … I don't know if I would be any more successful if I were working in men's clothes than I am working as a woman. But comparing myself to some of the people that I would consider real professional entertainers – people who are genuinely interested in the show as a show, and not just as I say, a street fairy, who wants to put on a dress and a pair of high heels to be seen and show off in public.

The stage impersonators are interested in 'billings' and publicity, in lighting and make-up and stage effects, in 'timing' and 'stage presence'. The quality by which they measure performers and performances is 'talent'. Their models in these matters are established performers, both in their performances and in their off-stage lives, insofar as the impersonators are familiar with the latter. The practice of doing 'impressions' is, of course, a very direct expression of this role modeling.

From this perspective, female impersonators are simply nightclub performers who happen to use impersonation as a medium. Many stage impersonators are drab in appearance (and sometimes in manner) off stage (see Newton 1972: 1–19). These men often say that drag is simply a medium or mask that allows them to perform. The mask is borrowed from female performers, the ethos of performance from show business norms in general.

The stated aspiration of almost all stage impersonators is to 'go legit', that is, to play in movies, television, and on stage or in respectable nightclubs, either in drag or (some say) in men's clothes. Failing this, they would like to see the whole profession 'upgraded', made more legitimate and professional (and to this end they would like to see all street impersonators barred from working, for they claim that the street performers downgrade the profession). T. C. Jones is universally accorded highest status among impersonators because he has appeared on Broadway (New Faces of 1956) and on television (Alfred Hitchcock) and plays only high-status nightclubs.

THE DRAG QUEEN

Professionally, impersonators place themselves as a group at the bottom of the show business world. But socially, their self-image can be represented (without the moral implications) in its simplest form as three concentric circles. The impersonators, or drag queens, are the inner circle. Surrounding them are the queens, ordinary gay men. The straights are the outer circle. In this way, impersonators are 'a society within a society within a society', as one impersonator told me.

A few impersonators deny publicly that they are gay. These impersonators are married, and some have children. Of course, being married and having children constitute no barrier to participation in the homosexual subculture. But whatever may be the actual case with these few, the impersonators I knew universally described such public statements as 'cover'. One impersonator's statement was particularly revealing. He said that 'in practice' perhaps some impersonators were straight, but 'in theory' they could not be. 'How can a man perform in female attire and not have something wrong with him?' he asked.

The role of the female impersonator is directly related to both the drag queen and camp roles in the homosexual subculture. In gay life, the two roles are strongly associated. In homosexual terminology, a drag queen is a homosexual male who often, or habitually, dresses in female attire. (A drag butch is a lesbian who often, or habitually, dresses in male attire.) Drag and camp are the most representative and widely used symbols of homosexuality in the English speaking world. This is true even though many homosexuals would never wear drag or go to a drag party and even though most homosexuals who do wear drag do so only in special contexts, such as private parties and Halloween balls.[1] At the middle-class level, it is common to give 'costume' parties at which those who want to wear drag can do so, and the others can wear a costume appropriate to their gender.

The principle opposition around which the gay world revolves is masculine-feminine. There are a number of ways of presenting this opposition through one's own person, where it becomes also an opposition of 'inside/outside' or 'underneath/outside'. Ultimately, all drag symbolism opposes the 'inner' or 'real' self (subjective self) to the 'outer' self (social self). For the great majority of homosexuals, the social self is often a calculated respectability and the subjective or real self is stigmatized. The 'inner/outer' opposition is almost parallel to 'back/front'. In fact, the social self is usually described as 'front' and social relationships (especially with women) designed to support the veracity of the 'front' are called 'cover'. The 'front/back' opposition also has a direct tie-in with the body: 'front' = 'face'; 'back' = 'ass'.

There are two different levels on which the oppositions can be played out. One is *within* the sartorial system[2] itself that is, wearing feminine clothing 'underneath' and masculine clothing 'outside'. (This method seems to be used more by heterosexual transvestites.) It symbolizes that the visible, social, masculine clothing is a costume, which in turn symbolizes that the entire sex role behavior is a role – an act. Conversely, stage impersonators sometimes wear jockey shorts underneath full stage drag, symbolizing that the feminine clothing is a costume.

A second 'internal' method is to mix sex-role referents *within* the visible sartorial system. This generally involves some 'outside' item from the feminine sartorial system such as earrings, lipstick, high-heeled shoes, a necklace, worn *with* masculine clothing. This kind of opposition is used very frequently in informal camping by homosexuals. The feminine item stands out so glaringly by incongruity that it 'undermines' the masculine system and proclaims that the inner identification is feminine.[3] When this method is used on stage, it is called 'working with (feminine) pieces'. The performer generally works in a tuxedo or business suit and a woman's large hat and earrings.

The second level poses an opposition between a one sex-role sartorial system and the 'self', whose identity has to be indicated in some other way. Thus when impersonators are performing, the oppositional play is between 'appearance', which is female, and 'reality', or 'essence', which is male. One way to do this is to show that the appearance is an illusion; for instance, a standard impersonation maneuver is to pull out one 'breast' and show it to the audience. A more drastic step is taking off the wig. Strippers actually routinize the progression from 'outside' to 'inside' visually, by starting in a full stripping costume and ending by taking off the bra and showing the audience the flat chest. Another method is to demonstrate 'maleness' verbally or vocally by suddenly dropping the vocal level or by some direct reference. One impersonator routinely tells the audience: 'Have a ball. I have two'. (But genitals must *never* be seen.) Another tells unruly members of the audience that he will 'put on my men's clothes and beat you up'.

Impersonators play on the opposition to varying extents, but most experienced stage impersonators have a characteristic method of doing it. Generally speaking, the desire and ability to break the illusion of femininity is the mark of an experienced impersonator who has freed himself from other impersonators as the immediate reference group and is working fully to the audience. Even so, some stage impersonators admitted that it is difficult to break the unity of the feminine sartorial system. For instance, they said that it is difficult, subjectively, to speak in a deep tone of voice while on stage and especially while wearing a wig. The 'breasts' especially seem to symbolize the entire feminine sartorial system and role. This is shown not only by the very common device of removing them in order to break the illusion, but in the command, 'tits up!' meaning, 'get into the role', or 'get into feminine character'.

The tension between the masculine-feminine and inside-outside oppositions pervades the homosexual subculture at all class and status levels. In a sense the different class and status levels consist of different ways of balancing these oppositions. Low-status homosexuals (both male and female) characteristically insist on very strong dichotomization between masculine-feminine so that people must play out one principle or the other exclusively. Low-status queens

are expected to be very nellie, always, and low-status butch men are so 'masculine' that they very often consider themselves straight.[4] (Although the queens
say in private that 'today's butch is tomorrow's sister'.) Nevertheless, in the
most nellie queens the opposition is still implicitly there, since to participate in
the male homosexual subculture as a peer, one must be male inside (physiologically).

Recently, this principle has begun to be challenged by hormone use and by
the sex-changing operation. The use of these techniques as a final resolution of
the masculine-feminine opposition is hotly discussed in the homosexual subculture. A very significant proportion of the impersonators, and especially the
street impersonators, have used or are using hormone shots or plastic inserts to
create artificial breasts and change the shape of their bodies. This development
is strongly deplored by the stage impersonators who say that the whole point
of female impersonation depends on maleness. They further say that these
'hormone queens' are placing themselves out of the homosexual subculture,
since, by definition, a homosexual man wants to sleep with other *men* (i.e., no
gay man would want to sleep with these 'hormone queens').

In carrying the transformation even farther, to 'become a woman' is
approved by the stage impersonators, with the provision that the 'sex changes'
should get out of gay life altogether and go straight. The 'sex changes' do not
always comply, however. One quite successful impersonator in Chicago had
the operation but continued to perform in a straight club with other impersonators. Some impersonators in Chicago told me that this person was now
considered 'out of gay life' by the homosexuals and could not perform in a gay
club. I also heard a persistent rumor that 'she' now liked to sleep with lesbians!

It should be readily apparent why drag is such an effective symbol of both
the outside-inside and masculine-feminine oppositions. There are relatively few
ascribed roles in American culture and sex role is one of them; sex role radiates
a complex and ubiquitous system of typing achieved roles. Obvious examples
are in the kinship system (wife, mother, etc.) but sex typing also extends far out
into the occupational-role system (airline stewardess, waitress, policeman,
etc.). The effect of the drag system is to wrench the sex roles loose from that
which supposedly determines them, that is, genital sex. Gay people know that
sex-typed behavior can be achieved, contrary to what is popularly believed.
They know that the possession of one type of genital equipment by no means
guarantees the 'naturally appropriate' behavior.

Thus drag in the homosexual subculture symbolizes two somewhat conflicting statements concerning the sex-role system. The first statement symbolized by drag is that the sex-role system really is natural: therefore homosexuals
are unnatural (typical responses: 'I am physically abnormal'; 'I can't help it, I
was born with the wrong hormone balance'; 'I am really a woman who was
born with the wrong equipment'; 'I am psychologically sick').

The second symbolic statement of drag questions the 'naturalness' of the sex-
role system *in toto*; if sex-role behavior can be achieved by the 'wrong' sex, it

logically follows that it is in reality also achieved, not inherited, by the 'right' sex. Anthropologists say that sex-role behavior is learned. The gay world, via drag, says that sex-role behavior is an appearance; it is 'outside'. It can be manipulated at will.

Drag symbolizes both these assertions in a very complex way. At the simplest level, drag signifies that the person wearing it is a homosexual, that he is a male who is behaving in a specifically inappropriate way, that he is a male who places himself as a woman in relation to other men. In this sense it signifies stigma. At the most complex, it is a double inversion that says 'appearance is an illusion'. Drag says, 'my "outside" appearance is feminine, but my essence "inside" [the body] is masculine'. At the same time it symbolizes the opposite inversion: 'my appearance "outside" [my body, my gender] is masculine but my essence "inside" [myself] is feminine'.

In the context of the homosexual subculture, all professional female impersonators are 'drag queens'. Drag is always worn for performance in any case; the female impersonator has simply professionalized this subcultural role. Among themselves and in conversation with other homosexuals, female impersonators usually call themselves and are called drag queens. In the same way, their performances are referred to by themselves and others as drag shows.

But when the varied meanings of drag are taken into consideration, it should be obvious why the drag queen is an ambivalent figure in the gay world. The drag queen symbolizes all that homosexuals say they fear the most in themselves, all that they say they feel guilty about; he symbolizes, in fact, *the* stigma. In this way, the term 'drag queen' is comparable to 'nigger'. And like that word, it may be all right in an ingroup context but not in an outgroup one. Those who do not want to think of themselves or be identified as drag queens under any circumstances attempt to disassociate themselves from 'drag' completely. These homosexuals deplore drag shows and profess total lack of interest in them. Their attitude toward drag queens is one of condemnation combined with the expression of vast social distance between themselves and the drag queen.

Other homosexuals enjoy being queens among themselves, but do not want to be stigmatized by the heterosexual culture. These homosexuals admire drag and drag queens in homosexual contexts, but deplore female impersonators and street fairies for 'giving us a bad name' or 'projecting the wrong image' to the heterosexual culture. The drag queen is definitely a marked man in the subculture.

Homosexuality consists of sex-role deviation made up of two related but distinct parts: 'wrong' sexual object choices and 'wrong' sex-role presentation of self.[5] The first deviation is shared by all homosexuals, but it can be hidden best. The second deviation logically (in this culture) corresponds with the first, which it symbolizes. But it cannot be hidden, and it actually compounds the stigma.

Thus, insofar as female impersonators are professional drag queens, they are evaluated positively by gay people to the extent that they have perfected a subcultural skill and to the extent that gay people are willing to oppose the heterosexual culture directly (in much the same way that Negroes now call themselves blacks). On the other hand, they are despised because they symbolize and embody the stigma. At present, the balance is far on the negative side, although this varies by context and by the position of the observer (relative to the stigma). This explains the impersonators' negative identification with the term *drag queen* when it is used by outsiders. (In the same way, they at first used masculine pronouns of address and reference toward each other in my presence, but reverted to feminine pronouns when I became more or less integrated into the system.)

THE CAMP

While all female impersonators are drag queens in the gay world, by no means are all of them 'camps'. Both the drag queen and the camp are expressive performing roles, and both specialize in transformation. But the drag queen is concerned with masculine-feminine transformation, while the camp is concerned with what might be called a philosophy of transformations and incongruity. Certainly the two roles are intimately related, since to be a feminine man is by definition incongruous. But strictly speaking, the drag queen simply expresses the incongruity while the camp actually uses it to achieve a higher synthesis. To the extent that a drag queen does this, he is called 'campy'. The drag queen role is emotionally charged and connotes low status for most homosexuals because it bears the visible stigmata of homosexuality; camps, however, are found at all status levels in the homosexual subculture and are very often the center of primary group organization.[6]

The camp is the central role figure in the subcultural ideology of camp. The camp ethos or style plays a role analogous to 'soul' in the Negro subculture (cf. Keil: 164–90). Like soul, camp is a 'strategy for a situation'.[7] The special perspective of the female impersonators is a case of a broader homosexual ethos. This is the perspective of moral deviance and, consequently, of a 'spoiled identity', in Goffman's terms. Like the Negro problem, the homosexual problem centers on self-hatred and the lack of self-esteem.[8] But if 'the soul ideology ministers to the needs for identity' (Keil: 165), the camp ideology ministers to the needs for dealing with an identity that is well defined but loaded with contempt. As one impersonator who was also a well known camp told me, 'No one is more miserable about homosexuality than the homosexual'.

Camp is not a thing. Most broadly it signifies a *relationship between* things, people, and activities or qualities, and homosexuality. In this sense, 'camp taste', for instance, is synonymous with homosexual taste. Informants stressed that even between individuals there is very little agreement on what is camp because camp is in the eye of the beholder, that is, different homosexuals like different things, and because of the spontaneity and individuality of camp,

camp taste is always changing. This has the advantage, recognized by some informants, that a clear division can always be maintained between homosexual and 'straight' taste. An informant said Susan Sontag was wrong about camp's being a cult,[9]

> and the moment it becomes a public cult, you watch the queens stop it. Because if it becomes the squares, it doesn't belong to them any more. And what will be 'camp art', no queen will own. It's like taking off the work clothes and putting on the home clothes. When the queen is coming home, she wants to come home to a campy apartment that's hers – it's very queer – because all day long she's been very straight. So when it all of a sudden becomes very straight – to come home to an apartment that any square could have – she's not going to have it any more.[10]

While camp is in the eye of the homosexual beholder, it is assumed that there is an underlying unity of perspective among homosexuals that gives any particular campy thing its special flavor. It is possible to discern strong themes in any particular campy thing or event. The three that seemed most recurrent and characteristic to me were *incongruity*, *theatricality*, and *humor*. All three are intimately related to the homosexual situation and strategy. Incongruity is the subject matter of camp, theatricality its style, and humor its strategy.

Camp usually depends on the perception or creation of *incongruous juxtapositions*. Either way, the homosexual 'creates' the camp, by pointing out the incongruity or by devising it. For instance, one informant said that the campiest thing he had seen recently was a midwestern football player in high drag at a Halloween ball. He pointed out that the football player was seriously trying to be a lady, and so his intent was not camp, but that the *effect* to the observer was campy. (The informant went on to say that it would have been even campier if the football player had been picked up by the police and had his picture published in the paper the next day.) This is an example of unintentional camp, in that the campy person or thing does not perceive the incongruity.

Created camp also depends on transformations and juxtapositions, but here the effect is intentional. The most concrete examples can be seen in the apartments of campy queens, for instance, in the idea of growing plants in the toilet tank. One queen said that *TV Guide* had described a little Mexican horse statue as campy. He said there was nothing campy about this at all, but if you put a nude cut-out of Bette Davis on it, it would be campy. Masculine-feminine juxtapositions are, of course, the most characteristic kind of camp, but any very incongruous contrast can be campy. For instance, juxtapositions of high and low status, youth and old age, profane and sacred functions or symbols, cheap and expensive articles are frequently used for camp purposes. Objects or people are often said to be campy, but the camp inheres not in the person or thing itself but in the tension between that person or thing and the context or association. For instance, I was told by impersonators that a homosexual clothes designer made himself a beautiful Halloween ball gown. After the ball he sold it to a wealthy society lady. It was said that when he wore it, it was very campy, but when she wore it, it was just an expensive gown, unless she had run around her ball saying she was really not herself but her faggot dress designer.

The nexus of this perception by incongruity lies in the basic homosexual experience, that is, squarely on the moral deviation. One informant said, 'Camp is based on homosexual thought. It is all based on the idea of two men or two women in bed. It's incongruous and it's funny'. If moral deviation is the locus of the perception of incongruity, it is more specifically role deviation and role manipulation that are at the core of the second property of camp, *theatricality*.

Camp is theatrical in three interlocking ways. First of all, camp is style. Importance tends to shift from what a thing *is* to how it *looks*, from *what* is done to *how* it is done. It has been remarked that homosexuals excel in the decorative arts. The kind of incongruities that are campy are very often created by adornment or stylization of a well-defined thing or symbol. But the emphasis on style goes further than this in that camp is also exaggerated, consciously 'stagey', specifically theatrical. This is especially true of *the* camp, who is definitely a performer.

The second aspect of theatricality in camp is its dramatic form. Camp, like drag, always involves a performer or performers and an audience. This is its structure. It is only stretching the point a little to say that even in unintentional camp, this interaction is maintained. In the case of the football player, his behavior was transformed by his audience into a performance. In many cases of unintentional camp, the camp performs to his audience by commenting on the behavior or appearance of 'the scene', which is then described as 'campy'. In intentional camp, the structure of performer and audience is almost always clearly defined.

Third, camp is suffused with the perception of 'being as playing a role' and 'life as theatre' (Sontag 1964: 529). It is at this point that drag and camp merge and augment each other. I was led to an appreciation of this while reading Parker Tyler's appraisal of Greta Garbo. Garbo is generally regarded in the homosexual community as 'high camp'. Tyler stated that '"Drag acts", I believe, are not confined to the declassed sexes. Garbo "got in drag" whenever she took some heavy glamour part, whenever she melted in or out of a man's arms, whenever she simply let that heavenly-flexed neck ... bear the weight of her thrown-back head' (Tyler: 12). He concludes, 'How resplendent seems the art of acting! It is all *impersonation*, whether the sex underneath is true or not' (Tyler: 28).

We have to take the long way around to get at the real relationship between Garbo and camp. The homosexual is stigmatized, but his stigma can be hidden. In Goffman's terminology, information about his stigma can be managed. Therefore, of crucial importance to homosexuals themselves and to non-homosexuals is whether the stigma is displayed so that one is immediately recognizable or is hidden so that he can pass to the world at large as a respectable citizen. The covert half (conceptually, not necessarily numerically) of the homosexual community is engaged in 'impersonating' respectable citizenry, at least some of the time. What is being impersonated?

The stigma essentially lies in being less than a man and in doing something that is unnatural (wrong) for a man to do. Surrounding this essence is a halo effect: violation of culturally standardized canons of taste, behavior, speech, and so on, rigorously associated (prescribed) with the male role (e.g., fanciful or decorative clothing styles, 'effeminate' speech and manner, expressed disinterest in women as sexual objects, expressed interest in men as sexual objects, unseemly concern with personal appearance, etc.). The covert homosexual must therefore do two things: first, he must conceal the fact that he sleeps with men. But concealing this *fact* is far less difficult than his second problem, which is controlling the *halo effect* or signals that would announce that he sleeps with men. The covert homosexual must in fact impersonate a *man,* that is, he must *appear* to the 'straight' world to be fulfilling (or not violating) all the requisites of the male role as defined by the 'straight' world.

The immediate relationship between Tyler's point about Garbo and camp/drag is this: if Garbo playing women is drag, then homosexuals 'passing' are playing men; they are in drag. This is the larger implication of drag/camp. In fact, gay people often use the word 'drag' in this broader sense, even to include role-playing which most people simply take for granted: role-playing in school, at the office, at parties, and so on. In fact, all of life is role and theater – appearance.

But granted that all acting is impersonation, what moved Tyler to designate Garbo's acting specifically as 'drag'? Drag means, first of all, role-playing. The way in which it defines role-playing contains its implicit attitude. The word 'drag' attaches specifically to the outward, visible appurtenances of a role. In the type case, sex role, drag primarily refers to the wearing apparel and accessories that designate a human being as male or female, when it is worn by the opposite sex. By focusing on the outward appearance of role, drag implies that sex role and, by extension, role in general is something superficial, which can be manipulated, put on and off again at will. The drag concept implies *distance* between the actor and the role or 'act'. But drag also means 'costume'. This theatrical referent is the key to the attitude toward role-playing embodied in drag as camp. Role-playing is *play*; it is an act or show. The necessity to play at life, living role after superficial role, should not be the cause of bitterness or despair. Most of the sex role and other impersonations that male homosexuals do are done with ease, grace, and especially humor. The actor should throw himself into it; he should put on a good show; he should view the whole experience as fun, as a camp.[11]

The double stance toward role, putting on a good show while indicating distance (showing that it is a show) is the heart of drag as camp. Garbo's acting was thought to be 'drag' because it was considered markedly androgynous, and because she played (even overplayed) the role of *femme fatale* with style. No man (in her movies) and very few audiences (judging by her success) could resist her allure. And yet most of the men she seduced were her victims because she was only playing at love – only acting. This is made quite explicit in the film *Mata Hari* in which Garbo the spy seduces men to get information from them.

The third quality of camp is its *humor*. Camp is for fun; the aim of camp is to make an audience laugh. In fact, it is a *system* of humor. Camp humor is a system of laughing at one's incongruous position instead of crying.[12] That is, the humor does not cover up, it transforms. I saw the reverse transformation – from laughter to pathos – often enough, and it is axiomatic among the impersonators that when the camp cannot laugh, he dissolves into a maudlin bundle of self-pity.

One of the most confounding aspects of my interaction with the impersonators was their tendency to laugh at situations that to me were horrifying or tragic. I was amazed, for instance, when one impersonator described to me as 'very campy' the scene in *What Ever Happened to Baby Jane?* in which Bette Davis served Joan Crawford a rat, or the scene in which Bette Davis makes her 'comeback' in the parlor with the piano player.

Of course, not all impersonators and not all homosexuals are campy. *The camp* is a homosexual wit and clown; his campy productions and performances are a continuous creative strategy for dealing with the homosexual situation, and, in the process, defining a positive homosexual identity. As one performer summed it up for me, 'Homosexuality is a way of life that is against all ways of life, including nature's. And no one is more aware of it than the homosexual. The camp accepts his role as a homosexual and flaunts his homosexuality. He makes the other homosexuals laugh; he makes life a little brighter for them. And he builds a bridge to the straight people by getting them to laugh with him'. The same man described the role of the camp more concretely in an interview:

> Well, 'to camp' actually means 'to sit in front of a group of people' . . . not on-stage, but you *can* camp on-stage . . . I think that I do that when I talk to the audience. I think I'm camping with 'em. But a 'camp' herself is a queen who sits and starts entertaining a group of people at a bar around her. They all start listening to what she's got to say. And she says campy things. Oh, somebody smarts off at her and she gives 'em a very flip answer. A camp is a flip person who has declared emotional freedom. She is going to say to the world, 'I'm queer'. Although she may not do this all the time, but most of the time a camp queen will. She'll walk down the street and she'll see you and say, 'Hi, Mary, how are you?' right in the busiest part of town . . . she'll actually camp, right there. And she'll swish down the street. And she may be in a business suit; she doesn't have to be dressed outlandishly. Even at work the people figure that she's a camp. They don't know what to *call* her, but they hire her 'cause she's a good kid, keeps the office laughing, doesn't bother anybody, and everyone'll

say, 'Oh, running around with Georgie's more fun! He's just more fun!'
The squares are saying this. And the other ones [homosexuals] are saying,
'Oh, you've got to know George, she's a camp'. Because the whole time
she's light-hearted. Very seldom is camp sad. Camp has got to be flip. A
camp queen's got to think faster than other queens. *This* makes her camp.
She's got to have an answer to anything that's put to her ...'[13]

Now *homosexuality* is *not* camp. But you take a camp, and she turns
around and she makes homosexuality funny, but not ludicrous: funny but
not ridiculous ... this is a great, great art. This is a fine thing ... Now
when it suddenly became the word ... became like ... it's like the word
'Mary'. Everybody's 'Mary'. 'Hi, Mary. How are you, Mary'. And like
'girl'. You may be talking to one of the butchest queens in the world, but
you still say, 'Oh, girl'. And sometimes they say, 'Well, don't call me
"she" and don't call me "girl". I don't feel like a girl. I'm a *man*. I just like
to go to bed with you girls. I don't want to go to bed with another man'.
And you say, 'Oh, girl, get you. Now she's turned butch'. And so you
camp about it. It's sort of laughing at yourself instead of crying. And a
good camp will make you laugh along with her, to where you suddenly
feel ... you don't feel like she's made fun of you. She's sort of made light
of a bad situation.

The camp queen makes no bones about it; to him the gay world is the
'sisterhood'. By accepting his homosexuality and flaunting it, the camp
undercuts all homosexuals who won't accept the stigmatized identity. Only
by fully embracing the stigma itself can one neutralize the sting and make it
laughable.[14] Not all references to the stigma are campy, however. Only if it is
pointed out as a joke is it camp, although there is no requirement that the
jokes be gentle or friendly. A lot of camping is extremely hostile; it is almost
always sarcastic. But its intent is humorous as well. Campy queens are very
often said to be 'bitches' just as camp humor is said to be 'bitchy'.[15] The
campy queen who can 'read' (put down) all challengers and cut everyone
down to size is admired. Humor is the campy queen's weapon. A camp queen
in good form can come out on top (by group consensus) against all the
competition.

Female impersonators who use drag in a comic way or are themselves comics
are considered camps by gay people. (Serious glamour drag is considered
campy by many homosexuals, but it is unintentional camp. Those who see
glamour drag as a serious business do not consider it to be campy. Those who
think it is ludicrous for drag queens to take themselves seriously see the whole
business as a campy incongruity.) Since the camp role is a positive one, many
impersonators take pride in being camps, at least on stage.[16] Since the camp
role depends to such a large extent on verbal agility, it reinforces the superiority of the live performers over record performers, who, even if they are
comic, must depend wholly on visual effects.

NOTES

1. In two Broadway plays (since made into movies) dealing with English homosexuals, *The Killing of Sister George* (lesbians) and *Staircase* (male homosexuals), drag played a prominent role. In *George,* an entire scene shows George and her lover dressed in tuxedos and top hats on their way to a drag party. In *Staircase,* the entire plot turns on the fact that one of the characters has been arrested for 'going in drag' to the local pub. Throughout the second act, this character wears a black shawl over his shoulders. This item of clothing is symbolic of full drag. This same character is a camp and, in my opinion, George was a very rare bird, a lesbian camp. Both plays, at any rate, abounded in camp humor. *The Boys* in *the Band,* another recent play and movie, doesn't feature drag as prominently but has two camp roles and much camp humor.

2. This concept was developed and suggested to me by Julian Pitt-Rivers.

3. Even one feminine item ruins the integrity of the masculine system; the male loses his caste honor. The superordinate role in a hierarchy is more fragile than the subordinate. Manhood must be achieved, and once achieved, guarded and protected.

4. The middle-class idea tends to be that any man who has had sexual relations with men is queer. The lower classes strip down to 'essentials', and the man who is 'dominant' can be normal (masculine). Lower-class men give themselves a bit more leeway before they consider themselves to be gay.

5. It becomes clear that the core of the stigma is in 'wrong' sexual object choice when it is considered that there is little stigma in simply being effeminate, or even in wearing feminine apparel in some contexts, as long as the male is known to be heterosexual, that is, known to sleep with women or, rather, not to sleep with men. But when I say that sleeping with men is the core of the stigma, or that feminine behavior logically corresponds with this, I do not mean it in any causal sense. In fact, I have an impression that some homosexual men sleep with men *because* it strengthens their identification with the feminine role, rather than the other way around. This makes a lot of sense developmentally, if one assumes, as I do, that children learn sex-role identity before they learn any strictly sexual object choices. In other words, I think that children learn they are boys or girls before they are made to understand that boys *only* love girls and vice versa.

6. The role of the 'pretty boy' is also a very positive one, and in some ways the camp is an alternative for those who are not pretty. However, the pretty boy is subject to the depredations of aging, which in the subculture is thought to set in at thirty (at the latest). Because the camp depends on inventiveness and wit rather than on physical beauty, he is ageless.

7. This phrase is used by Kenneth Burke in reference to poetry and is used by Keil in a sociological sense.

8. I would say that the main problem today is heterosexuals, just as the main problem for blacks is whites.

9. I don't want to pass over the implication here that female impersonators keep up with Susan Sontag. Generally, they don't. I had given the quoted informant Susan Sontag's 'Notes on "Camp"' to see what he would say. He was college educated and perfectly able to get through it. He was enraged (justifiably, I felt) that she had almost edited homosexuals out of camp.

10. Informants said that many ideas had been taken over by straights through the mass media, but that the moment this happened the idea would no longer be campy. For instance, one man said that a queen he knew had gotten the idea of growing plants in the water tank of the toilet. But the idea is no longer campy because it is being advertised through such mass media as *Family Circle* magazine. How to defend any symbols or values from the absorbing powers of the mass media? Jules Henry, I believe, was one of the first to point to the power of advertising to subvert

traditional values by appropriating them for commercial purposes. But subcultural symbols and values lose their integrity in the same way. Although Sontag's New York avant-garde had already appropriated camp from homosexuals, they did so in the effort to create their own aristocracy or integrity of taste as against the mass culture.

11. It is clear to me now how camp undercuts rage and therefore rebellion by ridiculing serious and concentrated bitterness.

12. It would be worthwhile to compare camp humor with the humor systems of other oppressed people (Eastern European Jewish, Negro, etc.).

13. Speed and spontaneity are of the essence. For example, at a dinner party, someone said, 'Oh, we forgot to say grace'. One woman folded her hands without missing a beat and intoned, 'Thank God everyone at this table is gay'.

14. It's important to stress again that camp is a pre- or protopolitical phenomenon. The anti-camp in this system is the person who wants to dissociate from the stigma to be like the oppressors. The camp says, 'I am not like the oppressors'. But in so doing he agrees with the oppressors' definition of who he is. The new radicals deny the stigma in a different way, by saying that the oppressors are illegitimate. This step is only foreshadowed in camp. It is also interesting that the lesbian wing of the radical homosexuals have come to women's meetings holding signs saying: 'We are the women your parents warned you against'.

15. The 'bitch', as I see it, is a woman who *accepts* her inferior status, but refuses to do so gracefully or without fighting back. Women and homosexual men are oppressed by straight men, and it is no accident that both are beginning to move beyond bitchiness toward refusal of inferior status.

16. Many impersonators told me that they got tired of being camps for their friends, lovers, and acquaintances. They often felt they were asked to gay parties simply to entertain and camp it up, and said they did not feel like camping off stage, or didn't feel competent when out of drag. This broadens out into the social problem of all clowns and entertainers, or, even further, to anyone with a talent. He will often wonder if he is loved for himself.

REFERENCES

Goffman, Erving, *Stigma*, Englewood Cliffs: Prentice-Hall, 1963.

Henry, Jules, *Culture Against Man*, New York: Random House, 1963.

Keil, Charles, *Urban Blues*, Chicago: U of Chicago P, 1966.

Tyler, Parker, 'The Garbo Image', in Michael Conway, Dion McGregor & Mark Ricci (eds.), *The Films of Greta Garbo* New York Citadel, n.d., 9–31.

6

IT'S BEING SO CAMP
AS KEEPS US GOING

Richard Dyer

Arguments have lasted all night about what camp really is and what it means. There are two different interpretations which connect at certain points – camping about is one, mincing and screaming. The other is a certain taste in art and entertainment, a certain sensibility.

Camping about has a lot to be said for it. First of all and above all, it's very us. It is a distinctive way of behaving and of relating to each other that we have evolved. To have a good camp together gives you a tremendous sense of identification and belonging. It is just about the only style, language and culture that is distinctively and unambiguously gay male. One of our greatest problems I think is that we are cut adrift for most of the time in a world drenched in straightness. All the images and words of the society express and confirm the rightness of heterosexuality. Camp is one thing that expresses and confirms being a gay man.

Then again camp is fun. It's quite easy to pick up the lingo and get into the style, and it makes even quite dull people witty. Fun and wit are their own justification, but camp fun has other merits too. It's a form of self-defence. Particularly in the past, the fact that gay men could so sharply and brightly make fun of themselves meant that the real awfulness of their situation could be kept at bay – they need not take things too seriously, need not let it get them down. Camp kept, and keeps, a lot of gay men going.

And camp is not masculine. By definition, camping about is not butch. So camp is a way of being human, witty and vital (for the whole camp stance is full

First published in *Playguy*, 1976, and reprinted in *The Body Politic Review Supplement* (Toronto), 10:36, September 1977.

of vitality), without conforming to the drabness and rigidity of the hetero male role. You've only got to think of the impact of Quentin Crisp's high camp (accurately enough charted in the Thames TV film *The Naked Civil Servant*) on the straight world he came up against, to see that camp has a radical/progressive potential: scaring muggers who know that all this butch male bit is not really them but who feel they have to act as if it is (Quentin showed that he knew they were screamers underneath it all); running rings of logic and wit round the pedestrian ideas of psychiatrists, magistrates and the rest; and developing by living out a high camp life-style a serenity and a sense of being at-one-with-yourself (caught in the beautifully camp line, 'I am one of the stately homos of Britain').

Identity and togetherness, fun and wit, self-protection and thorns in the flesh of straight society – these are the pluses of camp. Unfortunately there are also minuses, and they are precisely the opposite side of those positive features.

The togetherness you get from camping about is fine – but not everybody actually feels able to camp about. A bunch of queens screaming together can be very exclusive for someone who isn't a queen or feels unable to camp. The very tight togetherness that makes it so good to be one of the queens is just the thing that makes a lot of other gay men feel left out. One of the sadder features of the gay movement is the down so many activists have on queens and camp – on the only heritage we've got. But it can work the other way around too – some queens despise the straight-looking (or otherwise non-queenly) gays around them, as if camping about is the only way of being gay. You have to let people be gay in the way that's best for them.

The fun, the wit, has its drawbacks too. It tends to lead to an attitude that you can't take anything seriously, everything has to be turned into a witticism or a joke. Camp finds CHE (the Campaign for Homosexual Equality) too dull, GLF (the Gay Liberation Front) too political, all the movement activities just not fun enough. It's a fair point – up to a point CHE and GLF can be a bit glum and a bit heavy. But actually they've got quite a serious job to do. Life is not a bed of roses for gay men, still; sexism and our own male chauvinism are hard to understand, come to terms with, change. That does not always lend itself to fun and wit, but it needs to be done all the same.

Again, the self-mockery of self-protection can have a corrosive effect on us. We can keep mocking ourselves to the point where we really do think we're a rather pathetic, inferior lot. Phrases like 'silly Nelly', 'Chance'd be a fine thing' and 'It's too much for a white woman', funny though they are, have a lot that is self-hating about them – behind them linger such ideas as 'How stupid I am', 'I'm too wretched and ugly to attract anyone', 'I'm too sexually hung-up to be able to give myself physically' ... Camp can help us from letting the social, cultural situation of gays getting us down: but it is the situation that's wrong, not ourselves. Camp sometimes stops us seeing that.

Camping about then is good and bad, progressive and reactionary. Often it's very hard to disentangle these two aspects. For instance, I am very much in the habit of calling men 'she': a man with a large cock is 'a big girl'; to a man showing off, I'll say 'Get her!'; I welcome friends with 'It's Miss Jones' (or whatever the man's name is). In one way, this is a good habit. After all, I'm glad to be gay and I prefer straight women (i.e. most women) to straight men (i.e. most men). Calling gay men 'she' means I don't think of them, or myself, as straight men (with all that that implies). But given the actual situation of women in society, and given that however hard I try, there's still plenty of male chauvinism about me, there is something rather suspect about this habit. Isn't it tantamount to saying gay men are inferior to straight men, just as women are? Isn't it really a put-down of gay men, and of women? It's hard to decide, and in the end I think I'll go on doing it because I'd rather gay men identified with straight women than with straight men, since most of the values associated with masculinity in this society (aggressiveness, competitiveness, being 'above' tenderness and emotion) I reject. Yet the whole practice, like so much of camp, is deeply ambiguous. So much depends on what you feel about men and women, about sex, about being gay.

The context of camp is important too. Camp means a lot at a gathering of gay people, or used defiantly by open gays against straightness: but it is very easily taken up by straight society and used against us. We know two things about camp that straights, at any rate as the media and everyday jokes show it, don't – that it is nice to be a queen (can be, should be); and that not all gay men are queens. The straight media have taken up the queen image which we have created but use it against us. To a limited extent, they appreciate the wit, but they don't see why it was necessary. They pick up the undertow of self-oppression without ever latching on to the elements of criticism and defiance of straightness. And they just never seem to realize that camping is only one way of being gay. Camp queens are the inevitable image of gayness in art and the media. As I see it, this rather catches us in a cleft stick. We should defend camp, whether we're queens or not; at the same time, we've got to make it clear that we are not all camp all the same. That's a rather complicated argument for the straight media. It's also quite a complicated problem for us too – but ultimately I think we should be open about allowing each other to be queens or not as we feel, and should try to build on the anti-butch fun and wit legacy of camp as a way of building gayness into a better society.

What then of camp as a kind of taste or sensibility?

It is easy, and usual, to offer a list of camp things at the beginning of discussions of camp, so that we all know what we are talking about. Thus:

Nelson Eddy and Jeanette MacDonald
Aubrey Beardsley
Vienna waltzes
most classical ballet
Busby Berkeley
the Queen Mother

Ronald Firbank
velvet and brocade curtains
Marlene Dietrich.

Such lists are, however, a bit misleading, since camp is far more a question of how you respond to things rather than qualities actually inherent in those things. It's perfectly possible to take MacDonald and Eddy seriously as lovers in musicals, or the Queen Mother as an embodiment of Britannic royalty, or Beardsley as a draughtsman, and so on. Equally, you can find things camp which are, on the face of it, the very antithesis of camp – John Wayne, for instance, or Wagner. It's all a question of how you look at it.

How then to define the camp way of looking at things? Basically, it is a way of prising the form of something away from its content, of revelling in the style while dismissing the content as trivial. If you really believed in the emotions and stories of classical ballet, in the rightness and value of royalty, in the properness of supervirility and fascism, then you could not find *The Sleeping Beauty,* the Queen Mother, or John Wayne camp. What I value about camp is that it is precisely a weapon against the mystique surrounding art, royalty and masculinity – it cocks an irresistible snook, it demystifies by playing up the artifice by means of which such things as these retain their hold on the majority of the population.

It is interesting to speculate about why it is that camp should be the form that male gay culture has taken. Susan Sontag (1964b), in a marvellous essay, suggests that camp is the way gay men have sought to make some impression on the culture of the society they live in. Mastery of style and wit has been a way of declaiming that gays have something distinctive to offer society. This seems to me to be true. Gay men have made certain 'style professions' very much theirs (at any rate by association, even if not necessarily in terms of the numbers of gays actually employed in these professions) – hairdressing, interior decoration, dress design, ballet, musicals, revue. These occupations have made the life of society as a whole more elegant and graceful, and the show-biz end has provided the world at large with many pleasant evenings. At the same time hairdressing, interior decoration and the rest are clearly marked with the camp sensibility – they are style for style's sake, they don't have 'serious' content (a hairstyle is not 'about' anything), they don't have a practical use (they're just nice), and the actual forms taken accentuate artifice, fun and occasionally outrageousness – all that chi-chi and tat, those pinks and lace and sequins and tassels, curlicues and 'features' in the hair, satin drapes and chiffon scarves and fussy ornaments, all the paraphernalia of a camp sensibility that has provided gay men with a certain legitimacy in the world.

A certain legitimacy only. The very luxuriousness and 'uselessness' of these professions have also tended to reinforce the image of gay men as decadent, marginal, frivolous – above all, not involved in the real production of wealth (on the shopfloor or in the management offices) in society, just sterile parasites on the edges. And too the association of so much of the camp style professions with women is ambiguous. Although women in our society are involved in production, none the less their social role is seen as being adjuncts to men, not just to provide a man with a wife, servant and mother to 'his' kids, but also to display his wealth by her smartness, the frequency of her hair-dos, the number of her frocks. This applies above all to the wealthy of course, where the lady in her Paris fashions displays her husband's buying power and her access (by virtue of his position) to the canons of fashion and good taste. But in less spectacular forms it works further down the social scale. Most husbands expect their wives to 'look nice', to make an effort with their appearance when they take them out. It is only the poorest husband whose wife cannot afford a bouffant hair-do, some fake fur and a glass brooch for Saturday night out. And we gay men have been deeply involved in creating the styles and providing the services for the 'turn-out' of the women of the western world. This gives us legitimacy – but as parasites on women, who are themselves seen as subordinate to men and objects of luxury (however meagre). Moreover, the involvement of camp in objectifying women in this way (reaching its apotheosis in Busby Berkeley's production numbers – though I've never heard that he himself was gay) makes it something that anyone who cares about everyone's liberation should be wary of.

But that's a digression. Let's get back to the point about camp evolving because gay men have staked out a claim on society at large by mastery of style and artifice. That seems true, but the question still remains: why style and artifice rather than anything else? A reason is suggested by a German survey of gay people, the results of which were published in an early *Gay News* (London). They found that gays were extremely 'adaptable'; that is, we tend to find it easy to fit in to any occupation, or set-up, or circle of people. Or rather, and this is the point, we find it easy to appear to fit in, we are good at picking up the rules, conventions, forms and appearances of different social circles. And why? Because we've had to be good at it, we've had to be good at disguise, at appearing to be one of the crowd, the same as everyone else. Because we had to hide what we really felt (gayness) for so much of the time, we had to master the façade of whatever social set-up we found ourselves in – we couldn't afford to stand out in any way, for it might give the game away about our gayness. So we have developed an eye and an ear for surfaces, appearances, forms – style. Small wonder then that when we came to develop our own culture, the habit of style should have remained so dominant in it.

Looked at in this way, the camp sensibility is very much a product of our oppression. And, inevitably, it is scarred by that oppression. Some of the minuses of camp as a sensibility I've already mentioned – the relegation of its practitioners to licensed decorators on the edges of society, its involvement with the objectification of women. Other minuses resemble the drawbacks of camp behaviour.

The emphasis on surface and style can become obsessive – nothing can be taken seriously, anything deep or problematic or heavy is shimmied away from in a flurry of chic. Camp seems often unable to discriminate between those things that need to be treated for laughs and style, and those that are genuinely serious and important.

Besides this, camp is so beguiling that it has been adopted by many straights of late. (Think of the tone of much criticism of the arts these days – BBC2's *Film Night*, nostalgia books, the TV criticism of Clive James and Nancy Banks-Smith.) But something happens to camp when taken over by straights – it loses its cutting edge, its identification with the gay experience, its distance from the straight sexual world-view. Take the example of John Wayne. Many straight men find him camp now, but they love him just the same. Gay camp can emphasize what a production number the Wayne image is – the lumbering gait, drawling voice and ever more craggy face are a deliberately constructed and manufactured image of virility. In this way, gay camp can stop us from treating John Wayne as an embodiment of what it 'really' means to be a man. Straight camp puts a different emphasis. The authority, power and roughness of the Wayne image are still dear to the straight imagination, but they have been criticized heavily enough in recent years (by gays and camp among others) for there to be embarrassment about directly accepting or endorsing such qualities. Camp allows straight audiences to reject the style of John Wayne; but because it is so pleasant to laugh, it also allows for a certain wistful affection for him to linger on. However, affection for John Wayne can only be in reality affection for that way of being a man. Straight camp allows images of butchness to retain their hold even while they are apparently being rejected.

Of course, this twisting of camp away from its radical/progressive/critical potential is only possible because of the ambiguity of camp even within gay circles. (For instance, the drawings of Tom of Finland are at one level over-the-top camp, but also clearly a turn-on too.) Not all gay camp is in fact progressive, but none the less it does have the potential of being so. What camp can do is to demystify the images and world-view of art and the media. We are encouraged by schooling to be very solemn in the presence of art; and we are tempted by film and television to be drawn into the worlds they present as if they were real. Camp can make us see that what art and the media give us are not the Truth or Reality but fabrications, particular ways of talking about the world, particular understandings and feelings of the way life is. Art and the media don't give us life as it really is – how could they ever? – but only life as artists and producers think it is. Camp, by drawing attention to the artifices employed by artists, can constantly remind us that what we are seeing is only a view of life. This doesn't stop us enjoying it, but it does stop us believing what we are shown too readily. It stops us thinking that those who create the landscape of culture know more about life than we do ourselves. A camp appreciation of art and the media can keep us on our guard against them – and considering their view of gayness, and sexuality in general, that's got to be a good thing.

In his introduction to the first *Playguy* [The British gay magazine which originally commissioned this article in 1976] he edited, Roger Baker quoted

Dennis Altman's lovely phrase, 'Camp is to gay what soul is to black' (1971: 141). That's right – but push at the resemblance a bit and you get to the ambiguities of both camp and soul. Soul is not unequivocally a good thing. Certainly, it provides blacks (some blacks) with a definitely black culture; with its roots in religion, it provides an openness to irrational experience that white culture tends to play down; and with its connections to dance and ritual, it allows for a physical freedom, a being-at-home-in-your-body, that repressed white culture shies away from. But soul also reinforces notions of black people as mindless, superstitious and sex-obsessed – it may at times hold them back from making claims on the equally human and useful attributes of rationality and restraint. There is the same equivocality about camp – it does give us (some of us) an identity, it does undercut sex roles and the dominant world-view, it is fun; but it can also trap us if we are not careful in the endless pursuit of enjoyment at any price, in a rejection of seriousness and depth of feeling. What we've got to do is to activate the positive attributes of camp – mince in the streets, send up Kojak and Burt Reynolds and Colt models, come together for a camp, keep our oppression at bay with a scream and a joke – without letting them trap us.

You know those clenched fists you get on political badges (including women's liberation and GLF)? Well, why shouldn't it be a clenched fist on a limp wrist? Divine.

7

THE CINEMA OF CAMP
(AKA CAMP AND THE GAY SENSIBILITY)

Jack Babuscio

Camp and the gay sensibility have rarely been explored in relation to cinema. On the rare occasions when they have, analyses have tended to draw upon all the usual and demeaning stereotypes of gayness. The term 'camp' has been widely misused to signify the trivial, superficial and 'queer'. The original meaning and complex associations of the term (some of which are outlined below) are ignored. Thus, just as it has always been a sign of worthiness to speak out on behalf of any oppressed minority *other* than gays, so, too, there exists – even within our own community – a corresponding reluctance on the part of those who take the cinema seriously to regard camp as a means of heightening our appreciation of any particular performance, film or director. We have emerged, triumphant, from our closets only to leave camp, locked up, behind us.

Camp, as a product of the gay sensibility, has always existed on the same sociocultural level as the sub-culture from which it has issued. In other words, camp, its sources and associations, have remained secret in their most fundamental aspects, just as the inner life of gays remains a secret, still, in the arts, throughout the media, and in the consciousness of non-gays generally. Critics have appropriated the term 'camp' but without any understanding of its roots or significance within the gay community. The sub-cultural attitudes, catalysts and needs that have gone to produce camp as a creative expression of the gay sensibility are never considered. Yet camp is, essentially, one of that sensibility's highest forms of expression.

This expanded and revised version of 'Camp and the Gay Sensibility' (first published in Richard Dyer, ed., *Gays and Film*, London: British Film Institute, 1977) appeared in *Gay Sunshine Journal*, 35, Winter 1978.

The trouble with the speculations on what the critics have thought to term 'camp' (aside from the fact that most of it is not, or is straight-camp – a very different thing) is that they never illuminate the gay sensibility, but, rather, go far to reinforce those very standards of judgement and aesthetic excellence which are often antithetical to it. Even Susan Sontag virtually edited gays out of her otherwise brilliant 'Notes on Camp' (1964b), though she did acknowledge that 'homosexual estheticism and irony' *is* one of the 'pioneering forces of modern sensibility'.[1] The assumption remains, then, that camp has emerged from out of no intelligent body of sociocultural phenomena. To say this is not, however, to plead for the application of any narrow sociological analysis. Rather, it is a way of saying that the worth of camp can simply not be understood in critical terms unless some attention is first given to the attitudes that go to produce it – attitudes which spring from our social situation and which are crucial to the development of a gay sensibility.

The purpose of this essay, then, is to consider some of the ways in which individual films, stars and directors reflect a gay sensibility. In the course of this exploration, I hope to accomplish the following aims: to provide a more precise definition of what is, at present, a most confused area of response that goes under the vague label of 'camp'; to ascertain the relationship of camp and gayness; to consider some of the social patterns and mechanisms that make for the gay sensibility; to relate these considerations to cinema with the purpose of stimulating discussion of a hitherto neglected aspect of film; to promote solidarity and a greater sense of identification within our community; and finally, to remind ourselves that what we see in cinema is neither truth nor reality, but fabrications: individual, *subjective* perceptions of the world and its inhabitants.

CAMP AND THE GAY SENSIBILITY

I define the gay sensibility as a creative energy reflecting a consciousness that is different from the mainstream; a heightened awareness of certain human complications of feeling that spring from the fact of social oppression; in short, a perception of the world which is coloured, shaped, directed, and defined by the fact of one's gayness. Such a perception of the world varies with time and place according to the nature of the specific set of circumstances in which, historically, we have found ourselves. Present-day society defines people as falling into distinct types. Such a method of labelling ensures that individual types become polarised. A complement of attributes thought to be 'natural' and 'normal' for members of these categories is assigned. Hence, heterosexuality = normal, natural, healthy behaviour; homosexuality = abnormal, unnatural, sick behaviour. Out of this process of polarisation there develops a twin set of perspectives and general understandings about what the world is like and how to deal with it; for gays, one such response is camp.

The term 'camp' describes those elements in a person, situation, or activity that express, or are created by, a gay sensibility. Camp is never a thing or person per se, but, rather, a relationship between activities, individuals, situations and gayness. People who have camp, e.g. screen 'personalities' such as Bette Davis, Mae West, George Arliss, Edward Everett Horton, or who are in some way responsible for camp – Busby Berkeley, Josef von Sternberg, Edith Head, Tennessee Williams – need not be gay. The link with gayness is established when the camp aspect of an individual or thing is identified as such by a gay sensibility. This is not to say that all gays respond in equal measure to camp, or, even, that an absolute consensus could easily be reached within our community about what to include or emphasize. Hume's observation that beauty is 'not a quality inherent in things: it only exists in the mind of the beholder' is also true of camp. Yet tough camp is largely a matter of individual perception, there is an underlying unity of perspective among gays that gives to someone or something its characteristic camp flavour. Four features are basic to camp: irony, aestheticism, theatricality, and humour.

Irony

Camp is ironic insofar as an incongruous contrast can be drawn between an individual/thing and its context/association. The most common of incongruous contrasts is that of masculine/feminine. Some of the best examples of this are found in the screen personalities of stars whose camp attraction owes much to their androgynous qualities: Rudolph Valentino, in his independent-Paramount productions which emphasise the 'feminine' component in his personality (*Monsieur Beaucaire*, *A Sainted Devil*, and *Cobra*); Greta Garbo, in all her films, but particularly *Queen Christina*, where she masquerades as a man; David Bowie, in *The Man Who Fell to Earth*, where the pop star's persona is achieved through radical neutering via the elision of masculine/feminine 'signs'; other examples – Holly Woodlawn (*Trash*), Montgomery Clift (*Red River*), James Dean (*East of Eden*, especially), Julie Harris (*Member of the Wedding*), Edouard Dermit (*Les Enfants Terribles*), Mathieu Carrière (*Malpertuis*), Elizabeth Bergner (*As You Like It*), etc. Another inconguous contrast is that of youth/(old) age, particularly young man/old(er) woman: Bud Cort and Ruth Gordon in *Harold and Maude*; Mercedes McCambridge and George Hamilton in *Angel Baby*; and, especially, Gloria Swanson and William Holden in *Sunset Boulevard*, where Swanson's baroquely detailed performance as imperious, aging ex-star Norma Desmond ('I'm still big, it's the pictures that got small!') seems as much a criticism of contemporary (post-1929 'Talkies') Hollywood as a reflection of Swanson's own emphatic, sexually brazen brand of silent-screen acting. Other incongruous contrasts are the sacred/profane (*The Picture of Dorian Gray*; *I'm No Angel*); spirit/flesh (*Summer and Smoke*; *The Roman Spring of Mrs. Stone*); high/low status, as in dozens of rags-to-riches musicals (*The Countess of Monte Cristo*; *Gold Diggers of 1933*) and melodramas (*Ruby Gentry*; *Beyond the Forest*).

At the core of this perception of incongruity is the idea of gayness as a moral deviation. Sex/love between two men or two women is regarded by society as incongruous – out of keeping with the 'normal', 'natural', 'healthy', heterosexual order of things. The inner knowledge of our unique social situation has produced in us a heightened awareness of the discrepancies that lie between appearance and reality, expression and meaning. Again, gay partnerships are subversive of conventional morality, being less bound by the sort of social inequalities (age, money, class, etc.) so characteristic of *heterosexual* relationships. A partnership between two men or two women is, in terms of sex caste, an equal relationship, and therefore, an implicit 'threat' to the established order of things. This 'treat' may be understood by us on an instinctive or intellectual level, but it is understood, and internalised, nonetheless.

Aestheticism

The aesthetic element is also basic to camp, and like irony, constitutes a criticism of the world as it is. Irony, if it is to be effective, must be shaped. The art of camp therefore relies largely upon arrangement, timing, and tone. Similarly, the ironic events and situations which life itself presents will be more or less effective as camp, depending on how well the precision, balance, and economy of a thing is maintained. Camp is aesthetic in three interrelated ways: as a view of art; as a view of life; and as a practical tendency in things or persons: 'It is through Art, and through Art only, that we can shield ourselves from the sordid perils of actual existence' (Wilde).

Wilde's epigram points to a crucial aspect of camp aestheticism: its opposition to puritan morality. Camp is subversive of commonly received standards: it challenges the status quo. As Susan Sontag has said, there is something profoundly propagandistic about it: 'homosexuals have pinned their integration into society on promoting the aesthetic sense. Camp is a solvent of morality. It neutralizes moral indignation'. Consistently followed as a comprehensive attitude, aestheticism inevitably leads to an ingrown selfishness in life, and to triviality in art (see Johnson). As a means to personal liberation through the exploration of experience, it is an assertion of one's self-integrity – a means of accommodation with society in which art becomes, at one and the same time, an intense mode of individualism and a form of spirited protest. And while camp advocates the dissolution of hard and inflexible moral rules, it pleads, too, for a morality of sympathy. Its viewpoint suggests a detachment from the tyranny of conventional standards. Here again, as R. V. Johnson has pointed out, there is an aspect of aestheticism which diverges from 'a puritan ethic of rigid "thou shalt nots"', preferring, instead, to regard people and ideas with due consideration to circumstances and individual temperament.

A good example of this viewpoint is found in Jack Hazan's quasi-documentary portrait of artist David Hockney, *A Bigger Splash*. Here the director manages to convey the wry, distancing nature of his subject's visual humour as an integral part of a gay sensibility that is defiantly different from the mainstream. Because Hockney responds to his gay 'stigma' by challenging social and aesthetic conventions in life and art, Hazan's concern is to show the various ways in which his subject's private life affects his art – or how art records personal experience and determines our future. Thus, the film relates to the artist's work in much the same way as the paintings do to life. The presence of the unseen beneath the surface is no less important than what one actually sees.

This double aspect in which things can be taken is further emphasised by the semi-documentary nature of Hazan's film. Hockney and his friends appear as themselves, so that the relationships portrayed are much the same as in reality. But the reality is also rehearsed: Hazan occasionally suggests themes for his 'characters' to act out, and the line separating being and role-playing becomes blurred. This convention appears to suit Hockney, whose deceptive innocence and disorientating self-created face (platinum blonde hair, owl-rimmed spectacles) exhibit a special feeling for performance and a flair for the theatrical. And though the film remains, in the final analysis, a subjective record of *one* gay life in which the conjunction of fantasy and experience make common cause, it does effectively isolate the strong strain of protest that resides in the gay sensibility. By wit, a well-organised evasiveness, and a preference for the artificial, Hockney manages a breakthrough into creativity.

This detached attitude does not necessarily indicate an inability to feel or perceive the seriousness of life. In Hockney's case, it is a means of defiance: a refusal to be overwhelmed by unfavourable odds. When the world is a rejecting place, the need grows correspondingly strong to project one's being – to explore the limits to which one's personality might attain – as a way of shielding the inner self from those on the outside who are too insensitive to understand. It is also a method whereby one can multiply personalities, play various parts, assume a variety of roles – both for fun as well as out of real need.

In film, the aesthetic element in camp further implies a movement away from contemporary concerns into realms of exotic or subjective fantasies; the depiction of states of mind that are (in terms of commonly accepted taboos and standards) suspect; an emphasis on sensuous surfaces, textures, imagery, and the evocation of mood as stylistic devices – not simply because they are appropriate to the plot, but as fascinating in themselves. Such tendencies as these are consonant with the spirit of aestheticism in camp, and also go some way toward explaining the charm which particular film genres have for a certain section of our community.

The horror genre, in particular, is susceptible to a camp interpretation. Not all horror films are camp, of course; only those which make the most of stylish conventions for expressing instant feeling, thrills, sharply defined personality, outrageous and 'unacceptable' sentiments, and so on. In addition, the psychological issues stated or implied, along with the sources of horror, must relate to some significant aspect of our situation and experience; e.g. the inner drives which threaten an individual's well-being and way of life (Tourneur's *The Cat People*; Mamoulian's *Dr. Jekyll and Mr. Hyde*), coping with pressures to conform and adapt (Siegel's *Invasion of the Body Snatchers*), the masking of 'abnormality' behind a façade of 'normality' (Robson's *The Seventh Victim*,

Ulmer's *The Black Cat*), personal rebellion against enforced restrictions (Hartford-Davis's *Incense for the Damned*).

As a practical tendency in things or persons, camp emphasises style as a means of self-projection, a conveyor of meaning, and an expression of emotional tone. Style is a form of consciousness; it is never 'natural', always acquired. Camp is also urban; it is, in part, a reaction to the anonymity, boredom, and socialising tendencies of technological society. Camp aims to transform the ordinary into something more spectacular. In terms of style, it signifies performance rather than existence. Clothes and decor, for example, can be a means of asserting one's identity, as well as a form of justification in a society which denies one's essential validity.[2] Just as the dandy of the nineteenth century sought in material visibility (as Auden has said of Baudelaire) 'a way out of the corrupt nature into which he, like everyone else, is born', so many of our community find in the decorative arts and the cultivation of exquisite taste a means of making something positive from a discredited social identity. Hence, the *soigné* furniture and furnishings of the flat designed for Franz in Fassbinder's *Fox and His Friends*, or the carefully cluttered modishness of Michael's apartment in William Friedkin's film adaptation of Mart Crowley's *The Boys in the Band*. By such means as these one aims to become what one wills, to exercise some control over one's environment. But the emphasis on style goes further. Camp is often exaggerated. When the stress on style is 'outrageous' or 'too much', it results in incongruities: the emphasis shifts from what a thing or a person is to what it *looks* like; from what is being done to *how* it is being done. This stress on stylisation can also explain why the musical comedy, with its high budgets and big stars, its open indulgence in sentiment, and its emphasis on atmosphere, mood, nostalgia, and the fantastic, is, along with horror, a film genre that is saturated with camp. This can best be seen in the boldly imaginative production numbers of Busby Berkeley, whose work reveals a penchant for total extravagance, voyeurism, and sexual symbolism that is particularly blatant in 'The Lady in the Tutti-Frutti Hat' sequence of *The Gang's All Here*, with its acres of female flesh, outrageously phallic dancing bananas, and Carmen Miranda at her most aggressively self-assertive.

Before turning to the next element of camp, a distinction must be drawn here between kitsch and camp. The latter implies fervent involvement – an ability to strongly identify with what is perceived as camp. Not so the former, which refers to the artistically shallow or vulgar, and is marked by sensationalism, sentimentalism, and slickness. According to the definition provided in Knaur's *Encyclopedia*, kitsch is defined as a realisation of artistic motifs falsified by stylistic hypersentimentality or inadequacy. It corresponds, in part, to a reactionary attitude. Hence, kitsch can be seen in the German cinema of the 1930s and early 1940s, as well as the Italian cinema under the Fascists. As far as Nazi cinema is concerned, the work of Veit Harlan is saturated with kitsch, e.g. the antisemitic *Jüd Süss*, 1941, and the schmaltz-laden pastoral romance *The Great Sacrifice*, 1944, starring Harlan's wife, Kristina Soderbaum. Both these films illustrate the fatal Nazi mania for blond beauty, nature and innocence, but lack the irony and affection which would make them seem less cruel and cold. Kitsch also favours certain genres, e.g. 'religious' epics (*The Greatest Story Ever Told*), hardcore porn (*Teeny Tulip*, *Carmen Baby*), and films with famous persons as their subject (*Mahler*, *The Music Lovers*, *Lisztomania*). Like camp, kitsch is partial to horror; but the latter exploits the voyeurism of its audience, whereas camp encourages an affectionate involvement.

Theatricality

The third element of camp is theatricality. To appreciate camp in things or persons is to perceive the notion of life-as-theatre, being versus role-playing, reality and appearance. If 'role' is defined as the appropriate behaviour associated with a given position in society, then gays do not conform to socially expected ways of behaving as men and women. Camp, by focusing on the outward appearances of role, implies that roles, and, in particular, sex roles, are superficial – a matter of style. Indeed, life itself is role and theatre, appearance and impersonation.

Theatricality relates to the gay situation primarily in respect to roles. Gays do not conform to sex-role expectations: we do not show appropriate interest in the opposite sex as a possible source of sexual satisfaction. We are therefore seen as something less than 'real' men and women. This is the essence of gay stigma, our so-called 'failing'. Gayness is seen as a sort of collective denial of the moral and social order of things. Our very lifestyle indicates a rejection of that most cherished cultural assumption which says that masculinity (including sexual dominance over women) is 'natural' and appropriate for men, and femininity (including sexual submissiveness toward men) is 'natural' and appropriate for women. The stigma of gayness is unique insofar as it is not immediately apparent either to ourselves or to others. Upon discovery of our gayness, however, we are confronted with the possibility of avoiding the negative sanctions attached to our supposed failing by concealing information (i.e. signs which other people take for gay) from the rest of the world. This crucial fact of our existence is called 'passing for straight', a phenomenon generally defined in the metaphor of theatre, that is, playing a role: pretending to be something that one is not; or, to shift the motive somewhat, to camouflage our gayness by withholding facts about ourselves which might lead others to the correct conclusion about our sexual orientation.[3]

The art of passing is an acting art: to pass is to be 'on stage', to impersonate heterosexual citizenry, to pretend to be a 'real' (i.e. non-gay) man or woman. To pass is to recreate, or transform, the self. Such a practice of passing (which can be occasional, continuous, in the past or present) means, in effect, that one must be always on one's guard lest one be seen to 'deviate' from those culturally standardised canons of taste, behaviour, speech, etc. that are generally associated with the male and female roles as defined by the society in which we live. Because masculinity and femininity are perceived in exclusively heterosexual terms, our social stereotype (and often, self-image) is that of one who rejects his or her masculinity or femininity. Those unwilling to accept their socially defined roles are appropriately stigmatised. Proving one's 'manhood' or being a 'lady' is thus closely linked to the rejection of gay characteristics. In women, repression is often internalised; in men, it may be externalised in aggressive behaviour.

The experience of passing is often productive of a gay sensibility. It can, and often does, lead to a heightened awareness and appreciation for disguise, impersonation, the projection of personality, and the distinctions to be made between instinctive and theatrical behaviour. Films which touch on the passing experience of gays overtly – *Reflections in a Golden Eye*, *The Sergeant* – are never camp, while those that cast an ironic eye on the subject can be, and often are. An example of the latter is Anthony Asquith's 1952 film version of Oscar Wilde's play *The Importance of Being Earnest*. In this, Jack (Michael Redgrave) and Algernon (Michael Denison) are two dandies who date women as a means of covering up their secret 'sin', i.e. instinctive behaviour, or, as the characters choose to call it, 'bunburying' – socially illicit pleasures. There is an obvious connection here with Wilde's own secret 'sin' – the key fact about gays in Victorian England being their need to live a double life, to pass – a survival strategy which Wilde patterned into a style of life and art. The experience of passing would appear to explain the enthusiasm of so many in our community for certain stars whose performances are highly charged with exaggerated (usually sexual) role playing. Some of these seem (or are made to seem) fairly 'knowing', if not self-parodying, in their roles: Jayne Mansfield holding two full milk bottles to her breasts in *Will Success Spoil Rock Hunter?*; Bette Davis as the discontented housewife ('what a dump!') in *Beyond the Forest*; Anita Ekberg as a Swedish sex siren in *La Dolce Vita*; Mae West in all her films; Cesar Romero as the Cisco Kid. Others are apparently more 'innocent' or 'sincere': Jane Russell in *The Outlaw*; Raquel Welch; Mamie van Doren; Jennifer Jones in *Duel in the Sun* and *Ruby Gentry*; Johnny Weissmuller as Tarzan and Jungle Jim; Ramon Novarro, particularly in *Ben Hur* and *The Student Prince in Old Heidelberg*.

The time factor is also crucial to one's appreciation of camp theatricality. A good deal of the screen acting which only recently appeared quite 'natural' will, in the goodness of time, doubtless become camp for its high degree of stylisation (that is, if it is not already camp). Some examples would be: the 'method' acting of Rod Steiger and early Brando; the charming, 'dated' styles of George Arliss, Emil Jannings, Luise Rainer or Miriam Hopkins. Similarly, a number of personalities from the silent cinema, once revered for their sexual allure, now seem, in the 1970s, fairly fantastic: Theda Bara and Pola Negri. Men, as David Thomson has observed, have always had an insecure hold on the camera, so that male sex appeal, for example, in the case of Rudolph Valentino, vanished much more quickly than did the sway exerted by women. Finding such stars camp is not to mock them, however. It is more a way of

poking fun at the whole cosmology of restrictive sex roles and sexual identifications which our society uses to oppress its women and repress its men –
including those on screen. This is not to say that those who appreciate the camp
in such stars must, ipso facto, be politically 'aware'; often, they are not. The
response is mainly instinctive; there is something of those roles that each of us
is urged to play with such a deadly seriousness.

Thus, camp as a response to performance springs from the gay sensibility's
preference for the *intensities* of character, as opposed to its content: what the
character conveys tends to be less important than *how* or *why* it is conveyed.
Camp is individualistic; as such, it relishes the uniqueness and the force with
which personality is imbued. This is why actors and actresses regarded as camp
cannot usually be contained by the parts they play. A non-realistic style of
acting enables them to exceed the limits imposed by their films (which are
often termed 'vehicles' by the critics – vehicles for their personalities). Lytton
Strachey once remarked of Sarah Bernhardt that her extraordinary genius was
really to be seen at its most characteristic in work of inferior quality – this
gave her what she most wanted: opportunities for acting. This is true, too, in
the case of camp stars like Charles Laughton, who was best when recklessly
indulgent, as in *Rembrandt* and *I Claudius*; George Arliss, a distinguished
British actor of the 'old school' persuaded to act before the cameras in
Alexander Hamilton (when he was already well into his sixties, twice
Hamilton's age), *Disraeli*, *Voltaire*, *The Man Who Played God* (all of which
gave him parts well-suited to his histrionic style); Miriam Hopkins, a fero-
ciously proud performer seen to best effect in *Old Acquaintance*, *The Heiress*
and *The Chase* – the last of which would appear to confirm novelist Brigid
Brophy's remark that the nature of a great actress is rooted in an hysterical
personality. Laughton, Arliss and Hopkins are stars who, in their films, are
always themselves. Their roles provide the means whereby they can project
their hyperbolic personae. The more hackneyed the material, the easier it is for
them to find spaces within the framework of scene, situation and direction
wherein they can be themselves. There is no better proof of this than the career
of Bette Davis. Davis is camp by virtue of her intense theatricality. The clipped
voice, the strident walk, the raucous laugh, the hands that jab through space
with ash-laden cigarettes – these stylised touches project an image of emotional
authority, intelligence and 'masculine' self-sufficiency that serves as ironic
commentary on the roles Davis was forced to play. In the style, then, lies the
message.

This theatricalisation of experience, which is the key element of Davis's
camp, derives both from the passing experience (wherein, paradoxically, we
learn the value of the self while at the same time rejecting it) and from a
heightened sensitivity to aspects of a performance which others are likely to
regard as routine or uncalculated (see Goffman). It is this awareness of the
double aspect of a performance that goes a long way to explain why gays form
a disproportionately large and enthusiastic part of the audience of such stars as

Judy Garland. In part, at least, Garland's popularity owes much to the fact that she is always, and most intensely, herself. Allied to this is the fact that many of us seem able to equate our own strongly felt sense of oppression, past or present, with the suffering/loneliness/misfortunes of the star both on and off the screen. Something in Garland's personality allows for an empathy that colours one's whole response to the performer and the performance. As Vicki Lester in Cukor's *A Star is Born*, but, especially, as the concert singer in Ronald Neame's *I Could Go on Singing*, Garland took on roles so disconcertingly close to her real-life situation and personality that the autobiographical connections actually appeared to take their toll on her physical appearance from one scene to the next. Such performances as these solidified the impression, already formed in the minds of her most ardent admirers, of an integrity arising directly out of her great personal misfortunes.

Humour

The fourth characteristic of camp is its humour. This results from an identification of a strong incongruity between an object, person, or situation and its context. The comic element is inherent in the formal properties of irony. There is a basic contradiction or incongruity, coupled with a real or pretended innocence. But in order for an incongruous contrast to be ironic it must, in addition to being comic, affect one as 'painful' – though not so painful as to neutralise the humour. It is sufficient that sympathy is aroused for the person, thing, or ideal that constitutes the target of an incongruous contrast. To be affected in this way, one's feelings need to clash. It follows, then, that – as A. R. Thompson has argued in his study of irony, *The Dry Mock* – 'contrasts which conform exactly to the objective definitions of irony are not ironical at all when they do not arouse ... conflicting feelings'.

Humour constitutes the strategy of camp: a means of dealing with a hostile environment and, in the process, of defining a positive identity. This humour takes several forms. Chief of these is bitter-wit, which expresses an underlying hostility and fear. Society says to gays (and to all stigmatised groups) that we are members of the wider community; we are subject to the same laws as 'normals'; we must pay our taxes, etc.; we are, in short, 'just like everybody else'. On the other hand, we are not received into society on equal terms; indeed, we are told that we are unacceptably 'different' in ways that are absolutely fundamental to our sense of self and social identity. In other words, the message conveyed to us by society is highly contradictory: we are just like everyone else, and yet, we are not. It is this basic contradiction, this joke, that has traditionally been our destiny.

Not surprisingly, this contradiction has produced, in many, an identity-ambivalence that has found expression in our talk, our behaviour, our artistic efforts; in fact, our whole perception of the world and of our place in it. Like other oppressed groups, gays have developed skills out of much the same need to concentrate on strategy when the rules are stacked against us. Those of us who are sufficiently sensitive to criticism of ourselves may develop a commensurate ability to isolate, dissect, and bring into vivid focus the destructiveness and hypocrisy of others. It is thus that in much of our humour lies a strain of irony that is strongly flavoured with hostility for society, as well as for ourselves. As Erving Goffman has said: 'Given that the stigmatised individual in our society acquires identity standards which he applies to himself in spite of failing to conform to them, it is inevitable that he will feel some ambivalence about his own self'.

This tendency to see ourselves as others do is to some extent changing, and will continue to change as we come to define ourselves in terms that do not assume heterosexuality as the norm. In the past, however, and, to a lesser extent, in the present, our response to this split between heterosexual standards and self-demands has been a bitter-wit that is deeply imbued with self-hate and self-derogation. This can best be illustrated in films such as *Staircase*, *Boys in the Band*, and *The Killing of Sister George*, all of which are perhaps far too maudlin to be called camp, but whose characters do reflect, in exaggerated form, much of that bitter-wit that goes by the name of camp.

For example, in *Staircase*, directed by Stanley Donen, the humour is saturated with the sadness of those perceived as doomed to live their lives with 'unsuitable' emotions in a world where such feelings are tacitly recognised but officially condemned. Thus, throughout the film, the dialogue comments on the central couple's awful-funny confrontation with the 'normal' world outside; it is riddled with the self-hatred and low self-esteem of those who have successfully internalised straight society's opinion of us. Self-pity and an aching sense of loss are the prevailing themes: 'You've been a father', Charlie hisses at Harry, 'a privilege denied to thousands of us!' Such dialogue, geared for a 'superior' laugh, is squarely based on the tacit acceptance of the hegemony of heterosexual institutions. As for Donen's own patronising view of these proceedings, this finds its most appropriate metaphor in the maudlin tones of Ray Charles pleading in song (on the soundtrack) over the flickering images of gay *angst* to 'Forgive them for they know not what they do'. Finally, the very conventions of the commercial cinema provide their own language of lament via the presence of such big-name, belligerently straight-associated types as Rex Harrison (Charlie) and Richard Burton (Harry).

Camp can thus be a means of undercutting rage by its derision of concentrated bitterness. Its vision of the world is comic. Laughter, rather than tears, is its chosen means of dealing with the painfully incongruous situation of gays in society. Yet it is also true that camp is something of a protopolitical phenomenon. It assumes gayness to be a category that defines the self, and it steadfastly refuses to repudiate our long heritage of gay ghetto life. Any appreciation of camp, therefore, expresses an empathy with typical gay experiences, even when this takes the form of finding beauty in the seemingly bizarre and outrageous, or discovering the worthiness in a thing or person that is supposedly without value. Finally, camp can be subversive – a means of illustrating those cultural ambiguities and contradictions that oppress us all, gay and non-gay, and, in particular, women.

Yet because camp combines fun and earnestness, it runs the risk of being considered not serious at all. Usually overlooked by critics of the gay sensibility is camp's strategy of irony. Camp, through its introduction of style, aestheticism, humour, and theatricality, allows us to witness 'serious' issues with temporary detachment, so that only later, after the event, are we struck by the emotional and moral implications of what we have almost passively absorbed. The 'serious' is, in fact, crucial to camp. Though camp mocks the solemnities of our culture, it never totally discards the seriousness of a thing or individual. As a character in a Christopher Isherwood novel says: 'You can't camp about something you don't take seriously; you're not making fun *of* it; you're making fun *out* of it. You're expressing what's basically serious to you in terms of fun and artifice and elegance'.

CAMP AND 'THE SERIOUS'

As a way of illustrating camp in service of the serious, consider Rainer Werner Fassbinder's *The Bitter Tears of Petra von Kant*. Here, as in almost all of this director's work, the problem of how to make radical social commentary without alienating audiences is resolved by distancing the action – finding a common denominator to anchor the 'message'. In *Bitter Tears* the mannerist stylisation which dominates the *mise en scène*, the grand gestures, comic routines, and the melodramatic tendencies of the plot, constitute the strategy whereby Fassbinder aims to both distance and engage his audience. As Thomas Elsaesser has pointed out, Fassbinder's search for an 'unprovocative realism' has led the director to discover for the German cinema 'the importance of being artificial' as a strategy for forcing an audience to question its assumptions about society and its inhabitants.

This artificiality is the camp aspect of *Bitter Tears*. A highly theatricalised world devoid of the very passions that constitute its subject is provided by the director's formalised, almost Racinian dialogue; his elaborate, carefully calculated compositions locked into theatrical tableaux; the anachronistic costumes and mask-like makeup that reflect the psychological situation of the characters; the comic pop/classical music references – the incongruous juxtaposition of Verdi, the Platters, and the Walker Brothers; the stylised performances and ritualised division of the film into five acts, each heralded by the heroine's change of dress and wig; the expressive lighting effects that emphasise a world of masters and servants, predators and victims; and, generally, the formalised editing style which makes the most of the film's single set – a studio apartment that is dominated by a huge brass bed, a wall-sized mural-with-male-nude that bears ironic witness to the action below, and a scattered group of bald-pated mannequins whose poses are continuously rearranged as commentary on their human counterparts.

Each scene is so organised as to heighten the irony of Petra von Kant's (Margit Carstensen) inability to reconcile theory (a loving relationship must be free, honest, and nonpossessive) and practice. This failure is particularly apparent in Petra's sadomasochistic relationship with the omnipresent Marlene (Irm Hermann), a silent witness to her mistress's jealous possession of the sensual young model Karen (Hanna Schygulla), who ultimately rejects her benefactress in favour of her (Karen's) former husband. When, in the bitterly ironic final scene, an outrageous mixture of comedy and cruelty, the chastened Petra reverses roles and offers 'freedom and joy' to Marlene in return for companionship, the chalk-faced 'slave' dispassionately packs her bags and makes a hasty exit, pausing only to drop 'The Great Pretender' on the gramophone by way of vocal reply.

It is the very artificiality of Fassbinder's *Bitter Tears* that serves to support the characters and their emotions. The camp aspect of the work emerges in the use of calculated melodrama and flamboyant visual surfaces to accentuate the film's complex of interrelated themes: the interdependence of sex and power, love and suffering, pleasure and pain; the lover's demand for exclusive possession, which springs from vanity; the basic instability of love in the absence of a lover's sense of positive self-identity; the value of pose as an escape and protective shield; the inevitability of inequities within relationships so long as love, ego, or insights are distributed in unequal proportions. Such themes as these carry a special resonance for the gay sensibility. As outsiders, we are forced to create our own norms; to impose our *selves* upon a world which refuses to confront the arbitrariness of cultural conventions that insist on sexual loyalty, permanence, and exclusive possession. Fassbinder's film, by paying close attention to the ironic functions of style, aims to detach us, temporarily, from the serious content of the images – but which, later, encourages a more reflective analysis.

Whereas Fassbinder is only occasionally camp, there are directors – Luchino Visconti, King Vidor, Ernst Lubitsch, Josef von Sternberg, etc. – whose work, as a whole, has a very strong camp emphasis. Visconti's camp, like Fassbinder's, lies in the stress placed on artificiality as a means of conveying content. In his determination to demonstrate the unreality of cinema, Visconti remained detached from immediate concerns, preferring to pursue aesthetic, self-sufficient values. Even in *La terra trema* (1947), a contemporary study of social problems, Visconti is more concerned with his own personal situation of the historical process than in making direct contact with actuality, as did his neo-realist contemporaries. His approach is inward and reflective, as can be seen in the intensely operatic *Senso* (1954: with English dialogue by Tennessee Williams and Paul Bowles), where the images have the carefully chiselled beauty of an aesthetic that emphasises pictorial realism over analysis and narrative, and where the action unfolds, slowly, in a series of tableaux with unsung arias, duets and ensembles.

Further studies of the gay sensibility in relation to cinema will need to take account of the interaction of camp and auteur theory, genres, images of women, etc. What follows are two brief, tentative case studies concerning camp and the gay sensibility in relation to the work of a single director (Josef von Sternberg) and in various films based on the drama and fiction of Tennessee Williams.

CAMP IN THE FILMS OF JOSEF VON STERNBERG

To explain the relation of Sternberg to camp it is necessary to return, briefly, to the phenomenon of passing for straight. This strategy of survival in a hostile world has sensitised us to disguises, impersonations, the significance of surfaces, the need to project personality, the intensities of character, and so on. Sternberg's films – in particular, the Dietrich films from *Morocco* (1930) to *The Devil is a Woman* (1935) – are all camp insofar as they relate to those adjustment mechanisms of the gay sensibility. But they are also camp in that they reflect the director's ironic attitude toward his subject-matter – a judgement that says, in effect, that the content is of interest only insofar as it remains susceptible to transformation by means of stylisation. What counts in one's view of Sternberg's films as camp, then, is the perception of an underlying emotional autobiography – a disguise of self and obsessions by means of the artificial. One does not need to see these disguises in a strictly literal way. It is enough to sense the irony in the tensions that arise from Sternberg's anguish and cynicism, and his predilection for the most outrageous sexual symbolism as a means of objectifying personal fantasies.

Those who view camp either as a trivialisation of taste or as a cultural conspiracy will frown on any labelling of Sternberg as camp. Indeed, several of this director's staunchest admirers have already attempted to 'rescue' him from ridicule and replace his reputation in a suitably dignified light. For such critics neither the total experience nor the attitudes and emotional philosophy of the sensibility that produces camp are to be taken seriously. The validity of the camp statement, along with its cultural origins and associations, are regarded as of scant significance. Totally ignored is the fact that camp takes a radically different approach to the serious, one which relies heavily on aesthetic rather than moral considerations. Thus, to find camp in Sternberg is not to surrender to the joys of lover-decorated irrelevance. It is, rather, to appreciate the wit by which Sternberg renders his insights artificial; to sense something of an 'affaire' between Dietrich and her director; to perceive the deep significance of appearances – a sumptuous surface that serves not as an empty and meaningless background, but as the very subject of the films: a visual context for Sternberg's fantasies.

The style of Sternberg's films is the inevitable result of the director's need to impose himself upon his material; to control all the elements with which creative work concerns itself. Self-revelation is best accomplished when viewers are left undistracted by the storyline. The more hackneyed the material, the better the opportunities for self-projection. There is no place for spontaneity in such a scheme, as one needs always to be in total control of the information conveyed by camera, sets, actors, etc. Thus, the director demanded complete domination over every aspect of his films. Not only did the act of creation derive from him, but he, Sternberg, was also the object created: 'Marlene is not Marlene', he insisted, 'she is me'. Claire Johnston has said of *Morocco* that 'in order for a man to remain at the centre of the universe in a text which focuses on the image, the *auteur* is forced to repress the idea of woman as a social and sexual being [her Otherness] and to deny the opposition man/woman altogether. The woman as sign, then, becomes the pseudo-centre of the filmic discourse'.

The incongruous contrast posed by the sign is 'male/non-male', which the director established by disguising Dietrich in men's clothing. This is a masquerade which connects with the theme of sexual ambivalence, of central concern to the gay sensibility, and recurrent in Sternberg's work. Dietrich, then, functions principally as a primary motif. It is she, woman, who becomes the focus of Sternberg's symbolism, psychology, and sense of humour. As Amy Joly in *Morocco*; X-27, prostitute and spy, in *Dishonoured*, 1931; Shanghai Lily, prostitute, in *Shanghai Express*, 1932; Helen Faraday, nightclub entertainer and archetypal mother in *Blonde Venus*, 1932; Sophia Frederica, later Catherine II, in *The Scarlet Empress*, 1934; and Concha Perez in *The Devil Is a Woman* (1935), Dietrich as woman becomes a manifestation of Sternberg's fantasies. The man takes over; the woman recedes into myth and the details of the decor. The image that emerges is man-made. But it is also an integral part of the larger camp structure. Hence, the danger to which camp enthusiasts expose themselves is as inevitable as it is irreducible, i.e. the danger of surrendering to the corroboration of Sternberg's fantasies as each, in turn, is thrown back on us by the male-manufactured image of the star who illuminates the screen.

THE GAY SENSIBILITY IN THE FILMS OF TENNESSEE WILLIAMS

In the films based on the work of Tennessee Williams (I shall refer to these as 'Williams's films' since, even when the plays and fiction are adapted for the screen by someone other than the author, they retain the spirit of the original) the image of women is again of central concern in any consideration of camp and the gay sensibility.[4] The point I wish to take up here is one that various critics have used to denigrate both Williams's films and the gay sensibility; namely, that the typical heroine of these films is a 'drag queen'.[5]

This interpretation is nowhere more relentlessly pursued than in Molly Haskell's *From Reverence to Rape: The Treatment of Women in the Movies*. Haskell perceives Williams's women as products of the writer's own 'baroquely transvestised homosexual fantasies'. By no stretch of the imagination, she argues, can they conceivably be seen as 'real' women. Hence, Vivien Leigh's Blanche DuBois in *A Streetcar Named Desire* and Karen Stone in *The Roman Spring of Mrs Stone*; Geraldine Page's Alexandra Del Lago (the Princess Kosmonopolis) in *Sweet Bird of Youth* and Alma Winemiller in *Summer and Smoke*; Joanne Woodward's Carole Cutrere in *The Fugitive Kind*; Ava

Gardner's Maxine Faulk and Deborah Kerr's Hannah Jelkes in *The Night of the Iguana*; Elizabeth Taylor's Flora (Sissy) Goforth in *Boom!*, etc., etc. All these characters, Haskell argues, are 'hermaphrodites' who flow from out of 'the palpable fear and self-pity, guts and bravura of the aging homosexual'; the gay author, seething with repressed desires, dons his female mask (Blanche, Karen, etc.) and hungrily heads, in print as on screen, for a host of fantasy males of his own creation: Stanley Kowalski/Marlon Brando, Paolo/Warren Beatty, Chance Wayne/Paul Newman, etc. The 'cultured homosexual' (Williams) is thus seen as being compelled, 'often masochistically and against his taste' (Haskell), to love brutes and beachboys, natives and gigolos, primitives and peasants – as well as all the other unavailable prototypes of uninhibited sensuality.

There is some truth in all this, of course. Williams has 'used' women to his own advantage. There exists a certain conservatism in his work that is doubtless the product of passing. In *A Streetcar Named Desire*, *Summer and Smoke*, and *The Roman Spring of Mrs. Stone*, it is evident that Williams was as yet unprepared to parade his feelings as gay. Gayness thus found relief in the form of female guise: Blanche, Alma, Karen. These characters do express their creator's own 'unacceptable' emotions as a gay man. They all do declare the nature of Williams's own fantasy life at the time of their creation. In them the artist has found a means of dealing with the tensions that plagued and defined him – tensions that reside in such dualities as flesh/spirit, promiscuity/pride, youth/(old) age.

Yet it is also true that such a strategy of survival in a hostile world constitutes an imaginative act of which any artist is capable. Most male artists, whatever their sexual orientation, assume the habit of it as a necessary qualification in dealing with female emotions. What one needs to be concerned about is not the *fact* of an artist's fantasies; but, rather, the way in which these fantasies are *shaped* so that they speak to and for other people. Still, there remains the threat from certain critical quarters to reduce the whole of such problems of interpretation to generalities about the limitations of the gay artist. The central assumption of such criticism is that gays, generally, can know little of life as lived by those who take their place in the 'real' world of straight, rather than gay, relationships. This point is most succinctly expressed by Adelaide Comerford, who, writing in *Films in Review*, claims that when Williams is not dealing with 'sex degenerates or other psychopaths' his 'ignorance of life is boringly patent'.

This notion that the work of gay artists cannot be taken seriously because it deals with facts of feeling unknown to straights does have a certain awful logic to it.[6] People insufficiently sensitive to those aspects of our situation which give to an artist's work a measure of dignity surely cannot be expected to be open to the understandings that spring from our unique encounters with self and society. Those who malign or reject the existence of a gay sensibility will all too often overlook the fact that the feelings and creative productions of artists, gay or straight, are the sum total of their experiences – education, relationships, repressions, fortunes, and misfortunes – which have entered into their inner lives. To dismiss the creative efforts that spring from such influences on the ground that the artist is gay serves no useful purpose whatsoever. Certainly it is true enough that gays *do* develop a unique perception of the world, just as do all members of minority groups which have been treated, in essential respects, as marginal to society. And since sexuality can be divorced from no aspect of the inner workings of the human personality, it cannot be divorced from creativity. What one wants to know is this: given the nature of our unique situation, what special insights does the gay artist have to offer?

In defining the gay sensibility it is important to remember that gays are members of a minority group, and that minorities have always constituted some sort of threat to the majority. Thus, gays have been regarded with fear, suspicion, and, even, hatred. The knowledge of these attitudes has developed in us what I have referred to above as a unique set of perspectives and under-standings about what the world is like and how best we can deal with it. It is true that gay artists may at times protect themselves from the social pressures imposed upon them by our cultural contradictions and social prejudices. Hence, it may be that fantasies of revenge are sometimes transformed into art as a way of allowing vicarious play to erotic wishes renounced in the inter-ests of social acceptance; resentments are expressed over treatment received; appeals for sympathy are made through the demonstration of damage wrought by continued injustice and oppression; psychic wounds are recorded so that art becomes, as Williams has said of his own work, 'an escape from a world of reality in which I felt acutely uncomfortable' (*New York Times*, 8 March 1959); female masks are donned; charades enacted; false identities assumed.

But are not such forms of expression, such 'deceptions', everywhere the rule? In Freud's formulation of the creative impulse, the artist is originally one who turns away from reality out of a refusal to come to terms with the demand for his or her renunciation of instinctual satisfactions, and who then, in fantasy life, allows full play to erotic and ambitious wishes. Creativity is thus an inevitable outcome of repressed impulses or relationships. As such it constitutes a defiance against 'unlived life' (see Wenkart). True, the insights offered by so many of the female characters in Williams's films are the product of a gay sensibility. But then the gay artist is one who is graced with a double vision – a vision which belongs to all members of oppressed groups. Those on the outside better under-stand the activities of the insider than vice versa. As Benjamin DeMott has pointed out in his essay, 'But He's a Homosexual . . .', the gay artist often speaks more frankly than the straight on such matters as the tedium of marriage, the horrors of family life, the lover's exploitation of personality, and the slow erosion of character in promiscuity.

If we are not too rigid about drawing the line between thought and fantasy, but, rather, conceive of creative endeavour as encompassing a great range of

covert mental processes, then it should be possible to view more sympathetically Williams's female creations as important both to the conservation and
change of this artist's own sense of identity, as well as for what they reveal of
an aspect of love that is neither gay nor straight, but, simply, human. These are
facts of feeling which gays, who have early in life recognised irony in the
incompatible demands of gayness and society, cannot easily avoid. Yet these
are facts which can scarcely be understood by those oblivious to the peculia-
rities, past or present, of our situation in the general culture.

To say this is not to suggest that *only* gays can be objective about heterosexual institutions and arrangements. It is, rather, a way of saying that gays,
because of the demands constantly made upon us to justify our existence, have
never been able to simply accept, passively, the cultural assumptions that non-
gays may well take for granted. The insights provided by, for example, the
Deborah Kerr and Ava Gardner characters in *The Night of the Iguana* are not
those of 'drag queens'; rather, they spring from a gay sensibility that is not so
completely identified with its 'masculine' persona roles that it is incapable of
giving expression to its 'feminine' component. Such insights spring from a gay
sensibility that refuses to lapse into automatic acceptance of what others have
insisted is appropriate behaviour for two people in love. When the Deborah
Kerr character (Hannah Jelkes) speaks of her acceptance of the 'impermanence'
of relationships, Shannon (Richard Burton) chides her, offering up the metaphor of birds who build their nests 'on the very highest level'. To this Hannah
quickly replies: 'I'm not a bird, Mr Shannon, I'm a human being. And when a
member of that fantastic species builds a nest in the heart of another, the
question of permanence isn't the first or even the last thing that's considered'.
Echoing these sentiments precisely, the Ava Gardner character (Maxine Faulk)
tells Burton that sooner or later we all reach a point where it is important to
'settle for something that works for us in our lives – even if it isn't on the
highest kind of level'. This is the message advocated time and again by the
Williams female, and it is very much an insight of the gay sensibility.

NOTES

1. Sontag 1964b. A number of insights provided by Sontag in her seminal essay 'Notes
   on Camp' have been most helpful to me in formulating my own ideas on the subject
   of camp.
2. Esther Newton (1972) has explored the relationship of costume to female impersonators. I am much indebted to Newton for her insights on the style and humour
   systems of 'Drag Queens'.
3. I have developed these ideas at greater length in 'Passing for Straight' and in *We
   Speak for Ourselves*.
4. The *Memoirs* of Tennessee Williams have also been useful to me here for the light
   they throw on the ways in which the author's gayness has affected his creative
   output.
5. The instances of critics labelling a Williams heroine 'drag queen' are too numerous to
   cite. However, the most extended development of this particular line of interpretation can be found in Haskell, in Rothschild, where the reviewer speaks of Williams's
   'mal-formed females' and 'anti-female' imagination; see also Rosen; Hirsch; and

The Guardian, 27 October 1976; *Interview*, April 1973; *Gay Sunshine*, 29/30, Summer/Fall 1976.

6. Peter Dyer refers to the 'difficulty' of taking the film *Summer and Smoke* 'at all seriously', other than as 'a case-book study in arrested development'; similarly, Haskell writes: 'Williams's women can be amusing company if we aren't asked to take them too seriously' (251).

REFERENCES

Auden, W. H., 'Introduction' to Charles Baudelaire, *The Intimate Journals*, trans. Christopher Isherwood, London: Methuen, 1949.

Babuscio, Jack, 'Passing for Straight: The Politics of the Closet', *Gay News* 62, January 1974.

——, *We Speak for Ourselves: Experiences in Homosexual Counselling*, London: SPCK, 1976.

Comerford, Adelaide, *Films in Review* December 1962.

DeMott, Benjamin, *Supergrow: Essays and Reports on Imagination in America*, London: E. P. Dutton, 1970.

Dyer, Peter J., *Monthly Film Bulletin* 29:339.

Elsaesser, Thomas, 'A Cinema of Vicious Circles', in Tony Rayns (ed.), *Fassbinder*, London: BFI, 1976.

Freud, Sigmund, 'The Relation of the Poet to Daydreaming', in *Collected Papers*, Vol. 4, New York: Basic, 1959.

Goffman, Erving, *Stigma: The Management of Spoiled Identity*, Englewood Cliffs: Prentice-Hall, 1963.

Haskell, Molly, *From Reverence to Rape: The Treatment of Women in the Movies*, New York: Holt, Rinehart & Winston, 1973.

Hirsch, Foster, 'Tennessee Williams', *Cinema* (USA) 8:1, Spring 1973.

Hume, David, 'Of the Standard of Taste', in *Essays, Moral, Political and Literary*, Oxford: Oxford UP, 1963.

Johnson, R. V., *Aestheticism*, London: Methuen, 1969.

Johnston, Claire, 'Women's Cinema as Counter-Cinema', in *Notes on Women's Cinema*, London: SEFT, 1973.

Pehnt, Wolfgang (ed.), *Encyclopedia of Modern Architecture (Knaurs Lexicon der modernen Architektur)*, trans. Harold Meek et al., London: Thames & Hudson, 1963.

Rosen, Marjorie, *Popcorn Venus: Women, Movies, and the American Dream*, New York: Avon, 1974.

Rothschild, Elaine, *Films in Review* August-September 1964

Thompson, A. R., *The Dry Mock: A Study of Irony in Drama*, Berkeley: U of California P, 1948.

Thomson, David, *A Biographical Dictionary of the Cinema*, London: Secker & Warburg, 1975.

Wenkart, Antonia, 'Creativity and Freedom', *American Journal of Psychoanalysis* 23:2, 1963.

Wilde, Oscar, *The Decay of Lying*, London: Osgood, McIlvane & Co., 1891.

Williams, Tennessee, *Memoirs*, London: W. H. Allen, 1976.

8

FOR INTERPRETATION: NOTES AGAINST CAMP

Andrew Britton

Genet does not want to change anything at all. Do not count on him to criticise institutions. He needs them, as Prometheus needs his vulture. (Sartre, *Saint Genet*)

One. It almost seems at times to have become a matter of common acceptance that camp is radical; and the play *Men* by Noel Greig and Don Milligan provides a convenient example of the process by which I imagine that to have come about. *Men* offers itself as a polemic against 'the straight left' – an abstraction which it embodies in one of its two central gay characters, a shop steward in a Midlands factory and, in secret, the lover of Gene, a camp gay male for whom the play attempts to solicit a besotted and uncritical reverence. Their relationship is seen to be continuous with the dominant patterns of heterosexual relationships, and is presented as a synonym for them, though there is no attempt to consider, or even to acknowledge, the social pressures which have gone to produce the similarity. The play concludes that the political struggle in which Richard, the shop steward, is engaged at work can be assimilated to 'phallic' power drives (we are not allowed to forget that he is known to his fellow-workers as Dick), and offers, in Gene's plangent cry of 'Socialism is about me', what it takes to be the corrective emphasis. How 'socialism' is to be defined, or in what way, exactly, it can be said to be about Gene, are not matters which the play finds it proper to discuss, although it becomes clear enough that Richard's activities (from which women workers

Originally published in *Gay Left*, 7, Winter 1978/79.

are pointedly excluded except, in one instance, as the 'victims' of a strike-action) lie beyond the pale. Indeed, Gene's intimate relation to 'socialism' is very much taken as given. His ignorance of, and indifference to, politics is repeatedly stressed, yet he is somehow instinctively in line with the proper ends of political action; and in the final scene becomes the medium not only for a series of vague and tendentious aphorisms about patriarchy ('Men, like Nature, abhor a vacuum'), portentously delivered in a spotlight, but also for the savage, cruel and self-righteous scapegoating of Richard, who is endowed with the moral responsibility for his oppression. *Men* concludes that Richard should allow himself to become 'nervous, sensual and effeminate' – as dubious a set of Moral Positives as any one could reasonably demand – and indulges itself in a *Doll's House* ending which we are asked to take as a triumph of radical intelligence. Richard's confusion, desperation, self-oppression, are neither here nor there. It is all 'his fault', and we can take due satisfaction in his come-uppance: his guilty secret has been discovered by his workmates, and his just deserts are at hand.

The point I wish to make is that Gene's camp is taken as an automatic validation of the character. He has nothing to recommend him beyond a certain facile charisma and a few slick epigrams, yet his five-minute *tour de force* telephone monologue at the end of the first act is considered sufficiently impressive to 'place' the portrayal, in the preceding thirty minutes, of Richard's political involvement. *Men* arrives at its assessment of camp by a simple process of elision. The Richard/Gene relationship is 'like' a man/woman relationship. Therefore Gene's camp is continuous with woman-identification – is 'like' a feminist discourse against patriarchy. Therefore, camp is the means by which gay men may become woman-identified = radical = socialist, and we can carry on camping and 'being ourselves' with perfect equanimity (camp, of course, is always 'being oneself'), in the serene assurance that we are in the vanguard of the march towards the socialist future. The play does not seek at any point to *demonstrate* the validity of this spurious set of propositions. They are simply data, and as such relate significantly to certain characteristic assumptions of bourgeois feminism. Juliet Mitchell has argued, for example, that the 'political' and 'ideological' struggles are conceptually and practically distinct, the one to be fought by the working class and the other by the women's movement, and even goes so far as to suggest in *Woman's Estate*, that the revolution must now come from within the bourgeoisie. Gene, while ostensibly working class, is very much a mouthpiece for bourgeois aspirations; and *Men* compounds Mitchell's fallacy in its uncritical assimilation of camp to feminism, and its implicit assertion that there is no conceivable form of organised political activity which would not surreptitiously reiterate patriarchal power-structures.

Two. Camp always connotes 'effeminacy', not 'femininity'. The camp gay man declares – '"Masculinity" is an oppressive convention to which I refuse to conform'; but his non-conformity depends at every point on the preservation of the convention he ostensibly rejects – in this case, a general acceptance of what constitutes 'a man'. Camp behaviour is only recognisable as a deviation from an implied norm, and without that norm it would cease to exist, it would lack definition. It does not, and cannot, propose for a moment a radical critique of the norm itself. Being essentially a mere play with given conventional signs, camp simply replaces the signs of 'masculinity' with a parody of the signs of 'femininity' and reinforces existing social definitions of both categories. The standard of 'the male' remains the fixed point, in relation to which male gays and women emerge as 'that which is not male'.

Three. Camp requires the *frisson* of transgression, the sense of perversity in relation to bourgeois norms which characterises the degeneration of the Romantic impulse in the second half of the nineteenth century, and which culminates in England with Aestheticism and in France with the *décadence*. Camp is a house-trained version of the aristocratic, anarchistic ethic of transgression, a breach of decorum which no longer even shocks, and which has gone to confirm the existence of a special category of person – the male homosexual. Camp strives to give an objective presence to an imaginary construction of bourgeois psychology. The very term 'a homosexual' (of which, finally, the term 'a gay person' is only the recuperation, albeit a progressive one) defines not an object-choice of which any individual is capable, but a type with characteristic modes of behaviour and response. Sartre has analysed, in relation to Genet, the process by which a determinate social imperative ('I have been placed in such-and-such a role') can be transformed into existential choice ('Therefore I will take the initiative of adopting it'); and that process describes the fundamental complicity of what may appear to be an act of self-determination. Camp is collaborative in that sense.

Four. 'Subversiveness' needs to be assessed not in terms of a quality which is supposedly proper to a phenomenon, but as a relationship between a phenomenon and its context – that is, dynamically. To be Quentin Crisp in the 1930s is a very different matter from being Quentin Crisp in 1978. What was once an affront has now become part of life's rich pageant. The threat has been defused – and defused because it was always superficial. Camp is individualistic and apolitical, and even at its most disturbing asks for little more than living-room. Susan Sontag's remark that 'homosexuals have pinned their integration into society on promoting' the camp sensibility (Sontag 1964b, rpt. 1966: 292) seems to me exact, and in its exactitude quite damning. It is necessary, in making such a judgement, to dissociate oneself from any simple form of moralism.

Clearly, until very recently the ways of being gay have been so extraordinarily limited that the possibility of being radically gay has simply not arisen in the majority of cases. But in a contemporary context, gay camp seems little more than a kind of anaesthetic, allowing one to remain inside oppressive relations while enjoying the illusory confidence that one is flouting them.

Five. The belief in some 'essential' homosexuality produces, logically, Jack Babuscio's concept of 'the gay sensibility', of which camp is supposed to be the expression. 'I define the gay sensibility as a creative energy reflecting a consciousness that is different from the mainstream; a heightened awareness of certain human complications of feeling that spring from the fact of social oppression; in short, a perception of the world which is coloured, shaped, directed and defined by the fact of one's gayness' (Babuscio 1977: 40). This formulation contains two false propositions: (a) that there exists some undifferentiated 'mainstream consciousness' from which gays, by the very fact of being gay, are absolved; and (b) that 'a perception of the world which is ... defined by the fact of one's gayness' *necessarily* involves a 'heightened awareness' of anything (except, of course, one's gayness). I would certainly accept that oppression creates the *potential* for a critical distance from (and action against) the oppressing society, but one has only to consider the various forms of 'negative awareness' to perceive that the realisation of that potential depends on other elements of one's specific situation.

It is clearly not the case that the fact of oppression entails a conceptual understanding of the basis of oppression, or that the fact of belonging to an oppressed group entails ideological awareness. 'Consciousness' (which is, in itself, an unhelpful term) is not determined by sexual orientation, nor is there a 'gay sensibility'. The ideological place of any individual at any given time is the site of intersection of any number of determining forces, and one's sense of oneself as 'gay' is a determinate product of that intersection – not a determinant of it. It seems strange, in any case, to cite as exemplary of a gay sensibility a phenomenon which is characteristically male, and with which many gay men feel little sympathy.

Six. The failure to conceive of a theory of ideology is continuous with an untenable theory of choice. Susan Sontag, adopting a summarisingly crude behaviouristic model, remarks that 'taste governs every free – as opposed to rote – humam response' (Sontag 1964b, rpt. 1966: 278), and associates 'taste' with an ethereal individuality which transcends social 'programming'. Jack Babuscio develops the same line of argument: 'Clothes and decor, for example, can be a means of asserting one's identity, as well as a form of justification in a society which denies one's essential validity ... By such means as these one aims to become what one wills, to exercise some control over one's environment' (Babuscio 1977: 44). Neither writer seems aware that 'identity' and 'freedom' as used here are problematic terms. In order to explain the fact that gay men gravitate towards certain professions, one has to adduce the 'discredited social identity' (Ibid.) of gays as the determining factor of the choice rather than suggest that the choice alleviates the discredited social identity. The professions in which male gayness has been traditionally condoned (the theatre, fashion, interior decoration, and so on) are also those in which women have been able to command a degree of personal autonomy without threatening male supremacy in the slightest, since 'real men', by definition, would despise to be involved in them. It is scarcely permissible to explain the association of gay men with the 'luxury' professions in terms of a collection of individuals who discover, by some miraculous coincidence, that the assertion of their identity leads them to a single persona.

Seven. Whatever differences they may have on other points, the three most fully elaborated statements on camp to date (Sontag 1964b; Dyer 1976; Babuscio 1977) are all agreed that camp taste is a matter of 'style' and 'content', ignoring the fact that 'style' describes a process of meaning. The camp attitude is a mode of perception whereby artifacts become the object of an arrested, or fetishistic, scrutiny. It does not so much 'see everything in quotation marks' (Sontag 1964b, rpt. 1966: 289) as in parentheses; it is a solvent of context. Far from being a means for the 'demystification' of artifacts, as Richard Dyer asserts (1976), camp is a means by which that analysis is perpetually postponed. The passage from 'determinate object' to 'fetish' preserves the object safely and reassuringly in a vacuum.

Eight. All analysts of camp arrive eventually at the same dilemma. On the one hand, camp 'describes those elements in a person, situation or activity which express, or are created by, a gay sensibility' (Babuscio 1977: 40) (i.e. camp is an attribute *of* something). On the other hand, 'camp resides largely in the eye of the beholder' (Babuscio 1977: 41) (i.e. camp is attributed *to* something). The latter seems to me in most cases correct, and the generalising tendency indicates very clearly camp's essential facility. Camp attempts to assimilate everything as its object, and then reduces all objects to one set of terms. It is a language of impoverishment: it is both reductive and non-analytic, the two going together and determining each other. As a gay phenomenon, it is a means of bringing the world into one's scope, of accommodating it – not of changing it or conceptualising its relations. The objects, images, values, relations of oppression can be recuperated by adopting the simple expedient of redescribing them; and the language of camp almost suggests, at times, a form of censorship in the Freudian sense. There is, of course, a certain mode of contemporary aestheticism which is aware of the concept of camp, and whose objects are constructed from within that purview; but as a rule the conception of camp as a property either begs the question or produces those periodic insanities of Susan Sontag's essay, whereby Pope and Mozart can be claimed for the camp heritage as masters of rococo formalism.

Nine. According to Richard Dyer, John Wayne and Wagner can be camp. To perceive Wayne as camp is, on one level, simply too easy, and doesn't make any point about 'masculinity' which would not instantly earn the concurrence of any self-respecting reader of *The Daily Telegraph*. Of course Wayne's 'way of being a man' is a social construct, as are all 'ways of being a man', including the camp one – and to indicate as much doesn't seem particularly significant. On another level, which 'John Wayne'? The Wayne who advocates, on screen and off, Johnson's policy in Vietnam and McCarthyism, or the Wayne of Ford's westerns? Wayne 'means' very differently in the two cases, and while those meanings are intimately related, they cannot be reduced to one another. To perceive Wayne merely as an icon of 'butchness' which can be debunked from, apparently, a position of ideological neutrality, is either complacent or philistine. Similarly, to regard Wagner as camp is, on one level, only silly, and no more to be tolerated than any other kind of silliness because it masquerades as critical analysis. On another level, it pre-empts the discussion of the real problems raised by Wagner's music and the cult of Bayreuth (the discussion initiated by Nietzsche), and ends by corroborating the vulgar bourgeois critique of Wagner's 'overblown romanticism'. The 'camp insight', in these and many other cases, is little more than a flip variant of the worst kind of right-on liberalism.

Ten. In his essay, Jack Babuscio attempts to construct a relationship between camp and irony which, it transpires, turns on the same unresolved contradiction as that which afflicts the definition of camp itself. 'Irony is the subject matter of camp, and refers here to any highly incongruous contrast between an individual or thing and its context or association' (Babuscio 1977: 41). By the end of the paragraph, the irony has become a matter of the *'perception* of incongruity'. One should note, first, that irony is badly misdefined: it does not involve incongruity, and it is not, and can never be, 'subject-matter'. Irony is an operation of discourse which sets up a complex of tensions between what is said and various qualifications or contradictions generated by the process of the saying. Furthermore, it is difficult to see in what way any of the 'incongruous contrasts' offered as exemplary of camp irony relate either to camp, irony, or 'the gay sensibility'. Are we to assume that, because 'sacred/profane' is an incongruous pair, a great deal of medieval literature is camp? Most importantly, Jack Babuscio ignores the crucial distinction between the kind of scrutiny which dissolves boundaries in order to demonstrate their insubstantiality, or the value-systems which enforce them, and the kind of scrutiny which merely seeks to confirm that they are there. As a logic of 'transgression', camp belongs to the second class. If the transgression of boundaries ever threatened to produce the redefinition of them, the *frisson* would be lost, the thrill of 'something wrong' would disappear.

Eleven. Jack Babuscio quotes Oscar Wilde – 'It is through Art, and through Art only, that we can shield ourselves from the sordid perils of actual existence' – and adds, approvingly: 'Wilde's epigram points to a crucial aspect of camp aestheticism: its opposition to puritan morality' (1977: 42). On the contrary, the epigram is a supreme expression of puritan morality, which can almost be defined by its revulsion from the danger and squalor of the real. Puritanism finds its escape-clause in the aspiration of the individual soul towards God, in a relation to which the world is at best irrelevant and at worse inimical; and Wilde simply redefines the emergency-exit in aesthetic terms. Sartre remarks of Genet that 'beauty is the aesthete's dirty trick on virtue'. I would rephrase him to read: 'the isolation of style is the aesthete's dirty trick on the concept of value, and the constant necessity to analyse and reconstruct concepts of value'.

Twelve. Camp is chronically averse to value judgements, partly by choice (evaluation is felt to involve discrimination between various contents, and thus to belong to the realm of 'High Culture', 'Moral Seriousness', etc.) and partly by default: the obsession with 'style' entails both an astonishing irresponsiveness to tone and a refusal to acknowledge that styles are necessarily the bearers of attitudes, judgements, values, assumptions of which it's necessary to be aware, and between which it's necessary to discriminate. 'The horror *genre,* in particular, is susceptible to a camp interpretation. Not all horror films are camp, of course; only those which make the most of stylish conventions for expressing instant feeling, thrills, sharply defined personality, outrageous and "unacceptable" sentiments, and so on' (Babuscio 1977: 43).

What is 'instant feeling'? Or, for that matter, feeling which is not instant? And what are 'stylish conventions'? The conventions of the horror movie are complex and significant, and cannot be discussed in terms of a *chic* appendage to a content which is somehow separable from them. Certainly, horror films express 'unacceptable sentiments' – indeed, they exist in order to do so – but to read them as 'outrageous' in the camp sense is to protect oneself from their real outrageousness, to recuperate them as objects of 'good-bad taste' (which is what bourgeois critics do anyway). Once one has effected the impossible and meaningless distinction between 'aesthetic and moral considerations' (Babuscio 1977: 51) it becomes perfectly feasible to associate the critical intelligence of Von Sternberg movies with the coy, vulgar, sexist fantasising of Busby Berkeley musicals, or to confuse the grotesque complicity of the Mae West persona with the 'excess' of Jennifer Jones's performance in *Duel in the Sun* or Davis's in *Beyond the Forest* (Babuscio 1977: 51), where 'excess' is a function of an active critique of oppressive gender-roles. While ostensibly making demand for new criteria of judgement, camp is all the while quietly acquiescing in the old ones. It merely takes over existing standards of 'bad taste' and insists on liking them.

Thirteen. Camp has a certain minimal value, in restricted contexts, as a form of *épater les bourgeois*; but the pleasure (in itself genuine and valid enough) of shocking solid citizens should not be confused with radicalism. Still less should 'the very tight togetherness that makes it so good to be one of the queens', in Richard Dyer's phrase (1976, rpt. 1992: 136), be offered as a constructive model of 'community in oppression'. The positive connotations – an insistence on one's otherness, a refusal to pass as straight – are so irredeemably compromised by complicity in the traditional, oppressive formulations of that otherness; and 'camping around' is so often little more than being 'one of the boys' by pink limelight. We should not, *pace* Richard Dyer, feel it incumbent on us to defend camp, on charges of 'letting the side down' or wanting to be John Wayne. Camp is simply one way in which gay men have recuperated their oppression, and it needs to be criticised as such.

9

SEX AND ADDRESS IN *DYNASTY*

Mark Finch

Gay culture means something more specific than it pretends: a discursive system developed out of a metropolitan, white, middle-class and male gay community. Gay culture speaks from and to this position; it describes a socially-defined audience and an attendant cluster of texts. Derek Cohen and Richard Dyer distinguish four key roles for culture in constituting an audience: as identity, knowledge, propaganda, pleasure. Thus culture 'has a role that necessarily precedes any self-conscious political movement. Works of art express, define and mould experience and ideas, and in the process make them visible and available' (Cohen & Dyer 1980: 172).

In other words, gay culture is the prerequisite of political formation; it admits to our existence, interprets that fact in relation to the rest of the world, and provides us with pleasure in the process. Cohen and Dyer write about traditional and radical gay culture, and the consequent result of their collision. Traditional gay culture is neither necessarily produced by nor addressed to gay people: it is high straight culture or showbiz, and always an identification with the 'feminine': *Madame Butterfly*, Judy Garland and E. M. Forster. Radical gay culture is clearly allied to the expansion of gay liberation and women's movement, and sets up new terms of difference in, for example, *Word is Out*, *Fag Rag* and Gay Sweatshop's plays. The overlap has resulted in a new 'gay mainstream culture, operating in neither the alternative modes of the radical gay culture nor the subcultural language of the traditional' (184). But Cohen and Dyer hesitate

Originally published in *Screen*, 27:6, November–December 1986.

to describe, or confuse, the distillation of gay discourse into mainstream culture. Whereas traditional gay culture historically involves a grabbing at elements in straight culture, the latter now self-consciously claws back gay cultural terrain. It is no longer helpful to describe male pin-ups and coffee table books on camp in terms of a distinction between gay and straight culture; what has to be unravelled is the text's exact investment in either social group. What has the incorporation of gay discourse meant for contemporary mainstream texts? The weekly television serial *Dynasty*, 'seen on one hundred networks throughout the free world' (see Shapiro), represents a significant moment in this recuperative strategy, when the (ostensibly) most-watched mass media text becomes the latest addition to British and North American gay culture.[1]

ADDRESS (1): FORM AND GENDER

> It is a well-known fact that *Dynasty* makes more American women happy than any other show on American television. According to the A C Nielson Company, the series is consistently the viewing favourite of women aged from 18 to 54. (*Glasgow Herald*, 12 December 1984)

Like their North American counterparts, British women are assumed, in the absence of gendered demographics, to be pleased with *Dynasty*'s role models for real lives: 'Mature women everywhere have at last found a heroine their own age' (*Daily Mail*, 25 August 1984). It is this representational terrain, allied to the serial's association with soap opera form, which constitutes the popular assumption that *Dynasty* is more attractive to women than men. But single gendered address is complicated by conflicting contextual determinants.

> My husband Richard and I are asked often these days ... what we think the phenomenal appeal of *Dynasty* is based on ... We yearned for something we remembered from the movies we grew up with in the forties: stories where the audience pulled for men and women to fall in love and walk off in the sunset holding hands; stories with characters who dreamed of, pursued, and found their romantic ideal ... There seemed to be a renewed need for romance. Perhaps it had never left but was merely neglected in the necessary re-evaluation of more complex times. And so we set out to create the ultimate American fantasy family. (Shapiro, 2)

Producer Esther Shapiro turns the women's picture into a genre for both genders, by asserting her own married status (see also Aaron and Candy Spelling, producers, and Eileen and Robert Pollock, scriptwriters) and by forgetting the narrative problems which sustained those romantic texts. Shapiro remembers exactly the part that melodramatic continuous serials can never duplicate: the happy end. Certainly, *Dynasty* hinges upon heterosexual romance, centrally through Blake and Krystle; like the byline for the perfume 'Forever Krystle', it is a 'Love That Lives Forever'. But if that love is to live forever, if *Dynasty* is to reach its silver anniversary, there must always be a struggle to maintain that love. Romance fiction survives on this struggle, and Shapiro has picked upon a particularly complex example: 'It's the story of Daphne du Maurier's *Rebecca* retold with the wicked first wife still alive and kicking high and hard' (*Radio Times*, 21–27 July 1984). As Alison Light recalls, *Rebecca* is hardly an innocent text. For the unnamed heroine, Max De Winter's first wife presents, originally, an idea of a successful marriage which has room for female sexual desire, and, finally, the failure of this ideal and denial of a unified self. For Light, *Rebecca* is 'the crime behind the scene of Mills and Boon' (Light, 22). Two aspects of her model unravel *Dynasty*'s investment in gender: an unwillingness to read romance fiction as solidly oppressive, and a psychoanalytic frame which allows her to understand the textual construction of gendered subjectivity – a feminine point of view. The first aspect attends to the ambiguity of *Dynasty*'s response. In the serial form's perpetual postponement of closure, Krystle and Blake will always have problems about their relationship. In the first four series, Krystle left Blake four times, once each series; but if we always expect her to return, Blake is constructed with much less certainty. Linda Evans and John Forsythe previously appeared together in an American sitcom, *Bachelor Father*, the former playing the latter's adolescent niece. In *Dynasty*, Blake's role as father takes narrative and visual precedence over his role as husband; and the inflection is very often monstrous, if not incestuous. Forsythe's performance (Blake's mouth curls sarcastically, he moves abruptly, shouts, and 'stares through' characters) compounds a narrative which has him wilfully excluding his second wife in favour of Alexis, or threatening maniacally to keep the family together. In episode 7 he rapes Krystle when he finds she has been using birth control pills, an event that music and camera position register as traumatic. Of course, Blake's violence has been most pronounced with his son, Steven: they fight each other, physically (episodes 12 and 62) and in court (episodes 13, 63 and 64). In *Dynasty*, the struggle to maintain heterosexual romance and the family is articulated through forms of violence, particularly a *mise-en-scène* and soundtrack that generically codify emotional anguish.

Women's pictures are the only Hollywood texts regularly to explain the world (which becomes the domestic sphere) from an inscribed feminine perspective. Laura Mulvey, arguing from the same position as Light, and against auteurism, describes these melodramas in terms of a model which does not search 'beneath the surface' for authorial irony, but instead finds subversion in the practice of feminine exposition within a masculine cinema: 'Ideological contradiction is the overt mainspring and specific content of melodrama' (Mulvey, 'Sirk and Melodrama', 53). Henry Fenwick, in his *Radio Times* column, states a preference for *Dynasty*'s 'fragmented storylines, conspiracies and revelations, disappearances, reappearances, and reversals of fortune' compared to the 'stronger narrative thrust . . . more butch storyline' of *Dallas* (*Radio Times*, 15–21 September 1984). Are male viewers all occupying feminine subject positions? Address has to be understood – not in content study, like

Ellen Seiter's listing of television melodrama's male-centred stories – but in the negotiation between textual subject place and spectatorial social position.

ADDRESS (2): LOOKING AT MEN

Clearly, *Dynasty* is a cross-addressed text. A key location of this confusion is in the construction of desirable male bodies, a confusion which becomes coherent in a male gay context. If *Dynasty*'s women are Cosmo Girls (see Brunsdon) one decade on –

> The women of *Dynasty* would have lives and purposes. They would engage men competitively in business and with equal passion in bed. They too would be strong and goal-orientated. (Shapiro, 3)

– the serial's men are *Playgirl* pin-ups, with all the problems of diegetic dimensionality that implies. Mark Jennings is the best example, an opportunity for Alexis to declare how 'cute' he looks in tennis shorts. American television censorship reverses traditions of Hollywood cinema; women cannot be naked, but men can be seen in next to nothing. Of course, there are ways in which television can eroticise women, narratively and through editing, but women are differentiated, principally, in *Dynasty*, by costume. The familiar cinematic devices for eroticising women are used for male characters. Jeff, Dex, Adam, Steven and certain guest stars are shown in states of undress, whereas Blake, his lawyer and majordomo are not; the men available for romantic liaisons with characters are also available for *Dynasty*'s audience. This would seem to be a female audience, because undressed men are mostly introduced in the same shot as a female character (as in episode 86, where Sammy-Jo enters the gymnasium to find Adam there, in shorts), and because Steven's periods of homosexuality find him removed from this strategy, as if his gayness takes him away from the realm of desirable men. But an assumption that men can be constructed as sexual spectacle for women, using the same codes that have transformed women into spectacle for men is a naive one. When Mark steps out of the shower (episode 57), there is a play upon his near-nudity, transformed into total nudity by close-ups which cut off the towel around his waist; this device is 'commented upon' by Alexis's pretence of being nude in his bed, when the camera has shown that the quilt conceals her shoulderless dress. Laura Mulvey's vocabulary of fragmentation and fetishisation (see her 'Visual Pleasure') is appropriate for describing a visual strategy (white towel/tanned skin, disorientating close-ups of Alexis's pale hand on Mark's back and chest) but not, here, for mapping pleasure. It seems to me that the pleasure for female spectators is in seeing men treated like women, rather than the pleasure of seeing nudity in itself a textual equality to match representations of strong women.

Mulvey's use of pleasure here is psychoanalytically based; she neither engages with the distinct address of women's genres (though she addresses this in her 'Afterthoughts'), nor allows for extra-textual construction of the spectator, especially the determination of sexuality. Usually, when women are eroticised in a text, lesbian and heterosexual male spectators are most easily accommodated; the former's transgression is blurred by the fit of conspiring in the eroticisation of heroines. For female heterosexual spectators, a non-masculine position is an impossible one; along with gay men, they have to work to convert the hero's actions into spectacle. But women are not trained to objectify bodies as men are,[2] which implies that *Dynasty*'s codification of men along a *Playgirl/Cosmopolitan* discourse enables a gay erotic gaze at men through the relay of a woman's look.

A further problem with Mulvey's account is whether it is applicable to television at all, a medium which 'engages the look and the glance rather than the gaze' (Ellis, 128). Yet the system of spectacle is something *Dynasty* takes from cinema, even if, in a hierarchy of erotic pleasure, the gay male spectator who occupies a culturally-constituted feminine position is perhaps the only one to make the system work. In the same way, gay discourse 'makes sense' of aspects uncontainable within a dominant reading – like wit and representations of the male body – at the same time as *Dynasty* struggles to recuperate homosexuality.

By 'wit' I do not mean to ascribe a textual self-consciousness to *Dynasty*'s makers; I am interested in the conditions of its manifestation, and how it informs popular readings. Wit is primarily evident in dialogue, but in *Dynasty*, music is of more importance than in other genre serials. A musical narrative is constructed for the events leading to Fallon's car crash (episode 86), mixing elements of a familiar 'love theme', unusual (but easily understood) screeching strings, carousel music (referring back to episode 82), *Dynasty*'s frequent fast-paced dramatic theme, and ending on a repeated echo of her scream, teasingly over a black screen. For *Dynasty*'s regular viewers, this soundtrack makes sense without an accompanying image; together, they amount to a circuit of certainty about what is happening. Music sometimes makes the image ironic. An establishing shot of the mansion, from an unfamiliar angle (west wing in long shot, through trees) is coupled with an instrumental version of Michael Jackson's 'Thriller' – which turns out to be diegetically justified by Sammy-Jo's use of personal hi-fi (episode 85). And Sammy-Jo's seductions, of which there are two in episode 86, are underscored by a parodic jazz theme, as men declare (through lustful expressions and dialogue) their desire for her; that is to say, it's all an act. Dialogue is more frequently witty, but this is most often interpretable as characterisation, contained within conventions of mimetic drama: yet there are moments which sustain an uncertainty about *Dynasty*'s project, especially in a play upon viewer's knowledge of a diegetic history (Alexis often retorts, 'but that's all in the past!', as in episode 82), other serials (especially *Dallas*), and the actors' futures.

An example of the latter unfolded when Pamela Sue Martin left the series. For ten episodes before the season's end we were allowed to speculate on how her character, Fallon, would disappear, almost each one offering a different reason.

She becomes engaged to Peter (episode 76) and they plan a long honeymoon. Thirty minutes later, Peter has deserted, and Fallon is knocked down by a drunk driver. She isn't dead though, just paralysed (episode 77). Fallon completely recovers, only to suffer sudden blackouts (episode 79). Her doctor tells her it isn't a brain tumour, there is no danger (episode 81). Happy at last, Fallon accepts Jeff's proposal, but in the midst of her wedding she is seized with another migraine, drives away and collides with a truck (episode 86). That is still not the end: in the following series she is still alive (episode 87), and Jeff interviews someone who gave her a lift after the accident (episode 88); he discovers that she eloped with Peter after all (episode 89), only to be killed in a plane crash (episode 90). This playfulness is sealed when the female corpse cannot be positively identified, leaving a way for continued involvement, although Pamela Sue Martin has retired. The text flirts with our knowledge, prolonging the pleasure of speculation beyond the conventions of British soap opera and other melodramas. (Compare the death of Pam's fiancé in *Dallas*, drawn-out by that serial's standards, yet only involving an incurable disease and a plane crash.)

Of course, the play upon Pamela Sue Martin's departure is partly determined by Fallon's immense structural importance as a central character (the exits of Tracy and Kirby, in episodes 85 and 86, are far less elaborate). But it is as if the text takes this opportunity to be witty about conventions of television melo-drama. A similar strategy announces the change of actor who plays Steven, and shows how this is constructed by many formal aspects. The play around Fallon prioritises the part of plot development, melodrama's characteristically sudden narrative transformations. Steven's reappearance is primarily invested in visual codes. Before the accident, he is filmed from behind, in silhouette; as the camera moves to a frontal shot, he turns his head away, so we just miss seeing his (new) face (episode 44). This strategy is not to disguise the new actor, but declares the opposite by acknowledging that we are curious to see him. For a further six episodes he is filmed in full-face bandages, and the opening credit sequence refuses to name Jack Coleman (which would mean picturing him). The ban-dages come off (episode 50) and the camera looks over Steven's shoulder, but cannot see his reflection in the mirror he holds; finally, the camera pulls back and Steven stands to face us. *Dallas* has shown how the replacement of actors in order to continue with the same character can be constructed without explana-tion and without play. Viewers are not confused, of course, but they are not given any pleasure in the actual change: it is quickly asserted. *Dynasty* allows badinage, articulated textually and in conjunction with the special conditions of media gossip that the transatlantic time-lag facilitates.

LIBERAL GAY DISCOURSE (1): THE ORDINARY AND INDIVIDUAL HOMOSEXUAL

Dynasty is the site of competing discourses, two of which construct opposed homosexualities; these are the textual articulations of camp, and of the modern gay movement – or liberal gay discourse. Whereas with straight readings of

Dynasty there is an overwhelming amount of popular documentation, the status of the British gay community allows little access to the same machinery, so that what evidence there is of *Dynasty*'s importance exists primarily in the unrecorded gestures and dialogue of gay men. Within this terrain, there is scant evidence that the liberal discourse has been picked up, which suggests that it is not addressed to gay people at all.

Richard and Esther Shapiro are award-winning writers of 'social issue' television movies for PBS: *Sarah T, Portrait of an Alcoholic* (1975), *Intimate Strangers* and *The Cracker Factory*, about wife-beating and insanity (both 1979). Their liberal project is most clear in statements about *Dynasty*:

> If I had wanted to write a story from the point of view of a homosexual, there is no way that a mass audience would have taken it. But by using one ninth of the show to deal with Steven . . . over a number of years, I can deal with that thing, and that will become familiar to an American audience, without having to beat everybody over the head and say 'this is socially significant'. (Esther Shapiro, quoted in *The Sunday Express*, 1984)

Textually, this ambition translates into a notion of balance, informed by the message of the gay movement to straight America. Specifically, this is the gay movement at its most consumerist and acceptable after Stonewall (1968) but before AIDS (1980), and its message is that we are individuals, just like you.

> BLAKE: Steven, I'm about as Freudian as you could hope for in a capitalistic exploiter of the working classes. When I'm not busy grinding the faces of the poor, I even read a little. I understand about sublimation. I understand how you could try to hide sexual dysfunction behind hostility toward a father. I – I'm even prepared to say that I could find a little homosexual experimentation . . . acceptable – just as long as you didn't bring it home with you. Don't you see, son, I'm offering you a chance to straighten yourself out?
> STEVEN: Straighten myself out? I'm not sure I know what that means. I'm not sure I could if I wanted to. And I'm not sure I want to.
> BLAKE (*sarcastic*): Of course! I forgot the American Psychiatric Association has decided that it's no longer a disease. That's too bad. I could have endowed a foundation – the Steven Carrington Institute for the Treatment and Study of Faggotry. (*angry*) Now if you'll excuse me, I've got to go and get married.

This exchange, from episode 2, establishes some of the signifiers of the liberal discourse: the invocation of psychoanalysis, Steven's tentative assertiveness, the dissemination of 'facts' about homosexuality (it's not a disease). Conversely, the liberal project is upset by the suggestion, however parodic, of a political base to prejudice, and by Blake's sudden change of mood. I want first to expand upon the construction of liberal gay discourse, and then show how it suffers under the weight of contradiction.

One key way in which the text constructs balance is through dialogue. If someone (usually Blake or Sammy-Jo) says 'faggot', someone else in the same episode will say something tolerant (exceptionally, in the above example, Blake says both). Liberal gay discourse is maintained by opposition to these illiberal characters, rather than by residing in a single fixed source. Andrew can say 'There is no evidence that a child raised by a gay will turn out gay himself' (episode 62), not because this is his conventional position but because he is saying it to Blake, the consistent face of homophobia. Other non-regular characters who represent (what the text declares to be) anti-gayness are undermined by *mise-en-scène* or performance: the social worker who testifies in court that all homosexuals are 'antagonistic and over-emotional' (episode 63) is played by – in *Dynasty*'s terms – a physically unattractive woman. The notation of Blake's homophobia, though, is particularly complex, since he also has to be a credibly charismatic man. At the gay parenting trial (episode 63 and 64) he continually loses his temper and attacks a reporter; yet by episode 69 he has been sufficiently recovered by the text so that his proposal of remarriage will seem irresistible to Krystle.

The point is that what *Dynasty* finds unlikeable is prejudice, not Blake Carrington. With regard to 'social issues' the text constructs two sides, and shows both. In episode 12, Blake is depicted as the drunken master of an old dark house – two uncommon exterior shots coupled with ominous music establish that he is up (light on) late at night. But we have been prepared for this by scenes which illustrate his frustration at his failing marriage. So when he discovers that Steven is entertaining Ted in his bedroom, his anger is justified as 'the last straw'. Through parallel editing, the text offers both sides of what ends in murder. Travelling shots from Blake's point of view are coupled with dialogue which explains that Steven is saying goodbye to Ted, as Krystle has just done to Matthew (previous scene), a sad moment affirmed by a repeated musical theme. Blake's view of the embracing men is understandable, but mistaken. But so is Steven when he cries 'murder'. For the fight, the camera position keeps rapidly returning to the doorway, where Fallon, who is the only one to see what actually happens, stands; finally, we share her view of the incident. Thus, soap opera's subject position, 'a sort of ideal mother . . . who possesses greater wisdom than all her children' (Modleski, 92), becomes one of an ideal juror. 'Do you consider yourself a prejudiced man, Mr Carrington?' asks the defence lawyer (episode 63); prejudice is on trial, not homosexuality or homophobia (a specific form of prejudice). There is an insistence on free speech ('Opinions should be heard') set against the problem of human rights ('I won't change the way I live or my beliefs just to make life easier for Blake Carrington'). Therefore the hearing can only be concluded by Steven's sudden marriage (episode 65), an evasion of the issue of gay parenting which proclaims that the issue never was gay parenting.

The text has greater problems with the appearance of Steven, a central signifier of liberal gay discourse. He is what the gay movement in North

America argues gay men are like, and the sort of media representation the movement wishes for. He stands as a realist strategy to avoid stereotyping, but exactly because *Dynasty*'s form is melodrama and because of the cultural centrality of 'types' (see Dyer, 27–39) this strategy is confounded at almost every stage. According to *The Authorized Biography of the Carringtons*, Steven is 'a study in contradictions' (Shapiro, 73). Steven may conform to the serial's criteria of male attractiveness, but his association with literature and opera – his biography trails references to Ben Jonson, Emily Dickinson, Winston Churchill; his first love token to Claudia is a book; he quotes Robert Louis Stevenson at his wedding (episode 65); he remembers Pavarotti's 'nine high Cs' at the Metropolitan Opera (episode 2) – ties in, however faintly, with a tradition of homosexual aesthetes. Traditional gay culture's equation of the aesthetic with the feminine is also signalled by location and music: Ted and Steven go to a French restaurant, the soundtrack exploits the classical connotations of slow, 'melancholy' violins. Physiognomically, Al Corley contained this melancholy in features best described as 'brooding' (heavy brow, deep-set eyes, protruding lips); he played the part with his head down, and sometimes stammered. Similarly, Steven's past is used to explain his homosexuality; in court (episode 63), Alexis exclaims, 'Blake banished me from my own children! He deprived them of my own guidance, depriving them of everything a mother should give . . . ' At which point, Blake contests: 'Guidance! It was your guidance that did it! You had seven years to turn [Steven] into what he is. I've been fighting to make him into a man ever since!' Constant remarks that Steven is Alexis's favourite child sometimes amount to an incestuous competition with his romantic partners; in episode 66, Alexis phones Steven on his wedding night and has him check her apartment for intruders. A psychoanalytic explanation is thus proposed.

The prolongation of revealing Steven's new face is determined by its importance as the erasure of Al Corley's melancholy features and the substitution of Jack Coleman's far less troubled physiognomy. But this coup for liberal discourse's avoidance of stereotyping is sabotaged by the problem of how to involve Steven in stories that do not comment upon his sexuality. At the moment of recuperating homosexuality within the family, *Dynasty*'s generic requirement – that individuals are characterised by their transgression, like Fallon's promiscuity or Claudia's neurotic obsession, which become the sites for narrative problems – means that homosexuality will always be disruptive to the family's happiness and solidarity.

LIBERAL GAY DISCOURSE (2): GOING OFF BALANCE

The most recuperable part of the gay movement's message is that gay people are individuals who happen to be gay. When Steven forces his family to say out loud 'Steven is gay' (episode 34), the text is complexly acknowledging a personal issue that has to be defined socially. *Dynasty*'s liberal discourse is complicated by signifiers of a socially and politically defined homosexuality.

In episode 2, Steven and Claudia have individual liberationist speeches which disrupt (through pace and duration) preparations for Blake and Krystle's wedding. As representatives for what in *Dynasty*'s liberal frame are two easily elided discourses, the women's movement and gay movement, Claudia and Steven are perfect romantic partners. Claudia faces her husband with her sexual dissatisfaction ('What I'm trying to say is that women have sexual fantasies too'); Steven's confession of gayness is equally signalled as courageous, through performance and camera distance. This political alliance is heightened by Steven's accusations that oil companies like his father's have 'sold America out' by not developing alternative energy resources; 'Bolshevik', his sister jokes. Although Steven has lost this leftist inflection by *Dynasty*'s third series, in which he works as a controlling executive at rival Colbyco, episode 58 has Chris, his lawyer, come out as gay: 'Do you want to hear the story of my life? It's the same as yours'. Chris synopsises his gay romance, sham marriage, divorce and loneliness 'in the closet'; 'Are you surprised?' Steven answers for the viewer: 'I don't know ... I don't look for these things', but his astonished smile suggests he has been taken by surprise. Similarly, a man appears from out of a crowd in a New York bar and reminds Steven that they were college friends, flirtatiously proposing a dinner date (episode 85). *Dynasty*'s gay characters suggest a shared history and anonymity.

Steven's surprise on both meetings is partly the celebration of a liberal discourse which has, by repressing stereotypes, caught us off guard. At the same time, the text problematises the iconography of homosexuality. *Dynasty* foregrounds television's censorial inability to depict gay intimacy within realist codes by showing, melodramatically, how Steven's gayness is defined by a heterosexual gaze. Any display of affection is seized upon and translated into violence from other (straight) characters. Ted touches Steven's hand in a restaurant and is seen by a co-worker who later starts a fight (episode 5). Blake finds Chris in Steven's apartment and assumes they are lovers, initiating an argument (episode 62). Claudia, from a doorway, sees Luke adjusting Steven's tie and assumes they have made love (episode 94), causing her to sleep with another man. The diegetic spectator is wrong in assuming that Steven is sexually involved with these men. Chris insists that Steven tell his father that they are just friends (episode 63), but Steven will not do so 'on principle'. His implication is that this – Blake's misinterpretation and consequent custody trial – is a test case for all gay people. The catalogue of abrasions to liberal gay discourse suggest opposition to the concept that homosexuality is a personal issue, and opens up an area for gay address – not just in considering how we are identified by straight society, but in asking how we can be banished. This is central to a social group aware of its capacity for self-effacement.

> STEVEN: You know what Oscar Wilde said, 'Work is the curse of the drinking classes'.
> JEFF (*laughs*): Clever man, Oscar Wilde. Shame he was a homosexual.

STEVEN: Yeah, kind of makes you long for the good old days when they used to burn them at the stake.

JEFF: You know, I think that's a little rough, Steven – I mean, even for a joke.

STEVEN (*intense*): Oh, you mean 'Gay is Good'? 'Give a Cheer for a Queer'?

JEFF: No, I mean different strokes for different folks.

STEVEN: But you wouldn't want your brother to marry one?

When Steven moves from duplicity (episode 2) to fierce declaration (episode 34), the text attempts to extinguish his 'gay voice' by sending him to Singapore, or marrying him to Sammy-Jo and Claudia. Ted's death, Steven's facial reconstruction and Chris's inexplicable disappearance foreground the problem of erasing homosexuality from the text. Peter Buckman argues that, when dealing with 'social issues', continuous serials have the virtue of duration (69); *Dynasty* has, at the time of writing, had 84 episodes in which to discourse homosexuality, compared to a film melodrama like *Making Love* (directed by Arthur Hiller, 1982) or *Lianna* (directed by John Sayles, 1982). This is not to collapse into Shapiro's claim about using 'one ninth of the show', but to argue that in the other eight ninths, when *Dynasty* does not wish to deal with homosexuality and instead passes for straight, gaps and evasions in liberal discourse constitute an enquiry into the conditions of textual acceptance. This is complex enough to shore up a gay address also facilitated by representational problems about the male body; however, camp circulates as a second gay discourse, and has a more successful investment in a male gay audience.

CAMP DISCOURSE (1): CULTURAL CONTEXTS

Introducing *Dynasty*'s third season, *Radio Times* refers to 'dramatic death-dodging and dynamic derring-do' (4–11 April 1984); at the same time, the voice-over announcement before *Dynasty* prepares us for something less than serious, actually using the term 'camp' before episode 87. But British newspaper reviews noted *Dynasty*'s camp long before this, with the entrance of Joan Collins in episode 14. The *Guardian, Observer* and *Times* particularly use the serial to assert critical superiority, inflected differently from the tabloid papers' 'so funny, it's awful'. A two-paragraph review in *The Observer* (Conrad 1985) name-drops Wagner, Strauss, Jean Harlow, Lady Bracknell and Handel. *Dynasty* is employed to signal the reviewer's willingness to camp; this is a class-based discourse, an aspect often disregarded in attempts to define camp. The *Mirror* would never call *Dynasty* camp. The *Observer*'s reviewer also shows how camp is only a game, the end result of Susan Sontag's intellectual reclamation in 'Notes on Camp' and the mainstreaming of camp in texts like *The Rocky Horror Show* (1972) and *Hi-De-Hi* (1980). Two recent examinations of camp (Booth 1983 and Core 1984) are marketed as chic gift books. Today, 'camp is not necessarily homosexual. Anyone or anything can be camp. But it takes one to know one' (Core 1984: 7). And this is camp's problematic: neither a consistent theoretical perspective, nor a certain group of artifacts.

Arguments for camp's subversiveness, specifically in questioning culturally-constituted gender roles, are themselves questionable. Andrew Britton (1978) argues that 'being essentially a mere play with given conventional signs, camp simply replaces the signs of "masculinity" with a parody of the signs of "femininity" and reinforces existing social definitions of both categories'. Furthermore, the subversive argument is formalist in that it assumes a fixed relation between camp and gay culture, disregarding the historical specificity of that relation. When Richard Dyer (1986) defines camp as 'a characteristically gay way of handling the values, images and products of the dominant culture through irony, exaggeration, trivialisation, theatricalisation, and an ambivalent making fun of and out of the serious and respectable', he is actually describing pre-gay movement culture. Camp becomes important when it speaks to that historical experience. Bruce Boone (1982), for example, shows how Frank O'Hara's poetry uses camp discourse to oppose language colonised by liberal intellectuals, invested in an address to readers familiar with 1960s urban gay slang. Similarly if camp is considered subversive in *Dynasty*, it is to the extent that it displaces liberal gay discourse as the site for gay address; central in this operation is Joan Collins/Alexis, who – at specific instances – signifies a different level of enunciation from other figures in the text.

Dynasty's camp is most evident in conversation within the gay community, or in the paraphernalia of the community's bastions, gay clubs particularly, in Britain, between June and December 1984.[3] The Hippodrome Club (gay for one night each week) held a *Dallas* and *Dynasty* Ball on 16 July 1984, with over sixty look-alike contestants, mostly dressed as Alexis. The same club had been screening scenes from the two serials, giant-size, above the dance floor, since early June. When Krystle and Alexis fought in the lily-pond (episode 58), this was immediately and frequently screened in Heaven, 'Europe's largest gay discotheque'. Norma Lewis's Hi-Energy single, 'Fight for the Single Family', was accompanied by a video which pixillated and repeated images of the pond battle and studio fight (from episode 29), still screened in both clubs. These venues are pivotal in defining British gay culture: they are predominantly used by salaried, white 18–30 year old men. In the gay press, the Hippodrome Ball was considered one of 1984's 'highlights'; a disco single was released in November, marketed solely through the club and – like the venue itself – seemingly addressed to gay men who had enjoyed the Ball, while also accessible to a lesbian or straight audience. 'Dyna-Dall', 'a dream of *Dallas* and *Dynasty*', peculiarly conflates the two serials, and largely disregards the particular differences of each; it is most successful in reiterating melodrama's compression, inconsistency and (for the spectator) compulsiveness, in a fast beat, multiple percussion and actual lyrics:

Dallas and *Dynasty*, playing on my mind you see,
I'm always thinking of you.
Dallas and *Dynasty*, keep on taking over me,
Don't want to watch but we do . . .

Dallas and *Dynasty*, you provide the fantasy,
That's why we're so hooked on you.
Characters of different size disappear before my eyes,
And fade right back into view . . .

Is he with she or she with he?
I'm so confused it's hard to see
Just who is living with who.
And as we try to work it out
They change the storyline about,
Now that's not a nice thing to do!

The song goes on to imagine the excesses of mixing characters from each serial. Of course, Hollywood melodrama – and especially the women's picture – has always been the material of camp. 'Dyna-Dall' only articulates this interest as due to narrative incoherence and improbability. But *Dynasty* references the women's picture, like *The Women* (directed by George Cukor, 1939), through formal signifiers like costume (*Dynasty* designer Nolan Miller is 'in love' with Adrian's gowns for Crawford and MGM) and geography (confrontations take place in powder rooms, beauticians', boutiques). Other aspects of *Dynasty*, catalogued under 'excess', amount to 'irony, exaggeration, trivialisation, theatricalisation', which circulate about the figure of Joan Collins/Alexis.

CAMP DISCOURSE (2): ALEXIS, THE ENUNCIATOR

Of all *Dynasty*'s regular characters, Alexis is most closely matched by the performer's star persona. There are two key signifiers of this image: Britishness and bitchiness. From her work in the 1950s and 1960s (especially *Land of the Pharaohs* 1955, *The Opposite Sex* 1956, *Seven Thieves* 1960) Collins acquires the connotations of British Beauty, like Diana Dors. Joan Collins is 'our Joanie' (*Daily Star*, 23 June 1983). *Past Imperfect*, her autobiography, and *The Stud* (both 1978) confirm the signifiers of promiscuity and hardness that are deployed in earlier films (again *Land of the Pharaohs* and some of her 1970s horror films). Finally, she is indelibly associated with *The Bitch* (1979), a film which works to problematise that equation. *Dynasty* plays upon this image: 'I'm the best thing that *Dynasty* has got. It's because of me that the show became a hit' (Collins in *Nine to Five*, 16 July 1984).

There are endless signs which work to sustain 'that bitch' (*Sunday People*, 27 August 1984). She need no longer be referred to by name; when Krystle fights back, 'The Bitch is Ditched' (*The Sun*, 14 March 1984). A more innocuous version of this is the perfume, Scoundrel – but Joan is a bitch for refusing to join in *Dynasty*'s merchandising campaign, instead promoting a cheaper fragrance than Forever Krystle. Endlessly, the comparison is with Linda Evans, the serial's only other performer to be involved in a kind of fit between role and star image. Good-hearted Linda has 'inner beauty' (*Woman's Own*, 8 December 1984); Joan is hard, exterior. Gay culture responds to this hardness and innuendo: bitch becomes a term of endearment. Bradley and The Boys have recorded a special 'Bitch version' of 'Dyna-Dall': 'Dance, You Evil Witch!' Collins has played the witch in *Hansel and Gretel* for cable television (Collins, 303), and at Heaven's Christmas party an inverted fairy tale pantomime of insipid heroes and vivacious villains was brought to an end by video excerpts from *Dynasty*. Alexis is not far from a Wicked Witch of the West whose actions are directed against the happy monogamous couple – she originally arrived out of nowhere (a narrative surprise) to avenge her gay son's dead lover (episode 13).

> Underneath it all, she is a woman capable of great love, whose devotion to her children can result in a fierce protectiveness, which is often misinterpreted as cold brutality. Her toughened and guarded façade is merely armor for a core of vulnerability that lies deep within her. (Shapiro, 39)

Shapiro locates a final aspect which conflates role and star, but which works (ostensibly) against signifiers of bitchiness. Collins's daughter was close to death after being hit by a car in 1979:

> 'No!' I heard myself scream. 'No, no, no!' ... This was a nightmare. It must be a nightmare. 'Not my baby, not Katy!' I started to scream and thrash about. All my reason went. I became like an animal. I had no control – just unbearable agony and the frustration of being away from our beloved little girl at this dreadful time. (Collins, 307)

Like many parts of Collins's autobiography, this corresponds precisely with a scene from *Dynasty*. Fallon is hit by a car, and is in hospital, close to death; episode 78 ends, unusually, not with a new revelation of dramatic incident, but on a shot of Alexis's hysterical grief as she proclaims how much she loves Fallon, and the 'unbearable agony' of not being near her (she has been forbidden to see Fallon). *Dynasty* frequently constructs images of Alexis as an anxious mother.

The Alexis/Joan Collins conflation casts her as an outstanding figure. Rebecca Bailin describes how narrative is always enunciated 'by' a cluster of discourses and that, exceptionally, in *Marnie* (1964), one diegetic character becomes associated with the level of (hegemonic, patriarchal) enunciation. Similarly, Alexis's irony can be read as referring outside the diegesis. This is organised around two of Joan Collins's frequent claims: that she is really an actress who has her mind on better things than *Dynasty*, and that it was she who made the serial the success it is.

The close alliance of star and character biography implies that Collins is not acting, but playing out a role familiar to her. 'Men have used women for centuries. So why shouldn't it be our turn now?' she asks Tracy (episode 84), quoting from her autobiography (Collins, 323). And yet, despite the idea that this really is not acting, the way she plays Alexis emphasises performance; she completes her line to Tracy by grandly lighting a cigar. Often, Alexis ends her speeches with a deliberate gesture, like biting into a grape or turning her head away from the character she has been talking to (as in episode 59); these gestures are in excess of the non-naturalist performance melodrama demands. Alexis is at the centre of ambiguity about *Dynasty*'s project, re-cast as her intention: she asks Adam to defend her at the murder trial, and he consequently demands her utter honesty, to which she smilingly inquires (in medium close-up): 'When have I been anything but honest?' (episode 87). Alexis is always plotting. Characters are always reacting to her plots. Whether or not she succeeds, narrative change is brought about – sensationally, in the merger of Colbyco and Denver-Carrington (episodes 50–67) and Blake's bankruptcy (episodes 83–92). Frequently, Alexis is on the telephone to a private detective, discovering what we want to know. (Where is Krystle's first husband? Who was Kirby's mother?) She knows more than other characters. When Mark shouts 'You can't get rid of me', Alexis replies 'Just watch' (episode 84): he is dead in the next scene, although Alexis had nothing to do with it. Her 'knowledge' extends outside the diegesis.

Joan Collins/Alexis's irony is also directed at formal conventions. She is informed of Mark's death and insists, but casually, that it cannot be true: 'I left him only hours ago, and he was very much alive' (episode 84). The joke is that generic and serial conventions have conspired in his death. Equally, Alexis's retort to Dominique's 'Would you say these are the clothes and jewels of a journalist?' (episode 85) is 'Well ... anything can be rented nowadays', a joke about *Dynasty*'s expansive wardrobe. Of course, there is a fine distinction between irony within and without the diegesis. Other characters have witty dialogue; it is Collins's persona, performance, camera strategy and reactions of other characters which construct the special meaning of her words and gestures. Alexis of all characters comes closest to direct address; she has more lines to deliver as soliloquy. Krystle, Claudia and others are placed in reaction shots to her wit, threats and insults; they are shown to smile more often than look threatened or insulted – in admiration of Alexis's audacity, and also of her role.

I am not claiming that Alexis's irony consistently ruptures the diegesis, nor that the only spectator to understand this is a male gay one. But Alexis's construction (role as enunciator) makes sense of the text's wit, claims it for her own, and this is appreciable from a gay subject position. That Alexis is often allied to the level of enunciation is asserted by those moments when she is without knowledge. In scene four of episode 86, Alexis dares Kirby to shoot her – 'Go ahead, pull the trigger and watch me die' – calling on our knowledge of conventions which disallow Kirby to do exactly that. Yet scene 21 reverses her and our certainty: Alexis is arrested for murder. The police command to 'cuff the lady' enforces the loss of diegetic control.

CONCLUSION: THE DISCURSIVE BATTLEGROUND

According to Umberto Eco, mass media texts are most often closed texts. Unlike the fixed textual relations concealed by high art's seeming ambiguity, closed texts 'are in fact open to any possible aberrant decoding ... They seem to be structured according to an inflexible project. Unfortunately, the only one not to have been "inflexibly" planned is the reader' (5). But Eco does not show how 'aberrant decodings' are facilitated by specific textual strategies; he implies that they are little more than the consequence of perverse readers. Furthermore, Eco's formalism fails to account for the specific investments of mass media texts in both their own media and an inter-textual domain. Janet Wolff finds Eco's model to be entirely relativist: a text can mean whatever the reader wants. Wolff attempts to describe the reader's part in producing meaning without collapsing into relativism: 'The way in which the reader engages with the text and constructs meaning is a function of his or her place in ideology and society ... The role of the reader is creative but at the same time situated' (115).

A media text has to address itself to many different social groups in order to sustain its mass appeal. *Dynasty*'s contradictions and complexity allow the reader's 'creativity'. Of course, a male gay reading is constructed within the serial's preferred reading, but this is the discourse of a gay movement which inscribes a liberal heterosexual subject position. In Richard Dyer's words, 'While entertainment is responding to needs that are real, at the same time it is also defining and delimiting what constitutes the legitimate needs of people in this society' (1977: 7).

The 'legitimate needs' of gay men within gay culture are circulated within an oppositional discourse. Gay culture trains us to be alert to a particular conception of homosexuality which involves signifiers of 'femininity'. 'If there is such a thing as a gay sensibility', argues P.F. Grubb, ' ... it is to be found in a preparedness to find certain sign-material relevant for perception-forming processes related to homosexuality'. Aspects of *Dynasty*'s excess and compromised address cohere as camp discourse, which, through referencing Hollywood's melodramas/women's pictures touches on camp's historical alliance with homosexuality. Camp is what the liberal gay discourse/modern gay movement represses. This does not mean that camp is necessarily radical (any potential for subversion depends on the fixing of a contextual moment, and at least the questioning of its class specificity), but that it does enable Joan Collins/Alexis – in a supreme fit between character and star – sometimes to disrupt the diegesis (by plotting, joking, 'acting') and thus usurp the liberal discourse. The latter is itself insecure in that its notion of balance, avoidance of stereotyping, and affirmation of the individual is splintered by recognition that gayness is a political, collective issue; that definitions of homosexuality must be social; and that gayness keeps returning as potential disruption to the bourgeois family. In other words, when the text wants to pass for straight – turn its balancing act into a vanishing trick-camp discourse, associated with a different level of enunciation, draws out 'tell-tale' gaps and ruptures, just as if (and this was one of the sights at the Hippodrome's *Dallas* and *Dynasty* Ball) Steven Carrington, still in bandages and a dressing gown, had donned a tiara and drop ear-rings.

NOTES

1. Cohen & Dyer also establish the terms of my argument in their emphasis on male gay culture, which has a specificity apart from lesbian culture. As I go on to describe, *Dynasty*'s investment is exclusively in male gay culture. I can find no evidence that *Dynasty* addresses a lesbian audience to the same degree.
2. Rather than justify this argument with 'sociological' evidence (like the preponderance of 'sexual objectification' in the male gay community), I would want to point to textual evidence like *Saturday Night Fever* or *American Gigolo*, that is, films which pose the problem from a masculine perspective: the difficulty, for men, of being objectified.
3. Contemplating the determinants which act upon this lessening of interest would make an interesting aside: I'm not sure that it can be located in actual episodes, but it may have more to do with: (a) the BBC's continued promotion of *Dynasty* through Fenwick's column in *Radio Times* and its now settled place in the schedule – i.e., bringing the serial far more visibly into the mainstream; (b) the British launch of *Dynasty* merchandising directed, fundamentally, at wealthy married women; (c) the decline in London club attendance and the first wave of media panic about AIDS – i.e., dividing the gay community and eroding opportunities for gay cultural concretisation.

REFERENCES

Bailin, Rebecca, 'Feminist Readership, Violence, and Marnie', *Film Reader* 5, 1982, 24–36.

Brunsdon, Charlotte, 'A Subject for the Seventies', *Screen* 23:3–4, September-October 1982, 20–29.

Buckman, Peter, *All for Love*, London: Secker and Warburg, 1984.

Collins, Joan, *Past Imperfect*, revised edition, London: W. H. Allen, 1984.

Dyer, Richard (ed.), *Gays and Film*, London: British Film Institute, 1977.

Eco, Umberto, *The Role of the Reader*, London: Indiana UP, 1979.

Ellis, John, *Visible Fictions*, London, Routledge and Kegan Paul, 1982.

Grubb, P. F., 'You Got It from Those Books: A Study in Gay Reading', Gay Studies Conference, Amsterdam, 1982.

Light, Alison, 'Returning to Manderley: Romance Fiction, Female Sexuality and Class', *Feminist Review* 16, Summer 1984.

Miller, Nolan, interviewed by Russell Harty, *Harty Goes to Hollywood*, BBC2, 10 August 1984.

Modleski, Tania, *Loving With a Vengeance*, Connecticut: Shoe String Press, 1982.

Mulvey, Laura, 'Afterthoughts on "Visual Pleasure and Narrative Cinema" inspired by "Duel in the Sun" (King Vidor, 1946)', *Framework* 15/16/17, Summer 1981, 12–15.

——, 'Notes on Sirk and Melodrama', *Movie* 25, 1977.

——, 'Visual Pleasure and Narrative Cinema', *Screen* 16:3, Autumn 1975, 6–18.

Seiter, Ellen, 'Men, Sex and Money in Recent Family Melodramas', *Journal of the University Film and Video Association* 35:1, Winter 1983, 17–27.

Shapiro, Esther, *The Authorized Biography of the Carringtons*, London: Comet, 1984.

Wolff, Janet, *The Social Production of Art*, London: Macmillan, 1982.

10

HOMOSEXUAL SIGNS
(IN MEMORY OF ROLAND BARTHES)

Harold Beaver

Another inquiry into homosexuality? Best leave it to the experts: human rights activists, legal watchdogs, social historians, medical researchers even. Suitable for psychopathologists, of course. Good for gossip. But somehow, inherently, pornographic. The very attempt to attain a more elevated or abstract point of view, to grasp its implications in terms of language, conventions, or ritual codes must be considered ludicrous. As ludicrous as Proust's Baron de Charlus drawing himself up with a forbidding air to announce, 'To me, you understand, it is only general principles that are of any interest. I speak to you of this as I might of the law of gravitation' (*Captive*, 130).

The primal injunction was formulated long ago by none other than God: 'Be fruitful, and multiply'. Homosexuality defies that injunction; it transgresses against breeding. With cannibalism and incest, it appears the very incarnation of social self-destruction, seeking whom it may devour. Like cannibalism, it threatens to turn abundance to sterility. Like incest, it irrevocably defiles genital desire. But homosexuality alone achieves the dual distinction (and penalty) of simultaneously contravening both 'nature' and 'culture', fertility and the law. It transgresses not merely against breeding but against the institution of marriage and of the family.

Yet only partners in marriage – by committing incest or adultery, for example – can undermine that institution. Only those who have entered on a contract can break it. The homosexual has never submitted to a contract. He

An earlier version was published in *Critical Inquiry* 8:1, Autumn 1981.

is excluded, moreover, from all social contracts, all social bonds. Unlike formal engagements or dowries or wedding oaths, homosexual acts are never socially viewed as forms of exchange. It is only on the personal and symbolic plane that the phallus, for male homosexuals, becomes a token whose exchange fixes subjects in their mutual roles. What homosexuals defy is their legally confirmed *status,* intended to inhibit their freedom, not a contractual bond. If they transgress at all, it must be against the contract of language, what Roland Barthes called 'the controlled exchange on which the semantic process and collective life are based' (*Barthes,* 63). The homosexual's codes are countercodes. Like a cannibal, it might be charged, he exploits all ideas, messages, and roles by orgiastically wasting their content merely for the form, the vicarious fantasy, and then wearing them like a feather, or foreskin, in his cap.

Whatever the charge, the fundamental ethical problem is this: to recognize signs wherever they are, not to mistake them for natural phenomena, and to proclaim rather than conceal them. It was Ferdinand de Saussure (67–8) who made the revolutionary pronouncement that although the meanings of many actions may seem natural, they are always founded on shared assumptions or conventions; that what is obvious in the case of linguistic signs is also true of other signs. The social model, or aspiration, is all-pervasive.

In Judaic law, as until recently in the French penal code, that social model was the 'crime against nature'. As Paul, exhorting the Romans, put it: 'for even their women did change the natural use into that which is against nature: and likewise also the men, leaving the natural use of the women, burned in their lust one toward another'.[1] Yet homosexuality can neither be simply 'natural', because spontaneously generated, nor 'unnatural', degenerate because unregenerative. The term is parasitical, meaningful only within a specific cultural system or structured discourse. The ancient Greeks, though aware of every nuance of what we label 'homosexuality', had no nouns corresponding to our adjectival hybrids, 'a homosexual' and 'a heterosexual'. When Gide in *Corydon* attempted to construct, by means of a comparison with other species, a homosexuality which was biologically based, he was simply walking into a trap (see Hocquenghem, 48). *Homosexualität,* a German term coined in 1869, functions as a *social* concept disguised as a biological phenomenon. To this day an East German endocrinologist claims that by boosting the testosterone level in the amniotic fluid of pregnant women, he can save society.[2]

Proust, for all his evasions, was a good deal subtler than Gide. When Charlus and Jupien first meet in the courtyard of the Hôtel de Guermantes (part ogling, part posturing for, each other), he sums up their charade: 'The scene was not, however, positively comic; it was stamped with a strangeness, or if you like a naturalness, the beauty of which steadily increased' (*Cities,* 6). What is 'natural' is neither heterosexual nor homosexual desire but simply desire. Desire is innocent, though (for the innocent interloper) naturally comic. Desire is like the pull of a gravitational field, the magnet that draws body to body, plant to plant, or, as in the case of Charlus buzzing around Jupien, the bumble-bee to the orchid. Proust called it 'the visible stratagems of flowers'. The effeminate male reveals all the obstinate agility of a convolvulus, throwing out 'its tendrils wherever it finds a convenient post or rake', in his unconscious search for 'the masculine organ'. Proust described that initial encounter between the baron and the extailor in botanical terminology, as if demonstrating precise scientific laws of attraction and repulsion: 'I knew that this expectancy was no more passive than in the male flower, whose stamens had spontaneously curved so that the insect might more easily receive their offering; similarly the female flower that stood here, if the insect came, would coquettishly arch her styles, and, to be more effectively penetrated by him, would imperceptibly advance, like a hypocritical but ardent damsel, to meet him half-way'. Or again: 'I found the pantomime, incomprehensible to me at first, of Jupien and M. de Charlus as curious as those seductive gestures addressed, Darwin tells us, to insects by the flowers' (all quotations from *Cities*, 1–45).

As 'moral botanist' Proust defers to Darwin, with digressions on glow-worms and pistils and nectar and pollen and hermaphrodite flowers. The body obeys its own obscure laws, of which moral imagination and public censorship are only partial and ineffective witnesses. But the laws of homosexual desire are peculiarly obscure because they are so awkward and absurd. As Proust had pointed out in *Contre Sainte-Beuve*: 'Nature, as it has done for certain animals and flowers in which the organs of love are so badly placed that they almost never find pleasure, has certainly not spoiled them with regard to love' (260). Viewed in that light, the successful reconnoitre, engagement, and coupling of homosexual desire comes to seem positively miraculous.

But Proust emphatically denies that he has proved 'a relation between certain botanical laws' and 'homosexuality'. His 'conjunction' of terms is without any scientific basis. It is not even a hypothesis. It is simply 'a comparison of providential hazards'. Yet that comparison is the subject of the long exegesis which introduces the two volumes of *Sodome et Gomorrhe*. For as a bee ambiguously pollinates an orchid (Greek for 'testicles'), so Charlus physically penetrates and fertilizes Jupien. Only here, Proust adds, 'the word fertilize must be understood in a moral sense, since in the physical sense the union of male with male is and must be sterile, but it is no small matter that a person may encounter the sole pleasure which he is capable of enjoying, and that every "creature here below" can impart to some other "his music, or his fragrance or his flame"'.

Modern society, as Michel Foucault has shown in *La volonté de savoir*, cultivates its own peculiar perversion, not in repressing the deviant forms of sexual manifestation but in claiming to treat, control, and turn them to socially useful purposes. According to Foucault, Western culture is truly and genuinely perverse not because it is puritanical or hypocritical but because the principal forms of social control over the individual would be unthinkable without the cultivation of the category of 'the perverse'.

Since the seventeenth century the new human sciences of demography, medicine, psychiatry, psychoanalysis, penology, and pedagogy have systematically developed and enlarged this area of the perverse. Control of sexuality was less an instrument for subjecting the lower classes than a means for affirming bourgeois self-control. It was an investment in 'health'. Eugenics was linked to inheritance, and both were linked to capital. The new middle classes simply transformed the actual condition of their incestuous family structure into a social ideal. By defining the heterosexual monogamous couple as the very foundation of social life, bourgeois society was able to regard every other form of erotic relationship as *contre nature,* a threat to health as well as to society. Treatment of homosexuality, then, was intended merely to affirm the reality of the 'disease', to moderate symptoms without eliminating the causes of 'suffering'. The homosexual, like the impotent father, frigid wife, sadistic husband, or hysterical daughter, became a victim of sexual determinism as rigid as Marxist determinism regarding history or economics; but only the homosexual became a dangerous and surreptitious outcast: a rebel against the perverse psychiatrization of 'perverse' pleasures.

'Homosexuality' is not a name for a preexistent 'thing' but part of a network of developing language, on the model of 'male/female', 'man/beast', 'child/adult'. By the nineteenth century the matrimonial model needed, it seems, and so created its nonmarital counterpart in a seemingly unmotivated, nonprocreative, complementary form called the 'perverse'. At the same time industrial society compounded the conceptual dualism of the child/adult relationship by inventing a further nonprocreative, seemingly unmotivated sexual stage called 'adolescence'. Neither term was so much descriptive as it was a prescriptive self-definition of an ever-narrowing, exclusively matrimonial culture. Just as the adolescent was neither wholly a child nor an adult, so the homosexual was neither wholly male nor female.

This conceptual schema of homosexuality can never be *proved.* As long as the subject remains taboo, however, it is reinforced by vicious stereotypes. It is on stock gestures, as television quickly learned, that a self-defined heterosexual audience greedily feeds. For the pied piper is not readily spotted: in spite of the multiplicity of his signs, he remains a double-dealer, moving incognito through a heterosexual world – a marauding alien, an unscrupulous bogeyman plotting devious sexual revenge, a masked avenger (in drag), an invisible man, a secret agent crossing the shadow line of dreams. Like a bleached 'nigger' (or half-breed) he haunts the guilty heterosexual mind with threats of racial doom.

Just consider, for sheer paranoia, the range of synonyms when the mask is ripped, the silence broken, the deferment brutally concluded: angel-face, arse-bandit, auntie, bent, bessie, bugger, bum-banger, bum boy, chicken, cocksucker, daisie, fag, faggot, fairy, flit, fruit, jasper, mincer, molly, nancy boy, nelly, pansy, patapoof, poofter, cream puff, powder puff, queen, queer, shit-stirrer, sissie, swish, sod, turd-burglar, pervert. For Aristophanes, as for Norman Mailer and Mary Whitehouse, buggery equalled coprophagy: a corrupt, destructive, hypocritical, excremental, urban scatology. Heterosexuality equalled the fecund, rural norm. Aristophanes' diet for a giant dung beetle was turds from a buggered boy: 'he says he likes them well kneaded'.[3]

To this day degeneracy often seems to be just another code word for homosexuality, as does perversion and decadence; this very essay will seem to many a 'decadent' project. Nor would I balk at the term as long as it is interpreted in the French sense: intent on fulfilling Baudelaire's program of transforming the erotically passive to the intellectually active, the voluptuous to rational self-mastery. In Auden's words, 'To set in order – that's the task / Both Eros and Apollo ask' ('Letter', 162). Paradox, perversity, and semantic renewal go hand in hand.

Proust twice filled in questionnaires of the sort once treasured in family albums. The first he wrote at thirteen, the second at twenty. They included such questions as: What is for you the greatest unhappiness? Your ideal of earthly happiness? For what faults do you have the greatest indulgence? In what place would you like to live? To the last, at thirteen, he replied: 'In the land of the Ideal, or rather of my ideal'. At twenty: 'In the place where certain things I want would come to pass as if by enchantment – and where tender feelings would always be shared'.[4] The second answer explicates the first. However tentatively or coyly, by the age of twenty he had explored his homosexuality. In the real world, he realized, his tenderest feelings could seldom be shared. The real world seemed a mere masquerade whose aim was status or prestige. The real world was a fortress where prisoners, condemned to solitary confinement, unceasingly flashed their symbolic credentials from cell to cell, where 'certain things' must remain forever dreams.

For to be homosexual in Western society entails a state of mind in which all credentials, however petty, are under unceasing scrutiny. The homosexual is beset by signs, by the urge to interpret whatever transpires, or fails to transpire, between himself and every chance acquaintance. He is a prodigious consumer of signs – of hidden meanings, hidden systems, hidden potentiality. Exclusion from the common code impels the frenzied quest: in the momentary glimpse, the scrambled figure, the sporadic gesture, the chance encounter, the reverse image, the sudden slippage, the lowered guard. In a flash meanings may be disclosed; mysteries wrenched out and betrayed.

Even the Lambda badge remains a secret sign for a mainly secret fraternity. Homosexuals, like Masons, live not in an alternative culture but in a duplicate culture of constantly interrupted and overlapping roles. They must learn to live with ambiguity; and like any heterosexual lover they wrestle with that ambiguity. Every sign becomes the cause for elaborately inconclusive fantasizing. Every sign becomes duplicitous, slipping back and forth across a wavering line, once the heterosexual antithesis between love and friendship has been breached. The need to trace a compatible world becomes the urge to control one with an unceasing production of signs (the suede shoes amd cigarette holders of the 1950s, the leather and chain accoutrements of the

1960s, the key rings and pink triangles of the 1970s), as if nothing could be determined by trial, except the signature; nothing deduced from content, only hieroglyphs.

Most diverting, because most evasive, of all is the multiplication of signs. It seems an infinite world wholly devoted to a switching of signs based on shifting of context. A young fellow flouncing back to the bar to retrieve his duffle coat calls out, 'I forgot my mink!' The remark is addressed to no one; nothing in particular is validated; the sign is empty. Yet at a stroke the context is glossed with a tantalizing femininity. Queens need not necessarily be amusing nor even charming as long as their signs generate signs in constant mimicry from a circle of admirers, in a constant play of double entendres and innuendoes. Such exchanges are rituals designed to envelop an occasion with one controlling mood. Far from anticipating action or compelling thought, such signs are predatory, intent on invalidating specific gestures, usurping specific meaning, annulling specific thought. Though obviously referring to the duffle coat, 'my mink' does not denote the duffle coat. The duffle coat is displaced; it is replaced by the *sign* of the mink.

No wonder such chit-chat tends to seem disappointing, vacuous, even cruel – in a word, 'bitchy' – to outsiders: all coherent discourse is betrayed. All behaviour, too, as when Genet's Divine, taking his hand out of his pocket, means 'to extend her arm and shake her unfurled lace handkerchief. To shake it for a farewell to nothing, or to let fall a powder which it did not contain, a perfume' (110). Though female signifiers abound, females themselves are absent. The queens' vernacular masks this absence; but it also parades it. It is haunted by absence, by the impossibility of describing the truth by its own name. It entails a dual vision, in other words, that must withhold a truth (that the speakers are male), while affirming art. For queens are all accomplices in the art of fiction. Deprived of their own distinctive codes, homosexuals make art itself into their distinctive code. Aesthetic absorption is all. For Wilde (and his successors, Cocteau and Auden), it was no longer homosexuality that was duplicitous but its paradigm, art.[5] That is the revelation which all the paradoxes from Wilde to Barthes pursue. Art and sex are analogous activities since both are projections of fantasy. Their mutual term 'camp' reveals as much a sexual as an aesthetic norm of indirection, self-protection, and speculative irresponsibility.

'Human beings', Auden has written, 'are, necessarily, actors who cannot become something before they have first pretended to be it; and they can be divided, not into the hypocritical and the sincere, but into the sane who know they are acting and the mad who do not' ('Masque', 395–6). To be natural, as Wilde observed, is such a very difficult pose to keep up. The result is camp: the whole gay masquerade of men and women who self-consciously act; who flaunt incongruous allusions, parodies, transvestite travesties; who are still sanely aware of the gap between their feelings and their roles; who continue to proliferate a protean, and never normative, range of fantasies in social dramas of their own choosing. At its worst, camp is a joke aimed at the 'straight' who make the same or similar gestures unconsciously. But at its best, the laugh is on homosexuals themselves. For the real trick is not merely to don a mask; it is to mask the masquerade. Christopher Isherwood expressed it well: 'You can't camp about something you don't take seriously. You're not making fun of it; you're making fun out of it. You're expressing what's basically serious to you in terms of fun and artifice and elegance' (1954: 120).[6]

Camp is the desire of the subject never to let itself be defined as object by others but to reach for a protective transcendence, which, however, exposes more than it protects. Camp is a withdrawal into inverted commas, a flaunting by *self*-definition, a leap-frog of distancing. The delights of camp come from the call to interpretation that it issues. It was Wilde's most paradoxical pose to mask his homosexuality by outbidding W. S. Gilbert's caricature, outbunthorning Bunthorne in velvets and lilies and bows, to suggest that he could not be what he seemed to be, when that is exactly what he was. With Bosie in tow, this became a piece of brinkmanship designed as much to expose as to protect, in a compound and neutralizing measure that remains the quintessence of camp.

The very challenge of such revels is that of rebels: even the words are cognate. The essence of such freedom, as Thomas Mann's Felix Krull observed, is 'to live like a soldier but not as a soldier, figuratively but not literally, to be allowed in short to live symbolically' (115). Despite the catastrophe of his trials, despite *De Profundis*, Wilde remained to the end a Till Eulenspiegel, a triumphantly comic hero, spurning a world bridled by an alien law and substituting in its stead, to the best of his ample powers, a realm of bodily and spiritual freedom fabricated by fantasy in the shape of desire.

Those trials had exposed a desperate ideological struggle. For power and discourse are inseparable. Discourse, for Foucault, 'is not simply something that reveals (or conceals) desire; it is also itself the object of desire . . . the power one is trying to appropriate'.[7] Power is the right to formulate categories, to control the moral currency, to define the nature of 'nature'. Defeat is humiliation extorted as a confession. No law today would seem more alien to Wilde or his contemporary, Edward Carpenter, than that of Russia. The Marxist, at least in his Soviet guise, is a notorious antiaesthete and antipervert. Bourgeois art, like bourgeois affluence, is bound to appear to all such Marxists 'perverse', that is, resisting historical necessity. As the entrenched and isolated bourgeoisie resists the dialectic of history, so bourgeois art whimsically and self-indulgently attempts to transcend collective social necessity. The logical goal of such self-delusion (runs the argument) is the mass paranoia and bourgeois self-castration called fascism. Such paradoxical displays, based on capitalist self-interest, are bound not only to blind historical truth and distort universal human rights but to pervert nature. The antifascist, whether Marxist or committed Socialist, should stand firm on the self-evident necessities of history, of truth, and of nature – that is, of biologically explicit heterosexuality.

But in Soviet Russia there are spokesmen for the supreme presidium and for *Pravda* ready to defend as 'natural' the internment of so-called dissidents in psychological institutes and labour camps. To orthodox Marxists the Gulag Archipelago is not a depraved or lunatic cancer of Russian society, it is natural. That was Marx's definition of 'ideology': an established order which is masked as natural order; or rather, which pretends to operate by a sort of supernatural law dictated by Nature or History or God, as Yahweh dictated the law to Moses on Mount Sinai. To function it must consistently disguise its own artifice; for ideology can only function as a totality.

To Marxists, then, homosexual signs are counterrevolutionary; but to Westerners they merely seem a joke. If publicly gays serve to reinforce marital values and a society mortgaged for the upkeep of those values, surreptitiously they are cast in quite another role: that of actors, adolescents, lords of the life of misrule. In all forms of culture, Bakhtin observes in *Rabelais and His World*, everything serious had to have, and did have, its double. Just as in Saturnalia the jester doubled for the king and the slave for his master, so bourgeois culture has fixed such comic-double roles on the homosexual: as circus clown quaintly paralleling the serious and dangerous numbers on the program.

For men like Eduard Bernstein and Magnus Hirschfeld, however, these signs were revolutionary, even as spelled out in Carpenter's mild and plausible phrases:

> it is not unlikely that the markedly materialistic and commercial character of the last age of European civilized life is largely to be connected with the fact that the *only* form of love and love-union that it has recognized has been one founded on the quite necessary but comparatively materialistic basis of matrimonial sex-intercourse and child-breeding ... And in truth it seems the most natural thing in the world that just as the ordinary sex-love has a special function in the propagation of the race, so the other love should have its special function in social and heroic work, and in the generation – not of bodily children – but of those children of the mind, the philosophical conceptions and ideals which transform our lives and those of society.[8]

Nothing here of sadistic couplings – of vassalage and bondage and 'rough trade' – only the rhetoric of social and heroic ideals. Even Wilde, in *The Soul of Man under Socialism*, claimed to be a revolutionary of sorts. Both Wilde and Carpenter had found encouragement in Whitman; and it was Whitman who had made the decisive shift away from philosophical conceptions and ideals as a sign of transgression to sexual transgression itself viewed as a potent sign.

Those who rely on the notion of language as a rational system tend either to entrench themselves in the face of symbolic activities or to lump them indiscriminately with so-called deviant uses by children, poets, primitives, or neurotics. But all cultures breed their own internal tensions and self-contradictions. Descriptions of deviant practices, as Freud has shown, may well be displaced accounts of the symbolic needs of an entire culture. Deviance, by definition, is

that which cannot (for whatever reason) be confronted and directly compre-
hended. It poses a challenge; it sparks off anxiety; it is *too* serious. To become
nonserious it must first be condensed then systematically displaced in dreams,
ritual myths, and jokes.

Homosexuality poses a uniquely peculiar challenge to cultural stability
because it seems to threaten the genetic cycle itself and the whole elaborate
coding of binary sexuality. So it must be ruthlessly disarmed of its disruptive
power. Transformed to childish dreams and neurotic jokes, it ceases to be
serious. In this way its own transformative role is systematically repressed. Like
jokers, dreamers, poets, and neurotics, homosexuals too (we have seen) are
producers of signs. As Tzvetan Todorov has argued, it is the so-called deviants,
above all, who are the agents of culture, actively extending the rhetoric of sign
systems. They are the purveyors of change. Though relegated to the border-
lands and sick ghettos of bourgeois culture (with other scapegoats and victims),
the homosexual's role, far from parasitic, is central: as index of a cultural
complexity and self-awareness (in all symbolic activities, including language)
that floods traditional discourse with irrational needs and desires. It was
precisely through his investigation of dreams and jokes as archetypes of
condensation and displacement that Freud rediscovered the symbolic and
rhetorical structures of language in general. For that elaborate coding of binary
sexuality was transmitted to us through both the Greeks and the Hebrews.

The Greeks may have had no words for 'heterosexuality' or 'homosexuality';
yet even they distinguished between what was 'natural' and 'unnatural'. There
was sexual behaviour (for both sexes) that was natural. There was sexual
behaviour (for both sexes) that was unnatural. But for the Greeks it was not the
contexts that mattered so much as the *roles*. Their assumption was this: that
active roles were natural for men, passive roles for women. So a female
mounting her partner jockey-style behaved as unnaturally as a male performing fellatio or enjoying anal penetration (see Dover, 100–9). Only the weaker
sex permitted penetration because women lacked the political and military
virtues (moral insight and resolution). They were naturally fitted for passivity,
being dependent, subordinate, more sensual, and insatiable even in their sexual
cravings. But the submissive role unnaturally prostituted a male. A buggered
male had assimilated himself to women. He had *chosen* to be treated as an
object. He had voluntarily resigned from the citizen body. Pagan convention
was simple: the penetrator is victor; the penetrated his victim. Homosexual lust
was natural enough. Genital gratification was equally natural. Only to reci-
procate, or invite, that lust was unnatural and reprehensible. Indiscriminate
lust in adolescents was considered so unnatural that some *natural* explanation
had eventually to be found. A lateral leap had to be made from the (disguised)
social premise to a (hidden) biological cause.[9] But Plato went further. He
condemned even the active partner as unnatural. He was the first Greek to
declare natural only 'intercourse which procreates children': in *Laws* Plato
finally turned his back on the *Phaedrus,* the *Symposium,* and the rest of the

Socratic dialogues, dismissing the mystical flight of pederastic Eros for a beginner's course in biology. The case seems built mainly on the example of monogamous birds, like geese and swallows:

> Our citizens should not be inferior to birds and many other species of animals, which are born in large communities and up to the age of procreation live unmated, pure and unpolluted by marriage, but when they have arrived at that age they pair, male with female and female with male, according to their inclination, and for the rest of their time they live in a pious and law-abiding way, faithfully adhering to the agreements which were the beginning of their love.[10]

But even in *Laws* it is still the act not the appetite that is condemned. For Dante the appetite itself was unnatural. Sodomites in his hell are the very type of the 'violent against nature'. Even in purgatory they walk, to Dante's surprise, in a contrary direction, that is, against the natural way:

> for down the center of that fiery way
> came new souls from the opposite direction,
> and I forgot what I had meant to say.[11]

But Dante, of course, was also heir to Genesis: the myth of the cities of the plain and their fiery destruction.

Jean Soler has resolved the whole elaborate machinery of the Mosaic code to a single commandment: Thou shalt not mix. Thou shalt not mix gods. Thou shalt not mix marriages. Thou shalt not mix foods. Thou shalt not mix clothing. This is what links the dietary laws of Deuteronomy and Leviticus to their prohibitions against bestiality and incest. A man is a man or he is a god; he cannot be both at the same time. A man is a man or he is a beast; he cannot be both at the same time. So all human beings must either be men or women, they cannot be both at the same time. Homosexuality is outlawed.[12]

More than questions of masculinity and femininity are at stake. Since the taxonomy of all conceivable relationships is grounded on such dichotomies, the whole typology of roles based on female and (circumcised) male genitalia is affected. The Hebrew code uncompromisingly defines God, man, the animals, and the plants in a series of contrasting pairs, or antitheses.

> It is a matter of upholding the separation between two classes or two types of relationships. To abolish distinction by means of a sexual or culinary act is to subvert the order of the world. Everyone belongs to one species only, one people, one sex, one category. And in the same manner, everyone has only one God ... The keystone of this order is the principle of identity, instituted as the law of every being. (Soler, 136–7)

'Birds of the air' should not walk about on land (like the ostrich) or float about on water (like swans). They should stick to the rules. They should make up their minds. The hybrid, wherever discovered – as a mollusc, shell-fish, man-God, mixed marriage, cloth that is part linen part wool, an ox and ass yoked together, a vineyard sown with two kinds of seed – is unclean.[13] To subvert the antithesis is to challenge God. So homosexuality is unclean. It crosses categories; it defies the code; it is literally *unthinkable*.

All post-Hebrew religions perpetuate the taboo. Both Christians and Muslims succumbed to at least this aspect of the code. Yet Jesus openly defied Mosaic dietary laws. Peter personally broke them. The evangelists inaugurated a specifically *synthetic* age: of hybrid marriages and hybrid disciples and a hybrid priesthood, drinking a hybrid blood/wine, in chastely hybrid communion, to commemorate a hybrid man/God. Kosher and nonkosher, Jew and Gentile, male and female, were all commingled.[14] Only the homosexual taboo was, if anything, reinforced. But what is wrong with this vast and ever proliferating class that includes horses, hares, asses, camels, swine, grasshoppers, pelicans, herons, serpents, centipedes, weasels, mice, tortoises, ferrets, chameleons, lizards, snails, moles – and homosexuals? Are they all God's howlers? (see Leviticus 11; Deuteronomy 14).

The Hebrew code consciously assumes the continuity and regularity of all species. It is confident in the stability of the created world. In Genesis its Lord, once and for all, mapped their environment. But it is the irregularities, the breaks in continuity, that attract our attention. Our whole intellectual apparatus, since Darwin, is tuned to the monitoring of unexpected change. The whole notion of distinctive, ideal, and separate species (of walking, creeping, flying, swimming creatures, of Jews and Gentiles, males and females, hetero- and homosexuals) has been undermined. For it is no longer generic or sexual or dietary schemata that dominate us but experiences that shatter our hypotheses. Even a biblical Jew, after all, might have observed that hares do not 'chew the cud' and that masticating rodents are never 'ruminant'. But his religion was primarily intent on maintaining order: on stable social conduct in a stable world. Our own training, to the contrary, is wholly intent on deviations as revelations of disorder – on everything, in a word, he would have dismissed as 'unclean'.

What is called natural by one code may be pronounced unnatural by another. What is branded by one code unclean may be promoted by another to a transcendent status. What is suppressed may also exert a peculiar pull. Such are the zones which define distinction. They are magnetic zones; and the no man's land of sexuality is felt as a peculiarly dangerous erotic zone. Among Plains Indians, for example, the homosexual was cast as the marginal man, the mystic or shaman, at the culture's boundary. As if his protean need for transformation ushered in a timeless magical world, marked by a reversal of roles. That world has universal appeal. It was the ecstatic goal of Judaeo-Hellenic culture, its paradise regained and golden age restored: to discover a form of desire without utilitarian controls, without social classification, without consequences, without discourse even. No wonder such ministries of transport arouse fear! They conjugate mysteries of what is inexpressible with what has deliberately been left unexpressed. Like Janus or a heraldic eagle, back to back; or front to front, curled up together in bed; like an octopus:

> Que ne ressemblons-nous à cet aigle à deux têtes,
>   A Janus au double profil,
> Aux frères Siamois qu'on montre dans les fêtes,
>   Aux livres cousus par un fil?
>
> L'amour fait des amants un seul monstre de joie,
>   Hérissé de cris et de crins,
> Et ce monstre, enivré d'être sa propre proie,
>   Se dévore avec quatre mains.[15]

Only one peculiar myth expresses the dizzying reach of antithetical images capable of projecting the mystery of self in homosexual coupling: that of Narcissus by the poolside pining for his dim, mysterious lover. 'So he loves, yet knows not what he loves; he does not understand, he cannot tell what has come upon him; like one that has caught a disease of the eye from another, he cannot account for it, not realizing that his lover is as it were a mirror in which he beholds himself' (Plato, *Phaedrus*, 255d). It was not until the mid nineteenth century that the myth's logic was shifted from such impotent wilting (on land) to potent immersion (at sea), from the lure of metamorphosis to futile dissolution: 'And still deeper the meaning of that story of Narcissus, who because he could not grasp the tormenting, mild image he saw in the fountain, plunged into it and was drowned. But that same image, we ourselves see in all rivers and oceans. It is the image of the ungraspable phantom of life; and this is the key to it all'.[16] It is the key to Melville's Ishmael torn between phallic Queequeg and suicidal Ahab. It is the key to the major twentieth-century texts of homosexuality in France, America, and Japan: Genet's *Funeral Rites*; Burroughs' *Naked Lunch*; Mishima's *Forbidden Colours*.

To court the Narcissus myth is to invite alienation. The mirror image stares back startled or puzzled, recalcitrant or scowling. The self resists the probing scrutiny of the self. Squinting to catch a mirrored hint, it discovers only a foreboding, a stubborn, guarded resistance. Or self-infatuation is reduced to a fiasco of sexual heaving and detumescence. For Narcissus before his confiding mirror is condemned to a single pose: that of interloper inevitably (so he feels) disrupting 'the celebration of the mysteries' (Proust, *Guermantes*, 2:322). Such is Proust's comedy of the imagination, swelling in lust, wilting in attempted copulation, on exposure to the Narcissus double whose penetration must mean extinction. The quest for a loving double, as ego ideal or alter ego, may well be universal, though male homosexuals would seem to be its peculiar victims since their self-love is identified with mirror images that are not merely complementary but reciprocal. Each demands a fantasy role, as phallus, from the other; but each remains an observer before the mirror, recognizing and celebrating his discovery. From that perfect symmetry, that closed system of constituted objects and alienated subjects, that infinite dialectic of activity and passivity, there is no escape *outside language* (see Lacan).

'"Well, now that we *have* seen each other", said the Unicorn, "if you'll believe in me, I'll believe in you. Is that a bargain?" "Yes, if you like", said Alice'. It is a grudging reply, a merely polite assent. Alice is unwilling to admit that a corporate fiction can validate her private fiction; and that private fiction confronts the pervasive public fictions of social life. But all signs imply a system. It is the system alone that makes them significant. It is the system alone that sustains all subversive, or liberating, forces. So homosexual signs, too, must imply some sort of system. Plato, in the *Phaedrus* and the *Symposium,* elaborated one such system. Possibly Lacan today supplies another. Nothing else quite answers the need. On the contrary, the three most pervasive codes of the twentieth century deliberately aim at confounding such a system: Christianity by repressing homosexual desires (with a call to repentance); psychoanalysis by purging homosexual desires (with a call to sublimation); Marxism by ignoring homosexual desires altogether as irrelevant and unhistorical (and so unideological). Simply to declare homosexuality 'free', then, can never be enough. Without a political, intellectual, scientific, or even administrative system, homosexuality will remain inevitably trapped in empty gestures. As Barthes recalled:

> I had this nightmare of a loved one falling ill in the street and, in his agony, asking for drugs. But everyone passed by and sternly refused, despite my frantic comings and goings. His anguish mounted to such an hysterical pitch that I reproached him, only to realize, a little later, that this person was me. Of course. Of whom else does one dream? I implored all the languages (the systems) passing by, who ignored me. Vociferously, *shamelessly,* I appealed for a philosophy that would 'comprehend me' – would 'embrace me'. (*Fragments*, 250–1)

One way to independence – without formal declarations of independence – is to copy Jacques Derrida by using the word 'homosexuality' itself *sous rature* ('under erasure'): first to write the word then cross it out, leaving both word and deletion. Since the concepts embodied in homosexuality may well be misleading, it is crossed out; since (alas) it is necessary, it remains legible. It is the strategy of using the only available language while not subscribing to its premises. Derrida describes such strategy as 'discourse which borrows from a heritage the resources necessary for the deconstruction of that heritage itself' (*Writing*, 282). The reinvention of systems begins with demolition, like the inner wall of a house which becomes an outer wall after wars and devastation. Since the very language of homosexuality is incorporated in heterosexual discourse, its very principles have already been anticipated and categorized by the dominant side. It is not enough to work against ideology by pointing it out. Far more effective is subversion from within, sabotaging the machinery (like Soviet dissidents) by 'making it grind so that it can be heard, so that it will not be innocent, so that it will lose in fact that beautiful mask of innocence and of being natural' (Robbe-Grillet, 19).

The aim must be to reverse the rhetorical opposition of what is 'transparent' or 'natural' and what is 'derivative' or 'contrived' by demonstrating that the qualities predicated of 'homosexuality' (as a dependent term) are in fact a condition of 'heterosexuality'; that 'heterosexuality', far from possessing a privileged status, must itself be treated as a dependent term. By disqualifying the autonomy of what was deemed spontaneously immanent, the whole sexual system is fundamentally decentred and exposed.[17] For erotic arousal, much as verbal arousal, is not capable of functioning as unmediated or uncontrived expression. Neither verbal nor genital play is ever self-sufficient in this sense. Other objects are needed as signifiers in thought or deed for our fantasies of self-projection. The crisis of discharge, moreover, far from being transparent, cuts us off from even the least glimpse of ourselves since consciousness notoriously blanks out at the point of communication, in consummation or orgasm. Such climax is literally ecstatic, a jubilant dislocation or short-circuit of the self.

Not even masturbation is ever wholly unmediated. *All* forms of sexuality are triggered by a chain of indirection. Breaking the solipsist barrier, negotiating sensual images as texts of difference in a systematic play of deferment (*différance*), is an integral part of the sexual fun. The complexity of recording sexual acts is precisely that they are the functions neither of spontaneous presence (whether hetero- or homosexual) nor of formal absence (in private obsession) but, as Proust might witness, of a plenitude of absence infiltrating and flooding the present. 'Some day you will find, even as I have found', Wilde confessed to an undergraduate in 1885, 'that there is no such thing as a romantic experience; there are romantic memories, and there is the desire of romance – that is all. Our most fiery moments of ecstasy are merely shadows of what somewhere else we have felt, or of what we long some day to feel. So at least it seems to me' (letter to H. C. Marillier, 12 December 1885, in Hart-Davis, 64). All sexuality is experienced as an act of deconstruction in Derrida's sense: as a struggle with meaning, with a sense of uneasy loss in the undoing, the fragmentation, the disappearance of the subject. That is why Barthes identified his sense of *signifiance,* the play of signifiers, with *jouissance,* the thrill of 'coming' – of an assertive and spontaneous presence shattered by withdrawal and dissipation.

Only matrimony is exempted. Like the Holy Family, each family carries its own profundity within. Heterosexual matings promise a plenitude, a fulfillment derived from that hidden centre, that seedbed, that core which defines value by identifying the mystery of one man's and one woman's copulation. This alone constitutes its significance. Their offspring, if any, do not constitute that significance; though children are a revelation of the inner truth that predetermined their existence. Homosexuals, by definition, are excluded from this sign. Their couplings lack that promised plenitude of seedbed and core, of an ultimate mystery that reveals the hidden principles of truth, value, life, of 'reality' itself. In copying woman, furthermore, 'in assuming her position on the other side of the sexual barrier' (Barthes, *S/Z*, 66), the homosexual not only transgresses morphology, grammar, discourse; he is charged with castrating creative play, with literally castrating society's generative forces. Without centre he must turn in an endless circulation of forms (bodies, faces, words) in a language of signs, of gestures, of mutual indications at play, which remains vacant of all ultimate meaning (no Virgin, no Christ Child), revealing in a dazzling succession only a further vista of signs behind signs behind signs.

In the knowledge of that proliferation of signs dawns an enlightenment freed of secret profundities and values. In this landscape, which Barthes called Japan, 'the empire of signifiers is so vast, so far in excess of speech, that the exchange of signs constitutes a density, a mobility, a subtlety, which is spell-binding despite the opaqueness of the idiom, sometimes even because of it' (*Empire*, 18–20). The attraction of structuralism for Barthes was precisely this elaborated emphasis on form over content. 'In fact the whole of Japan is a pure invention', wrote Wilde. 'There is no such country, there are no such people . . . The Japanese people are, as I have said, simply a mode of style, an exquisite fancy of art' ('Decay of Lying', 315). In place of truth or value the homosexual tradition proposes elegance, style, art. 'The only criterion of an act is its elegance', proclaimed Genet; which Sartre brilliantly expounded as 'the quality of conduct which transforms the greatest quantity of being into *appearing*' (379). Barthes consciously echoed Genet, transforming his camp ethics into a camp poetics:

> It can be seen that we deal in no way with a harmony between content and form, but with an *elegant* absorption of one form into another. By *elegance* I mean the most economical use of the means employed. It is because of an age-old abuse that critics confuse *meaning* and *content*. The language is never anything but a system of forms, and the meaning is a form. (*Mythologies*, 133)

Should not our sexual codes, too, be less compromised by physiological distinctions? Should not the semantics of sex be capable of a similar alternation, like the opposing spirals of Yin and Yang, or the glyph '69', incorporating flows of expansion and contraction in dynamic equilibrium? So it seemed to one semiotician in a grammarian's daydream: 'as if we were the vocabulary of a strange, new language, in which it was freely permitted to substitute one term for another. Coupling would be limitless, not through boundless proliferation, but through the indifferent play of their permutations' (Barthes, *Fragments*, 269). For it is our sexual roles, not our genitalia, that are reversible. It is sex roles that constitute a network of forever negative differences.[18]

Sade, in this sense, re-*produced* reality. He constructed a revolutionary grammar based not on sexual preferences but on sexual functions. In his erotic vocabulary anyone can, and must, in turn be agent and patient, whipper and whipped.

This is a cardinal rule, first because it assimilates Sadian eroticism into a truly formal language, where there are only classes of actions, not groups of individuals, which enormously simplifies its grammar, ... second, because it keeps us from basing the grouping of Sadian society on the particularity of sexual practices (just the opposite of what occurs in our own society; we always wonder whether a homosexual is 'active' or 'passive'; with Sade, sexual preferences never serve to identify a subject). (Barthes, *Sade, Fourier, Loyola*, 30)

Everyone can be either sodomizer or sodomized, agent or patient, subject or object since pleasure is possible anywhere, with victims as well as masters. This art is revolutionary, Barthes argued, not as a myth of virility but as a new language of signs. The sadistic novel is rhapsodical, picaresque, defiant of logical, natural, organic order; resisting conclusion; alternating erotic scene and explication in an infinite, self-generating series. The diagrams of pornography demand (as Sade's Juliette is informed in front of the frescoes of Herculaneum) 'a great disorder of the imagination' (*Sade*, 136). In lieu of Narcissus, mirrors yield the multiple reflection of an orgy.

Chaos is worse confounded by the proliferating semantic confusion, a verbal incest transgressing the decencies of lexical categories. 'So libertinage appears: a fact of language'. Such is the revolutionary act: an assistant who can as readily be a victim as a wife; a daughter who is at once a grand-daughter and a niece. Defiance of nature is dissolved in linguistic defiance: 'the act *contra naturam* is exhausted in an utterance of counter-language' (*Sade*, 137–8). In merging Derrida with Lacan, Barthes moved beyond the constraints even of this paradoxical need for perversity. 'What is difficult', he wrote, 'is not to liberate sexuality, according to a more or less libertarian project, but to release it from meaning, including from transgression as meaning' (*Barthes*, 136). 'Confrontations and paradigms must be dissolved', he concluded, 'both the meanings and the sexes pluralized: meaning will tend toward its multiplication, its dispersal (in the theory of the Text); and sex will be taken into no typology (there will be, for example, only *homosexualities*, whose plural will baffle any constituted, centralized discourse, to the point where it seems to him virtually pointess to talk about it)' (*Barthes*, 73).

A plurality of signs constitutes Sodom; or rather, Sodom becomes wholly a matter of the plurality of signs. The development of a system for undermining the popular concept of what is natural, Barthes argued, is bound to centre on the sign. For the sign alone may be celebrated (as well as denounced) for its arbitrariness, its multiplications, its transgressions, and so ultimately its dispersal and dissolution. The neutrality he favoured was not some statistical mean between active and passive, possessor and possessed. It was what he once called a to-and-fro oscillation '*at another link of the infinite chain of language*, the second term of a new paradigm, of which violence (combat, victory, theatre, arrogance) is the primary term'. If Barthes was oppressed by nightmares of exclusion, as we have seen, he could also daydream; and as dreamer he was haunted by signs. Perhaps he even experienced the panic-struck suspension of codes, the blank that blots out linguistic control, the break of that interior monologue which formed his identity, the *loss* of meaning that Zen calls *satori*. The mind of the perfect man, says a Taoist master, is like a mirror. It reaches out for nobody, but repulses nobody. Like a mirror it promiscuously receives all others, without conserving or perpetuating others. Certainly by the end Barthes had glimpsed a vision, a prophetic vision, an exuberant vision, as he expressed it in his semiotic way: 'Once the antinomy is rejected, once the paradigm is blurred, utopia begins: meaning and sex become the object of free play, at the heart of which the (polysemant) forms and the (sensual) practices, liberated from the binary prison, wlll achieve a state of infinite expansion' (*Barthes*, 136–7).[19]

NOTES

1. Romans 1:26–7. Homosexuality was not an offence under the *Code Napoléon* drafted by Cambacérès; but the penal code introduced by the Pétain regime in Nazi-occupied France was confirmed by de Gaulle in 1945.
2. Havelock Ellis first naturalized the term 'homosexuality' in *Sexual Inversion* (1897). The term 'homoerotism' was coined by Ernest Jones in 1916. From genital size and hip contours attention has shifted recently to the structure of the brain. According to a Dr. Dorner, a low level of testosterone in a sample of amniotic fluid drawn during pregnancy is a sure sign of female-type cervical nodes forming to control an otherwise male physique. By injecting a homosexual with estrogen, he claims, he can 'test' this 'phantom womb'; for the brain will be fooled into reacting like a woman's. 'I think there may be the possibility in the future', he is reported as saying, 'to correct homosexuality' (interview on the BBC program *Horizon*, 21 May 1979).
3. Literally, 'a *hetairekos* boy': male prostitute, or boy-friend (Aristophanes, *Peace* 11). So much for the Socratic educational idea of pederasty. At Plato's *Banquet* (*Symposium* 212c), 'Socrates took his seat amid applause from everyone but Aristophanes' (my translation). As Freud pointed out: 'Where the anus is concerned it becomes still clearer that it is disgust which stamps that sexual aim as a perversion. I hope, however, I shall not be accused of partisanship when I assert that people who try to account for this disgust by saying that the organ in question serves the function of excretion and comes in contact with excrement – a thing which is disgusting in itself – are not much more to the point than hysterical girls who account for their disgust at the male genital by saying that it serves to void urine' (30–31).
4. Cited in Shattuck, 19. 'Experience', Walter Pater argued, 'already reduced to a swarm of impressions, is ringed round for each one of us by that thick wall of personality through which no real voice has ever pierced on its way to us, or from us to that which we can only conjecture to be without. Every one of those impressions is the impression of the individual in his isolation, each mind keeping as a solitary prisoner its own dream of a world'.
5. So Henry James again and again affirmed the mystery of what is absent (in ghosts or death or art) against that overassertive imposture, what is present. So Melville's *Moby Dick* wheels round and round that riddling negation, that ambiguous abstention of meaning, the *whiteness* of the whale. So Proust's *A la Recherche du temps perdu* is a quest transcending the evasions and frustrations of immanent experience itself through the plenitude of art.
6. Cf. Barthes: 'le vrai jeu n'est pas de masquer le sujet, mais de masquer le jeu lui-même' (*Barthes*, 145).

7. Foucault, inaugural lecture at the Collège de France, 1970.

8. Carpenter, 343–4. The second sentence echoes Francis Bacon's paraphrase of the *Symposium*: 'The best works and of greatest merit for the public have proceeded from the unmarried and childless man, which both in affection and means have married and endowed the public'. For the earliest defense of homosexuality as revolutionary politics, see Pausanias' speech on the triad pederasty, sport and philosophy as guardian of democracy against despotism (Plato, *Symposium*, 182bc). Eduard Bernstein, a German Social Democrat exiled in England, wrote two articles on the trials of Oscar Wilde in *Die Neue Zeit* (1895) before the final verdict. Magnus Hirschfeld founded the Scientific Humanitarian Committee (1897) that published a Yearbook for Intermediate Sexual Types (*Jahrbuch für Sexuelle Zwischenstufen*) from 1899 to 1923. In 1918 he founded the Magnus Hirschfeld Foundation for Sex Research.

9. For example, that seminal fluid was secreted in the anus so that anal friction alone gave (temporary) relief (Pseudo-Aristotelian *Problemata*, 4.26, cited by Dover, 169–70).

10. Plato, *Laws*, 838e and 840de, cited in Dover, 166–7. Dover adds: 'This argument is weak, if only because Plato knew virtually nothing about animals'.

11. Dante, *Purgatorio*, 26.28–30. It was Thomas Aquinas who first called homosexual behaviour 'the abominable and detestable crime against nature not to be named among Christians'.

12. Homosexual acts are declared an 'abomination' and capital offense in Leviticus 18:22 and 20:13.

13. See Deuteronomy 7:3 and 22:9–11.

14. So Paul: 'There is neither Jew nor Greek, there is neither bond nor free, there is neither male nor female: for ye are all one in Christ Jesus' (Galatians 3:28).

15. Cocteau, 170; my translation: 'Don't we look like that twin-headed eagle, / Like Janus with his double profile, / Like the Siamese twins exhibited at fairs, / Like books stitched together with one thread? // Love makes of lovers a single monster of joy, / Bristling with cries and with hair, / And this monster, drunk at being its own prey, / Devours itself with four hands'.

16. Melville, 95. Cf. Ovid, *Metamorphoses*, 3. 486–88.

17. On masturbation as a 'supplement' of normal sexuality, see Derrida, *Grammatology*, chap. 2.

18. The ultimate law of language, according to Saussure, is that nothing can ever reside in a single term: 'It is precisely because the terms *a* and *b* as such are radically incapable of reaching the level of consciousness – one is always conscious of only the *a/b* difference – that each term is free to change according to laws that are unrelated to its signifying function' (118).

19. Two years later (7 January 1977), in his inaugural lecture from the chair of Literary Semiology at the Collège de France, he added: 'This freedom is a luxury which every society should afford its citizens: as many languages as there are desires – a utopian proposition in that no society is yet ready to admit the plurality of desire. That a language [*langue*], whatever it be, not repress another; that the subject may know without remorse, without repression, the bliss of having at his disposal two kinds of language [*instances de langage*]; that he may speak this or that, according to his perversions, not according to the Law' ('Lecture', 37)

REFERENCES

Alighieri, Dante, *The Divine Comedy*, trans. John Ciardi, New York, 1961.

Auden, W. H., 'New Year's Letter' (1940), & 'The Masque', in Edward Mendelson (ed.), *Collected Poems*, London, 1976.

Bakhtin, Mikhail, *Rabelais and His World*, trans. Helene Iswolsky, Cambridge, Mass., 1968.

Barthes, Roland, *L'Empire des signes*, Geneva, 1970.
——, *Fragments d'un discours amoureux*, Paris, 1977.
——, 'Lecture', trans. Howard, *Oxford Literary Review*, Autumn 1979.
——, *Mythologies*, trans. Annette Lavers, London, 1972.
——, *Roland Barthes*, Paris, 1975; trans. Richard Howard, New York, 1977.
——, *Sade, Fourier, Loyola*, trans. Richard Miller, London, 1971.
——, *S/Z*, trans. Richard Miller, New York, 1974.
Carpenter, Edward, *Homogenic Love and Its Place in a Free Society* (1894), rpt. in Brian Reade (ed.), *Sexual Heretics: Male Homosexuality in English Literature from 1850 to 1900*, London, 1970.
Cocteau, Jean, 'Un ami dort', in *Poèmes, 1916–1955*, Paris, 1956.
Derrida, Jacques, *Of Grammatology*, trans. Gayatri Chakravorty Spivak, Baltimore and London, 1974.
——, *Writing and Difference*, trans. Alan Bass, Chicago, 1978.
Dover, K. J., *Greek Homosexuality*, London, 1978.
Foucault, Michel, *La volonté de savoir*, Paris, 1976.
Freud, Sigmund, 'The Sexual Aberrations', in *Three Essays on the Theory of Sexuality*, trans. James Strachey, 1905; London, 1949.
Genet, Jean, *Our Lady of the Flowers*, trans. Bernard Frechtman, New York, 1966.
Hart-Davis, Rupert (ed.), *Selected Letters of Oscar Wilde*, Oxford, 1979.
Hocquenghem, Guy, *Homosexual Desire*, trans. Daniella Dangoor, London, 1978.
Lacan, Jacques, *The Language of the Self: The Function of Language in Psychoanalysis*, trans. Anthony Wilden, Baltimore, 1968.
Mann, Thomas, *Confessions of Felix Krull, Confidence Man*, trans. Denver Lindley, London, 1955.
Melville, Herman, *Moby Dick; or, The Whale* (1851), London, 1972.
Pater, Walter, 'Conclusion', in *The Renaissance: Studies in Art and Poetry*, London, rev. ed., 1888.
Proust, Marcel, *La Prisonnière*, 1923; *The Captive*, trans. C. K. Scott Moncrieff, Part Two, London, 1941.
——, *Sodome et Gomorrhe*, I, Paris, 1921; *Cities of the Plain*, trans. Moncrieff, Part One, London, 1941.
——, *Contre Sainte-Beuve*, Paris, 1954.
——, *The Guermantes Way*, trans. Moncrieff, 2 vols., Paris, 1921.
Robbe-Grillet, Alain, 'Order and Disorder in Film and Fiction', trans. Bruce Morrissette, *Critical Inquiry* 4, Autumn 1977.
Sartre, Jean-Paul, *Saint Genet: Actor and Martyr*, trans. Bernard Frechtman, New York, 1963.
Saussure, Ferdinand de, *Course in General Linguistics*, trans. Wade Baskin, New York, 1959.
Shattuck, Roger, *Proust*, London, 1974.
Soler, Jean, 'The Semiotics of Food in the Bible', in Robert Forster & Orest Ranum (eds.), *Food and Drink in History*, Baltimore, 1979, 126–38.
Todorov, Tzvetan, 'Le langage et ses doubles', in *Théories du symbole*, Paris, 1977.
Wilde, Oscar, 'The Decay of Lying', in Richard Ellmann (ed.), *The Artist as Critic: Critical Writings of Oscar Wilde*, London, 1970.

11

FORGERY

Neil Bartlett

A forger of no mean or ordinary capability.

After 25 May 1895 ('Guilty') Wilde could no longer pass. Everyone knew that Oscar was a forgery, a fake. He was not what he had appeared to be. It was no defence that he himself had never claimed to be anything other than both forger and forgery. ('The first duty in life is to be as artificial as possible'.) He had modelled himself on the liars, the comedians, the critics – 'the fool, the fraud, the knave' – anyone who had signed no contract with truth; the embroiderers and inventers of the truth, the prostitutes. *He was entirely lacking in wholeness and completeness of nature*. He wished, in fact, to be completely unnatural. He was a creator of copies, borrowing and reprocessing fragments of his own and other people's works. He assiduously composed his public life as father, husband, and moralist, and he created a career for himself as a playwright whose plays are littered with the wrecks of fathers, husbands, and moralists struggling to prove that they are who and what they say they are. His 'private' homosexual life was an elaborate drama of deception, lies and, most of all, inspired invention. He could not, even in 1895, after concealment had failed, reveal his true nature. There was no real Oscar Wilde, if by real we mean homosexual. He did not, like us, have the alibi of 'being like that'. London in 1895 had no conception of a man being 'naturally homosexual'. A man who loved other men could only be described as an invert, an inversion of something else, a pervert, an exotic, a disease, a victim, a variation. Wilde was an artist as well. He was entirely uninterested in authenticity.

Reprinted from *Who Was That Man? A Present for Mr Oscar Wilde*, London: Serpent's Tail, 1988.

One can fancy an intense personality being created out of sin.

After his release from Reading Gaol, on 19 May 1896, Oscar Wilde ceased to exist. His place was taken by a Mr Sebastian Melmoth. Reggie Turner gave him a dressing case, stamped with the initials S.M. In 1897 mail was forwarded to the Hotel Sandwich, Dieppe (the first of many such hotels) c/o Monsieur Sebastian Melmoth. Carrington's 1905 Paris edition of Barbey D'Aurevilly's *What Never Dies* attributed the translation (falsely) to *Sebastian Melmoth (O.W.)*.

This was not the first transformation. Changes of costume were not just metaphors for these men; they were bone-deep. Oscar Fingal O'Flahertie Wills Wilde, a big, strong, heavy, virile Irishman, had become a London queen. In the 1890s, the 'Oscar' of the back streets had changed back into 'Mr Wilde' by the time the cab reached Chelsea. Some men spoke of a scarcely human character known as 'The O'Flaherty'. Boulton and Park had emerged from their dressing rooms at 13 Wakefield Street as Mrs Fanny Graham and Lady Clinton. Alfonso Conway had strolled along the seafront with Mr Wilde dressed up and no doubt feeling just like a gentleman's son, which, since he sold newspapers for a living, was not his natural state. Jack Saul, also from Dublin, had made the same change when he had left town after the persecution of 1884 and moved in with Hammond at 19 Cleveland Street. John Gray had ceased to be the eldest son of a family of nine children in Woolwich and was to become the consort of the wealthy Marc-André Raffalovich; that Canon Gray for whom Raffalovich built a church where, once a year, a mass was said for the repose of the soul of Paul Verlaine. Lord Alfred Douglas became, when his beloved wrote in despair from Holloway on 3 May 1895, *Prince Fleur de Lys*, and was then to be just *Bosie*, a lord no longer, when he received *De Profundis*. Simeon Solomon had become a successful exhibitor at the Royal Academy, then a Bohemian, then finally a criminal, insane, alcoholic, perverted pavement artist. I've seen photographs of myself four years ago, and I hardly recognize myself.

When this man chose his new name, which could not be discarded at the end of an evening (I've met a Vera who is Steve by daytime, and I know a Blanche who is always Blanche, but he never appears in the daylight), he did so with care, undaunted by Lady Bracknell's warning that an adult baptism is both *grotesque and irreligious*. *Sebastian*, we may suppose, is from the saint of the same name, whose life is an appropriate blend of fact and homosexual fantasy. The title is fitting, since the subject was now sitting for his Portrait of the Artist as an Old Man; it was to be an altarpiece, with the offstage violence of British justice dignified by the suggestion that the criminal is a martyr. The body displayed in such pictures is always handsome, the martyrdom always more or less sexual, the arrows inflicting multiple, anonymous penetrations on the half-desiring flesh. *Melmoth* is from *Melmoth the Wanderer*, the Gothic horror novel by Charles Maturin, our hero's maternal great-uncle. The name maintains a tenuous link with the lost family, the lost country; but the hero of the novel is the antitype of the Celtic, Ossianic heroes whose names were borrowed by an idealistic, nationalistic mother for her son's first christening – Oscar, Fingal. For his second christening, the profligate son inverted the glamour of his heritage. He took the name of a hideous, heartless man, condemned to wander the earth, homeless for eternity, in penance for some hideous, unnamed, unnameable crime.

The choice of names indicates the bitterness and the care with which the new personality was to be forged. What had in fact been imposed (exile, loss of family, being a criminal) was made to appear chosen, a chosen role.

One name is as good as another, when one has no right to any name.

Mr Sebastian Melmoth travelled Europe supported by his friends until his death in 1900. He enjoyed and endured a combination of pleasures and miseries entirely appropriate to the role of exiled Queen, until he chose to announce his personal *fin de siècle*, unable to face the prospect of enduring into a new century. He was always on the make, making things up, wearing make-up. He wasn't destroyed, denuded or stripped down to his 'real' personality. He was nothing if not inconsistent. He was reunited with his one True Love, the only man who could make sense of his life ('I feel that it is only with you that I can do anything at all'), the man to whom he addressed the thousands of terrible, agonized, sincere words of *De Profundis* – and he fell in love again, fell out of love, lived with him in a Neapolitan villa, left him several times.

Meanwhile he corresponded happily with English public schoolboys and a Harvard undergraduate. He fell madly in love (usually for three days or less) with all the boys of Rome, Naples, Paris and Genoa, and was quite unable or unwilling to distinguish between the services of prostitutes and lovers. (1 January 1899: 'I am practically engaged to a fisherman of quite extraordinary beauty, aged eighteen.') His letters, now that he had nothing to lose, blossom with boys, flowers, obscenities, wines, the small delights of European travel. He lived entirely for pleasure, but also found time to write two signed and serious letters to the *Daily Chronicle*, arguing with informed compassion for practical reforms in the English prison system. The first was written just nine days after his release. It is about the systematic maltreatment of children and the mentally disturbed in Reading Gaol. Surely these are not the writings for which 'Oscar Wilde' is famous. And just three years after the première of *The Importance of Being Earnest* he published *The Ballad of Reading Gaol*, his hardest, darkest fiction, and not under his old name but as C33, his cell number in Reading, as if that conferred dignity enough on the text. ('He who lives more lives than one / More deaths than one must die', he wrote.) On 9 September 1900 he was reading Edward Carpenter's *Civilization, Its Cause and Cure*, as if the author of *The Soul of Man Under Socialism* was finally taking himself seriously, now that he was experiencing real material and financial need for the first time in his life. In April, knowing that he was the antiChrist of Europe, he had made a point of having himself blessed by the Pope on Easter Day, occasioning religious sentiments of such sincerity and ludicrousness as to make both Firbank and Rolfe seem quite sane:

> I have again seen the Holy Father. Each time he dresses differently; it is most delightful. Today over his white and purple a velvet cape edged with ermine, and a huge scarlet and gold stole. I was deeply moved as usual ...
> I have become very cruel to boys, and no longer let them kiss me in public.

He also attributed the Pope with the power of curing his food poisoning, and of inspiring an appreciation of Bernini. Was he serious? Were his religious affectations, after the pieties of the cell in Reading, merely being sent up to Heaven in a final, sacrificial pantomime? Who was the *real* Sebastian Melmoth? What was his life like?

In four years he lived the lives of several men.

On 16 November 1891 he wrote: 'My existence is a scandal'.

> Insincerity is simply a method by which we can multiply our personalities.

The characteristic name for the heroic life of things or people which have no right to exist was invented, along with so many other features of our lives, during the life and times of Mr Oscar Wilde. It is a word that we still use. We still consider inventing a new life to be an ordinary, even inevitable activity. If you can't be authentic (and you can't), if this doesn't feel like real life (and it doesn't), then you can be *camp*.

Mr Wilde himself never committed the word to writing, although the first traceable record we have of it used as part of a gay language dates from his schooldays. On 21 November 1869, Frederick Park wrote to Lord Arthur Clinton:

> I should like to live to a green old age. Green did I say? Oh, *ciel!* The amount of paint that will be required to hide that very unbecoming tint. My campish undertakings are not at present meeting with the success they deserve. Whatever I do seems to get me into hot water somewhere. But *n'importe*. What's the odds so long as you're happy?
> Believe me,
> your affectionate sister-in-law,
> Fanny, Winifred, Park.

For Fanny the word does not indicate a decorative set of gestures or enthusiasms, but an *undertaking*, a serious activity. The 1972 Supplement to the Oxford English Dictionary assures us that the word is derived from the French *se camper*, and is invariably associated with 'exceptional want of character', by which it presumably means publicly gay men, Harrap's French/English Dictionary notes that a painter may camp (pose) his subject, as may an author too: *Voilà votre homme campé en peu de mots* – there you have him in a nutshell. *Bien campé* – well built, well set up. Rachilde's *Monsieur Venus* gives us another implicitly gay use of the word in 1884, when we see her hero Jaques, whose effeminate beauty is such that only his large hands give him away as a man (ah, how true!), sitting surrounded by flowers in the luxurious apartment bought for him by an admirer, *se campant vis-à-vis la glace qui lui renvoyait, multipliées, toutes les splendeurs de son paradis*. How am I to translate that? Either Jaques is 'posing himself before the mirror which reflected and multiplied all the splendours of his paradise' – or 'he is sitting in front of the mirror in his luxurious apartment and camping it up'. The pose of Mr Sebastian Melmoth is best described as camp. Remember that the initial charge had been that he had posed – *To Oscar Wilde, posing as a somdomite* [sic]. From 1894 to 1900 he was posing, camping not just to save his life, but to find out if any life at all was possible.

A new life! That was what he wanted.

To forge can mean two things. Forgery is 'the making of a thing in fraudulent imitation of something'. To forge is to make a copy, a fake which, when detected, alarmingly reveals that a fake has just as much life, as much validity as the real thing – until detected. It is then revealed as something that has no right to exist. It puts into question authenticity. It even has the power to damage, specifically and effectively, certain specific forms of authentication. Wilde, for instance, was married, and from the same class as his judges. But he invited Parker back to Tite Street while the children were asleep; he enjoyed sharing his money, body and conversation with working-class men. So what sense could the words 'married' and 'gentleman' retain when applied to Oscar Wilde? Wilde's plays bore all the hallmarks of successful comedies; but when, in the spring of 1895, they suddenly revealed an entirely unsuspected new set of meanings, they were hurriedly closed down. They all conclude with happy marriages, but they also catalogue the pains of innocent wives, husbands touched by horrible scandals, obscurely threatening, and unmarried, fashionable men. One society lady idly remarks, 'The secret of life is to appreciate the pleasure of being terribly, terribly deceived', but the audience did not agree. Oscar Wilde was exposed as a forger. The scandal of his existence was not simply that he had lied, but that he had effectively debased the very values which he had appeared to endorse.

To forge can also mean to hammer out, to create in a forge, to create something new with fire and ingenuity and amidst flying sparks. The dazzling career was not interrupted by being exposed; Mr Sebastian Melmoth was to be the most brilliant forgery yet.

Something that is forged has no intrinsic value. Rather it has the value with which the forger himself manages to invest his creation. There is no intrinsic value to homosexuality. There is no 'real' us, we can only ever have an unnatural identity, which is why we are all forgers. We create a life, not out of lies, but out of more or less conscious choices; adaptations, imitations and plain theft of styles, names, social and sexual roles, bodies. The high camp of

Sebastian Melmoth's life is a true model for us, not because we are all devastated upper class queens, or want to be, but because we too must compose ourselves. We may not talk like him, but we still rephrase everything, we give new meanings to things, wear the wrong clothes in the wrong places, refuse to have any but the most provisional form of integrity. Could you possibly summarize the daily fluctuations in your physical appearance with a single name? Which is it to be – the casually dressed citizen, or the well-dressed nightclubber? Or will it be the naked lover, as 'spontaneous', for once, as the half-remembered boy? Select a photograph to send me, to introduce yourself to a stranger. Choose something from the stuffed wardrobe, all those versions of yourself acquired since that moment when you reduced yourself to zero by announcing, 'I am gay'. Choose carefully, since it is only now that you realize that you are leading just one particular gay life among many. You have moved from the impossibility of that life in a small town to the possibilities of this city life. And now, what traces of authenticity, of the man you were supposed to 'grow into' (as if the fitting had already been made), what traces remain, and where in your face or body can you find them, those remains of the heterosexual child they thought you were? Oscar Wilde was a queen, an invert, a pervert, a sodomite, an Uranian, a simisexual, a homosexual and a Maryanne. Each word describes a different creature. We can never say of any man that he was (or is) a homosexual, and leave it at that. Consider your own variety of poses over the last four years. Or make your own list of the extraordinarily various forms we've taken in the last forty years: since coming home from the war, we have been The Flaming Queen (Fitzrovia, 1959; *Bolts* or *Benjys* 1979), The Speed Queen (Soho, 1963; Leicester Square, 1986), Leather Boys (c. 1960 to the present day), the Macho Man (*Subway* ad infinitum), The Clone. Our reading has included 'sensitive' novels, *Jeremy, Mister, Him* and *Gay News*; we have read in the papers about Alan Turing, Wildeblood, Wolfenden, Thorpe and Trestrail; there has been life before, during and 'after' Gay Liberation; we've enjoyed True Love, Fucking Around, Boy George and Safe Sex. My summary of our identities might describe a procession of mannequins, a chronology of exhibits, a genealogical tree in whose privileged shade you stretch out. Or it may describe the transformations of a single, literal body, someone you know. We never arrive. There is no single story in this city, where your (his) narrative may be punctuated by, but never quite conclude with, friendship, or independence, with several loves, or few or none. Nobody I know cares to remain constant.

Who wants to be consistent? What kind of integrity is that?

We are all fakes, all inventions. We are making this all up as we go along.

> To invent anything at all is an act of sheer genius, and, in a commercial age like ours, shows considerable physical courage.

12

TOWARD A
BUTCH-FEMME AESTHETIC

Sue-Ellen Case

In the 1980s, feminist criticism has focused increasingly on the subject position: both in the explorations for the creation of a female subject position and the deconstruction of the inherited subject position that is marked with masculinist functions and history. Within this focus, the problematics of women inhabiting the traditional subject position have been sketched out, the possibilities of a new heterogeneous, heteronomous position have been explored, and a desire for a collective subject has been articulated. While this project is primarily a critical one, concerned with language and symbolic structures, philosophic assumptions, and psychoanalytic narratives, it also implicates the social issues of class, race, and sexuality. Teresa de Lauretis reviews the recent excavations of the subject position in terms of ideology, noting that much of the work on the subject, derived from Foucault and Althusser, denies both agency and gender to the subject. In fact, many critics leveled a similar criticism against Foucault in a recent conference on postmodernism, noting that while his studies seem to unravel the web of ideology, they suggest no subject position outside the ideology, nor do they construct a subject who has the agency to change ideology (see 'Postmodernism'). In other words, note de Lauretis and others, most of the work on the subject position has only revealed the way in which the subject is trapped within ideology and thus provides no programs for change.

For feminists, changing this condition must be a priority. The common appellation of this bound subject has been the 'female subject', signifying a

An earlier version was published in *Discourse*, 11:1, Fall–Winter 1988–89.

biological, sexual difference, inscribed by dominant cultural practices. De Lauretis names her subject (one capable of change and of changing conditions) the feminist subject, one who is 'at the same time inside and outside the ideology of gender, and conscious of being so, conscious of that pull, that division, that doubled vision' (10). De Lauretis ascribes a sense of self-determination at the micropolitical level to the feminist subject. This feminist subject, unlike the female one, can be outside of ideology, can find self-determination, can change. This is an urgent goal for the feminist activist/theorist. Near the conclusion of her article (true to the newer rules of composition), de Lauretis begins to develop her thesis: that the previous work on the female subject assumes, but leaves unwritten, a heterosexual context for the subject and this is the cause for her continuing entrapment. Because she is still perceived in terms of men and not within the context of other women, the subject in heterosexuality cannot become capable of ideological change (17–18).

De Lauretis's conclusion is my starting place. Focusing on the feminist subject, endowed with the agency for political change, located among women, outside the ideology of sexual difference, and thus the social institution of heterosexuality, it would appear that the lesbian roles of butch and femme, as a dynamic duo, offer precisely the strong subject position the movement requires. Now, in order for the butch-femme roles to clearly emerge within this sociotheoretical project, several tasks must be accomplished: the lesbian subject of feminist theory would have to come out of the closet, the basic discourse or style of camp for the lesbian butch-femme positions would have to be clarified, and an understanding of the function of roles in the homosexual lifestyle would need to be developed, particularly in relation to the historical class and racial relations embedded in such a project. Finally, once these tasks have been completed, the performance practice, both on and off the stage, may be studied as that of a feminist subject, both inside and outside ideology, with the power to self-determine her role and her conditions on the micropolitical level. Within this schema, the butch-femme couple inhabit the subject position together – 'you can't have one without the other', as the song says. The two roles never appear as ... discrete. The combo butch-femme as subject is reminiscent of Monique Wittig's 'j/e' or coupled self in her novel *The Lesbian Body*. These are not split subjects, suffering the torments of dominant ideology. They are coupled ones that do not impale themselves on the poles of sexual difference or metaphysical values, but constantly seduce the sign system, through flirtation and inconstancy into the light fondle of artifice, replacing the Lacanian slash with a lesbian bar.

However, before all of this *jouissance* can be enjoyed, it is first necessary to bring the lesbian subject out of the closet of feminist history. The initial step in that process is to trace historically how the lesbian has been assigned to the role of the skeleton in the closet of feminism; in this case, specifically the lesbian who relates to her cultural roots by identifying with traditional butch-femme role-playing. First, regard the feminist genuflection of the 1980s – the catechism of 'working-class-women-of-color' feminist theorists feel impelled to invoke at the outset of their research. What's wrong with this picture? It does not include the lesbian position. In fact, the isolation of the social dynamics of race and class successfully relegates sexual preference to an attendant position, so that even if the lesbian were to appear, she would be as a bridesmaid and never the bride. Several factors are responsible for this ghosting of the lesbian subject: the first is the growth of moralistic projects restricting the production of sexual fiction or fantasy through the antipornography crusade. This crusade has produced an alliance between those working on social feminist issues and right-wing homophobic, born-again men and women who also support censorship. This alliance in the electorate, which aids in producing enough votes for an ordinance, requires the closeting of lesbians for the so-called greater cause. Both Jill Dolan and Alice Echols develop this position in their respective articles.

Although the antipornography issue is an earmark of the moralistic 1980s, the homophobia it signals is merely an outgrowth of the typical interaction between feminism and lesbianism since the rise of the feminist movement in the early 1970s. Del Martin and Phyllis Lyon describe the rise of the initial so-called lesbian liberatory organization, the Daughters of Bilitis (DOB), in their influential early book, *Lesbian/Woman* (1972). They record the way in which the aims of such organizations were intertwined with those of the early feminist, or more precisely, women's movement. They proudly exhibit the way in which the DOB moved away from the earlier bar culture and its symbolic systems to a more dominant identification and one that would appease the feminist movement. DOB's goal was to erase butch-femme behavior, its dress codes, and lifestyle from the lesbian community and to change lesbians into lesbian feminists.

Here is the story of one poor victim who came to the DOB for help. Note how similar this narrative style is to the redemptive, corrective language of missionary projects: 'Toni joined Daughters of Bilitis . . . at our insistence, and as a result of the group's example, its unspoken pressure, she toned down her dress. She was still very butch, but she wore women's slacks and blouses . . . one of DOB's goals was to teach the lesbian a mode of behavior and dress acceptable to society . . . We knew too many lesbians whose activities were restricted because they wouldn't wear skirts. But Toni did not agree. "You'll never get me in a dress", she growled, banging her fist on the table'. The description of Toni's behavior, her animal growling noise, portrays her as uncivilized, recalling earlier, colonial missionary projects. Toni is portrayed as similar to the inappropriately dressed savage whom the missionary clothes and saves. The authors continue: 'But she became fast friends with a gay man, and over the months he helped her to feel comfortable with herself as a woman' (77). Here, in a lesbian narrative, the missionary position is finally given over to a man (even if gay) who helps the butch to feel like a woman. The contemporary lesbian-identified reader can only marvel at the conflation of gender identification in the terms of dominant, heterosexual culture with the adopted gender role-playing within the lesbian subculture.

If the butches are savages in this book, the femmes are lost heterosexuals who damage birthright lesbians by forcing them to play the butch roles. The authors assert that most femmes are divorced heterosexual women who know how to relate only to men and thus force their butches to play the man's role, which is conflated with that of a butch (79). Finally, the authors unveil the salvationary role of feminism in this process and its power to sever the newly constructed identity of the lesbian feminist from its traditional lesbian roots: 'The minority of lesbians who still cling to the traditional male-female or husband-wife pattern in their partnerships are more than likely old-timers, gay bar habituées or working-class women'. This sentence successfully compounds ageism with a (homo)phobia of lesbian bar culture and a rejection of a working-class identification. The middle-class upward mobility of the lesbian feminist identification shifts the sense of community from one of working-class, often women-of-color lesbians in bars, to that of white upper-middle-class heterosexual women who predominated in the early women's movement. The book continues: 'the old order changeth however' (here they even begin to adopt verb endings from the King James Bible) 'as the women's liberation movement gains strength against this pattern of heterosexual marriages, the number of lesbians involved in butch-femme roles diminishes' (80).

However, this compulsory adaptation of lesbian feminist identification must be understood as a defensive posture, created by the homophobia that operated in the internal dynamics of the early movement, particularly within the so-called consciousness-raising groups. In her article with Cherríe Moraga on butch-femme relations, Amber Hollibaugh, a femme, described the feminist reception of lesbians this way: 'the first discussion I ever heard of lesbianism among feminists was: "We've been sex objects to men and where did it get us? And here when we're just learning how to be friends with other women, you got to go and sexualize it" ... they made men out of every sexual dyke' (402). These kinds of experiences led Hollibaugh and Moraga to conclude: 'In our involvement in a movement largely controlled by white middle-class women, we feel that the values of their culture ... have been pushed down our throats ...', and even more specifically, in the 1980s, to pose these questions: 'why is it that it is largely white middle-class women who form the visible leadership in the anti-porn movement? Why are women of color not particularly visible in this sex-related single issue movement?' (405).

When one surveys these beginnings of the alliance between the heterosexual feminist movement and lesbians, one is not surprised at the consequences for lesbians who adopted the missionary position under a movement that would lead to an antipornography crusade and its alliance with the Right. Perhaps too late, certain members of the lesbian community who survived the early years of feminism and continued to work in the grass-roots lesbian movement, such as Joan Nestle, began to perceive this problem. As Nestle, founder of the Lesbian Herstory Archives in New York, wrote: 'We lesbians of the 1950s made a mistake in the 1970s: we allowed ourselves to be trivialized and reinterpreted by feminists who did not share our culture' (23). Nestle also notes the class prejudice in the rejection of butch-femme roles: 'I wonder why there is such a consuming interest in the butch-fem lives of upper-class women, usually more literary figures, while real-life, working butch-fem women are seen as imitative and culturally backward ... the reality of passing women, usually a working-class lesbian's method of survival, has provoked very little academic lesbian-feminist interest. Grassroots lesbian history research is changing this' (23).

So the lesbian butch-femme tradition went into the feminist closet. Yet the closet, or the bars, with their hothouse atmosphere have produced what, in combination with the butch-femme couple, may provide the liberation of the feminist subject – the discourse of camp. Proust described this accomplishment in his novel *The Captive*:

> The lie, the perfect lie, about people we know, about the relations we have had with them, about our motive for some action, formulated in totally different terms, the lie as to what we are, whom we love, what we feel in regard to those people who love us ... – that lie is one of the few things in the world that can open windows for us on to what is new and unknown, that can awaken in us sleeping senses for the contemplation of universes that otherwise we should never have known. (213, cited in Sedgwick)

The closet has given us camp – the style, the discourse, the *mise en scène* of butch-femme roles. In his history of the development of gay camp, Michael Bronski describes the liberative work of late-nineteenth-century authors such as Oscar Wilde in creating the homosexual camp liberation from the rule of naturalism, or realism. Within his argument, Bronski describes naturalism and realism as strategies that tried to save fiction from the accusation of daydream, imagination, or masturbation and to affix a utilitarian goal to literary produc-tion – that of teaching morals. In contrast, Bronski quotes the newspaper *Fag Rag* on the functioning of camp: 'We've broken down the rules that are used for validating the difference between real/true and unreal/false. The controlling agents of the status quo may know the power of lies; dissident subcultures, however, are closer to knowing their value' (1984: 41). Camp both articulates the lives of homosexuals through the obtuse tone of irony and inscribes their oppression with the same device. Likewise, it eradicates the ruling powers of heterosexist realist modes.

Susan Sontag, in an avant-garde assimilation of camp, described it as a 'cer-tain mode of aestheticism ... one way of seeing the world as an aesthetic phenomenon ... not in terms of beauty, but in terms of the degree of artifice' (1964b, rpt. 1966: 275). This artifice, as artifice, works to defeat the reign of realism as well as to situate the camp discourse within the category of what can be said (or seen). However, the fixed quality of Sontag's characteristic use of camp within the straight context of aestheticization has produced a homo-sexual strategy for avoiding such assimilation: what Esther Newton has des-cribed as its constantly changing, mobile quality, designed to alter the gay camp sensibility before it becomes a fad (1972: 105). Moreover, camp also protects homosexuals through a 'first-strike wit' as *Fag Rag* asserts: 'Wit and irony provide the only reasonable modus operandi in the American Literalist Terror of Straight Reality' (Bronski 1984: 46).

Oscar Wilde brought this artifice, wit, irony, and the distancing of straight reality and its conventions to the stage. Later, Genet staged the malleable, multiple artifice of camp in *The Screens*, which elevates such displacement to an ontology. In his play, *The Blacks*, he used such wit, irony, and artifice to deconstruct the notion of 'black' and to stage the dynamics of racism. *The Blacks* displaced the camp critique from homophobia to racism, in which 'black' stands in for 'queer' and the campy queen of the bars is transformed into an 'African queen'. This displacement is part of the larger use of the closet and gay camp discourse to articulate other social realities. Eve Sedgwick attests to this displacement when she writes:

> I want to argue that a lot of energy of attention and demarcation that has swirled around issues of homosexuality since the end of the nineteenth century ... has been impelled by the distinctly indicative relation of homosexuality to wider mappings of secrecy and disclosure, and of the private and the public, that were and are critically problematical for the gender, sexual, and economic structures of the heterosexist culture at large.... 'the closet' and 'coming out' are now verging on all-purpose phrases for the potent crossing and recrossing of almost any politically charged lines of representation ... The apparent floating-free from its gay origins of that phrase 'coming out of the closet' in recent usage might suggest that the trope of the closet is so close to the heart of some modern preoccupations that it could be ... evacuated of its historical gay specificity. But I hypothesize that exactly the opposite is true.

Thus, the camp success in ironizing and distancing the regime of realist terror mounted by heterosexist forces has become useful as a discourse and style for other marginal factions.

Camp style, gay-identified dressing, and the articulation of the social realities of homosexuality have also become part of the straight, postmodern canon, as Herbert Blau articulated it in a special issue of *Salmagundi*: 'becoming homosexual is part of the paraphilia of the postmodern, not only a new sexual politics but the reification of all politics, supersubtilized beyond the unnegotiable demands of the sixties, from which it is derived, into a more persuasive rhetoric of unsublimated desire' (233). Within this critical community, the perception of recognizable homosexuals can also inspire broader visions of the operation of social codes. Blau states: 'there soon came pullulating toward me at high prancing amphetamined pitch something like the end of Empire or like the screaming remains of the return of the repressed – pearl-white, vinyl, in polo pants and scarf – an englistered and giggling outburst of resplendent queer ... what was there to consent to and who could possibly legitimate that galloping specter I had seen, pure ideolect, whose plunging and lungless soundings were a full-throttled forecast of much weirder things to come?' (221-22). Initially, these borrowings seem benign and even inviting to the homosexual theorist. Contemporary theory seems to open the closet door to invite the queer to come out, transformed as a new, postmodern subject, or even to invite straights to come into the closet, out of the roar of dominant discourse. The danger incurred in moving gay politics into such heterosexual contexts is in only slowly discovering that the strategies and per-spectives of homosexual realities and discourse may be locked inside a homophobic 'concentration camp'. Certain of these authors, such as Blau, even introduce homosexual characters and their subversions into arguments that conclude with explicit homophobia. Note Blau's remembrance of things past:

> thinking I would enjoy it, I walked up Christopher Street last summer at the fag end of the depleted carnival of Gay Pride Day, with a disgust unexpected and almost uncontained by principle ... I'll usually fight for the right of each of us to have his own perversions, I may not, under the pressure of theory and despite the itchiness of my art, to try on yours and, what's worse, rather wish you wouldn't. Nor am I convinced that what you are doing isn't perverse in the most pejorative sense (249).

At least Blau, as in all of his writing, honestly and openly records his personal prejudice. The indirect or subtextual homophobia in this new assimilative discourse is more alluring and ultimately more powerful in erasing the social reality and the discursive inscriptions of gay, and more specifically, lesbian discourse.

Here, the sirens of sublation may be found in the critical maneuvers of heterosexual feminist critics who metaphorize butch-femme roles, transvestites and campy dressers into a 'subject who masquerades', as they put it, or is 'carnivalesque' or even, as some are so bold to say, who 'cross-dresses'. Even when these borrowings are nested in more benign contexts than Blau's, they evacuate the historical, butch-femme couples' sense of masquerade and cross-dressing the way a cigar-store Indian evacuates the historical dress and behavior of the Native American. As is often the case, illustrated by the cigarstore Indian, these symbols may only proliferate when the social reality has been successfully obliterated and the identity has become the private property of the dominant class. Such metaphors operate simply to display the breadth of the art collection, or style collection, of the straight author. Just as the French term *film noir* became the name for B-rate American films of the 1940s, these notions of masquerade and cross-dressing, standing in for the roles of working-class lesbians, have come back to us through French theory on the one hand and studies of the lives of upper-class lesbians who lived in Paris between the wars on the other. In this case, the referent of the term Left Bank is not a river, but a storehouse of critical capital.

Nevertheless, this confluence of an unresolved social, historical problem in the feminist movement and these recent theoretical strategies, re-assimilated by the lesbian critic, provide a ground that could resolve the project of constructing the feminist subject position. The butch-femme subject could inhabit that discursive position, empowering it for the production of future compositions. Having already grounded this argument within the historical situation of butch-femme couples, perhaps now it would be tolerable to describe the theoretical maneuver that could become the butch-femme subject position. Unfortunately, these strategies must emerge in the bodiless world of 'spectatorial positions' or 'subject positions', where transvestites wear no clothes and subjects tread only 'itineraries of desire'. In this terrain of discourse, or among theorized spectators in darkened movie houses with their gazes fixed on the dominant cinema screen, 'the thrill is gone' as Nestle described it. In the Greenwich Village bars, she could 'spot a butch 50 feet away and still feel the thrill of her power' as she saw 'the erotic signal of her hair at the nape of her neck, touching the shirt collar; how she held a cigarette; the symbolic pinky ring flashing as she waved her hand' (21–2). Within this theory, the erotics are gone, but certain maneuvers maintain what is generally referred to as 'presence'.

The origins of this theory may be found in a Freudian therapist's office, where an intellectual heterosexual woman, who had become frigid, had given way to rages, and, puzzled by her own coquettish behavior, told her story to Joan Rivière sometime around 1929. This case caused Rivière to publish her thoughts in her ground-breaking article entitled 'Womanliness as a Masquerade' that later influenced several feminist critics such as Mary Russo and Mary Ann Doane and the French philosopher Jean Baudrillard. Rivière began to 'read' this woman's behavior as the 'wish for masculinity' which causes the woman to don 'the mask of womanliness to avert anxiety and the retribution feared from men' (303). As Rivière saw it, for a woman to read an academic paper before a professional association was to exhibit in public her 'possession of her father's penis, having castrated him' (305–6). In order to do recompense for this castration, which resided in her intellectual proficiency, she donned the mask of womanliness. Rivière notes: 'The reader may now ask how I define womanliness or where I draw the line between genuine womanliness and the "masquerade" . . . they are the same thing' (306). Thus began the theory that all womanliness is a masquerade worn by women to disguise the fact that they have taken their father's penis in their intellectual stride, so to speak. Rather than remaining the well-adjusted castrated woman, these intellectuals have taken the penis for their own and protect it with the mask of the castrated, or womanhood. However, Rivière notes a difference here between heterosexual women and lesbian ones – the heterosexual women don't claim possession openly, but through reaction-formations; whereas the homosexual women openly display their possession of the penis and count on the males' recognition of defeat (312). This is not to suggest that the lesbian's situation is not also fraught with anxiety and reaction-formations, but this difference in degree is an important one.

I suggest that this kind of masquerade is consciously played out in butch-femme roles, particularly as they were constituted in the 1940s and 1950s. If one reads them from within Rivière's theory, the butch is the lesbian woman who proudly displays the possession of the penis, while the femme takes on the compensatory masquerade of womanliness. The femme, however, foregrounds her masquerade by playing to a butch, another woman in a role; likewise, the butch exhibits her penis to a woman who is playing the role of compensatory castration. This raises the question of 'penis, penis, who's got the penis', because there is no referent in sight; rather, the fictions of penis and castration become ironized and 'camped up'. Unlike Rivière's patient, these women play on the phallic economy rather than to it. Both women alter this masquerading subject's function by positioning it between women and thus foregrounding the myths of penis and castration in the Freudian economy. In the bar culture, these roles were always acknowledged as such. The bars were often abuzz with the discussion of who was or was not a butch or femme, and how good they were at the role (see Davis & Kennedy). In other words, these penis-related posturings were always acknowledged as roles, not biological birthrights, nor any other essentialist poses. The lesbian roles are underscored as two optional functions for women in the phallocracy, while the heterosexual woman's role collapses them into one compensatory charade. From a theatrical point of view, the butch-femme roles take on the quality of something more like a character construction and have a more active quality than what Rivière calls a reaction-formation. Thus, these roles qua roles lend agency and self-determination to the historically passive subject, providing her with at least two options for gender identification and with the aid of camp, an irony that allows her perception to be constructed from outside ideology, with a gender role that makes her appear as if she is inside of it.

Meanwhile, other feminist critics have received this masquerade theory into a heterosexual context, retaining its passive imprint. In Mary Ann Doane's influential article entitled 'Film and the Masquerade: Theorizing the Female Spectator', Doane, unfortunately, resorts to a rather biologistic position in constructing the female spectator and theorizing out from the female body. From the standpoint of something more active in terms of representation such as de Lauretis's feminist subject or the notion of butch-femme, this location of critical strategies in biological realities seems revisionist. That point aside, Doane does devise a way for women to 'appropriate the gaze for their own pleasure' (77) through the notion of the transvestite and the masquerade. As the former, the female subject would position herself as if she were a male viewer, assimilating all of the power and payoffs that spectatorial position offers. As the latter, she would, as Rivière earlier suggested, masquerade as a woman. She would 'flaunt her femininity, produce herself as an excess of femininity – foreground the masquerade', and reveal 'femininity itself ... as a mask' (81).

Thus, the masquerade would hold femininity at a distance, manufacturing 'a lack in the form of a certain distance between oneself and one's image' (82). This strategy offers the female viewer a way to be the spectator of female roles while not remaining close to them, nor identifying with them, attaining the distance from them required to enter the psychoanalytic viewing space. The masquerade that Doane describes is exactly that practiced by the femme – she foregrounds cultural femininity. The difference is that Doane places this role in the spectator position, probably as an outgrowth of the passive object position required of women in the heterosexist social structures. Doane's vision of the active woman is as the active spectator. Within the butch-femme economy, the femme actively performs her masquerade as the subject of representation. She delivers a performance of the feminine masquerade rather than, as Doane suggests, continue in Rivière's reactive formation of masquerading compensatorily before the male-gaze-inscribed-dominant-cinema-screen. *Flaunting* has long been a camp verb and here Doane borrows it, along with the notion of 'excess of femininity', so familiar to classical femmes and drag queens. Yet, by reinscribing it within a passive, spectatorial role, she gags and binds the traditional homosexual role players, whose gender play has nothing essential beneath it, replacing them with the passive spectatorial position that is, essentially, female.

Another feminist theorist, Mary Russo, has worked out a kind of female masquerade through the sense of the carnivalesque body derived from the work of Mikhail Bakhtin. In contrast to Doane, Russo moves on to a more active role for the masquerader, one of 'making a spectacle of oneself'. Russo is aware of the dangers of the essentialist body in discourse, while still maintaining some relationship between theory and real women. This seems a more hopeful critical terrain to the lesbian critic. In fact, Russo even includes a reference to historical instances of political resistance by men in drag (3). Yet in spite of her cautions, like Doane, Russo's category is once again the female subject, along with its biologically determined social resonances. Perhaps it is her reliance on the male author Bakhtin and the socialist resonances in his text (never too revealing about gender) that cause Russo to omit lesbian or gay strategies or experiences with the grotesque body. Instead, she is drawn to depictions of the pregnant body and finally Kristeva's sense of the maternal, even though she does note its limitations and problematic status within feminist thought (6). Finally, this swollen monument to reproduction, with all of its heterosexual privilege, once more stands alone in this performance area of the grotesque and carnivalesque. Though she does note the exclusion, in this practice, of the 'the already marginalized' (6), once again, they do not appear. Moreover, Russo even cites Showalter's notion that feminist theory itself is a kind of 'critical cross-dressing', while still suppressing the lesbian presence in the feminist community that made such a concept available to the straight theorists (8). Still true to the male, heterosexual models from which her argument derives, she identifies the master of *mise en scène* as Derrida. Even when damning his characterization of the feminist as raging bull and asking 'what kind of drag is this', her referent is the feminist and not the bull ... dyke (9). This argument marks an ironic point in history: once the feminist movement had obscured the original cross-dressed butch through the interdiction of 'politically incorrect', it donned for itself the strategies and characteristics of the role-playing, safely theorized out of material reality and used to suppress the referent that produced it.

In spite of their heterosexist shortcomings, what, in these theories, can be employed to understand the construction of the butch-femme subject on the stage? First, how might they be constructed as characters? Perhaps the best example of some workings of this potential is in Split Britches' production of *Beauty and the Beast*.[1] The title itself connotes the butch-femme couple: Peggy Shaw as the butch becomes the Beast who actively pursues the femme, while Lois Weaver as the excessive femme becomes Beauty. Within the dominant system of representation, Shaw, as butch Beast, portrays a bestial woman who actively loves other women. The portrayal is faithful to the historical situation of the butch role, as Nestle describes it: 'None of the butch women I was with, and this included a passing woman, ever presented themselves to me as men; they did announce themselves as tabooed women who were willing to identify their passion for other women by wearing clothes that symbolized the taking of responsibility. Part of this responsibility was sexual expertise ... this courage to feel comfortable with arousing another woman became a political act' (21). In other words, the butch, who represents by her clothing the desire for other women, becomes the beast – the marked taboo against lesbianism dressed up in the clothes of that desire. Beauty is the desired one and the one who aims her desirability at the butch.

This symbolism becomes explicit when Shaw and Weaver interrupt the Beauty/Beast narrative to deliver a duologue about the history of their own personal butch-femme roles. Weaver uses the trope of having wished she was Katharine Hepburn and casting another woman as Spencer Tracy, while Shaw relates that she thought she was James Dean. The identification with movie idols is part of the camp assimilation of dominant culture. It serves multiple purposes: (1) they do not identify these butch-femme roles with 'real' people, or literal images of gender, but with fictionalized ones, thus underscoring the masquerade; (2) the history of their desire, or their search for a sexual partner becomes a series of masks, or identities that stand for sexual attraction in the culture, thus distancing them from the 'play' of seduction as it is outlined by social mores; (3) the association with movies makes narrative fiction part of the strategy as well as characters. This final fiction as fiction allows Weaver and Shaw to slip easily from one narrative to another, to yet another, unbound by through-lines, plot structure, or a stable sense of character because they are fictional at their core in the camp style and through the butch-femme roles. The instability and alienation of character and plot is compounded with their own personal butch-femme play on the street, as a recognizable couple in the lower

East Side scene, as well as within fugitive narratives onstage, erasing the difference between theater and real life, or actor and character, obliterating any kind of essentialist ontology behind the play. This allows them to create a play with scenes that move easily from the narrative of beauty and the beast, to the duologue on their butch-femme history, to a recitation from *Macbeth*, to a solo lip-synched to Perry Como. The butch-femme roles at the center of their ongoing personalities move masquerade to the base of performance and no narrative net can catch them or hold them, as they wriggle into a variety of characters and plots.

This exciting multiplicity of roles and narratives signals the potency of their agency. Somehow the actor overcomes any text, yet the actor herself is a fiction and her social self is one as well. Shaw makes a joke out of suturing to any particular role or narrative form when she dies, as the beast. Immediately after dying, she gets up to tell the audience not to believe in such cheap tricks. Dies. Tells the audience that Ronald Reagan pulled the same trick when he was shot – tells them that was not worth the suturing either. Dies. Asks for a Republican doctor. Dies. Then rises to seemingly close the production by kissing Weaver. Yet even this final butch-femme tableau is followed by a song to the audience that undercuts the performance itself.

Weaver's and Shaw's production of butch-femme role-playing in and out of a fairy tale positions the representation of the lesbian couple in a childhood narrative: the preadolescent proscription of perversity. Though they used *Beauty and the Beast* to stage butch-femme as outsiders, the quintessential childhood narrative that proscribes cross-dressing is *Little Red Riding Hood*, in which the real terror of the wolf is produced by his image in grandmother's clothing. The bed, the eating metaphor, and the cross-dressing by the wolf, provide a gridlock closure of any early thoughts of transgressing gender roles. Djuna Barnes wrote a version of this perspective in *Nightwood*. When Nora sees the transvestite doctor in his bed, wearing women's nightclothes, she remarks: 'God, children know something they can't tell; they like Red Riding Hood and the wolf in bed!' Barnes goes on to explicate that sight of the cross-dressed one: 'Is not the gown the natural raiment of extremity? ... He dresses to lie beside himself, who is so constructed that love, for him, can only be something special ...' (78–80).[2] *Beauty and the Beast* also returns to a childhood tale of taboo and liberates the sexual preference and role-playing it is designed to repress, in this case, specifically the butch-femme promise. As some lesbians prescribed in the early movement: identify with the monsters!

What, then, is the action played between these two roles? It is what Jean Baudrillard terms *séduction* and it yields many of its social fruits. Baudrillard begins his argument in *De la séduction*, by asserting that seduction is never of the natural order, but always operates as a sign, or artifice (10). By extension, this suggests that butch-femme seduction is always located in semiosis. The kiss, as Shaw and Weaver demonstrate in their swooping image of it, positioned at its most clichéd niche at the end of the narrative, is always the high camp kiss. Again, Baudrillard: seduction doesn't 'recuperate the autonomy of the body ... truth ... the sovereignty of this seduction is transsexual, not bisexual, destroying all sexual organization ' (18). The point is not to conflict reality with another reality, but to abandon the notion of reality through roles and their seductive atmosphere and lightly manipulate appearances. Surely, this is the atmosphere of camp, permeating the *mise en scène* with 'pure' artifice. In other words, a strategy of appearances replaces a claim to truth. Thus, butch-femme roles evade the notion of 'the female body' as it predominates in feminist theory, dragging along its Freudian baggage and scopophilic transubstantiation. These roles are played in signs themselves and not in ontologies. Seduction, as a dramatic action, transforms all of these seeming realities into semiotic play. To use Baudrillard with Rivière, butch-femme roles offer a hypersimulation of woman as she is defined by the Freudian system and the phallocracy that institutes its social rule.[3]

Therefore, the female body, the male gaze, and the structures of realism are only sex toys for the butch-femme couple. From the perspective of camp, the claim these have to realism destroys seduction by repressing the resonances of vision and sound into its medium. This is an idea worked out by Baudrillard in his chapter on pornography, but I find it apt here. That is, that realism, with its visual organization of three dimensions, actually degrades the scene; it impoverishes the suggestiveness of the scene by its excess of means (49). This implies that as realism makes the spectator see things its way, it represses her own ability to free-associate within a situation and reduces the resonances of events to its own limited, technical dimensions. Thus, the seduction of the scene is repressed by the authoritarian claim to realistic representation. This difference is marked in the work of Weaver and Shaw in the ironized, imaginative theatrical space of their butch-femme role-playing. Contrast their freely moving, resonant narrative space to the realism of Marsha Norman, Beth Henley, Irene Fornes's *Mud*, or Sam Shepard's *A Lie of the Mind*. The violence released in the continual zooming-in on the family unit, and the heterosexist ideology linked with its stage partner, realism, is directed against women and their hint of seduction. In *A Lie of the Mind*, this becomes literally woman-battering. Beth's only associative space and access to transformative discourse is the result of nearly fatal blows to her head. One can see similar violent results in Norman's concerted moving of the heroine toward suicide in *'night, Mother* or Henley's obsession with suicide in *Crimes of the Heart* or the conclusive murder in Fornes's *Mud*. The closure of these realistic narratives chokes the women to death and strangles the play of symbols, or the possibility of seduction. In fact, for each of them, sexual play only assists their entrapment. One can see the butch Peggy Shaw rising to her feet after these realistic narrative deaths and telling us not to believe it. Cast the realism aside – its consequences for women are deadly.

In recuperating the space of seduction, the butch-femme couple can, through their own agency, move through a field of symbols, like tiptoeing through the two lips (as Irigaray would have us believe), playfully inhabiting the camp space of irony and wit, free from biological determinism, elitist essentialism, and the heterosexist cleavage of sexual difference. Surely, here is a couple the feminist subject might perceive as useful to join.

NOTES

1. There is no published version of this play. In fact, there is no satisfactory way to separate the spoken text from the action. The play is composed by three actors, Deborah Margolin along with Shaw and Weaver. Margolin, however, does not play within the lesbian dynamics, but represents a Jewish perspective. For further discussions of this group's work see Davy; Dolan; and Case.
2. My thanks to Carolyn Allen, who pointed out this passage in Barnes to me in discussing resonances of the fairy tale. In another context, it would be interesting to read the lesbian perspective on the male transvestite in these passages and the way he works in Barnes's narrative. 'The Company of Wolves', a short story and later a screenplay by Angela Carter, begins to open the sexual resonances, but retains the role of the monster within heterosexuality.
3. The term *hypersimulation* is borrowed from Baudrillard's notion of the simulacrum rather than his one of seduction. It is useful here to raise the ante on terms like artifice and to suggest, as Baudrillard does, its relation to the order of reproduction and late capitalism.

REFERENCES

Barnes, Djuna, *Nightwood*, New York: New Directions, 1961.

Baudrillard, Jean, *De la séduction*, Paris: Galilée, 1979.

Blau, Herbert, 'Disseminating Sodom', *Salmagundi* 58–59, 1983, 221–51.

Case, Sue-Ellen, 'From Split Subject to Split Britches', in Enoch Brater (ed.), *Contemporary Women Playwrights*, Oxford, 1989.

Davis, Madeline & Elizabeth Lapovsky Kennedy, 'Oral History and the Study of Sexuality in the Lesbian Community: Buffalo, New York, 1940–1960', *Feminist Studies* 12:1, 1986, 7–26.

Davy, Kate, 'Constructing the Spectator: Reception, Context, and Address in Lesbian Performance', *Performing Arts Journal* 10:2, 1986, 43–52.

de Lauretis, Teresa, *Technologies of Gender,* Bloomington: Indiana UP, 1987.

Doane, Mary Ann, 'Film and the Masquerade: Theorizing the Female Spectator', *Screen* 23, 1982, 74–87.

Dolan, Jill, 'The Dynamics of Desire: Sexuality and Gender in Pornography and Performance', *Theatre Journal* 39:2, 1987, 156–74.

Echols, Alice, 'The New Feminism of Yin and Yang', in Ann Snitow, Christine Stansell, and Sharon Thompson (eds.), *Powers of Desire: The Politics of Sexuality,* New York: Monthly Review Press, 1983, 440–59.

Hollibaugh, Amber & Moraga, Cherríe, 'What We're Rollin' Around in Bed With: Sexual Silences in Feminism', in Ann Snitow, Christine Stansell & Sharon Thompson (eds.), *Powers of Desire: The Politics of Sexuality,* New York: Monthly Review Press, 1983, 395–405.

Martin, Del, and Phyllis Lyon, *Lesbian/Woman*, New York: Bantam, 1972.

Nestle, Joan, 'Butch-Fem Relationships: Sexual Courage in the 1950s', *Heresies* 12, 1981, 21–24.

'Postmodernism: Text, Politics, Instruction', International Association for Philosophy and Literature, Lawrence, Kansas, April 30–May 2, 1987.

Rivière, Joan, 'Womanliness as a Masquerade', *International Journal of Psycho-Analysis* 10, 1929, 303–13.

Russo, Mary, 'Female Grotesques: Carnival and Theory'. Working Paper no. 1, Center for Twentieth Century Studies, Milwaukee, 1985.

Sedgwick, Eve, 'The Epistemology of the Closet', 1987, manuscript, revised and published in Sedgwick 1990.

Wittig, Monique, *The Lesbian Body,* trans. David LeVay, New York: William Morrow, 1975.

SECTION III
GENDER, AND OTHER SPECTACLES

INTRODUCTION

The varying (institutional, social, cultural) contexts that mark the 'coming of age' of gay criticism in the 1980s coincide with the giving up of the totalizing definitional enterprise. Readings, more or less explicitly, restricted the object of their analysis to *one* aspect, one mode, one *wing* of camp, in a 'localising' attitude promoted by the acknowledgement of its inherent elusiveness – what Dollimore announces by limiting his discussion to 'that mode of camp which undermines the categories which exclude it [...] through parody and mimicry' ('Post/modern', reprinted here). In the late 1980s, in fact, camp drew its significance on the critical scene precisely from the parodic mode of gender deconstruction that Dollimore refers to, and gay studies were progressively accompanied by gender studies and queer theory as its most necessary and relevant perspectives. The second section of this Reader, in fact, ends with Sue-Ellen Case's 1988 essay, with its timely intervention on the possible (if not intrinsically necessitated) alliance between camp and feminist reading strategies. Case's move was related to the unburdening of a lesbian feminist practice of camp; and yet, the development of 'second wave' feminism, or historicism of gender, offered a context in which gay camp too – after the 1970s critique moved by gay activists and feminist commentators to its investment in the stigma of 'effeminacy', with its derogatory (self-hating and misogynous) implications investing gay men just as women – may be politically valuable in a feminist framework.

Sontag herself, a decade after writing 'Notes on "Camp"', felt it necessary to address the alleged complicity of camp with the patriarchal order of culture, and to reassess the implications of the 'amoral' camp disengagement she had celebrated in her former essay. In doing so, Sontag suggested such protofeminist value, pointing to 'the camp taste for the theatrically feminine' as 'help[ing] undermine the credibility of certain stereotyped femininities' (Boyers & Bernstein 1975, rpt. 1982: 339). What in 1964 had been ascribed to an aristocratic detachment and irresponsibility, could be reframed as a demystifying detachment from one's self, a *dis*identification within the self as culturally constituted, participating in those power relations that are inscribed in stereotypes, and deconstructed by camp's 'inverted commas'.[1]

Once again, this reassessment proceeds in concert with a reconstruction of camp, one that identifies in it a common ground for social formations whose marginality has been intertwined with 'the theatrical'. It might be claimed that even in Newton's *Mother Camp*, ascribing to 'the homosexual beholder' the activation of a camp relationship, what funds camp is not so much the homosexuality of the perceiving/performing subject, but rather the cohesive effect of the theatrical (self-)representation of a stigmatized self.[2] And in a non-deterministic paradigm, in fact, the link between homosexuality and the 'aesthetic sense', histrionic behaviour and theatricality posited by essentialist theories – be those in the suggestions of a 'gay sensibility' or in the pathologising/patronising bourgeois constructions of homosexuality – should be dismissed in favour, as Sinfield (1991: 43–44) suggests, of a materialist reading starting from the historical convergence of theatre and illicit sexualities in a common inner-city territory – the 'free port' for vagrant sexualities and 'forged' subjectivities. Newton, in 1993, traced the origins of the 'camp/theatrical' sensibility in 'the anti-Puritanism of the Elizabethan and Restoration London theatrical scene and the underground world of prostitution' (84), offering 'the conjunction of a relatively safe social space and the power of "make-believe"' (85), and 'the community feeling of play that is the theater, and the laughter and fantasy world and costumes' (86). Such conjunction was constituting – we might say – *a camp*, a space of alternative order, plausibility and belonging. This tradition is in fact, says Newton, 'cousin to lesbian butch/femme identities' (85); and under the aegis of queer theatricality camp has come to refer no longer to the limited field of gay 'effeminacy', but to the whole apparatus of theatricalised performance of gender signs and gender roles.

'Effeminacy' itself may in fact be inscribed in a history of semiotic derogation (on whose rearticulations the must-read is Sinfield 1994), one that voided the bourgeois male self of its permanence, stability, authenticity – a history within which it is highly significant that in the already mentioned 1909 Ware dictionary of late Victorian slang (cf. the Introduction) *camp* refers to 'persons of exceptional want of character' – to *queer* (of-questionable-character, not-in-a-normal-condition, forged) people. It is precisely through the inscription of effeminacy within 'the theatrical' that it seems legitimate to include among camp(ed up) feminist subjectivities not only the otherness of the butch-femme duo, or – as Pamela Robertson's *Guilty Pleasures* (1996, excerpted here) suggests – of heterosexual same-sex (female) mimicry. This inscription is in fact legitimated, within gay culture, by the inclusion of the very opposite of 'effeminacy', that is to say the macho, leathered clone, who in his excess of masculinity always merges (just think of the Village People or Freddie Mercury) with the 'effeminacy' nuances brought about by the excessively 'theatrical' and theatrically excessive.[3]

In this sense, camp as a 'gay sensibility' may be called, as Dollimore does, an oxymoron, for camp works through the parodic evacuation of the essential depth implied by the very notion of 'sensibility'. Camp does not simply hollow it out by dispensing with its features of depth, though. This mode of camp works through the *transgressive reinscription* of parodic displacement; it 'undermines the depth model of identity from inside' by performing it to excess; by rendering 'gender a question of aesthetics',[4] and sensibility – as argued in Eve Kosofsky Sedgwick's *Epistemology of the Closet*, excerpted here – a question of *spectacle*. Sedgwick opposes camp-*recognition* to Kitsch-*attribution*, unlike which it doesn't pass a judgement on the object and its audience based on objectivism (the negativity of Kitsch, its failure, being 'inherent') while respecting the cultural hierarchies of authority inscribed in the very notion of taste. Instead, camp recognition enacts an overcodifying question – *what if* – and an explicitly 'creative' perception, one that disregards the rules of 'correct' (faithful, coherent, permanent: *straight*) interpretation and value judgement. The camp recognising *eye/I* fantasies over a potential queer community and field of plausibility, wondering if 'the resistant, oblique, tangential investments of attention and attraction that I am able to bring to this spectacle are actually uncannily responsive to the resistant, oblique, tangential investments of the person, or of some of the people, who created it'; and if 'others whom I don't know or recognize can see it from the same "perverse" angle'. Such a reading, in other words, mediated by the lens of the camp 'perverse' spectacles, deviates the perception and stages its object, turns it into a fancy-dress party, into a performance – into a spectacle.

In its aristocratic detachment, and in the ludic or playful quality of its legitimate misreading and deviant decoding, camp spectacularises both subject and object of perception, performing the narcissistic (and self-deflating) glorification of the camp eye/I. And yet, the camp theatricality in itself takes part in the representation of the power it debunks. Not just because the theatre, as 'new historicist' research has explored in great detail and powerful argumentation in the last twenty years, embodies the site for assertion and challenge to the cultural order, investing the very modality through which power ratifies itself, and showing it as (empty) spectacle and performative act. As a highly ritualised and codified space, the camp theatrical reproduces the discursive conditions of its enactment, it *stages* indeed power by its 'perverse' relationship with the categories that ratify an order of truth and authenticity, and it does so – being a *queer* performativity – with a potentially *denaturalising* gesture. In fact, the ludic disrespect of camp for textual intentions and depth might be claimed to enact a demystifying theatricalisation of the violence lurking behind the respectable façade of liberal-humanist theory and practice of 'non-ideologically determined' (im/partial, respectful in its supposed neutrality of the full immanent transcendence of the text) interpretation. But in order to challenge such imperative by staging it, the imperative must be evoked and thus present, however *in absentia*, in the spectacles (both senses) of camp. As a *crossing* gesture, camp requires its transgressed principle of norm-ality, which is precisely what constitutes the dynamic of assimilating exclusion, of inversion between the authentic and the inauthentic (the 'drag'), and of transgression of a doxastic limit (a factual example may be offered in the outrageous Joe Orton–Edna Welthorpe 'debate' discussed by Dollimore).

From different perspectives and with different critical objects, Linda Mizejewski's 'Camp Among the Swastikas', June Reich's 'Genderfuck: The Law of the Dildo', also published in 1992, and Pamela Robertson's 1996 *Guilty Pleasures*, of which the introductory, axiomatic essay is excerpted here, find a common ground in precisely such queer enactment of the power relations activated by the camp spectacles, and in their exposure. Mizejewski's piece deals with Christopher Isherwood's camp queen Sally Bowles (from *Goodbye to Berlin*), whose history of stage and screen adaptations is explored at length in her *Divine Decadence* (1992). But the Weimar Germany setting of that short story inscribes the gender parody of the protagonist into the wider frame of the camp *mise en scène* of transgression and its containment, framing Sally Bowles, the Nazi swastikas and the spectator/reader in the refraction-play of twisted mirrorings. The totalitarian deployment of the spectacle, in its highly coded rituals, hypnotic fascination with hierarchy, uniforms and parades, contributes to the *display* (self-enactment/demystification) *of power* at the very core of the camp 'frivolity'. The grotesque performance of gender thus takes part in an intertwined representation of aestheticism, power and eroticism, as embodied in the Nazi society of the spectacle – what Sontag (1975) ascribed in fact to the queer 'fascination' of fascist theatricality.

The camp scene of Weimar Germany envisioned through the mirroring spectacles of Sally Bowles can in fact be traced, Mizejewski suggests, to the Bakhtinian carnivalesque. Another related (albeit distinct) suggestion offered in the 'Queering the Camp' introduction to this volume is that camp draws its constitutive element from the deployment of 'ephemeral apparatuses', whose historical situation – from the Baroque celebrations, with stage effects and false façades, to its retrieval within postmodern architecture – shows them as inextricably coupled to the visual enactment or display of power, its exposure as exhibition, and the challenge to the institutional 'architectures' of signification. With, indeed, all the ambiguity entailed by that display, echoing the ambiguity of the Bakhtinian carnivalesque as a space of 'authorised transgression', and the 'double-dealing' highlighted in parody by its duplicitous prefix (*para* meaning both 'against' and 'beside'). Within such a framework it may be possible to read June Reich's butch-femme 'genderfuck', the camp destabilisation of the Symbolic which constitutes an alternative, queer order of signification by means of the performance, or *erection*, of the dildo as 'forged' Lacanian phallus. But it also enables us to read, as queer fellow-travellers of Reich, and of other theorists of camp whose work we have met so far, the whole complex relationship of camp to visual culture, the filmic experience, and the psychoanalytic theories of female masquerade to which Pamela Robertson's essay offers an excellent overview,[5] positing the theoretical basis for the analysis of the feminist camp practice enacted by the same-sex mimicry of Mae West, Joan Crawford, and Madonna (three major figures in the camp gallery of female queens), conducted in *Guilty Pleasures*.

It is in the ambiguity of the ephemeral and parodic, inscribed in the camp performance of power, that we may finally place the closing essay of this section, Piggford's 'Who's That Girl?'. Piggford points to a tradition of 'female androgyny', overlapping with the one drawn by Robertson, spanning from its alleged origins in Virginia Woolf's queer biography, *Orlando*, to the altogether distant (and not just temporally) case of the pop singer Annie Lennox, whose mid-80s music videos and public 'drag acts' enact on a different stage the ephemeral apparatuses of both masculine and feminine power. Piggford grounds his oxymoronic 'female androgyny' on the context-boundness of all camp effect; and the context for Lennox's performances, in fact, is the mass-marketed 'transgression' that Madonna has so aptly mastered, which plunges us disorientingly into the complex scenario of the postmodern – and in so doing, Piggford's essay announces the scenario dealt within the next section.

NOTES

1. Sontag inferred that 'the diffusion of camp taste in the early 1960s should probably be credited with a considerable if inadvertent role in the upsurge of feminist consciousness in the late 1960s'.
2. 'Now, *homosexuality* is *not* camp. But you take a camp, and she turns around and she makes homosexuality funny, but not ludicrous; funny, but not ridiculous', says one of Newton's informants.
3. On the clone and on the masculinity camp see especially Segal 1990; Bredbeck 1993; Harper 1994; Michasiw 1994; Levine 1998. The campiness of the hypermasculine male is no 'novelty', though – both Sontag 1964 and Dyer 1976 included figures such as Victor Mature and John Wayne among their examples of camp excess.
4. Dollimore develops Beaver's 1981 suggestion on the Wildean double transgression (aesthetical and sexual) as a deviance from the principles (the real, the true, the right, and the authentic) of straight *norm*-ality.
5. Psychoanalitic theories of female masquerade with specific reference to camp have been mainly developed in studies in visual culture and film criticism (cf. Penley 1988; Modleski 1990; Ross 1990; Doane 1991; Tyler 1991, reprinted here; de Lauretis 1994; Moltke 1994, reprinted here; Benshoff 1997; and the essays in Gledhill 1991; Telotte 1991; Gever, Greyson & Parmar 1993; Wilton 1995; Horne & Lewis 1996) – just like, in fact, a significant bulk of criticism on camp, from the 1960s and 1970s writings of Susan Sontag, Andrew Sarris, Richard Schickel, John Simon, Parker Tyler, Jack Babuscio, Richard Dyer and Vito Russo.

13

FROM 'WILDE, NIETZSCHE, AND THE SENTIMENTAL RELATIONS OF THE MALE BODY'

Eve Kosofsky Sedgwick

SENTIMENTAL/ANTISENTIMENTAL

One night in Ithaca in the mid-1970s, I happened to tune into a country music station in the middle of a song I had never heard before. An incredibly pretty male voice that I half recognized as Willie Nelson's was singing:

> And he walks with me, and he talks with me,
> And he tells me I am his own.
> And the joy we share, as we tarry there,
> None other has ever known.
>
> He speaks; and the sound of his voice
> Is so sweet the birds hush their singing.
> And the melody that he gave to me
> Within my heart is ringing.
>
> And he walks with me, and he talks with me,
> And he tells me I am his own.
> And the joy we share, as we tarry there,
> None other has ever known.
>
> I'd stay in the garden with him
> Though the night around me be falling,
> But he bids me go through the voice of woe.
> His voice to me is calling . . .

Excerpted from *Epistemology of the Closet*, Berkeley-Los Angeles: California University Press, 1990.

This blew me away. I had already listened to a lot of Willie Nelson's songs about Waylon Jennings, which I always interpreted as love songs, but I never thought I was meant to; and nothing had prepared me for a song in which the love and sensuality between two men could be expressed with such a pellucid candor, on AM shit-kicker radio or maybe anywhere.

A decade later, I noted an article by J. M. Cameron in the *New York Review* about religious kitsch, which, he says, 'presents us with a serious theological problem and stands, far beyond the formal bounds of theology, for something amiss in our culture' ('Reply'):

> Kitsch must include more than the golden-haired Madonnas, the epicene statues of Jesus, the twee pictures of the infant Jesus … It must also include music, and the words of the liturgy, and hymns as well … [An] example is:
>
>> I come to the garden alone,
>> While the dew is still on the roses.
>> And the voice I hear,
>> Falling on my ear,
>> The Son of God discloses.
>> And He walks with me and He talks with me,
>> And He tells me I am his own.
>> And the joys we share, as we tarry there,
>> None other has ever known. ('The Historical Jesus', 21)

Cameron considers it important not only to

> describe … this as sentimental … but … discuss it as what it surely is, a terrible degradation of religion not simply as a purveyor of the false and the unworthy but as a kind of nastily flavored religious jello, a fouling of the sources of religious feeling. It is as though the image of Jesus is caught in a cracked, discolored distorting mirror in a fun house. (22)

Let me remark on two possible sources for Cameron's ostentatious disgust here, one topical, regarding the *subject* of sentimentality, and the other grammatical, regarding its *relations*. Topically, I have to wonder if a certain erotic foregrounding of the male body, what made the song so exciting to me, may not be tied to the stigmatization of these verses as sentimental and kitsch. I have mentioned the difficult kind of cynosure that proliferating images of Jesus, what Cameron refers to as the 'epicene statues', create within a homophobic economy of the male gaze. This scandal might account for the discomfort of a J. M. Cameron with the hymn, but it does leave us with questions about the local specifications of the sentimental, and in particular about its gender: if the sentimental, as we have been taught, coincides topically with the feminine, with the place of women, then why should the foregrounded *male* physique be in an indicative relation to it?

If indeed, however, as I want to hypothesize, the embodied male figure is a distinctive, thematic marker for the potent and devalued categories of kitsch and the sentimental in this century, then it is only the equivocal use of the first person ('And he tells me I am his own') – the first person that could be your grandmother but could be Willie Nelson, too, or even a distinguished professor of religion at the University of Toronto – that lends such a nasty flavor to the gender-slippage of this morsel of religious 'jello' down the befouled and violated gullet of Mr. J. M. Cameron. The gender-equivocal first person, or the impossible first person – such as the first person of someone dead or in process of dying – are common and, at least to me, peculiarly potent sentimental markers: my goose bumps, at any rate, are always poised for erection at 'She walks these hills in a long black veil, / Visits my grave when the night winds wail', and my waterworks are always primed for 'Rocky, I've never had to die before', or letters to Dear Abby purporting to be from seventeen-year-olds who were too young to die in that after-school car crash. Arguably, indeed, the *locus classicus* of this tonally and generically unsettling, ingenuous-disingenuous first-person mode, other versions of which can be found in any high school literary magazine, is the ballad that ends *Billy Budd*:

> No pipe to those halyards. – But aren't it all sham?
> A blur's in my eyes; it is dreaming that I am.
> A hatchet to my hawser? All adrift to go?
> The drum roll to grog, and Billy never know?
> But Donald he has promised to stand by the plank;
> So I'll shake a friendly hand ere I sink.
> But – no! It is dead then I'll be, come to think.
> I remember Taff the Welshman when he sank.
> And his cheek it was like the budding pink.
> But me they'll lash in hammock, drop me deep.
> Fathoms down, fathoms down, how I'll dream fast asleep.
> I feel it stealing now. Sentry, are you there?
> Just ease these darbies at the wrist,
> And roll me over fair!
> I am sleepy, and the oozy weeds about me twist. (1435)

These knowing activations of the ambiguities always latent in grammatical person as such, at any rate, point to the range of meanings of sentimentality that identify it, not as a thematic or a particular subject matter, but as a structure of relation, typically one involving the author- or audience-relations of spectacle; most often, where the epithet 'sentimental' itself is brought onto the scene, a discreditable or devalued one – the sentimental as the *insincere*, the *manipulative*, the *vicarious*, the *morbid*, the *knowing*, the *kitschy*, the *arch*.

To begin with the question of thematic content. In recent feminist criticism, particularly that involving nineteenth-century American women's fiction, a conscious rehabilitation of the category of 'the sentimental' has taken place, insofar as 'the sentimental' is seen as a derogatory code name for female bodies and the female domestic and 'reproductive' preoccupations of birth, socialization, illness, and death (see, for example, Tompkins). The devaluation of 'the sentimental', it is argued, has been of a piece with the devaluation of many aspects of women's characteristic experience and culture: in this view 'the sentimental', like the very lives of many women, is typically located in the private or domestic realm, has only a tacit or indirect connection with the economic facts of industrial marketplace production, is most visibly tied instead to the 'reproductive' preoccupations of birth, socialization, illness, and death, and is intensively occupied with relational and emotional labor and expression. Since one influential project of recent popular feminist thought has been to reverse the negative valuation attached to these experiences, emphases, and skills by both high culture and marketplace ideology, an attempted reversal of the negative charge attached to 'the sentimental' has been a natural corollary.

It would make sense to see a somewhat similar rehabilitation of 'the sentimental' as an important gay male project as well – indeed, one that has been in progress for close to a century under different names, including that of 'camp'. This gay male rehabilitation of the sentimental obviously occurs on rather different grounds from the feminist one, springing as it does from different experiences. The kid in Ohio who recognizes in 'Somewhere Over the Rainbow' the national anthem of a native country, his own, whose name he's never heard spoken is constructing a new family romance on new terms; and for the adult he becomes, the sense of value attaching to a 'private' realm, or indeed to expressive and relational skills, is likely to have to do with a specific history of secrecy, threat, and escape as well as with domesticity. A very specific association of gay male sexuality with tragic early death is recent, but the structure of its articulation is densely grounded in centuries of homoerotic and homophobic intertextuality;[1] the underpinnings here have long been in place for both a gay male sentimentality and, even more, a sentimental appropriation by the larger culture of male homosexuality as spectacle.

I have been arguing that constructions of modern Western gay male identity tend to be, not in the first place 'essentially gay', but instead (or at least also) in a very intimately responsive and expressive, though always oblique, relation to incoherences implicit in modern male *hetero*sexuality. Much might be said, then, following this clue, about the production and deployment, especially in contemporary US society, of an extraordinarily high level of self-pity in nongay men. Its effects on our national politics, and international ideology and intervention, have been pervasive. (Snapshot, here, of the tear-welling eyes of Oliver North.) In more intimate manifestations this straight male self-pity is often currently referred to (though it appears to exceed) the cultural effects of feminism, and is associated with, or appealed to in justification of, acts of violence, especially against women. For instance, the astonishing proportion of male violence done on separated wives, ex-wives, and ex-girlfriends, women just at the threshold of establishing a separate personal space, seems sanctioned and guided as much as reflected by the flood of books and movies in which such violence seems an expression not of the macho personality but of the maudlin. (One reason women get nervous when straight men claim to have received from feminism the gift of 'permission to cry'.) Although compulsively illustrated for public consumption (see, on this, the *New York Times*'s 'About Men', passim, or for that matter any newspaper's sports pages, or western novels, male country music, the dying-father-and-his-son stories in *The New Yorker*, or any other form of genre writing aimed at men), this vast national wash of masculine self-pity is essentially never named or discussed as a cultural and political fact; machismo and competitiveness, or a putative gentleness, take its place as subjects of nomination and analysis. Poised between shame and shamelessness, this regime of heterosexual male self-pity has the projective potency of an open secret. It would scarcely be surprising if gay men, like all women, were a main target of its scapegoating projections – viciously sentimental attributions of a vitiated sentimentality.

The sacred tears of the heterosexual man: rare and precious liquor whose properties, we are led to believe, are rivaled only by the *lacrimae Christi* whose secretion is such a specialty of religious kitsch. What charm, compared to this chrism of the gratuitous, can reside in the all too predictable tears of women, of gay men, of people with something to cry about? Nietzsche asks scornfully: 'Of what account is the pity of those who suffer!' But, he explains, 'a man who can do something, carry out a decision, remain true to an idea, hold on to a woman, punish and put down insolence ... in short a man who is by nature a *master* – when such a man has pity, well! *that* pity has value!' (*Beyond*, 198). Both the mass and the high culture of our century ratify this judgment, by no means stopping short at such a man's pity for himself. Cry-y-yin' – lonely teardrops, teardrops cryin' in the rain, blue velvet through the tracks of my tears, the tears of a clown, maybe Cathy's clown, the Red Skelton clown by whose tears every show of lowbrow art must be baptized, the Norman Mailer or Harold Bloom buffoon by whose tears ...

If these modern images borrow some of their lasting power from the mid-nineteenth-century association of sentimentality with the place of women, what their persistence and proliferation dramatize is something new: a change of gears, occupying the period from the 1880s through the First World War, by which the exemplary instance of the sentimental ceases to be a woman per se, but instead becomes the body of a man who, like Captain Vere, physically dramatizes, *embodies* for an audience that both desires and cathartically identifies with him, a struggle of masculine identity with emotions or physical stigmata stereotyped as feminine. Nietzsche says, 'With hard men, intimacy is a thing of shame – and' (by implication: therefore) 'something precious' (*Beyond*, 87). This male body is not itself named as the place or topos of sentimentality, the way the home, the female body, and female reproductive labor had been in the mid-nineteenth century. Rather, the relations of figuration and perception that circulate around it, including antisentimentality, might instead be said to enact sentimentality as a trope.

How, then, through the issue of sentimentality can we bring to Nietzsche questions that Wilde and the reading of Wilde may teach us to ask? Gore Vidal begins a recent essay on Wilde: 'Must one have a heart of stone to read *The Ballad of Reading Gaol* without laughing?' (1063). The opening points in only too many directions. Between it and the same remark made by Wilde himself, a century earlier, about the death of Little Nell, where to look for the wit-enabling relation? One story to tell is the historical/thematic one just sketched: that whereas in the nineteenth century it was images of women in relation to domestic suffering and death that occupied the most potent, symptomatic, and, perhaps, friable or volatile place in the sentimental *imaginaire* of middle-class culture, for the succeeding century – the century inaugurated by Wilde among others – it has been images of agonistic male self-constitution. Thus the careful composition of *The Ballad of Reading Gaol*, where Wilde frames his own image between, or even as, those of a woman-murdering man and the Crucified, sets in motion every conceivable mechanism by which most readers know how to enter into the circuit of the sentimental:

> Alas! it is a fearful thing
> To feel another's guilt!
> For, right, within, the Sword of Sin
> Pierced to its poisoned hilt,
> And as molten lead were the tears we shed
> For the blood we had not spilt.
>
> And as one sees most fearful things
> In the crystal of a dream,
> We saw the greasy hempen rope
> Hooked to the blackened beam,
> And heard the prayer the hangman's snare
> Strangled into a scream.
> And all the woe that moved him so
> That he gave that bitter cry,
> And the wild regrets, and the bloody sweats,
> None knew so well as I:
> For he who lives more lives than one
> More deaths than one must die. (732, 735)

Think of the cognate, ravishing lines of Cowper –

> We perished, each alone,
> But I beneath a rougher sea
> And whelmed in deeper gulfs than he
> (lines 64–66)

– and the cognate sentimental markers (the vicariousness, the uncanny shifting first person of after death, the heroic self-pity) that give them their awful appropriateness, their appropriability, to the narrow, imperious, incessant self-reconstitution of, say, Virginia Woolf's paterfamilias Mr. Ramsay. Yet the author of *Reading Gaol* is also the creator of 'Ernest in town and Jack in the country' and of Mr. Bunbury, of men whose penchant for living more lives than one, and even dying more deaths, not to speak of having more christen-ings, seems on the contrary to give them a fine insouciance about such identity issues as the name of the father – which his sons, who have forgotten it, have to look up in the Army Lists. 'Lady Bracknell, I hate to seem inquisitive, but would you kindly inform me who I am?' *(Earnest*, 181). At the same time, the precise grammatical matrix of even the most anarchic Wildean wit still tends toward the male first-person singular in the mode of descriptive self-definition. 'None of us are perfect. I myself am peculiarly susceptible to draughts'. 'I can resist anything except temptation'. 'I have nothing to declare except my genius'. The project of constructing the male figure is not made any the less central by being rendered as nonsense; in fact, one might say that it's the candor with which Wilde is often capable of centering this male project in the field of vision that enables him to operate so explosively on it.

The squeam-inducing power of texts like *De Profundis* and *Reading Gaol* – and I don't mean to suggest that they are a bit the less powerful for often making the flesh crawl – may be said to coincide with a thematic choice made in each of them: that the framing and display of the male body be placed in the explicit context of the displayed body of Jesus. One way of reading *The Picture of Dorian Gray* would tell the same story, since the fall of that novel from sublime free play into sentimental potency comes with the framing and hanging of the beautiful male body as a visual index of vicarious expiation.

That the circumference of sentimental danger in Wilde's writing should have at its center the image of a crucified man would have been no surprise to Nietzsche. Nietzsche oriented, after all, his own narrative of the world-historical vitiation of the species around the fulcrum point of the same dis-played male body; appropriately his meditations concerned, not the inherent meaning of the crucifixion or the qualities of the man crucified, but instead the seemingly irreversible relations of pity, desire, vicariousness, and mendacity instituted in the mass response to that image.

Evidently Nietzsche's ability to describe the relations around the cross from a new perspective depends on an Odyssean trick: blindfolding himself against a visual fixation on the focal figure aloft, deaf to the aural penetration of his distant appeal, Nietzsche (like the jello-phobic J. M. Cameron) gives himself over, in his discussions of Christianity, to the other three senses – taste, touch, smell, those that least accommodate distance, the ones that French designates by the verb *sentir* – and in the first place to the nose. 'I was the first to sense – *smell* – the lie as a lie ... My genius is in my nostrils' *(Ecce*, 126). Possessing 'a perfectly uncanny sensitivity of the instinct for cleanliness, so that I perceive physiologically – *smell* – the proximity or – what am I saying? – the innermost parts, the "entrails", of every soul' 48–9), Nietzsche is alive to 'the complete lack of psychological cleanliness in the priest' (*Anti*, 169), is able 'to *smell* what dirty fellows had [with Christianity] come out on top' (183). He gags most on the proximity into which this spectacle of suffering draws the men who respond to it: 'pity instantly smells of the mob' (*Ecce*, 44). And in this pheno-menon he finds the origin of virtually every feature of the world he inhabits. 'One who smells not only with his nose but also with his eyes and ears will notice everywhere these days an air as of a lunatic asylum or sanatorium ... so paltry, so stealthy, so dishonest, so sickly-sweet! Here ... the air stinks of secretiveness and pent-up emotion'.[2]

Nietzsche, then, is the psychologist who put the scent back into sentimen-tality. And he did it by the same gesture with which he put the rank and the rancid back into rancor. The most durably productive of Nietzsche's psycho-logical judgments was to place the invidious, mendacious mechanism rather mysteriously called *ressentiment* – re-sniffing, one might say as much as 'resent-ment', or re-tonguing, re-palpating – at the center of his account of such ordinary anno Domini virtues as love, goodwill, justice, fellow-feeling, egali-tarianism, modesty, compassion. *Ressentiment* was for Nietzsche the essence of Christianity and hence of all modern psychology ('there never was but one psychology, that of the priest');[3] and the genius of his nostrils repeatedly reveals these apparently simple and transparent impulses as complex, unstable lami-nates of self-aggrandizement and delectation with self-contempt and abnega-tion, fermented to a sort of compost under the pressure of time, of internal contradiction, and of deconstructive work like Nietzsche's own. The *re*-prefix of *ressentiment* marks a space of degeneration and vicariousness: the nonsin-gularity of these laminates as *re*doublings of one's own motives, and their nonoriginality as *re*flexes of the impulses of others. Thus the sentimental mis-naming, in the aftermath of the crucifixion, of its observers' sensuality and will-to-power as pity becomes the model for the whole class of emotions and bonds of which Nietzsche was the privileged analyst:

> At first sight, this problem of pity and the ethics of pity (I am strongly opposed to our modern sentimentality in these matters) may seem very special, a marginal issue. But whoever sticks with it and learns how to ask questions will have the same experience that I had: a vast new panorama will open up before him; strange and vertiginous possibilities will invade him; every variety of suspicion, distrust, fear will come to the surface; his belief in ethics of any kind will begin to be shaken. (*Genealogy*, 154)

Sentimentality, insofar as it overlaps with *ressentiment* in a structure we would not be the first to call ressentimentality, represents modern emotion itself in Nietzsche's thought: modern emotion as vicariousness and misrepresentation, but also as sensation brought to the quick with an insulting closeness.

DIRECT/VICARIOUS; ART/KITSCH

It would be hard to overestimate the importance of vicariousness in defining the sentimental. The strange career of 'sentimentality', from the later eighteenth century when it was a term of high ethical and aesthetic praise, to the twentieth when it can be used to connote, beyond pathetic weakness, an actual principle of evil – and from its origins when it circulated freely between genders, through the feminocentric Victorian version, to the twentieth-century one with its complex and distinctive relation to the male body – is a career that displays few easily articulable consistencies; and those few are not, as we have seen, consistencies of subject matter. Rather, they seem to inhere in the nature of the investment by a viewer in a subject matter. The sacralizing contagion of tears was the much reenacted primal scene of the sentimental in the eighteenth century. If its early celebrants found it relatively (only relatively) easy to take for granted the disinterestedness and beneficence of the process by which a viewer 'sympathized' with the sufferings of a person viewed, however, every psychological and philosophic project of the same period gave new facilities for questioning or even discrediting that increasingly unsimple-looking bond (on this, see Marshall; and Caplan). Most obviously, the position of sentimental spectatorship seemed to offer coverture for differences in material wealth (the bourgeois weeping over the spectacle of poverty) or sexual entitlement (the man swooning over the spectacle of female virtue under siege) – material or sexual exploitations that might even be perpetuated or accelerated by the nonaccountable viewer satisfactions that made the point of their rehearsal. The tacitness and consequent nonaccountability of the identification between sufferer and sentimental spectator, at any rate, seems to be the fulcrum point between the most honorific and the most damning senses of 'sentimental'. For a spectator to misrepresent the quality or locus of her or his implicit participation in a scene – to misrepresent, for example, desire as pity, *Schadenfreude* as sympathy, envy as disapproval – would be to enact defining instances of the worst meaning of the epithet; the defining instances, increasingly, of the epithet itself. The prurient; the morbid; the wishful; the snobbish;[4] the knowing; the arch: these denote subcategories of the sentimental, to the extent that each involves a covert reason for, or extent or direction of, identification through a spectatorial route. As Nietzsche says of Renan (with whom he has so much in common), 'I can think of nothing as nauseating as such an "objective" armchair, such a perfumed epicure of history, half priest, half satyr ... [S]uch 'spectators' embitter me against the spectacle more than the spectacle itself' (*Genealogy*, 294).

   It follows from this that the description of scenes, or even texts, as intrinsically 'sentimental' (or prurient, morbid, etc.) is extremely problematical, not least because such descriptions tend to carry an unappealable authority: the epithet 'sentimental' is *always* stamped in indelible ink. 'Sentimental' with its quiverful of subcategories: don't they work less as static grids of analysis against which texts can be flatly mapped than as projectiles whose bearing depends utterly on the angle and impetus of their discharge? Elsewhere, we discussed 'worldliness' as an attribution whose force depended, not on its being attached firmly to a particular person or text, but on its ability to delineate a chain of attributive angles of increasing privilege and tacitness (cf. Sedgwick 1990: 91–130); a 'worldly' person, for instance, is one whose cognitive privilege over a world is being attested, but the person who can attest it implicitly claims an even broader angle of cognitive privilege out of which the 'worldly' angle can be carved, while a silent proffer to the reader or auditor of a broader angle yet can form, as we discussed, the basis for powerful interpellations. 'The sentimental' and its damning subcategories work in an analogous way. Themselves descriptions of relations of vicariousness, the attributive career of each of these adjectives is again a vicariating one. For instance, it is well known that in Proust the snobbish characters are easy to recognize because they are the only ones who are able to recognize snobbism in others – hence, the only ones who really disapprove of it. Snobbism, as René Girard points out, can be discussed and attributed only by snobs, who are always right about it except in their own disclaimers of it (72–73). The same is true of the phenomenon of 'the sentimental' as a whole and of its other manifestations such as prurience and morbidity. *Honi soit qui mal y pense* is both the watchword and the structural principle of sentimentality-attribution. What chain of attribution is being extended, under pretense of being cut short, when Nietzsche exclaims, 'O you sentimental hypocrites, you lechers! You lack innocence in your desire and therefore you slander all desire' (*Zarathustra*, 122–23)? What tacit relations of prurient complicity are compounded under the prurience-attribution of Nietzsche's discussion of the *Law-Book of Manu*:

> One sees immediately that it has a real philosophy behind it, *in* it . . . – it gives even the most fastidious psychologist something to bite on . . . All the things upon which Christianity vents its abysmal vulgarity, procreation for example, women, marriage, are here treated seriously, with reverence, with love and trust. How can one actually put into the hands of women and children a book containing the low-minded saying 'To avoid fornication let every man have his own wife, and let every woman have her own husband . . . for it is better to marry than burn'? And is it *allowable* to be a Christian as long as the origin of man is Christianized, that is to say *dirtied*, with the concept of the *immaculata conceptio*? . . . I know of no book in which so many tender and kind remarks are addressed to woman as in the Law-Book of Manu; these old graybeards and saints have a way of being polite to women which has perhaps never been surpassed. 'A woman's mouth' – it says in one place – 'a girl's breast, a child's prayer, the smoke of a sacrifice are always pure'. Another passage: 'There is nothing purer than the light of the sun, the shadow of a cow, air, water, fire and a girl's breath'. A final passage – perhaps also a holy lie – : 'All the openings of the body above the navel are pure, all below impure. Only in the case of a girl is the whole body pure'. (*Anti*, 176)

Vidal's score off Wilde, 'Must one have a heart of stone . . . ?', seems to depend on the same structure. If the joke were that the Wilde who took advantage of the enormous rhetorical charge to be gained from hurling at Dickens the aspersion of sentimentality also at another time, perhaps later in his life when the hideous engines of state punishment had done their work of destroying the truth and gaiety of his sensibility, developed a proneness to the same awful failing, that would be one thing. Perhaps, though, the point is that there isn't a differentiation to be *made* between sentimentality and its denunciation. But then we are dealing with a joke that can only be on Gore Vidal himself, whose hypervigilance for lapses in the tough-mindedness of others can then only suggest that he in turn must be, as they say, insecure about his own. It may be only those who are themselves prone to these vicariating impulses who are equipped to detect them in the writing or being of others; but it is also they who for several reasons tend therefore to be perturbed in their presence.

By 'they' here I definitionally mean 'we'. In order to dispense with the further abysmal structuring of this bit of argument through an infinity of insinuating readings of 'other' writers, let me try to break with the tradition of personal disclaimer and touch ground myself with a rapid but none the less genuine guilty plea to possessing the attributes, in a high degree, of at the very least sentimentality, prurience, and morbidity. (On the infinitesimally small chance that any skepticism could greet this confession, I can offer as evidence of liability – or, one might say, of expert qualification – the pathos injected into the paraphrase of *Esther* (see Sedgwick 1990), which I loved composing but which is rendered both creepy and, perhaps, rhetorically efficacious by a certain obliquity in my own trail of identifications. As a friend who disliked those paragraphs put it acidly, it's not me risking the coming out, but it's all too visibly me having the salvational fantasies.)

Clearly, this understanding of 'sentimentality' makes problems for a project, whether feminist- or gay-centered, of rehabilitating the sentimental. The problem is not just that the range of discrediting names available for these forms of attention and expression is too subtle, searching, descriptively useful, and rhetorically powerful to be simply jettisoned, though that is true enough. A worse problem is that since antisentimentality itself becomes, in this structure, the very engine and expression of modern sentimental relations, to enter into the discourse of sentimentality at any point or with any purpose is almost inevitably to be caught up in a momentum of essentially scapegoating attribution.

The attempt to construct versions of the present argument has offered, I might as well say, startlingly clear evidence of the force of this momentum. Given a desire to raise the questions I'm raising here, it's all too easy to visualize the path of least resistance of such an argument. The ballistic force of the attribution of 'sentimentality' is so intense today that I've found it amazingly difficult to think about any analytic or revaluative project involving it that wouldn't culminate its rehabilitative readings with some yet more damning unmasking of the 'true', and far more dangerous, sentimentality of an author not previously associated with the term. This would be congruent with a certain difficult-to-avoid trajectory of universalizing understandings of homo/heterosexual definition – Irigaray's writing about the 'hom(m)osexual' is the *locus classicus* of this trajectory, although feminist thought has no monopoly on it – according to which authoritarian regimes or homophobic masculinist culture may be damned on the grounds of being *even more homosexual* than gay male culture (see Owens on this point). And each of these trajectories of argument leads straight to terrible commonplaces about fascism. In the case of Nietzsche and Wilde, the most readily available – the almost irresistibly available – path of argument would have been to use the manifestly gay Wilde as a figure for the necessity and truth of a 'good' version of sentimentality, then to prove that the ostensibly heterosexual and antisentimental Nietzsche was, like Wilde, maybe even more actively than Wilde because unacknowledgedly, and in ways that could be shown to have implications for his writing and thought, 'really' homosexual, and at the same time 'really' sentimental.

Why should it be so hard to think about these issues without following an argumentative path that must lead to the exposure of a supposed fascist precursor as the *true* homosexual, or especially as the *true* sentimentalist? I have tried to avoid that path of exposure, for four reasons. First, of course, Nietzsche, like Whitman, is a cunning and elusive writer on whose self-ignorance one never does well to bet the mortgage money. Second, though, such a trajectory of argument presupposes that one has somewhere in reserve a stable and intelligible definition for both what is 'really homosexual' and what is 'really sentimental', while our historical argument is exactly the opposite: that those definitions are neither historically stable in this period nor internally coherent. Third, obviously, that argument necessarily depends for its rhetorical if not its analytic force on the extreme modern cultural devaluations of both categories, the homosexual and the sentimental – a dependence that had better provoke discomfort, however much Nietzsche's own writing may sometimes be complicit in those fatal devaluations. And finally, the most productive questions we can ask about these definitional issues must be, I think, not 'What is the true meaning, the accurate assignment of these labels?' but, rather, 'What are the relations instituted by the giving of these labels?' In that case, any enabling analytic distance we might have would be vitiated to the degree that our argument was so aimed as to climax with this act of naming.

The categories 'kitsch' and 'camp' suggest, perhaps, something about how the formation of modern gay identities has intervened to reimagine these potent audience relations. Kitsch is a classification that redoubles the aggressive power of the epithet 'sentimental' by, on the one hand, claiming to exempt the speaker of the epithet from the contagion of the kitsch object, and, on the other, positing the existence of a true *kitsch consumer* or, in Hermann Broch's influential phrase, 'kitsch-man' (Broch, 295). Kitsch-man is never the person who uses the word 'kitsch'; kitsch-man's ability to be manipulated by the kitsch object and the kitsch creator is imagined to be seamless and completely uncritical. Kitsch-man is seen either as the exact double of the equally unenlightened producer of kitsch or as the unresistant dupe of his cynical manipulation: that is to say, the imagined kitsch-producer is *either* at the abjectly low consciousness level of kitsch-man or at the transcendent, and potentially abusive, high consciousness level of the man who can recognize kitsch when he sees it. In the highly contestative world of kitsch and kitsch-recognition there is no mediating level of consciousness; so it is necessarily true that the structure of contagion whereby it *takes* one to *know one*, and whereby any object about which the question 'Is it kitsch?' can be asked immediately *becomes* kitsch, remains, under the system of kitsch-attribution, a major scandal, one that can induce self-exemption or cynicism but nothing much more interesting than that.

Camp, on the other hand, seems to involve a gayer and more spacious angle of view. I think it may be true that, as Robert Dawidoff suggests, the typifying gesture of camp is really something amazingly simple: the moment at which a consumer of culture makes the wild surmise, 'What if whoever made this was gay too?'[5] Unlike kitsch-attribution, then, camp-recognition doesn't ask, 'What kind of debased creature could possibly be the right audience for this spectacle?' Instead, it says *what if*: What if the right audience for this were exactly me? What if, for instance, the resistant, oblique, tangential investments of attention and attraction that I am able to bring to this spectacle are actually uncannily responsive to the resistant, oblique, tangential investments of the person, or of some of the people, who created it? And what if, furthermore, others whom I don't know or recognize can see it from the same 'perverse' angle? Unlike kitsch-attribution, the sensibility of camp-recognition always sees that it is dealing in reader relations and in projective fantasy (projective though not infrequently true) about the spaces and practices of cultural production. Generous because it acknowledges (unlike kitsch) that its perceptions are necessarily also creations,[6] it's little wonder that camp can encompass effects of great delicacy and power in our highly sentimental-attributive culture.

Neither rehabilitation nor rubbishing, wholesale, is a possible thing to do, then, with these representational meanings of 'sentimental', 'antisentimental', or even 'ressentimental'; they stand for rhetorical – that is to say, for relational – figures, figures of concealment, obliquity, vicariousness, and renaming, and their ethical bearings can thus be discussed only in the multiple contexts of their writing and reading. Though each could be called a form of bad faith, each can also be seen as a figure of irrepressible desire and creativity – if only the sheer, never to be acknowledged zest of finding a way to frame and reproduce the pain or the pleasure of another. 'Good', Nietzsche remarks, but his affect here may be rather enigmatic, 'is no longer good when your neighbour takes it into his mouth' (*Beyond*, 53).

NOTES

1. One might look, for instance, to Achilles and Patroclos, to Virgilian shepherds, to David and Jonathan, to the iconography of St. Sebastian, to elegiac poetry by Milton, Tennyson, Whitman, and Housman, as well as to the Necrology of Vito Russo's *Celluloid Closet*...

2. 'What noble eloquence flows from the lips of these ill-begotten creatures! What sugary, slimy, humble submissiveness swims in their eyes!' Nietzsche, *Genealogy*, 258–9.

3. Paraphrased in Deleuze & Guattari, 110.

4. I mean 'snobbish', of course, not in the sense of a mere preference for social altitude, but in the fuller sense explicated by Girard, the one whose foundational principle is Groucho Marx's 'I wouldn't belong to any club that would have me as a member': it is the tacit evacuation of the position of self that makes snob relations such a useful model for understanding sentimental relations. See Girard, 53–82, 216–28.

5. Personal communication, 1986. Of course, discussions of camp have proliferated since Susan Sontag's 'Notes on "Camp"'. One of the discussions that resonates most with this book's emphasis on the open secret is Core 1984.

6. 'CAMP depends on where you pitch it ... CAMP is in the eyes of the beholder, especially if the beholder is camp'. Core 1984: 7.

REFERENCES

Broch, Hermann, *Einer Bemerkungen zum Problem des Kitsches*, in *Dichten und Erkennen*, vol. I, Zurich: Rhein-Verlag, 1955.

Cameron, J. M., 'The Historical Jesus', *New York Review of Books*, 33, 13 February 1986, 21.

——, Reply to a letter, *New York Review of Books*, 33, 29 May 1986, 56–7.

Caplan, Jay, *Framed Narratives: Diderot's Genealogy of the Beholder*, Minneapolis: U of Minnesota P, 1986.

Cowper, William, 'The Castaway', in H. S. Milford (ed.), *Complete Poetical Works*, Oxford: Humphrey Milford, 1913.

Deleuze, Gilles & Felix Guattari, *Anti-Oedipus: Capitalism and Schizophrenia*, New York: Viking, 1977.

Girard, René, *Deceit, Desire, and the Novel: Self and Other in Literary Structure*, Baltimore: Johns Hopkins UP, 1965.

Marshall, David, *The Surprising Effects of Sympathy: Marivaux, Diderot, Rousseau, and Mary Shelley*, U of Chicago P, 1989.

Nietzsche, Friedrich, *The Anti-Christ*, in *Twilight of the Idols / The Anti-Christ*, New York: Viking Penguin, 1968.

——, *Beyond Good and Evil*, New York: Viking Penguin, 1973.

——, *Ecce Homo*, New York: Penguin, 1979.

——, *The Genealogy of Morals*, in *The Birth of Tragedy and The Genealogy of Morals*, New York: Doubleday Anchor, 1956.

——, *Thus Spoke Zarathustra*, New York: Viking Compass, 1966.

Owens, Craig, 'Outlaws: Gay Men in Feminism', in Alice Jardine & Paul Smith (eds.), *Men in Feminism*, New York: Methuen, 1987, 219–32.

Tompkins, Jane P., *Sensational Designs: The Cultural Work of American Fiction, 1790–1860*, New York: Oxford UP, 1985,

Vidal, Gore, 'A Good Man and a Perfect Play', *Times Literary Supplement*, 28 October 1987, 1063.

Wilde, Oscar, *The Ballad of Reading Gaol*, in *The Complete Works*, Twickenham, Middlesex: Hamlyn, 1963.

——, *The Importance of Being Earnest*, in *The Complete Works*, Twickenham, Middlesex: Hamlyn, 1963.

14

POST/MODERN: ON THE GAY SENSIBILITY, OR THE PERVERT'S REVENGE ON AUTHENTICITY

Jonathan Dollimore

To be really modern one should have no soul. (Oscar Wilde)

Will he force me to think that homosexuals have more imagination than the ... others? No, but they are more frequently called upon to exercise it. (André Gide)

THE ELUSIVE HOMOSEXUAL SENSIBILITY

Separately and in different ways, Susan Sontag and George Steiner have suggested that a (or 'the') homosexual sensibility is a major influence in the formation of modern culture. In 1964 Sontag wrote that 'Jews and homosexuals are the outstanding creative minorities in contemporary urban culture. Creative, that is, in the truest sense: they are creators of sensibilities. The two pioneering forces of modern sensibility are Jewish moral seriousness and homosexual aestheticism and irony'. She seeks to substantiate this claim in the famous essay from which it is taken (1964b, rpt. 1966: 290).

For Steiner homosexuality is if anything even more central to, and definitive of, the modern. 'Since about 1890', he believes, 'homosexuality has played a vital part in Western culture'. Whereas 'heterosexuality is the very essence of ... classic realism', a 'radical homosexuality' figures in modernity, particularly in its self-referentiality and narcissism; indeed 'homosexuality could be construed as a creative rejection of the philosophic and conventional realism, of the *mundanity* and extroversion of classic and nineteenth century feeling'. Further,

Reprinted from *Sexual Dissidence: Augustine to Wilde, Freud to Foucault*, Oxford: Clarendon, 1991.

homosexuality in part made possible 'that exercise in solipsism, that remorseless mockery of philistine common sense and bourgeois realism which is modern art' (Steiner 1975, rpt. 1978: 115, 117, 118). Steiner's association of homosexuality with narcissism, solipsism, and the refusal of referentiality obviously suggests reservations about both modernism (as he conceives it) and the efficacy of the homosexual influence upon it,[1] and it comes as no surprise that in his most recent book he launches a strong attack on the former. Steiner now contends that two historical moments, the one epitomized in Mallarmé's 'disjunction of language from external reference', and the other in Rimbaud's 'deconstruction of the self' – *je est un autre* (I is (an)other) – splinter the foundations of the Western tradition and precipitate it into the crisis of modernity. Rimbaud would seem to be especially culpable since 'the deconstructions of semantic forms, the destabilizations of meaning, as we have known them during the past decades, derive from Rimbaud's dissolution of the self'. Compared to these two cultural moments, 'even the political revolutions and great wars in modern European history are, I would venture, of the surface' (Steiner, 101, 94–6).

Steiner and Sontag are in a sense correct about the centrality of homosexuality to modern culture. But the argument of this book is that its centrality is quite otherwise than they suggest. Steiner's ludicrous generalizations stem in part from the very notion of defining cultures and history in terms of a sensibility. Even a cursory look at gay history and culture suggests that the sweep and conclusions of his argument are questionable at virtually every turn, as indeed is the very notion of a homosexual sensibility.[2]

Sontag's article at least has the virtue of tentativeness; it is in the form of notes (dedicated to Oscar Wilde), and acknowledges the difficulty of defining a sensibility, especially one as 'fugitive' as this (277). But still questions abound: is this sensibility transcultural, or historically rooted in the (varying) histories of the representation of homosexuality? Is it a direct expression of homosexuality, or an indirect expression of its repression and/or sublimation? Is it defined in terms of the sexuality of (say) the individual or artist who expresses or possesses it – and does that mean that no non-homosexual can possess/express it? I shall suggest that there is a sense in which the very notion of a homosexual sensibility is a contradiction in terms. I am interested in an aspect of it which exists, if at all, in terms of that contradiction – of a parodic critique of the essence of sensibility as conventionally understood.

Michel Foucault argues that in the modern period sex has become definitive of the truth of our being (see Dollimore 1991: 219–27). As such, sexuality in its normative forms constitutes a 'truth' connecting inextricably with other truths and norms not explicitly sexual. This is a major reason why sexual deviance is found threatening: in deviating from normative truth and the 'nature' which underpins it, such deviance shifts and confuses the norms of truth and being throughout culture. Wilde's transgressive aesthetic simultaneously confirmed and exploited this inextricable connection between the sexual and the (apparently) non-sexual, between sexual perversion and social subversion, and does so through Wilde's own version of that connection: 'what paradox was to me in the sphere of thought, perversity became to me in the sphere of passion' (*De Profundis*, 466).

If I had to give a single criterion of that dubious category, the homosexual sensibility, it would be this connection between perversity and paradox – if only because it suggests why that sensibility does not exist as such. As we have seen (see Dollimore 1991: 3–17, 39–63), Wilde's transgressive aesthetic writes desire into a discourse of liberation inseparable from an inversion and displacement of dominant categories of subjective depth (the depth model). It is from just these categories that notions of sensibility traditionally take their meaning. Additionally for Wilde, perverse desire is not only an agency of displacement, it is partly constituted by that displacement and the transgressive aesthetic which informs it. Just as in reverse discourse the categories of subordination are turned back upon the regimes of truth which disqualify, so this 'other' sensibility is in part affirmed as an inversion and absence of sensibility's traditional criteria. Perverse desire is transvalued, socially, sexually, and aesthetically. *Dorian Gray* describes moments when 'the passion for sin, or for what the world calls sin' is utterly overwhelming

> and conscience is either killed, or, if it lives at all, lives but to give rebellion its fascination, and disobedience its charm. For all sins, as theologians weary not of reminding us, are sins of disobedience. When that high spirit, that morning-star of evil, fell from heaven, it was as a rebel that he fell. (210)

Law and conscience are subjected to the perverse dynamic, being made to enable and intensify the rebellion they were supposed to prevent; likewise with Wilde's transgressive aesthetic in the realm of desire and culture.

Wilde lived an anarchic and a political homosexuality simultaneously. Richard Ellmann describes him as 'conducting, in the most civilized way, an anatomy of his society, and a radical reconsideration of its ethics ... His greatness as a writer is partly the result of the enlargement of sympathy which he demanded for society's victims' (xiv). I agree, and this can stand as a cogent if incomplete description of what is meant by a political homosexuality. But Wilde also fashioned his transgressive aesthetic into a celebration of anarchic deviance, and this is yet another factor which makes it difficult to identify the sensibility involved. There is a positive desire to transgress and disrupt, and a destructiveness, even a running to one's own destruction, paradoxically creative. Though in a different way, what we have seen to be true of Gide was also true of Wilde: 'running foul of the law in his sexual life was a stimulus to thought on every subject ... His new sexual direction liberated his art. It also liberated his critical faculty' (Ellmann, 270).

Conformity angered and bored Wilde. It is not clear which, the anger or the boredom, was thought to be the more insulting, but both were expressed as that arrogance for which he was often hated. Yeats recalls receiving a letter from Lionel Johnson 'denouncing Wilde with great bitterness'; Johnson believed that Wilde got a 'sense of triumph and power, at every dinner-table he dominated, from the knowledge that he was guilty of that sin which, more than any other possible to man, would turn all those people against him if they but knew' (cited in Yeats, 285). Maybe Johnson was paranoid; that does not stop him being correct. Gide at the end of his life remarked that Wilde only began to live after dark as it were, away from most of those who knew him (*So Be It*, 27). But the point here is that Wilde also lived in terms of the discrepancy between his 'public' and 'private' selves, and took pleasure from it – from having a sexual identity elsewhere at the same time as being socially 'here'.

The anarchic and the political, the anger and the boredom, are all active in Wilde's transgressive aesthetic, and most especially when the survival strategies of subordination – subterfuge, lying, evasion – are aesthetically transvalued into weapons of attack, but ever working obliquely through irony, ambiguity, mimicry, and impersonation.

Which brings us to camp, considered by some to be the essence of the homosexual sensibility, by others, both within and without gay culture, as virtually the opposite: the quintessence of an alienated, inadequate sensibility. The definition of camp is as elusive as the sensibility itself, one reason being simply that there are different kinds of camp. I am concerned here with that mode of camp which undermines the categories which exclude it, and does so through parody and mimicry. But not from the outside: this kind of camp undermines the depth model of identity from inside, being a kind of parody and mimicry which hollows out from within, making depth recede into its surfaces. Rather than a direct repudiation of depth, there is a performance of it to excess: depth is undermined by being taken to and beyond its own limits. The masquerade of camp becomes less a self-concealment than a kind of attack, and untruth a virtue: many a young man, says Wilde, 'starts with the natural gift of exaggeration which, if encouraged could flourish. Unfortunately he usually comes to nothing, either falling into the bad habit of accuracy, or frequents the society of the aged and well informed' ('Decay of Lying', 294). Compare John Mitzel: 'gay people are, I have learned, in the truest sense of the word, *fabulous* ... The controlling agents of the status quo may know the *power* of lies; dissident sub-cultures, however, are closer to knowing their value' (cited in Bronski 1984: 41).

The hollowing-out of the deep self is pure pleasure, a release from the subjective correlatives of dominant morality (normality, authenticity, etc.) – one reason why camp also mocks the *Angst*-ridden spiritual emptiness which characterizes the existential lament. Camp thereby negotiates some of the lived contradictions of subordination, simultaneously refashioning as a weapon of attack an oppressive identity inherited *as* subordination, and hollowing out dominant formations responsible for that identity in the first instance. So it is misleading to say that camp is the gay sensibility; camp is an invasion and subversion of other sensibilities, and works via parody, pastiche, and exaggeration.

Jack Babuscio has suggested that the homosexual experience of passing for straight leads to a 'heightened awareness and appreciation for disguise, impersonation, the projection of personality, and the distinctions to be made between instinctive and theatrical behaviour' (1977: 45). Richard Dyer remarks, in relation to Babuscio, that the gay sensibility 'holds together qualities that are elsewhere felt as antithetical: theatricality and authenticity . . . intensity and irony, a fierce assertion of extreme feeling with a deprecating sense of its absurdity' (1986: 154). I would add that camp is often also a turning of the second set of categories – theatricality, irony, and a sense of the absurdity of extreme feeling – onto the first, such that the latter – authenticity, intensity, the fierce assertion of extreme feeling – if they remain at all, do so in a transformed state. In this respect camp, as Andrew Ross observes, anticipated many of the recent debates of sexual politics: 'in fact, camp could be seen as a much earlier, highly coded way of addressing those questions about sexual difference which have engaged non-essentialist feminists in recent years' (1988, rpt. 1989: 161).

Camp integrates this aspect of gender with aesthetics; in a sense it renders gender a question of aesthetics. Common in aesthetic involvement is the recognition that what seemed like mimetic realism is actually an effect of convention, genre, form, or some other kind of artifice. For some this is a moment of disappointment in which the real, the true, and the authentic are surrendered to, or contaminated by, the factitious and the contrived. But camp comes to life around that recognition; it is situated at the point of emergence of the artificial from the real, culture from nature – or rather when and where the real collapses into artifice, nature into culture; camp restores vitality to artifice, and vice versa, deriving the artificial from, and feeding it back into or as, the real. The reality is the pleasure of unreality. And the primacy of fantasy: as the inheritor of a religious impulse, 'modern' sexual desire seeks to universalize and naturalize itself. Camp knows and takes pleasure in the fact that desire is culturally relative, and never more so than when, in cathecting contemporary style, it mistakes itself, and the style, for the natural.

Camp is not the same as gender inversion, but it often connects with it, and with good reason. Like cross-dressing (see Dollimore 1991: 284–306), gender inversion remains controversial because it allegedly only inverts, rather than displaces, the gender binary. But again, in (historical) practice to invert may also be to displace. Mario Mieli quotes an unnamed gay writer: 'we [gay men] demand our "femininity", the same thing that women reject, and *at the same time* we declare that these roles are devoid of sense' (46). An appropriate inversion becomes a deconstructive displacement.

So it is futile to try to define the homosexual sensibility according to the standards of conventional sensibility: first because the latter has sought to exclude the former; second because, in retaliation, the former has often worked to undermine the latter and, in the process, challenged the very nature of the aesthetic, fashioning in the process new and sometimes oppositional mutations of it. The search for the nature of the distinctively gay sensibility can be productively redirected as an exploration of the limitations of the aesthetic as conventionally understood, especially the way it is said to transcend the socio-political, and used in support of the proposition that discrimination is the essence of culture.[3] Further, rather than seeking such a sensibility in an 'inner condition', we might more usefully identify it outwardly and in relation to other strategies of survival and subversion, especially the masquerade of femininity, and the mimicry of the colonial subject. What it might be found to share with the first is a simultaneous avoidance and acting out of the ambivalence which constitutes subordination, and a pushing of that ambivalence to the point of transgressive insight and possibly reinscribed escape.[4] As for the colonial context, Homi Bhabha argues that here mimicry is both a strategy of colonial subjection – an appropriation, regulation, and reform of the other – and, potentially, a way of menacing colonial discourse in and through an inappropriate imitation by the native, one which reveals the normative structure of colonial control. As such, mimicry becomes, in Bhabha's memorable phrase, 'at once resemblance and menace' (199).

KNOWLEDGE AND PLEASURE IN JEAN GENET

In so many respects utterly different from Wilde, Genet nevertheless also subverts the depth model of identity via the perverse dynamic, and perhaps more so than any other writer since Wilde. Like the latter, Genet inverts and subverts the surface/depth binary, confirming and exploiting the connections between the paradoxical and the perverse, and turning them against the regimes, heterosexual and otherwise, which outlaw the deviant. Genet, also like Wilde, produces both anarchic pleasure and subversive knowledge inseparably.

Charles Marowitz once identified a crucial characteristic of Genet's work:

> In perhaps one of the most shocking hypotheses ever put forward in the drama, Genet suggests that the only thing that distinguishes the sexual pervert who masquerades as priest, king, or hero from his legitimate social counterpart, is a certain timidity. The sexual pervert lives his fantasies in private and is therefore harmless; whereas the social personages play out their roles in public. (173)

This facilitates and in part constitutes the challenge of the perverse:

> the highest ideal in *The Balcony* is for characters to attain that point of social definition at which others desire to impersonate them. Reality corresponds to the density of one's artifice. When a man achieves his highest reality he can serve as a fantasy for another man; and in a frightening Genetic turnabout, both then become equal. (173)

They become equal because fictions of selfhood are transvalued. Genet said of himself: 'Dehumanizing myself is my own most fundamental tendency' (*Our*

Lady, 82). The transgressive drive in his work is not a quest for the authentic self, but almost the reverse:

> The mechanism was somewhat as follows (I have used it since) to every charge brought against me, unjust though it be, from the bottom of my heart I shall answer yes. Hardly had I uttered the word – or the phrase signifying it – than I felt within me the need to become what I had been accused of being ... I owned to being the coward, traitor, thief and fairy they saw in me. *(The Thief's Journal*, 145)

To be sure, the characteristics of the transcendent self remain in play: to become what others saw him as being required great self-discipline 'similar to spiritual exercises'; eventually he aspires to a classical stoic independence of spirit, a kind of sainthood (146). But then in *Our Lady of the Flowers* 'the gesture of solitude that makes you sufficient unto yourself' is not abstinence or retreat, but masturbation (124). Inversion and substitution are intensely narcissistic; despite that – or rather because of it, since Genet also transvalues narcissism – they extend far beyond the self. Of Divine, the anti-hero/ine drag queen of *Our Lady*, it is said:

> her carnal pleasures never made her fear the wrath of God, the scorn of Jesus, or the candied disgust of the Holy Virgin ... for as soon as she recognized the presence within her of seeds of these fears (divine wrath, scorn, disgust), Divine made of her loves a god above God, Jesus, and the Holy Virgin, to whom they were submissive like everyone else. (138)

Here, the figures who act as transcendent foils to a mundane inauthenticity, abjection, and subjection are themselves brought low, made to submit to what they once subjected. Notions of the freedom and autonomy of the self are at one and the same time inverted and used to pervert the ethical and metaphysical values which such a self is or was supposed to instantiate. Authentic selfhood is denied and then reconstituted in a perverse, parodic form – and then perhaps denied again, transformed from other to same and then back to a (different) other. Genet reinscribes himself within the violent hierarchies of his oppression, installing himself there relentlessly to invert and pervert them.

He writes in *Our Lady*: 'We are, after all, familiar enough with the tragedy of a certain feeling which is obliged to borrow its expression from the opposite feeling so as to escape from the myrmidons of the law. It disguises itself in the trappings of its rival' (113). Such incorporation facilitates a specific kind of transgressive reinscription. As in this passage, Genet not only disguises himself in terms of the law, but internalizes the disguise. What transpires is not the sacrilege which pays testimony to the sacred (i.e. containment), but a sacrilege inscribed within the sacred. Inside the church

> the [priest's] sprinkler is always moist with a tiny droplet, like Alberto's prick which is stiff in the morning and which has just pissed.

> The vaults and walls of the chapel of the Virgin are white-washed, and the Virgin has an apron as blue as a sailor's collar.
>
> Facing the faithful, the altar is neatly arranged; facing God, it is a jumble of wood in the dust and spider webs. (161)

In the description of the sprinkler and the apron, and especially the altar, the internalization of law (as disguise) results in this sacrilege within reverence, an intimacy with law which can blow apart its ideological effect (revealing the hidden side of the altar) – and with a strange knowing innocence strangely inseparable from that intimacy.[5]

ORTON'S BLACK CAMP

Joe Orton, so different again from Wilde or Genet, nevertheless shares their transgressive commitment to inversion and the critique of authenticity. His *What the Butler Saw* (1969) becomes a kind of orgy of cross-dressing, gender confusion, and hierarchical inversion. It is also an angry repudiation of sexual repressiveness as enforced by the ideology of authentic, normal sexuality, now ratified by state law and the medical professions. But once again anger works through irony, parody, and pastiche, and is held together not by a unified dramatic voice but by a stylistic blankness, a kind of black camp. Here, as in his and Halliwell's notorious defacement of library books (for which they were imprisoned), and in Orton's theory of montage, there is an anticipation of that effect of pastiche which Fredric Jameson identifies as a defining criterion of the post-modern:

> Pastiche is, like parody, the imitation of a peculiar or unique style, the wearing of a stylistic mask, speech in a dead language: but it is a neutral practice of mimicry, without parody's ulterior motive, without the satirical impulse, without laughter, without that still latent feeling that there exists something *normal* compared to which what is being imitated is rather comic. Pastiche is black parody, parody that has lost its humor. (114)

The difference is that Orton's pastiche *is* comic but in a way which interrogates rather than presupposes the norm. As Jane Feuer points out, camp involves a kind of sensibility in which 'blank mimicry and a critical edge may coexist', and thereby resembles that form of postmodern parody which Linda Hutcheon defines as a 'repetition with critical distance that allows ironic signalling of difference at the very heart of similarity' (cited by Feuer 1986: 455–6). Thereby camp may also, either implicitly or directly, interrogate the norm which, according to Jameson, traditional parody assumes. This is only one respect in which camp delights in the selfsame artifice which others distrust.

Orton's intention was to outrage. Had he been alive he would doubtless have been delighted at the response of the leading conservative theatre critic Harold Hobson to *What the Butler Saw* (1969): 'Orton's terrible obsession with perversion, which is regarded as having brought his life to an end [alluding to the fact that Orton was beaten to death by his lover] and choked his very high talent, poisons the atmosphere of the play. And what should have been a piece of gaily irresponsible nonsense becomes impregnated with evil'. Perhaps Hobson spoke truer than he knew, for the play is a kind of gay non-sense:

> [DR] RANCE: When Dr Prentice asked you to pose as a woman did he give a reason?
> NICK: No.
> RANCE: Didn't you consider his request strange?
> NICK: No.
> RANCE: Have you aided other men in their perverted follies?
> NICK: During my last term at school I was the slave of a corporal in the Welsh Fusiliers.
> RANCE: Were you never warned of the dangers inherent in such relationships?
> NICK: When he was posted abroad he gave me a copy of 'The Way to Healthy Manhood'.

By insisting on the arbitrariness and narrowness of gender roles, and that they are socially ascribed rather than naturally given, Orton expresses a central motif in the sexual politics of that time. *What the Butler Saw* becomes an orgy of confused and *refused* gender identities:

> GERALDINE: [*dressed as a boy*]. I must be a boy. I like girls.
> RANCE: I can't quite follow the reasoning there.
> PRENTICE: Many men imagine their preference for women is, *ipso facto*, a proof of virility.

Cross-dressing leads to wholesale gender confusion, while Dr Rance's precisely inappropriate assumptions about madness, the natural, and 'the order of things' discredit the claims of psychiatry:

> RANCE: Were you present when Dr Prentice used this youth unnaturally?
> NICK: What is unnatural?
> RANCE: How disturbing the questions of the mad can be. (*To Nick* [*disguised as a girl*]) Suppose I made an indecent suggestion to you? If you agreed something might occur which, by and large, would be regarded as natural. If, on the other hand, I approached this child – (*he smiles at Geraldine* [*disguised as a boy*]) – my action could result only in a gross violation of the order of things.

In the 1960s psychiatry was attacked for being a form of social policing which, with the aid of pseudo-scientific categories, mystified socially desirable behaviour as natural, and undesirable behaviour as the result of abnormal psychosexual development (a deviation from 'The Way to Healthy Manhood'). R. D. Laing wrote in *The Divided Self*:

> Psychiatry can so easily be a technique of brainwashing, of inducing behaviour that is adjusted, by (preferably) non-injurious torture ... I would wish to emphasize that our 'normal' 'adjusted' state is too often the abdication of ecstasy, the betrayal of our *true potentialities*, that many of us are only too successful in acquiring a false self to adapt the false realities. (12; my emphasis)

Orton goes further than Laing, for his plays transgress accepted norms at every point yet refuse to replace them with 'our true potentialities'; Laing is still preoccupied with the authentic self, the repressed human essence. Orton refuses that long-established kind of transgression which, in the very sincerity of its non-conformity, revalidates society's lapsed moral integrity. As John Milton put it centuries before: 'Men of most renowned vertu have sometimes by transgressing, most truly kept the law' (75).

A significant contemporary manifestation of that belief, and a vivid instance of how 'modern' sexuality became a surrogate religion, somewhere for an essentially religious notion of integrity to survive in a mutated and displaced form, was at the prosecution for obscenity of D. H. Lawrence's *Lady Chatterley's Lover* (1960). In that trial the author was defended on the grounds that he had to transgress moral respectability in order to be moral at a deeper, more authentic level dictated by personal conscience.[6] Even the indignation of satire might assume the same moral perspective as that of the order being challenged, or at least an alternative to it. But, as his diaries indicate, Orton's indignation was too anarchic to be recuperated in such terms. In *What the Butler Saw*, sexuality, like language, becomes decentred and therefore radically contingent: it not only escapes from, but disorientates the medical and legal attempts to define and regulate it.

Not surprisingly, Orton's anarchic irresponsibility was thought by some to go too far, not just in what he actually *did*, but in the refusal in his work to confront established morality with an earnest moral alternative. What we find instead is a kind of delinquent black camp. In the article referred to at the outset, Susan Sontag remarks that camp 'is a solvent of morality. It neutralizes moral indignation, sponsors playfulness' (275, 280, 290). Orton's camp is indeed constituted by playfulness and it acts as a solvent of morality – but it does this to provoke rather than disarm moral indignation. 'No first night of the sixties was more volcanic than that of *What the Butler Saw*', says Orton's biographer, John Lahr; while Stanley Baxter, who played Dr Prentice, has recalled the 'militant hate' of the audience, some of whom 'wanted to jump on the stage and kill us' (Lahr 1978: 333–4).

HOSTILE EROTICISM

As a style, and even more as a politics, the transgressive reinscriptions practised by such writers have proved controversial, especially when grounded in the celebration of a perverse inauthenticity disturbingly implicated in authenticity itself, as in Genet. On the positive side there are those like Kate Millett who find in Genet's deviants a subversive inversion of dominant heterosexuality, especially its masculine component.[7] Thus inverted, these structures are shorn of their ideological legitimation; in effect the world of normality, beyond which Genet lives in exile, is ridiculed and contradicted in the very process of being imitated. Genet's femininity for instance 'is, as Sartre phrases it, a "hostile eroticism", delighted to ridicule and betray the very myth of virility it pretends to serve' (Millett, 18, 349). All this means that, for Millett, Genet is 'the only living male writer of first class literary gifts to have transcended the sexual myths of our era' (22). Conversely, for Hans Mayer, Genet's commitment to inversion makes him deeply conservative: 'Genet's books are the exact opposite of a literature of indignation and rebellion. The author has no intention of making accusations or unmasking society. He is a true believer in the bourgeois order, not a critic.[8] More critical still are those like Walter Heist who conclude that Genet is pervaded with fascism (cited by Mayer, 255, who dissents from the view).

Certainly there is a crucial sense in which Genet presupposes what he would challenge: 'I am steeped in an idea of property while I loot property. I recreate the absent proprietor', he says in *The Thief's Journal* (129); and in a 1975 interview: 'I would like the world, and pay attention to the way I'm saying it, I would like the world not to change so that I can be against the world' (Fichte, 79).

There is an ambivalence in Genet which his critic always misread and his defenders often overlook. Such ambivalence often figures within transgressive reinscription, and is one reason why it rarely approximates to a straightforwardly 'correct' political attitude. Consider two kinds of ambivalent transgressive reinscription within gay culture, camp and machismo. As styles they are very different, virtual alternatives in fact. But both have been regarded as politically reprehensible, camp because allegedly insulting to women, machismo because allegedly aping the masculinity oppressive of women (lesbian and straight) and gays. Defenders of camp and machismo point out that they are parodic critiques – in the first case of what is allegedly insulted (femininity), in the second of what is allegedly aped (masculinity). Certainly both gay camp and gay machismo can and do problematize femininity and masculinity as traditionally understood. Thus Richard Dyer has argued of gay machismo that, by taking the traditional signs of masculinity and 'eroticising them in a blatantly homosexual context, much mischief is done to the security with which "men" are defined in society, and by which their power is secured' (1981: 61).

Throughout *Gender Trouble* Judith Butler offers – and for, rather than against, feminism – a similar defence of practices like drag, cross-dressing, and, in lesbian culture, butch/femme sexual stylization. She contests the view that these practices are 'either degrading to women, in the case of drag and cross-dressing, or an uncritical appropriation of sex-role stereotyping from within the practice of heterosexuality, especially in the case of butch/femme lesbian identities' (Butler 1990a: 137). Thus she reads drag as playing with a threefold distinction: anatomical sex, gender identity, and gender performance:

> If the anatomy of the performer is already distinct from the gender of the performer, and both of those are distinct from the gender of the performance, then the performance suggests a dissonance not only between sex and performance, but sex and gender, and gender and performance ... *In imitating gender drag implicitly reveals the imitative structure of gender itself – as well as its contingency.* (137)

Butler sees deviant sexualities more generally as involving this same process of denaturalizing, as parodic subversive repetitions which displace rather than consolidate heterosexual norms. The parody of deviant sex, far from presupposing and ratifying an original natural sexuality, exposes it as a fiction. Thus 'gay is to straight *not* as copy is to original, but, rather, as copy is to copy' (31). Additionally, the parody encourages a 'proliferation and subversive play of gendered meaning' (33). Most controversially of all, this argument has been extended to sado-masochistic sexuality which, far from ratifying the 'real' violence of society, theatricalizes and demystifies it.

In certain respects this argument replays for a post/modern politics Wilde's transgressive aesthetic and the gay (anti)sensibility which it helped inaugurate. It also resembles the strategy of the early modern female cross-dresser for whom sexual difference was not derived from natural and divine law, but produced by 'custom', that is, culture. Here then is a continuity between the early modern and the post/modern, one often overlooked when we concentrate on the differences in the way sexuality is conceptualized in the two periods. But crucial differences remain, and it was because the early modern transvestite was not conceptualized in terms of a pathological sexual subjectivity – the modern 'homosexual' – that her transgression was regarded, albeit with paranoia, as more social than sexual. The connections between gender and class were apparent enough in the early modern period, and if the transvestite was a pervert or invert it was precisely in the pre-sexological senses of these ideas; whether actually or only in the paranoid imagination of the dominant, she was regarded as upsetting the entire social domain, even when her sexual 'orientation' was not the issue.

So when it is argued today that the sexual deviant challenges sexual difference by denaturalizing it through parody, the realization of the early modern transvestite that both the deviant and the difference are effects of culture rather than nature is being revived and sophisticated. But a residual effect of the 'privatizing' of sexuality, and in particular of the construction of sexual deviance as an identity, a pathology of being, rather than a kind of behaviour in principle open to all, is that the challenge to this construction often itself remains imprisoned by the public/private dichotomy. So while the whole point of the argument, and rightly, is that when gender is understood as culture rather than nature we see that gender is implicated in all aspects of culture, in practice the argument rarely gets off the bed. As we shall see shortly, the way out of the bedroom is via the wider cultures, rather than the specific sexual acts, of transgressive reinscription – for example, the writings of Wilde, Genet, and others, the subculture from which they emerge and help to form and transform.

First there is another objection to be considered: do deviant identities and sexualities really denaturalize through theatrical parody as straightforwardly as is sometimes suggested? Leo Bersani thinks not, at least where camp and gay machismo are concerned. He concedes a potentially subversive dimension to camp, but one inseparable from a more problematic and ambivalent relation to both femininity and women:

> the gay male parody of a certain femininity, which, as others have argued, may itself be an elaborate social construct, is both a way of giving vent to the hostility toward women that probably afflicts every male (and which male heterosexuals have of course expressed in infinitely nastier and more effective ways) *and* could paradoxically be thought of as helping to deconstruct that image for women themselves ... The gay male bitch desublimates and desexualizes a type of femininity glamorized by movie stars, whom he thus lovingly assassinates with his style.

Of the subversive claims for gay machismo, Bersani is even more sceptical, since he regards it as involving not a parodic repudiation of straight machismo, but a profound respect for it. But, crucially, and this reminds us of Genet, Bersani locates a challenge inseparable from a certain ambivalence: if gay males threaten male heterosexual identity, it is not because they offer a detached parody of that identity, but rather because 'from within their nearly mad identification with it, *they never cease to feel the appeal of its being violated*' (1987: 208–9). Bersani arrives at this position because he sees gay male sexuality as enacting insights into sexuality *per se* which heterosexual culture has to repress ruthlessly.

The cultural dynamics of transgressive reinscription suggest how both positions are correct: identification with, and desire *for*, may coexist with parodic subversion *of*, since a culture is not reducible to the specific desires of the individuals comprising it – desires which anyway differ considerably – and even less to the 'truth' of desire itself. Gay culture is in part constituted by a self-reflexive, ironic representation of desire itself, gay and straight, and of the objects of desire, again both gay and straight. This is especially so of its involvement with masculinity. In one and the same gay milieu one is likely to encounter identification with, desire for, and parodies of masculinity. Among numerous other things, gay *subcultures* (as opposed to the illusory 'truth' of a unitary homosexual *desire*) include all three, and sometimes indistinguishably. And if those subcultures discredit any notion of an essential or unitary gay desire, they also constitute a crucial enabling condition of transgressive reinscription. More than that, they help constitute it. This is why transgressive reinscription should not be understood in terms of discrete transgressive acts which 'succeed' or 'fail' in some immediate sense. Reinscription is an oppositional practice which is also a perspective and language (sensibility?) constantly interpreting and re-presenting all sections of a culture including its dominant and subordinate fractions, its conventional (e.g. heterosexual) as well as deviant (e.g. homosexual) identities. Butler remarks the importance of *repetition* in the process of resistance and transformation: 'The task is ... to repeat and, through a radical proliferation of gender, to *displace* the very gender norms that enable the repetition itself' (Butler 1990a: 148). Certainly, but that displacement can only occur if it is also a struggle in and for representation – specifically, the representation of the repetition *as* re-presentation/inversion/displacement of the norm. In short, the displacing repetition still has to be culturally construed as such. In the process the transgression and the norm are both re-presented. And this, far from being a containment (transgression presupposing and thereby ratifying the norm it contravenes), is one condition of the norm's undoing.

Transgressive reinscription will always remain controversial, if only because it raises such disturbing questions about desire itself, making it profoundly social and thereby asking equally disturbing questions about culture, representation, and social process. This is even more so when, as I have argued with homosexuality, so many dimensions of a culture have been displaced and/or condensed into the identity of the transgressor. But then there is no transgression from the position of the subordinate that is not controversial; it is a virtually inevitable consequence of the disempowered mounting a challenge at all.

[...]

Notes

1. We might recall that there have been even more curious versions of this argument for the connection between homosexuality and modernity. Some in the nineteenth century thought that the modern age, bringing as it did, steam, speed, electricity, 'unnatural' city existence, and so on, encouraged decadence and degeneration, and these were in part a surrender to it. Mosse writes: 'for many physicans as well as racists, departures from the norm were caused by the surrender to modernity'; some thought the 'vibrations of modernity' led *to* homosexuality (136).
2. See especially Altman 1982, ch. 5, and Bronski 1984.
3. Connecting the gay sensibility to cultural politics also invites crucial questions about whether either can operate within a reformist vision, or whether they entail a more radical vision. See Bronski 1984: 38–9, 197ff. esp. 213–4.
4. On masquerade and femininity see Rivière; Irigaray, who also explores femininity in relation to mimicry); Heath; Modleski; Ross 1988; Butler 1990a: 46–54 (who includes a thoughtful discussion of the links berween the masquerading woman and the homosexual man).
5. In an elaboration of his theory of how a system is abolished only by pushing it into hyperlogic, Jean Baudrillard has spoken of how the 'masses' express 'a false fidelity to the law, an ultimately impenetrable simulation of passivity and obedience ... which in return annuls the law governing them' (33, 46). Genet might be understood to have elaborated the potential of such a strategy and in a way which showed in advance the absurdity of its generalization in relation to the 'masses'.

6. See Sinfield 1990b: 268–71. For a fuller discussion of the Chatterley trial along these lines, see Dollimore 1983.
7. Millett, esp. 16–22 and ch. 8; for other feminist identifications with Genet's work see Cixous, 97–8 and 255–6, and Santellani's reading of a passage from Genet's *Miracle of the Rose* (95–7).
8. Mayer, 255. For a more perceptive and helpful introduction to Genet, see Adams, 182–205.

References

Adams, Stephen, *The Homosexual as Hero in Contemporary Fiction*, London: Vision, 1980.

Baudrillard, Jean, *In the Shadow of the Silent Majorities ... or the End of the Social and Other Essays*, trans. Paul Foss, Paul Patton & John Johnston, New York: Semiotext(e), 1983.

Bhabha, Homi, 'Of Mimicry and Man: The Ambivalence of Colonial Discourse', in James Donald & Stuart Hall (eds.), *Politics and Ideology*, Milton Keynes: Open UP, 1986.

Cixous, Hélène, 'Sorties,' in E. Marks & I. de Courtivron (eds.), *New French Feminisms*, Brighton: Harvester, 1981.

Ellmann, Richard, *Oscar Wilde*, London: Hamish Hamilton, 1987.

Fichte, Hubert, 'Interview with Jean Genet', in Winston Leyland (ed.), *Gay Sunshine Interviews*, Vol. 1, San Francisco: Gay Sunshine, 1978, 67–94.

Genet, Jean, *Our Lady of the Flowers* (1943), trans. Bernard Frechtman, London: Panther, 1966.

——, *The Thief's Journal* (1949), trans. Bernard Frechtman, Harmondsworth: Penguin, 1967.

Gide, André, *So Be It, or: The Chips are Down* (1952), trans. Justin O'Brien, London: Chatto, 1960.

Heath, Stephen, 'Joan Rivière and the Masquerade', in Victor Burgin, James Donald, and Cora Kaplan (eds.), *Formations of Fantasy*, London: Methuen, 1986.

Hobson, Harold, *Christian Science Monitor*, 19 March 1969.

Irigaray, Luce, *This Sex Which is not One*, trans. Catherine Porter with Carolyn Burke, Ithaca: Cornell UP, 1985.

Jameson, Fredric, 'Postmodernism and Consumer Society', in Hal Foster (ed.), *The Anti-Aesthetic: Essays on Postmodern Culture*, Washington: Bay Press, 1983.

Laing, R. D., *The Divided Self*, Harmondsworth: Penguin, 1965.

Marowitz, Charles, 'The Revenge of Jean Genet' (1961), in Charles Marowitz et al. (eds.), *The Encore Reader: A Chronicle of the New Drama*, London: Methuen, 1965.

Mayer, Hans, *Outsiders: A Study in Life and Letters*, trans. Denis M. Sweet, Cambridge: MIT Press, 1982.

Mieli, Mario, *Homosexuality and Liberation: Elements of a Gay Critique* (1977), trans. David Fernbach, London: Gay Men's Press, 1980.

Millett, Kate, *Sexual Politics*, London: Virago, 1977.

Milton, John, *Tetrachordon*, in Don M. Wolfe (ed.), *Complete Prose Works*, New Haven: Yale UP, 1953–82 (Vol. iv).

Modleski, Tania, 'Femininity as Mas[s]querade: A Feminist Approach to Mass Culture', in Colin MacCabe (ed.), *High Theory/Low Culture: Analysing Popular Television and Film*, Manchester: Manchester UP, 1986.

Mosse, George L., *Nationalism and Sexuality: Respectable and Abnormal Sexuality in Modern Europe*, New York: Howard Fertig, 1985.

Rivière, Joan, 'Womanliness as Masquerade' (1929), in Victor Burgin, James Donald & Cora Kaplan (eds.), *Formations of Fantasy*, London: Methuen, 1986.

Santellani, Violette, 'Jean Genet's *The Miracle of the Rose*', in S. Sellers (ed.), *Writing Differences*, Milton Keynes: Open UP, 1988.

Steiner, George, *Real Presences: Is There Anything in What We Are Saying?*, London: Faber, 1989.

Wilde, Oscar, 'The Decay of Lying' (1889), in Richard Ellmann (ed.), *The Artist as Critic: Critical Writings of Oscar Wilde*, London: W. H. Allen, 1970.

——, *The Picture of Dorian Gray* (1891), Harmondsworth: Penguin, 1949.

——, *De Profundis* (1897), in Rupert Hart-Davis (ed.), *The Letters of Oscar Wilde*, New York: Harcourt Brace, 1962.

Yeats, W. B., *Autobiographies*, London: Macmillan, 1955.

15

CAMP AMONG THE SWASTIKAS: ISHERWOOD, SALLY BOWLES, AND 'GOOD HETER STUFF'

Linda Mizejewski

INTRODUCTION: DIVINE DECADENCE

In Bob Fosse's 1972 film *Cabaret*, Liza Minnelli as Sally Bowles introduces herself with a theatrical flash of green fingernails and enthusiastic wickedness: 'Divine decadence!' she exclaims. Along with the sleazy nail paint, Minnelli wears Louise Brooks's bobbed hair, mama Judy Garland's frazzled would-be glamour, and rings of eyeliner that match that of the emcee character, Joel Grey. When she dons her black boots and garters to perch on a high-back chair at the Kit Kat Klub, the Dietrichesque touch completes her capsulation of camp touchstones and codes: licentious Weimar Berlin, drag-queen iconicity, gay cult celebrity, and divinely shocking taste.

Ten years ago, when I wrote 'Good Heter Stuff' as part of a longer work about the many versions of the character Sally Bowles, the Academy Award winning film with Minnelli was probably the most widely known. Since that time, two successful Broadway revivals of the 1966 musical *Cabaret* have brought Sally to cultural center stage once more, most recently with Natasha Richardson in 1998. Although Sally's tale has never been a straightforward one, it has taken multiple detours since its appearance in Christopher Isherwood's 1939 story collection *Goodbye to Berlin*. John Van Druten's 1951 stage play *I Am a Camera* and the 1955 Henry Cornelius film of the same name cleaned up Sally's milieu so that only in-the-know audiences would pick up the more decadent implications of the Kit Kat Klub and her oddly asexual male roommate. The

Excerpted from *Divine Decadence: Fascism, Female Spectacle, and the Makings of Sally Bowles*, Princeton: Princeton UP, 1992, pp. 37–84.

1966 Joe Masteroff stage musical lovingly restored the kinkiness, but not until the Fosse film in 1972 was the 'secret' sexual identity of the Chris/Christopher/ Herr Issyvoo character revealed. His characterization is integral to Sally's, because her need for a leading man and the text's need for a hero have been key elements in the campy subtexts of the adaptations. In the 1980s and 1990s stage productions, his character is bisexual, so Sally's outrageous performances of female heterosexuality have been given progressively more ironic distance as her story is revised through the century – a story that apparently retains cultural fascination and significance.

The larger problem has been how audiences should love or distance themselves from Sally's endearing, funny, but frightening excesses. In every version of the story, she embraces Berlin cabaret life and impassively ignores the rotten 1933 political scene, which the putative hero understands and renounces. Since 1966, the adaptations have cranked up the presence of both the Weimar camp carnivalesque and the Nazis. In turn, Sally's comedy has grown darker and more uneasy, the character's borderline grotesqueries more pronounced. While Minnelli's Sally is a fabulous singer who gets a dazzling exit number among the swastikas, Richardson's is a coke addict who trembles through her last song and stumbles away from the microphone in despair.

In short, the Sally Bowles character continues to raise questions about camp's political meanings, in particular, questions about the vampy, Dietrich-esque cabaret singer in relationship to Nazism. Meanwhile, in the decade since I wrote about Isherwood's Sally, critical thinking about both camp and sexuality has enriched and complicated the ways she can be interpreted. Seen through queer theory's explorations of parody and performance, for example, Sally can be understood as a transvestite figure along the lines of Tennessee Williams' Blanche du Bois or Truman Capote's Holly Golightly (a tribute to Isherwood and Sally) – a strategy of gay male writers in an era when homosexual identities had to be repressed. A flamboyant construction of breathless dialogue, the Sally character comically asks us to imagine an impossible body and thus is perhaps always ill-served in adaptations in which she is embodied by a female actress. As a self-conscious homosexual discourse, Isherwood's Sally Bowles story arguably illustrates a queer, oppositional sensibility channeled into a recognizable, compulsory category – what Isherwood called 'good heter stuff'.

However, the Sally Bowles character has always been associated with a much more specific historical interpretation: the 'spectacle' of Nazism, its 'fascinating' allure for passive spectators, and a 'decadent' Weimar that staged a triumphant Third Reich. Such a judgmental framework restrains an explanation of this character as the queer, anti-categorical transvestite. The following essay traces the Sally character's complicated inscription – alternately comic, affectionate, hostile – in the original Isherwood story. My argument is that her campiness emerges from intersecting histories of popular culture, Nazism, and sexual identity, beginning with a group of 1930s gay male British writers in Berlin and their friendship with the woman-who-would-be-Sally Bowles.

Thinking about camp through these narratives, we can ground poststructuralist issues of performance and parody in problems of censorship, exile, abortion laws, and boundaries of mainstream and marginal literary material. My argument also emphasizes cinema history as a context for the development of camp humor, for Sally Bowles as an outrageous spectacle was, even in her first materialization, the object of a camera.

Christopher Isherwood's most famous sentence, beginning 'I am a camera . . .' is the opening of the second paragraph of *Goodbye to Berlin*. When Isherwood was working on this book in the mid-1930s, he had good reasons to think of stories set up for cameras. A self-described film fan throughout his lifetime, he had already done screenplay work and would continue to do so during the following decades after moving to Hollywood. The camera metaphor in *Goodbye to Berlin* also served a practical, political purpose. Its positioning of the narrator as a nearly invisible outsider to the action defers to the pressures on Isherwood, at the time of publication, to publicly conceal his homosexuality. *Goodbye to Berlin*'s would-be femme fatale, Sally Bowles, originates in these intersecting conditions of repression and visual culture, as well as Isherwood's stated intention to produce a popular, mainstream text about a heterosexual character.

Isherwood's ambiguous relationship to the Sally Bowles material resembles and in fact overlaps with his relationship to the classic Hollywood cinema of the 1930s, an institution which was overwhelmingly mainstream/heterosexual in its representations and politics. Sally's character is constituted through the special vision or codings of camp, which has long been a gay access to mainstream cinema as both a reading strategy and as stylistic markings of gay workers behind and in front of the camera. Produced from the context of compulsory heterosexuality, the story 'Sally Bowles' nattily satirizes female sexiness as a commodity with specific market value, suggesting the artifice of other culturally defined sexualities. Yet this campy stylization does not account for the long-playing cultural life of the Sally Bowles character, whose association with Weimar cabaret life and in turn with Nazism has deeply inflected and darkened her comedy. While post-1939 history has given Sally's Berlin story a particularly menacing twist, her inscription in the Isherwood text is already poised between glamour and grotesquery, and between endearing humor and hostile satire.

The Sally character begins with Isherwood and his friends in what would become their legendary Berlin days. It was a legend they would build deliberately for themselves, though its most popular version remains Isherwood's two novels in that setting, *The Last of Mr. Norris* (1935) and *Goodbye to Berlin* (1939), frequently cited together as *The Berlin Stories* since their joint publication under that title in 1954. In *Goodbye to Berlin*, the story 'Sally Bowles' is positioned among much more serious texts: the grim framing sketches 'A

Berlin Diary 1930' and 'A Berlin Diary 1932–33'; the unhappy homosexual affair, coded as a 'friendship', described in 'On Reugen Island'; the working class sketch 'The Nowaks', which ends with the gloomy sanitarium scene; and 'The Landauers', which recounts the narrator's friendship with the charming Jewish department-store owner who refuses to acknowledge the imminent danger of the Nazis. Within this ominous context, the comedy and theatricality of Sally and her adventures take on an uneasy edge. Likewise, the serious abortion sequence in 'Sally Bowles' is oddly located between the two major jokes that make up the narrative: the jilting of Sally by the wealthy, drunken American Clive, and the tricking of Sally by the fake movie-agent/con man.

As with most of the other narratives in this book, these events are freely based on Isherwood's experience in Berlin, including his interactions with Jean Ross, the spunky British woman who was the model for Sally Bowles. Both Isherwood and his friend Stephen Spender later came forth with supporting details about her. Spender clarified that it was he, not Isherwood, who set Ross up with a con man, and he noted how 'impressed' he was with the fact that Ross had an abortion (138–9). In his 1972 memoir *Christopher and His Kind*, Isherwood recalls of Ross that 'Like Sally, she boasted continually about her lovers' to the point that he thought she was exaggerating. 'Now I am not so certain', he adds (61).

Ross herself, whose photo images from that era align her with the masculinized Weimar New Woman, in later years contradicted the accounts of Isherwood and his friends except to confirm that, like them, she was in Berlin as a young rebel: 'Chris's story was quite, quite different from what really happened. But we were all utterly against the bourgeois standards of our parents' generation. That's what took us to Berlin' (Johnstone, 33–4). Jean Ross returned to England for an active career as a newspaper correspondent and film critic, but after the Sally Bowles character was adapted to stage and screen, she was besieged by journalists looking for the 'real' story of 'Berlin in the Thirties'. As Ross complained later, 'they don't want to know about the unemployment or the poverty or the Nazis marching through the streets – all they want to know is how many men I went to bed with' (Caudwell, 28). That is, sexual politics displaces national politics; the sensational personal story overshadows sensational public story. Furthermore, while the politics of the Sally Bowles character in *Goodbye to Berlin* range dubiously from apathy to anti-Semitism, Jean Ross became a political activist against fascism, making the fictionalization an embarrassment to her cause.

A major issue here is Isherwood's frankly autobiographical methodology and its subsequent romanticizations, especially by his own crowd – Spender, W. H. Auden, Edward Upward, John Lehmann. These writers, who were also each others' critics and advisors, did 'what looks like deliberate legend-building to self-consciously set themselves up as the Next Generation (after Joyce, Huxley and Eliot)', critic Colin Wilson points out (312–13). Jean Ross is not the only person to be appropriated in Isherwood's conflations of friendship and fiction. His crowd appears as figures in his books from the 1930s (*Lions and Shadows, All the Conspirators*) to the 1960s (*Down There on a Visit*); for anyone unable to break the code, Isherwood supplies a who's who throughout *Christopher and His Kind*.

The result of all this is a remarkably incestuous circle of writers-readers-characters who shared not just common cultural codes (their class and university background, and the shadow of fathers who had experienced the Great War) but private ones as well. The American writer Paul Bowles remarked that when he met Isherwood and Spender in Berlin, they were like 'two members of a secret society constantly making references to esoteric data not available to outsiders' (110). Through these elaborate, divisive codes, outsiders were either rejected or transformed into the multiple fictions and allusions which this set of colleagues kept in circulation.

The subculture which Isherwood and his friends constructed for themselves was specifically homosexual. Isherwood explains in *Christopher and His Kind* that he and Auden were in Germany from 1929 to 1933 not in idealistic self-exile from their stuffy upper-class British world, but because in certain sections of Berlin, they could practice more openly the homosexuality that was illegal in their own country: 'Berlin meant Boys'. (2). In the same memoir, Isherwood points out the awkward moments that occurred at times with the only hetero-sexual member of his group, Edward Upward. Speaking of sexual matters, 'Christopher was conscious that Edward trod carefully. When he spoke of "buggers" and "buggery" . . . he did so in exactly the right tone of voice' (47–8).

Thus Sally Bowles, one of literature's most raucously heterosexual char-acters, was produced in the immediate conditions of a close-knit, homogeneous group of gay male intellectuals who were bonded not just through the literature they were producing, but through private loyalties to each other, and the identification of themselves as both criminal and consciously opposed to the ideology of heterosexuality, as Isherwood makes clear in his memoirs.[1] The status of Jean Ross within this group is unfortunately romanticized and obscured in their own memoirs, mainly because she has been so overwhel-mingly identified as Isherwood's Sally and the Sally of the adaptations. Isher-wood himself admits he can no longer clearly remember Ross because she has been recreated by so many later actresses, but he maintains that he and Ross were affectionate friends and 'truly intimate' as 'brother and sister' (*Christo-pher and His Kind*, 63). In his 1951 recounting of the Berlin days, Stephen Spender gives Ross only a few walk-on descriptions as one of the 'characters' who would appear sometimes in Isherwood's flat. But in his 1974 essay on Berlin, he confesses that Jean Ross's language 'repelled' him, being explicitly 'physiological' in a way that could not be reproduced by Isherwood for publi-cation in the 1930s (138). If Edward Upward felt that he had to use 'exactly the right tone of voice' to make sexual references in this group, then the presence of Jean Ross with her casual conversations about lovers would have indeed created a dissonant note in Isherwood's milieu.

In fictionalizing his outspoken female friend, however, Isherwood was contending with much more than her colorful language. John Lehmann, the editor at Hogarth working with the story, points out that because of the abortion sequence, Isherwood needed Ross's permission to publish in order to avoid a libel suit. Though he himself was 'fascinated' by the abortion story, Lehmann was 'nervous whether our printers – in the climate of those days – would pass it'. When he warned Isherwood about this and encouraged him to drop the sequence, Isherwood's reply in a 1937 letter is telling: 'It seems to me that Sally, without the abortion sequence, would just be a silly little capricious bitch. Besides, what would the whole thing lead up to? And down from? The whole idea of the study is to show that even the greatest disasters leave a person like Sally essentially unchanged' (Lehmann, 28–9).

The 'climate of those days' to which Lehmann refers was one in which the abortion issue in Great Britain had become particularly sensitive. Though abortion had been illegal and punishable by life imprisonment (in theory, for both the mother and the doctor) since 1861, few cases had been brought to trial. But beginning in 1934, roughly a hundred inquests a year were carried out in cases in which women had died in illegal abortion procedures. At the time Isherwood was writing 'Sally Bowles', the topic of abortion had become both public and controversial. So the stakes for Ross were quite different than for Isherwood in being identified with private, illegal activity. While the gay identity of characters is repressed or occluded in *Goodbye to Berlin*, Ross's abortion becomes public text and justified as the 'whole point' of her story.

Isherwood's biographer Jonathan Fryer explains that 'Anyone who knew Jean Ross during the 1930s would have had very little trouble in recognizing her as the basis for Sally Bowles'. Though Ross eventually gave her permission for publication, she had changed quite a bit in the meantime, unlike 'Sally', having returned to London and gotten involved with serious left-wing politics, partially in response to growing fascist sentiment in Great Britain. 'Several of Jean's friends were shocked by the book', reports Fryer, 'and . . . she avoided all possible publicity connected with it. She was a brave and kind woman, by now deeply committed to left-wing causes, and the book did not help her image much among those comrades who realized she was the model' (164).

The other problem of fictionalizing Jean Ross was the heterosexual codings of popular literature. Sally Bowles is recognizable as the young, attractive, upper-class heroine of mainstream fiction; her world revolves around men, love affairs, and the relationships of these to money – plotline codes that are dependent upon heterosexual desire. Critics have pointed out how her character departs from Isherwood's previous work – that is, how he had refrained from using these codes. In a 1936 letter to Lehmann while he was working on the story 'Sally Bowles', Isherwood specifically names a literary precedent he used for inspiration: 'It's rather like Anthony Hope: "The Dolly Dialogues". It is an attempt to satirize the romance-of-prostitution racket. Good heter stuff' (Lehmann, 27).

Isherwood's reference here is a telling clue to the sort of 'heter stuff' he had in mind. British writer Anthony Hope's *Dolly Dialogues* had been serialized in 1892 and published in 1899; these sketches were still in circulation in the 1920s, broadcast on British radio. By pinpointing as precedent a character instantly recognizable in popular culture, Isherwood was also naming his own project to appeal to a mainstream audience. Clearly, he and his friends had no intention of creating a cult or underground art. Lehmann recalls Spender's description of their group as a 'heroic band who were out to create an entirely new literature' (Lehmann, 8). And they succeeded. Beyond their presence in the literary anthologies, they are acknowledged as *the* writers of the 1930s, honored in 1976 by an exhibit at the National Portrait Gallery in London, which Isherwood criticized because 'nowhere was it mentioned that so many of the leading figures of that literary generation had been homosexual or bisexual' (Fryer, 287). The result of this contention between mainstream and marginal location of desires is the curious representation of female eroticism and hetero-sexuality found in the story 'Sally Bowles'.

While the trajectory or tension of *The Dolly Dialogues* is dependent upon the mutual sexual attraction of narrator and character (will they confess their desire? will they act on it?), Isherwood's story relates the interaction of the desirable, accessible woman and the narrator who is wholly without desire for her, in spite of strong fictional codes requiring their attraction. In a 1975 interview, Isherwood explains that using a homosexual narrator in the 1930s would have introduced a subject more controversial and distracting than any-thing else in the book. He also confesses that he had to sacrifice some of the comedy that resulted from his actual relationship with 'Sally' – 'how, at one time I had no money, we actually shared our room and slept in the same bed, and, of course, the relations between my boy friends and her! It would have created comedy, certainly, but at what a cost. It would have become tiresome, because it's not what the book is *about*' (Stoop, 62).

My argument is that the repression of one kind of comedy here – and the repression of homosexuality, in fact – causes the book to be 'about' other dis-sonances and posturings. Beyond being 'a satire of the romance-of-prostitution racket', 'Sally Bowles' satirizes and reveals the entire construction of female sexiness as performance, theater, elaborate 'sham', to use Isherwood's word. A distinctive relationship between narrator and character is deployed to maintain this effect. While the Dolly character in her flirtations is at times just as thea-trical and posturing as Sally Bowles, the *Dolly* narrator is willing to take on the proper role and engage in this sexual theater, though with some archness and irony, because he has a stake in it: his own desire. But in 'Sally Bowles', that stake or interest is missing; Sally's exaggerations and poses, her bids for atten-tion and sexual interest, are played out to a narrator for whom it is only theater.

Describing Sally's behavior and voice, the narrator Chris continually plays up their theatrical artifice: her 'little stage-laugh' (23); her deliberate settling of herself into a 'pose' for effect (27); her ability to spontaneously come up with 'some really startling lies' that she 'half-believed' herself (35). Her flirtation on the telephone is a 'performance' not only for the person she is calling, but to her observers: '"Hilloo", she cooed, pursing her brilliant cherry lips as though she were going to kiss the mouthpiece: "Ist dass Du, mein Liebling?" Her mouth opened in a fatuously sweet smile. Fritz and I sat watching her, like a performance at the theatre' (22–3).

In the economy of desire (the heterosexual codes of mainstream fiction) and the great sexual energy suggested by the narrative (Sally's promiscuity), something has been displaced or gone awry. What should be sexy is only 'sexy'. What poses as passion – for example, Sally's description of a lover – cannot possibly be taken seriously: 'He was so marvellously primitive: just like a faun. He made me feel like a most marvelous nymph, or something, miles away from anywhere, in the middle of the forest' (39). The awkward qualification of her descriptions – 'or something' – points at once to the borrowing of this discourse from other sources, and also her own inability to generate a more original or sincere way to speak of desire; but it is also a comic way to deflate the grandiose pronouncements. Sally's language comically trips on its own attempts at drama or tension: 'I feel all marvelous and ethereal', Sally gushes about her newest lover, 'as if I was a kind of most wonderful saint, or something' (39) Even her complaints about the sexual-monetary contract are undermined by her own acquiescence in it: 'He wants me to be his mistress, but I've told him I'm damned if I will till he's paid all my debts. Why are men always such beasts?' (24).

Sally is always on an imaginary stage; the narrator describes her attempts to be serious as 'a kind of theatrically chaste effect, like a nun in grand opera' (27). Likewise, her language is constantly puffed with flamboyant hyperbole, a conscious acting-out of 'sexiness': '"That's the man I slept with last night', she announced. 'He makes love marvellously. He's an absolute genius at business and he's terribly rich – "' (23). And this very quality of sex-in-quotation-marks reveals not just its parodic nature, but its affinity to similar posturings in other texts which approach heterosexuality ironically. The combination of humor, ironic distance, and satire of sex and gender role in this discourse is recognizable as camp. In fact, the imaginative origin of the Bowles character may have been a campy play with sex and gender identity; Jean Ross suspected that Sally Bowles was based on a male friend of Isherwood, and Isherwood himself admits that he named the character for Paul Bowles, whose 'looks' he had liked.[2]

At least one critic has pointed out that Sally's campy comedy works at odds with the growing political urgency in *Goodbye to Berlin*; eventually, these stories are no longer funny because of the outrageous political scene, in which the camp sensibility of exaggeration has been out-parodied by the far-from-amusing Nazis.[3] The question indeed is how and when Sally stops being comic, or how her comedy is distanced by its ugly political context. At some point, the affectionate comedy takes on a sharp edge, and Isherwood's campy, ironic distancing from the cultural 'sexual woman' permits a conflation with the other necessary distancing in this text – from Nazism.

The comic structure of the short story 'Sally Bowles' suggests this conflation. The narrative is based on a series of jokes revealing the contrast between Sally's supposedly worldly sexual economics and her failures at actually transacting any profit from them. Early in the story, the narrator observes that Sally is not a very effective gold digger when he sees her at a club flirting with a gentleman 'who would obviously have preferred a chat with the barman' (26). The joke here is about a presumed universal heterosexuality. Later in the plotline, when Sally is ditched by the wealthy Clive, who leaves her only a few hundred marks, she is momentarily disillusioned by the sex-money market and declares, 'I'm sick of being a whore. I'll never look at a man with money again' (51). Even Sally's meager earnings as a 'whore' with Clive bring her no joy, for she has to use the money to get an abortion for her pregnancy by Klaus. The closure of the story and the major episode after the abortion is a final joke on Sally which is set up by the narrator: her manipulation and theft by someone claiming to be an American film agent who turns out to be a sixteen-year-old, mentally disturbed Polish con man.

Beginning with the abortion, the humor around Sally's sexuality becomes more strained and points to an uneasy tension between a campy send up of gold digging and a more hostile positioning of female sexuality which is demystified and put in its place. As Freud reminds us in *Jokes and Their Relation to the Unconscious,* jokes have considerable power in the dynamics of aggression: 'A joke will allow us to exploit something ridiculous in our enemy which we could not, on account of obstacles in the way, bring forward openly or consciously' (103). In addition, these jokes are qualified by the problematic historical context and disturbing metonymic crises of Weimar politics and the emergence of the Third Reich.

First, the comedy of Sally's vampiness is explicitly reversed and inscribed within a troubling historical framework through a series of anti-Semitic references. When Sally's gold digging with Clive backfires, the effect is comic and campy. But there is another effect altogether when she describes one of her exploits in anti-Semitic terms in a later scene: 'And then there's an awful old Jew who takes me out sometimes. He's always promising to get me a contract; but he only wants to sleep with me, the old swine' (31). Later in the story, we hear an echo of this racist discourse through one of the narrator's co-lodgers. A music-hall *jodlerin*, who had been specifically identified as a Nazi, comes forward with a warning when Sally is about to go off to the nursing home for the abortion: '"The doctor isn't a Jew, I hope?" Frl. Mayr asked me sternly. "Don't you let one of those filthy Jews touch her. They always try to get a job of that kind, the beasts!"' (53). It is impossible not to hear in this language Sally's remark about the 'awful old Jew', and also her previous comic railing about men as 'beasts'. In the later story 'The Landauers', Sally makes a cameo appearance when Chris arranges, as an 'experiment' (160), a meeting with the prudish, elegant Natalia, a member of the prominent Jewish family. Sally's social lapse upon her arrival is too offensive to be amusing. 'I've been making love to a dirty old Jew producer', she says. 'I'm hoping he'll give me a contract – but no go, so far' (161). In all the postwar adaptations of this story, these episodes and dialogues are retained but the anti-Semitic slurs are cut, so that Sally is not as directly connected with the discourse prevalent in Third Reich ideology; with full postwar knowledge of Hitler's agenda, it would have been impossible to impute this casual racism to Sally without wholly alienating her character.

Sally's previous camp language and poses are similarly foiled by uncomfortable elements in the abortion subplot. When Sally tells the nurse a fake, melodramatic story about her pregnancy, she admits she does it because the real story (being jilted by Klaus) 'isn't particularly flattering' (53). Later, Sally likewise uses her customary, overdramatic language to explain her sadness and moodiness about the operation: 'Having babies makes you feel awfully primitive, like a sort of wild animal or something, defending its young' (55). Rather than amusing the narrator, this conversation disturbs him so much that he suddenly decides to leave Berlin: 'It was partly as the result of this conversation that I suddenly decided, that evening, to cancel all my lessons, leave Berlin as soon as possible, go to some place on the Baltic and try to start working' (56).

Significantly, then, the turning point in the narrator's relationship with Sally is paralleled by a turning point in his relationship to Berlin and to his writing. It is also the framework of an historical turning point; he returns in mid-July 1931 to witness the major financial débâcle and closing of the banks. The headline he sees in the newspaper reads, 'Everything Collapses!' (58). But the comedy of Sally's promiscuity has collapsed, too. When he next sees Sally, her gold digging has shifted into something more serious; she is set up in a fashionable apartment and apparently is 'moving in financial circles' (60). Their interaction is bristly and unpleasant; the 'racket' of her sexual life is no joke when it is successful. At the same time, the text's references to Nazism and the political situation escalate; the ensuing stories in *Goodbye to Berlin* move away from comedy entirely, and in the last section, the Third Reich is in power.

The encroaching Nazi reality hinted at in the 'Sally Bowles' story operates in relation to two other dynamics that problematize the camp comedy: the issue of language versus image, and the question of a normative discourse. While sexual tension is displaced by comedy/parody, the structuring jokes of the narrative retain a distinctly sexual anxiety about Sally as body and materiality. This tension is in turn displaced as a challenge to the narrator's ability to tell the story at all. The conflict shifts to the narrator's status as a writer as opposed to Sally's status as a would-be actress, gold digger, and self-proclaimed 'whore'. While the latter is a camped-up parody of Sally's poses, lies, and theatrics, the former is posited as not only 'real', but as the means of understanding Sally as comic and camp.

Mikhail Bakhtin's analysis of parody in *The Dialogic Imagination* is useful in depicting this dynamic. Here Bakhtin describes parody as language 'used "with conditions attached", every word enclosed in intonational quotation marks' (76). Looking at the novel as a '*system* of languages that mutually and ideologically interanimate each other' (47), Bakhtin suggests that parody arises to show the limitations of a certain discourse. Parody can be understood, then, as a resistance against a single, monolithic understanding of reality. It resists by suggesting repressed or unarticulated alternatives; it points to contradictory languages and meanings.

Bakhtin makes useful distinctions between the 'two languages' involved in parody. He points out that what appears in the text as parody is not the thing itself, but its representation, its style. The Sally Bowles character is not a parody of female sexuality, but the stylizations of its representations – the vamp, the *femme fatale,* Anthony Hope's Dolly. But if these are the representations being parodied, we are left with the question of what is doing the parodying. Bakhtin differentiates between 'the language being parodied' and 'the language that parodies', the positing or suggestion of a norm against which the parody is played. And this is the troubling question about the Sally character in the Isherwood story and in the subsequent adaptations: the identification of what Bakhtin calls 'an actualizing background for creating and perceiving' (75–6). While camp comedy often depends on the privileging of a gay authority and point of view – the deliberate subversion of the binary, heterosexual sign system – this is not the authority of the narrator in *Goodbye to Berlin*, whose gay identity is repressed and whose authority stems from the much more traditional status of 'author'.

In *Goodbye to Berlin,* a good deal of the comedy, in fact, involves a play of normative versus theatrical language: Sally's exaggerations and hyperboles against which the normative language of the narrator is played for effect. The narrator's position in the plot as a writer, an authority with language, is brought to the fore as topic of discussion and contention throughout this story. Chris is the deconstructor of Sally's language who can tell her coolly that her 'shocking' talk is a 'trick' forcing strangers to 'violently' approve or disapprove of her (33). Most importantly, the issue of Chris's writing precipitates the final turn in the plotline of 'Sally Bowles', the set-up with the Polish con man which occurs after the abortion and which undermines Isherwood's claim that the abortion sequence is the narrative fulcrum, the 'whole point' of 'Sally Bowles'. If the 'point' is to show that 'even the greatest disasters leave a person like Sally essentially unchanged', then what is 'unchanged' in Sally is revealed in the two remaining and troubling episodes, her argument with the narrator and his revenge.

This crisis between Sally and Chris concerns an article that Sally asks him to compose for her on 'The English Girl', an ironic self-reference to the status of the text 'Sally Bowles'. Sally rejects his article because it is 'not nearly snappy enough' (62). In the ensuing quarrel about the value of his writing, Sally's attack is vicious; his kind of artistic posing, she says, makes her 'sick' (63). The Sally that emerges in this scene is no campy showgirl, but classic castrating woman, aiming directly for the source of authority in this text, which is certainly Phallic in the Lacanian sense. 'What an utter little bitch she is', Chris comments furiously (64). After the argument, he reflects on 'The awful sexual flair women have for taking the stuffing out of a man!' (65). His rationalization about the source is no comfort: 'It was no use telling myself that Sally had the vocabulary and mentality of a twelve-year-old schoolgirl, that she was altogether comic and preposterous; it was no use – I only knew that I'd been somehow made to feel a sham' (65). But his retaliation for this threat and humiliation provides the closure for the Sally narrative; approached by the Polish con man, Chris deliberately sends him to Sally, 'perhaps, out of malice', he admits (67). As a result, Sally's threat is diminished. She is wholly fooled, sexually exploited, and robbed, thus properly punished by a 'comic' scenario which restores her to Chris's good graces by the end of the story.

One might ask what questions are answered by this happy ending. Sally, characterized by language that is consistently empty or inappropriate, is situated throughout the text as body, materiality, theatricality, but also as specific threat: 'The awful sexual flair women have for taking the stuffing out of a man!' Positioned opposite her is the narrator whose introduction of himself as a 'camera' suggests objectivity, while Sally's status as would-be actress is continually undermined as part of her comic discourse. The authority of his own language reveals the emptiness of hers. More than that, it serves as the demystification of her sexuality; Chris can locate her sexiness as a 'trick' (33) but also can know her – as she apparently cannot know herself – as someone who can be tricked with the flimsiest kind of appeal.

Sally attacks this authority of Chris as writer – an authority which in fact denies her own subjectivity, her own ability to know. But this sexual threat is diminished by an elaborate humiliation which is the final joke of a narrative that aims, after all, for comedy. The narrative can literally move across Sally's body – signified constantly as economic stake, as surface, as site of fecundity posited opposite Chris's 'fertility' as a writer – but can ultimately disavow its sexual power – strictly speaking, in Lacanian terms, its threat of lack, castration – because Sally's sexuality has been recontained by the symbolic order in which it cannot speak itself but can be spoken – here, quite literally as a joke.

Such an analysis, a fairly standard feminist semiotic treatment of this dynamic, takes this study outside the realm of materialist study and into a radically ahistorical framework. I would instead relocate this argument within the 1930s and Isherwood's group of gay exiles by considering Isherwood's appeal to a modern sensibility familiar with a particular apparatus and spectatorship: 'I am a camera'. The dynamics outlined above, of body/image versus narrative authority, and female sexual threat disavowed by punishment or humiliation, parallel feminist film theory's descriptions of classic Hollywood cinema. In Laura Mulvey's famous psychoanalytic formulation, the woman in this cinema functions as the image across which the authoritative male narrative is constructed (11–12). For my own purposes, the psychoanalytic framework is not as useful as a materialist one, but it can provide evidence of how Isherwood's experience with the 'good heter stuff' of mainstream cinema influenced his constitution of the vampy Sally Bowles.

In *Lions and Shadows*, Isherwood describes himself not just as a 'born film fan' but as a writer whose methodology has clearly been influenced by this medium. The cinema, he says, coincides with his fascination for 'the outward appearance of people – their facial expressions, their gestures, their walk, their nervous tricks', and in imagining a fictional scene, 'it is simplest to project it on to an imaginary screen. A practised cinema-goer will be able to do this quite easily' (85–6). Moreover, Isherwood had accumulated some direct experience with filmmaking by the time he was writing *Goodbye to Berlin*. He had taken a short-lived job as an extra for a film at Lasky Studios during his university days, and in 1933–4 wrote the screenplay for Berthold Viertel's *The Little Friend* (an opportunity arranged by Jean Ross). His friendship with Viertel, a Hollywood director, led him to further screenplay work with MGM and eventually with Warner Brothers and Paramount on films such as *Rage in Heaven* (1941), *A Woman's Face* (1941), and *Crossroads* (1942). By choosing to remain in major studios rather than work with experimental or avant-garde filmmakers, Isherwood was restricted by the Production Code of the Motion Picture Producers and Distributors Association in those days, and thus committed to an institutionalized censorship of the topic of his own sexual identity.

His situation here is not unique. As Richard Dyer and others have pointed out, the Hollywood business of illusion making and role playing has special relevance for the gay who often must play straight as a survival tactic. Cinema provides more subversive tactics as well, as Dyer explains: 'We could pilfer from straight society's images on the screen such that would help us build up a subculture' (1–2). Camp is of course a major discourse in this subculture, and has important connections to cinema, not only in its openly subversive moments but with the possibility of a campy reading-against-the-grain of classic film. An example of this kind of reading actually occurs in 'Sally Bowles', when Sally and Chris go to see 'a film about a girl who sacrificed her stage career for the sake of a Great Love, Home and Children. We laughed so much that we had to leave before the end' (42).

Sally Bowles as a camp figure has affinities to the excesses of Mae West, for example, but while the 'too-muchness' of West points ironically to artificial gender construction, the pointing is done with her own authority. In contrast, the character Sally Bowles operates as parodic and excessive in relationship to *another* authority or 'actualizing background' – the narrator of *Goodbye to Berlin*. Her comic power to unsettle gender/sex boundaries is displaced back to a male authorship that has been organized as more 'real' than hers – and certainly more politically valid. Leo Bersani has suggested that all male camp parody may paradoxically both help deconstruct gender images but also give 'vent to the hostility toward women that probably afflicts every male (and which male heterosexuals have of course expressed in infinitely nastier and more effective ways)' (1987: 208).

Like the carnivalesque grotesque which is a traditional part of camp humor, Sally is the character who repeatedly makes a spectacle of herself, whether in her grand entrances and shocking announcements, or with her painted green fingernails and odd costumes: 'Everybody stared at Sally, in her canary yellow beret and shabby fur coat, like the skin of a mangy old dog' (44). As a sexual construction, she often shows the seams: 'She had very large brown eyes', the narrator relates upon first meeting Sally, 'which should have been darker, to match her hair and the pencil she used for her eyebrows' (22). While the green fingernails and mangy coat may only suggest Sally's eccentricity, she is described at other times in much harsher terms: 'I noticed how old her hands looked in the lamplight. They were nervous, veined and very thin – the hands of a middle-aged woman. The green finger-nails seemed not to belong to them at all; to have settled on them by chance – like hard, bright, ugly little beetles' (29). When Sally first suspects she is pregnant, she drinks so much that 'sometimes her eyes looked awful, as though they had been boiled. Every day the layer of make-up on her face seemed to get thicker' (46). It is not difficult to find in these passages traditional Western cultural dread of female biology. Certainly this play of the grotesque, as comic and/or threatening, is climaxed by Sally's pregnancy, abortion, and most of all, her subsequent expression of a wish for the child, threatening to enact the grotesquery of pregnancy. This is the conversation which most dramatically interrupts the text, sending the narrator out of the city and beginning the break in his relationship with Sally.

Sally's ambivalence as a camp construction becomes most disquieting in its relationship to the exaggerating, posturing, threatening political problem which is the subtext of *Goodbye to Berlin*: Nazism. For while the narrator represents a linguistic and phallic norm against which Sally is drawn and disavowed as body and threat, a parallel dynamic operates in regard to the narrator's relationship to the other developing spectacle in these stories, the rise of the Third Reich.

Here, too, the narrator is established not just as objective observer but as political norm against which Nazism is characterized as morally and physically grotesque. The Nazi *jodlerin* Frl. Mayr, who makes the anti-Semitic remark about doctors and abortions, is described by Isherwood's narrator with specific physical detail: 'The muscles of Frl. Mayr's nude fleshy arms ripple unappetisingly', he tells us (9). In the next scene she listens with sadistic glee as the Jewish woman downstairs is beaten by her boyfriend because of Frl. Mayr's fraudulent interference (11). In 'On Ruegen Island', the story immediately following 'Sally Bowles', the Nazi menace is the 'ferrety' doctor at the beach who uses scientific justifications for putting away non-Aryans and all 'criminal' types, including the young working-class Otto, perhaps because of his homosexuality (89). In the final two sections of *Goodbye to Berlin*, 'The Landauers' and 'A

Berlin Diary (Winter 1932–3)', the hints of grotesquery erupt into actual violence as the narrator witnesses anti-Jewish riots and harassment, sees Nazi street violence, and loses his friend Bernhard Landauer to Nazi persecution.

Two factors in the structure of *Goodbye to Berlin* link the Sally Bowles character with Nazism as parallel spectacles that first seem only 'comic and preposterous'. First, though the sketches are not presented in strict chronological order, there is a progression from the first 'Diary' section of 1930 to the last 'Diary' of 1932–3, and the interweaving events of the stories in between are chronologically related. 'On Ruegen Island', for example, is clearly the story of the months when Chris had left Berlin after Sally's abortion, related in 'Sally Bowles'. In this structuring, it is also clear that the two stories 'Sally Bowles' and 'The Landauers' overlap, or are parallel stories; Sally makes her cameo appearance in the latter story and shocks Natalia with her sexuality and her anti-Semitism. This intertextual relationship, and the connecting narrative event of Sally's meeting with Natalia, underscores the parallel relationship of two threatening phenomena witnessed by the narrator – Sally Bowles and the development of Nazism and anti-Semitism. Persecution of Jews, the most obvious sign of the development of Nazism in Berlin, is also the element closely connected to Sally's most unflattering characteristics: her political apathy/ignorance, as seen in her bored response to the political funeral (48–9), her tendency to stereotype and exaggerate, and her language which aims at effect rather than meaning.

An incident in 'The Nowaks' demonstrates this latter characteristic as an anti-Semitic strategy. Frau Nowak engages in some clichés about her Jewish tailor which obviously reflect anti-Jewish propaganda, but she does not understand the implications of what she is saying: 'When Hitler comes, he'll show these Jews a thing or two. They won't be so cheeky then', she says. The narrator points out that 'when Hitler comes', he will remove her neighbor altogether. She seems startled – though, ironically, for entirely selfish reasons: 'Oh, I shouldn't like that to happen. After all, he makes very good clothes' (117).

This gap between surface effect (or performance) and meaning is the second major link between the camp parody and comedy of 'Sally Bowles' and the positioning of Nazism in the last two sections of *Goodbye to Berlin*. The escalating violence becomes progressively unreal as history and comprehensible only as spectacle – like film spectacle, in fact, overdramatic, staged, not to be taken seriously. When the narrator learns of a street shooting that had taken place while he was at Bernhard's lawn party, he understands its impact as particularly cinematic and even comic in its combination of high drama and incongruity: 'I thought of our party lying out there on the lawn by the lake, drinking our claret-cup while the gramophone played; and of that police-officer, revolver in hand, stumbling mortally wounded up the cinema steps to fall dead at the feet of a cardboard figure advertising a comic film' (177). Like a Hollywood gangster, the policeman falls against a cardboard backdrop; here, the backdrop, an advertisement, is part of a 'real' scenario publicizing a popular illusion. Yet the drama on the street exceeds the drama of what is shown on the screen, so the boundaries of illusion/reality are deliberately blurred.

The problem is that the illusion business of the Nazis, like the illusion business of cinema, seems too overblown and even self-parodic to be taken seriously. In the next sequence, the narrator tries to warn Bernhard about the Nazis. However, the menacing letter which Bernhard has received is couched in too many Hollywood-gangster clichés to alarm him: 'We are going to settle the score with you and your uncle and all the other filthy Jews. We give you twenty-four hours to leave Germany' (178). Bernhard's response is to laugh.

The narrator cautions Bernhard that there is more to the Nazis than comic overdramatization: 'The Nazis may write like schoolboys, but they're capable of anything. That's just why they're so dangerous. People laugh at them, right up to the last moment' (179). This passage uncomfortably echoes the narrator's previous description of the language of Sally Bowles: 'Sally had the vocabulary and mentality of a twelve-year-old schoolgirl'. The subsequent description of the Nazis in this later story confirms the narrator's opinion of their dangerous, innocuous effect. The SA boys in uniform stand outside a Jewish department store to urge a boycott: 'The boys were quite polite, grinning, making jokes among themselves. Little knots of passers-by collected to watch the performance – interested, amused or merely apathetic' (183).

In the final sketch, 'Berlin Diary (Winter 1932–33)', Isherwood makes an explicit connection between the dynamics of spectatorship and the development of the Third Reich. Describing the fascinated crowds watching the obviously fake wrestling match at the fairgrounds, the narrator concludes, 'The political moral is certainly depressing: these people could be made to believe in anybody or anything' (190). But spectatorship involves more than gullibility, as the next sequences make clear. Witnessing shootings, riots, and the harassment of Jews on the street almost daily, spectators grow progressively more numb, passive, less surprised. During one incident in which a crowd sees a young man beaten by the Nazis, the narrator notices that 'They seemed surprised, but not particularly shocked – this sort of thing happens too often, nowadays' (201). The cushioning of this 'shock' is directly related to Walter Benjamin's concept of the shocks of modernity in relation to the camera; a particular mode of perception has developed, and what has become incomprehensible as politics or history is comprehensible as the witnessing of a spectacle.

In this last 'Diary', brief, separate incidents are described without connecting narrative, like separate shots or photographs. In the final paragraphs, describing the narrator's last day in Berlin, the pleasant sight of the Kleiststrasse seems to contradict history: 'The sun shines, and Hitler is master of this city'. The city is located not in real time, but as its own representation: the people and streets have 'striking resemblance to something one remembers as normal and pleasant in the past – like a very good photograph'. The concluding sentences more explicitly deny history: 'No. Even now I can't altogether believe that any of this has really happened ...' (207).

Postwar struggles to understand Nazism in terms of performance and spectatorship, the triumph of image over language, are evident in subsequent adaptations of *Goodbye to Berlin*. In the 1972 Fosse film, Sally Bowles is part of the spectacle on-stage which visually 'mirrors' the swastika armbands in the audience. Isherwood's construction of Sally is a great deal more more complex. Fashioned in the comic, parodic strategies of camp, this character is certainly no straightforward, mirror image of the history Isherwood witnessed in the 1930s in Berlin. But she is also situated as the threat of image over language, in an uneasy parallel with Nazi strategy, and her power must be disavowed with a laugh that grows more uneasy through the *Berlin* stories and the adaptations. Isherwood's project to produce 'good heter stuff' thus crosses larger, multiple cultural projects dealing with sexual and historical anxieties.

NOTES

1. Isherwood reports that in those days, the world was dualistically divided between their own allies versus 'The Others' – who could be, for example, the 'mere merchants' who might decline to publish one's books. See *Christopher and His Kind*, 80. Also see Isherwood's description of his conscious rejection of heterosexuality in his youth and his characterization of his resistance against 'the will of Nearly Everybody', 12.
2. See Caudwell, 28, and Isherwood, *Christopher and His Kind*, 60–1.
3. As Peter Thomas (1976: 130) puts it, 'The Nazi reality is Camp without comedy'.

REFERENCES

Bakhtin, Mikhail, *The Dialogic Imagination: Four Essays*, ed. Michael Holquist, Austin: U of Texas P, 1981.
Bowles, Paul, *Without Stopping*, New York: Peter Owen, 1972.
Caudwell, Sarah, 'Reply to Berlin', *The New Statesman*, 3 October 1986, 28–9.
Dyer, Richard, 'Introduction', in Richard Dyer (ed.), *Gays and Film*, New York: Zoetrope, 1984.
Freud, Sigmund, *Jokes and Their Relation to the Unconscious*, trans. James Strachey, New York: Norton, 1960.
Fryer, Jonathan, *Isherwood: A Biography of Christopher Isherwood*, New York: Doubleday, 1978.
Isherwood, Christopher, *Berlin Stories: The Last of Mr. Norris and Goodbye to Berlin*, New York: New Directions, 1954.
——, *Christopher and His Kind, 1929–1939*, New York: Farrar, Straus & Giroux, 1976.
——, *Lions and Shadows* (1947), New York: Pegasus, 1969.
Johnstone, Iain, 'The Real Sally Bowles', *Folio* Autumn 1975, 32–8.
Lehmann, John, *Christopher Isherwood: A Personal Memoir*, New York: Henry Holt, 1987.
Mulvey, Laura, 'Visual Pleasure and Narrative Cinema', *Screen* 16, 1975, 6–18.
Spender, Stephen, 'On Being a Ghost in Isherwood's Berlin', *Mademoiselle*, September 1974, 138–9+.
Stoop, Norma McLain, 'Christopher Isherwood: A Meeting by Another River', *After Dark* 7, 1985, 60–5.
Wilson, Colin, 'An Integrity Born of Hope: Notes on Christopher Isherwood', *Twentieth-Century Literature* 22, 1976, 312–31.

16

GENDERFUCK:
THE LAW OF THE DILDO

June L. Reich

> To revolt outright against patriarchy is to affirm its authority. To right-
> eously confront it is to see patriarchy as a monolithic whole free of
> contradiction and more powerful than it is. Such righteousness means denial
> that patriarchy is part of us, and thus forces us to define ourselves *in contrast
> to*. Better to acknowledge patriarchy and undermine from within, gently
> erode, recognize discrepancies, play with the roles, the language and the
> symbols, and let the play itself rob them of their terrifying power. (Carol
> LeMasters, 28)

> Alex extracted her [Michael's] cock. Kay was already at her elbow with a
> can of Crisco and a towel. 'Room service', she grinned. 'Oh, yeah, slick it up,
> stud, get that big fuckpole ready to do that fine piece a favor. Gonna fuck
> that slut right offa those high-heeled shoes'. (Pat Califia, 120)

This is an essay on boys and girls, or those who would-be-boys and those who
would-be-girls. It's the parable of genderfuck, a little prick living in a capitalist,
postmodern world.

Genderfuck: Susie Bright says, 'When we want to compliment someone's
visual menu, we say "genderfuck" instead of androgynous' (9). She wrote this
in 1989, in her 'Toys For Us' column of the fifth-anniversary issue of *On Our
Backs*. Although she was talking about fashion, not theory, her definition
condenses a history of discourse and materialism that touches on how we live
our lives as queers and straights, girls and boys, and consumers of culture.

In the 'Toys for Us' essay, 'A Star is Porn', Bright predicted for the gay or
'post gay' 1990s a sexual liberation theme of 'Get Over Yourself' (8). What is

Originally published in *Discourse*, 15:1, Fall 1992.

this 'get over yourself' call to arms? The end of identity politics? Yes. Are we defined by who we are, or by what communities we are part of? No . . . 'To get over yourself' is counter-identity politics. It's the modus operandi: we are defined not by who we are but by what we do. This is effectively a politics of performance. It neither fixes nor denies specific sexual and gendered identifications but accomplishes something else. This paper is an exploration of the imperative of that something else.

As many theorists have argued, sexuality and gender are interrelated but distinctive cultural constructions, and sexuality, in particular, must be thought of as irreducible to gender.[1] There are contradictions that inhere, let's say, in the difference between myself in the shower (as a woman – gendered) and myself in bed (as a femme – sexualized) that need to be articulated through a theory of genderfuck, which 'deconstructs' the psychoanalytic concept of difference without subscribing to any heterosexist or anatomical truths about the relations of sex to gender (you remember the binarisms, male = masculine, female = feminine, masculine = aggressive, feminine = passive, etc.) Instead, genderfuck structures meaning in a symbol-performance matrix that crosses through sex and gender and destabilizes the boundaries of our recognition of sex, gender, and sexual practice.

In the fall of 1989, already out as a lesbian and a femme, I began coming out as a 'genderfucker'. What this means, basically, is that I began a reinvigorated reading of the discontinuity between sex and gender, during sex, in my performance as a 'girl' on the streets, and in intellectual pursuits in the realms of phallogocentrism.

Although I don't want to theorize lesbian sexuality as the privileged site of genderfuck and feminist political practice, I understand genderfuck most clearly within the context of butch/femme role playing. Butch/femme offers a rich history for talking about bodies, identities, and agential politics in a way that hopefully furthers the work of breaking down multiple oppressions.

BUTCH/FEMME HISTORY: CONDENSED

Butch/femme has been a recognizable lesbian practice for a very long time. Masculine and feminine women couples historically have been recognized as lesbians when less conspicuous sisters passed (as straights, or unnoticed) on the streets. Consequently, because of their visual recognizability, butch/femme codes have enjoyed various sociopolitical meanings. In the 1950s, with underground lesbian social organizations (like the Daughters of Bilitis) and publications beginning surreptitious discussions about sex, butch/femme was often criticized for not conforming with mainstream fashion. Joan Nestle has eloquently documented the 1950s as, among other things, assimilationist times for lesbians:

> Butch-femme was an erotic partnership serving both as a conspicuous flag of rebellion and as an intimate exploration of women's sexuality. It

was not an accident that butch-femme couples suffered the most street abuse and provoked more assimilated or closeted Lesbians to plead with them not to be so obvious ...

The butch-femme couple embarrassed other Lesbians (and still does) because they made Lesbians culturally visible, a terrifying act for the 1950s ... The desire for passing, combined with the radical work of survival that the *Ladder* [published from 1956 to 1972] was undertaking, was a paradox created by the America of the fifties ... To survive meant to take a public stance of societal cleanliness. But in the pages of the journal itself all dimensions of Lesbian life were explored including butch-femme relationships. The *Ladder* brought off a unique balancing act for the 1950s. It gave nourishment to a secret and subversive life while it flew the flag of assimilation. (101–2)

Nestle's essay, which she says took forty years to write, is part of a huge body of literature and sweat that foregrounds the conflicts between lesbianism and feminism. In *Daring to Be Bad: Radical Feminism in America, 1967–1975,* Alice Echols argues that lesbianism from the beginning constituted a '"problem" for feminism':

Until late 1969, opponents of women's liberation were more apt to raise the issue of lesbianism than were many radical feminists – many of whom were initially befuddled by the conjoining of these seemingly disparate issues. Of course, some radical feminists did allude to sexual preference, if only obliquely in the context of sexual liberation. While most early radical feminists believed that the sexual revolution of the '60s was in many respects more exploitative than liberating, they nonetheless envisioned feminism dismantling the edifice of sexual repression ...

But many radical feminists, especially those who viewed women's liberation and sexual liberation as mutually exclusive, were often skittish if not hostile toward lesbianism. Most commonly, they dismissed lesbianism as sexual rather than political. Thus Roxanne Dunbar of Cell 16 [an early radical feminist group] argued that the task of feminism was to get women out of bed rather than change the gender of their partners ... A number of radical feminist agreed [also] that lesbians were too attached to sex roles, in the form of butch-femme roles, to be likely or desirable recruits to feminism. Many also feared that lesbianism could become a refuge from feminist activism.

But at the same time that many radical feminists were rushing to disassociate feminism from lesbianism, many others – both politicoes and radical feminists – were discovering that they felt sexually attracted toward one another ... (211–12)

Eventually a strain of feminism and lesbianism cohered to become a lesbian-feminist movement (part of cultural feminism, which eventually superseded radical feminism as a mainstream political institution). This of course is not the end of the story (I still haven't entered the lesbian-feminist debate or even come out yet). Butch/femme continued to be disparaged, through the 1970s and 1980s, especially, in what has come to be known as the 'sex wars' (see, for example, Vance). Arguing that butch/femme role-playing was 'heteropatriarchal' and oppressive to women, cultural feminists began a campaign of sexual censorship, based on a philosophy that sexual representations and sex itself were transparent agents of women's oppression (rather than complex cultural expressions). Butch/femme became to some symbolic extent more dangerous than it had in the 1950s, at least in terms of feminist debate: role-playing became s&m (a conflation that distorts a continuum of sexual practices), and s&m was vilifed. But by this time, the pornographic and erotic works of lesbians, and discussions of their meanings and values, became more public; and in the 1980s popular critical theories by and for a sophisticated 'queer' audience began popping up, so that the semiotics of fashion and sex codes, postmodernism, and a host of other topics enjoyed a vogue that is still prevalent. (I came out by this time.)[2]

FRAMING THE PHALLUS

I begin my theory of genderfuck with the dildo. It is, in fact, my *raison d'être,* my personal philosophy, akin to religion. But before I follow this all-important theoretical vein, I would like to frame the phallus in its psychoanalytic (Lacanian) and literary contexts, briefly, in order to engage the slippery theoretical practice of reading and writing the body.

The phallus, broadly speaking, forces a subject into the Symbolic, the realm of language, signification, and culture. In theory it is not an object, or an organ, but an experience of difference (even, or especially, primary sexual difference), initiating a subject into desire, which is an experience of lack. The phallus, as 'point zero' in psychoanalytic theory, determines meaning by filling in absences, covering over the split it creates between object and concept. The logic of signification demands that a concept and object be identical to one another. And yet the phallus, as the determining figure in signification, like a zero, does not really exist. The zero institutes the process of numerical progression, but it signifies nothing. It assures, however, that $1 = 1$ because of its place/function as zero ($1 + 0 = 1$; but 1 is, nevertheless, the second point on the number line, and is therefore always already displaced) (Miller; for more on 'suture', see also Heath). Through a theoretically analogous process, the phallus signifies a pretended or fantasmatic unity, suturing object and concept in a dialectical relationship with a subject.

Unity could be thought of as a consensus of meaning, or of referentiality. In the traffic of signifiers and signifieds, there is potentially unlimited play that prevents meaning from settling into one cozy, specific definition. But, as the process of interpretation forces an inevitable rest at signified, political interference at the point of representation is critical. The phallus has for too long been associated with being or not being the penis (this is heterosexism), even in abstract mathematical theory, and often most vehemently when this connection is being disavowed (see Gayle Rubin's critique of psychoanalysis). In this respect, the phallus can deconstruct itself into total nothingness without upsetting sex/gender binarisms and privileging male constructions of desire. If it is possible, through genderfuck, however, to interrupt the referentiality of the phallus, a theory of subjectivity and desire could be expounded without making phallogocentrism an accusation of exclusive (that is, male-centered) practice, but one process (among many) that produces meaning and knowledge. Because, as I hope to expose, women already possess the phallus, though how, where, why, and to what extent we do is hotly contested.

THE DILDO*

(*Dildos are measured from their bases to their heads, making allowances for slight loss in length if they are to be used with a harness. I would appreciate if this system were applied to my essay when determining its desirability. Please measure concepts from base of page to header, and observe safe reading practices when moving from one section to another. Borders are permeable.)

The question fueling this investigation of genderfuck is: 'What is the difference between a woman with a strap-on and a man?' Assuming that the symbolic man wants to fuck and not be fucked (which I would assume makes him femme), I would argue that in a libidinal economy there is no structural difference. Butch/femme relations are constructed around difference, or heterosexuality, if you like (though this is not to say 'straight' sex).

'Subject positions' have consumed much recent feminist theory, building on psychoanalytic and ideological critiques in order to elucidate a point from where women can act without being erased or posited as non-subjects, or the negative of the 'masculine'. Sue-Ellen Case, in 'Toward a Butch-Femme Aesthetic', argues that butch-femme subject positions allow an articulation of agency in a way heterosexual female positions fail to. Beginning with Teresa de Lauretis's 'feminist subject', who accomplishes a 'sense of self-determination at the micropolitical level' (1988, rpt. 1989: 282), Case proposes for feminism coupled butch-femme subjects that 'do not impale themselves on the poles of sexual difference or metaphysical values, but constantly seduce the sign system, through flirtation and inconstancy into the light fondle of artifice, replacing the Lacanian slash with a lesbian bar' (283). Taking up Case's aesthetic argument, I would like to forward the coupled butch-femme subject into the explicit realm of the phallic.

Case's aesthetic hinges on artifice and the discourse/performance of camp. She argues first that psychoanalysis has hegemonically consigned femininity to a passive performance of 'masquerade', a position that is purely negative excess. Then, building upon the history of feminist masquerade theories themselves based on Joan Rivière's watershed reading of a frigid intellectual woman patient, Case maintains that feminine masquerade remains passive only within the construct of assumed heterosexuality. Rivière's argument is this: the intellectual frigid woman, having symbolically castrated her father by virtue of her intellectual acumen, assumes feminine behavior as a reaction-formation against this taboo. Rivière notes that 'heterosexual women don't claim possession [of the penis] openly, but through reaction formations; whereas the homosexual women openly display their possession of the penis and count on the males' recognition of defeat' (cited in Case 1988, rpt. 1989: 291). Case maintains that this open display is 'consciously played out in butch-femme roles':

> The butch is the lesbian woman who proudly displays the possession of the penis, while the femme takes on the compensatory masquerade of womanliness. The femme however, foregrounds her masquerade by playing to a butch, another woman in a role; likewise, the butch exhibits her penis to a woman who is playing the role of compensatory castration ... [Because] there is no referent [for the penis] in sight, the fictions of penis and castration become ironized and 'camped up' ... These women play on the phallic economy rather than to it. (291)

Heterosexual masquerade theories stabilize the feminine = passive/masculine = active equation in biological terms, so that 'women' are only able to assume an active position by taking on a male perspective. This has proven to be problematic for feminist theorists, who have been forced to argue, as a logical consequence, that active pleasure can only be taken by men or women acting like men. A way out of this bind has been to foreground, by 'camping it up', the irony of the masculine and feminine positions themselves, so that the cultural constructions of gender are highlighted. Case maintains that in butch = femme camp, both partners are performers, because the penis is conspicuously absent and women are playing to each other. And while she maintains, rightfully so, that this move both highlights and subverts cultural constructs of gender, it does not alter the masquerade, which necessitates a *distance* between a performer herself (whatever that is – even if it is argued that there is no essential self) and the construct she performs. While the players have shifted from male-female (penis present) to butch-femme (penis absent), the distance between the gendered body and sexual role playing has remained structurally equal. I would like to argue that foregrounding the distance between the phallus and *its* performance as penis or dildo would ironize the prescriptive constructs of femininity and masculinity without necessarily distancing the gendered body from its sexual materiality in performance. This strategy hopefully reinstates an embodiment that is sorely lacking in current deconstructive and performative theories.

Case's definition of the butch-femme subject position bears repeating here, because it is at this juncture that I would like to push some of its consequences: 'These are not split subjects, suffering the torments of dominant ideology. They are coupled ones that do not impale themselves on the poles of sexual difference or metaphysical values ...' (283). For one thing, her definition assumes an awareness about butch-femme relations that is necessary for camp but not always the lived experience of many butch and femme women. I find it interesting that most butch women I've talked with knew themselves as lesbians first and women second, while many femmes understood their identity foremost as womanly and most often tried on hetero relationships before acting on their lesbian desires. Furthermore, Case's couple dances around penetration, the phallic act *par excellence*. She has ignored the dildo, and what our dynamic duo may be doing offstage, for a micropolitically safe space outside ideology. I am not arguing that this space doesn't exist or isn't useful (it's essential) for political change, but I wonder about what is glossed in the theoretics, specifically concerning the symbolic politics of penetration, fucking, phallic aggression, etc.

As a prosthesis, the dildo has often been accused of being the literalization of women's lack, a substitute penis, the object of women's desire. Desire for an other is confused with heterosexuality so-called[3] when the penis is the referent for the phallus, and the dildo becomes a subordinate and stand-in for man. Consequently, lesbian penetration is confused with heterosexual so-called practice, rather than being constituted as a unique, or different, instance of meaning. This misunderstanding not only fuels straight misconceptions of lesbianism but has led to censorship within the feminist community, mostly by Lesbian Separatists who outlaw s&m practices at women-only functions, and anti-pornography feminists, who claim in various degrees that sex hurts women.

The dildo is a sutured phallus. Quite literally. Symbolically, however, it could be conceived of as *the* phallus. The dildo, by itself, is a funny-looking piece of molded silicone or rubber. But in context, it is a powerful fucker. It is the law of the Daddy Butch. As a phallus, it assures difference without essentializing gender. And, I would argue, it could irreparably alter any inter-sex (or gendered) relations when the libidinal paradigm is shifted from gender-identity to sexuality-performance. When we inspect the dildoed-girl and the dicked-boy for meaningful differences, I must insist that there is some substantive difference between them (there is a preference in who we take to bed, for instance). The consequence of this difference is the gendering of desire, since in structural terms the two figures are the same. So I might offer the hypothesis that 'boys' like to fuck and 'girls' like to be fucked and situate these two positions, masculine and feminine, as extremes or poles of a gender/sexuality spectrum. The anatomical binarism male-female figures here as a kind of limit-text, one which works to undermine genderfuck if we insist on recognizing biological 'realness' ('naturalness') on the one hand, but which genderfucks if 'realness' (as defined in *Paris Is Burning*)[4] works strictly at the level of the performance of dominant stereotypes without 'corresponding' genitalia revealed. To my mind, these two situations figure the extremes of the anatomical axis.

A word about transsexuality: it works to stabilize the old sex/gender system by insisting on the dominant correspondence between gendered desire and biological sex. The feelings of acute discontinuity that lead to cosmetic alternation need theorizing apart from genderfuck. Pepper LaBajia, reigning Mother of the House of LaBajia and somewhat of a superstar because of the box-office success of *Paris Is Burning*, described the politics of anatomy best when she said she never wanted a sex-change. A vagina is no guarantee of security or happiness.

The consequences of the dildo-as-phallus are potentially far reaching for emancipating theory from the appeal to Truth. At the very least, the dildo schema announces the arbitrariness of the hegemonic phallus = penis construction, while attending to the rigid logic of the phallic economy. At its most radical, the dildo, as an equal-opportunity accessory, and as a simulacrum (an object circulating without origin), undermines the penis as a meaningfully stable organ, denaturalizing the body without erasing its materiality.

Using the dildo as an interpretive as well as a sexual device opens the field of identification to all sorts of contradictory constructions. My femininity, for example, is an instance of drag performance (that is, genderfucked). Not only are there positions for feminine women and masculine men, manly women and womanly men (these can be accomplished through masquerade theories), there is also space for queer or straight butch and femme identities that traverse the theoretically spacialized continuum more than once. For instance, I know a butch woman who likes to be penetrated by a butch lover, pretending they are both gay men. Why should that be perverse?

CAMP: 'A HOLIDAY FOR CONSENTING ADULTS'[5]

> It's embarrassing to be solemn and treatise-like about Camp. One runs the risk of having, oneself produced a very inferior piece of Camp. (Sontag 1964b, rpt. 1966: 277)

My genderfuck sensibility has me questioning the self-conscious performance of virtually everyone I see on the streets or on the bus, although I am aware that not only are not many of these folks queer, gay, or straight, they probably have no notion of how radically different the economy of their desires would be in a relation of dildoic-phallic signification. In an effort to keep this paradigm in perspective, then, I will attempt a shift from the reading to the writing of the body. Both are discursive acts, public in nature but privatized ideologically. Reading practices generally are used in performative theories, but I think writing demands a specificity that makes generalizing the body more difficult. It also constructs the micropolitically safe space needed for positive agential politics.

I will contextualize reading/writing by utilizing butch/femme relations once again. As a femme, I am in a privileged position in relation to dominant culture because, while my object-choice may be thought to be perverse, my performance of myself is allied with dominant notions of femininity. My butch lover, on the other hand, constructs herself as a boy. To reconcile this dominant contradiction I would insist that she is a boy, in bed, and perhaps in varying degrees on the streets. This turns upside down not only cultural binarisms of sex and gender in sexual relationships, but also the dominant assumptions of who has the power to inscribe meaning on the bodies of others. As a femme, I do the writing, and I read, insuring not only my own non-erasure but also authorizing the noncontradiction of a butch's gender/sexual performance.

Yet performative politics are cooptable, or at least subject to easy misinterpretation. How is my femininity different than that of the straight woman with little self-consciousness of her gendered construction; or, for that matter, what difference does it make if dominant culture can read her and me as essentially the same?

The language of performance, critical to the theoretics of postmodern bodies, usually constructs subject and object as spectator (reader) and performer (read) in a dualism that either forecloses or negativizes agentic possibilities. Without an alternative critical language, however, theories of performance are still preferable to those of identity. The crux of agentic possibility in performative language could be thought of as 'presence', where the apparent paradox of mimesis, or the representation of the construction of representation (a self-conscious performance) is worked out within the limits of 'verisimilitude', or what I have been calling 'realness'. Mimicry problematizes the real by representing both the presence and absence of a construction. It's hard to keep it up, though, as meaning is an excess, an effect the performer cannot control.

An aesthetics of pleasure, more precisely, offers no guaranteed effects, but involves a 'leap of faith', a reading and writing that must take place with the consent of subjects. The dildo performance is 'queer' not because it is part of gay or lesbian sex but because it doesn't respect the distinctions of a hetero/homosexual dichotomy. What limits an anything-goes in interpretation, however, is a politics of radical materiality, where the construction of the semiotic system on the body is accounted for.

Does the genderfuck performance, a mimicry, unmask the psychoanalytic constructions of feminine and masculine sexuality? The answer, it seems, relies on the referential position of the phallus. At the very least, repositioning the phallus as dildo radically alters the meanings of 'being' and 'having' in such a way that the constructions of sexuality cannot be reducible to anatomy, even though we can acknowledge primary sexual difference. The point is that difference, in itself, signifies nothing but needs an interpretation to effect meaning.

To ask, once again, some rude but important questions: does the site of woman's primary sexual difference constitute a lack or is it just a vagina? What does a woman with a vagina and with a dildo represent? A man, a masculine woman, the denaturalization of masculinity? If phallic homosexual practice were a mimicry of heterosexual genital-to-genital practice (and it could be conceived this way without being derogatory), its perversion is not the performative act but the subversion of the construction that naturalizes or normalizes heterosexual so-called practice. Sexual practices are mimicry, differenced from themselves as concepts and objects. We are sutured, dildoed folks.

Camp is the celebration of passionate failures. The triumph of theatricality over substance, it is cynical, ironic, sentimental, pleasure-seeking, naively inno-cent, and corrupting. More importantly, it accomplishes more than mere inver-sion and duplicity; it alters traditional sensibilities altogether. Sontag (1964b, rpt. 1966) fingers a few really insightful aspects of camp, which I would sum up if I were only as erudite:

> 34. Camp taste turns its back on the good-bad axis of ordinary aesthetic judgment. Camp doesn't reverse things. It doesn't argue that the good is bad, or the bad is good. What it does is to offer for art (and life) a different – a supplementary [!] – set of values. (286)
>
> 55. Camp taste is, above all, a mode of enjoyment, of appreciation – not judgment. Camp is generous. It wants to enjoy. It only seems like malice, cynicism. (Or if it is cynicism, it's not a ruthless but a sweet cynicism.) Camp taste doesn't propose that it is in bad taste to be serious; it doesn't sneer at someone who succeeds in being seriously dramatic. What it does is to find the success in certain passionate failures.
>
> 56. Camp taste is a kind of love, love for human nature. It relishes, rather than judges, the little triumphs and awkward intensities of 'character' ... Camp taste identifes with what it is enjoying. People who share this sensibility are not laughing at the thing they label as 'a camp', they're enjoying it. Camp is a tender feeling. (291–2)

Camp is also very homosexual; while it's not exclusively so, it was, as Case says, born in the closet (287). Where Sontag fails to grasp the political ramifi-cations of camp, many gay theorists have picked it up. I hope genderfuck will be seen as another quixotic incarnation.

In formulating my genderfuck theory I had three options, as I saw it, in camp territory: (1) the dildo most certainly is camp. Following this argument led me smack into Sue-Ellen Case's lap (not a bad place to be, I should think). The dildo is nothing if not pure artifice, a 'supplement' to the 'natural' body. With butch/femme, 'a strategy of appearances replaces a claim to truth. Thus, butch-femme roles evade the notion of "the female body" as it predominates in feminist theory, dragging along its Freudian baggage and scopophilic transub-stantiation. These roles are played in signs themselves and not in ontologies. Seduction, as a dramatic action, transforms all of these seeming realities into semiotic play' (297). However, I wanted to reclaim *some* body (anybody) and also challenge lesbianism as theory. So the dildo as camp isn't the whole picture, as I see it.

This brings me to (2) the penis as a camp object. As a dyke with no grudge against boys, I have little trouble with this deduction. By arguing that the dildo is more phallic than the penis, the male organ (to use a Senate Judiciary Committee turn-of-phrase) is somewhat depleted of its powers. In the light of the dildo it is not hard to see the penis as another masquerade of the phallus, ready-made with a 'dildo envy' complex, and to subsequently foreground cultural constructions of masculinity.

And (3) the phallus itself must be camp, in relation to the dildo and in relation to itself. Here is the triumph of 'instant character' over content, and also passionate failure. When the dildo denudes the penis it reincarnates the phallus in its image, not vice versa. Dildo phallocracy maintains that dildo, penis, and phallus are all camp entities.

GENDERFUCK

Genderfuck could be said to be the effect of unstable signifying practices in a libidinal economy of multiple sexualities. The production of a recognizable genderfuck paradigm, effected by camp 'realness', alters the contextual process of signification by foregrounding the gap between sex and gender and producing different models of interpretation through different writing/reading practices. Genderfuck, as a mimetic, subversive performance, simultaneously traverses the phallic economy and exceeds it.

This process is the destabilization of gender as an analytic category, though it is not, necessarily, the signal of the end of gender (whose binarisms I have grown quite fond of in some respects). The play of masculine and feminine, on the body and/as (note the 'lesbian bar') the text, subverts the possibility of possessing a unified subject position. Once woman, a symbol and construction, no longer equals female in any meaningful way – that is, once the split between anatomy and the semiotic is recognized in the process of interpretation – the economy of desire for an Other does not have to follow a heterosexist matrix. The ambiguity of the system is its interplay and constant negotiation between the meaningful productions of sex/gender, on the one hand, and gender/sexual performance, on the other. It is a discourse of pleasure, producing desire in a subject who is able to get over herself and have it make a difference.

What is a genderfuck body? It is, to steal a phrase from Roland Barthes, a '*drag* anchor' (66; emphasis added). Drag: a performance that interrupts the circulation of the phallus in its attempt to fix, that is, anchor, signification. A drag anchor, far from centering a soul, casts a body loose in a queer sea of love.

NOTES

I would like to take this opportunity to thank a few folks: Judith Halberstam, Michelle Lekas, Carol Mason, Kitty Millet, John Mowitt, and Paula Rabinowitz. Also, for his interest and encouragement, David Halperin, and my friends from the 'Flaunting It' conference, Cheryl Kader and Thomas Piontek. It's been a ball.

1. This argument was recently advanced by Sedgwick (1990, especially chapter 1): 'Ultimately, I do feel, a great deal depends – for all women, for lesbians, for gay men, and possibly for all men – on the fostering of our ability to arrive at understandings of sexuality that will respect a certain irreducibility in it to the terms and relations of gender' (16).
2. I don't know when exactly 'queer theory' began, but the distinction 'queer', as opposed to 'lesbian/gay', marks a shift in theory.

3. I have borrowed the idea of the hyphenated heterosexuality *so-called* from Abelove. He talks about 'cross-sex genital intercourse' as 'sexual intercourse *so-called*'. This makes apparent the constructedness of sexual intercourse or heterosexuality, when dominant culture would have us believe its being is natural or normal, or that its meaning is clear and uncontested.

4. *Paris Is Burning* (Off White Productions, 1990), a film by Jennie Livingston, documents the balls of New York's black and Latino gay male underground.

5. Core 1984: 7.

REFERENCES

Abelove, Henry, 'Some Speculations on the History of Sexual Intercourse during the Long Eighteenth Century in England', *Genders* 6, Fall 1989, 125–30.

Barthes, Roland, *The Pleasure of the Text*, trans. Richard Miller, New York: Noonday, 1975.

Bright, Susie, 'A Star is Porn', *On Our Backs* October-November 1989, 8–9.

Califia, Pat, 'The Calyx of Isis', in *Macho Sluts*, Boston: Alyson, 1988, 84–176.

Echols, Alice, *Daring to Be Bad: Radical Feminism in America, 1967–1975*, Minneapolis: U of Minnesota P, 1989.

Heath, Stephen, 'Film and System: Terms of Analysis, Part I', *Screen* 16:1, 1975, 7–77; 'Part II', *Screen* 16:2, 1975, 91–113.

LeMasters, Carol, 'S/M and the Violence of Desire', *Trivia: A Journal of Ideas* 16, Fall 1989, 17–30.

Miller, Jacques-Alain, 'Suture (Elements of the Logic of the Signifier)', *Screen* 18:4, 1977–78, 24–47.

Nestle, Joan, 'Butch-Femme Relationships: Sexual Courage in the 1950s', in *A Restricted Country*, Ithaca: Firebrand, 1987, 100–9.

Rubin, Gayle, 'The Traffic in Women: Notes on the 'Political Economy' of Sex', in Karen V. Hansen & Ilene J. Philipson (eds.), *Women, Class, and the Feminist Imagination*, Philadelphia: Temple UP, 1990, 74–113.

Vance, Carole S. (ed.), *Pleasure and Danger: Exploring Female Sexuality*, London: Pandora, 1989.

17

WHAT MAKES THE FEMINIST CAMP?

Pamela Robertson

[...] Many critics [...] claim that camp represents a critical political practice for gay men: they equate camp with white, urban, gay male taste to explore camp's effectiveness as a form of resistance for that subculture. Richard Dyer (1986: 115), for instance, attributes a past-tense politics to camp when he claims that for gay men the use of camp constituted 'a kind of going public or coming out before the emergence of gay liberationist politics (in which coming out was a key confrontationist tactic)'. This reading of camp, which links it to gay identity and cultural politics, has become dominant with the rise of gay activist politics and gay and queer studies in the academy.

While recognizing camp's appeal for 'straights', most critics argue that 'something happens to camp when taken over by straights – it loses its cutting edge, its identification with the gay experience, its distance from the straight sexual world view' (Dyer 1976, rpt. 1992: 145). In part, this is a historical claim, positing the 1960s 'outing' of camp as a betrayal of 'true' gay camp. In this light, straight camp, almost an oxymoron, flattens into what Fredric Jameson has labeled postmodern 'blank parody' or pastiche, the heterogeneous and random 'imitation of dead styles, speech through all the masks and voices stored up in the imaginary museum of a now global culture' (1984: 65). According to Jameson, postmodern pastiche, which he equates with camp, lacks the satiric impulse of parody, and equalizes all identities, styles, and images in a depthless ahistorical nostalgia. Linda Hutcheon, in contrast, argues

Excerpted from *Guilty Pleasures: Feminist Camp from Mae West to Madonna*, Durham-London: Duke University Press, 1996.

that postmodernism effects a denaturalizing critique through parody that is not nostalgic or dehistoricizing, but critical and subversive. But Hutcheon, similar to Jameson, differentiates between high postmodern parody and the 'ahistorical kitsch' of camp.

However, the postmodern equation of camp and pastiche is itself ahistorical. As a form of ironic representation and reading, camp, like Hutcheon's high parody, 'is doubly coded in political terms; it both legitimates and subverts that which it parodies' (1989, 93, 8, 101). Whereas postmodern pastiche may privilege heterogeneity and random difference, camp is productively anachronistic and critically renders specific historical norms obsolete. What counts as excess, artifice and theatricality, for example, will differ over time. As Andrew Ross has noted, 'the camp effect' occurs at the moment when cultural products (for instance, stars, fashions, genres, and stereotypes) of an earlier moment of production have lost their power to dominate cultural meanings and become available, 'in the present, for redefinition according to contemporary codes of taste' (1988, rpt. 1989: 139). Camp redefines and historicizes these cultural products not just nostalgically but with a critical recognition of the temptation to nostalgia, rendering both the object and the nostalgia outmoded through an ironic, laughing distanciation. In the postmodern moment, 'contemporary codes of taste' may have rendered camp's form of critique outmoded so that camp has been recoded as pastiche. But if we understand camp to have been always already mere 'blank parody', we simply dehistoricize and 'postmodernize' camp's parodic and critical impulse.

In addition, and prior even to the historical claim about post-1960s camp, the argument against straight camp presumes that camp's aestheticism is exclusively the province of gay men. In particular, women have been excluded from discussions of pre-1960s camp because women, lesbian and straight, are perceived to 'have had even less access to the image- and culture-making processes of society than even gay men have had'.[1] We tend to take for granted that many female stars are camp and that most of the stars in the gay camp pantheon are women: consider Garland, Streisand, Callas, Dietrich, Garbo, Crawford, just to name a few. We also take for granted gay men's camp appropriations of female clothing, styles, and language from women's culture: consider drag and female impersonation, or gay camp slang such as calling one another 'she' or using phrases like 'letting one's hair down' and 'dropping hairpins', and even 'coming out' (appropriated from debutante culture) (see Chauncey 1994). Most people who have written about camp assume that the exchange between gay men's and women's cultures has been wholly one-sided; in other words, that gay men appropriate a feminine aesthetic and certain female stars but that women, lesbian or heterosexual, do not similarly appropriate aspects of gay male culture. This suggests that women are camp but do not knowingly produce themselves as camp and, furthermore, do not even have access to a camp sensibility. Women, by this logic, are objects of camp and subject to it but are not camp subjects.

Assuming this one-way traffic between gay men's and women's cultures, critics emphasizing those aspects of camp most closely related to Isherwood's 'low' camp have criticized camp for preferring images of female excess that are blatantly misogynistic. Most of the answers to this charge have been unsatisfactory. For instance, Mark Booth justifies the misogynist slant of camp by claiming that because gay men have been marginalized, camp commits itself to and identifies with images of the marginal and that women simply represent the primary type of the marginal in society (1983: 18). This justification simply underlines camp's potential for affirming patriarchal oppression.

Even worse is Wayne Koestenbaum's reply, in his essay on Maria Callas, to Catherine Clement's statement that the gay male identification with female stars is 'vampiristic' (28). According to Koestenbaum, Clement recycles the myth (which he links with the 'fag hag' stereotype) 'that a man's projection of glamour and flamboyance onto a woman is febrile, infantile, and poisonous, and that such attentions harm the woman thus admired'. He then sloughs off the criticism, stating that female stars, 'as images adrift in the culture, lend themselves to acts of imaginative borrowing and refurbishing' and that these images 'were not placed on the market at gay men's instigation' (13–14).

Like Booth, Koestenbaum's response begs the question: The question is not whether gay men put these images on the market, but rather how they deployed these images and whether that deployment partakes of misogyny. While cultural studies broadly considered and star studies, in particular, depend on the idea that texts are 'adrift in the culture' and can be put to different uses by different audiences and spectators, we nonetheless need to be able to account for how texts get taken up – not simply to accept any and all appropriations as equally valid, but instead to explore how and why certain texts get taken up in certain ways by certain groups.

Koestenbaum's response sounds curiously like the familiar cliché deployed in the justification of rape. To state that female stars are 'adrift in the culture' and, consequently, ripe for 'refurbishing' is simply an academic form of blaming the victim: 'What was she doing walking alone at night?' 'Why did she wear that sexy outfit?' Not only do these remarks compound the misogyny of gay camp, but they also limit themselves to a justification of camp's misogyny for gay men only, without asking whether or how heterosexual men and women, or even lesbians, might use these images.

We can, however, reclaim camp as a political tool and rearticulate it within the theoretical framework of feminism. To counter criticisms of camp's misogyny, for instance, some critics have articulated a positive relationship between the camp spectator and images of female excess. Andrew Ross notes that camp's attention to the artifice of these images helps undermine and challenge the presumed naturalness of gender roles and to displace essentialist versions of an authentic feminine identity (1988, rpt. 1989: 161). By this account, the very outrageousness and flamboyance of camp's preferred representations would be its most powerful tools for a critique, rather than mere affrmations of stereotypical and oppressive images of women. Thus, despite camp's seemingly exclusive affiliation with gay men and misogynist tendencies, camp offers feminists a model for critiques of gender and sex roles. Camp has an affinity with feminist discussions of gender construction, performance, and enactment; we can thereby examine forms of camp as feminist practice.

Clearly, it would be foolish to deny camp's affiliation with gay male sub-culture or to claim that women have exactly the same relation to camp as gay men do. But it seems rash to claim that women have no access to camp. If the exchange between gay men and women has been wholly one-sided, how do we account for stars like Mae West and Madonna who quite deliberately take on aspects of gay culture? Are they merely exceptions to the rule? Are there other 'exceptions'? What about Texas Guinan? Bette Davis? Marlene Dietrich? Eve Arden? Agnes Moorehead? Dolly Parton? Furthermore, if camp is exclusively the province of gay men, how do we account for the pleasure women take in camp artifacts like musicals, or Dietrich, or *Designing Women*? What are we assuming about identification if we presume that women take their stars 'straight'? Do gay men automatically have a critical distance from roles and stereotypes that women blindly inhabit?

Most troubling is that women's frequent exclusion from the discourse about camp has meant not just that these questions have not been fully addressed but that they have not even been asked. At the very least, would it not be important to determine why women enjoy so many of the same cultural texts as gay men? Asked another way: Why do gay men like so many of the same cultural texts as women? By not posing the latter question, what are we assuming about gay men? Inversion? Misogyny? By viewing the exchange between women and gay men as a two-way street we could begin to better understand gay male camp and stop taking for granted camp's reliance on feminine images and styles (as if these acts of appropriation were 'natural').

We could also begin to break down some of the artificial barriers between audiences and between subcultures that theories of spectatorship and cultural studies have unwittingly advanced [...]. By thinking about subcultures in constellation, we would necessarily rethink some of our assumptions about textual address and also which subculture we discuss in relation to which kind of text. To take an example pertinent to this project, many critics acknowledge a gay male audience for the musical but ignore the genre's popularity among women;[2] alternately, much work has been done on the female spectator of the woman's film, without considering that genre's popularity among gay men. If, however, we considered gay men as spectators of the women's film (a genre chock full of eventual camp idols) or women as spectators of the musical (it seems so obvious), we would have to reconsider issues of textual address, identification, subcultures, resistance, and domination.

By looking at the links between gay men and women across cultural texts we could also begin to better understand the many close ties and friendships shared by women and gay men, which we have, as yet, almost no way to talk about – despite their very routineness, their 'of-courseness'. Certainly, there are stereotypes. There is the figure of the 'beard', the lesbian or hetero-sexual woman who serves as heterosexual cover for the closeted gay man (just as men have served as 'beards' for lesbians).[3] Colloquially, we also have the 'fag hag', an epithet hostile to both the 'fag' and the 'hag'. Rather than describe the love and friendship between women and gay men, the fag hag stereotype often seems to presume a failed object choice on the part of the woman, the 'hag' – that is, the fag hag chooses gay men because she 'can't get a man' (she is stereotypically unattractive) and/or because she desires a man who doesn't want her (she is stereotypically secretly, desperately attracted to gay men; see, for example, Robert Rodi's novel, *Fag Hag*). At the same time, it diminishes the man in the relationship, the 'fag'. While the term recognizes that at least some women do not share the dominant culture's disparagement of gay men, in naming the friendship this way, the term (used inside gay culture as well as being imposed from without) reinforces the initial devalua-tion of gay culture.[4]

We also have a new media stereotype: the gay neighbor, who provides local color to urban settings but participates little in the plot (see, for example, *Frankie and Johnny* and *The Prince of Tides*). The gay neighbor is kin to what I will call the gay enabler, the gay man whose primary function is to help the heterosexual lovers resolve their conflicts (see, for example, *Burn This*, *Melrose Place*, and *Mrs. Doubtfire*). While there might be some value in having at least this minimal acknowledgment of the friendships between women and gay men, these newly minted stereotypes, no less than other, overtly pejorative ones, seem a far cry from representing the routine richness of these friendships.

Part of the difficulty in talking about women's friendships with gay men can probably be blamed on the problematic formulation 'some of my best friends' (given a new twist in Seinfeld's quip, 'not that there's anything wrong with it'). But the fact that we don't talk about friendships between gay men and women reflects, I think, the larger academic divisions that obtain between gay and feminist theory, as well as lesbian and gay, and heterosexual and lesbian feminist, theory. Academic politics and identity politics are such that instead of seeking points of overlap between gay men and women and between lesbian and heterosexual women, we increasingly focus on differences.

In part, this is for good reason, as it represents a greater attention to the specificity of gendered and sexed experiences and seeks to counter the problem of being 'spoken for' that, for instance, many lesbians feel with respect to both feminist and gay theory. But oftentimes we seem to be addressing ourselves only to the already converted – or, worse, to be self-defeating, proving the lie that only gays should be interested in gay issues or insisting on a single and singular identification (one difference at a time). Lesbians, especially, have often been forced to choose between identifying, as women, with feminist theory and politics (which tends to privilege [white] heterosexual women) and identifying, as homosexuals, with gay theory and politics (which tends to privilege [white] gay men). It thus becomes more difficult to form alliances between feminism and gay theory and politics as we focus on points of divergence.[5]

Any discussion of women's relation to camp will inevitably raise, rather than settle, questions about appropriation, co-optation, and identity politics. But as an activity and a sensibility that foregrounds cross-sex and cross-gender identifications, camp provides an opportunity to talk about the many points of intersection, as well as the real differences, between feminist and gay theory, and among lesbians, heterosexual women, and gay men. I argue that women, lesbian and heterosexual, have historically engaged in what I call feminist camp practices. This tradition of feminist camp, which runs alongside – but is not identical to – gay camp, represents oppositional modes of performance and reception. Through my analysis of feminist camp I reclaim a female form of aestheticism, related to female masquerade and rooted in burlesque, that articulates and subverts the 'image- and culture-making processes' to which women have traditionally been given access.

Although I argue for the crucial role of heterosexual women as producers and consumers of camp, I hesitate to describe feminist camp as 'straight' and suggest instead that camp occupies a discursive space similar to the notion of 'queer' described by Alexander Doty: 'the terms "queer readings", "queer discourses", and "queer positions", ... are attempts to account for the existence and expression of a wide range of positions within culture that are 'queer' or non-, anti-, or contra-straight' (1993: 3). In Doty's sense, 'queer' refers to a variety of discourses that have grown up in opposition to or at variance with the dominant, straight, symbolic order. This sense of queerness includes gay- and lesbian-specific positions as well as non-gay and non-lesbian ones. Unlike Moe Meyer (1994b), who also describes camp as a queer discourse but clearly states that queer means exclusively gay and lesbian (and lumps all other forms of camp under the category of the 'camp trace'),[6] I take camp to be a queer discourse in Doty's sense, because it enables not only gay men, but also heterosexual and lesbian women, and perhaps heterosexual men, to express their discomfort with and alienation from the normative gender and sex roles assigned to them by straight culture. Feminist camp, then, views the world 'queerly': that is, from a non- or anti-straight, albeit frequently non-gay, position.

This is not to say that camp or the mobile notion of queerness I am describing will always include all non- or anti-straight viewpoints. Doty points out that not all queer texts are gay (citing *The Silence of the Lambs* as an example). Similarly, gay camp might be misogynist and feminist camp may or may not be antihomophobic. Although both feminists and gay men engage in discourses that are at variance with the dominant culture, those discourses are not always identical. 'Queer' then functions for me as an explanatory term connoting a discourse or position at odds with the dominant symbolic order, the flexibility and mobility of which helps account for instances of overlap among the interests and points-of-view of heterosexual women, lesbians, and gay men, but which, at the same time, can account for feminist aesthetics and interpretations that are simultaneously non-gay and not stereotypically straight.

CAMP AND GENDER PARODY

For feminists, camp's appeal resides in its potential to function as a form of gender parody. Feminist theorists working in a variety of disciplines have turned to gender parody as a critical tool and a promising means of initiating change in sex and gender roles. For example, at the end of her *The Desire to Desire*, Mary Ann Doane argues that women need to map themselves in the 'terrain of fantasy' in order to denaturalize representations of women. She claims that the woman's film stylizes femininity, narrativizing and making acceptable stereotypical feminine scenarios. 'What is needed', she contends, 'is a means of making these gestures and poses *fantastic*, literally *incredible*' (180).

Doane believes that the credibility of images of the feminine can be undermined by a 'double mimesis' or parodic mimicry. Parodic mimicry, Doane claims, allows one to disengage from the roles and gestures of a seemingly naturalized femininity: 'Mimicry as a political textual strategy makes it possible for the female spectator to understand that recognition is buttressed by misrecognition' (182). In other words, the mimicry of stereotypical images demonstrates the female spectator's recognition of herself in those images, while it also allows the spectator to misrecognize herself, to see that her 'self' does not exist prior to the mimicry but is always already a construction.

Judith Butler similarly emphasizes the significance of parody for feminist politics. Butler accounts for the cultural construction of gender and identity as a collective activity of 'gendering' and questions how gender identities might be constructed differently. She asks: 'What kind of subversive repetition might call into question the regulatory practice of identity itself?' and claims that 'genders can be rendered thoroughly and radically incredible' through a politics of gender parody (1990a: 32, 141).

Although both Doane and Butler seek a means to render gender identities 'incredible' through parody, Doane roots her notion of 'double mimesis' in the concept of the 'feminine masquerade', while Butler begins her discussion of feminist parody with a description of homosexual drag. Butler argues that 'in imitating gender, drag implicitly reveals the imitative structure of gender itself – as well as its contingency' (137). As Esther Newton says in her book on female impersonation, 'if sex-role behavior can be achieved by the "wrong" sex, it logically follows that it is in reality also achieved, not inherited, by the "right" sex' (1972: 103).

Butler's provocative linkage in *Gender Trouble* between homosexual drag and feminist gender parody has been construed as a claim that drag subversively displaces gender norms. However, as Butler makes clear in her later work, *Bodies That Matter*, drag is subversive only 'to the extent that it reflects on the imitative structure by which hegemonic gender is itself produced and disputes heterosexuality's claim on naturalness and originality' (125). To be sure, drag reveals the performative status of gender identity, but it cannot effectively dismantle gender identity. The surprise and incongruity of drag depends upon our shared recognition that the person behind the mask is really another gender. (Consider the drag performer's ritual of removing his wig and/ or baring his chest at the end of the show.) While the 'naturalness' of gender identities is destabilized through this practice, that destabilization might merely effect a regulatory system of identifying 'unnatural' identities – for example, the stereotype of the effeminate homosexual man or the masculinized woman.

Doane has argued that in opposition to transvestism, the concept of female masquerade offers a more radical parodic potential. Joan Rivière's 1929 essay, 'Womanliness as a Masquerade', has been taken up in feminist theory as a divining rod pointing to the 'performative status' and 'imitative structure' of the feminine.[7] Rivière's essay describes intellectual women who 'wish for masculinity' and then put on a 'mask of womanliness' as a defense 'to avert anxiety and the retribution feared from men' (35). In other words, the woman takes on a masculine 'identity' to perform in the intellectual sphere, then takes on a feminine 'identity' to placate the Oedipal father whose place she has usurped. In a now famous passage, however, Rivière casually challenges the very notion of a stable feminine identity: 'The reader may now ask how I define womanliness or where I draw the line between genuine womanliness and the "masquerade". My suggestion is not, however, that there is any such difference; whether radical or superficial, they are the same thing' (38). Stephen Heath sums up the way in which Rivière's statement points to the absence of 'natural' identities: 'In the masquerade the woman mimics an authentic – genuine – womanliness but then authentic womanliness is such a mimicry, is the masquerade ("they are the same thing")' (49). The masquerade mimics a constructed identity in order to conceal that there is nothing behind the mask; it simulates femininity to dissimulate the absence of a real or essential feminine identity.

Despite the theatricality of the term, masquerade can never be merely theatrical but is always also social. The trope of the masquerade deepens our sense of the activity of gendering as enactment and acting-out. Doane suggests that 'a woman might flaunt her femininity, produce herself as an excess of femininity, in other words, foreground the masquerade' in order to 'manufacture a lack in the form of a certain distance between oneself and one's image' ('Film and the Masquerade', 25, 26). Doane uses the example of Stella Dallas's self-parody as an instance of 'double mimesis' or self-conscious masquerade. When Stella effectively parodies herself, pretending to be an even more exaggeratedly embarrassing mother than she is in the rest of the narrative, she demonstrates her recognition of herself as a stereotype (a pose, a trope) while making the excessiveness of her role visible and strange, depriving the initial mimesis of its currency. Like Doane's notion of 'double mimesis', the self-conscious masquerade discovers a discrepancy between gesture and 'essence' and not simply between anatomy and costume. It makes the 'natural' 'un-natural' – cultural or historical.

In opposition to drag, the surprise and incongruity of same-sex female masquerade consists in the identity between she who masquerades and the role she plays – she plays at being what she is always already perceived to be. This might consist in the exaggeration of gender codes by the 'right' sex, in a female masquerade of femininity or a male masquerade of masculinity, similar to lesbian 'femme' role-play or the hyperbolic masculinization of gay 'macho' Levi's-and-leather culture. The concept of the masquerade allows us to see that what gender parody takes as its object is not the image of the woman, but the idea – which, in camp, becomes a joke – that an essential feminine identity exists prior to the image. As Butler observes, 'the parody is *of* the very notion of an original' (1990a: 138).

Gender parody would utilize masquerade self-consciously in order to reveal the absence behind the mask and the performative activity of gender and sexual identities. It would have to be a parody of the masquerade so that masquerade would no longer serve as a placating gesture but instead would become a gesture of defiance toward the assumption of an identity between the woman and the image of the woman. Gender parody, therefore, doesn't differ in structure from the activity of the masquerade but self-consciously theatricalizes masquerade's construction of gender identities.

In using Doane and Butler to open up my discussion of feminist camp, I do not mean to claim that they advocate camp in their discussions of 'double mimesis' or gender parody, nor do I believe that camp is the only interpretation available for a politics of gender parody.[8] Rather, I consider camp to be a likely candidate for helping us explore the appeal of and reason for a politics of gender parody. Conversely, I want to use the notion of gender parody as a paradigm for defining a specifically feminist form of camp spectatorship.

CAMP AND FEMALE SPECTATORSHIP

The often fraught and contested concept of the female spectator has been central to feminist film theory since the 1970s.[9] The concept can be traced back to 1970s semiotic and psychoanalytic theories of spectatorship, represented by the work of Christian Metz and the journal *Screen*, along with the earliest feminist psychoanalytic interventions, especially as articulated by Stephen Heath and Julia Lesage and crystallized by Laura Mulvey in her famous 'Visual Pleasure' essay. Feminist film theorists have grappled with Mulvey's provocative claims about the 'male gaze', often in contention with her bleak assessment of the female spectatorial position. Psychoanalytically informed debates initially focused on the female spectator constructed through textual address in analyses, for instance, of the female melodrama or feminine spectacle in film noir. Increasingly, feminist film theorists, influenced by the Frankfurt School and British Cultural Studies, have attempted to give the concept of the female spectator historical specificity and/or ethnographic precision in order to account for different kinds of readings and possible forms of sub-cultural resistance. While the debate about the nature of female spectatorship continues and models proliferate, some of the most crucial problems facing feminist film theorists today are still those prompted by Mulvey's critique: the need to (1) rescue some forms of pleasure for the female viewer; (2) concept-ualize spectatorship as a process mediating between the textually constructed 'female spectator' and the female audience, constructed by socio-historical categories of gender, class, and race; and (3) rethink ideas of ideology, resist-ance, and subversion.

Miriam Hansen describes 'the greater mobility required of the female spec-tator – a mobility that has been described in terms of transvestitism, masquer-ade and double identification' as 'a compensatory one, responding to the patriarchal organization of classical cinematic vision and narration'. She links the 'structurally problematic' nature of spectatorship for women to that of 'other, partly overlapping groups who are likewise, though in different ways, alienated from dominant positions of subjectivity – gays and lesbians, or racial and ethnic minorities' (173). Camp foregrounds this structural problem of female viewing. The camp spectator, in a sense, ironically enacts the female spectator's mobility through a double identification that is simultaneously critical of and complicit with the patriarchal organization of vision and narration. Camp, as a performative strategy, as well as a mode of reception, commonly foregrounds the artifice of gender and sexual roles through literal and metaphoric transvestism and masquerade. Since camp has been primarily conceived of as a gay male subcultural practice, its articulation with the concept of female spectatorship will enable us to explore the degree to which the female camp spectator shares her liminal status with another alienated group and also to explore what kind of subcultural resistances are available to women.

Although Doane locates distanciation primarily in the text, rather than reception, she underlines the masquerade's potential usefulness for understand-ing the spectator's activity as well as the performer's: 'What might it mean to masquerade as a spectator? To assume the mask in order to see in a different way?'[10] Here, Doane begins to articulate a relationship between gender parody and a theory of spectatorship that, while not exactly about pleasure, offers a specific route to camp. In opposition to the female's presumed overidentifica-tion with or absorption in the image, camp necessarily entails assuming the mask as a spectator – to read against the grain, to create an ironic distance between oneself and one's image. Camp not only allows for the double nature of masquerade (the spectator in disguise will always see through two pairs of eyes) but also accounts for the pleasure of the masquerade (typically unacknow-ledged), its status as amusement and play for both the masquerading viewer and the performer.

The trope of the masquerade, then, helps describe camp's negotiation between textual address and the viewer. As Christine Gledhill explains, the concept of negotiation implies an ongoing process of give-and-take: 'It suggests that a range of positions of identification may exist within any text; and that, within the social situation of their viewing, audiences may shift subject positions as they interact with the text' (73; see also Hall). One way to imagine the audience shifting positions is to consider subject positions as different masks, different 'identities'. Most theories figure the female spectator's activity as an either/or hopscotch between positions of identification; they picture the female spectator shifting unconsciously between an active masculine and a passive feminine identity, like Rivière's intellectual women or Mulvey's transvestite moviegoer. Camp offers a slightly different model of negotiation to account for the overlap between passivity and activity in a viewer who sees through, simultaneously perhaps, one mask of serious femininity and another mask of laughing femininity.

Most importantly, examining camp in relation to the female spectator opens up new possibilities for describing the kinds of pleasure a female spectator might take in mass-produced objects that seem to support an oppressive patriarchal sexual regime. Too often, spectatorship studies, and (sub)cultural studies more generally, tend to reify pleasure, particularly female pleasure, as either a consciously resistant activity or a wholly passive manipulation. Judith Mayne discerns in this either/or tendency the impulse 'to categorize texts and readings/responses as either conservative or radical, as celebratory of the dominant order or critical of it' (1993: 93). According to Mayne, while the first position ascribes an unqualified power to the text ('dominant'), the second ascribes that power to viewers ('resistant').

This either/or tendency is produced by the utopian desire to activate a difference between constructed and essential identities. The 'dominant' model (often associated with the Frankfurt School and political modernists) argues that texts interpellate viewers into essentialist positions of subjecthood and thus believes that the ties to those texts must be broken by creating new texts that will displace essentialist identities and stereotypes. Doane and Butler, for instance, offer a concept of distanciation that echoes the Brechtian concept of estrangement, which renders the 'natural' strange, and distances the viewer from his or her everyday 'normal' assumptions. For them, estrangement must entail a destruction of some forms of pleasure as advocated programmatically by Mulvey.

The 'dominant' model rightfully points out the problem with unexamined pleasure, its complicity with an oppressive sexual regime. Still, these models do not provide a way in which to name the pleasures taken by performers and viewers. Doane and Butler's discounting of pleasure, for example, underrates not only the communal and pleasurable aspects of performance and spectatorship but also the viewer's sense of humor and interpretive capability. Although both Doane and Butler envision the formation of gender identities as a cultural practice, neither seems to regard pleasure as an activity in which we all engage as cultural agents. Instead, like many cultural critics and political modernists from Adorno to Foucault, they view pleasure as a form of cultural domination, passively imbibed, that renders us all cultural dupes.

On the other side of the debate, however, the 'resistance' model's assumption that the activity of making meaning resides solely with viewers falls into a similar determinism. American cultural studies, in particular, has been identified with the resistance model, which valorizes pleasure as redemptive. Often, as Elspeth Probyn argues, 'versions of (sub)cultural analysis tend to turn out rather "banal" descriptions of cultural resistance' (52).[11] Meaghan Morris sums up the typical mode of argument in this 'banal' 'vox pop style': 'People in modern mediatized societies are complex and contradictory, mass cultural texts are complex and contradictory, therefore people using them produce complex and contradictory culture' (30). In ascribing unqualified power to viewer response, this model suggests that, rather than interpellating viewers, the text produces a multiplicity of meanings from which the viewer can choose his or her point of identification. If the conservative model reifies pleasure by seeing texts as 'dominant' and audiences as dupes, the viewer-oriented model similarly reifies pleasure by ignoring the force of dominant ideology in favor of a free-for-all textual and cultural ambiguity. In ascribing an unqualified power to viewers' pleasure, this model often fails to account for the ways in which pleasure can merely affirm the dominant order and pre-empt even the possibility of resistance as the subject goes laughing into the shopping mall.

Each of these models has its own seductive appeal. Nonetheless, neither one seems to accurately capture the deep complexities of texts and audiences, much less the contradictions of pleasure itself. Camp, however, reveals the porousness of pleasure, its locally overlapping features of passivity and activity, affirmation and critique. Rather than wilfully posit what Mayne refers to as a 'happy integration' of these two extreme models, I explore camp's negotiation of these two extremes in order to account for both the 'complex and contradictory' nature of camp spectatorship and its deep complicity with the dominant. Through my discussion of camp as a 'guilty' pleasure, I seek to challenge the basic determinism of spectator studies, especially as this determinism applies to the female spectator. With Susan Rubin Suleiman, who, like Doane and Butler, locates the potential for feminist subversion of patriarchal norms in parody (179), I would like to imagine women playing and laughing.[12] At the same time, I want to avoid reifying pleasure as wholly resistant. I would like to claim camp as a kind of parodic play between subject and object in which the female spectator laughs at and plays with her own image – in other words, to imagine her distancing herself from her own image by making fun of, and out of, that image – without losing sight of the real power that image has over her.

By examining the complexity and contradictions of camp's guilty pleasures, its two-sidedness, we can begin to move beyond this debate to explore what Mayne points to as 'the far more difficult task of questioning what is served by the continued insistence upon this either/or, and more radically, of examining what it is in conceptions of spectators' responses and film texts that produces this ambiguity in the first place' (Mayne 1993: 93). We can begin to broach these questions by complicating our sense of how dominant texts and resistant viewers interact to produce camp, and by reconceptualizing resistance and subversion to account for the way in which camp's simultaneous pleasures of alienation and absorption refuse simplistic categories of dominant-versus-resistant readings.

Camp necessarily entails a description of the relationship between the textually constructed spectator and her empirical counterparts. Although camp tends to refer to a subjective process – it 'exists in the smirk of the beholder' (Hess 1965: 53) – camp is also, as Susan Sontag points out, 'a quality discover-able in objects and the behavior of persons' (1964, rpt. 1966: 277). Further-more, camp is a reading/viewing practice which, by definition, is not available to all readers; for there to be a genuinely camp spectator, there must be another hypothetical spectator who views the object 'normally'.

Camp further demands a reconceptualization of subcultures so as to make clear that subcultures are variable communities that are not always well-defined and easily identifiable (through, for instance, fashion) but can have differing individuated practices. Although camp has been almost wholly associ-ated with a gay male subculture, that subculture has not necessarily always participated in camp as a group or even recognized itself as a group. While there have been public gay camp rituals (e.g., drag shows and parties, im-personation and transvestism, Judy Garland concerts), camp consists also of individual and private, even closeted, moments of consumption.[13]

[...] Camp must be understood as not only a means of negotiating subject positions, but also as a socio-historical cultural activity that negotiates between different levels of cultural practices. Rather than emphasize either performance or reception, we need to understand masquerade as both a performative strat-egy and a mode of reception in order to sort through the difficulty of attributing camp to texts. Camp is most often used as an adjective, referring to a quality or qualities found in an object. But camp can also be a verb (from the French *se camper* – to posture or to flaunt). Like the masquerade, the activity of producing camp can be located at both the level of performance and at the level of spectatorship – and the line between the two activities will not always be clear. A performer might produce camp as an aesthetic strategy, as my readings of Mae West and Madonna in *Guilty Pleasures* emphasize. At the same time, a spectator creates a camp effect in reading texts as camp whether those texts intentionally produce camp or not, as I suggest in my readings of *Johnny Guitar* and *Gold Diggers of 1933*. And, as the examples of recycled camp informed by camp spectatorship demonstrate, camp blurs the line between the seemingly distinct categories of production and reception. Alexander Doty, discussing the difficulty of attributing queerness to texts, writes: 'The complexity and vola-tility of mass culture production and reception-consumption often make any attempt to attribute queerness to only (or mostly) producers, texts, or audiences seem false and limiting' (1993: xiii). Similarly, attributing camp to any text requires an understanding of not only textual address but also audience, production history, and the more general historical context of a text's reception.

Unlike gay camp, typically identified as an upper-class sensibility, feminist camp tends to speak from and to a working class sensibility.[14] Therefore, in *Guilty Pleasures* I examine textual representations of working-class women, gold diggers, and prostitutes, and I relate these images to extracinematic discourses (e.g., Progressive Era antiprostitution discourse, Friedan's analysis of the 'feminine mystique') that negotiate attitudes toward women and work. Produced at moments of antifeminist backlash, the particular texts I have chosen use anachronistic images to challenge dominant ideologies about women's roles in the economic sphere and to revitalize earlier (seemingly outmoded) feminist critiques.

Since camp has been linked with gay subcultural practice, most camp objects have taken on general associations related to sex and gender roles, but I limit my discussion of camp to the practice and reception of audiovisual representations of women. These relate most closely to those aspects of gay camp culture involving drag, female impersonation, and the gay reception of female stars. By limiting my discussion in this way, I emphasize the crucial role women have played as producers and consumers of both gay and feminist camp.

I have deliberately excluded any discussion of male stars. In part, I simply want to focus on female performers as a corrective to notions that female stars are camp but do not knowingly produce themselves as camp. In addition, I believe that a discussion of male stars would detract somewhat from the model of female spectatorship I put forward. Women might take camp pleasure in the hypermasculine masquerade of Arnold Schwarzenegger or Victor Mature, and that pleasure might be described as feminist. It seems to me, however, that a description of female identification with these figures would inevitably return to a model of transvestism, until further explorations are made of heterosexual men's relation to the camp sensibility.

[...] I emphasize reception in my analyses of camp texts. However, without unmediated access to fans' own comments about these texts, and suspicious of strict ethnographic audience surveys, I seek primarily to recreate the conditions of reception that create different camp effects. To determine the historical conditions of reception that cause some objects to be taken as camp, I analyze archival materials related to cinematic, institutional, and fan discourses.

[...] Throughout, I consider not only how feminist camp articulates the overlapping interests of women and gay men but also how it fails to do so. In my chapter on Mae West, for instance, I argue that West's appeal to women and to gay men is virtually identical. In contrast, I regard as antifeminist Crawford's transformation into a camp grotesque from the 1950s to the present and offer a feminist reading of her role in *Johnny Guitar* that depends on fans residual identification with Crawford as a working woman's star. My analysis of Madonna questions whether the mainstreaming of camp taste obscures real difference and reduces gay politics to a discourse of style.

While I acknowledge camp's limitations as a sensibility more committed to the status quo than to effecting real change, I emphasize feminist camp's utopian aspects. By reclaiming camp as a political tool and rearticulating it within the framework of feminism, we can better understand not only female production and reception but also how women have negotiated their feelings of alienation from the normative gender and sex roles assigned to them by straight culture. If, in Richard Dyer's words, 'it's being so camp as keeps us going', then perhaps, by retrieving this aspect of our cultural history, we can better understand where we have been and help move the feminist camp forward.

NOTES

1. This quotation comes from a footnote to the 1977 reprint of Dyer 1976. This note no longer appears in the 1992 reprint, nor does any discussion of women's access to camp.
2. Shari Roberts offers an analysis of the female audience for musicals in *Seeing Stars*.
3. Perhaps not surprisingly, when I looked online for books on gay male friendships with women, the only title that came up with 'women' and 'gay men' in it was a book, Whitney's *Uncommon Lives*, about marriages between gay men and straight women.
4. Dawne Moon analyzes the use of the term 'fag hag' among gay men and finds that the term is used sometimes to mark certain women's exclusion from gay male culture and, contradictorily, to mark others' acceptance by gay men. I am also grateful to Eve Kosofsky Sedgwick for helping me sort through the meanings of this term.
5. Some critics seek to bridge the gap between feminist and gay theory. Eve Kosofsky Sedgwick, in particular, has consistently and elegantly negotiated feminist and gay theory and has demonstrated the joint articulations of antifeminist and homophobic discourses in a variety of contexts. Richard Dyer, as well, seems exemplary in his attention to the intersections of sex and gender oppression. And the shift toward 'queer' theory, as I discuss below, may encourage more alliances.
6. Meyer dismisses not only pop camp as camp trace but also, explicitly, criticizes Dyer's analysis of Judy Garland for not 'addressing the problem of her nongay sexual identity, and without a political analysis of the relationship between gay discourse and nongay producers of camp'.
7. For the introduction of the concept into film studies, see Mary Ann Doane, 'Film and the Masquerade' and 'Masquerade Reconsidered'; Johnston; Heath; and Butler 1990a: 43–57.
8. Doane, for example, would resist camp and discounts her own model of masquerade due to its overlapping passivity and activity. She says that there is a 'pronounced difficulty in aligning the notion of masquerade with that of female spectatorship' due to 'the curious blend of activity and passivity in the masquerade' and 'the corresponding blurring of tbe opposition between production and reception'. Doane, 'Masquerade Reconsidered', 39.
9. See Bergstrom & Doane, 16–17. See also Pribram; Gamman & Marshment; and Stacey. For an overview of theories of spectatorship in film studies generally, see Mayne 1993.
10. Doane, 'Film and the Masquerade', 26. For a critique of Doane's emphasis on the text, see Modleski, 310.
11. Both Mayne and Probyn cite John Fiske, in particular, as exemplary of this tendency in cultural studies. I would argue, and I think they would agree, that the redemptive model is much more widespread.
12. On comedic forms of female transgression and women's laughter, see Rowe 1995.

13. Richard Dyer, for example, describes a letter he received while researching his piece on Garland and gay men in which the author tells a story about himself and another young boy defending Garland in a high school class, each unaware that the other was gay and unaware of Garland's association with gay subcultures. Dyer 1986: 193.

14. My description of these class sensibilities are not meant to describe economic or power relations. Rather, I take it to be true that, through camp, gay men of different classes identify with a perceived or imaginary upper-class sensibility and that women of different classes identify with a perceived or imaginary working-class position.

REFERENCES

Bergstrom, Janet & Mary Ann Doane, 'The Female Spectator: Contexts and Directions', *Camera Obscura* 20–21, May-September 1989.

Butler, Judith, *Bodies That Matter: On the Discursive Limits of 'Sex'*, New York: Routledge, 1994.

Clement, Catherine, *Opera, or the Undoing of Women*, trans. Betsy Wing, Minneapolis: U of Minnesota P, 1988.

Doane, Mary Ann, *The Desire to Desire: The Woman's Films of the 1940s*, Bloomington: Indiana UP, 1987.

——, 'Film and the Masquerade: Theorizing the Female Spectator' (1982), and 'Masquerade Reconsidered: Further Thoughts on the Female Spectator' (1988–89), rpt. in Doane 1991: 17–32, 33–43.

Gamman, Lorraine & Margaret Marshment (eds.), *The Female Gaze: Women as Viewers of Popular Culture*, Seattle: Real Comet Press, 1989.

Gledhill, Christine, 'Pleasurable Negotiations', in E. Deidre Pribram (ed.), cit.

Hall, Stuart, 'Encoding/Decoding', in Stuart Hall et al. (eds.), *Culture, Media, Language*, London: Hutchinson, 1980, 128–39.

Hansen, Miriam, Individual response to questionnaire, *Camera Obscura* 20–21, May-September 1989.

Heath, Stephen, 'Joan Riviere and the Masquerade', in Victor Burgin, James Donald & Cora Kaplan (eds.), *Formations of Fantasy*, London: Methuen, 1986, 45–61.

Johnston, Claire, 'Femininity and the Masquerade: *Anne of the Indies*' (1975), rpt. in E. Ann Kaplan (ed.), *Psychoanalysis and Cinema*, New York: Routledge, 1990, 64–72.

Koestenbaum, Wayne, 'Callas and Her Fans', *Yale Review* 79:1, May 1990.

Morris, Meaghan, 'Banality in Cultural Studies', in Patricia Mellencamp (ed.), *Logics of Television: Essays in Cultural Criticism*, Bloomington: Indiana UP, 1990.

Modleski, Tania, 'Rape versus Mans/laughter: Hitchcock's *Blackmail* and Feminist Interpretation', *PMLA* 102:3, May 1987.

Moon, Dawne, 'Insult and Inclusion: The Term "Fag Hag" and Gay Male "Community"', *Social Forces* 74:2, December 1995.

Mulvey, Laura, 'Afterthoughts on "Visual Pleasure and Narrative Cinema" inspired by King Vidor's *Duel in the Sun*', in *Visual and Other Pleasures*, Bloomington: Indiana UP, 1989, 29–38.

Pribram, E. Deidre (ed.), *Female Spectators: Looking at Film and Television*, New York: Verso, 1988.

Probyn, Elspeth, *Sexing the Self: Gendered Positions in Cultural Studies*, New York: Routledge, 1993.

Rivière, Joan, 'Womanliness as a Masquerade' (1929), rpt. in Victor Burgin, James Donald & Cora Kaplan (eds.), *Formations of Fantasy*, London: Methuen, 1986, 35–44.

Roberts, Shari, *Seeing Stars: Spectacles of Difference in World War II Hollywood Musicals*, Durham: Duke UP, forthcoming.

Stacey, Jackie, *Star Gazing: Hollywood Cinema ond Female Spectatorship*, New York: Routledge, 1994.

Suleiman, Susan Rubin, *Subversive Intent: Gender, Politics ond the Avant-Garde*, Cambridge: Harvard UP, 1990.

Whitney, Catherine, *Uncommon Lives: Gay Men ond Straight Women*, New York: New American Library, 1990.

18

'WHO'S THAT GIRL?' ANNIE LENNOX, WOOLF'S *ORLANDO*, AND FEMALE CAMP ANDROGYNY

George Piggford

According to Judith Butler, gender may be understood as a performance, as 'a kind of persistent impersonation which passes as the real'. The genders masculine and feminine are for her not natural or essential, and are not directly connected to a widely perceived sexual binary of male and female. Men have traditionally been encouraged in Western societies to be aggressive, protective, dominant, and generally active, whereas women have often felt compelled to be defensive, nurturing, submissive, and generally passive. In Butler's feminist model, these cultural imperatives are seen as simplistic, oppressive, and unfair, especially to those who desire to cross gender, to be feminine men or masculine women. Drag performance – men dressing as women and vice versa – might usefully be seen, she further argues, as a strategy of resistance and subversion, for drag is not an 'imitation of gender' but instead 'dramatize[s] the signifying gestures through which gender itself is established' (1990a: viii).

Closely associated with drag is camp, a kind of delight in the outrageous that has frequently been associated with homosexual – usually gay male – subcultures, as in the estheticist dandyism of Oscar Wilde and his circle. Camp has recently been an important subject for many theorists who work within a Butlerian model of gender identity. Camp theory, beginning with Susan Sontag's seminal essay 'Notes on "Camp"' (1964b), serves as a useful addition to Butler's gender theory because a reading of a performance or text that focuses on camp allows for an examination of gender in particular historical and

Originally published in *Mosaic*, 30:3, September 1997.

cultural contexts. While Butler's theory often seems ahistorical and, particularly in the case of *Gender Trouble*, uninterested in cultural specificity, camp theory relies heavily on an understanding of context in order for a performer or author to communicate his/her attitude toward gender to a viewer or a reader.

In this essay I wish to extend this emphasis upon particular circumstances by arguing for the existence of a specific female tradition of camp, whose central figure is what I will call the 'female androgyne'. Although this term might seem oxymoronic, when used in the context of camp it serves to suggest that the biological sex of the performer is an important aspect of the attempt to unsettle notions of gender, especially in cultures in which the male is regarded as the norm. These female/androgynous figures do not simply dress as men; rather, they are women who dress, perform, write, appear as gendered identities that might be placed in a range between masculine and feminine. These women employ a camp sensibility – a code of appearance and behavior that mocks and ironizes gender norms – in order to undermine the gender assumptions of their specific cultures.

In order to explore concretely the implications of this sensibility, I will begin by looking at a significant, fairly recent example of a camp androgyne: Annie Lennox, and particularly her appearance as Elvis Presley at the 1984 Grammy Awards ceremony. Then I will return to Butler and general theories of camp. Finally, I will move back to the early twentieth century and an important literary critique of conventional notions of sexual identity in which the female camp androgyne arguably first appears: Virginia Woolf's *Orlando: A Biography* (1928). Such a retrospective procedure will allow recent performance and theory to comment, as it were, on earlier texts, while at the same time highlighting differences and thus emphasizing the importance of reading any instance of camp in its specific historical context. Similarly, by connecting Woolf with more recent music-video performance, I hope to identify a tradition of female camp whose history might run from *Orlando* – and the model for its protagonist, Vita Sackville-West – through Marlene Dietrich and Mae West, and ultimately to Lennox.

By early 1984, Annie Lennox, the vocalist for the pop duo Eurythmics, was well-known as a distinctly androgynous figure in British and American popular culture. She established her distinctive look in the promotional video for the number one single 'Sweet Dreams (are made of this)' (1983), in which she wears a conservative, dark business suit and sports a flaming red crew cut along with incongruous thickly-applied make-up and lipstick. Though much of this look is based on male-associated coding, she is also recognizable in the video as 'essentially' female; that is, it is clear that Annie is a woman performing androgyny. Her use of androgyny allows for a fluidity between perceived cultural stereotypes of masculinity, emblematized by accoutrements of male power (the conservative suit and a suspiciously phallic baton) and those of femininity (the use of eye make-up, rouge, and glossy lipstick).

In the group's second North American video release, 'Love is a Stranger' (1983), the androgynous-looking Lennox performs two kinds of drag: in the first half of the video she appears as two feminine types; wearing first a platinum-blonde wig, long false eyelashes, and a mink coat and later a long black wig, heavy lipstick, and a shiny black dress. In the second half she wears a dark business suit and mirrored sunglasses, with no discernible facial make-up. It is not clear from viewing the video whether Lennox is a man in female drag (in the first part of the video) or a woman in male drag (in the second half). This video certainly had a disorienting effect at least on the censors of MTV, who terminated the transmission of the video in the middle of its first broadcast. They even went so far as to ban all Eurythmics videos from American television until Lennox proved that she was in fact a woman and not 'an American-youth-corrupting transvestite' (Randall, 45). In this video, she became the androgyne successively playing at being both feminine and masculine, but for MTV's censors, this playfulness clearly posed some sort of perceived threat to an assumedly stable and proper relationship between biological sex and gender performance.

These performances were only the precursors of what might be called an iconic camp moment: Lennox's appearance at the 1984 Grammys as the reincarnation of Elvis Presley. Her choice of Elvis was apt: he remains an immediately recognizable rock icon whose own gender performances – which involved elaborate, often sequined, costumes and his infamous gyrating pelvis – continue to be the site of both sexual desire and gender anxiety. Lennox came onto the stage in men's clothes, with a Presleyesque coiffure and the stubble of facial hair. The immediate effect on the audience, like that which her 'Love is a Stranger' performance had on MTV's censors, was one of disorientation: who was this? As soon as she began to sing the familiar 'Sweet Dreams', however, her identity became clear. The publicity stunt worked. The video for Eurythmics' next single, 'Who's That Girl?' (1984), features Lennox both as an Elvis look-alike and as a blonde-wigged torch singer. Through a trick of special effects at the end of the video, Elvis-Annie kisses torch singer-Annie passionately on the lips, in a moment of narcissistic fulfillment. The song quickly ascended the pop charts, and the video for it played in heavy rotation on MTV for weeks after Eurythmics' infamous Grammy performance. Annie Lennox became an instant camp diva through this gender-bending appearance witnessed by millions of television viewers.

Drag performances such as Lennox's direct our attention to what Judith Butler calls the performative nature of all gender identities, their dependence on repetitive and stylized actions: 'the gendered body ... has no ontological status apart from the various acts which constitute its reality ... [since] acts and gestures, articulated and acted desires create the illusion of an interior and organizing gender core' (1990a: 136). From a Butlerian perspective, Lennox's male drag in 'Love is a Stranger' and especially her performance at the 1984 Grammys were disorienting and unsettling precisely because they threatened the traditional 'ontological status' of the gendered body, by undermining the 'illusion' of an 'organizing gender core', at least momentarily.

Butler's theory, while important for understanding the role of performativity in the formation of gender roles, has been widely criticized for ignoring the culturally perceived 'biological body' as a key factor in the construction of gender and thereby for ahistoricizing gender. Recently, in her *Bodies that Matter*, Butler has responded to the first attack by discussing the 'process of materialization that stabilizes over time to produce the effect of boundary, fixity, and surface we call matter' (9) and thereby attempting to make bodies 'matter', or signify. She has responded to the second criticism by utilizing Foucault's notion of 'regulatory power', which functions to police discourses of subjectivity through a process of Althusserian 'interpellation' (*Bodies* 10, 121). The problem, however, is that her gestures toward materiality and history are informed by a dominantly Derridian theorization of gender, and Derridian deconstruction has been criticized for its rejection of the material and for its unapologetic ahistoricism.

For example, Butler associates performativity with citationality, invoking Derrida's 'Signature, Event, Context'. For Butler, as for Derrida, any signifier of identity, any signature, is citation: discourse can be neither original nor authoritative. Butler defines citationality as follows: 'every [speech] act is itself a recitation, the citing of a prior chain of acts which are implied in a present act and which perpetually drain any "present" act of its presentness' (244). The performative is always citational in that it is 'always derivative' (13). Citationality is predicated upon a notion of 'historicity' in which history is perceived as a function of discourse. That is, although a 'sedimentation of conventions' (282) infuses performative actions with meaning, the process of sedimentation that has produced the body is always-already completed. Indeed, the title of her work – *Bodies that Matter* – must necessarily be read ironically; 'biological bodies' as material entities remain untheorizable elements in her gender theory because Butler subsumes materiality under the umbrella of 'speech acts', or discursivity.

Butler's own explanation for the 'abjection' or exclusion of the material body from her gender theory is that 'To "concede" the undeniability of "sex" or its "materiality" [the body] is always to concede some version of "sex", some formation of "materiality"' (10); this concession is precisely what her Derridian theorization of gender as citational and performative seeks to avoid. It is the presumed undeniability of 'sex' as a biological given that Butler critiques in *Bodies that Matter*. Following the lead of Foucault's introduction to *Herculine Barbin*, Butler seeks to put to rest once and for all the widely held notion that sexual identity is self-evident and stable, although she does admit that the 'bodies' cause her 'some anxiety' (10).

Butler also acknowledges that not all drag subverts dominant cultural assumptions about gender identity and sex; some drag, in fact, helps to solidify and reinforce those assumptions. As she explains in *Bodies that Matter*, 'there is no necessary relation between drag and subversion . . . drag may very well be used in the service of both the denaturalization and reidealization of hyperbolic heterosexual gender norms' (125). Drag performance, therefore, does not necessarily disorient its viewer or destabilize its viewer's assumptions about sexual identity and gender. For example, while Annie Lennox's Elvis drag at the 1984 Grammys was disorienting, the drag performed by her hard-rock contemporaries – Twisted Sister, Kiss, Motley Crue – can usefully be seen as 'tied to a certain construction of American masculinity' (Ross 1988, rpt. 1989: 165). This latter form of drag can be understood as supportive of the dominant gender system because it accentuates the grotesqueness and inappropriateness of men in feminine attire and makeup. The performance of these groups might best be described as clownish, in contrast to the dead-on parody of gender norms performed by Annie Lennox. What separates Lennox's performance from the hard-rock version of drag is its androgynous aspect, a quality, I would argue, that is closely associated with a camp sensibility.

The association of camp with androgyny is not new. In her seminal 'Notes on Camp', published in 1964, Susan Sontag argues that the androgyne 'is certainly one of the great images of Camp sensibility' (1964b, rpt. 1966: 279). For Sontag, camp is something ephemeral, difficult to define – a 'sensibility' rather than a mode or style; it is also closely associated for her with androgyny. Indeed, the androgynous nature of camp seems almost obvious, particularly if one accepts Carolyn Heilbrun's definition of this 'ancient Greek word – from *andro* (male) and *gyn* (female)': 'a condition under which the characteristics of the sexes, and the human impulses expressed by men and women, are not rigidly assigned. Androgyny seeks to liberate the individual from the confines of the appropriate' (x). If androgyny signifies the fluidity of sexual characteristics, then it can be associated only in a very general way with a drag performance that involves a mere sartorial switch. As in the case of Lennox's performance, the camp androgyne both performs drag and produces a deliberate 'camp effect' – a period of disorientation that encourages its viewer to question his/her assumptions about the relationship between gender performance and biological sex.

Sontag posits two different kinds of camp: 'naive', or accidental, and 'deliberate'. For her, although both kinds are 'apolitical', 'Pure Camp is always naive. Camp which knows itself to be Camp . . . is usually less satisfying' (277, 282). In contrast, most recent theorists of the subject have argued that all 'pure' camp is deliberate and that camp at least might be political. Andrew Ross, for example, locates the sensibility in an elite camp 'cognoscenti' who 'celebrate .. alienation, distance, and incongruity', who consciously produce camp by calling attention to their difference from the norm (1988, rpt. 1989: 146). These he contrasts to the 'ignoranti', or the general population, who are unable to read camp. More recently, Moe Meyer has gone so far as to *define* camp as the 'strategies and tactics of queer parody' (9). Following Sontag's lead, however, most theorists have hesitated to provide a denotative definition for the slippery term 'camp'; for, as she argues, camp is 'something of a private code, a badge of identity even, among small urban cliques', and to break the code *in toto* is impossible. According to Sontag codedness or indecipherability is a central attribute of the sensibility, and 'To talk about Camp is therefore to betray it' (275).

Sontag's preference for naive camp suggests that anyone can be campy, not just the cognoscenti. In contrast, by privileging deliberate camp, theorists such as Ross and Meyer attempt to keep camp in the space of its original production: small, urban coteries, whose populations include many self-identified homosexuals who use camp to celebrate their distance and alienation from the dominant culture. Meyer argues that 'Sontag killed off the binding referent of Camp – the Homosexual – and the discourse began to unravel as Camp became confused and conflated with [other] rhetorical and performative strategies' (1994b: 7). Whereas for Sontag camp is 'almost, but not quite, ineffable' (276), for Meyer camp is a practical political strategy.

The danger of Meyer's reading, however, is that he loses sight of the fact that camp signifies polyvalently, that humor and irony are as intrinsic to the sensibility as its potential political effects. As Lee Edelman has persuasively shown, no one can ever know the outcome of his/her particular political 'strategy', particularly homosexuals: 'we must recognize that "our" "activist" discourse is only a *mutation* of "their" "master discourses" and that its effect on them, though certain, is always unpredictable' (1994: 111). Indeed, camp might best be understood as a parodic mutation, a sensibility that is both political and playful and that often employs drag to expose the arbitrary and artificial media – clothes, makeup, hair – through which gender and sex signify in contemporary culture.

Understood at least partially as a political act, camp drag produces an effect that will critically comment on or at least inflect the gender system of a particular historical/cultural moment in unpredictable, but readable, ways. Whereas Sontag suggests that drag approaches ontology itself as a performance – it affirms 'Being-as-Playing-a-Role ... life as theatre' (280) – later theorists have placed this threat to ontological assumptions specifically within the frame of a threat to the reality of gender in society. Esther Newton, for example, argues that camp performance asserts that 'the entire sex-role behaviour [system] is a role – an act' (1972: 101); Ross contends that camp plays 'a crucial role in the redefinition of masculinity and femininity' (1988, rpt. 1989: 148); David Bergman thinks that 'camp constantly plays with notions of inside and outside, masculine and feminine, it does not locate truth in these polarities' (1993c: 94–5). These theorists do not deny the extra-discursive reality of biological bodies; for them, bodies perform camp. Likewise, camp performance does not eliminate the category of gender; rather, it dissociates the category of biological sex from roles that women and men are coerced into playing in a particular society.

It is also because camp functions within particular societies in particular periods in specific ways that no generic definition of camp will ultimately suffice. Sontag notes that 'the canon of Camp can change. Time has a great deal to do with it' (285), and according to Ross, camp has 'different uses and meanings ... for different groups, subcultures, and elites' (56). Thus Annie Lennox's camp performance at the 1984 Grammys is readable as a by-product of the process of commodification of gay culture that can be traced back to the Stonewall riot. The drag queens who fought with the police at the Stonewall bar in New York in 1969 were the victims of discriminatory laws; their widely publicized resistance to police harassment provided both a new impetus for gay political action in the US and increased visibility for both drag and gay culture. As these cultures became more visible, however, their modes and styles were more accessible to the larger culture, Ross's ignoranti, who often imitated the mode without necessarily taking on the sexual identity. What were once potentially subversive accoutrements – earrings, leather jackets, makeup for men, men's suits for women – became chic commodities for the dominant culture.

The way that this process of commodification borrows elements of a homosexual sensibility and attempts to de-homosexualize them is evident in the case of Lennox: once her biological sex was definitely determined by the censors at MTV and others, Lennox made it clear that she was not only a woman but also, according to interviews in *Rolling Stone* and other popular periodicals, a heterosexual woman. At the same time that Lennox's performance disrupts the connection between homosexuality and drag, however, it ironizes and thereby destabilizes the hegemony of the gender binary. Lennox's performance cannot be removed from the consumerist system that circumscribes it, but it nevertheless provides an important example of what I have labelled 'camp androgyny', focusing its irony on a dominant gender system that refuses to acknowledge the possibility of a gender identity displaced from biological sex.

Annie Lennox's performances as a camp androgyne offer interesting parallels to Virginia Woolf's serially dual-sexed Orlando, the protagonist of *Orlando: A Biography*. *Orlando* includes photos and illustrations of its fictional subject, the most striking of which is a photograph of Vita Sackville-West facing p. 126, the 'real-life' inspiration for the title character of Woolf's biography. In the photograph, Sackville-West's feminine (long, curly) hair is contrasted with a facial expression that suggests British masculine-imperialist hubris. Because photographs of Sackville-West and her family had appeared with regularity in the society pages of Britain's major newspapers throughout the 1920s, her face – and the fact that she was a woman – was well known to her contemporaries. The photograph of her in *Orlando*, entitled 'Orlando as Ambassador' represents, like Annie Lennox's 'Sweet Dreams', a female camp performer, the camp androgyne who exhibits both masculine and feminine characteristics.

The photographic representations of Sackville-West as the androgynous Orlando in the pages of Woolf's novel suggest the possible beginnings of a specifically female tradition of androgynous gender performance. Sackville-West, like Lennox, does not appear as an hermaphroditic body dressed in various clothes – in neither performance is the viewer perceiving an organism that possesses the sex organs of both sexes. Rather, it is the tension between perceived biological sex and the style of self-presentation that creates a moment of disorientation and uncertainty, the 'camp effect' of their respective andro-gynous performances. In *Orlando*, Woolf's descriptions of characters are designed to inscribe the same kinds of uncertainties that are suggested by the inclusion of the images of Sackville-West. The 'body' of Woolf's text presents a kind of camp performance akin to Sackville-West's and Lennox's.

In her theoretics of writing and gender, A *Room of One's Own*, Woolf makes two pronouncements that are directly relevant to her textual – and sexual – project in the roughly contemporaneous *Orlando*. The first passage provides a warning: 'it is fatal for any one who writes to think of their sex. It is fatal to be a man or woman pure and simple; one must be woman-manly or man-womanly' (104). Whether an author is a man or a woman biologically, it is his/her job to transcend his/her sex. In other words, as Woolf puts it, 'a great mind is androgynous' (98); the character Orlando, who gains insights into both maleness and femaleness throughout his/her extended life, provides an example of just such a great mind. Woolf's emphasis on androgyny does not, however, suggest that sex evaporates or disappears for writers, as she makes clear in a second assertion, that female authors should 'think back through our mothers' (76). Woolf suggests that the female author should write 'as a woman, but as a woman who has forgotten that she is a woman' (93), if she wants to talk in any relevant way about the topic of sexuality. As in Lennox's performance at the Grammys and the representation of Sackville-West in 'Orlando as Ambassador', Woolf's characterization of Orlando fore-grounds androgyny; at the same time, *Orlando* is inescapably a female text, written by a woman and a feminist.

In order to understand and to read lucidly the specific effects of the inscrip-tion of the camp androgyne into *Orlando*, it is first necessary to situate the text within its historical/cultural context. To this end, two frames become necessary for an understanding of *Orlando* as camp: a psychological frame in order to examine the ways that Woolf's text functions as a critique of contemporary discourses of sexuality, and a biographical frame – a reading of the text as a biography of Vita Sackville-West.

Orlando should be understood as a camp text situated specifically in the late 1920s, a text that comments upon gender constructions and restrictions within Woolf's privileged, bourgeois culture. Elaine Showalter once dismissed *Orlan-do* as 'tedious high camp' (1977: 291), as, implicitly, an apolitical romp; conversely, it has been read persuasively as a kind of lesbian-feminist manifesto by critics such as Sherron E. Knopp and Elizabeth Meese. This essay, in contrast, seeks to read it as an instance of high camp that Woolf employed to interrogate Freudian theories of sexual identity.

By the time of Virginia Woolf's composition of *Orlando* (1927–28), theories of sexuality developed by sexologists such as Havelock Ellis and Richard von Krafft-Ebing and through the psychoanalytic method of Sigmund Freud had saturated the cultural consciousness of England. Some critics have argued that Woolf was particularly well acquainted with the sexological theories of Ellis because of her involvement with the obscenity trial of Radclyffe Hall's *The Well of Loneliness*, a lesbian novel that is heavily influenced by Ellis's theories and for which he wrote a laudatory preface. Jane Marcus, for example, identifies the character Judith Shakespeare in Woolf's *A Room of One's Own* with the self-proclaimed 'invert' Radclyffe Hall, and she describes the narrator as 'speaking in the voice of Mary (Llewelyn), Stephen Gordon's lover in *The Well of Loneliness*' (163). By reading *Room* as a rewriting of Hall's novel, Marcus aligns Woolf's understanding of sapphism with Hall's conception of inverted lesbianism as famously theorized by Ellis: 'a man trapped in a woman's body'.

Although it is very likely that the sexology of Ellis was discussed by members of Woolf's immediate Bloomsbury circle, particularly during the *Well* trial, one should also note that Woolf apparently did not begin to read Ellis until approximately twelve years after she finished writing *Orlando*. At no time, moreover, did Woolf express any particular interest in Ellis's theories. A mention of Ellis appears in a diary entry of 1926, in which Woolf generally expresses a desire to read 'Dante, Havelock Ellis, & Berlioz' (*Diary*, 3: 103); there is no indication in any of her published papers that she fulfilled this desire any time before 1940, when, according to a letter to Ethel Smyth, Woolf was 'going asleep over' a book by Ellis (*Letters*, 6: 386). Similarly, she was apparently uninterested in Hall's 'meritorious dull book' (*Diary*, 3: 193), which she also called 'that Well of all that's stagnant and lukewarm' (*Letters*, 3: 555).

Judging from her personal writings, Woolf was more familiar with Freud's psychoanalytic theory than with the sexologists' theories of inversion. Significantly, the Woolfs' Hogarth Press had been publishing the *Collected Writings* of Freud since 1924 (*Letters*, 3: 119). Freud's notions of sexual identity might have been introduced to Woolf through her brother Adrian Stephen and his wife Karin, both of whom graduated from the University College Hospital in London as psychoanalysts in 1926. It is also possible that her first discussions about Freudian psychoanalysis might have been with her close friend the biographer Lytton Strachey – who had been a member of the British Society for the Study of Sex and Psychology (*Diary*, 1: 110) – or with Strachey's brother James and James's wife Alix, who had been analyzed by Freud and who were in the process of translating Freud's *Complete Works* in the 1920s (Holroyd, 724, 825). Finally, Woolf's husband Leonard was a self-avowed Freudian. In 1914 he published a highly favorable review of Freud's

The Psychopathology of Everyday Life; and in his autobiography Leonard later wrote that he was 'rather proud of having in 1914 recognized and understood the greatness of Freud and the importance of what he was doing at a time when this was by no means common' (167). At the very least, Virginia Woolf must have been aware of her husband's unbridled enthusiasm for Freudian psychoanalysis.

Although Woolf was certainly aware of Freudian theory, however, she was at best ambivalent and at worst hostile to it at the time when she was writing *Orlando*. According to Ellen Goldstein, this attitude persisted at least until the late 1930s. Goldstein also notes that even though psychoanalysis 'was available in London' as early as 1913, Woolf never underwent psychoanalysis in order to treat her periodic bouts of insanity, invariably enduring instead the 'rest cures' prescribed by her doctors (444–5). In addition, in a review of J. D. Beresford's novel *An Imperfect Mother*, Woolf expresses an ambivalent – albeit very well-informed – attitude toward Freudian theories. In the review, entitled 'Freudian Fiction', Woolf suggests that Beresford, in attempting to apply Freudian theories to his novel, has produced an esthetic that oversimplifies and is unfaithful to the experience of human life, because 'the new key [of Freudian theory] is a patent key that opens every door. It ... detracts rather than enriches' (154). Woolf criticizes Beresford for not allowing his characters to be individuals, choosing instead to present them as psychoanalytic 'cases'; this, she argues, is why the novel must be labelled 'a failure' (153).

Given Woolf's dislike of Freud, one senses some sarcasm in her observation in a letter of 1924 that the Freudian texts the Hogarth Press was publishing were 'dumped in a fortress the size of Windsor castle in ruins upon the floor' of the Woolfs' flat *(Letters*, 3: 119). Further, when in a letter to Molly MacCarthy of the same year Woolf does admit to reading few lines of Freud, her observations are hardly laudatory:

> [W]e are publishing all Dr. Freud's, and I glance at the proof and read how Mr. A. B. threw a bottle of red ink on to the sheets of his marriage bed to excuse his impotence to the housemaid, but threw it in the wrong place, which unhinged his wife's mind, – and to this day she pours claret on the dinner table. We could all go on like that for hours; and yet these Germans think it proves something – besides their own gull-like imbecility *(Letters*, 3: 134–5).

As this comment suggests, Woolf's hostility seems to be directed at Freud's male-centered reading of a woman's neurosis, his assertion that a wife's sanity must hinge upon her husband's virility and his accurate aim when throwing bottles of red ink.

Unlike Ellis, whose work induced somnolence, Freud's writings tended to trigger intense anger in Woolf. She does not attack other psychoanalytic theorists in her writing, and, as Elizabeth Abel notes, she is actually fairly sympathetic with the work of the psychoanalyst Melanie Klein (9–20). To Abel,

'Woolf's objections to psychoanalysis are specific to Freud', and her narratives are designed to 'interrogate Freud' (18, 3). It is in this sense that Abel regards Freudian psychoanalysis as an important context for reading Woolf, a context that is also key for reading sexuality in *Orlando* – a text that Abel, however, does not discuss in any detail.

To appreciate Woolf's use of camp in *Orlando* to undermine Freud's psychoanalytic model, we might look first at the succinct version of his theory of sexuality, which appears in his 'On Narcissism' (1924):

> We have discovered, especially clearly in people whose libidinal development has suffered some disturbance, such as perverts and homosexuals, that in their later choice of love-objects, they have taken as a model not their mother but their own selves. They are plainly seeking *themselves* as a love-object and are exhibiting a type of object choice which must be termed 'narcissistic'. In this observation we have the strongest of the reasons which have led us to adopt the hypothesis of narcissism. (88)

In contrast to this kind of narcissistic 'pervert', Freud posits the 'normal' or 'anaclitic' person, who takes for his/her love-object an 'other' rather than him/herself (87).

This simplistic theory is critiqued most clearly through the abrupt transformation that the protagonist of Woolf's *Orlando* undergoes, which is described by a narrative voice whose tone is humorous and playful: 'He stretched himself. He rose. He stood upright in complete nakedness before us, and while the trumpets pealed Truth! Truth! Truth! we have no choice left but to confess – he was a woman' (137). This transformation can be read as a critique of Freud's theory of sexual orientation, in that Orlando changes from an anaclitic male (a male who desires women) to a narcissistic female (a woman who desires women, a pervert). On board a ship returning from the mysterious East, where her sex change occurred, the now-female Orlando realizes that her sex-object choice has not altered along with her body:

> as all Orlando's loves had been women, now, through the culpable laggardry of the human frame to adapt itself to convention, though she herself was a woman, it was still a woman she loved; and if the consciousness of being of the same sex had any effect at all, it was to quicken and deepen those feelings which she had had as a man. (161)

Though her sex has changed, her gender identification remains the same – she becomes an anaclitic male in a female's body – almost the very definition, for Freud, of the narcissistic female. Gender becomes in this text much too complicated for the Freudian model, which depends on the permanency of a particular biological sex in a single subject.

Moreover, even to those of us for whom a particular biological sex at least *appears* to be a permanent condition, gender is much more slippery than Freud imagined. The narrative voice of Woolf's text explains:

> In every human being a vacillation from one to the other takes place, and often it is only the clothes that keep the male or female likeness, while underneath the sex is the very opposite of what it is above. Of the complications and confusions which thus result every one has had experience. (189)

Through cross-dressing Orlando illustrates these 'complications and confusions'. As a young man, Orlando dresses in (historically appropriate) fashions that do 'something to disguise' his sex (13). Likewise, after transforming into a woman, Orlando often dresses as 'a young man of fashion', looking 'the very figure of a noble Lord' (215). Just as the male Orlando is feminized by his clothing, so the female Orlando is masculinized by hers; each wears clothing that serves to disguise his/her sex.

Other instances in the text suggest that these 'complications and confusions' are related to sexual object-choice. For example, though Orlando the male desires women, his most significant erotic obsession is focused on an androgynous figure: Sasha, the Russian princess. When he first sees her, 'he beheld, coming from the pavilion of the Muscovite Embassy, a figure, which, whether boy's or woman's, for the loose tunic and trousers of the Russian fashion served to disguise the sex, filled him with the highest curiosity'. The narrator then proceeds to describe the exact appearance of this figure, finally concluding: 'But these details were obscured by the extraordinary seductiveness which issued from the whole person' (37). It would seem, therefore, that what arouses Orlando's desire is a figure of ambiguous gender.

Another example of Orlando's attraction to androgynous figures occurs, of course, much later in the form of her love affair with Marmaduke Bonthrop Shelmerdine, or Shel, to whom Orlando professes her 'passionat[e] . . . love'. In the moment following this admission of love, however, 'an awful suspicion rushed into both their minds simultaneously', which they both immediately articulate:

> 'You're a woman, Shel!' she cried.
> 'You're a man, Orlando!' he cried.
> Never was there such a scene of protestation and demonstration as then took place since the world began. (252)

Orlando and Shel are more than just Freudian narcissists; the complicated notion of gender articulated in Woolf's text overdetermines the Freudian model by radically disconnecting sex and gender. This disconnection plays a large part in making *Orlando*, according to numerous critics, a 'difficult' text (see Wilson, 170). The separation of sex and gender produces a particular disorientation in the reader in regard to socially prescribed gender roles, and creates what I would like to call the 'camp effect' of *Orlando*: its deliberate subversion of the dominant sexual discourse – represented in this frame by Freud – through gender performance.

One might protest that *Orlando* is just a text, and moreover a fantastic one, so that any attempt to compare the 'real' people upon which Freud based his theories and Woolf's fictional protagonist must necessarily be faulty. Orlando, however – like the Freudian case studies that provided the evidence for Freud's contentions in 'On Narcissism' – was based on a close study of a 'real' individual: Vita Sackville-West. The association between Sackville-West and the fictional Orlando provides a second necessary frame for reading *Orlando* as camp: biography.

Commenting on the genesis of *Orlando* in his edition of her letters, Nigel Nicholson notes: 'On 5 October [1927] Virginia wrote in her diary: "And instantly the usual exciting devices enter my mind: a biography beginning in the year 1500 and continuing to the present day, called Orlando: Vita; only with a change about from one sex to another"' (*Letters*, 3: 427n1). When Virginia asked Vita if she would give her permission to be the subject of this unusual biography, Vita replied, on 11 October 1927:

> My God, Virginia, if ever I was thrilled and terrified it is at the prospect of being projected into the shape of Orlando. What fun for you; what fun for me ... You have my full permission. Only I think that having drawn and quartered me, unwound and retwisted me, or whatever it is that you intend to do, you ought to dedicate it to your victim. (*Letters* 3: 429n1)

A number of critics have examined *Orlando* as a fantastical biography of Vita Sackville-West, beginning with Frank Baldanza in a 1955 *PMLA* essay. More recently, in her *Vita and Virginia* Suzanne Raitt contends that 'the writing of the book was bound up with [Woolf's] desire for Sackville-West ... The writing of *Orlando* injected a new energy and tension into their relationship, sustaining it and in a way *becoming* it' (17–18). According to Raitt's reading, *Orlando* derives its energy from Woolf's sapphic (or, roughly, lesbian) desire for Vita Sackville-West.

This sapphic energy provides an impetus for undermining gender types in *Orlando*. Woolf's text parodies a Freudian discourse of sexual identity that framed Virginia and Vita's sapphic relationship; it thereby challenges that discourse. *Orlando* suggests that homosexual desire functions in contradictory and even paradoxical ways that are not accounted for in Freud's notion of 'narcissistic cathexis' – a model that is insufficient both in its oversimplification of desire and in its male-centered formulation, as Woolf points out in her essays and letters. In addition, through its biographical structure, *Orlando* reveals the ways that the dominant overly simple gender system limited the possibilities of subjects circumscribed by it, particularly women and implicitly lesbian women.

The limitations placed upon sapphic women are exemplified through the lawsuit against which the female Orlando must defend herself in order to retain her property and her titles. In a conversation with Shel, Orlando reads the outcome of this legal battle:

'The lawsuits are settled . . . Children pronounced illegitimate (they said I had three sons by Pepita, a Spanish dancer). So they don't inherit, which is all to the good . . . Sex? Ah! what about sex? My sex', she read out with some solemnity, 'is pronounced indisputably, and beyond the shadow of a doubt (what was I telling you a moment ago, Shel?) Female. The estates which are now desequestrated in perpetuity descend and are tailed and entailed upon the heirs male of my body, or in the default of marriage . . . but there won't be any default of marriage, nor of heirs either, so the rest can be taken as read'. (255)

The very idea of Orlando as a definably gendered and sexed subject is here undermined. Orlando asks Shel 'what was I telling you a moment ago. . .?' before she pronounces her legal sex: 'Female'. Had she been telling Shel that she was a woman or that she was a man? Woolf's narrator does ironically suggest that Shel makes Orlando feel like a 'real woman', at least for a moment. But we are provided only with 'a great blank' in the passage leading up to this episode (253); we are prevented from knowing what exactly Orlando was telling Shel 'a moment ago'. Thus, Woolf continues to suggest the ambiguity of Orlando's sexual identity. Also emphasized here are the legal effects of the dominant, binaristic system of gender construction, which oppresses women by transferring their material possessions to their male children, and which further oppresses women who are 'violently Sapphic' (Woolf, *Letters*, 3: 155) by requiring them to marry and produce children in order to allow the transferal to take place.

Importantly, Vita Sackville-West was involved in a parallel lawsuit that established her father's position as legal heir of the Sackvilles' ancestral home, Knole. Vita's own situation was similar to Orlando's, and the reference to her grandmother Pepita points the reader directly to Vita's biography. Sackville-West's own plight, however, differed from Orlando's in two important ways: first, though she engaged in numerous female-female sexual relationships – most notably with Violet Trefusis and of course Virginia Woolf – she did produce two legitimate sons by Harold Nicholson; second, it was Vita herself who was disinherited, who would never inherit Knole because of her own 'essential' femaleness. Thus, although Orlando bears a close resemblance to Vita Sackville-West in certain ways, Woolf's protagonist is in other ways a fantastic invention, and this aspect is central to Woolf's project. Woolf, that is, uses the figure of Orlando first to disrupt simplistic notions of gender, and then to associate that disruption with the 'real-life' figure of Vita Sackville-West, who lost her family home through a legal system based largely on the very same simplistic notions of gender and sexual identity. This text relates its fantastic protagonist – whose biological sex is mystically reversed – to Sackville-West without confusing the two. By presenting Orlando as a camp androgyne – both male and female, both real and imagined – Woolf's text thematizes gender as subversive performance.

A last question arises in turn: can women produce deliberate camp? Though many theorists associate self-conscious camp with gay maleness, others have allowed women also to engage in the fun. Moe Meyer (1994b), for example, associates it with queerness generally, and Pamela Robertson suggests that women might employ it for feminist ends: 'Camp ... offers feminists a model for critiques of sex and gender roles' (1993, rpt. 1993: 156). Because the role of women as producers of camp has been undertheorized, it is understandable that Lytton Strachey's biographical style has been described as 'camp Mandarin' (Spurr 1990: 31), but that Woolf has not typically been read as camp. Yet if, as David Bergman has argued, in camp 'the very excessiveness in style cues the reader' (1993c: 96), then a text such as Woolf's that foregrounds and thematizes an excess of gender signification can be read as camp, whether written by a male or by a female. Woolf's very femaleness, however, is important to her use of camp. Abel claims that the 'weighting of androgyny toward the maternal is in fact implicit throughout Woolf's discussion' of androgyny in *A Room of One's Own* (87). If the androgyny of Orlando is read with this female emphasis, then Woolf's text can be understood as inaugurating a tradition of female camp androgyny that attempts to play with and thereby threaten the gender system that writes meaning onto the bodies of 'real' people through the fictions of psychoanalytic narratives.

Importantly, camp functions within a particular historical/cultural frame to undermine the gender assumptions of particular societies. Sontag asserts that 'the Camp eye has the power to transform experience. But not everything can be seen as Camp. It's not *all* in the eye of the beholder' (277). Following Eve Kosofsky Sedgwick, I would like to suggest that camp is in the performance, a performance that presupposes a certain sensibility – a certain eye – that can decode its excesses; Sedgwick labels this phenomenon 'camp-recognition' (1990: 156). Camp celebrates alienation and distance because it moves beyond the boundaries outlined by dominant ways of understanding identity, gender, and sexuality. Those who cannot read the camp in a performance (whether framed by a text or not) are bound to become disoriented, mystified, frustrated – an effect that *Orlando* has produced in many of the 'ignoranti'. Those who can read the camp will also be disoriented; the difference is that they will revel in and celebrate the sensation.

Because the cultural codes embedded in camp are quite socially and historically specific, the particulars of Lennox's performance as Elvis and Woolf's inscription of Vita Sackville-West as Orlando should be read within disparate contexts that must be examined closely in order to recreate their camp effects. Lennox's performance should be understood in terms of the commodification of gay culture that was well underway by the 1980s, whereas Woolf's should be seen as part of a struggle against the pathologizing and psychologizing models of sexuality proposed by thinkers such as Freud. By situating these performances historically, it is possible to understand the relationship between performativity and the culturally-situated 'body'.

What Lennox's and Woolf's projects have in common, however, is that they both undermine their respective cultures' assumptions about the stable connection between biological sex and gender through the use of female camp androgyny. Camp functions within a relationship between a performance and a viewer; it is produced through a coded, ironic 'wink', a knowing glance shared between a cognizant perceiver – who can read and appreciate this wink – and a performative agent. In the cases of both Lennox's Elvis and Woolf's Orlando, those viewers and readers willing to revel in gender disorientation will be able to break the code of the camp androgyne.

I would like to thank Gregory W. Bredbeck for his stimulating comments on the Bloomsbury Group and Freud, which proved invaluable as I was working out Woolf's relationship to psychoanalysis. Heartfelt thanks also to Henry Abelove for his very helpful commentary on an earlier draft and to Robert K. Martin, whose careful interrogation of previous versions of this essay greatly aided me in rethinking aspects of my argument.

REFERENCES

Abel, Elizabeth, *Virginia Woolf and the Fictions of Psychoanalysis*, Chicago: U of Chicago P, 1989.

Baldanza, Frank, '*Orlando* and the Sackvilles', *PMLA* 70, 1955, 274–9.

Butler, Judith, *Bodies That Matter: On the Discursive Limits of 'Sex'*, New York: Routledge, 1993.

Derrida, Jacques, 'Signature Event Context', in *Limited Inc.*, Evanston: Northwestern UP, 1988.

Freud, Sigmund, 'On Narcissism: An Introduction', *The Standard Edition of the Complete Psychological Works of Sigmund Freud*, ed. and trans. James Strachey, Vol. 14, London: Hogarth, 1957, 73–102.

Goldstein, Jan Ellen, 'The Woolfs' Response to Freud: Water Spiders, Singing Canaries, and the Second Apple', *Psychoanalytic Quarrerly* 43, 1974, 438–76.

Heilbrun, Carolyn G., *Toward a Recognition of Androgyny* (1964), New York: Norton, 1982.

Holroyd, Michael, *Lytton Strachey: A Biography*, London: Book Club, 1973.

Love, Jean O., '*Orlando* and its Genesis: Venturing and Experimenting in Art, Love, and Sex', in Ralph Freedman (ed.), *Virginia Woolf: Revaluation and Continuity*, Berkeley: U of California P, 1980, 189–218.

Marcus, Jane, *Virginia Woolf and the Languages of Patriarchy*, Bloomington: Indiana UP, 1987.

Raitt, Suzanne, *Vita and Virginia*, Oxford: Clarendon, 1993.

Randall, Lucian, *Annie Lennox*, London: Carlton, 1994.

Strachey, James, 'Editor's Note', in *The Standard Edition of the Complete Psychological Works of Sigmund Freud*, Vol. 14. London: Hogarth, 1957, 69–71.

Wilson, J. J., 'Why is *Orlando* Difficult?' in Jane Marcus (ed.), *New Feminist Essays on Virginia Woolf*, London: Oxford, 1981, 170–84.

Woolf, Leonard, *Beginning Again: An Autobiography of the Years 1911 to 1918*, New York: Harcourt, 1964.

Woolf, Virginia, *The Diary of Virginia Woolf*, ed. Anne Olivier Bell., 5 vols., London: Hogarth, 1977–81.

——, 'Freudian Fiction' (1920), in Leonard Woolf (ed.), *Contemporary Writers*, London: Hogarth, 1965.

——, *The Letters of Virginia Woolf*, ed. Nigel Nicholson, 6 vols. London: Hogarth, 1975–80.
——, *Orlando: A Biography* (1928), San Diego: Harcourt, 1973.
——, *A Room of One's Own* (1929), San Diego: Harcourt, 1989.

SECTION IV
POP CAMP, SURPLUS COUNTER-VALUE, OR THE CAMP OF CULTURAL ECONOMY

INTRODUCTION

If not the 'sensibility of an era', 'Notes on "Camp"' certainly captured the ultimate sensation of the 1960s, projecting its subject-matter and author to intellectual and public stardom – Sontag being 'packaged' at one and the same time with her 'product' under the name of 'Miss Camp' and 'the Camp Girl' (cf. White 1966: 71). Within just a few months, major US and British periodicals – the *New Statesman*, *Time*, *Holiday*, the *Observer*, *Art News* and the *New York Times* (both supplement and magazine) – gave a significant portion of their columns to articles on the 'new taste' celebrated by Sontag. Days after the publication of the 'Notes', Tom Wolfe depicted the high (hip and hyped) camp of an 'Andy Warhol meets the Rolling Stones' party in 'The Girl of the Year', a piece of 'new journalism' for *New York* (the *New York Herald Tribune* Sunday supplement), and Calvin Trillin wrote a 'camp love story' for the *New Yorker*. It's hard to underestimate the currency value the term gained during the rest of the decade, so that – as a reader wrote in the Letters section of the *New Statesman* – 'no literary review or posh Sunday supplement [could] manage for long without [...] this indispensable and compendious monosyllable' (Shaw et al. 1967: 759). In August 1966 the *Observer* had camp on the front cover of its colour supplement: a year before that, a furniture sale could still be advertised in the *New York Times* as a 'Great New Camp Site'. Isherwood's disconcertion at its absence from public discourse had been fully satisfied; but in becoming 'an indispensable and compendious monosyllable', and part of the mainstream cultural economy of the 1960s, *camp* also became a high rate *selling* cultural product.

The camp mania of the mid-1960s, in fact, mirrors the craze for the pop scene and icons it referred to. The terms *camp* and *pop*, as George Melly recorded at the end of the decade, were 'interchangeable' in relation to 'an irreverent revival of certain humble or popular objects from the past' (1970: 147), to the 'fleamarket' nostalgic mode and the swinging venue of Carnaby Street in London, with its complex aesthetic of the transient, the disposable, and the endearingly 'poor' taste turned into a sign of (new) cultural capital. But such intertwined existence of camp and pop can't be reduced to a flattening of the former on the latter: the popularity of camp was spinned by its expendability within spheres of cultural life as separate as a Marcel Duchamp exhibition (cf. Hess 1965) and the *Batman* TV series (cf. Torres 1996, reprinted here; see also Medhurst 1991, and Spigel & Jenkins 1991). Not that the 1960s camp scene can be reduced to homogeneity, split as it is between the New York liberal setting that expressed 'the Camp Girl' herself, and the British scene, with its Oxbridge educated tradition and overtones of queer sexuality, co-opted by countercultures such as the Teds (wearing suede shoes and other tokens from queer Edwardian sartorial codes) and the 'lambretta & Union Jack' self-styled Mods. Camp circulated at the time with the excitement induced by a movement across boundaries, both those of the high vs. pop culture dychotomy, and of the commercialized, 'new', supermarket(ed) American culture vs. the European cultural 'nobility' opposition undermined by the US 'colonisation' of Europe, and Europe's 'striking back' with the colonial trophies of the pop music and fashion 'British invasion' of America in 1964.

The euphoria inscribed in the 'contradictory concept' of pop camp (camp being 'an "in" idea, a property of a minority', Melly 1970: 192) was spun, in fact, precisely by the possibility that camp offered to muddle up categories and to mix audiences, in the exhilaration brought forth by the simultaneous challenge to the settled hierarchies of taste *and* sexuality (gender being, we have seen in Section III, an *aesthetical* issue). As the campy *bricolage* of upper class 'effeminacy' was adopted by juvenile countercultures and by glam rock stars, censorship was undergoing a severe critique, and homosexuality and the drag scene were themselves in the process of coming out. The underground scene was gaining access to an unprecedented visibility: Andy Warhol brought drag queens to superstardom, and Pop Art was moving from the supermarket to the highbrow galleries. In that extraordinary dialectic of progressive and reactionary positions (with camp as a theatre for the confrontation between the Joe Ortons and the Edna Whelthorpes), in other words, society at large was getting somehow queerer;[1] and at the same time, with gay attempts at assimilation to the mainstream (be those in the egalitarian mode or, yes, through pop camp),[2] homosexuality was willing to give up some of its *radical* queerness. Of course, this means acknowledging that in the process camp might have lost to some degree its cutting edge for the gay culture whose construction it had both enabled and constrained, its use for gay solidarity and resistance, along with its co-optation as a fashionable phenomenon. But this isn't paramount to saying that postwar appropriations voided camp of its alleged original, univocally progressive, politics – for progressiveness was *not* inherent to, and necessitated by, the 'original' deployment of camp within gay culture.

Within the most significant (gay, lesbian, queer, cultural) critical discourse, in fact, the reassessment of the 1960s mainstreaming of camp coincides no longer with the 'reclaiming' enterprise, with its orientation so grounded in (and justified within) gay identity politics, but rather in an archaeological effort to map the queer circulation of the camp discourse within both gay and hetero-sexual settings: to map its uses as a means to different ends, and to assess its logic of circulation, the interests mobilised by that exuberant field of reference, and its intersections with issues of sexual and cultural politics. Andrew Ross's 'Uses of Camp' (1988) posits such a framework and offers the unavoidable starting point for a reconsideration of the 'cultural economy' of camp.

Ross discusses the postwar camp challenge to categories of taste, value and sexuality by inscribing them in the *surplus* logic of camp. When he describes camp as 'the re-creation of surplus value from forgotten forms of labor', Ross is not only unfolding the camp nostalgic mode as 'more than just a remembrance of things past'. He is also pointing to the logic of the parasitical and of the supplement enacted by what I have called the camp ephemeral apparatuses – be they those of the dildo, of signs of gendered power, of the investment in sartorial codes and outward 'appearance' of the subject's essence, or of the paratextual. The camp effect requires in fact, both as a performance and as a decoding act, the setting up of a stage: a whole 'venue' and surplus *semiotic* value come into being through the camp 'deviant' decoding. Ross's essay follows Sontag's and Booth's suggestion in placing camp within a history of aristocratic taste *vis-à-vis* bourgeois domination, whose late twentieth-century *mise en scène* is the 'superior' stand of the camp performing/decoding subject (a queer superiority, in fact, in concert with the exclusion from the power of representation, and an assertion of divinely decadent superiority through the 'perverse' reinscription). The dandy of recycled and mass culture was thus an icon for a variety of religions, all of them claiming counter-cultural status.

The camp logic of surplus value may in fact be framed as a logic of surplus *counter*-value, for the re-creation of surplus value from forgotten forms of labour was no mere, straight nostalgia: camp enacts a perversion of nostalgia itself, twisting the original circulation and intentions of its objects, reframing them so as to direct them against those very portions of the social body who were 'originally' represented by them, thus turning them into powerful signs of oppositional identities (so that Victoriana and the Union Jack, once the signs of the British domination, were adopted as signs of fake power – the power of forgery). And yet, the extraordinary significance of camp within the 1960s scene is inexorably linked not only to its oppositional value, but also to its availability as a weapon of containment – to its *counter*-value as an opposi-tional strategy inherently haunted by its otherness, the specter of complicity. Ross discusses, in fact, the conservative implications of the 1960s adoption of camp by intellectuals, who 'were able to "pass" as subscribers to the throw-away Pop aesthetic', while preserving – via the camp elitism – their cultural authority inscribed in 'the traditional panoply of tastemaking powers which Pop's egalitarian mandate had threatened'.

Sasha Torres's excellent 'The Caped Crusader of Camp' challenges such argument, whilst following Ross in the analysis of the 1960s camp contradict-ory and multilayered cultural economy. Torres's reading of the *Batman* series aired by the ABC network in 1966 shows the intertwined existence of pop and camp as both, at once and the same time, challenging and 'sanitising' elements at work one against the other. In dealing with *Batman*, Torres addresses in fact a central icon of the pop 1960s and a most popular gay (sub)text, along with the whole swinging set of heroes-in-disguise celebrated by Ronald Bryden in 1966 on the front cover of the *Observer* – from James Bond, sent on a mission 'in drag' by Cyril Connolly in 'Bond Strikes Camp' (1963), to the British series *The Avengers* (cf. Andrae 1996) and to the popular TV program *The Man from U.N.C.L.E.*, spoofed in the gay pulp fiction of *The Man from C.A.M.P.* written by Victor Banis under the (appropriate) disguise of a pseudonym (Don Holli-day) between 1966 and 1968. If the threat of Pop to the panoply of tastemakers could be redeemed by marketing Batman as camp, Torres's argument goes, the gay nuances of the super-hero brought forth through its 'outing' in the mid-1950s by the outrageously homophobic (and pretty campy himself) psychiatrist Fredric Wertham, required the de-sexualising 'sanitation' endorsed by Pop. Torres thus develops the often refrained thesis of degayfication enabled by pop camp, but she gives it new critical poignancy acknowledging the mutually appropriative existence of camp and pop, echoing that of 'high' and 'mass' culture. If Ross's essay concludes reminding us the extent to which the cultural economy of camp, despite its *frisson* of transgression, 'was tied to the capitalist logic of development that governed the mass culture industries', a text such as *Batman*, in its activation of the double challenge and containment of pop and camp, enacts the queer relation of the two terms as both queer aesthetical currency and queer members of the 1960s social contract. Which brings us to Andy Warhol, the site of friction between pop, camp, and a third freightful term also intervening at the time – the 'postmodern' – and the object of a recent wave of criticism, of which Matthew Tinkcom's essay reprinted here is a good specimen, devoted to contrast the dehomosexualisation of his figure and work that occurred along their trajectory between the underground New York scene and the empyrean of High Culture.[3]

While the relationship between camp and the postmodern has not yet been fully addressed in all its complexity, the striking convergence of the two notions has produced a constant, if unsystematic, referral to both camp as a feature of the postmodern, and to postmodernism as camp – most notably by Fredric Jameson, whose Marxist critique of the 'logic of late capitalism' places the postmodern theory and depthless reality under the derogatory label of 'camp or "hysterical" sublime' (1984: 76–7).[4] The postmodernist crisis of the depth model, in Jameson's account, entails the downfall of aesthetical and epistemo-logical hierarchies, the voiding of identity and agency, suspension of the foun-dational character of reality, and loss of historicity, induced by a camp historicism (celebrating 'the random cannibalization of all the styles of the past', 65) and by a 'nostalgia mode' (66) that abolishes the concreteness of its object of desire, its referent. What is left is a mall, an artificial Eden offering itself to the consumer's 'appetite for a world transformed into sheer images of itself and for pseudo-events and "spectacles"' (66). As to the parodic impulse appreciated by postmodern and camp practitioners alike, what remains is in fact a parody 'without a vocation', a *pastiche* 'devoid [...] of any conviction that alongside the abnormal tongue you have momentarily borrowed, some healthy linguistic normality still exists' (65). Jameson contrasts in fact Warhol's *Diamond Dust Shoes* (1980) to the 'modernist' pair of Van Gogh's *Old Shoes with Laces* (1886), showing how the failure, in the former, of the 'hermeneu-tical gesture' willing 'to restore to these oddments [its] whole larger lived context' constitutes it as a fetish, while 'the Van Gogh footgear are a hetero-sexual pair, which allows neither for perversion nor for fetishization' (60).

This orthodox Marxist mourning of the categories of textual and ontological depth suspended by postmodern theory and practice all too suspiciously recalls similar liberal humanist lamentations,[5] and one cannot but contrast it with the counter-cultural, challenging character of camp by means of a stylistic *brico-lage* and a conspicuous consumption oriented to a semiotic subcultural guer-rilla (as theorised in Hebdige 1979, and Beaver 1981, reprinted here). Jameson is in fact denying any radical character to queer representation, which, in the perversion of the 'healthy linguistic normality', in the twisting of the direction inscribed in 'vocation', and in the subversion of the heterosexual – and hermeneutically (re)productive – imperative, finds its political and aesthetical worth. As to the alleged frustration, in the spectator of Warhol's acrylic figures and glossy images, to 'complete the hermeneutical gesture', Tinkcom's essay gives Marxist theory a 'gay twist' in a heterodox attempt to restore its 'larger lived context'. In resorting to camp as peculiarly deployed within the male gay tradition, and as a form of *gay labour* (camp thus being 'the alibi for gay-inflected labour to be caught in the chain of value-coding within capitalist political economies'), Tinkcom frames Warhol's work as informed by his appreciation of gay responses to industrialisation, *besides and against* the avant-garde redefinition of sexualities within metropolitan reality.

Warhol's camp can in fact be framed as a *queer currency*, a perverted form of production that surreptitiously 'infects' commodity culture and the bourgeois modes of production, pushing them to implosion – turning them into a spectacle. And yet, Jameson's lament cannot just be dismissed as in its turn an hysterically normative humanist failure to cope with the queer challenge of the camp 'perverse' semiotic. If only Jameson's mourning should invite us to acknowledge what he seems not to – that 'postmodernism', just like 'camp' and 'pop', is *not* a unitary phenomenon, whose configuration and implications can be assessed without taking into account their specific articulation in time and space. As Andreas Huyssen's splendid mapping of postmodernism shows (1986: 179–221), it is at least ingenuous to acritically celebrate the camp (and postmodern tongue-in-cheek), unstably ironic 'subversion', just as it may seem reactionary to deny their potential, or historical, progressive value. In both cases, the wishful thinking or depression of the present flattens the local specificity of that strategy; and a better reading might start by looking at the *difference* between the present and the past (say, between the postmodern anarchism of the 1980s/90s, and the camp exuberance of the 1960s, and between that and the Wildean anarchism of the 1890s), not simply in order to complain about how 'transgression' has been rendered ineffective by making the *norm* itself mobile enough to *resist* transgression. Even in the event that present situation allowed us to reassess the 1960s transgression itself as a euphoric phase within which the depoliticised postmodern was already lurking, we might still invest that assessment towards the identification of a better strategy.

NOTES

1. During the camp popular 'craze', Vivian Gornick pointed out that in fact the dispersal of the 'origins' of camp, when it was 'the private property of American and English homosexuals', went in concert with the way homosexuals had accepted their marginal role *within* bourgeois society – popular culture being, through camp, 'in the hands of the homosexuals', whose 'temperament [. . .] is guiding the progress of Pop Art' (1966: 1).
2. This process is charted in Van Leer 1995. But see also Clark 1991, who offers an excellent assessment of the commodification of lesbianism.
3. See also Smith 1986; Shaviro 1993; R. Meyer 1994; Cagle 1995; Doyle, Flatley & Muñoz 1996; Suárez 1996.
4. The relationship of camp and postmodernism is touched upon, if not discussed, in Huyssen 1986; McRobbie 1986; Hake 1988; Wilson 1988; Hutcheon 1989: 10; Anderson 1990; Weinstein et al. 1990; Hoesterey 1991; Ceserani 1992, 1997b; Coombe 1992; Huskey 1992; Kalaidjian 1992; Dainotto 1993; Dellamora 1994; Kellner 1994; Sinfield 1994; J. Collins 1995; Dickinson 1995; Wheale 1995; Cleto 1996a, 1997; Leitch 1996; Smigiel 1996; Walters 1996; Roth 1998, and the relevant essays included in Doan 1994; O'Donnell 1995a. Such convergence was in fact embedded in the very access of camp to public discourse, when Sontag described it as an 'unmistakably modern' sensibility (cf. Section I); and possibly under the influence of that proposal *camp* circulated as referring to practices also labelled 'postmodern', especially (but not exclusively) within arts and architectural criticism. See Jencks 1973a&b, 1980; Smith 1977; Kramer 1982, 1984b; see also Fiedler 1969; Hassan 1971; Calinescu 1977.
5. A close analysis of that critique, of course, can't be undertaken here: see the excellent discussion in Dellamora 1994; Feuer 1986, and Dollimore's essay reprinted here.

19

USES OF CAMP

Andrew Ross

'It's beige! *My* color!'
(Elsie De Wolfe, on facing the Parthenon for the first time)

Take four iconic moments from the 1960s:

1961: In *What Ever Happened to Baby Jane?* (Robert Aldrich) – according to Bette Davis, the first 'women's picture' for over ten years, bringing together for the first time the aging, uncrowned royalty of classic Hollywood – Davis and Joan Crawford. 'Baby Jane' Hudson, ex-child-star, now grotesquely made-up (at Davis's own inspirational insistence) like a pantomime Ugly Sister, serves up steamed rat for lunch to her wheelchair-bound sister Blanche, a big film star in the 1930s, whose career was tragically cut short by a car accident. Blanche spins in terror in her wheelchair, shot from above; Jane laughs from the belly up, her face twitching with glee. Their House of Usheresque present refracts the Babylonish history of Hollywood stardom, while it creates a new horror film subgenre for the new decade.

1964: A different Baby Jane, in a New York photographer's studio in the year of the British invasion – Baby Jane Holzer, in Tom Wolfe's 'Girl of the Year', cavorting at her twenty-fourth birthday party which doubled as a publicity event for her star guests, the Rolling Stones. Back from the London 'Pop' summer of 1963, sporting the Chelsea Look, and talking Cockney ('Anything beats being a Park Avenue housewife'), Holzer, for Wolfe, for *Vogue,* and for Andy Warhol, is the living symptom of the new, pluralistic, 'classless'

First published in *Yale Journal of Criticism*, 2:1, fall 1988. A longer version appears in Andrew Ross, *No Respect: Intellectuals and Popular Culture*, New York-London: Routledge, 1989.

melting pot culture, where socialites – though not only the Social Register type – enthusiastically took up the styles and subcultural idioms of arriviste 'raw-vital proles' (the party's theme was Mods vs. Rockers) by way of the exotic British import of 'East End vitality' ('they're all from the working class, you know').

1969: The evening of the funeral of Judy Garland (a long time gay icon), members of the New York City Vice Squad come under fire, from beer cans, bottles, coins, and cobblestones, as they try to arrest some of the regulars at the Stonewall inn in Christopher Street. The mood of the protesters, many of them street queens in full drag, had changed from that of reveling in the spectacle of the arrest, even posing for it, to one of anger and rage, as one of the detainees, a lesbian, struggled to resist her arrest. Within minutes, the police were besieged within the burning bar. Some of those present thought they heard the chant 'Gay Power', while others only saw a more defiant than usual show of posing; it wasn't clear whether this confrontation was 'the Hairpin Drop Heard Around the World' or the 'Boston Tea Party' of a political movement.

Later in 1969: A different scene of conflict at the Altamont free festival, the dark sequel to Woodstock, and the Stones again. Jagger is up front, berobed and mascara'd, swishing, mincing, pouting, and strutting before a huge audience barely in check, while on every side of the stage are posted Hell's Angels, confrontation dressers all – the sometime darlings of radical chic, which saw in them an aggressive critique of the counterculture's 'male impotence'. Here employed as soft police, they stare, bluntly and disdainfully, at the effeminate Jagger, some of them mocking his turns and gyres, while the off-stage violence escalates, to end soon in the death of eighteen-year old Meredith Hunter, caught on film in *Gimme Shelter*, the Stones's blatant attempt at self-vindication, in which Jagger poses the rhetorical question: 'Why does something always happen when we start to play that song?' – 'Sympathy for the Devil'.

There are many 1960s themes that could serve to link each of these highly mediated moments together. And for those who like to tell the 'story' of the 1960s, such moments would probably mark significant points in the stock narrative of rise and fall, of hope and disillusion, which has become the dominant or favored media version of that decade's events. The purpose they serve here is to introduce particular aspects of the history of *camp*, that category of cultural taste, which, more than anything else, shaped, defined, and negotiated the way in which 1960s intellectuals were able to 'pass' as subscribers to the throwaway Pop aesthetic, and thus as patrons of the attractive world of immediacy and disposability created by the culture industries. On the importance to the 1960s of this category of taste, George Melly, the English jazz musician and Pop intellectual, was adamant: camp was 'central to almost every difficult transitional moment in the evolution of pop culture ... [it] helped pop make a forced march around good taste' (1970: 160–1).

But if there is a story to tell about the transitional function of camp as an *operation of taste*, then it will be a story of unequal and uneven development. It will demonstrate the different uses and meanings camp generated for different groups, subcultures, and elites in the 1960s. The exercise of camp taste raised different issues, for example, for gay people, *before* and *after* 1969; for gay males and for lesbians; for women, lesbian and straight, before and after the various movements for sexual liberation; for straight males, before and after the call to androgyny had been fully sounded; for traditional intellectuals (obliged now, in spite of their prejudices, to go 'slumming') and organic intellectuals (whose loyalty to the Pop ethic of instant gratification and expendability left little space for political philosophy or discriminations of resistance); for dis-advantaged working-class subcultures (whose relation to Pop culture was a glamorous, and seldom inadequate, semiotic of their aspirations and dreams of social mobility and leisure) and the middle-class counterculture (whose whole-sale withdrawal from the everyday commodity world thrived upon a heady, premodernist fantasy of self-sufficiency).

While it would be wrong to see camp as the privileged expression of any of these groups, even the traditional pre-Stonewall, gay male culture for which the most legitimate claim can be made, there are certain common conditions which must be stressed. Just as the new presence of the popular classes in the social and cultural purview of the postwar state had required a shift in the balance of *containment* of popular democracy, so too, the reorganization of the capitalist bases of the culture industries, the new media technology and the new modes of distribution that accompanied that shift necessarily changed the aesthetic face of categories of taste. New markets – youth and swinging 'Playboy' males in the 1950s (to be followed by women in the 1960s and gays in the 1970s) – had produced massive changes in the patterns of consumption. These changes, in turn, produced the affluence and the material social conditions out of which the newly constructed, interlocking subcultures of the 1950s emerged in the 1960s as visible phenomena in the writing of Tom Wolfe and Pop intellectuals. The changes in cultural technologies had quite specific effects, which I shall discuss, in turn, with respect to the four iconic moments with which I began.

What triggers the narrative action and the new sadistic-jealous mood of 'Baby Jane' Hudson is the showing of one of Blanche's old movies on television. The most recent version of Old Hollywood was in decline, the star-system had foundered, and the whole corporate economy of the studio system had been challenged, outpaced, and largely outdated by the television industry. The late 1950s and early 1960s saw the recirculation of classic Hollywood films on television, giving rise to a wave of revivalist nostalgia, and supplementing the cult of Hollywoodiana – with all of those necrophilic trappings that embellish its decadent fascination with the link between glamor and death.[1] No longer was this a taste reserved for members of film societies and clubs; or for avant-garde filmmakers like the celebrated Jack Smith, who had studied every frame of certain 1930s films, and whose cult of

Maria Montez, one of the most cherished of the pantheon of camp screen goddesses, was to irradiate important sectors of the early 'Underground' film scene.

True to the Hollywood logic, of course, the stylized morbidity of this cult had long been an institution – a horror film subgenre – in its own right. In Billy Wilder's *Sunset Boulevard* (1950), Hollywood had produced its own baroque funeral elegy for silent film. Joe Gillis (William Holden), the young, down-on-his-luck scriptwriter and heel, recognizes the mark of movie history beneath the faded glamor of Norma Desmond (Gloria Swanson): 'You used to be in silent pictures. You used to be big'. Desmond shoots back: 'I *am* big. It's the pictures that got small'. In a sense Desmond is correct (in spite of Gillis's crass, authoritative voiceover, Norma is almost always correct). But her outrageous self-conceits and her tirades against 'words', 'writing', and 'dialogue' can only produce their truly camp effect in a film, like Wilder's, which relies so heavily upon words and dialogue, and in which the new Hollywood – the 'smallness' of today's pictures – is represented by the no-nonsense, professional earnestness of Betty Schaefer (Nancy Olson), a scriptreader who finds 'social interest' themes to develop in the scripts of the noirish gigolo Gillis.

The cult meaning of Norma Desmond's *grande damerie* is generated out of a contemporary predicament, which is suggested here by the incongruous juxtaposition of the present with the trauma of the passing of silent film. By 1950, the studio star system, already in trouble with television, was about to enter its last phase – the Monroe phase. The anxiety of that moment is ironically figured in the other great camp film of that year, Joseph Mankiewicz's *All About Eve*, in which a young Monroe plays the role of a talentless ingénue in hot pursuit of a career in one of the vacuums created by the retirement of a great Broadway actress (played by Bette Davis), while the traditional hierarchy of prestige between Broadway and Hollywood is broadened to include a third, and much despised third term – television (as the theater critic in the film, Addison De Witt, affirms: 'That's all television is, my dear, nothing *but* auditions'). As Hollywood is passing out of its 'bourgeois' moment, the origins of that moment are invoked in the spectacle of Norma Desmond, a residual survivor of the prebourgeois age of screen gods and goddesses, whose crumbling aristocracy now serves, in the 1950s, as a displaced symptom of the current, further decline (or increased democratization) of the film medium. It is the historical incongruity of this displacement which creates the world of tragic-ironic meanings that camp exploits.

Over a decade later, a similar collision of meanings ensures the success of the macabre tragicomedy of *What Ever Happened to Baby Jane?* The conclusion of this film is more incongruous yet. Where Norma Desmond noirishly basks, at the ending of *Sunset Boulevard*, in the garish light of camera flashes, and in the knowledgeable attention of a crowd of reporters and voyeurist hangers-on, Jane Hudson strikes up her blithe child-star routine in the beach heat of a California sun, surrounded by an oblivious group of teenagers.

The camp effect, then, is created not simply by a change in the mode of cultural production (and the contradictions attendant on that change), but rather when the products (stars, in this case) of a much earlier mode of production, which has lost its power to produce and dominate cultural meanings, become available, in the present, for redefinition according to contemporary codes of taste.

A similar relation to disempowered modes of production can be seen in the importance of the so-called British invasion to the Pop version of camp. For here was the first evidence of a foreign culture making sense of the American popular culture which had been widely exported since the war. For Britons, the importation of American popular culture, even as it was officially despised, contained, and controlled, brought with it guaranteed immunity to those traditional 'European' judgments of elitist taste to which it was structurally oblivious.[2] By the early 1960s, the 'success' of this wave of American exports among British tastemakers was such that they were able to set the final seal of approval on the formation and acceptance of Pop taste in the US itself. Thus, the British version of Pop (always an *imaginary* relation to a foreign culture – James Hadley Chase, for example, invented the America of his many best-selling novels, after one short visit to Florida as a tourist) (cited in Chambers 1986: 40) was somehow needed to legitimize American pop culture for Americans in accord with the higher canons of European taste to which they were still, in some way, obliged to defer.

The 'camp' moment in this complex process, however, is the ironic recognition of the eclipsed capacity of real British power to play the imperialist game of dominating foreign taste. That is why the British flag, for Mods and other subcultures, and Victoriana, for the later Sergeant Pepper culture, became camp objects; precisely because of their historical association with a power that was now spent. The Stars and Stripes, and Americana, by contrast, could only be kitsch, because its serious intentions were still the historical support of a culture that holds real imperialist power in defining the shape of foreign cultures. It makes sense, then, to find in 'Girl of the Year' that the 'supermarvellous' Baby Jane Holzer plays her part opposite a group of Cockney primitives, or Teen Savages, among whom Jagger is described as almost not human, 'with his wet giblet lips', speaking a deformed language, a slurred, incomprehensible 'Bull Negro' when he is not mumbling a forcibly inarticulate native Cockney. At the very moment when the balance of a transatlantic taste is being redefined, it is only fitting that Wolfe invoke terms and images from the historical discourse of colonial subjugation. (Elsewhere he describes the natives of his 'discovered' Californian subcultures as 'Easter Islanders' (*Kandy-Kolored*, 86) – Who are they and how did they achieve this level of civilization?)

But what was the meaning of this newly proclaimed 'classless' culture? The purist Pop intellectual like Warhol simply proclaimed that everyone (and everything) was equal: 'It was fun to see the Museum of Modern Art people next to the teeny-boppers next to the amphetamine queens next to the fashion editors' (Warhol & Hackett 1980: 162). Others, like Wolfe, made righteous claims about the new cultural power of the disenfranchised – 'now high style comes from low places ... the poor boys ... teenagers, bohos, camp culturati ... have won by default' – and went on to emphasize the pioneering risks they themselves were taking to champion those who had neither 'stature nor grandeur': the 'petty bureaucrats, Mafiosi, line soldiers in Vietnam, pimps, hustlers, doormen, socialites, shyster lawyers, surfers, bikers, hippies and other accursed Youth, evangelists, athletes...' (Wolfe & Johnson, 38). While for intellectuals like Susan Sontag, with more traditional knee-jerk avant-garde tastes, it meant a passport from the top down (but not necessarily from the bottom up) to all corners of a cultural garden of earthly delights: 'From the vantage point of this new sensibility, the beauty of a machine or of the solution to a mathematical problem, of a painting by Jasper Johns, of a film by Jean-Luc Godard, and of the personalities and music of the Beatles is of equal access' (Sontag, 304).

Each of these responses pays tribute in its own way to the official national ideology of liberal pluralism; a heterogeneous set of culturally diverse groups with 'special interests', ranged together in harmonious coexistence. The non-committal, 'documentary' stance of many Pop intellectuals, while it was an important break with the morally charged paternalism of their forebears, did little to expose what the liberal pluralist model had excluded – all of the signs of conflict generated by the uneven development of the 'affluent society', and the antagonism of huge numbers of oppressed people excluded by or marginalized within the new pluralist conjuncture. In fact, Wolfe's use of the term 'subculture' as a 'statusphere' appealed to a simple, functionalist description of an autonomous group seeking its share of the pie. There was no consideration of the conflicts and contradictions that result from the antagonistic relation of any single subculture to a parent culture, or from its relation to other subcultures, or from multiple membership in different groups and subcultures.[3]

That the existence of a pluralistic range of subcultures does not spell harmony, and that even a counterhegemonic bloc of oppositional subcultures will be riven with internal contradictions proved to be one of the 'lessons' of the 1960s. Hence the mock-heroic anger and frustration of Wolfe at the turn of events in the later 1960s, when a law-and-order, or 'control', society was hurriedly being put in place to contain the antiwar movement. Appearing in a symposium at Princeton with Paul Krassner, Günter Grass, Allen Ginsberg, and Gregory Markopoulos, he is blithely offended by their talk of police repression, 'the knock on the door' and other strategies of coercion. 'What are you talking about?' he said. 'We're in the middle of a Happiness Explosion' (*Gang*, 14).

The deficiencies of the liberal pluralist model can be seen more clearly in the examples of Altamont and Stonewall, where subcultures within the evolved 'counterculture' are at odds with each other. The Pop slogans of immediate gratification, hedonism, and accessibility had informed a grammar of achievement and mobility for working-class cultures. For the middle-class counterculture, they had also come to generate a vocabulary of dissent and antiauthoritarianism, wielded against the guardians of a system struggling to resolve, through consumerism, its long crisis of overproduction. As a result, the discourses of hedonism began to outstrip the limits of the controlled structures of consumer society, and soon a wholesale ideology of disaffiliation from the institutions of Establishment culture was in place, complete with its own alternative structures (in the areas of family, education, labor, media, taste, lifestyle, and morality), founded upon utopian premises. Loosely incorporating the dominant white student faction of the New Left (itself divided between sectarian political elements and, increasingly, along gender lines), this countercultural bloc was obliged, largely by the pressure of the media's definition of its aims, to recognize its alternative culture heroes (its own organic intellectuals) as leaders *even as* it proclaimed its self-reliance (that is, reliance on grass-roots community organizations), and thus its opposition to vanguardist leadership.[4]

One example of this contradiction was the running battle, from the mid-1960s on, with the youth-oriented entertainment industries who sought to absorb, assimilate, and exploit countercultural values for profit, and whose management of this process increasingly demanded the celebrification of rock stars as culture hero-leaders. The free music festival became a privileged symbol of this struggle, a test of the capacity to mobilize the alternative networks in support of a vast noncommercial celebration of the 'liberated' sector of the population. At Altamont, planned as little more than an end-of-tour publicity stunt for the Rolling Stones, the violence, associated with the 'retarded' masculinity of the Hell's Angels, and the 'bad vibes', associated with exploitative drug trafficking, came to be seen as symptomatic of the contradictions of the counterculture. In fact, it is important to see that the Angels, recruited as alternative 'police', represented a different, working-class, ethic of *delinquency*, which, unlike the counterculture, had never sought to devolve itself entirely from the parent culture, and which retained its suspicion and resentment of the libertarian privileges of student and other middle-class cultures. Although they found it offensive to be cast as 'police', and were right in thinking they were being patronized (no properly countercultural group would play this role), they were in fact more likely to be found marching against the students (as happened in Berkeley) and with the real riot police, with whom they shared a common, if uneasy, class constituency.[5]

At Stonewall, where a traditionally persecuted minority group fought back and made history, but not under conditions of its own making, a more clearcut picture of the new 'control' society emerges. The immediate local problem at stake in the Stonewall 'riots' was as much Mafia control of gay bars as routine acts of police repression (Marotta, 70–99). Thus, the commercial control of a gay subculture that existed hitherto as a network of codes of concealment was *already* an issue in the founding moment of the overtly *identified* subculture that was soon to emerge under the aegis of Gay Pride, Gay Power, and the Gay Liberation Front (GLF). Formed explicitly on the model of the civil-rights movement for blacks, the gay liberation movement was committed to going beyond the reformist aims – polite integration – of the liberal homophile politics that had been urged since the early 1950s by the Mattachine Society and the Daughters of Bilitis.[6] Inheriting the irreverent but militant style of the New Left, and following the example of community organizing fostered in the South by the Student Nonviolent Coordinating Committee (SNCC), gay leaders contended that the liberation movement could not simply be a question of gay businessmen taking control of the bars, stores, and clubs; alternative institutions had to be created. The success of the lesbian community in creating such a network of institutions (along with its crucial participation in the women's movement) has been seen as the most positive legacy of this movement. For gay males – one of the prime target, higher-income, cachet groups that were ripe for new consumer marketing in the 1970s – the gains have been less certain. Today, gay intellectuals who were active in the GLF or the Gay Activists Alliance view with ambivalence the commercial development of the gay scene and the complicity of gay communities in the creation of that scene.[7] Today's gay male is the 'new model intellectual' of consumer capitalism, at the forefront of the business of shaping and defining taste, choice, and style for mainstream markets. So too, the sexual freedoms won by the liberation movements are often inseparable from the commodification of sex, on the one hand, and the use of categories of sexuality to socially control and quarantine groups identified by sexual orientation, on the other.

It is in this dialectic between sexual *liberation* and corporate-State *regulation* that we can locate the problems faced by gay cultural politics, today, in a control society reinforced by its capacity to define the 'threat' of AIDS on its own terms. How does a subculture make sense of this dialectic? This is where the question of 'camp', which is often posed as an embarrassment to post-Stonewall gay culture ('the Stepin Fetchit of the leather bars') (Melly 1984), becomes political all over again, not only because of its articulate engagement with the (commodity) world of popular taste, but also because camp contains an explicit commentary on feats of *survival* in a world dominated by the taste and interests of those whom it serves.

CAMP *OBLIGE*

In her seminal 'Notes on Camp' (1964b), Susan Sontag raises the question of survival in a quite specific way: 'Camp is the answer to the problem; how to be a dandy in an age of mass culture' (rpt. 1966: 188). Her formula – one among many memorable aperçus to be found in her essay – suggests that what is under attack in an age of mass culture is precisely the power of taste-making intellectuals to patrol the higher canons of taste, and that the significance of the 'new sensibility' of camp in the 1960s is that it presents a means of salvaging that privilege.

The pseudoaristocratic patrilineage of camp can hardly be overstated. Consider the etymological provenance of the three most questionable categories of American cultural taste: schlock, kitsch, and camp. None is of Anglo origin, although it is clear, from their cultural derivation, where they belong on the scale of prestige: *Schlock*, from Yiddish (literally, 'damaged goods' at a cheap price), *Kitsch*, from German, petty bourgeois, and *Camp*, more obscurely from the French *se camper*, with a long history of upper-class English usage. While schlock is truly unpretentious – nice things in nice taste – and is designed primarily to fill a space in people's lives and environments, kitsch has serious pretensions to artistic taste, and, in fact, contains a range of references to high or legitimate culture which it apes in order to flatter its owner-reader-consumer. Its seriousness about art, and its aesthetic chutzpah is associated with the class aspirations and upward mobility of a middlebrow audience, deemed 'insufficient' in cultural capital to merit access to legitimate culture (see Sternberg 1971, Brown 1975).

Of course, kitsch is no more a fixed category than schlock or camp. These categories are constantly shifting, their contents are constantly changing; what is promoted one year may be relegated again the next. What is important is their persistently subordinate relation to the dominant culture, by which they are defined as examples of 'failed taste'. Neither can they be regarded as categories defined with equal objectivity but which signify different value, since schlock and kitsch are more often seen as categories of objects, while camp tends to refer to a subjective process: Camp, as Thomas Hess put it, 'exists in the smirk of the beholder' (1965: 53). If certain objects and texts tend to be associated with camp more readily than others, they are often described as 'campy', suggesting a self-consciousness about their lack of pretension which would otherwise, and more accurately, be attributed to the sophisticated beholder. Not surprisingly, Sontag downgrades this self-consciousness, reserving her purist praise for the category of *naïve* camp, presumably because, with the latter, it is the critic and not the producer who takes full cultural credit for discerning the camp 'value' of a text.

It is clear, at any rate, that the division between kitsch and camp partially reflects a division between manual and mental labor, or, in camp's own terminology, between ignoranti and cognoscenti. The producer or consumer of kitsch either is unaware of the extent to which his or her intentions or pretensions are alienated in the kitsch text, or else is made to feel painfully aware of this alienation in some way. Camp, on the other hand, involves a celebration, on the part of cognoscenti, of the alienation, distance, and incongruity reflected in the very process by which it locates hitherto unexpected value in a popular or obscure text. Camp would thus be reserved for those with a high degree of cultural capital. It belongs to those who have the accredited confidence to be able to devote their idiosyncratic attention to the practice of cultural slumming in places where others would feel less comfortable.

Just as it is absurd to speak of a lasting canon or pantheon of camp texts, objects, and figures (though such exclusive lists do exist, temporarily, for certain groups who 'use' camp), universal definitions of camp are rarely useful. In Philip Core's encyclopedia of camp, for example, camp is defined as 'the lie that tells the truth' or as 'the heroism of people not called upon to be heroes' (1984: 5), while Christopher Isherwood finds that camp is a matter of 'expressing what's basically serious to you in terms of fun and artifice and elegance' (1954: 214). This is why Sontag chose to write her essay about this 'fugitive sensibility' in the form of notes or jottings, although her decision to do so has as much to do with her unpolitical conviction that there are 'almost, but not quite, ineffable' causes which give rise to a 'logic of taste', as it has to do with her expressed anxiety about writing something ridiculous – 'a very inferior piece of camp', as she puts it. More useful is Mark Booth's expanded and exhaustive account of Sontag's 'pocket history of camp' (her note no. 14 – embracing rococo, mannerism, *les précieux*, Yellow Book aestheticism, art nouveau), a history that is polemically governed by his thesis that 'to be camp is to present oneself as being committed to the marginal with a commitment greater than the marginal merits' (1983: 18). The advantage of this formulation is that it clearly defines camp *in relation to the exercise of cultural power*. Booth argues, for example, that camp, far from being a 'fugitive sensibility', belongs to the history of the 'self-presentation' of arriviste groups. Because of their marginality, because they lack inherited cultural capital, and thus the accredited power to fully legitimize dominant tastes, these groups parody their subordinate or uncertain social status in 'a self-mocking abdication of any pretensions to power' (1983: 29).

Unlike the traditional intellectual, whose function is to legitimize the cultural power of a ruling group, or the organic intellectual, who promotes the interests of a rising class, the marginal (or camp) intellectual expresses his impotence as the dominated fraction of a ruling bloc in order to remain there (i.e., as a non-threatening presence) while he distances himself from the conventional morality and taste of the growing middle class. The nineteenth-century camp intellectual may well be a parody or negation of dominant bourgeois forms: anti-industry, proidleness; antifamily, probachelorhood; antirespectability, proscandal; antimasculine, profeminine; antisport, profrivolity; antidecor, proexhibitionism; antiprogress, prodecadence; antiwealth, profame. But his aristocratic affectations are a sign of his *disqualification*, or remoteness from power, because they comfortably symbolize, to the bourgeois, the deceased power of the aristocrat, while they are equally removed from the threatening, embryonic power of the masses.

Hitherto associated with the high-culture milieu of the theater, camp intellectuals become an institution in the twentieth century, within the popular entertainment industries, reviving their role there as the representative or stand-in for a class that is no longer in a position to exercise its power to define official culture. So too, they maintain their parodic critique of the properly educated and responsibly situated intellectual who speaks with the requisite tone of moral authority and seriousness as the conscience and consciousness of society as a whole (i.e., as the promoter of ruling interests).

Thus it is ironic that Sontag chooses to link her account of the (largely homosexual) influence of camp taste with the intellectual successes of Jewish moral seriousness, as the two 'pioneering forces of modern sensibility' (note no. 51). More than any other publication, her essay (and the book in which it appeared, *Against Interpretation*), signaled the challenge to, if not the demise of, the tradition of Jewish moral seriousness that had governed the cultural crusading of the cold-war liberal. Not that Sontag herself is willing to jettison entirely the prerogative of the liberal's act of judgment; in fact, she is careful to record her ambivalence about camp – 'a deep sympathy modified by revulsion'. Nonetheless, the importance of her own critical intervention in the mid-1960s was in the service of pleasure and erotics, and against judgment, seriousness, interpretation; against, in short, the hermeneutics of depth with which established intellectuals – the New Critics and the New York Intellectuals alike – had dictated literary taste since the war.

Camp, in the form in which it came to be received and practiced in the 1960s, symbolized an important break with the style and legitimacy of the old liberal intellectual. I shall now examine two important contexts of this break: first, Pop, and its reorientation of attitudes toward mass culture; and second, the question of sexual liberation, the redefinition of masculinity, and the concomitant rise of the gay movements.

POP CAMP

In England in the 1950s, the fledgling studies of Pop by members of the International Group at the Institute of Contemporary Art had come directly out of the postwar mass culture debates. Against the cold-war 'consensus' thesis about manipulation, standardization, and lobotomization, Reyner Banham and others argued that the consumers of mass culture were experts, trained to a high degree of connoisseurship in matters of consumer choice and consumer use; for them, there was no such thing as an 'unsophisticated consumer'. Lawrence Alloway wrote passionately against the received wisdom that mass culture produced a passive, undifferentiated audience of dupes:

> We speak for convenience about a mass audience but it is a fiction. The audience today is numerically dense but highly diversified. Just as the wholesale use of subception techniques in advertising is blocked by the different perception capacities of the members of any audience, so the mass media cannot reduce everybody to one drugged faceless consumer. Fear of the Amorphous Audience is fed by the word 'mass'. In fact, audiences are specialized by age, sex, hobby, occupation, mobility, contacts, etc. Although the interests of different audiences may not be rankable in the curriculum of the traditional educationist, they never-

theless reflect and influence the diversification which goes with increased industrialization. (42)

In the drab cultural climate of Britain in the 1950s, popular culture and mass media were much more than a functional and necessary guide to modern living; they were, in Alloway's eloquent phrase, 'a treasury of orientation, a manual of one's occupancy of the twentieth century'. To the paternalist Establishment culture, they represented the specter of 'Americanization'. To the working-class consumer, they brought a taste of glamor, affluence, immediate gratification, and the dream of a pleasure-filled environment to transcend the workaday drudgery of their circumstances. To middle-class aficionados, American popular culture was a Cockaigne of the perverse intellect, a fantasy of taste turned upside down with which to avenge themselves against the tweedy sponsors of European tradition. The very idea of Richard Hamilton's painting 'Hommage à Chrysler Corp', for example, exudes the bittersweet flavor of camp – a highly wrought conceit of the European as a fake American.

While the American experience of commercial, popular culture was, of course, much more *lived* and direct, we should not fall into the trap of assuming that it was less mediated or less fantasmatic. The uses made of comic strips, science fiction, 'Detroit' auto styling, Westerns, rock 'n' roll, and neon advertising by different social groups cannot be read as if they were spontaneous responses to real social conditions. On the contrary, they represent an *imaginary relation* to these conditions, and one which is refracted through the powerful lens of the so-called Great American Dream – a pathologically seductive infusion of affluence, ordinariness, and achieved utopian pleasure. The American as a dream American.

Pop's commitment to the new and everyday, to quantity and to the throwaway was a direct affront to those who governed the boundaries of official taste. Nothing could be more execrable to a tradition of taste held together by the precepts of 'universality', 'timelessness', and 'uniqueness' than a culture of obsolescence: that is, designed not to endure. Camp, however, offered a negotiated way by which this most democratic of cultures could be partially 'recognized' by intellectuals. In fact, Pop camp, as Melly argues, is a contradiction in terms, because camp is the 'in' taste of a minority elite (Melly 1970: 174). Pop, on the other hand, was supposed to declare that everyday cultural currency had value, and that everything had more or less equal value. Culture was to be described and enjoyed, not prescribed like a dose of medicine by those with the cultural capital to decide 'what's good for you'.

In fact, Pop could no more shut out history than the sublime Coke bottle could escape its future as an empty but *returnable* commodity item. For the immediacy and self-sufficiency of the consumption of the Pop experience *already contains the knowledge that it will soon be outdated* – spent, obsolescent, or out of fashion. A throwaway culture, even a disposable culture, moreover, is not one which simply disappears once its meaning has been consumed;

whether it figures as waste, to be recycled, or as detritus, to lie in wait until it is tastefully redeemed twenty years hence, it contains messages about the historical *production* of the material and cultural conditions of taste.

This knowledge about history is the precise moment when camp takes over, because camp is a rediscovery of history's waste. Camp irreverently retrieves not only that which had been excluded from the serious high-cultural 'tradition', but also the more unsalvageable material that has been picked over and found wanting by purveyors of the 'antique'. For the camp liberator, as with the high modernist, history's waste matter becomes all too available as a 'ragbag', but irradiated, this time around, with glamor, and not drenched with tawdriness by the mock-heroism of Waste Land irony. But, in 'liberating' the past in this way, it also bolsters the economy whereby objects and discourses of disdain are transformed into collector's items. Camp, in this respect is more than just a remembrance of things past, it is the *re-creation of surplus value from forgotten forms of labor.*

By the late 1960s, this parasitical practice had become a survivalist way of life for the counterculture, whose patronage of flea markets was a parody of the hand-me-down working-class culture of the rummage sale. The flea-market ethos, like most countercultural values, paid its respects to a notion of prelapsarian authenticity. In an age of plastic, authentic value could only be found in the 'real' textures of the past, along with traces of the 'real' labor that once went into fashioning clothes and objects. By sporting a whole, exotic range of preindustrial, peasant-identified, or non-Western styles, the students and other denizens of the counterculture were confronting the guardians (and the workaday citizens) of commodity culture with the symbols of a spent historical mode of production, or else one that was 'Asiatic', or 'underdeveloped'. By doing so, they signaled their complete disaffiliation from the semiotic codes of contemporary cultural power. In donning gypsy and denim, however, they were also patronizing the current aspirations of those social groups for whom such clothes called up a long history of poverty, social exclusion, and oppression. And in their maverick Orientalism, they romanticized other cultures by plundering their stereotypes. By contrast, the confrontation dressing of the later punk subculture was staged in the readily accessible, contemporary milieu of consumer culture, and was loosely organized around the tactic of reappropriating and redefining the current meanings of its objects and discourses, rather than invoking historical signifiers already saturated with the unequal opportunities accorded to class, race, sex, and nationhood.

The earlier phase of Pop camp arose directly out of the theatrical encounter of a culture of *immediacy* with the experience of history's amnesia. In reviving a period style, or elements of a period style that were hopelessly, and thus 'safely', dated, camp acted as a kind of *memento mori*, a reminder of Pop's own future oblivion which, as I have argued, Pop cannot help but advertise. For the Pop intellectual, camp was also a defense against the threat of being stripped of the traditional panoply of tastemaking powers which Pop's egalitarian mandate poses. Camp was an antidote to Pop's contagion of obsolescence. It is no surprise, then, to find that Sontag had been contemplating an essay on death and morbidity before she decided to write 'Notes on Camp' (cf. Boyers & Bernstein 1975, rpt. 1982: 338–9). The switch in her mind from thinking about 'mortuary sculpture, architecture, inscriptions and other such wistful lore' to the sociability of camp wit was, perhaps, triggered by a quite understandable flight from the realms of chilled seriousness to the warmer climate of theatrical humor. It is symptomatic, however, of the necrophilic economy that underpins the camp sensibility, not only in its resurrection of deceased cultural forms, but also in the way in which it serves an ambivalent notice of mortality to the contemporary intellect.

When Sontag associates the camp sensibility with the principle of 'the equivalence of all objects' (note no. 47), she is making claims for its 'democratic esprit'. What Sontag means, however, is that camp declares that anything, given the right circumstances, could, in principle, be redeemed by camp. Everything thereby becomes fair game for the camp cognoscenti to pursue and celebrate *at will*. This is a different thing altogether from the 'democratic' proposition of Pop philosophy, which simply *complies* with, rather than exploits, the principle of general equivalence. Sontag no doubt acknowledges this difference when she characterizes Pop as 'more flat and more dry' ('ultimately nihilistic') than camp, and when she describes camp, by contrast, as 'tender', 'passionate', and nurtured 'on the love that has gone into certain objects and personal styles' (notes 55–6). While Pop tries to disavow the traces of production behind its objects of attention, and concentrates on surface immediacy, camp cultivates an attitude toward the *participation* of the producers, past and present. In effect, the Pop intellectual is the new technocratic recruit, committed to accepting the realm of creative consumerism as the new site of cultural power. Camp, by contrast, celebrates the survival of the avant-garde intellectual, who patronizes and liberates by mobilizing attention to labor as the productivist site of cultural power.

A striking example of what I mean is the inexorable process by which *bad taste* – Sontag's formulation of 'the ultimate Camp statement; it's good because it's awful' – has come to be accepted as a semilegitimate expression of its own, and consequently, as a commercial market unto itself. There is no question that camp's patronage of bad taste, which thrives today in the work of John Waters and on the cult 'bad film' circuit, was as much an assault on the established canons of taste as Pop's eroticization of the everyday had been. This, however, was by no means a clean break with the logic of cultural capital, for it must also be seen from the point of view of those whom it indirectly patronized, those lower-middle-class groups who, historically, have had to bear the stigma of 'failed taste'. The *objet retrouvé* of camp's bad taste could hardly shake off its barbaric associations with the social victimization of its original audience. In fact, this process of camp rehabilitation, which cannot avoid the exploitation of these barbaric associations, lies at the root, today, of that vast and lucrative sector of the culture industry devoted to the production of 'exploitation' fare. Camp apologists will say that the initial aim of 'bad taste' was to ridicule the institutional solemnity with which social groups were linked to hierarchical cultural categories. There is a thin line, however, between the political appeal of this directed satire and the more unsavory caricature of social taste with which it runs parallel and with which it infrequently joins forces in the fully commercialized forms of bad taste. The fun and pleasure created by camp is often only enjoyed at the expense of others, and this is largely because camp's excess of pleasure, finally, has very little to do with the (un)controlled hedonism of a consumer; it is the work of a producer of taste, and 'taste' is only possible through exclusion *and* depreciation.

If we want to look beyond specialized taste, however, then it is in the realm of performance rock, pop, and rock 'n' roll that camp's penchant for the deviant has crossed over the threshold of restricted consumption into the mass milieux of homes, schools, colleges, clubs, and workplaces all over the country. But the outrageousness of performance rock has, among other things, always been something of a family affair – the object of what teenagers (and record-company producers) imagine is every good parent's worst fantasy. It is almost impossible, then, to talk about the history of that ever-shifting pageant of eroticized spectacle, from Elvis's gyrating hips to Annie Lennox's gender-blurred sangfroid, without first giving an account of how sexual difference was articulated, from the late 1950s onward, in ways that redefined the social categories of masculinity and femininity, inside and outside the family.

PRISONERS OF SEX

Female and male impersonation, representations of androgyny, and other images of gender-blurring have all played an important historical role in cinema's creation of our stockpile of social memories. For most spectators, whose voyeuristic captivity (as captors *and* prisoners) of the cinema image is an eroticized response to a psychic scenario on the screen, the suggestive incidence of cross-dressing among those memories is readily explicable. It has proved much more difficult, however, to provide a systematic account of how 'masculine' and 'feminine' positions of spectatorship are assumed as part of the process of reading and responding to these ambiguous images.

Molly Haskell has argued that the overwhelming disparity of images of female to male impersonation in films can be explained by the fact that, historically, male impersonation is a source of power and aggrandizement for women, while the theatrical adoption of female characteristics by men is a process of belittlement. Male impersonation is serious and erotic, while female impersonation is simply comical (61). In a book about cross-dressing in Hollywood cinema, Rebecca Bell-Metereau argues that Haskell's serious/comical distinction no longer applies, by pointing to the change in attitudes toward female impersonation that have occurred in the last two decades – with its range of 'legitimate' and sometimes popular, female impersonators of 'women of power'. So too, in the pre-1960 examples, 'tragic' or 'comic' readings of a film's treatment of cross-dressing are not simply the result of gender alignment. More important is whether the male or female imitation is 'willingly performed and sympathetically accepted by the social group within the film' (Bell-Metereau 1985: 117ff).

Just as the reading of these images is inflected by the complex interplay between spectacle and narrative, or between transgressive display and social judgment, there is no guarantee that what is *encoded* in these film scenarios will be *decoded* in the same way by different social groups with different sexual orientations. This is nowhere more obvious than in the highly developed gay subculture that evolved around a fascination with classical Hollywood film and, in particular, with film stars like Judy Garland, Bette Davis, Mae West, Greta Garbo, Marlene Dietrich, Joan Crawford, and performers like Barbra Streisand, Diana Ross, and Bette Midler. Denied the conventional 'masculine' and 'feminine' positions of spectatorship, and excluded by conventional representations of male-as-hero or narrative agent, and female-as-image or object of the spectacle, the gay male and lesbian subcultures express their lived spectatorship largely through imaginary or displaced relations to the images and discourses of a straight, 'parent' culture.

Unlike Pop or countercultural camp, the gay camp canon of film stars has very little to do with transformations of taste. In its pre-Stonewall heyday (before 'gay' was self-affirming), it was part of a survivalist culture that found, in certain fantasmatic elements of film culture, a way of imaginatively expressing its common conquest of everyday oppression. As with persecuted or economically subordinate groups, the fantasy possibilities of life on the screen allowed the utopian privilege of imagining a better world. In the gay camp subculture, glamorous images culled from straight Hollywoodiana were appropriated and *used* to make sense of the everyday experience of alienation and exclusion in a world socially polarized by sexual labels. Here, a tailored fantasy – which, by definition, never 'fits' the real – is worn in order to suggest an imaginary control over circumstances.

Gay male identification with the power and prestige of the female star was, first and foremost, an identification with women as *emotional* subjects in a film world in which men 'acted' and women 'felt'.[8] In this respect, camp reasserted, for gay males, the 'right to ornamentation and emotion, that Western and particularly Anglo-Saxon society has defined as feminine preoccupations' (Altman 1982: 154). Since these are qualities rarely emphasized by the legitimate representations of masculine sexuality, there are few male culture heroes in the camp pantheon; gay-identified actors like Montgomery Clift and Tab Hunter are an exception, but for obvious reasons, while the emotional sensitivity of Brando and Dean was more of a focus of interest for women in a pre- or protofeminist conjuncture.

The identificatory envy of the female film star's own 'power' is not, of course, without its contradictions, since that power is not unconditionally granted, and since its exercise in the service of some transgression of male-defined behavior is usually directly met with punishment and chastisement. As Michael Bronski argues, however, the mere idea that sexuality brings with it a degree of power, 'albeit limited and precarious, can be exhilarating' for the gay male who 'knows that his sexuality will get him in trouble'.[9] But what can the relation of this everyday triumph of the will to the commodity-controlled spectacle of a major star's 'sexuality' tell us about the power exercised by the institution of sexuality itself? This is the question gay politics has come to ask of camp.

In answering that question, it is important always to bear in mind that the traditional gay camp sensibility was an *imaginary* expression of a relation to real conditions, both past and present – an ideology, if you like – just as it still functions today, in the 'liberated' gay and straight world, as a kind of imaginary challenge to the new *symbolic* conditions of gay identity. Whether as a pre-Stonewall, utopian, survivalist fantasy, or as a post-Stonewall return of the repressed, camp transforms, destabilizes, and subverts the existing balance of acceptance of sexual identity and sexual roles. It never proposes a *direct* relation between the conditions it speaks to – everyday life in the present – and the discourse it speaks with – usually a bricolage of features pilfered from conditions of the past.

This knowledge might help us to answer the charge of misogyny that is often brought to bear upon camp representations of 'feminine' characteristics.[10] It could be argued that the camp idolization of female film starts contributes to a radical desexualization of the female body. In the context of a social spectacle where the female has little visible existence outside of her being posed as the embodiment of the sexual, any reading that defetishizes the erotic scenario of woman-as-spectacle is a progressive one. In the classic camp pantheon, film stars are celebrated for reasons other than their successful dramatization of erotic otherness. Here, camp joins forces with feminist appraisals of the 'independent' women of Hollywood – West, Davis, Crawford, and Garbo – who fought for their own roles, either against the studios themselves, or in the highly mannered ways in which they acted out, acted around, or acted against the grain of the sexually circumscribed stereotypes they were contracted to dramatize.

In a 1975 interview, Sontag has suggested that the diffusion of camp taste in the earlier part of the 1960s ought to be credited 'with a considerable if inadvertent role in the upsurge of feminist consciousness in the late 1960s'. In particular, she claims that the fascination with the 'corny flamboyance of femaleness' in certain actresses helped to 'undermine the credibility of certain stereotyped femininities – by exaggerating them, by putting them between quotation marks' (cf. Boyers & Bernstein 1975, rpt. 1982: 338–9). In acknowledging this, Sontag was clearly withdrawing from one of her controversial positions in 'Notes on Camp' – that camp was essentially 'apolitical', and that it was essentially an 'aesthetic' (especially pertinent to the times) of 'failed seriousness'. While gay intellectuals have long challenged this view (see Babuscio

1977, Bronski 1984), its flaws became increasingly visible as a full-blown sexual politics began to explore and criticize existing definitions of femininity and masculinity. Much of the ensuing debate has focused on questions camp had already highlighted, about the relation between 'artifice' and 'nature' in the construction of sexuality and gender identity. In fact, camp was a highly developed way of talking about what nonessentialist feminism has come to call sexual difference.

To nonessentialist feminism and to the gay camp tradition, the importance of particular film stars lies in their various challenges to the assumed 'naturalness' of gender roles. Each star presents a different way, at different historical times, of living with the 'masquerade' of femininity.[11] Each demonstrates how to *perform* a particular representation of womanliness. And the effect of these performances is to demonstrate, in turn, why there is no 'authentic' femininity, why there are only representations of femininity, socially redefined from moment to moment. So too, the 'masculine' woman, as opposed to the androgyne, represents to men what is unreal about masculinity, while actors whose masculinity is overdone and dated (Victor Mature is the classic camp example, not least, I think, because of the symmetry of his names) invoke the dialectic between (past) imprisonment and (present) liberation that helped to inspire the sexual politics of the late 1960s.

The politics of camp assumes that there is no easy escape from these definitions, and in this respect, it is opposed to the search for alternative, utopian, or essentialist identities that lay behind many of the countercultural and sexual liberation movements. Because of its zeal for artifice, theatricality, spectacle, and parody, camp has often been seen as pre-political, even reactionary. In its commitment to the mimicry of existing cultural forms, and its refusal to advocate wholesale breaks with these same forms, the politics of camp fell out of step and even into disrepute (as a kind of blackface) with the dominant ethos of the women's and gay liberation movements. Nonetheless, its survival, and its crossover presence in straight, masculine culture, has been directly responsible for the most radical changes in the constantly shifting, or hegemonic, definition of masculinity in the last two decades.

As make-up and dressing-up became a common feature of the flamboyant counterculture, 'drag', hitherto the professional conscience of camp, took on the generalized meaning, for straight culture, of all forms of everyday role-playing.[12] Countercultural liberation for men was one moment in the two decades of 'permissiveness' (the right-wing definition) that began with the swinging *Playboy* ethic of the mid-1950s and ended with the stirrings of the neoconservative backlash in the mid-1970s. Barbara Ehrenreich has argued that the 1950s 'male revolt' against the suburban bondage of breadwinning, announced by the consumerist *Playboy* lifestyle, also delivered men from suspicions of homosexuality that had hitherto been attached to those who shunned marriage.[13] So too, the 'ethnicization' of homosexuality, which gay liberation had brought about in the 1970s by advocating the policy of 'coming out', meant that straight men could pursue their exploration of androgyny without the fear of their heterosexuality being questioned. The new macho man was gay. The radical 'moment' of bisexuality was lost.

The privileges of androgyny, however, were not available for women until well into the 1970s, and only *after* gender-bending had run its spectacular, public course through a succession of musical youth heroes: David Bowie (the first and the best, although Jagger and Lou Reed of the Velvet Underground had been pioneers), Alice Cooper, the New York Dolls, Elton John, Iggy Pop, Marc Bolan, and other dandies of glam rock. It was not until punk ushered in a newer and more 'offensive' kind of oppositional drag that women fully participated in the confrontational strategies of iconoclastic posing and transgressing: Patti Smith, trash-princess; Siouxsie Sue, Wendy O. Williams, and the ebullient Poly Styrene.

To look for today's most socially threatening expressions of camp and drag, we must go to the outrageously spectacular heroes of the youth heavy metal (Cock Rock) scene, a subculture that is also supposed to harbor and perpetuate the most retarded features of traditional working-class masculinity. In heavy-rock culture today, the most 'masculine' images are spliced with miles of manicured long hair, risqué costumes, elaborate make-up, and a whole range of fetishistic body accessories, while it is the cleancut, close-cropped, 1950s-style Euro crooners who are seen as lacking masculine legitimacy. It is ironic, then, to consider that when, in 1984, the affable and nonthreatening Boy George received a Grammy Award on network television, he told his audience: 'Thank you, America, you've got style and taste, and you know a good drag queen when you see one'. Behind this ambiguous compliment, there was a long history of smug European attitudes toward American puritanism. But what does Boy George's comment mean in the age of Motley Crue, Twisted Sister, Kiss, Ratt, and Bon Jovi, whose use of drag is synonymous with a certain kind of American masculinity? There are more than just class differences at stake here, although it is important to recognize that heavy metal is as much a critique of middle-class masculinity as it is an affirmation of working-class sexism. It is also a question of international relations. The violence associated with heavy-metal 'drag' speaks, in its own way, to the legitimate power of American masculinity in the world today. By contrast, the jolly decorum of Boy George transmits the cheerful European features of a masculinity in the twilight of its power. One is emboldened and threatening, the other is genial and peaceloving.

POSTSCRIPT: WARHOL'S BOTTOM LINE

I have suggested that camp can be seen as a *cultural economy* at work from the time of the early 1960s. It challenged, and, in some cases, helped to overturn legitimate definitions of taste and sexuality. But we must also remember to what extent this cultural economy was tied to the capitalist logic of development that governed the mass culture industries. Nowhere is this more obsessively demonstrated than in the following remarks of Warhol, tongue-in-cheek certainly, but religiously devoted nonetheless to the 'idea' of his philosophy of work:

> I always like to work on leftovers, doing the leftover things. Things that were discarded and that everybody knew were no good, I always thought had a great potential to be funny. It was like recycling work. I always thought there was a lot of humor in leftovers ... I'm not saying that popular taste is bad so that what's left over is probably bad, but if you can take it and make it good or at least interesting, then you're not wasting as much as you would otherwise. You're recycling work and you're recycling people, and you're running your business as a byproduct of other businesses. Of *other directly competitive* businesses, as a matter of fact. So that's a very economical operating procedure. It's also the funniest operating procedure because, as I said, leftovers are inherently funny. (Warhol, 93)

Warhol here reveals what he knows about camp's re-creation of surplus value; the low risks involved, the overheads accounted for, and the profit margins expected. This at least was one artist's way of talking about the massive reorganization of cultural taste that took place in the course of the 1960s. It was a way of talking that offended some intellectuals because it suggested, even if Warhol never seemed to mean what he said, that its attention to 'economy' was more than just a metaphor for the critique of capitalism that, in their eyes, all art must surely deliver. On the contrary, it suggested that art had something more directly to do with conditions of production and consumption than it had to do with the aesthete's idea of a windless realm of 'taste'.

As for what Warhol calls the 'inherent funniness' of leftovers, that is the other side of camp – the creamy wit, the wicked fantasies, and the *gaieté de coeur*. All that was, and still is, priceless.

NOTES

1. No one has pursued more assiduously the task of exposing the seedy and tragic side of Hollywood's own celebration of this cult than Kenneth Anger, in his *Hollywood Babylon* and *Hollywood Babylon II*.
2. For accounts of the postwar British experience and reception of American popular culture, see Hebdige ('Cartography' and 'In Poor Taste'); Melly 1970; Nuttall; and Chambers 1986.
3. The use of the term 'subculture' in the context of delinquent youth groups dates from Albert Cohen. The most developed version of this tradition is in the work produced at the Birmingham Center for Contemporary Cutural Studies. The classic exposition can be found in Hall & Jefferson.
4. Todd Gitlin examines at length the contradictions of a student movement that was pledged to democratically redefine 'leadership' but that was forced to produce celebrities in order to gain access to the press.
5. For an analysis of the biker subculture, see the British study by Paul Willis. Also see Hunter S. Thompson's exercise in participatory journalism.
6. The best history of this period is D'Emilio. Also, see Katz.

7. Altman 1982, and Altman; Bronski 1984; Weeks 1985.
8. Bronski 1984: 95. While a case for the lesbian relation to camp has been made, it is the gay male 'possession' of that culture which has been stressed most often. See, however, Sheldon, 5–26; Riddiough 1980: 21–2. It has often been pointed out, however, that the subaltern position of lesbians in traditional gay culture enabled them to construct a more successful autonomous 'liberation' culture than did gay males.
9. Bronski 1984: 96. Also see the study of Judy Garland in Dyer 1986.
10. Garland, Davis, and the other queens of Hollywood are one thing. Maria Montez, Tallulah Bankhead, Carmen Miranda, and Eartha Kitt are another. If they are also figures celebrated by gay camp, then it is not for their thespian talents or for their stylized parodies of femininity. On the contrary, the widespread cultivation of these exploited actresses (*Myron*'s cult of Montez, in Gore Vidal's novel, is representative) is inevitably tinged with ridicule, derision, even misogyny. Their moments in the camp limelight cannot fail to conceal a 'failed seriousness' that is more often pathetic and risible than it is witty or parodic. So too, it is difficult to finally justify those Warhol films like *Lupe*, which depicts Lupe Velez's death by drowning in the toilet bowl after taking a Seconal overdose, or *Ecstasy and Me*, about the shoplifting tribulations of Hedy Lamarr. Michael Bronski asks the relevant questions of this cult practice: 'It would be absurd to want to pretend that any of these women had a great talent, but what does it mean for a large group of gay men to like a female performer expressly because of the fact that she is terrible?' Bronski 1977, rpt. 1978: 210.
11. In the psychoanalytic tradition, the classic essay (1929) on the 'masquerade' of femininity is Joan Rivière's 'Womanliness as Masquerade', incisively commented by Heath, who sets out the choices for feminist film theory in the light of Riviere's arguments. See also Doane.
12. On the history of drag, see Kris Kirk & Ed Heath's (1984) fascinating oral history; Ackroyd; and Newton 1972.
13. Ehrenreich concludes, in fact, that the antifeminist backlash of the late 1970s was an attack, not on feminism itself, but on the 'male revolt' that had threatened to dispense with the breadwinner ethic altogether, and deprive married women of the privilege of living off their husband's incomes.

REFERENCES

Ackroyd, Peter, *Dressing Up: Transvestism and Drag*, New York Simon & Schuster, 1979.

Alloway, Lawrence, 'The Long Front of Culture', in Suzi Gablik & John Russell (eds.), *Pop Art Redefined*, New York: Praeger, 1969.

Altman, Dennis, 'What Changed in the Seventies?' in Gay Left Collective 1980: 52–63

Anger, Kenneth, *Hollywood Babylon*, New York: Bell, 1975; and *Hollywood Babylon II*, London: Arrow, 1986.

Banham, Reyner, 'Who is This "Pop"?', in Penny Sparke (ed.), *Design by Choice*, New York Rizzoli, 1981, 94–6.

Cohen, Albert, *Delinquent Boys*, Glencoe, Ill.: Free Press, 1955.

D'Emilio, John, *Sexual Politics, Sexual Communities: The Making of a Homosexual Minority in the United States 1940–1970*, Chicago: U of Chicago P, 1983.

Doane, Mary Ann, 'Film and the Masquerade: Theorizing the Female Spectator', *Screen* 23:3–4, 1982.

Ehrenreich, Barbara, *The Hearts of Men: American Dreams and the Flight from Commitment*, Garden City: Doubleday, 1983.

Gitlin, Todd, *The Whole World is Watching: Mass Media in the Making and Unmaking of the New Left*, Berkeley: U of California P, 1980.

Hall, Stuart & Tony Jefferson (eds.), *Resistance through Rituals: Youth Subcultures in*

Postwar Britain, London: Hutchinson, 1975.

Haskell, Molly, *From Reverence to Rape*, New York: Holt, Rinehart & Winston, 1973.

Heath, Stephen, 'Joan Riviere and the Masquerade', in Victor Burgin, James Donald & Cora Kaplan (eds.), *Formations of Fantasy*, London: Methuen, 1986.

Hebdige, Dick, 'Towards a Cartography of Taste: 1936–1962', in Bernard Waites, Tony Bennett & Graham Martin (eds.), *Popular Culture: Past and Present*, London: Croom Helm and Open University, 1982, 194–218.

——, 'In Poor Taste: Notes on Pop', *Block* 8, 1983, 54–68.

Katz, Jonathan (ed.), *Gay American History: Leshians and Gay Men in the U.S.A.*, New York: Thomas Crowell, 1976.

Marotta, Toby, *The Politics of Homosexuality*, Boston: Houghton Mifflin, 1981.

Nuttall, Jeff, *Bomb Culture*, London: Paladin, 1970.

Rivière, Joan, 'Womanliness as Masquerade' (1929), rpt. in Victor Burgin, James Donald & Cora Kaplan (eds.), *Formations of Fantasy*, London: Methuen, 1986.

Sheldon, Caroline, 'Lesbians and Film: Some Thoughts', in Richard Dyer (ed.), *Gays and Film*, London: BFI, 1977, 5–26.

Sontag, Susan, 'One Culture and the New Sensibility', in Sontag 1966: 293–304.

Thompson, Hunter S., *Hell's Angels: A Strange and Terrible Saga*, New York Random House, 1966.

Warhol, Andy, *The Philosophy of Andy Warhol (From A to B and Back Again)*, New York: Harcourt Brace Jovanovich, 1975.

Willis, Paul, *Profane Culture*, London: Routledge & Kegan Paul, 1978.

Wolfe, Tom, *The Kandy-Kolored Tangerine-Flake Streamline Baby*, New York: Farrar, Straus & Giroux, 1965.

——, *The Pump-House Gang*, New York: Farrar, Straus & Giroux, 1968.

Wolfe, Tom & E. W. Johnson (eds.), *The New Journalism*, New York: Harper & Row, 1973.

20

THE CAPED CRUSADER OF CAMP: POP, CAMP, AND THE *BATMAN* TELEVISION SERIES

Sasha Torres

In this essay, I explore the mutually appropriative relations between 'high' and 'mass' culture in the 1960s, through a reading of the deployment of the terms 'Pop' and 'camp' in the popular press reception of the *Batman* television series. I take queerness to be the most important point of intersection in the cultural nexus I describe here; it energizes not only the series but also the extensive public debates about the meanings of the series and of Pop and camp.

To understand the density of these debates, it is crucial to recall the moment, in 1954, when Batman and Robin were 'outed' by New York psychiatrist Fredric Wertham. Wertham claimed, in a book called *Seduction of the Innocent*, that the Batman comics depicted a gay relationship or, in his words, represented 'a wish-dream of homosexuals living together'.[1] In 'I Want to Be a Sex Maniac', a chapter analyzing the effects of comics on the psychosexual development of children, Wertham asserts that 'only someone ignorant of the fundamentals of psychiatry and of the psychopathology of sex can fail to realize a subtle atmosphere of homoeroticism which pervades the adventures of the mature "Batman" and his young friend "Robin"' (190).

As I argue at greater length elsewhere, Wertham's account has had consistently organizing effects on Batman representation ever since the mid-1950s, because he managed, in his bumbling, homophobic way, to voice Batman narrative's open secret: that the elements of Batman representation that invite speculation about Batman's sexuality are so deeply structuring of that representation that they can't be excised (see Torres). The presence of Robin is the

Originally published in Jennifer Doyle, Jonathan Flatley and José Esteban Muñoz (eds.), *Pop Out: Queer Warhol*, Durham-London: Duke University Press, 1996.

most obvious but also the most expendable of these elements. More crucial in continually reintroducing these questions of homo-hetero definition with respect to Batman are two foundational elements of all narratives about him: the originary and traumatic replacement of Bruce Wayne's heterosexual nuclear family with a series of all-male parenting relations, and the homologous relation between having a secret identity as a crime fighter and having a secret identity as a closeted homosexual.

Batman emerges in response to a familial tragedy that significantly disrupts both gender and sexual identity for Bruce Wayne; indeed, the Batman origin story, which has been reproduced obsessively throughout Batman's history, is most centrally about the status of gender and sexuality within these narratives.[2] Batman is born, we are told, the night young Bruce Wayne's parents are mugged. The thief wants Martha Wayne's necklace; her husband tries to intervene and is shot and killed. Martha Wayne calls for the police and is also shot. Bruce vows to bring their killer to justice and to fight 'all criminals'. Obviously, this is a story about the relative efficacy of the men within it: the mugger, Dr. Wayne, Bruce. Martha Wayne serves merely as the excuse for urban class warfare and male violence – both the violence of the mugger and the violent stupidity of her rich husband, who could presumably have afforded another necklace and kept them both alive. That this story is only about masculine agency is confirmed by the self-evidentness with which it presents Bruce Wayne's choice to become a vigilante crime fighter as a solution to the loss of his parents. For Bruce to have adopted a more private solution would have meant that he had missed the point of the story.

Because the insistent repetition of the origin story in Batman representation continually reinscribes the connection between Bruce Wayne's personal loss and his public career, it's important to specify what exactly gets lost in this scene. Crucially, this moment marks a shift, for Bruce, out of a heterosexual nuclear family in which traditional gender arrangements still obtain, to a male parenting configuration in which he is raised by Alfred, his butler. Bruce/Batman's crime fighting is motivated, therefore, not only by the child's anger at and fear of separation from his parents but also by nostalgia for the conventional versions of gender and sexuality that the nuclear family is supposed to install – and for the conventional version of heterosexual masculinity to which Bruce might have otherwise had relatively unproblematic access. Instead, given that this moment inaugurates Bruce/Batman's participation in a series of all-male families – not only Alfred with Bruce but also Bruce with his ward, Dick Grayson, and Batman with Robin – Bruce's masculinity and heterosexuality are inescapably compromised: in a culture that sees the nuclear family as the proper route to normative gender and sexual identity, Batman representation's insistence on these alternative familial configurations raises real questions about the possibility of straight masculinity for its characters.

Further, in its persistent play with secret identities, Batman narrative instantiates the structure Eve Kosofsky Sedgwick identifies, in the titular essay of

Epistemology of the Closet, as 'the distinctively indicative relation of homo-sexuality to wider mappings of secrecy and disclosure' (1990: 71). Indeed, since Bruce and Batman both encode a cultural stereotype of the male homosexual – Bruce is a fairy, and Batman is a secretive, hypermasculine character who spends a lot of time prowling city streets at night – the Bruce/Batman dyad is *itself* a figure for a gay couple, in which the ontological impossibility of their ever being in the same place at the same time recapitulates in extreme form the logic of the closet.[3] Even Mark Cotta Vaz, who wrote the DC-endorsed history of Batman for the fiftieth anniversary of the character, is forced to admit, in the chapter 'The Loves of Batman', that Batman has often 'inhibited the flowering of love' in Bruce Wayne's 'romantic entanglements' (125). Batman performs such inhibition because he is the man to whom Bruce Wayne has a secret connection and because this connection fully structures Bruce's public and private lives.[4]

When Wertham opened the door to Batman's closet, the Batman industry panicked, going so far, in the early 1960s, as to kill off Alfred the butler (to quash speculation about three adult men living together in Bruce Wayne's mansion) and to add Batwoman and Batgirl as appropriate heterosexual love interests for Batman and Robin. Given its post-Wertham timing, then, the *Batman* series, with its self-conscious appropriations of Pop and camp, has been read, by Batman fans and producers, as a major setback in the project of Batman's redemptive heterosexualization.[5]

In the rest of this essay I take up the oscillation of rumor and recuperation that the problem of Batman's sexual identity continually produces and ask what it has to do with the industrial practice that produces the television series and with the show's reception in the popular press. In particular, I will consider the ways in which 'camp' and 'Pop', as categories of taste and as codes for – rumors of – queerness, are deployed both by the series and by the larger cultural discourse that the series generated. And since the definitional elusiveness of camp and Pop produces contortions and elisions in the popular discourses not unlike those evident in the academic debates about these categories, I will revisit some of the latter as well.

On January 13, 1966, the *New York Times* ran an article covering some of the local hoopla surrounding the premiere of the *Batman* television show. The article, written by Val Adams and entitled 'Discotheque Frug Party Heralds Batman's Film and TV Premiere', makes clear how hard ABC, *Batman*'s network, was working to position the series to cash in on the capital – cultural and otherwise – that Pop was so successfully attracting.[6] As Adams's lead puts it, 'An attempt to establish a Batman society whose primary function would be to work for a high Nielsen rating was begun here last night by the American Broadcasting Company'. The 'attempt' consisted of cocktails and dancing at Harlow's and a bus ride to the York Theater to see the world premiere of *Batman*, commercials and all. Jackie Kennedy was invited but didn't come.

Harold Prince, Tammy Grimes, and Burgess Meredith did, though. And, despite the fact that *Batman* owes more, visually, to Lichtenstein, 'Andy Warhol, the pop artist, was there'. When the company reached the York, they found 'Batman drawings and stickers that said "authentic pop art"', but as one observer remarked, 'The real pop art are the people who are attending this party'.

The *Times* leaves open the question of whether the Pop mavens at ABC might have understood 'authentic pop art' ironically. The article's own stance, however, is clear with regard to Batman's mass-cultural appropriation of Pop, a high-cultural style that appropriates mass culture. In noting that 'there was no applause when the world premiere of *Batman* ended', whereas 'guests in the theater cheered' at a cornflakes commercial, Adams situates Pop's apparent celebration of consumer culture and ABC's crass pursuit of ratings on the same bat-continuum.[7] Awash in the fluidity Pop encourages among distinctions like art/commodity, art/television, and authenticity/copy, Adams casts about for that category of taste pressed into service, by intellectuals or TV critics with high-cultural aspirations to solidify such distinctions: camp. How else to read camp's cameo appearance here – '*Batman* has been around since the 1930s, but now ABC is out to make him the caped crusader of high camp' – than as the life preserver clutched by a drowning arbiter of mass culture discernment?

I allude to Andrew Ross's 'Uses of Camp', in which he argues that 'camp was ... a defense against the decease of the traditional panoply of tastemaking powers which Pop's egalitarian mandate had threatened' (1988, rpt. 1989: 152). Contending that 'for intellectuals, the espousal of Pop represented a direct affront to those who governed the boundaries of taste', because 'Pop arose out of problematizing the question of taste itself', Ross situates camp as an elitist solution to the problems posed by Pop (149). He further suggests that, by claiming to 'discover' the American landscape of the everyday that Pop celebrated and by salvaging the artifacts of the throwaway culture Pop refigures and always itself risks becoming, 'camp intellectuals' in the 1960s tried to manage 'Pop's commitment to the new and the everyday, to throwaway disposability, to images with an immediate impact but no transcendent sustaining power' (149).

In their discussion of the contemporary press garnered by *Batman*, Lynn Spigel and Henry Jenkins (1991) follow Ross's lead by situating camp as a reception strategy that allowed television critics and other arbiters of mass taste to manage Pop's disquieting self-alignment with precisely those elements of television which they had always disdained most. Arguing that influential critics such as Jack Gould of the *New York Times* valued the 'intimacy, immediacy and presence' of realist, live, Golden-Age drama, Spigel and Jenkins read Pop as rejecting these values in favor of 'cartoonish characters, cheap industrial tools, gimmicky special effects, a flattened-out and exaggerated sense of color, repetitious imagery, and factory-like production' (121–2).

For Spigel and Jenkins, Pop thus endorses precisely those elements of 'television's dominant practice' with which 1960s critics were most uncomfortable (122). Even worse, they suggest:

> *Batman* precipitated a questioning of critical hierarchies because it self-consciously placed itself within the Pop art scene. While shows like *Bewitched*, *Mr. Ed* and *My Favorite Martian* stretched the limits of TV's realist aesthetic, *Batman* laughed in the face of realism, making it difficult for critics to dismiss the program as one more example of TV's puerile content. *Batman* presented these critics with the particularly chilling possibility that this childish text was really the ultimate in art circle chic. (123)

In Spigel and Jenkins's account, then, camp allowed critics another way to approach *Batman*. Referring to Newton Minow's 1961 influential assessment of US television as a 'vast wasteland', they contend that 'the camp sensibility' afforded viewers 'who had previously displayed disdain for mass culture' a comfortable distance from the show's comic book materials, because it reworked the aesthetics of Popism in a way more in line with the firmly entrenched 'wasteland critique' (124).[8]

But if Ross, Spigel, and Jenkins read camp as a solution to the crisis of taste which Pop inaugurates, another *New York Times* article (Stone 1966) suggests that, given the history of Batman representation, 'camp' raises as many problems for the makers of the series as it might solve. The article, an interview with *Batman* cast and crew by Judy Stone, quotes series producer William Dozier as saying: 'In Hollywood they're calling me the "King of Camp". I hate the word "Camp". It sounds so faggy and funsies'. Stone uses the problem of 'camp', with its attendant (for Dozier, at least) associations with homosexuality, as the central organizing principle of this article, polling writers, producers, and actors for their reaction to reminders of the Caped Crusader's outing by Wertham. With the exception of Lorenzo Semple, a writer for the series, who charmingly remarks that 'on a very sophisticated level, [the show] is *highly* immoral, because crime seems to be fun' (emphasis in original), most of those involved with the production blanch. But Ward, for example, responds testily that 'Batman and Robin represent the wish-dream to do good, to be a morally good person. I don't think it's wrong to go out and catch crooks'. And Dozier replies 'severely' that 'I never saw anything like that in the comic book. There will be no doubt on TV that Batman and Robin like girls, even though they may be too busy fighting crime to have much time for them'.

Dozier combats potentially contaminating insinuations about Batman's sexual identity, insinuations for which camp serves as the most discursively present code, by redefining the problem of the series as a problem of taste. And, in a structure precisely the opposite of that suggested by Ross, Spigel, and Jenkins, the solution to this problem is 'Pop'. For Dozier, the show's appropriation of Pop is both a marketing mechanism and a way to circumvent

Batman's associations with low culture and children's entertainment. As a marketing mechanism, Pop allows *Batman* to bridge the gap between children and adult viewers or, in the words of the *Times*, 'to transform the comic into the number one TV choice of everyone from the milk to the martini set'. As Stone puts it, Dozier 'decided to apply the pop art technique of the exaggerated cliché, laying it on to the point where it becomes amusing to adults'. Simultaneously, Dozier is able to align Pop's cachet high cultural with his high-concept programming *coup* and thus explain away the apparent disparity between his past work, as a producer of 'quality television' like *Playhouse 90*, *Studio One*, and *You Are There*, and his current endeavor. As Stone informs us, Dozier 'was stupefied when ABC asked him to develop the program'. Stupefied, presumably, because of the distance between the high seriousness of Golden-Age drama and this bit of kiddie fluff, *Batman*. Thus, as a synecdoche for adult, even avant-garde taste, 'Pop' performs multiple functions here: it allows Dozier to define, and thus promote, his crossover programming strategy; it grants him distance from his ephemeral material; and it diverts, if only momentarily, the course of Judy Stone and her readers toward the dangerous territory of 'camp'.[9]

The first lesson to be learned from Stone's article is that Pop and camp bear multiple relations to each other in the public discourse of the period and that any account of camp's 'management' of Pop is insufficient to describe the richness and multiplicity of these relations. As Dozier's rhetorical two-step suggests, each was potentially unsettling, and under the right conditions, each had the capacity to assuage some of what was troubling about the other. But in several other 1966 discussions of *Batman*, the two terms appear to be so closely linked as to be almost synonymous with each other. Shana Alexander (remember her?), for example, included 'High Camp and Low Camp, pop art and op art' as part of a long list of reasons she wouldn't ordinarily watch *Batman* (Alexander 1966). Robert Terwilliger, an Episcopalian minister whose reading of Batman as a 'messianic' figure received enough attention to be written up in the *New York Times* twice, said in his well-covered sermon that camp, 'this elusive, undefinable "in" term, signifies a new "Pop" aestheticism' (Terwilliger 1966). In *Life*, Tom Prideux suggested that 'Pop art and the cult of camp have turned Superman and Batman into members of the intellectual community' (1966: 23). *Time* called camp 'a sort of tongue-in-cheek philosophy of pop culture' and hinted that 'there is ... every expectation that grown men will be showing up at Andy Warhol's next party dressed like the Batman' (Anon. 1996b). And in Jack Gould's review of the series (1966), camp and Pop collapse into each other completely: 'The point about *Batman*, of course, is that the show has been construed as a belated extension of the phenomenon of pop art to the television medium. And contrary to the mournful misgivings of some who felt this act was a ghastly affront to culture, it could be an unseen blessing of major proportions'. A 'blessing' because what Gould calls 'non-events in the arts' – which I take to be a reference to Pop and particularly to Warhol, who is mentioned in this article's lead – have succeeded because they have been 'shielded against over-exposure'. Surrounded by enormous publicity, Batman will perform a service because, as Gould puts it, 'the only way to eradicate a non-event is to let it wear everybody out'. But his next sentences make clear that for Gould, camp is of a piece with Pop, not an antidote to it: 'The secret answer to camp is exhaustion, not protest. *Batman* promises to be a real help'.

Warhol keeps showing up in this discourse, not only because commentators may have been familiar with his own forays into Batman representation – particularly in the 1964 film *Batman Dracula*, on which he collaborated with Jack Smith and which mined the homoerotic resources of these legends, featuring walk-ons in aluminum foil-covered jockstraps – but also because the popular press knew in 1966 what is elided by the determination of later commentators to situate Pop and camp in opposition: that Warhol's work, an important engine of Pop's development, was during this period as deeply informed by the styles and sensibilities of camp practice as it was by the acuity of his reading of commodity culture. His work thoroughly articulated this relation by this point. Think, for example, of the collation of glamour, power, and death to be found in the early *Marilyns* (1962) and in *Sixteen Jackies* (1964). Or think of his refiguration of the pin-up boy at about the same time (for example *Troy Donahue* in 1962). The imbrications of Pop and camp, of which Warhol's work during the early- to mid-1960s reminds us, brings me to the second lesson to be learned from Stone's article, a lesson having to do more specifically with camp.

Dozier's phobic defense against the *word* 'camp', let alone the attendant chain of associations that suggests itself so easily even to the readers of the *New York Times*, should remind us that the failure – or refusal – to really theorize the queer valences of camp's history, to understand the thorough-going and persistent connection, in the everyday 'uses' of the term, between camp and gay subcultural tastes, performances, and persons, is a very basic conceptual failure: it is the failure to account for the complexities of the interface between subcultural style and its more 'mainstream' appropriations. More specifically it is the failure – or refusal – to ask fairly obvious historical questions about the role of gay taste not only in the important political and artistic moments of the 1960s counterculture, like Pop, but also in the mass-cultural popularizations and cannibalizations of those moments, like *Batman*. And this failure – or refusal – is rendered all the more perplexing – or suspicious – by camp's unrelenting presence as the key modifier in accounts of the *Batman* series, since Batman representation, in the wake of Wertham's scandalous accusations, has been organized not only by the generic obsessions that are the superhero's stock in trade – the promise of technology, the limits of masculine agency, the role of the vigilante in the ideology of law and order – but also by the difficulties of managing the question of homo-hetero definition that Batman continually begs.

This failure is, of course, as old as Susan Sontag's 'Notes on "Camp"', with its bland assurance that even though homosexuals have been its vanguard, Camp taste is *much more than* homosexual taste. Obviously, its metaphor of life as theater is peculiarly suited as a justification and projection of a certain aspect of the situation of homosexuals. (The Camp insistence on not being 'serious', on playing, also connects with the homosexual's desire to remain youthful.) *Yet one feels that if homosexuals hadn't more or less invented Camp, someone else would.* (Sontag 1964b, rpt. 1966: 262; emphasis mine)

D. A. Miller has characterized this moment as 'that unblinking embrace of counterfactuality' that allows Sontag to imagine that she herself might have invented camp, and indeed, Miller is perfectly right to remind us, in his reading of this passage, of the opening of Sontag's essay, in which she 'justified her phobic de-homosexualization of Camp as the necessary condition for any intelligent discourse on the subject' (1989: 93). In Sontag's by-now-infamous formulation:

> I am strongly drawn to Camp, and almost as strongly offended by it. That is why I want to talk about it, and why I can. For no one who wholeheartedly shares in a given sensibility can analyze it; he can only, whatever his intention, exhibit it. To name a sensibility, to draw its contours and to recount its history, requires a deep sympathy modified by revulsion. (278)

Though I certainly share Miller's revulsion, I am less interested in Sontag's reinscription of herself as camp's inventor than I am in what that reinscription prevents her from theorizing. That is, I am less concerned with why she might make recourse to the counterfactual than in what the effects of that recourse might be. It seems to me that Sontag's de-gaying of camp itself *performs* what it most crucially fails to *explain*. Even as she enacts the straight appropriation of camp with her assertion that 'Camp taste is much more than homosexual taste', she renders invisible the most interesting and elusive thing about camp: its placement at the borderlines of gay and non-gay taste. In this regard, it becomes possible to read Sontag's refusal of the essay form – a form that might require her actually to argue her assertions – in favor of 'jottings', as another way in which this writing anticipates, formally, the seemingly haphazard processes of non-gay appropriations of camp, processes this essay inaugurates and makes possible, even as it tries to make them theoretically irrelevant.[10]

Though Ross makes more conceptual room than Sontag does for gay camp as part of the range of 'uses' to which camp was put in the 1960s, he, too, fails to chart the articulations of gay uses with those of others. As I have suggested, Ross is most interested, in this essay, in situating camp's effectivity for intellectuals challenged by Pop's assault on categories of taste. But in his discussion of gay camp, Ross admits that 'unlike the histories of Pop and camp which I have discussed, the gay camp fascination with Hollywood had much less to do with transformations of taste. In its pre-Stonewall heyday ... [i]t was part of a survivalist culture which found, in certain fantasmatic elements of film culture, a way of imaginatively communicating its common conquest of everyday oppression' (157). The question Ross entertains, in his final section on Warhol, but declines, finally, to answer is what difference these two 'uses of camp' might have made for each other.[11]

This problem of how to understand camp's placement at the intersections of gay and non-gay style during the period of *Batman*'s production is solved no more satisfyingly, alas, by Andy Medhurst's (1991a) explicitly gay-affirmative reading of Batman, 'Batman, Deviance, and Camp'. Medhurst, in 'offer[ing] a gay reading of the whole Bat-business', usefully traces the history of attempts by the producers of Batman narrative to close down the questions about Batman's sexuality that have been opened up by readers such as Wertham. But his attention to the definitional constraints imposed by the larger homophobic markets in which Batman narrative circulates stops short when he discusses the TV series. Medhurst claims that the televisual *Batman*, produced during what he calls 'the decade in which camp swished out of the ghetto and up into the scarcely prepared mainstream', was an example of what Sontag would call 'deliberate camp': according to Medhurst, it 'employed the codes of camp in an unusually public and heavily signalled way' (155). By camp, Medhurst clearly means gay camp. Alongside the show's parodic hyperseriousness, that is, Medhurst discerns more or less explicit, if 'joking', reference to Batman and Robin's 'relationship':

> The Batman/Robin relationship is never referred to directly; more fun can be had by presenting it 'straight', in other words, screamingly camp. Wertham's reading of the Dubious Duo had been so extensively aired as to pass into the general consciousness, it was part of the fabric of Batman, and the makers of the TV series proceeded accordingly. (156–7)

As evidence for this claim, Medhurst offers canny readings of several episodes, including one guest-starring Tallulah Bankhead as the Black Widow. As Medhurst (158) puts it:

> Best of all, and Bankhead isn't even in this scene but the thrill of having her involved clearly spurred the writer to new heights of camp, Batman has to sing a song to break free of the Black Widow's spell. Does he choose to sing 'God Bless America?' Nothing so rugged. He clutches a flower to his Bat chest and sings Gilbert and Sullivan's 'I'm Just a Little Buttercup'.

Now, however convincing one finds Medhurst's account of this particular episode, it still begs the larger question of what the producers of the series might have been up to when they broadcast this show – and others – to what Medhurst himself calls 'the scarcely prepared mainstream'. It is telling that Medhurst goes right from a direct assertion of the producers' camp intentions to the texts of the program itself, rather than, say, to any of the many statements those producers made to the press during the series' run. Many of those statements gleefully use the term 'camp', but none of them, except for the Judy

Stone interview I've quoted, situates camp's gay associations in relation to Batman's post-Wertham history.

But I do find Medhurst's readings convincing, and so the question – the same question I've been asking about camp's interstitial status, now posed in a more specific form – becomes, Why would the makers of the *Batman* series risk self-consciously deploying the codes and icons of gay camp in the context of their massively popular network TV show? The answer lies in all those other, 'straight' responses to the show, which talk about the show as camp but which have in mind definitions of the term very different from Medhurst's, definitions that have little to do with gay subcultures. In the public discourses generated by *Batman*, camp is defined variously as 'nostalgic' (Terwilliger 1966); as that which brings forth 'accumulations of debris from the recent past . . . to be admired, reproduced and treasured' (Cuneo 1966); as 'tongue in cheek' (Ace 1966); as 'involv[ing] a wry sophistication' (LeShan 1966); as 'a sneering fake enthusiasm for whatever is pretentious and not quite successful'; as 'contempt set in code' (Skow 1966); and, most often, as that which 'decrees that anything that is really bad must be awfully good' (Anon. 1966b).

Even if we entertain the characterization of camp as 'so bad it's good' as a densely encoded (and widely and unself-consciously circulated) reference to gay identifications and practices, the range of connotative associations Batman discourse generated about camp – from 'faggy and funsies' to 'nostalgic' to 'contempt set in code' – is still sufficiently wide as to suggest that it was precisely the term's ambiguity that made it attractive to the show's producers. 'Camp' was a way for them both to shut down and to open up Batman's gayness, a way for them both to dispense with Batman's history and to realize its potential in an unprecedented way. Camp was paradoxically useful in effacing popular memory of Wertham's reading of Batman because, in the wake of Sontag's account, it was going through the same de-gaying that Batman was, saddled – as he was in the early 1960s – with the tiresome Batwoman and Batgirl. Camp thus serves as a perfectly condensed marker for the simultaneous admission and denial of Batman's queerness. But, of course, the makers of the series were also unable to purge camp of its connotative associations with gay culture. And there is some evidence to suggest that they didn't want to: Adam West (who played Batman) quips in the Stone article that 'with the number of homosexuals in this country, if we get that audience, fine. Just add 'em to the Nielsen ratings'. It would be a mistake, I think, to discount this joke, because I suspect that *Batman* succeeded quite well in garnering a gay audience and because West's off-the-cowl remark is on to something crucial about Batman and about 1960s television: in voicing this 'hypothetical' appeal to a gay audience, West, I suggest, demonstrates an almost uncanny connection to the mass-cultural zeitgeist and actually manages to identify the *Batman* series with what was most pleasurable about both.

A lot of the pleasure Batman offers his consumers – gay and straight, male and female – comes precisely from his sexual undecidability. Arguably, Batman narrative's oblique articulation of questions about gender and sexuality has at least contributed to – if not constituted – the character's enduring appeal. As evidence in favor of this hypothesis, I submit Dick Giordano's recollections of his childhood encounters with the early Batman. Giordano, vice president of DC Comics (the division of Warner Communications that publishes Batman comics) and a former editor and illustrator of Batman stories, describes these encounters in the introduction to *The Greatest Batman Stories Ever Told*:

> There were many ... elements that added to the appeal of the character – his alter ego Bruce Wayne being rich and pretending to be an ineffectual playboy was part of the fun. I felt like an 'insider' when I saw Bruce acting silly at a party because I knew he was The Batman and before long he would put aside his foppish ways, don cape and cowl and bring the bad guys to justice, returning to the role of useless playboy before the story ended. (9)

Giordano suggests that the 'fun' of reading Batman comics lay in charting Bruce Wayne/Batman's dichotomous, contradictory relation to heterosexual masculinity; his description of Bruce – 'foppish', 'ineffectual', 'useless' – evokes both femininity and effeminacy, while Batman represents pure masculine effectivity, 'bringing the bad guys to justice'. The pleasure Giordano depicts in this passage seems to come not only from identifying these differing relations to hegemonic masculinity and sexuality but also, and perhaps more important, from seeing them coexist in the same person. Bruce/Batman, as Giordano describes him, enables a fantasy of being at once passive and active, silly and serious, leisured and hardworking, feminine and masculine, gay and straight – with the latter term always comfortingly available to recuperate the former.

And a lot of the pleasure 1960s television offers its consumers – gay and straight, male and female – comes from its covert critiques of life in the suburban nuclear family. This was, after all, the moment in which television gave us the anti-familial grousing of Samantha Stevens's mother, Endora, and the grim and pathetic attempts at suburban assimilation by poor old Herman Munster.[12] And it wasn't unprecedented for such critiques to be aligned with gay-coded characters. Batman actually aired opposite *Lost in Space*, which, as you surely recall, featured the unrelentingly savage commentary of 'Dr. Smith', forced to spend his foreseeable future marooned on another planet with a nice nuclear family that might, under other circumstances, have lived out their days quite happily next door to Ward and June Cleaver.[13] I like to imagine that it might have been difficult, in those days before the VCR, for some viewers, those who belonged to the community whose idiom *Lost in Space* and *Batman* borrowed, to choose between them.

The *Batman* series understood these simple truths about the enduring appeal of its source material and the emergent pleasures of its medium. The circulation of camp's gay meanings allowed its producers to mine the resources of both, and its straight flow allowed them to cash in – almost – without risk.

NOTES

I am grateful to Siobhan Burns for research assistance and to Michèle Barale, Judith Frank, Annelise Orleck, Eve Kosofsky Sedgwick, and the editors of this volume (Jennifer Doyle, Jonathan Flatley and José Esteban Muñoz) for their comments on earlier drafts of this essay.

1. Wertham, 190. Wertham's larger agenda was to link comics to juvenile delinquency; his book participated in growing national hysteria about comics' effects on their readers, hysteria which prompted Senate hearings and industry self-censorship (in the form of the 'Comics Code Authority') and which prefigured the Dodd committee's congressional hearings in the early 1960s on the relation between television and juvenile delinquency. Wertham's rantings, in other words, lassoed Batman representation for the first time, but not the last, into the arena in which the meanings and functions of childhood, and especially of children's sexuality, are contested. On the comics scare, see Gilbert, and Rasula. These concerns about Batman's effects on children were revived and widely circulated in strikingly similar form in relation to the television series. See, for example, LeShan 1966. She writes, 'if camp involves a wry sophistication, an adult grasp of subtleties in language and point of view, does it matter that children watching this program take it absolutely literally?' LeShan's claim that viewing Batman produced particularly violent play in children she observed, because the children were unable to distinguish between 'real' and 'camp' violence, serves as a cover, I think, for other fears about Batman's possible production of queer children. LeShan is more deeply worried, I think, that children might understand camp than she is that they might not.
2. The original story was first disseminated in November 1939 in *Detective* #33. More recent versions appear in Tim Burton's 1989 film, *Batman*, and in the following, all published by DC Comics: *The Dark Night Returns*, story and pencils by Frank Miller, inks by Klaus Janson and Frank Miller, colors by Lynn Varley (1986); *Batman: Year One*, written by Frank Miller, illustrated by David Mazzucchelli, colored by Richmond Lewis (1988): *Arkham Asylum*, written by Grant Morrison, illustrated by Dave McKean (1989); and *Gotham by Gaslight*, written by Brian Augustyn, pencils by Michael Mignola, inks by P. Craig Russell, coloring by David Hornung (1989).
3. I owe this formulation to Jeff Nunokawa.
4. Most of the other comic book superheroes also lead secret double lives; if we assume, with Sedgwick, that closetedness of any kind always contains within it at least an allusion to problems of homo/hetero definition, then Superman, the Green Hornet, and others might also be read along the lines I read Batman here. But I think that Batman narrative is particularly available to such reading (that is, perhaps more so that the others), both because of the persistence of the Robin function and because of the determining effects that Wertham's account of Batman had on subsequent visions of the character.
5. See Vaz, for one version of how this narrative tends to go. In 'Television, Homosexuality, and the History of Batman', I read at length the two major interpretations of Batman produced in the 1980s – Frank Miller's 1986 graphic novel, *The Dark Knight Returns*, and Tim Burton's 1989 film, *Batman* – arguing that the hostility to television manifest in both these texts simultaneously inscribes and displaces a more specific animosity, that toward the *Batman* series and its queering of the Caped Crusader. The violent remasculinization of Batman that takes place in both these representations is thus also a violently homophobic attempt to de-gay the character.
6. Adams 1966. Andrew J. Edelstein notes that the Batman industry's efforts to appropriate Pop might be discerned in the comics as well as in the television series: 'In the mid-'60s Batman comic book, one panel said "At the Gotham City Museum, Bruce Wayne, millionaire sportsman and playboy, and young ward Dick Grayson attend a sensational 'Pop Art' show"' (188).

7. Adams here anticipates Christin Mamiya's argument that 'the [Pop Art] movement not only appropriated the images and strategies from consumer culture but also was itself absorbed into the established institutional matrix, thereby rendering it ineffective as a critique and neutralizing any potential for bringing about significant change' (4).

8. Newton Minow, FCC chairman under Kennedy, gave the 'vast wasteland' speech to the National Association of Broadcasters in 1961. As Spigel and Jenkins remind us, 'Minow's reform plans centered around the aesthetic hierarchies of the Golden Age critics, calling for more reality-based, educational programs, and fewer game shows, sitcoms, and westerns' (1991: 122). See also Boddy.

9. If Pop served for Dozier at this point in *Batman*'s publicity cycle as the counter to the series' childishness, it is important to recognize that precisely this role was later filled by camp. This is, camp came to serve as the crucial mechanism by which the show's dual address to children and adults was both assured and managed: formulations like 'To the kids it's real, to the adults it's camp' were repeated so often in the popular press that they became a kind of public interpretive mantra. To chart the development of this explanatory tic, see, for example: Anon. 1966b; Alexander 1966; Cuneo 1966, p. 63s; LeShan 1966; Thompson 1966; Hyers 1967 and Anon. 1968.

10. Sontag writes: 'To snare a sensibility in words, especially one that is alive and powerful, one must be tentative and nimble. The form of jottings, rather than an essay (with its claim to a linear, consecutive argument) seemed more appropriate for getting down something of this particular *fugitive* sensibility' (278; emphasis mine).

11. This question is begged as well by Core's suggestion that 'camp was a prison for an illegal minority; now it is a holiday for consenting adults' (Core 1984: 7). What happened, exactly, to make that insouciant semicolon possible?

12. See Spigel, who argues that 'fantastic family sit-coms', like *Bewitched*, *I Dream of Jeannie*, and *The Munsters,* voiced, with other popular media of the period, widespread disillusionment with the suburban ideal that had been promoted by earlier sitcoms such as *Leave It to Beaver* and *The Donna Reed Show. Batman*, which aired from 1966 to 1968, appeared just as the suburban family sitcoms disappeared. The fantastic family subgenre, which had begun to gain ground in the early part of the decade, was well on its way to being the hegemonic sitcom form by 1966.

13. I am indebted here to Nunokawa's discussion of Dr. Smith in 'The Sun Always Shines on TV'.

REFERENCES

Boddy, William, *Fifties Television: The Industry and Its Critics*, Champaign: U of Illinois P, 1990.

Edelstein, Andrew J., *The Pop Sixties*, New York: World Almanac, 1985.

Gilbert, James, *A Cycle of Outrage: America's Reaction to the Juvenile Delinquent in the 1950s*, New York: Oxford UP, 1986.

Giordano, Dick, *The Greatest Batman Stories Ever Told*, New York: DC Comics, 1988.

Mamiya, Christin J., *Pop Art and Consumer Culture: American Super Market*, Austin: U of Texas P, 1992.

Nunokawa, Jeff, 'The Sun Always Shines on TV: Television Culture and the Resistance to Patriarchy in Margaret Atwood's The *Handmaid's Tale*', paper presented at the MLA Conference, Washington, DC, 1989.

Rasula, Jed, 'Nietzsche in the Nursery: Naive Classics and Surrogate Parents in Postwar American Cultural Debates', *Representations* 29, Winter 1990, 50–77.

Spigel, Lynn, 'From Domestic Space to Outer Space: The 1960s Fantastic Family Sitcom', in Constance Penley et al. (eds.), *Close Encounters: Film, Feminism, and*

Science Fiction, Minneapolis: U of Minnesota P, 1991, 205–35.

Torres, Sasha, 'Television, Homosexuality, and the History of Batman', unpublished essay.

Vaz, Mark Cotta, *Tales of the Dark Knight*, New York: Ballantine, 1989.

Wertham, Fredric, *Seduction of the Innocent*, New York: Rinehart, 1954.

21

WARHOL'S CAMP

Matthew Tinkcom

Upon its opening in the spring of 1994, the Andy Warhol Museum was heralded by a Pittsburgh gay newspaper as the 'largest museum in the world devoted to a gay artist'.[1] This statement was at odds with the Museum's own publicity, which described Warhol as 'the most influential artist of the second half of the twentieth century' whose importance lay in the fact that 'the power of his work comes from its concentration on fundamental human themes – the beauty and glamour of youth and fame, the passing of time, and the presence of death'.[2] This contest between local gay activism and international art discourses reveals a significant fissure between what each wanted to claim in the name (or in the disappearance) of sexuality and artistic production, but it was not clear what was to be gained by either affirming or denying Warhol's status as a gay man. Once Warhol had been claimed as a gay artist, the question arose of how that was to be witnessed in his production. The question, from the point of fine-art production, became how to situate Warhol within a longer tradition of art in the twentieth century, namely the avant-garde.

This moment introduces the problem of what might seem a nagging insistence upon avant-garde artistic production by gays as in some way being inflected by their sexuality, and I will address the work of Andy Warhol in terms of the gay camp aesthetic in order to wonder how the idea of the avant-garde has neglected, at least in many of its critical descriptions, the vital

Originally published in Colin MacCabe, Mark Francis and Peter Wollen (eds.) *Who is Andy Warhol?* London: BFI; Pittsburgh: The Andy Warhol's Museum, 1997.

importance of dissident sexualities in the historical project of ascertaining the 'avant-garde'. Avant-garde production can be understood as a radical response to the reorganisation of life under capitalist political economies, and has frequently been allied with leftist politics in order to interrogate and demystify the reshaping of everyday life under capital. A significant feature of the avant-garde has been its attention to the redefinition of sexualities within the industrial metropolis. Yet, as we well know, it has frequently been marked by a preoccupation with the powerful heterosexual tropes of desire; we need look only at Léger's *Ballet mécanique*, Salvador Dali's depictions of the female form, or more recently, the exercises of Jeff Koons to remember this. The effect has often been to equate the politics of the avant-garde legacy with *only* a radical heterosexuality, leaving open the question of whether gay, lesbian and other dissident sexualities might play a significant role in the avant-garde opposition to bourgeois culture.

In light of this, the task of underscoring Warhol's homosexuality as a vital force for the critical dimensions of his work is difficult to take up, particularly when we recall that the artist never depicted his work as interested in interrogating the dynamics of contemporary life from a leftist or Marxist interest. By this, I mean that critical and historical accounts of the avant-garde are bereft of any way of seeing how gay sexualities and sensibilities might inform the works of artists like Warhol. Ironically, despite the occlusion of gay themes and styles from idealisations of avant-garde practices, Warhol's artistic output was informed by his appreciation of gay responses to industrialisation, and this appearance of a gay sensibility within the avant-garde itself turns upon an important relation between gay subcultures and commodity culture, namely that of camp ironic practices. That is, what is most avant-garde about Warhol's work may also be what's most camp about it.

Recently, there have been many attempts to analyse and to theorise camp, but allow me here to offer my own definition. Camp is the alibi for gay-inflected labour to be caught in the chain of value-coding within capitalist political economies. By terming camp an 'alibi', I want to retain the notion that somehow a crime is being perpetrated, a crime upon value which involves gays passing off their labour as *not* differentiable so that they might enjoy the rewards of their work without being offered for nomination as participating in dissident sexual practices. At the same time, the trace of gay labour, which resides upon the commodity-form in its camp valences, also figures in this alibi because this trace allows for some consumers to wonder at the commodity's production ('did a gay have some hand in its making?') and, simultaneously, for others not to have to engage in any such speculation. By definition, an alibi (indeed, its Latin root) maintains the claim to having been elsewhere while the crime was being perpetrated; this does not mean that one did not participate in it, but that, as a suspect, one has the claim to being somewhere else, doing something besides being a criminal. This sense of camp's alibi preserves the tension of gay work as being produced under conditions where it is frequently a hazard to risk being named as gay, either by self-proclamation or through the act of being 'outed' by others.

Where camp's motives differ from those of the avant-garde might best be outlined in terms of the conditions under which each stance has arisen. Peter Bürger reminds us that the avant-garde is most powerfully understood as a set of institutions, ones that promulgate the notion that art is autonomous from the workings of capital in contemporary life. By autonomous, Bürger means that the avant-garde can claim to investigate our ways of looking and hearing only by accepting that, in some measure, avant-garde production is irrelevant to more dominant economies of representation; taking his cue from Theodor Adorno, Bürger sets the avant-garde against popular culture. Yet, Bürger suggests that the apparent autonomy of the avant-garde is an illusion, one based upon the idea that, sanctioned from the noise of popular culture, the avant-garde artist can more fully perceive the operations of mystification which inhere to bourgeois cultural production. Reciting Adorno's claim that 'it is impossible to conceive of the autonomy of art without covering up work' (Adorno, 9), Bürger then suggests that 'like the public realm, the autonomy of art is a category of bourgeois society that both reveals and obscures an actual historical development' (36). It is my claim that an actual historical development which idealisations of the avant-garde obscure, at least in the case of Warhol, is a gay camp sensibility as it had a measurable influence upon him. The 'covering up' of work, which Adorno describes and which bolsters avant-garde claims to autonomy, becomes more apparent for us in a discussion of Warhol when we consider Warhol's artistic training, not within the realm of fine-art production, but within the gay demimonde of New York fashion retailing and advertising during the 1950s. For, in terms of that setting we might perceive the artist's talents to navigate the treacherous waters of a homophobic America and the conditions of its popular cultural production.

By raising the question of gay camp in the context of Warhol's subsequent work, particularly in cinema, I am suggesting that revisionings of his work in the name of the avant-garde have often cleaved gay camp apart from his output. And, by the way, there's every indication that Warhol understood the risks of articulating camp and homosexuality, witness the conversations with Emile de Antonio recorded in *POPism: The Warhol '60s*, where Warhol describes the animosity felt towards him by such Hemingway-esque straight-dude artists of the 1950s as Pollock or de Kooning. (For a particularly fervent denunciation of gay tastes, see Vivian Gornick's pungent commentary in her *Village Voice* piece: Gornick 1966) But, ironically, it may be that the avant-garde disavowal of gay camp, which preserves the fictive autonomy about which Bürger warns us, occurs as much through the hostility of the avant-garde to popular culture as it does from any homophobia. Thus, if we should historicise Warhol in relation to the appearance of camp practices in post-war American commodity culture, it is not necessarily in order to preserve or apologise for the inadequacy of the idea of avant-garde production. That said, I would add that a specific feature of some avant-garde projects has been to pay attention to the proliferation of commodities and the social relations that they embody, a hallmark shared by camp. The question then becomes: what do avant-garde antagonisms and camp ironies share?

Let us remind ourselves of the avant-garde interest in the commodity form through Walter Benjamin. Benjamin sensed the power of capital's fresh energies to redefine consciousness when he described industrialism's 're-enchantment' of the social arena. For Benjamin, even to embark upon a critique of the social organisation of capital meant confronting the profusion of goods arrayed within the metropolis, where 'the commodities are suspended and shoved together in such boundless confusion, that [they appear] like images out of the most incoherent dreams'.[3] In order to confront the vibrant experiences to be had at the dawning of the age of consumerism, Benjamin's impulse was to consider the dream as a metaphor for the waking confusions which inhere to the experiences of commodity proliferation. These confusions (or, more helpfully, contradictions) account for the social formations and daily habits to which commodity-production gives form. As Susan Buck-Morss formulates this approach:

> Here was a fundamental contradiction of capitalist-industrial culture. A mode of production that privileged private life and based its conception of the subject on the isolated individual had created brand new forms of social existence – urban spaces, architectural forms, mass-produced commodities, and infinitely reproduced 'individual' experiences – that engendered identities and conformities in people's lives, but not social solidarity, no new level of collective consciousness of the commonality and thus no way of waking up from the dream in which they were enveloped. (261)

We should note from Buck-Morss's reading of Benjamin that the subsumption of social consciousness within the realm of commodity-production is total and complete (as dreaming and waking become one in her analysis). While in general we might agree to the power of capital over those whose primary relation is that of wage-earner and consumer, it is not so immediately evident that the meanings to which the commodities give rise are always the same. Working from the notion that capital *engenders* its subjects, what of those subjects whose gendering works at cross-purposes to the total subsumption of their consciousness: what of the experiences and responses, for example, of some gays?

Benjamin sounds the call for us to pay attention to the proliferation of commodities, for in them we discover the reification of the historical development of capital. What Benjamin did not anticipate was that the circulation of commodities could take them into social settings that might redefine how and what those commodities mean. When we think of Benjamin gazing through the shop windows of the Paris arcades at the array of new goods, we might also remember that Warhol (and many of his contemporaries in New York, Rauschenberg and Johns among them) were originally window-dressers. The appearance of the Germanic critical eye on one side of the window may be met by its counterpart on the other, the camp gay artist organising the goods to be beheld in the spectacle of the window. Karl Marx, meet Oscar Wilde.

Most powerful among Benjamin's insights into the changing value of artistic production was his claim about the disappearance of aura from the artwork. For Benjamin, this occurred at the moment that the work no longer seemed singular and divinely remote and, of course, he was addressing the power of serial production to undermine a piece's sanctified status. Bürger powerfully reads Benjamin as having missed the strength of his own argument by insisting on periodisation; according to Bürger, the loss of aura is less helpfully debated in terms of a moment in which artistic aura might have faded (the appearance of non-sacral art, or the ascent of the bourgeoisie after the French Revolution), and more convincingly seen in terms of the processes of production and reception that were changed by industrial production. Bürger writes that

> the explanation of the change in the mode of reception by the change in reproduction techniques acquires a different place value. It can no longer lay claim to explaining a historical process, but at most to being a hypothesis for the possible *diffusion* of a mode of reception that the dadaists were the first to have intended. (29)

Bürger indicates that reproducibility and seriality do not necessarily beget habits of critique commensurate with these new features of cultural production. While, in Bürger's reading of Benjamin, industrial techniques spelled the death of aura, this did not necessarily entail radical new forms of viewing, especially of works reproduced serially (i.e. popular culture). Such new, and critical, viewing practices would only appear when the avant-garde made demands of its audiences by upsetting and bewildering them. Yet, in camp we witness viewing practices (Bürger's 'diffusion of modes of reception') which do insist on reading both avant-garde art and popular culture for their limits and contradictions; the problem is that the gay marginality that gave rise to camp has never been understood as being in any way radical in the sense that a leftist avant-garde might wish it. And it would seem that camp has had an upsetting and bewildering effect upon its critics; for this we might look at Stanley Kaufmann's repeated broadside attacks upon Tennessee Williams's plays during the 1950s and 1960s, where Williams's heroines become for Kaufmann an attack upon proper American femininity.

These problems within the avant-garde are important for situating Warhol's cinematic output, because Warhol's films did not necessarily depict the relation between artist and world, or critic and world, that the avant-garde tradition bequeathed to him. Responding to the overwhelming presence of Hollywood film in modern America, Warhol sought to use the materials of Hollywood in order to critique it. In particular, it was his great insight that film was like

Duchamp's bottle-drier and snow-shovel; it circulated within the same domains of producer and consumer as virtually everything else made in industrial settings, and yet it did not restrict how its viewers could respond to it. (Nor for that matter did most commodities, as Duchamp's found objects sought to demonstrate.) As such, film could be both a powerful tool for demystifying everyday life and it could be a source of pleasure in the process. And, while this insight itself rested upon a contradiction: namely, that film in the twentieth century has within the American setting been overwhelmed by Hollywood, to the exclusion of other kinds of film-making, Warhol's film-work breaks with a tradition, beginning with Horkheimer and Adorno, and continuing within the United States in the work of Clement Greenberg and Dwight MacDonald, in which popular culture was vilified as so much kitsch or 'ersatz high culture'.

Despite the saturating presence of Hollywood, which Warhol dreamed of in his Pittsburgh youth and, indeed, dreamed of all his life, his films demonstrated the dual bind of camp in that they were so alien to the very Hollywood product which they seemed to emulate. Warhol's cinema took its shape as a response to, but not a rejection of, the presence of Hollywood. Yet, how does camp function as a critique of the industries? Moe Meyer has recently claimed that camp 'is a suppressed and denied oppositional critique embodied in the signifying practices that processually constitute queer identities' (1994b: 1). Although I agree with Meyer's impulse to see camp as embodying an oppositional stance, I would suggest that camp is more productively seen in relation to what it says about bourgeois representation (and its tendencies to exclude gays) than in whatever help it lends in the formation of identities. In fact, if camp were only instrumental in the formation of yet another identity (or as part of the trajectory whereby 'queer' replaces 'gay and lesbian' replaces 'homosexual') there would seem to be little to say about where those identities are embedded in current social arrangements. It is more important to ascertain how camp critiques capitalist social organisation in its analysis of the work involved in producing representations that exclude same-sex desiring subjects, and how camp's energies are devoted to a constant reinsertion of gay tastes into the consumption and recirculation of 'straight' imagery. In order to ground this claim, I would focus upon one feature of Hollywood which Warhol's camp visions worked upon: namely glamour.

If not invented by the Hollywood studios, certainly the phenomenon of glamour in the twentieth century must be one of Hollywood's most significant achievements. Loosely defined, we might say that glamour is the sense that an image achieves what could never be secured in our own everyday efforts; we are held in the thrall of the glamorous image because it depicts people and lives that are not our own. Not only is this because we are prohibited from imitating the glamorous image by virtue of our various physical shortcomings, but because we have little sense of the complicated efforts demanded in the enhancement of stars through make-up, costuming, lighting and film-stocks. Glamour, then, is profoundly a mystification. When we behold the image of a star, say in the voluptuous surfaces of a photograph by Hurrell or the renderings of Dietrich as captured by Von Sternberg, the glamorous image entreats us to defer to its power without recourse to understanding under what circumstances the image was made. We are subsequently prevented from an analysis of glamour because glamour is antithetical to labour; the failure of such an analysis to appear can be remarked upon in the primary metaphor of fans' responses to movie-stars. The fan is rendered helpless in the sight of the star's image.

Warhol's films of the underground period sought to emulate the feel of Hollywood, not by emulating conventional narrative patterns, but by creating their own versions of glamour. In large measure, camp interest in Hollywood cinema is driven by spectacle and glamour, over and above narrative and identification. By spectacle, I mean that the cinematic image, be it the flickering light on the film screen or the 8×10 glossy of the movie star, is frequently arrested from its bond with the narrative and fixed in other sets of meanings. In this sense, the camp registers of Warhol's films accentuate the production of Hollywood and its related industries *as production by its spectators*, at least to the extent that they show how the media of popular culture can be manipulated to produce meanings probably unintended by the industries themselves.

The impulse by camp viewers to emphasise Hollywood's production of spectacle, *vis-à-vis* glamour, stems from the all-too-frequent perception of how gay life has been mostly excluded from Hollywood films, except for the occasional depiction of pathological homosexuality or a 'sympathetic' account of the miseries of gay life. (And, for an example of both those things, I would direct you to the blockbuster hit *Philadelphia*, whose own depiction of an opera queen embeds the gay man's attention to diva-glamour as a symptom of his own bathos-laden destruction.) Rather than ignore Hollywood because of its censorship of dissident sexualities, the camp underpinnings of Warhol's films take up Hollywood iconography at the moment in which it departs from narrative, in the form of the glamorous star icon.[4]

Richard Dyer discusses the power of star-iconography in terms of 'charisma'. Dyer offers Max Weber's formulation of charisma, 'a certain quality of an individual personality by virtue of which he [*sic*] is set apart from ordinary men and treated as endowed with supernatural, superhuman or at least superficially exceptional qualities', and reads the power described in Weber's definition in terms of how stars are ideological embodiments of particular historical notions of femininity, beauty, morality and so on. Vital for my treatment of Warhol's films is Dyer's suggestion that, 'star charisma needs to be situated in the specificities of the ideological configurations to which it belongs', and that 'virtually all sociological theories of stars ignore the *specificities* of another aspect of the phenomenon – the audience'. He adds, 'I would point out the absolutely central importance of stars in gay ghetto culture' and that 'if these star-audience relationships are only an intensification of the conflicts and exclusions experienced by everyone, it is also significant that, in any discussion of "subversive" star images, stars embodying adolescent, female and gay images play a crucial role' (59). The ways that stars may embody gay images, though, has been notoriously complex to document, especially given the ways that many gays have *identified* with female stars (Garland, Taylor, Crawford, Davis and Monroe) while *desiring* male stars (Hudson, Clift, Dean and Brando).

As we know, Warhol was a fan all his life, beginning in Pittsburgh, where he filled in colouring books of stars while he was home from school, writing letters to Truman Capote during the 1950s and taking photos of stars at the Factory and Studio 54 when he himself had become a star. These moments help to describe the link between gays and female stars as occurring through a perception on the part of the gay fan that glamour marks the achievement of becoming, through the expense of labour, something that one is not. For the female star, that 'something else' is perceived to be the star as in possession of an exceptional beauty that is further enhanced by clothing and make-up (which indeed would not exist without the clothing and make-up), while for the gay fan it comments upon the exclusion of many gays from cinematic/cultural depictions of seduction and heterosexual union. Sometimes, gay camp critique takes the form of drag, but it also appears through the intense devotion of the gay fan to one female star who embodies strength, vulnerability or humour and a defence against that exile from representation.

Even if the effect of glamour is that it seems to involve a complete lack of effort, that the star simply *is* glamorous, the achievement of glamour requires an immense expenditure of time, investment and effort on the part of the studio.[5] Indeed, we should take pains to remember that, apart from glamour's concealed labour, some versions of cinematic spectacle do encourage audiences to sit in awe at the expense of money and labour. For example, in the creation of immense sound-stages for historical epics or action-pics (such as De Mille's Roman Circuses or the *Die Hard* films' exploding buildings), spectacle often demands our wonder at the magnitude of the project's undertaking. In contrast, glamour seldom seeks to portray equally enormous undertakings; audiences are seldom called upon to marvel at the fact that a star has been rendered even *more* beautiful. But it was this spectacle which Warhol sought to make even more spectacular. Remembering Warhol's comment that he wanted $1,000,000 from Hollywood to make a movie, I can only hazard that the final product might have looked like *Terminator II* with RuPaul playing the hero.

Warhol's films, then, depict glamour as a lever which refigures Hollywood through the gay camp spectator's reading. This involves reversing glamour, from being a form of concealed labour, to becoming a spectacle of its own conditions of production. For Warhol, this reversal would take the form of sustaining glamour by making remarkably marginalised figures into Factory stars. Warhol's work takes up the production of glamour in the everyday, in which non-stars produce themselves to be looked at.

Now, in a longer project I will explore this dynamic more fully through the course of Warhol's film-making career, but in the present context allow me to take up this motif of camp, labour and glamour in reference to one film only. In *Haircut* (a silent production from 1964), three men are seen; one carefully cuts another's hair, while the third packs a pipe with what appears to be marijuana and takes long, hypnosis-inducing drags from it.[6] With no edits save the reel changes, they go about the work of snipping and combing, all the while chatting casually and ignoring the presence of the camera. As they groom themselves, they pose themselves within the frame, forming at moments abstracted compositions; even in a domesticated moment such as this, we see them taking pains to remember their appearances. The effect of *Haircut* is that it drives us back into the realm of the mundane, only to reveal the efforts required of us to appear within that quotidian life: even if we don't function as stars, star culture functions within us as we go about preparing ourselves for the world. At the film's conclusion, the figures fix their gazes directly upon the camera, seeming to respond to some unheard request from the director and in this final tableau they display their handiwork. Finally, they begin to laugh, as if on cue, and we are left with this silent and ambiguous gesture that could be a mockery of us or an entreaty to share their pleasure. Particularly striking about this final segment is the serenely detached way in which they fix our gaze: these are expressions seemingly taken directly from the Hollywood icon. Cool and remote, like Harlow or Crawford, the stars of *Haircut* share with us the pleasures of being seen and *knowing* that one is being seen.

We can hardly ignore, though, in *Haircut* the fact that the action takes place in a rather squalid loft, and is lighted by a glaring lightbulb within the frame. Freddy Herko, one of the figures, is nude, and the clothing of the others displays the tattered flourishes of bohemian style, at the time signalled by their comparatively long hair. In this setting, it becomes apparent that we are nowhere near the glamour-mills of a Hollywood studio, and the film then presents us with the question of what impulse would drive the minute attentions given by these men to their appearance. I would hazard that, in part, the film serves to remind us of the immense difference between those whom Hollywood cinema understood itself as appealing to and, in this particular case, the inadvertent gay fans who model themselves upon it.

To conclude: I began this essay with the suggestion that Andy Warhol's films, as they have been subsumed to the avant-garde, operate in distinct tension to what the avant-garde is said to be capable of showing us. And perhaps it is not the case that what Warhol's cinematic visions depict is that different from the claims of avant-gardism as enumerated by its promoters and critics: if anything, we might all agree that a different sense of how we could look at the world might arise through inventive reuses of film in non-corporate settings of production. Yet Warhol sought to extend the capacities of film for a camp re-visioning of the world *through* his attentions to popular media in ways that make it difficult for us to understand the project of an avant-garde. The films strain avant-garde definitions in two respects: first, they honour the power of Hollywood film for the gay men who campily respond to it, and second, they indicate how much work is required in forging the camp response.

Given that Warhol departed from hands-on film-making after 1968, it is worth remembering these things for several reasons. For one thing, Warhol was commenting on processes of cultural production and dissemination that continue: Hollywood's place in the popular imagination is arguably stronger than ever and the dynamics which the underground film could imitate, mock, disavow and embrace are still central to our lives. Second, the processes of cultural appropriation work on both sides of production and critique: if Warhol used the icons and methods of Hollywood to explore the margins of its viewership, it was only a matter of time within the dynamics of mass-cultural production that his works would come to be imitated. Hollywood could (and did) reappropriate those very notions of the marginal for its own purposes, and one reads with a certain sadness the passages in POPism where the Factory members sense, upon the release of John Schlesinger's Midnight Cowboy, an ill-judged euphoria over their future access to Hollywood, an access which never came for them. So much for that moment of capital's re-enchantment. Further, the fact of camp contestations over the functions of popular culture continue; the Oscar given in 1995 to Priscilla, Queen of the Desert for its splendid costuming signals camp's fascination with glamour as a now more central issue for popular cinema, while Bruce LaBruce's recent release Super 8½ foregrounds Warhol's continuing importance for new visions of queer cinema. These lessons only affirm the importance of gay camp contributions to the avant-garde project *and* to popular forms, contributions which now, more than ever, continue to delight and challenge us.

NOTES

1. *Planet Queer* (Pittsburgh), Spring 1994.
2. *The Andy Warhol Museum* (Pittsburgh: The Carnegie Museum of Art, Carnegie Institute, 1992); a promotional brochure distributed to schools and museums in advance of the museum's debut.
3. Walter Benjamin, quoted in Susan Buck-Morss, 254. I am here relying upon Buck-Morss's reconstruction of Benjamin's unfinished *Passagen-Werk*, a monumental project in which Benjamin sought to account for the social organisation of the modern city that gave rise to the profusion of goods witnessed in the arcades of 20s Paris.
4. Camp fascination with glamour, as exploited in the work of Warhol, takes off from a perception of star imagery similar to that of Laura Mulvey in 'Visual Pleasure and Narrative Cinema'. Mulvey described the tendency of the female star to arrest, however temporarily, the narrative momentum of a Hollywood film, and her primary interest was to theorise the dynamics of patriarchal pleasure, i.e. how heterosexual male spectators were positioned to gaze upon the sight of the star. Interestingly, Mulvey's subsequent addendum to her essay addressed *female* (both heterosexual and lesbian) spectatorial pleasure, but did not provide an account of how the male homosexual might respond to the same image. See also Mulvey's 'Afterthoughts'.

5. The work demanded to achieve glamour, we should remember, is highly regimented and co-ordinated, and frequently in Hollywood, performed by women. While some of this labour is rendered glamorous in itself (as in accounts of Cecil Beaton's work, for example), more often it has taken the form of sweatshop labour. See Nielsen.

6. Freddy Herko, one of the stars of *Haircut*, was an important figure for Warhol in his transition to the underground scene in New York; Herko brought many of the 'A-men' (amphetamine users) to the early Factory and put Warhol in touch with many of the figures who would populate the Factory. Warhol later wrote, 'The people I loved were the ones like Freddy, the leftovers of show business, turned down at auditions all over town. They couldn't do something more than once, but their one time was better than anyone else's. They had star quality, but no star ego – they didn't know how to push themselves. They were too gifted to lead "regular lives", but they were also too unsure of themselves to ever become real professionals'. Warhol & Hackett 1980: 56.

REFERENCES

Adorno, Theodor W., *Asthetische Theorie,* edited by Gretel Adorno & R. Teidemann, Frankfurt: Suhrkamp, 1970.

Buck-Morss, Susan, *The Dialectics of Seeing: Walter Benjamin and the Arcades Project,* Cambridge: MIT Press, 1990.

Bürger, Peter, *Theory of the Avant-Garde,* trans. Michael Shaw, Minneapolis: U of Minnesota P, 1984.

Dyer, Richard, 'Charisma', in Gledhill 1991.

Mulvey, Laura, 'Visual Pleasure and Narrative Cinema', *Screen* 16:3, Autumn 1975.

—— , 'Afterthoughts on "Visual Pleasure and Narrative Cinema" inspired by *Duel in the Sun*', *Framework* 6:15–17, 1981.

Nielsen, Elizabeth, 'Handmaidens of the Glamour Culture: Costumers in the Hollywood Studio System', in Jane Gaines & Charlotte Herzog (eds.), *Fabrications: Costume and the Female Body,* New York: Routledge, 1990, 160–79.

SECTION V
THE QUEER ISSUE

INTRODUCTION

The late 1980s unfolded and celebrated the critical subversiveness enacted by the camp spectacles; the scene of the 1990s, though, offers a virtually opposite picture as regards the *practice*, if not the theory, of camp in the aftermaths of its 'pop' euphoria. The co-optation of its marginality within the heart of dominant culture (the bourgeois, North American, male, white, upper-middle class whose 'straight camp' is celebrated in the 1993 *Esquire* article discussed in the main Introduction), while eloquent on the reformulation of the self-ratifying devices posited by 'the dominant' itself, seems to tell the lie of pop camp, and the sad truth about how poorly transgressive that mass transgression was. This 1990s scene seems to give poignancy to Fredric Jameson's critique (cf. Section IV) of the 'camp or "hysterical" sublime' of postmodernism, with its winking, smirking and self-undermining statement, with its 'irony epidemic' (see Rudnick & Anderson 1989) and citational consumerism, as the cultural logic indeed of late capitalism, rather than the tool for its challenge and erosion. The only site for an undisputed subversiveness of 1990s camp might thus appear to be its gay and lesbian activist deployment (what in fact, although without validating it, frames the mid-1990s contradictory essentialist reclaiming of gay political camp discussed at some length in the Introduction). And yet, in the very years that produced the 'death of camp', as Daniel Harris (1996c) tags the decay of traditional 'gay culture', critical readings have been enacting an increasingly problematic approach to the issue as a *queer* issue.

The 1990s, in fact, had been inaugurated by Judith Butler's *Gender Trouble* (1990), whose remarkably lucid analysis of the gay drag demystification of the gender binary grounds the very performative 'theory' of camp that this Reader has suggested, and a significant number of the essays it includes. If the vast majority of post-1990 writings refer to it, Newton's 1972 *Mother Camp* is explicitly acknowledged by Butler herself as seminal, and other equally consonant earlier formulations, such as Babuscio's, have been pointed out (cf. Graham 1995: 165). As gay drag enacts an incongruous juxtaposition of feminine and masculine features, one contradicting the other in a virtually endless *mise en abyme* of surfaces, Newton argued, the sex/gender system might be demystified as an artifice; and Butler develops that suggestion by showing how gay drag stages and erodes the process of subjectivation as subjection, and the heterosexual construction of coherence. As such, the secondariness of drag, by imitatively displacing the bourgeois 'original', transgresses it, and makes heterosexual gendered identities an 'incredible' performative fabrication devoid of ontological priority – a copy, just like drag. Those who had an investment in camp for theory and practice (intellectually, politically, or even just for the sake of the *frisson* that its mainstreaming, however we value this process, has surely watered down), could not but welcome this restoring of its rightful worth, definitive as it seemed for the powerful elucidation it had eventually received.

The political, aesthetic and intellectual *worth* of camp thus seemed to coincide with its *lesbian and gay context*, the one element that turns imitation into a transgressive reinscription of the heterosexual original. But such subversiveness, simultaneous with its localisation in a gay setting, is of course neglecting the radical ambiguity of parody, and the always already compromised status of camp as gay drag – the early 1990s celebration of drag was in fact, as Carole-Anne Tyler timely pointed out in her excellent 'Boys Will Be Girls' (1991; excerpted here), so suspiciously excessive as to end up being camp itself. In her later work Butler felt it necessary to address the limits to drag subversiveness, which may offer an illusory relief from that hegemonic gender prescription it claims to dispute. But even in the passage from *Gender Trouble* excerpted here, Butler pointed out an usually disregarded limitation to the 'subversiveness' claim, stating that '[p]arody by itself is not subversive' and invoking a non-typological (insufficient, she says – inadequately normative, we may add) approach to 'understand what makes certain kinds of parodic repetitions effectively disruptive, truly troubling, and which repetitions become domesticated and recirculated as instruments of cultural hegemony'.

It is reasonable, though, to remark that Butler does not give the same emphasis that Newton did to the conservative potential of gay drag (that normative horizon that you can't dispense with if you subvert something), which in its 'unnatural' dissonance of inside/outside appearance might *as well* be taken to authorise the rightfulness of stigma and the reinforcing of the heterosexual priority. Still, in its apparent invitation to camp followers to circumvent their subversive practice to gay drag, Butler appropriately points to the scenario developed by Tyler, drawing the contours of the gay drag camp as a site of *radical crisis* both for heterosexual culture and for drag advocates, enacting contradictory intentions, identities, and pragmatical effects. A 'rara avis' indeed in 1991, Tyler forcefully reads the psychoanalytical nexus of 'transvestic fetishism', and shows that the outcome is queerer than most critics would allow. Tyler reminds us, in fact, that drag only operates insofar as the performer's biological sex – the 'body' (the identity-grounding corpo*reality*) 'underneath' – is made visible, and that such unavoidable *presence* may also bring forth a spectatorial identification that does not subvert phallic identities, but rather works to 'resecure masculine identity', and bring the gender 'incredible' back to its reality effect. In staging drag in its context of necessarily presupposed difference, Tyler shows a manifold set of ambivalently deployed differences, that camp 'subversion' may in fact reproduce and reinforce in the very process of their subversive 'reinscription'. Just like the theories of female mimicry are shown to 'reinscribe white, middle class femininity as the real thing, the (quint)essence of femininity', Tyler argues, gay drag is grounded in a white, bourgeois, and masculine symbolic economy. The context-related imaginary of differences that drag activates invokes *in its turn* a demystification, requiring in gay and feminist critics alike an acknowledgement of 'their positioning in a number of discourses besides those of gender and sexuality' and the acceptance of difference – including their own.

Tyler argues that among the other 'dragged differences' of the drag culture camp one should also take into account not only issues of class, on which criticism had already shown some degree of awareness, but also of *race*, that neglected issue within camp studies, thus pointing to an accomplished queer theory, however possible that may be, one that addresses the complex system of subordination on the axes of gender, class and ethnicity/race as simultaneously operative. Years after Tyler's invitation, in fact, the great part of critical work on 'racial camp' remains to be done, having been (usually, less than centrally) addressed in a restricted number of writings (see Clark 1993; Roberts 1993; Román 1993; Smith 1993; Cruz-Malavé 1995; Halberstam 1997). Pamela Robertson's 'Mae West's Maids: Race, "Authenticity", and the Discourse of Camp', included here, finds its stimulus in this persistent absence, one that her 1996 *Guilty Pleasures* had addressed in the introductory essay as an open question that exceeded that particular volume's necessary field delimitation while being evoked by its very subject (cf. Section III).

Mae West, the 'queen of camp' (Hamilton 1995) whose female burlesque and same sex impersonation point to a tradition of marginal camp different from the gay male tradition, also enacts a form of 'racial camp', crossing the borderlines of 'black' and 'white' and performing the intertwinedness of race and gender in her films and theatre. And as her same sex-mimicry promoted the non-normative deployment of queer camp on the sex/gender axis, West's icon is read as a starting point for an analysis that fulfils Tyler's invitation, an analysis that makes the most of queer in breaking the barriers between subculturally marked audiences in their confrontation with dominant culture – those barriers which enforce their subordination. In Robertson's reading of *I'm No Angel*, framed with other 'black performances' by West, the role of authentification assumed in gay drag by the exposure of the 'true identity', of the real sex 'beneath', is invested in the otherness of West's black maids, whose relation to 'the queen' incessantly wavers from proximate (their common position on the gender axis) to distance (their class position, reducing their gender 'sameness'); as to the racial otherness of the maids, it operates at once as a trigger to the racial fluidity embodied by West herself, and as a frame of stable blackness that marks the queen's whiteness in the very movement of her flirting with 'othered', 'real' blacks. If camp is 'the lie that tells the truth', as Philip Core wrote in 1984 (cf. Section I), well, such telling may assert the arbitrary status of the very category of 'truth' – but it may also be its contradictory statement: the way, that is to say, by which the challenged 'truth' affirms and reinforces itself.

Robertson's piece invites us to consider the unmarked whiteness within which the camp spectator is textually constructed and the unsettling effect that a consideration of an African-American spectatorial position may have on that 'natural' spectatorship. Her piece thus also solicits the appraisal of the 'spectatorial position' that the critic of camp assumes, in its gendered, raced, class-related specificity – and we may add another item, possibly even less accounted for, to the list: nationality. Johannes von Moltke's 'Camping in the Art Closet: The Politics of Camp and Nation in German Film' further complicates this question as the critic addresses it by staging Fassbinder's cinema through John Waters's camp 'spectacles' – the prerequisite brought forth by camp, and in camp, being critical spectatorship (if not, in this 'postmodern' phase of ours, American spectatorship). In von Moltke's reading, Fassbinder's cinema fluctuates between the two poles, invoked in film theory and in New German Cinema criticism, of an American (deterritorialised, aestheticised) 'reception' vs. German (original, text-inscribed, political) 'address', making these poles 'impossible alternatives', whose perennial tension is made explicit by the camp, queer, *across* movement. Von Moltke's argument thus espouses the derivative camp, following the authenticity-restoring path to the German alleged address and 'inscribed audience', in order to show this as fictional construct 'produced at least in equal measure by the critical discourse surrounding the films as by the films themselves' – *as copy is to copy*, Butler would phrase it. Which is to say that the borders crossed by camp may work as a reminder not only of the pragmatic effects of the camp subversion (potentially contradicting progressive intentions), but also of the pragmatic conditions in which we construe the camp spectacles through *our own* spectacles. As such a reminder, though, camp delegitimises any ambition to stabilise the answers to the questions it poses, starting with the one of our own self-awareness as its critical constructors, of our own partiality and specificity. If von Moltke's camp framing of Fassbinder's cinema capitalises the uncertainty of intentionality and address as inherent to an 'original' context, it also makes clear the ambiguous political value of the German 'address' itself, placing as it potentially does 'the allegedly subversive potential of the New German Cinema in the service of a revisionist discourse', a discourse which in recovering history's waste highlights the constructedness of history itself and the artificiality of the historical referent; a discourse that in staging the lure of the Third Reich produces, oh well, the 'surplus value' of fascist spectacle. The one duty we owe to history is to rewrite it, said Oscar Wilde; to what ends, that has to be settled – and will remain so for a while.

It seems appropriate to bring this Reader to its end by addressing the alleged 'death of camp', repeatedly proclaimed 'oncoming' whenever a shift in its modes of enactment has taken place, and which was powerfully sanctioned in 1997 by Daniel Harris's *The Rise and Fall of Gay Culture*, a collection of his 1990s writings. (The proclamation has been common since the late 1970s, but it is not without significant antecedents: as early as December 1964, for instance, Jan Brunvand announced its death due not so much to its popularisation, but to the 'disappearance' of Edwardian-styled British camp, as the sexually indeterminate youth were no longer modelled on the Oxbridge-educated queer and stylish example, but rather on the 'butch', American-derived androgyny of the cheap, unisex clothing.) In the wake of what we have seen so far, it won't be surprising to discover, however, that Caryl Flinn's included 'The Deaths of Camp' is not in fact an epitaph at all. In reading the construction of death and bodily decay within camp representations, and within camp itself, Flinn faces the whole nexus of questions that has accompanied the critical apprehension of the issue: the questions of consumption, time elapsing, failure, decline, semiotic cannibalism, how they are enacted by camp, and what implications for material bodies the camp disjointed, grotesque body (of knowledge) may have. In its final invitation to face the 'crucial challenge for gay, lesbian, and queer theorists and all feminists to reconvene discussions of the body and body practices like camp and drag, along with any attendant claims to subversion', Flinn's essay eventually refuses to indulge in the epistemic closure that the 'death of camp' grants, along with an undeniably elegiac, decadent, end-of-the-line pleasure, and points to its potential path of relentless questioning of 'the historical sphere of material, social, sexed bodies and cultures'. So, the appropriate conclusion with the 'death of camp' may be reformulated into a different – less reconciling, inconclusive – conclusion. It may probably be even more queerly appropriate to the theory, history and practice of camp whose framework it has attempted to delineate, in fact, that this Reader ends where it all began, if only etymologically speaking: pointing to a sinuous path drawing a half circle that abruptly breaks its curvilinear regularity to follow a transversal, disunified direction – well, isn't that a question mark?

22

FROM INTERIORITY TO GENDER PERFORMATIVES

Judith Butler

In *Discipline and Punish* Foucault challenges the language of internalization as it operates in the service of the disciplinary regime of the subjection and subjectivation of criminals.[1] Although Foucault objected to what he understood to be the psychoanalytic belief in the 'inner' truth of sex in *The History of Sexuality*, he turns to a criticism of the doctrine of internalization for separate purposes in the context of his history of criminology. In a sense, *Discipline and Punish* can be read as Foucault's effort to rewrite Nietzsche's doctrine of internalization in *On the Genealogy of Morals* on the model of *inscription*. In the context of prisoners, Foucault writes, the strategy has been not to enforce a repression of their desires, but to compel their bodies to signify the prohibitive law as their very essence, style, and necessity. That law is not literally internalized, but incorporated, with the consequence that bodies are produced which signify that law on and through the body; there the law is manifest as the essence of their selves, the meaning of their soul, their conscience, the law of their desire. In effect, the law is at once fully manifest and fully latent, for it never appears as external to the bodies it subjects and subjectivates. Foucault writes:

> It would be wrong to say that the soul is an illusion, or an ideological effect. On the contrary, it exists, it has a reality, it is produced permanently *around*, *on*, *within*, the body by the functioning of a power that is exercised on those that are punished (29; my emphasis).

Reprinted from *Gender Trouble: Feminism and the Subversion of Identity*, London-New York: Routledge, 1990.

The figure of the interior soul understood as 'within' the body is signified through its inscription *on* the body, even though its primary mode of signification is through its very absence, its potent invisibility. The effect of a structuring inner space is produced through the signification of a body as a vital and sacred enclosure. The soul is precisely what the body lacks; hence, the body presents itself as a signifying lack. That lack which *is* the body signifies the soul as that which cannot show. In this sense, then, the soul is a surface signification that contests and displaces the inner/outer distinction itself, a figure of interior psychic space inscribed *on* the body as a social signification that perpetually renounces itself as such. In Foucault's terms, the soul is not imprisoned by or within the body, as some Christian imagery would suggest, but 'the soul is the prison of the body' (30).

The redescription of intrapsychic processes in terms of the surface politics of the body implies a corollary redescription of gender as the disciplinary production of the figures of fantasy through the play of presence and absence on the body's surface, the construction of the gendered body through a series of exclusions and denials, signifying absences. But what determines the manifest and latent text of the body politic? What is the prohibitive law that generates the corporeal stylization of gender, the fantasied and fantastic figuration of the body? We have already considered the incest taboo and the prior taboo against homosexuality as the generative moments of gender identity, the prohibitions that produce identity along the culturally intelligible grids of an idealized and compulsory heterosexuality. That disciplinary production of gender effects a false stabilization of gender in the interests of the heterosexual construction and regulation of sexuality within the reproductive domain. The construction of coherence conceals the gender discontinuities that run rampant within heterosexual, bisexual, and gay and lesbian contexts in which gender does not necessarily follow from sex, and desire, or sexuality generally, does not seem to follow from gender – indeed, where none of these dimensions of significant corporeality express or reflect one another. When the disorganization and disaggregation of the field of bodies disrupt the regulatory fiction of heterosexual coherence, it seems that the expressive model loses its descriptive force. That regulatory ideal is then exposed as a norm and a fiction that disguises itself as a developmental law regulating the sexual field that it purports to describe.

According to the understanding of identification as an enacted fantasy or incorporation, however, it is clear that coherence is desired, wished for, idealized, and that this idealization is an effect of a corporeal signification. In other words, acts, gestures, and desire produce the effect of an internal core or substance, but produce this *on the surface* of the body, through the play of signifying absences that suggest, but never reveal, the organizing principle of identity as a cause. Such acts, gestures, enactments, generally construed, are *performative* in the sense that the essence or identity that they otherwise purport to express are *fabrications* manufactured and sustained through corporeal signs and other discursive means. That the gendered body is performative suggests that it has no ontological status apart from the various acts which constitute its reality. This also suggests that if that reality is fabricated as an interior essence, that very interiority is an effect and function of a decidedly public and social discourse, the public regulation of fantasy through the surface politics of the body, the gender border control that differentiates inner from outer, and so institutes the 'integrity' of the subject. In other words, acts and gestures, articulated and enacted desires create the illusion of an interior and organizing gender core, an illusion discursively maintained for the purposes of the regulation of sexuality within the obligatory frame of reproductive heterosexuality. If the 'cause' of desire, gesture, and act can be localized within the 'self' of the actor, then the political regulations and disciplinary practices which produce that ostensibly coherent gender are effectively displaced from view. The displacement of a political and discursive origin of gender identity onto a psychological 'core' precludes an analysis of the political constitution of the gendered subject and its fabricated notions about the ineffable interiority of its sex or of its true identity.

If the inner truth of gender is a fabrication and if a true gender is a fantasy instituted and inscribed on the surface of bodies, then it seems that genders can be neither true nor false, but are only produced as the truth effects of a discourse of primary and stable identity. In *Mother Camp: Female Impersonators in America*, anthropologist Esther Newton (1972) suggests that the structure of impersonation reveals one of the key fabricating mechanisms through which the social construction of gender takes place. I would suggest as well that drag fully subverts the distinction between inner and outer psychic space and effectively mocks both the expressive model of gender and the notion of a true gender identity. Newton writes:

> At its most complex, [drag] is a double inversion that says, 'appearance is an illusion'. Drag says [Newton's curious personification] 'my "outside" appearance is feminine, but my essence "inside" [the body] is masculine'. At the same time it symbolizes the opposite inversion; 'my appearance "outside" [my body, my gender] is masculine but my essence "inside" [myself] is feminine'. (130)

Both claims to truth contradict one another and so displace the entire enactment of gender significations from the discourse of truth and falsity.

The notion of an original or primary gender identity is often parodied within the cultural practices of drag, cross-dressing, and the sexual stylization of butch/femme identities. Within feminist theory, such parodic identities have been understood to be either degrading to women, in the case of drag and cross-dressing, or an uncritical appropriation of sex-role stereotyping from within the practice of heterosexuality, especially in the case of butch/femme lesbian identities. But the relation between the 'imitation' and the 'original' is, I think, more complicated than that critique generally allows. Moreover, it gives us a clue to the way in which the relationship between primary identification – that is, the original meanings accorded to gender – and subsequent gender experience might be reframed. The performance of drag plays upon the distinction between the anatomy of the performer and the gender that is being performed. But we are actually in the presence of three contingent dimensions of significant corporeality: anatomical sex, gender identity, and gender performance. If the anatomy of the performer is already distinct from the gender of the performer, and both of those are distinct from the gender of the performance, then the performance suggests a dissonance not only between sex and performance, but sex and gender, and gender and performance. As much as drag creates a unified picture of 'woman' (what its critics often oppose), it also reveals the distinctness of those aspects of gendered experience which are falsely naturalized as a unity through the regulatory fiction of heterosexual coherence. *In imitating gender, drag implicitly reveals the imitative structure of gender itself – as well as its contingency.* Indeed, part of the pleasure, the giddiness of the performance is in the recognition of a radical contingency in the relation between sex and gender in the face of cultural configurations of causal unities that are regularly assumed to be natural and necessary. In the place of the law of heterosexual coherence, we see sex and gender denaturalized by means of a performance which avows their distinctness and dramatizes the cultural mechanism of their fabricated unity.

The notion of gender parody defended here does not assume that there is an original which such parodic identities imitate. Indeed the parody is *of* the very notion of an original; just as the psychoanalytic notion of gender identification is constituted by a fantasy of a fantasy, the transfiguration of an Other who is always already a 'figure' in that double sense, so gender parody reveals that the original identity after which gender fashions itself is an imitation without an origin. To be more precise, it is a production which, in effect – that is, in its effect – postures as an imitation. This perpetual displacement constitutes a fluidity of identities that suggests an openness to resignification and recontextualization; parodic proliferation deprives hegemonic culture and its critics of the claim to naturalized or essentialist gender identities. Although the gender meanings taken up in these parodic styles are clearly part of hegemonic, misogynist culture, they are nevertheless denaturalized and mobilized through their parodic recontextualization. As imitations which effectively displace the meaning of the original, they imitate the myth of originality itself. In the place of an original identification which serves as a determining cause, gender identity might be reconceived as a personal/cultural history of received meanings subject to a set of imitative practices which refer laterally to other imitations and which, jointly, construct the illusion of a primary and interior gendered self or parody the mechanism of that construction.

According to Fredric Jameson's 'Postmodernism and Consumer Society', the imitation that mocks the notion of an original is characteristic of pastiche rather than parody:

> Pastiche is, like parody, the imitation of a peculiar or unique style, the wearing of a stylistic mask, speech in a dead language but it is a neutral practice of mimicry, without parody's ulterior motive, without the satirical impulse, without laughter, without that still latent feeling that there exists something *normal* compared to which what is being imitated is rather comic. Pastiche is blank parody, parody that has lost it humor. (114)

The loss of the sense of 'the normal', however, can be its own occasion for laughter, especially when 'the normal', 'the original' is revealed to be a copy, and an inevitably failed one, an ideal that no one *can* embody. In this sense, laughter emerges in the realization that all along the original was derived.

Parody by itself is not subversive, and there must be a way to understand what makes certain kinds of parodic repetitions effectively disruptive, truly troubling, and which repetitions become domesticated and recirculated as instruments of cultural hegemony. A typology of actions would clearly not suffice, for parodic displacement, indeed, parodic laughter, depends on a context and reception in which subversive confusions can be fostered. What performance where will invert the inner/outer distinction and compel a radical rethinking of the psychological presuppositions of gender identity and sexuality? What performance where will compel a reconsideration of the *place* and stability of the masculine and the feminine? And what kind of gender performance will enact and reveal the performativity of gender itself in a way that destabilizes the naturalized categories of identity and desire?

If the body is not a 'being', but a variable boundary, a surface whose permeability is politically regulated, a signifying practice within a cultural field of gender hierarchy and compulsory heterosexuality, then what language is left for understanding this corporeal enactment, gender, that constitutes its 'interior' signification on its surface? Sartre would perhaps have called this act 'a style of being', Foucault, 'a stylistics of existence'. And in my earlier reading of Beauvoir (cf. Butler 1990a: 111–28), I suggest that gendered bodies are so many 'styles of the flesh'. These styles all never fully self-styled, for styles have a history, and those histories condition and limit the possibilities. Consider gender, for instance, as *a corporeal style*, an 'act', as it were, which is both intentional and performative, where *'performative'* suggests a dramatic and contingent construction of meaning.

Wittig understands gender as the workings of 'sex', where 'sex' is an obligatory injunction for the body to become a cultural sign, to materialize itself in obedience to a historically delimited possibility, and to do this, not once or twice, but as a sustained and repeated corporeal project. The notion of a 'project', however, suggests the originating force of a radical will, and because gender is a project which has cultural survival as its end, the term *strategy* better suggests the situation of duress under which gender performance always and variously occurs. Hence, as a strategy of survival within compulsory systems, gender is a performance with clearly punitive consequences. Discrete genders are part of what 'humanizes' individuals within contemporary culture; indeed, we regularly punish those who fail to do their gender right. Because there is neither an 'essence' that gender expresses or externalizes nor an objective ideal to which gender aspires, and because gender is not a fact, the various acts of gender create the idea of gender, and without those acts, there would be no gender at all. Gender is, thus, a construction that regularly conceals its genesis; the tacit collective agreement to perform, produce, and sustain discrete and polar genders as cultural fictions is obscured by the credibility of those productions – and the punishments that attend not agreeing to believe in them; the construction 'compels' our belief in its necessity and naturalness. The historical possibilities materialized through various corporeal styles are nothing other than those punitively regulated cultural fictions alternately embodied and deflected under duress.

Consider that a sedimentation of gender norms produces the peculiar phenomenon of a 'natural sex' or a 'real woman' or any number of prevalent and compelling social fictions, and that this is a sedimentation that over time has produced a set of corporeal styles which, in reified form, appear as the natural configuration of bodies into sexes existing in a binary relation to one another. If these styles are enacted, and if they produce the coherent gendered subjects who pose as their originators, what kind of performance might reveal this ostensible 'cause' to be an 'effect'?

In what senses, then, is gender an act? As in other ritual social dramas, the action of gender requires a performance that is *repeated*. This repetition is at once a reenactment and reexperiencing of a set of meanings already socially established; and it is the mundane and ritualized form of their legitimation (see Turner; and Geertz). Although there are individual bodies that enact these significations by becoming stylized into gendered modes, this 'action' is a public action. There are temporal and collective dimensions to these actions, and their public character is not inconsequential; indeed, the performance is effected with the strategic aim of maintaining gender within its binary frame – an aim that cannot be attributed to a subject, but, rather, must be understood to found and consolidate the subject.

Gender ought not to be construed as a stable identity or locus of agency from which various acts follow; rather, gender is an identity tenuously constituted in time, instituted in an exterior space through a *stylized repetition of acts*. The effect of gender is produced through the stylization of the body and, hence, must be understood as the mundane way in which bodily gestures, movements, and styles of various kinds constitute the illusion of an abiding gendered self. This formulation moves the conception of gender off the ground of a substantial model of identity to one that requires a conception of gender as a constituted *social temporality*. Significantly, if gender is instituted through acts which are internally discontinuous, then the *appearance of substance* is precisely that, a constructed identity, a performative accomplishment which the mundane social audience, including the actors themselves, come to believe and to perform in the mode of belief. Gender is also a norm that can never be fully internalized; 'the internal' is a surface signification, and gender norms are finally phantasmatic, impossible to embody. If the ground of gender identity is the stylized repetition of acts through time and not a seemingly seamless identity, then the spatial metaphor of a 'ground' will be displaced and revealed as a stylized configuration, indeed, a gendered corporealization of time. The abiding gendered self will then be shown to be structured by repeated acts that seek to approximate the ideal of a substantial ground of identity, but which, in their occasional discontinuity, reveal the temporal and contingent ground-lessness of this 'ground'. The possibilities of gender transformation are to be found precisely in the arbitrary relation between such acts, in the possibility of a failure to repeat, a de-formity, or a parodic repetition that exposes the phan-tasmatic effect of abiding identity as a politically tenuous construction.

If gender attributes, however, are not expressive but performative, then these attributes effectively constitute the identity they are said to express or reveal. The distinction between expression and performativeness is crucial. If gender attributes and acts, the various ways in which a body shows or produces its cultural signification, are performative, then there is no preexisting identity by which an act or attribute might be measured; there would be no true or false, real or distorted acts of gender, and the postulation of a true gender identity would be revealed as a regulatory fiction. That gender reality is created through sustained social performances means that the very notions of an essential sex and a true or abiding masculinity or femininity are also constituted as part of the strategy that conceals gender's performative character and the performative possibilities for proliferating gender configurations outside the restricting frames of masculinist domination and compulsory heterosexuality.

Genders can be neither true nor false, neither real nor apparent, neither original nor derived. As credible bearers of those attributes, however, genders can also be rendered thoroughly and radically *incredible*.

NOTE

1. Parts of the following discussion were published in two different contexts: in my 'Gender Trouble, Feminist Theory, and Psychoanalytic Discourse', and 'Performa-tive Acts and Gender Constitution'.

REFERENCES

Butler, Judith, 'Gender Trouble, Feminist Theory, and Psychoanalytic Discourse', in Linda J. Nicholson (ed.), *Feminism/Postmodernism*, New York: Routledge, 1989.
——, 'Performative Acts and Gender Constitution: An Essay in Phenomenology and Feminist Theory', *Theatre Journal*, 20:3, Winter 1988.
Foucault, Michel, *Discipline and Punish: the Birth of the Prison*, trans. Alan Sheridan, New York: Vintage, 1979.
Geertz, Clifford, 'Blurred Genres: The Refiguration of Thought', in *Local Knowledge: Further Essays in Interpretive Anthropology*, New York: Basic, 1983.

Jameson, Fredric, 'Postmodernism and Consumer Society', in Hal Foster (ed.), *The Anti-Aesthetic: Essays on Postmodern Culture*, Port Townsend, WA.: Bay Press, 1983.

Turner, Victor, *Dramas, Fields and Metaphors*, Ithaca: Cornell UP, 1974.

23

BOYS WILL BE GIRLS:
DRAG AND TRANSVESTIC FETISHISM

Carole-Anne Tyler

'Girls will be boys and boys will be girls / It's a mixed up muddled up shook up world except for Lola', the Kinks sang in 1970, asserting that the gay man in drag was the only sane person in a crazy world. That rock group's revaluation of camp and masquerade is currently shared by many theorists on the left, who advocate it as a postmodern strategy for the subversion of phallogocentric identities and desires. Their now radical chic has made the likes of Dolly Parton and Madonna (and their satin queen or Wanna-Be parodies or imitations) more than chicks with cheek. They have become draped crusaders for the social constructionist cause, catching gender in the act, as an act, so as to demonstrate there is no natural, essential, biological basis to gender or heterosexuality. Postmodern critics argue that because both gender and sexuality are organized around the phallus in our culture, there can be no escaping phallic effects. Any appeal to identities or desires beyond or before the phallus and its signifiers is both too utopic and essentialist. According to this logic, drag is just postmodern pragmatism, deconstructing identity from within so as not to sacrifice desire to an outmoded, purist, and Puritan essentialism.

Not so long ago camp languished, theorized as the shameful sign of an unreconstructed, self-hating, and even woman-hating, homosexual. Now not only femininity but even macho masculinity is read as drag and, therefore, radical. Such a literal re-habilitation of sexual difference seems almost too camp to be sincere. The stories we tell about the gender acts of others tell something

A longer version of this essay originally appeared in Diana Fuss (ed.), *Inside/Out: Lesbian Theories, Gay Theories*, New York: Routledge, 1991. It has been revised for this anthology to abridge rather than update or significantly alter its arguments.

about our own as they position subjects and objects with respect to symbolic castration and what signifies lack. If there is a desire for camp, expressed in drag fantasies, there is no camping up desire, which we cannot 'put on' or put off with the masquerades which are its symptoms. What is revealed – or concealed – by the desire for drag, whether to perceive or perform it? In whose eyes is what chic radical when all gender is an act and not an expression of an essence? Does a camp relation to identity subvert or support phallocentric hierarchies of difference?

CAMP, HOMOPHOBIA, AND MISOGYNY

Andrew Ross (1988, rpt. 1989: 144) suggests that after Stonewall camp was an embarrassment to the gay community, the sign of a pre-political gay identity. But other historians of drag have argued that gay and lesbian activists were uncomfortable with it long before then, at least since the 1950s. Both the Daughters of Bilitis and the Mattachine Society disapproved of it and parti- cipated in the consolidation of a distinction between gender and sexual 'devi- ance' which resulted in the separation of transvestism and transsexualism from homosexuality, according to Dave King.[1] The impulse behind the devaluation of camp was the apparent complicity of the latter with the sexual inversion model of homosexuality. Inversion theory, and most 'third sex' theories, assert that the invert or 'uranian' has the psyche of one gender (or perhaps both) and the body of the other, so that what looks like a homosexual object choice is in effect heterosexual. Thus, if men desire men, they do so as a women, as Freud explains: 'they identify themselves with a woman and take *themselves* as their sexual object. That is to say, they proceed from a narcissistic basis, and look for a young man who resembles themselves and whom *they* may love as their mother loved *them*'. Similarly, among women, 'the active inverts exhibit masculine characteristics, both physical and mental, with peculiar frequency and look for femininity in their sexual objects ...' (*Three Essays*, 11).

This model reinscribes heterosexuality within homosexuality itself, as Judith Butler (1990a: 54–5), among others, has argued. However, in doing so, it is unable to account for the apparently 'normally' gendered partner in homo- sexual object choices. Freud recognized there was a certain amount of 'ambi- guity' about masculine inversion (if not about lesbianism):

> There can be no doubt that a large proportion of male inverts retain the mental quality of masculinity, that they possess relatively few of the secondary characteristics of the opposite sex and that what they look for in their sexual object are in fact feminine mental traits ... A strict con- ceptual distinction should be drawn according to whether the sexual character of the object or that of the subject has been inverted. (*Three Essays*, 10)

He sometimes describes the subject of homosexual desire as feminine, in search of a masculine object, and sometimes as masculine, in search of a feminine object. In both cases he explains desire heterosexually; his inversion cannot account for the butch gay man or the lesbian femme. Confronting the theoretical impossibility of their existence, gay men and lesbians affirmed both their desire and their gender, refusing to assimilate homosexuality to heterosexuality but repudiating drag and butch-femme roles as deviations from gender norms. For the Daughters of Bilitis and the Mattachine Society, gay men and lesbians, despite their object choices, were really just like heterosexual men and women. Even more recent theorists have also been wary of drag, asserting that embracing gender norms is not assimilationist but radical, given the public's common-sense model of homosexuality, which is still indebted to the inversion model; for example, Martin Humphries writes, '[b]y creating amongst ourselves [gay men] apparently masculine men who desire other men we are refuting the idea that we are really feminine souls in male bodies' (1985: 84).[2] If the logical conclusion of inversion theory is the claim that homosexuality is really transsexualism, the extreme form of the reaction against it, the inverse of inversion theory, is the belief that transsexualism is only a defense against homosexuality. To reject either is to court charges of homophobia or transphobia, but it is the former which accounts for the gay community's rejection of camp and butch-femme roles (though it is important to recognize that there was never a feminization of lesbian culture as a counter to charges of masculine inversion comparable to the rise of gay machismo in the 1960s and 1970s).

Transphobia takes the very specific form of misogyny when femininity is devalued, which may be why even drag queens often insist they should not be mistaken for women. The emphasis on gay masculinity might be a defense against the feminization our culture has persistently linked to homosexuality, and not just a counter to heterosexist inversion theory. Hypermasculinity can allay the castration anxiety evoked by man objectified as spectacle, as film theorists have argued (cf. Dyer; Flitterman-Lewis; Neale). Thus John Marshall is right to underline that the association of gender inversion with homosexuality has been used to police masculine and feminine roles, for example, through homophobic questions like, 'What are you – a fag?' (153–4). However, because he privileges sexuality rather than gender when defining gay identity, he does not discuss the common misogynist corollary, 'What are you – a girl?'.

Being called a fag or queer, a sissy, and a girl, are closely in Western culture, but as Craig Owens indicates, homophobia and misogyny are not the same thing – as Owens emphasizes by arguing that it is possible for feminists, like Luce Irigaray, to be homophobic. He therefore contradicts himself when he cites Jacques Derrida as authority for the assertion that gay men are not gynephobic because they do not suffer from castration anxiety (219–20). It does not follow that because gay men are unafraid of being seen as gay, they are unafraid of being seen as feminine (or castrated, in a patriarchal fantasmatic) unless they 'really' are already feminine or castrated, ruled out from the moment homophobia and misogyny – or homosexuality and gender inversion

– are made disjunct. The fear that homosexuality robs a man of his virility and feminizes him, which Freud saw in Leonardo Da Vinci, conjoins homophobia and misogyny and impacts on both straight and gay culture (*Leonardo*, 88). Denigration of drag queens in gay culture may be a rejection of the heterosexist stereotype of the effeminate invert, who is contrasted with the 'real thing', the gay-identified masculine man, but it also may be a misogynist rejection of the feminine. The queens in literature or film are often traject or abject, as in John Rechy's *City of Night* or Hubert Selby, Jr.'s *Last Exit to Brooklyn*. Those interviewed in *Men in Frocks* are defensive – like Harvey Fierstein's Arnold in the movie *Torch Song Trilogy* (1987), who announces that he is a female impersonator to his soon-to-be-lover Alan with a bravado that suggests he believes he is being provocative if not downright offensive.[3] The major premise of the cult hit *Outrageous!* (1977), starring Craig Russell, is that his character's drag is just that, outrageous. 'It's one thing to be gay, but drag—' his gay boss tells him at one point, and later fires him for refusing to give it up. Even one of Robin's lovers says, 'I don't usually make it with drag queens – none of the guys do'.

Gay theory's affirmation of the properly gay man as a masculine man may also coincide with a misogynist critique of drag and camp effeminacy:

> The gay male parody of a certain femininity . . . is both a way of giving vent to the hostility toward women that probably afflicts every male . . . *and* could also paradoxically be thought of as helping to deconstruct that image for women themselves. A certain type of homosexual camp speaks the truth of that femininity as mindless, asexual, and hysterically bitchy, thereby provoking, it would seem to me, a violently anti-mimetic reaction in any female spectator. The gay male bitch desublimates and desexualizes a type of femininity glamorized by movie stars, whom he then lovingly assassinates with his style, even though the campy parodist may himself be quite stimulated by the hateful impulses inevitably included in his performance. The gay-macho style, on the other hand, is intended to excite others sexually, and the only reason that it continues to be adopted is that it frequently succeeds in doing so. (Bersani 1987: 208)

Leo Bersani here assigns women the place of lack as bitches, actual and potential, in need of the rather violent 'help' that drag queens are best equipped to offer them. But drag queens themselves are also the victims of a misogyny for which Bersani would make them responsible, represented as just as bitchy and narcissistic as the 'real thing', too self-involved to be stimulating to anybody else, unlike the altruistic macho man.[4] Asserting that neither the 'glamorized' movie star nor the queen are desirable (they are 'asexual', despite the evidence of star fan clubs and Chicks-with-Dicks phone sex numbers), Bersani condemns them to/for masturbation.

However, he rehabilitates drag when it is dressed up as 'feminine masochism' rather than bitchy sadism:

> It is possible to think of the sexual as, precisely, moving between a hyperbolic sense of self and a loss of all consciousness of self. But sex as self-hyperbole is perhaps a repression of sex as self-abolition. It inaccurately replicates self-shattering as self-swelling, as psychic tumescence. If ... men are especially apt to 'choose' this version of sexual pleasure, because their sexual equipment appears to invite by analogy, or at least to facilitate, the phallicizing of the ego, neither sex has exclusive rights to the practice of sex as self-hyperbole. For it is perhaps primarily *the degeneration of the sexual into a relationship that condemns sexuality to becoming a struggle for power.* As soon as persons are posited, the war begins. It is the self that swells with excitement at the idea of being on top ... (218)

Bersani argues that promiscuous best realizes self-shattering *jouissance*. What could be more threatening to the heterosexist media, he asks, than 'the sexual act [which] is associated with women but performed by men and ... [which] has the terrifying appeal of a loss of the ego, of a self-debasement?' (220). His conclusion implicitly answers what is only a rhetorical question: 'if the rectum is the grave in which the masculine ideal (an ideal shared – differently – by men *and* women) of proud subjectivity is buried, then it should be celebrated for its very potential for death' (222).

Though Bersani admits that the ways in which sex politicizes are 'highly problematical', he nevertheless reifies one kind of sex as politically progressive because dephallicizing. But do all attenuated intersubjective engagements necessarily fail to function as 'relationships'? Freud stressed the relative stability of the fantasies which structure a subject's psyche and characteristic defenses; promiscuity might be defensive and as much a part of that fantasy life as any other type of object choice. Furthermore, in a persuasive analysis of T.E. Lawrence's writings ('White Skin, Brown Masks'), Kaja Silverman demonstrates that masochism is not inconsistent with phallic narcissism and may even be a crucial component of masculinity and leadership in general. Being the bottom can be a means to being on top. If Bersani is right to insist that women, like men, can experience a phallicizing of the ego, despite what some feminist theorists assert, he is surely wrong to imagine that promiscuous anal sex is a greater guarantee of the self-shattering death of the subject than another kind of sex, including the vaginal sex he has asserted it recalls by association.[5] In this essay, a 'feminizing' promiscuous anal sex has a phallicizing function, swelling the ego of the theoretical impersonator (as 'feminine masochist') at the expense of women. Gay men are the better women, represented as better equipped to undo identity. When the rectum is a grave, the vagina is evidently a dead end.

THE PHALLIC WOMAN

The gay man in drag in Bersani's essay is sometimes misogynist and sometimes a victim of misogyny, a self-swelling phallic sadist and a shattered and castrated masochist. Too often, feminists have been unable to see that the penis is not the phallus – perhaps not surprisingly, given that patriarchal culture promotes such a misrecognition. Though no one has the phallus and the omniscience, omnipotence, and wholeness that it signifies, in patriarchy woman often figures as the mirror in which man sees himself whole, through the regressive defense mechanisms of projection, sadism, voyeurism, and fetishism. For many feminists the gay man in drag is just another misogynistic representation of woman. Radical lesbian feminist Marilyn Frye argues that gay camp effeminacy 'is a casual and cynical mockery of women, for whom femininity is the trappings of oppression, but it is also a kind of play, a toying with that which is taboo. It is a naughtiness indulged in ... more by those who believe in their immunity to contamination than by those with any doubts or fears' (137). Judith Williamson writes that men in drag undermine 'female characteristics' and satirize women (47–54), while Erika Munk argues that female impersonators are like whites in blackface, 'hostile and patronizing' (89), and Alison Lurie asserts that 'men who wear women's clothes, unless they are genuine transsexuals, seem to imitate the most vulgar and unattractive sort of female dress, as if in a spirit of deliberate and hostile parody' (258). They believe drag is a defense against femininity and the lack it signifies. The femininity of the female impersonation is a put-on, not the real thing, signalling he has what women lack: the phallus.

Psychoanalysis offers the same explanation of most cross-dressing, which is labeled transvestic fetishism.[6] The transvestite feminizes himself only in order to 'masculinize' or phallicize himself through the erection the cross-dressing causes. Masquerading as the phallic woman, he is able to have (the illusion of having) the phallus. 'I was in Toronto once, and the only female impersonator they had was a woman', the star of a drag act in *Outrageous!* jokes, which is why so many feminists have found drag outrageous, though no laughing matter. By insisting on their difference from 'real girls' ('r.g.'s', in transvestic slang) impersonators can defend themselves against the castration the latter are made to signify. Like other men in a patriarchal symbolic, the female impersonator may feel whole at woman's expense, misrecognizing her difference as lack and fetishistically disavowing even that.

Andrew Ross has argued that camp is radical because it defetishizes the erotic scenario of woman-as-spectacle (1988, rpt. 1989: 159). But as Freud points out, the fetishist both worships and castrates the fetish object, romanticizing and reviling it for its differences – differences the fetishist himself makes meaningful or invents, like the 'shine on the nose' one of Freud's patients could see in certain women even when others could not ('Fetishism', 219, 214). The details that mark an impersonation as such function fetishistically, signs of the ambiguous difference between phallic women and r.g.'s. Drag routines generally reveal the body beneath the clothes, which is made to serve as the ground of identity.[7] Joking in double entendres, dropping the voice, removing the wig and falsies, exposing the penis all work to resecure masculine identity by effecting a slide along a chain of signifiers which are in a metaphoric and metonymic relationship with one another and with the transcendental signifier, the phallus.

The pleasure of transvestism is like the pleasure of the Western, in which we see men mutilated, castrated, and restored, rendered whole again.[8] It is exhibitionistic as well as voyeuristic, and may invite identification with rather than disidentifcation from the hero/victim. Powerful female characters like *Dynasty*'s Alexis Carrington Colby Dexter, serve as a conduit for a gay look, according to Mark Finch (1986). Such phallic women solicit not only a transvestic gaze but a transvestic identification, as they are both the subjects and the objects of the gaze and phallic mastery, as transvestite pornography makes clear. Lola, 'tall, dark and hung', and Pasha, 'the Polynesian Bombshell', are consistently described and imaged as phallic women in *Drag Queens* (4:3, 1986: 2). Lola has 'the right equipment for either sex ... [she] loves to play it both ways, and she knows she's got what it takes to make it work', the magazine claims and verifies that with photos drawing attention to Lola's breasts and erect nipples and to her partially erect penis (40). Both shots and writing emphasize fetishism: 'Lola loves to show it all off. The slow striptease is her favorite. Wearing lace, nylons, and high heeled shoes, she hides her meaty truth. At the right moment, she unveils her cock. The shock is erotic and irresistible. Lola is unique!' (7). Phallic narcissism is suggested by the many photos of Lola masturbating and by captions which describe her as 'the seducer of herself, a woman capable of turning herself in to [sic] a rigid and throbbing man!' (7). The text makes clear the queen's penis is king, continually reinscribing patriarchal gender hierarchies, describing Lola's feminine 'half' as 'turning on the man below', 'desir[ing] to please', 'giv[ing] way to the long thick cock', etc. (7, 23, 11). And although Lola is never shown having sex with anyone, she is frequently represented masturbating to pornography in which another black man in drag is seen anally penetrating a white man. If Lola is a woman, she is one with a very special difference; after all, 'she can take her man where no woman has taken him before' (32). Represented as active, masterful, and complete, Lola is obviously the phallic woman.

Pink Flamingos (1972) also plays with the power of the queen. In one sequence, the voyeuristic pleasure of Raymond in a beautiful woman is suddenly disrupted when she lifts her skirt to reveal her penis. The spectator, aligned by the camera with Raymond, can only laugh by disidentifying from him; otherwise, s/he is the butt of the joke too. The transvestite's gesture in this sequence is almost literally a punch-line, as the look at a shocked and visibly displeased Raymond in the reverse shot reveals. The laughter of the viewer is a defensive response to the castration anxiety suddenly evoked and evaded by making what is literally a transvestic identification with the phallic woman. Such scenes point to the presence of a desire Freud never discusses when he elaborates on the negative oedipus: the boy's active, sadistic, and masculine wish to penetrate the father, rather than his passive, masochistic, and feminine wish to be penetrated by him, a desire that undermines the father's alignment with the phallus.

I am not suggesting that spectators are always encouraged to identify with the man in drag, only that such an identification is possible and may not subvert phallic identities. Of course, it is far more common for distancing effects to be maintained by representing the transvestite as mastered and lacking object, rather than potent subject, of the gaze, which suggests that Marilyn Frye's critique of what she calls the 'phallophilia' of gay men and drag is neither fair nor accurate (128–51). For example, *The Queens*, a 'photographic essay' by George Alpert, tells a story of pathos and horror. It incorporates many photos of older comic and ugly 'dames', whose failure of femininity is suggested by contrast with the young 'glam' queens included, who are usually not photographed in extreme close-up or in unflattering lights or poses, and are sometimes even seen in romantic soft focus, like women. But they are also often photographed against or behind doors and windows, sometimes barred, or in corners, suggesting they are tragically trapped by their 'perverse' inclinations. The opening and closing series in particular convey this effect. The first ends with a close-up of 'Baby' looking pensive; on his cheek glistens what appears to be a tear, though it could just be a drop of water left after washing off make-up. The final picture of the last sequence is of 'the twins' sadly trying to peer out over the sill or through the frame of what could be a window which partially obstructs their faces. The photo suggests the pain of being caught in 'their' world, barred definitively from 'ours'. This book does not confuse the queen's penis with the phallus. It envisions the female impersonator as symbolically castrated, tragically – even horribly – lacking, a point of view which is not necessarily (or only) heterosexist, since it is also available to homosexuals.

MASOCHISM

When *Torch Song*'s 'Virginia Ham' (Arnold/Harvey Fierstein) drops her voice to tell her gay audience, 'You can't become a dame until you've knelt before a queen', she constitutes herself as a phallic woman, invested with an erotic power denied by Bersani and others. Though spectators might identify with her, her punning address to us invites us to pay her homage in an act that both feminizes and ennobles. The spectacle of queen makes a lady of her supplicant; she is the phallic woman who offers the ambiguous pleasures of masochism. As D.N. Rodowick has pointed out, Mulvey's almost biologizing insistence on aligning the cinematic gaze with masculinity and an active and controlling voyeurism and fetishism blinds her to the possibility of a passive component of vision, one in which fetishism coincides with masochism rather than sadism. Interested in theorizing a feminine pleasure in films Mulvey seems to rule out, Rodowick considers Freud's essay on the beating fantasy to extend to film its notion of multiple enunciations for a single utterance. He does not discuss what we can infer, that the gaze directed toward the heroine at those moments when she is most fetishized could be masochistic rather than sadistic. Nor does Rodowick discuss whether the masochistic spectator might fetishize the male hero he argues can be viewed as an erotic object by women and men (though Rodowick does not elaborate a homoerotic gaze, his theory, unlike Mulvey's, implicitly includes it). Bound by the Freudian logic he used to question Mulvey, he does not theorize the significance of difference other than gender for the gaze, desire, and subjectivity, differences which may well come into play in fetishism.

Some recent feminist work shares Rodowick's conviction that the phalli can solicit a masochistic, rather than sadistic, gaze. Griselda Pollock argues that one of Dante Gabriel Rossetti's paintings of women, *Astarte Syriaca* (1877), transcends the 'repetitious obsessive fetishization' of most of his art in order to represent 'a figure before which the masculine viewer can comfortably stand subjected . . . a fantasy image of the imaginary, maternal plenitude and phallic mother' (Pollock, 153). Berkeley Kaite arrives at a similar conclusion about pornographic images, asserting that the look at the fetishized woman who looks back – whether that woman's investment with the phallus is 'literal' (the transvestite or 'tv') or vestiary (the r.g.) – provides the pleasure of the surrender to the penetrating 'cut', the moment when the subject is severed from the phallic M/Other and accedes to difference and a fantasy of self-possession (Kaite, 158).[9] And in a series of essays devoted to the topic of masochism itself, Kaja Silverman explores at length the eroticization of lack and subordination for men. She notes that the conscious heterosexuality of the male masochists Freud discusses in 'A Child Is Being Beaten' 'constitutes a "feminine" yet heterosexual male subject', one whose identification with the phallus is disrupted by installing the mother in the dominant place. (Freud himself subordinates that fantasy to the unconsious and homosexual desire to be beaten by the father) ('Masochism and Male Subjectivity', 36).[10] Like Kaite and Pollock, she privileges the relation to the phallic M/Other who 'precedes' the symbolic, which subordinates her and the child to the father. She does so to make the radical claim that the male masochist 'cannot be reconciled to the symbolic order or to his social identity' because his sexuality is 'devoid of any possible productivity or use value' ('Masochism', 58).

Whereas Silverman's emphasis is on the male masochist, just a few years earlier Jane Gallop and others had focused on the subversive force of the phallic woman or mother who undoes the logic of ideological solidarity between phallus, father, power, and man.[11] Yet when Freud discusses the phallic woman, for example in the 'Wolf Man' case or the essay on the taboo on virginity in 'primitive cultures', he suggests she is phallic on the same terms as the man, having acquired a penis or what stands for it, perhaps from a man with whom she has had intercourse ('Infantile Neurosis', 256, 258; 'Taboo of Virginity', 76–8). It is therefore revealing that Sade's archetypal phallic woman, the eponymous heroine of *Juliette*, explains her desire as a reactive copy of masculine desire: 'My lubricity, always modeled after men's whims, never is lit except by fire of their passion; I am only really inflamed by their desires, and the only sensual pleasure I know is that of satisfying all their deviations'.[12] When the active, desiring woman still reflects man's desire, the mirrors of the patriarchal imaginary are not shattered.

The fantasy of the phallic mother is the topic of a great deal of feminist writing on mother-daughter relations.[13] This work has focused on the difficulty of difference for the daughter, who cannot quite distinguish herself from her mother in a symbolic which requires that confusion. Woman is theorized as unable to represent lack for herself because she must represent it for men by becoming, through identification, their lost object of desire. She cannot enter the symbolic, too close to the mother whom she is unable to give up or give up being, because for her, having nothing to lose, castration poses no 'real' threat. The daughter's response to this lack of a lack and difference is paranoia, a defense associated with psychosis and foreclosure of symbolic castration. The mother is phallic because she is invested with the power to free her little girl, to divest herself of her phallus-child.

This paranoid fantasy about the phallic mother is a cornerstone of object-relations theory, for which the boy's accession to masculinity is a problem, rather than the girl's to femininity, as in the Freudian/Lacanian paradigm. Object-relations theorists assume masculinity and femininity are there from the start, rather than produced through the resolution of the castration complex and the separation from the mother. They suppose a boy is destined for masculinity even though he begins in a 'feminine' dependence on and identification with the mother. She is presumed phallic in that she is blamed for men's 'gender identity disorders', like transsexualism, which according to well-known expert Dr. Robert Stoller results from too much mother and too little father. The phallic mother will not let boys be boys.

This phallic mother is at once castrating and castrated. When the fantasy is paranoid and the lack of difference figured as fearful, it cannot be progressive for women; it contributes to the repudiation of femininity patriarchy already engenders and realigns women with the maternal as a role they can never adequately perform. However, when the fantasy is also fascinating and pleasurable, it maintains the subject on the edge of subjection and self-(dis)possession. Berkeley Kaite argues that transvestism does just that, providing the pleasure of self-dispossession as castration and the death of desire through the death of the subject, who lacks a lack in or difference from the phallic M/Other. Yet Kaite critiques Francette Pacteau for associating androgyny with just such a death of desire, which follows from Pacteau's assertion that androgyny represents the narcissistic desire for wholeness in the phallic M/Other, beyond the lack that motivates desire and so beyond difference itself, including sexual difference. According to Kaite, the tv or androgyne expresses a desire for repression rather than a repression (or, more properly, foreclosure) of desire (164). Kaite wants to retain for transvestism and fetishism the radicality of a refusal of the symbolic and its hierarchies of difference and without giving up the recognition of castration, difference, and lack accession to the symbolic is supposed to generate. Kaite's beliefs about fetishism are as contradictory as the fetishist's about the mother's phallus: fetishistic disavowal will (not) make him/her whole. The fetishist at once knows and refuses to acknowledge his lack or castration, his self-difference. The perversion has a defensive function, even if it also has a subversive impulse. In this, fetishism is like what Julia Kristeva has called abjection, which can re-fashion 'his majesty the ego' by storming the fortress in which he reigns, described by Lacan as the 'orthopaedic ... armour of an alienating identity' (Lacan, *Ecrits*, 4–5). But the emperor's new clothes threaten to expose him utterly, leaving him defenseless against the phallic M/Other, prey to the psychotic failure of subjectivity itself. For Kristeva, the loss of the subject abjection threatens is not without its liabilities, even if a rigidly defensive ego is also a liability.

Gendering feminine such a tantalizing/terrifying loss reveals the defensive nature of masculinity itself. Silverman says that the beating fantasy Freud discusses, and masochistic fantasies in general, attest to the need to be boys to be girls, so that even the female 'feminine masochist' has a masculinity complex, albeit one in which she makes an identification with the homoerotic man, wishing to be passive and masochistic rather than active and sadistic. Castration or divestiture, Silverman argues, 'can only be realized at the site of male subjectivity because it is there that the paternal legacy is stored' ('Masochism', 62). The woman has nothing to lose; it is the male subject's self-fetishizing phallic imposture which provides him with the signifiers of lack: the penis and all that signals the power and privilege accruing to man in a patriarchal culture. Man appears to have the phallus by exhibiting what signifies having the phallus, that which is metaphorically or metonymically linked to it. One such substitute is the woman herself, the fetishized M/Other, who 'masquerades' as the phallus so that man can 'parade' his phallus, the woman whose lack he needs to feel complete. In the Lacanian paradigm, man, like woman, only comes into being when 'photo-graphed', fixed by the look of the phallic M/Other, who reflects for him an image of wholeness with which he jubilantly identifies (*Four Fundamental Concepts of Psychoanalysis*, 104). Both man and woman literally appear to be subjects. Their relations revolve around having or being the phallus for one another, which is never more than *appearing* to have or be the phallus for the other who can be duped by the performance ('The Meaning of the Phallus', 83–5).

However, man's fetishistic misrecognition of the organ upon which his identity hangs is legislated by the patriarchal symbolic, so that it seems to be the real thing. The subject who desires to take up the position of being the phallus for the phallic M/Other, the hole in her whole, must be castrated, feminized. This leads to the curious conclusion that only men can become real women (in fact, Moustapha Safouan asserts just that about transsexuals, and it is implicit in Bersani's and Silverman's work on masochism). Masochists – and even theorists of masochism – have been duped by the penis-fetish when they fail to distinguish between it and the phallus, even if such a misrecognition apparently does not serve man's phallic narcissism. Masochistic fantasies may include 'scenes' in which the male genitals, the symbol of man's identification with the father as bearer of the phallus, are beaten or cut off, but this does not preclude the belief that the phallic mother is phallic because she has castrated the father and retained his penis.

In a classic essay on transvestism which ties it to masochism, Otto Fenichel notes that the little boy can desire to have the mother's baby just as a little girl might desire to have the father's baby (214–15). Freud emphasizes that the wish for a child points to an unconscious equation made between the penis and the baby. The daughter's desire to be a mother, expressed in playing with dolls, is motivated by penis envy (*Introductory Lectures*, 113). The same might be said of the expectant son, who anticipates the gift of the phallus in sexual relations, even masochistic relations, because they are are all structured around phallic exchange. If a world with such sexual relations would be an inversion of those current in Western patriarchy, the meaning of the phallus and its 'privileged' signifiers would nevertheless remain unanalyzed.

DRAGGING THE DIFFERENCES

Luce Irigaray reads the little girl's interest in dolls differently, seeing in it not an expression of penis envy but a desire for a 'feminine' mastery of the mother/child relationship by playing with an image of the self (*Speculum*, 73–80). Playing with dolls is a variant of what Irigaray calls 'mimicry', in which the woman masters 'her' image, the fetishistic masquerade, putting it on so as to signify it is a put on and can easily be taken off (*This Sex*, 76). Irigaray suggests mimicry signifies a distance between woman and her image which is necessary for knowledge and hinges on disidentification and difference. Woman cannot know 'woman' if she is too close to her image to see it with a critical eye. Transvestism also may express such mimicry, in which the son plays with his image like a doll, dressing it up to signal his distance – and difference – from lack. If femininity, like masculinity, can be a defense, a phallic imposture, a literal castration, as in transsexualism, it may not effect a symbolic castration. The fact that men can assume femininity (and castration) in order to disidentify from it (as lack) has distressed feminists who have discussed drag. Yet the possibility of assuming it to disidentify from it has excited feminists who theorize a *female* female impersonation or mimicry. The mimic can know 'woman' because she does not have to be her and does not have to make a transvestic identification with man in order to have some perspective on her image. Mimicry provides an alternative to adopting a masculine point of view, without necessitating a naive idealist or essentialist belief in the ability to access a 'genuine' femininity beyond patriarchy.

Paradoxically, feminists praise in female female impersonation or mimicry what they condemn in female impersonation or drag: its distancing effects. This contradiction is symptomatic, but not necessarily of homophobia. Rather, it points to the significance of differences other than those of gender or sexual orientation, which have to be 'dragged' into drag and its theories. Though feminist theorists of mimicry and lesbian and gay theorists of drag generally do not comment on the work of the other camp, both privilege the tactic of assuming an identity as a false identity. For both any identity is 'assumed' or false and alienated, unreal, fictional – what Lacan terms 'masquerade' or 'parade'. There is no authentic, 'real' self beyond or before the process of its social construction, so our identitites must be subverted from within.

As Judith Butler explains, drag promotes

> a subversive laughter in the pastiche-effect of parodic practices in which the original, the authentic, and the real are themselves constituted as effects. The loss of gender norms would have the effect of proliferating gender configurations, destabilizing substantive identity and depriving the naturalizing narratives of compulsory heterosexuality of their central protagonists: 'man' and 'woman'. (1990a: 146–47)

Sue-Ellen Case suggests that butch-femme lesbians camp up the fiction of castration, ironizing it, while Jack Babuscio, Richard Dyer, Jeffrey Escoffier, Andrew Ross, and Vito Russo all discuss drag as a parodic or ironic exaggeration or hyperbolization of gender.[14] These are the very terms and phrases which feminist theorists use when they write about mimicry. To be a mimic, according to Irigaray, is to 'assume the feminine role deliberately ... so as to make 'visible', by an effect of playful repetition, what was supposed to remain invisible ...' (*This Sex*, 76). To play the feminine is to 'speak' it ironically, to italicize it, in Nancy Miller's words, to hyperbolize it, in Mary Ann Doane's words, or to parody it, as Mary Russo and Linda Kauffman describe it.[15] The mimic and the drag queen 'camp up' ideology in order to undo it, producing knowledge about it, that gender and the heterosexual orientation presumed to anchor it are unnatural and even oppressive.

For theorists of drag and mimicry, irony and parody set them off from the masquerade or parade of those who play gender straight. But if all identities are alienated and fictional, what makes one credible and the other incredible, an obvious fake? The answer, it seems, is the author's intention: parody is legible in the drama of gender performance if someone meant to script it, intending it to be there. Any potential confusion of the two is eliminated by a focus in the theories on production rather than reception or perception. Sometimes, however, one is ironic without having intended it, and sometimes, despite one's best intentions, no one gets the joke. When, as Lacan points out, the 'real thing' is already a comedy what passes for passing for or impersonating a gender must be analyzed ('Meaning of the Phallus', 84).

In theories of camp, butch-femme drag is visible as such because of an essential 'gay sensibility', invoked to keep straight the difference between gay and heterosexual gender impersonation. Some theorists, like Babuscio (1977: 41) and Russo (1976: 208), explicitly refer to it as the ground of camp, explaining that 'passing' sensitizes gays and lesbians to both the oppressiveness and artificiality of gender roles. But as Andrew Britton suggests, such gay essentialism is problematic because it is obvious that the experience of homophobic oppression does not necessarily lead to an understanding of it (1978: 12). Gayatri Spivak has made a similar point about oppression in general, arguing that theorists like Michel Foucault are too ready to credit the oppressed with the power to know and articulate their oppression directly when the very fact of oppression can make that impossible, since consciousness itself may be dominated and, indeed, constituted by hegemonic ideology ('Can the Subaltern Speak?', 273–6).

Other theorists of drag only implicitly invoke a 'gay sensibility', which manifests itself in the difficulty they have demonstrating the difference between butch-femme and inversion, on the one hand, and butch-femme and straight gender roles, on the other. It is a difficulty apparent in Freudian theory too, which cannot explain the desire of the femme for the butch lesbian or, conversely, of the butch gay man for the queen – they are too gay to be straight inversions.[16] Camp theory has difficulty with the same two roles, which are too straight to be gay parodies or drag. Butler, Babuscio, and Oscar Montero suggest that butches and queens mark their impersonations as such through the use of incongruous contrasts, signs of a double gender identity, and through parodic excess (for example, Ross says the queen dresses 'over the top').[17] 'Excess' is what prevents drag from being mere inversion or a heterosexual role when there are no incongruous contrasts and confused gender signs, as with lesbian femmes and butch gay men. When Butler discusses the play of difference and desire in lesbian camp she argues that the butch does not assimilate lesbianism into heterosexuality as inversion because being a woman recontextualizes masculinity through the confusion of gender signs. She says it is exactly this confusion the femme finds desirable: 'she likes her boys to be girls' (1990a: 123). Butler discusses the butch as the subject of gender play but the object of desire, which enables the lesbian to be consistently associated with transvestic subversion. The femme's being a woman does not obviously recontextualize femininity, nor does it sound particularly radical to suggest the butch likes her girls to be girls. Yet just a few lines later Butler insists the femme displaces the heterosexual scene as if she embodied the same shifting of sexed body as ground and gender identity as figure that the butch does. Similarly, when Case (1988, rpt. 1989: 294) writes that the femme 'aims her desirability' at the butch, she inscribes as active a potentially passive fem-ininity so that it can appear as distinct from femininity.[18]

What ultimately makes the femme different from the r.g. for both theorists is that she plays her role for another woman, which they claim makes it excessive and incongruous by 'recontextualizing' or 'reinterpreting' it (an argument that provides an additional safeguard against butch roles as mere inversion by asserting the legibility of the butch's womanliness despite the confusion of gender signs). This is an essentialist tautology: butch-femme or drag is gender play because it is gay; it is gay because it is gender play. An implicit 'gay sensibility' determines in advance what counts as gender play, keeping straight the difference between enlightened drag and unenlightened masquerade or parade. It is not surprising that the tautology fails, as Lisa Duggan reveals in an article tellingly titled, 'The Anguished Cry of an 80s Fem: 'I Want to be a Drag Queen': 'When lesbians sponsor strip shows, or other fem erotic performances, it is very difficult to "code" it as lesbian, to make it feel queer. The result looks just like a heterosexual performance, and lesbian audiences don't respond to it as subversively sexual, specifically ours' (64). In fact, the photo of two women in corsets illustrating this article is by Annie Sprinkle, who has appeared in similar tv pornography which has a straight audience. The picture or fantasy has two different enunciations, one that is heterosexual and masculine, and one that is lesbian.[19] Teresa de Lauretis underlines this dilemma when she writes that the femme cannot appear in most contexts '[u]nless ... she enter [sic] the frame of vision *as* [sic] *or with* a lesbian in male drag' (1988: 177). Clearly only something like a gay sensibility would enable one to recognize a femme in butch drag.

Perhaps the most troubling consequence of such essentialism is its paradoxical reinforcement of the idea that the 'authentic' or 'natural' self is heterosexual, even as it inverts the hierarchy by proclaiming the 'fake' or artificial gay self to be the 'better', smarter – more smartly dressed – self, which deconstructs itself by knowing its difference from itself and the gender role it only assumes like a costume. This erects the gay self as the upright self, properly non-identical by comparison with the straight self which also, therefore, lacks gay *jouissance*. Such uses of *jouissance* make it 'stiffen into a strong, muscular image', according to Jane Gallop; it becomes phallic, a sign of 'an ego-gratifying identity' in which 'fear or unworthiness is projected outward ...' ('Beyond the *Jouissance* Principle', 114). Gays and lesbians are no more free from castration anxiety than anyone else, as this defensive maneuvre suggests. Like straight men – and women – they can disavow castration through projection and fetishism, including the self-fetishism of phallic imposture which may not be inconsistent with camp. For when roles are already alienated and unreal, the problem is maybe not how one holds them at a distance but how one responds to that distance. In transvestic drag, it is fetishized: the impersonator assumes a phallic identity through an apparent identification that is, in fact, a disidentification, signified by the incongruous contrasts and ironic excess s/he sees – and those who share that point of view see – in that gender act, which constitute it as camp.

It is also fetishized in mimicry, as I have argued in 'The Feminine Look'. Theories of mimicry reinscribe white, middle-class femininity as the real thing, the (quint)essence of femininity. This is implicit in the feminist critiques of drag I have discussed, which define its style as sign of a hostile burlesque through contrasting it with that of a 'natural' femininity, whose understated good taste is a sign of the genuine article. If boys will be girls they had better be ladies. A real woman is a real lady; otherwise, she is a female impersonator, whose 'unnaturally bad' taste – like that of working-class women or women of color – marks the impersonation as such. The mimic flaunts or camps up lack by fetishistically projecting it on to some 'other' woman, from whom she distances herself through a disidentification that takes the form of an apparent identification, as with the impersonator.

Feminist theorists of mimicry distinguish themselves from 'other' women even as they assimilate the latter by romanticizing them, assuming the 'other' has a critical knowledge about femininity because of her difference from what counts as natural femininity: white, Anglo, bourgeois style. It is only from a middle-class point of view that Dolly Parton looks like a female impersonator; from a Southern working-class point of view she could be the epitome of genuine womanliness. Something similar can be said of Divine in *Polyester* (1981), whose polyester marks his impersonation as such for those who find it in unnaturally bad taste, since Divine never gives any (other) indication he is 'really' a man.[20] Mimicry is distinguished from masquerade on the basis of differences between women which white, middle-class feminists fetishistically disavow whenever they talk of 'the' feminine, as if it were only one thing.

Some women can 'have' the phallus in our culture because it is not just the penis but all the other signs of power and privilege, which stand in a metaphoric and metonymic relation not only to 'penis' but also to 'white' and 'bourgeois', the signs of a 'proper' racial and class identity. Relations between members of different races and classes, like those between genders, can be structured by the imaginary and characterized by fetishism, in which the signs of difference signify phallic lack or wholeness. The symbolic is more than a masculine imaginary; it is also a white and bourgeois imaginary, which explains the potentially oppressive effects of mimicry and drag when they constitute the other as what must be repudiated (the inverse complement, a symptom of lack and ignorance) or what can make one whole (the supplement, the phallic M/Other who guarantees full self-presence and knowledge). Feminists have shown that talk of a 'common humanity' is only a masculinist ruse disguising oppression. The utopic vision of a common femininity and of women free from the effects of symbolic castration and the unconscious it produces, the source of the desires and fears that motivate us, has been made possible by an indifference to the significance of differences other than gender. The same can be said of relations between gays, which may not be characterized by the perfect reciprocity and equality that Harold Beaver, Craig Owens, and other gay theorists imagine they are.[21]

Homosexuality, like femininity, is marked by the effects of castration anxiety. Gay men, like women (including lesbians), are in the symbolic as much as heterosexual men are by virtue of a phallic imposture which they can use to defend themselves from the psychosis with which both homosexuality and femininity have been associated in psychoanalysis since Freud's analysis of Schreber (in 'Psycho-Analytic Notes'). As Eve Sedgwick points out, gay theorists must acknowledge the significance of differences within the gay community, differences which can be activated defensively and oppressively in gay relationships and identities, including camp (54–5). Race and class fetishism can operate in homosexual as well as heterosexual eros, since forms of otherness between men or women can have a phallic significance which all too often has been overlooked. Sunil Gupta, Kobena Mercer, Isaac Julien, and Thomas Yingling, among others, have written about the potential for the replication of racism in gay relationships through fantasies about the black or Asian man's sex, while Jane Gallop has described a lesbian relationship in which the working-class woman functioned as the phallus for her middle-class lover just as women in general function as the phallus for men.[22] If they are at stake in fetishistic masochism, race and class differences can give the fantasy a symbolic productivity or use value even when the subject subverts phallic gender norms.

The fantasy Homi Bhabha locates at the heart of racism, the 'primal scene' he claims to derive from Frantz Fanon, centers on a fascinating and fearful interracial rape that could be a permutation of the fetishistic/masochistic beating fantasy analyzed by Freud. In the scene, a little white girl 'fixes Fanon in look and word' as she turns from him to identify with her mother, saying, 'Look, a negro … Mamma, *see* the Negro! I'm frightened. Frightened'. Fanon describes the experience as 'an amputation, an excision'. Its violence is that of a castration, as in the retrospective understanding of the sexual primal scene. In each, subjects take up one of two, antithetical positions. One has or lacks color; one has or lacks the penis. However, in the racial primal scene's confluence with the sexual primal scene, the other is figured as frighteningly different not because he lacks but because he has the organ, though one which is monstrous.

While Bhabha genders the subject of this drama, Fanon himself does not explicitly mark the sex of the child who speaks of being afraid of him (though later he implicitly does by discussing as the white man's fantasy the fear that 'his' women are 'at the mercy of the Negroes').[23] The fantasy, therefore, could have a white masculine as well as a feminine enunciation, just as the beating fantasy has two gendered enunciations. Freud's exploration of the effects of the primal scene in his analysis of the 'Wolf Man' implies just this possibility because in it differences besides gender figure importantly. What the Wolf Man is afraid of is the big, bad dick, symbolized by the well-endowed dream wolves with their over-grown tails ('Infantile Neurosis', 213, 216). The Wolf Man wants to be loved like a woman by his father, but he is afraid it means he will be castrated (221, 228). He also wants to be a gentleman like his father and, therefore, different from the maids and male estate workers he might imagine are castrated (because they too seem to have a passive, feminine attitude toward his father). Paradoxically, his very identification with his father also means he will be castrated, since he believes his mother retains his father's penis after intercourse (210, 278–9). This fetishistic circuit of pleasure, displeasure, identification, and disidentification is condensed in the image of the wolves, who represent both the father and the Wolf Man as at once phallic (their tails are big) and castrated (their tails are too big, obvious fakes or prostheses disguising their lack).

At stake in the Wolf Man's castration anxiety fantasies are not only his gender but also his class identity. Peter Stallybrass and Allon White make this clear when they discuss his predilection for 'debased' women like Grusha, his nursery maid, as typical for the bourgeois man of his time:

> The opposition of working-class maid and upper-class male ... depended upon a physical and social separation which was constitutive of desire. But it was a desire which was traversed by contradictions. On the one hand, the 'lowness' of the maid reinforced antithetically the status of the gentlemen ... But on the other hand ... she was a figure of comfort and power. (156)

These women represent what has to be repudiated by the middle-class child as s/he grows up: improper dress, manners, speech, and hygiene, all the signs of someone with no class. At the same time, they threaten the bourgeois subject with the return of the lack he has lost, which accounts for their fearful fascination.

Though Stallybrass and White discuss this as abjection, Homi Bhabha terms the similar psychic mechanism at work in the racial primal scene and stereotyping 'fetishism' (159). Fetishism also seems to characterize the gay bourgeois 'sexual colonialism' Jeffrey Weeks documents, in which 'working class' equals 'masculine' equals 'closeness to nature' – for better or worse, as with the racial 'primitive other' (121–2). Such fetishism helps reproduce race and class differences, as well as gender differences, in all their ambivalence.

The fetishistic gaze at the 'other' may be masochistic, and not just sadistic; Fanon's primal scene offers both enunciations. Race and class differences regularly figure in masochistic fantasies. Joan Rivière discusses a case that seems to anticipate Fanon, in which a (Southern) white woman fantasizes being attacked by a black man from whom she defends herself by having him make love to her so she can – eventually – turn him over to justice (a scenario remarkably like that in the many popular film versions of *King Kong*) (212). Silverman describes one in which a man imagines himself a Portuguese prisoner of the Aztecs who is eventually skinned alive, another in which a middle-class woman is beaten by 'rough' and 'ignorant' working class women, and yet another in which she is beaten and loved as a male 'savage' by a domineering Robinson Crusoe figure ('Masochism', 55, 60–1). Transvestite pornography often includes stories, sketches, and photos of both men and women who serve a dominatrix as a slave or maid does a mistress.[24] Even the Kinks' domineering queen Lola has 'a dark brown voice', a synethesia suggesting she is black.

What is remarkable about these fantasies is their subjects' fluid shifting not only of gender but also of racial and class identities in ways which simultaneously subvert and sustain phallic identifications complexly articulated through differences in gender, race, and class. It is not always necessary for the masochist (whether male or female) to fantasize being a man in order to be beaten and loved 'like a woman' and thereby symbolically castrated. There are a number of ways to be divested of the phallus in our symbolic which do not center on the penis as the mark of power and privilege. Phallic divestiture by one means can even be congruent with phallic investiture by another, functioning defensively so as to distinguish the subject from the phallic Other (mother or father) whose (mis)recognition s/he solicits and shares in order to be a subject at all.

Furthermore, the fantasy of the 'other' as phallic Other is not necessarily radical, since s/he may be phallic in exactly those terms a sexist, racist, and classist symbolic legitimates, and the fantasizing subject may identify with that position of omnipotence and omniscience, rather than imagine s/he is excluded from it, as occurs in theories of camp and mimicry. Finally, even when the subject does feel excluded from that place, and his/her fetishism is an anxious response to a sense of lack, the object/other still remains only a phallic fantasy. S/he does not exist as such: s/he does not exist for the subject (who wants to be whole through him/her), and s/he is not what s/he seems to be for the subject (since s/he has desires the subject cannot know). Theorists of camp and mimicry have not concerned themselves with the subjectivity of their 'others' except as it seems to guarantee their own status as phallic Others who know what they are about. The irony in mimicry and camp is all too often at the other's expense, a defense against castration anxiety. Thus, while it is perfectly possible to imagine a white male transvestic and camp identification with the heroine in *King Kong*, for example, it would not be particularly progressive for black men, made once again the bearers of the big, bad dick that has figured so prominently in the history of race relations structured by fantasies of miscegenation and all too real lynchings.

CONCLUSION

Camp (like mimicry) functions complexly by dragging in many differences at once that are all too easily articulated with phallic narcissism in a symbolic which functions as a white, bourgeois, and masculine fetishistic imaginary. This narcissism needs to be analyzed, its phallic impostures unveiled as such. Gay theorists – like feminist theorists – must recognize their positioning in a number of discourses besides those of gender and sexuality and accept difference, including self-difference and lack. While camp may not always facilitate such recognition and acceptance, it is not essentially at odds with it. Indeed, though Zora Neale Hurston's Janie Mae Crawford says, 'You got tuh *go* there *tuh* know there' (183), Gayatri Spivak points out that 'knowledge is made possible and is sustained by irreducible difference, not identity' (*In Other Worlds*, 254). The play of identification and disidentification in drag could be the very condition of autocritique.

I would argue that it does make possible self-criticism for one very fragile moment in *City of Night*, when the first-person narrator, a hustler, briefly accepts his castration by identifying with the beautiful queen Kathy, whom he understands to be castrated, paradoxically, because she has (rather than lacks) a penis; it is what prevents her from being a whole (and phallic) woman. His self-knowledge (which promotes our self-knowledge, since we have been asked to identify with him) is revealed in his response to a scene he witnesses in New Orleans during Carnival, when Kathy directs one of the heterosexual male tourists who has come on to her to grope her crotch:

> The man's hand explores eagerly. Kathy smiles fiercely. The man pulled his hand away violently, stumbling back in astonishment. Kathy follows him with the fading eyes. Now Jocko [a hustler friend] smiles too.
>
> I turn away quickly from the sign. I feel gigantically sad for Kathy, for the dropped mask – sad for Jocko – for myself – sad for the man who kissed Kathy and discovered he was kissing a man.
>
> Sad for whole rotten spectacle of the world wearing cold, cold masks.

'Minutes later', the narrator says, 'my own mask began to crumble'. He tells two scores he is not what they think he is, 'tough', 'the opposite from them' (Rechy, 254). In effect, he acknowledges his virile 'parade' is a masquerade, a charade of having something valuable to give (the penis as phallus) to those others who can afford to pay for it, who can 'afford' to be castrated for him, as the Wolf Man could not for this father. He understands that like Kathy he is only a man and not what he must seem to be in the comedy of sexual relations. At that moment, he recognizes sex could be something other than an exchange of the phallus, though he is not quite sure how. But as the rest of the novel reveals, he resumes hustling and refuses the painful knowledge of castration that nevertheless returns to haunt him as the feeling that heaven is unfairly barred to some. The 'solution' to anxiety about fetishistic phallic imposture proves to be more fetishism, not surprising, since the symbolic itself legislates the repudiation of lack. Disrupted by camp, the camp moment does not last; misrecognition follows upon recognition, and incredible acts, unfortunately, begin to seem credible once more.

NOTES

1. See also Marshall, 150–1; Escoffier 1985: 133–42; Mager, 32–6; and Case 1988, rpt. 1989: 284–6.
2. See also Blachford (1981: 200), who argues that gay macho 'may be an attempt to show that masculine or "ordinary" men can be homosexual too ...'.
3. Sometimes, the interviewees in *Men in Frocks* are defensive about their masculinity, as I indicated above; sometimes, they are defensive about their femininity and discuss the denigration of queens in the gay community – see, for example, Terri Frances, 110, and Rebel Rebel, 120 (in Kirk & Heath 1984).
4. The transvestic slang, 'r.g.', ('real girl') is useful for suggesting that even the 'real thing' needs to be written in quotation marks, since she is only a product of certain gender codes which privilege the body as essential ground of gender identity, codes which the transvestite contests – but also uses, if the impersonation is fetishistic, involving an apparent identification with femininity which is, in fact, a disidentification, through

the appeal to the body beneath the clothes as sign of the truth of gender. I discuss this double strategy later in the essay. See Butler (1990a) for a deconstructive critique of the ontology of the body.

5. See my 'The Feminine Look' and 'The Supreme Sacrifice?'

6. The classic psychoanalytic essay on transvestism is Fenichel's 'The Psychology of Fetishism'. Also relevant are Freud, 'Fetishism', and Lacan & Granoff, 265–76. See also Silverman, *Acoustic Mirror*, 1–42, and my 'Feminine Look', 201–10.

7. Annette Kuhn suggests that films with cross-dressers offer the promise of a multiplicity of gender relations but tend to renege on it ultimately by exposing the body beneath the clothes as the 'truth' of gender (56–7).

8. Neale, 8–10.

9. I have used the term 'phallic M/Other' because the place of phallic omnipotence and omniscience can be filled by the fantasy of the phallic mother or the primitive father, since neither is imagined to be subject to castration. I will suggest later in the essay that the phallic Other may appear to have the phallus by virtue of his/her class or racial difference as well as because of his/her gender, since such differences signify lack or having with respect to the power and privileges which accrue to the phallic subject. Women are not the only ones who do not exist except as a phallic fantasy in the symbolic.

10. See especially this essay for the subversiveness of masochism, but see also her 'White Skin, Brown Masks'.

11. For discussions of the literature on de Sade, see Gallop, *Intersections*, and Carter.

12. Quoted in Gallop, *Intersections*, 57.

13. Two excellent, representative essays are in Doane, *The Desire to Desire*, 123–54, and in Gallop, *Daughter's Seduction*, 113–30.

14. Case 1988, rpt. 1989: 287, 291–2; Babuscio 1977: 41, 44, 47–9; Dyer 1981: 60–1; Escoffier 1985: 140–1; Ross 1988, rpt. 1989: 162; Russo 1979: 205.

15. Miller, 38; Doane, 'Film and the Masquerade', 82; Russo, 217, 224; Kauffman, 294–5, 298.

16. Once again, I want to stress that is a problem for theory, and not necessarily for real people.

17. Butler 1990a: 123; Babuscio 1977: 41; Montero, 40–1; Ross 1988, rpt. 1989: 162.

18. At p. 291 she claims that playing the gender roles between women recontextualizes them and 'foregrounds' them as myths.

19. See 'A Touch of Class in the Hourglass', which features Annie Sprinkle (and other women) in corsets (Sprinkle first appears solo on page 22).

20. Both Case and Ross note that class differences may be a factor in camp, but neither elaborates on the observation or makes it as central to camp as I am suggesting it is. See Case 1988, rpt. 1989: 286, and Ross 1988, rpt. 1989: 146.

21. Beaver 1981: 113–14; Owens, 228; see also my discussion above about the implication for egalitarianism of a subjectivity free from castration anxiety, as Owens (and, he maintains, Derrida) assume homosexuality to be (219). With regard to the question of the radicality of camp, Bersani (1987: 207) points out that a distinction must be made between its effects on the gay couple, who may not have subversive intentions, and its effects on heterosexuals. While I believe any politics of consciousness is suspect – as I hope to demonstrate here, the effects, not the intentions, of camp are what count – Bersani's statement does at least suggest the importance of context. Britton (1978: 12) also notes the importance of context when he says that subversion is not intrinsic to a phenomenon but to its context, its reception.

22. Gallop, 'Annie Leclerc'. I discuss Gallop's essay in 'The Feminine Look', 207–8.

23. Fanon, 157. The child's fear of the black man is described on 112.

24. For example, see *Reflections*.

REFERENCES

'A Touch of Class in the Hourglass', *Reflections* 9:1 (1986), 21–29.

Bhabha, Homi, 'The Other Question: Difference, Discrimination, and the Discourse of Colonialism', in Francis Barker et al. (eds.), *Literature, Politics, and Theory: Papers from the Essex Conference, 1976–1984*, London: Methuen, 1986, 148–72.

Carter, Angela, *The Sadeian Woman and the Ideology of Pornography*, New York: Harper Colophon, 1988.

Doane, Mary Ann, *The Desire to Desire: The Woman's Film of the 1940s*, Bloomington-Indianapolis: Indiana UP, 1987.

——, 'Film and the Masquerade: Theorising the Female Spectator', *Screen* 23:3–4, 1982.

Dyer, Richard, 'Don't Look Now', *Screen* 23:3–4, 1982, 61–73.

Duggan, Lisa, 'The Anguished Cry of an 80s Fem: "I want to be a drag queen"', *Out/Look* 1:1, 1988.

Fanon, Frantz, *Black Skin, White Masks*, New York: Grove, 1967.

Fenichel, Otto, 'The Psychology of Transvestism', Hendrik M. Ruitenbeek (ed.), *Psychoanalysis and Male Sexuality* (1930); New Haven: College and University Press, 1966, 203–10.

Flitterman-Lewis, Sandy, 'Thighs and Whiskers: The Fascination of "Magnum PI"', *Screen* 26:2, 1985, 42–58.

Freud, Sigmund, 'Fetishism', in *Sexuality and the Psychology of Love*, New York: Collier, 1963, 214–19.

——, 'From the History of an Infantile Neurosis' (1918), in *Three Case Histories*, trans. James Strachey; New York: Collier, 1963.

——, *Leonardo Da Vinci* (1916), trans. A. A. Brill, New York: Vintage, 1944.

——, *New Introductory Lectures on Psychoanalysis* (1933), trans. James Strachey, New York: W. W. Norton, 1965.

——, 'Psycho-Analytic Notes on an Autobiographical Account of a Case of Paranoia' (1911), in *Three Case Histories*, trans. James Strachey; New York: Collier, 1963, 1–82.

——, 'The Taboo of Virginity', in *Sexuality and the Psychology of Love*, New York: Collier, 1963, 76–78.

——, *Three Essays on the Theory of Sexuality* (1905), trans. James Strachey, New York: Basic, 1975.

Frye, Marilyn, *The Politics of Reality: Essays in Feminist Theory*, Trumansburg: Crossing Press, 1983.

Gallop, Jane, 'Annie Leclerc Writing a Letter with Vermeer', in Nancy Miller (ed.), *The Poetics of Gender*, New York: Columbia UP, 1986, 137–56.

——, 'Beyond the *Jouissance* Principle', *Representations* 7, 1984.

——, *Intersections: A Reading of Sade with Bataille, Blanchot and Klossowski*, Lincoln: U of Nebraska P, 1980.

——, *The Daughter's Seduction: Feminism and Psychoanalysis*, Ithaca: Cornell UP, 1982.

Gupta, Sunil, 'Black, *Brown*, and White', in Simon Shepherd & Mick Wallis (eds.), *Coming on Strong: Gay Politics and Culture*, London: Unwin Hyman, 1989, 163–79.

Hurston, Zora Neale, *Their Eyes Were Watching God* (1937), New York: Harper & Row, 1990.

Irigaray, Luce, *Speculum: of the Other Woman*, trans. Gillian Gill, Ithaca: Cornell UP, 1985.

——, *This Sex Which Is Not One*, trans. Catherine Porter, Ithaca: Cornell UP, 1985.

Kaite, Berkeley, 'Transgression is the Law', in Arthur & Marilouise Kroker (ed.), *Body Invaders: Panic Sex in America*, New York: St. Martin's, 1987.

Kauffman, Linda, *Discourses of Desire: Gender, Genre, and Epistolary Fictions*, Ithaca: Cornell UP, 1986.

King, Dave, 'Gender Confusion: Psychological and Psychiatric Conceptions of Transvestism and Transsexualism', in Kenneth Plummer (ed.), *The Making of the Modern Homosexual*, Totowa: Barnes & Noble, 1981, 155–83.

The Kinks, 'Lola', *Part One: Powerman, Lola Versus and the Moneygoround*, Burbank: Warner Bros. Records, R56423, 1970.

Kristeva, Julia, *The Powers of Horror: An Essay on Abjection*, trans. Leon Roudiez, New York: Columbia UP, 1982.

Kuhn, Annette, *The Power of the Image: Essays on Representation and Sexuality*, New York-London: Routledge & Kegan Paul, 1985.

Lacan, Jacques, *Ecrits: A Selection* (1949), trans. Alan Sheridan, New York: Norton, 1977.

——, *The Four Fundamental Concepts of Psychoanalysis*, trans. Alan Sheridan, ed. Jacques-Alain Miller, New York: Norton, 1978.

——, 'The Meaning of the Phallus', in Jacqueline Rose & Juliet Mitchell (ed.), *Feminine Sexuality*, trans. Jacqueline Rose, New York: Norton, 1982.

Lacan, Jacques & Wladimir Granoff, 'Fetishism: The Symbolic, the Imaginary and the Real', in Sandor Lorand (ed.), *Perversion*, New York: Gramercy, 1956, 265–76.

Lurie, Alison, *The Language of Clothes*, New York: Random House, 1983.

Mager, Don, 'Gay Theories of Gender Role Deviance', *Sub-Stance* 46, 1985.

Marshall, John, 'Pansies, Perverts and Macho Men: Changing Conceptions of Male Homosexuality', in Kenneth Plummer (ed.), *The Making of the Modern Homosexual*, Totowa: Barnes & Noble, 1981.

Mercer, Kobena & Isaac Julien, 'True Confessions', *Ten.8* 22 (no date), 4–9.

Miller, Nancy, 'Emphasis Added: Plots and Plausibilities in Women's Fiction', *PMLA* 96, 1981.

Montero, Oscar, 'Lipstick Vogue: The Politics of Drag', *Radical America* 22:1, 1988, 40–1.

Mulvey, Laura, 'Visual Pleasure and Narrative Cinema', in Constance Penley (ed.), *Feminism and Film Theory*, New York-London: Routledge, 1988, 57–68.

Munk, Erika, 'Drag: 1. Men', *Village Voice*, 5 February, 1985.

Neale, Steve, 'Masculinity as Spectacle: Reflections on Men and Mainstream Cinema', *Screen* 24:6, 1983, 2–16.

Owens, Craig, 'Outlaws: Gay Men in Feminism', in A. Jardine & P. Smith (ed.), *Men in Feminism*, London: Methuen, 1987.

Pollock, Griselda, *Vision and Difference: Femininity, Feminism, and the Histories of Art*, London-New York: Routledge, 1988.

Rechy, John, *City of Night*, New York: Grove, 1963.

Rivière, Joan, 'Womanliness as a Masquerade' (1929), in Hendrick M. Ruitenbeek (ed.), *Psychoanalysis and Female Sexuality*, New Haven: College and University Press, 1966, 209–20.

Rodowick, D. N., 'The Difficulty of Difference', *Wide Angle* 5, 1982, 7–9.

Russo, Mary, 'Female Grotesques: Carnival and Theory', in Teresa de Lauretis (ed.), *Feminist Studies/Critical Studies*, Bloomington-Indianapolis: Indiana UP, 1986.

Safouan, Moustapha, 'Contribution à la psychanalyse du transsexualisme', *Scilicet* 4, 1983, pp.150–52.

Sedgwick, Eve Kosofsky, 'Across Gender, Across Sexuality: Willa Cather and Others', *South Atlantic Quarterly* 88:1, 1989: 53–61.

Selby, Hubert Jr., *Last Exit to Brooklyn* (1957), New York: Grove, 1986.

Silverman, Kaja, *The Acoustic Mirror: the Female Voice in Psychoanalysis and Cinema*, Bloomington: Indiana UP, 1988.

——, 'Masochism and Male Subjectivity', *Camera Obscura* 17, 1988.

——, 'White Skin, Brown Masks: The Double Mimesis, or With Lawrence in Arabia', *differences* 1:3, 1989, 30–37.

Spivak, Gayatri, 'Can the Subaltern Speak?' in Cary Nelson & Lawrence Greenberg (eds.), *Marxism and the Interpretation of Culture*, Urbana: U of Illinois P, 1988.
——, *In Other Worlds: Essays in Cultural Poetics*, New York-London: Methuen, 1987.
Stallybrass, Peter & Allon White, *The Politics and Poetics of Transgression*, Ithaca: Cornell UP, 1986.
Stoller, Robert, *Presentations of Gender*, New Haven: Yale UP, 1985.
Tyler, Carole-Anne, 'The Feminine Look', in Martin Kreiswirth & Mark Cheetham (ed.), *Theory Between the Disciplines: Authority/Vision/Politics*, Ann Arbor: U of Michigan P, 1990, 191–212.
——, 'The Supreme Sacrifice?' TV, "TV", and the Renée Richards Story', *differences* 1:3, 1989.
Weeks, Jeffrey, 'Inverts, Perverts, and Mary-Annes: Male Prostitution and the Regulation of Homosexuality in England in the Nineteenth and Early Twentieth Centuries', *Journal of Homosexuality* 6:1–2, 1980–81.
Williamson, Judith, *Consuming Passions: The Dynamics of Popular Culture*, London: Marion Boyars, 1986.
Yingling, Thomas, 'How the Eye is Caste: Robert Mapplethorpe and the Limits of Controversy', *Discourse* 12:2, 1990, 3–28.

24

MAE WEST'S MAIDS:
RACE, 'AUTHENTICITY', AND
THE DISCOURSE OF CAMP

Pamela Robertson

In recent years, subcultural studies have merged increasingly with academic identity politics. But while much work has been done on queer and camp representation and also on racial stereotypes, subcultural studies have unwittingly advanced artificial barriers between audiences and between subcultures such that we often tend to talk about only one audience, one subculture at a time, and only in relation to the in-that-instance Other, dominant culture (one gender/race/ethnicity/class, one category, one difference at a time). Most analyses of camp do not, therefore, remark upon the relation between camp's sexual politics and race discourse. Moe Meyer (1994b: 5–7), for instance, discusses the controversy over African American drag queen Joan Jett Blakk's 1991 bid for mayor of Chicago as Queer Nation candidate as exclusively a debate in gay politics about the effectiveness of camp, without once mentioning Blakk's race as potentially affecting the debate or mentioning what the politics of running an African American drag queen are for a Queer Nation.

Alternately, in discussions of *Paris is Burning* – a film which foregrounds the links between queerness, camp, and racial discourse – critics tend to treat the African American and Hispanic use of camp to gain access to fantasies of whiteness as a special case, without fully acknowledging the degree to which the film's invocation of 'realness' testifies to how inextricably race and sex are intertwined, and without considering whether or how race discourse operates in camp generally. An important exception is bell hooks' essay 'Is Paris Burning?'.

Included in Henry Jenkins, Jane Shattuc, Tara McPherson (eds.), *Hop on Pop: The Pleasures and Politics of Cultural Studies*, Durham-London: Duke University Press, forthcoming.

hooks views the film as a graphic documentary of the way in which colonized black people (in this case black gay brothers, some of whom were drag queens) worship at the throne of whiteness, even when such worship demands that we live in perpetual self-hate, steal, lie, go hungry, and even die in pursuit (149).

hooks claims, however, that, rather than interrogating whiteness, the entertainment value of the film obscures its 'more serious critical narrative', a narrative of the pain and sadness behind the camp spectacles. For hooks, the white filmmaker and white audience both evade the race politics of *Paris is Burning* in their focus on and pleasure in the film's camp effect. But, by mapping the relationship between the film's race politics and its camp effect onto a narrative vs. spectacle paradigm, hooks similarly masks the link between race and camp in the film. She suggests that the film is really about race and not camp. She, therefore, maintains the barrier between race discourse and camp discourse by viewing camp spectacle as being in the service of white pleasure and at a remove from 'the more serious narrative' about blackness.

Most discussions of camp, whether about gay men, lesbians, or heterosexuals, assume the adjective 'white'. Because whiteness, as Richard Dyer says, 'secures its dominance by seeming not to be anything in particular' (141), representations of normative whiteness foreground race and ethnicity as categories of difference. Queer and camp Western representations though non-normative in terms of sex and gender, are still consistently defined through categories of racial difference and especially blackness.

This racial specificity becomes clear in the frequent analogies made between camp and blackness. Dennis Altman, for instance, says, 'Camp is to gay what soul is to black' (1971: 141). Describing post-Stonewall attitudes toward camp, Andrew Ross refers to camp falling into disrepute 'as a kind of blackface' (1988, rpt. 1989: 143), and George Melly dubs camp 'the Stepin Fetchit of the leather bars, the Auntie Tom of the denim discos' (1984: 5). We could ask why Uncle Tom and blackface haven't been recuperated as camp clearly has (by queer identity politics and in academic discourse). If this question seems problematic, and it should, it points out how thin these analogies are, and it also points to the fact that the flexibility of sex and gender roles promised by theories of camp performativity does not yet extend to race. In part these analogies suggest, as David Bergman says, the fact that camp raises the issues of any minority culture – issues having to do with appropriation, representation, and difference (1993b: 10). But the consistency of the category 'black' as the counterpart to camp (as opposed to other racial or ethnic categories) not only signals the degree to which camp is assumed to be white but also mirrors the way tropes of blackness operate in much white camp as an authenticating discourse that enables the performance of sex and gender roles.

This essay focuses on Mae West and how she enlists racial difference in the service of queer performativity. Elsewhere, I have argued that West created a form of feminist camp through her dual appropriations of the live entertainment traditions of female impersonation and female burlesque. My interest in that earlier essay was in locating the role women have played as producers and consumers of camp, 'to de-essentialize the link between gay men and camp, which reifies both camp and gay male taste; and to underline camp's potential for asserting the overlapping interests of gay men and women, lesbian and straight' (1993: 57). Like other theorists of camp, I ignored the racial specificity of West's queer and feminist performativity. Emphasizing how West forged a feminist camp character from gay male and heterosexual female traditions, I dodged the question of how West's simultaneous appropriation of African American music and her characters' interactions with African American performers complicated or delimited the flexible and porous model of queer identity I saw in West's films. Yet, neither aberrant nor exceptional, West's use of blackness as an authenticating discourse is a trope that runs through white camp in general and needs to be taken into account to fully understand camp.

This essay, then, attempts to correct or complement my previous analysis of West. Hopefully, however, this essay can do more than fill a gap in my analysis and will instead provide a point of entry into a discussion of the seemingly contradictory reliance in camp and queer discourse on tropes of racial authenticity and will enable us to rethink camp as a discourse that is exclusively about sex and gender to consider how codes of sex and gender intersect with racial codes. Using West as an example and a point of departure, then, this essay examines the racial dimension of camp, by considering 1) how tropes of blackness are used in camp performance; 2) the degree to which the camp spectator is textually constructed as white; and 3) how a consideration of an African American spectatorial position modifies our understanding of camp practice.

LITTLE EVA

In his piece on West, John Kobal mentions that West's earliest theatrical experiences were as Little Eva in *Uncle Tom's Cabin* and as a 'coon shouter'. Kobal mistakenly identifies 'coon shouter' as an old vaudeville term for African American singers who perform for white audiences not in blackface or whiteface, but 'as themselves'. In fact, the term 'coon shouter' or 'coon singer' was used to describe white, often Jewish, performers, like Fanny Brice, Sophie Tucker, Eddie Cantor, and Al Jolsen, who sang, not only in Negro dialect, but also in blackface (Sochen, 45).[1] Eliding the links between 'coon shouting' and blackface, as well as the links to Jewish entertainment traditions, and aligning it instead with African American performers, Kobal describes the 'Mae West character' as 'the first white woman with a black soul'. And he wistfully posits the unfounded assertion that West has 'a touch of colour in her blood' (154). Thus, in Kobal's narrative, West is identified simultaneously with the white child Harriet Beecher Stowe says is representative of her race, with black singers, and with blackness itself. If we take into account the more accurate definition of 'coon shouting', Kobal's narrative also links West with blackface. If camp is, as Melly says, an 'Auntie Tom', it may be appropriate to think of

West as camp's Little Eva, Tom's dearest friend; but, more importantly, I want to use Kobal's odd narrative to suggest that the Mae West character is not just a white woman with a black soul, but manages to be both representative of her race and of camp style because she identifies so closely with blackness and especially black music.

Kobal's account differs from most accounts of West's early career which tend to focus on her early role as Little Lord Fauntleroy and suggest that she dropped her imitation of black styles when she adopted the style of female impersonation and white female burlesque. However, as much as West aligned herself with gay male culture both by borrowing aspects of gay style and by writing anti-homophobic plays about gay life, she also aligned herself with African American culture. In addition to her potential cross-sex, cross-gender identification as a female female impersonator, West also participates in complicated cross-racial identifications with blackness which are key to her transgressive image.

As Kobal suggests, West appropriated black musical styles and she also adopted the shimmy after seeing it in a Harlem nightspot. In addition, she wrote a novel, *The Constant Sinner*, about an interracial love affair. According to Clarence Muse, West gave him money for an anti-lynching campaign. West frequently featured African American performers in her films, including Louis Armstrong, Hazel Scott, and Duke Ellington, whose band she forced Paramount to sign for *Belle of the Nineties*. And West garnered extremely positive receptions in the African American press. One article in *The Chicago Defender*, for instance, applauds her for being more attentive to the African American journalists than Hazel Scott, who is accused of being 'high hat' with them (see LaMae).

But, although West affiliated herself with black performers, and, to a degree, race issues, the roles of African Americans in her films are still quite limited. The musical performers in her films do not figure in the plot and are typical of African American specialty acts in Hollywood films. The African Americans who do figure prominently in her films play maids and include Gertrude Howard, Louise Beavers, Hattie McDaniel and Libby Taylor, who played the role both on and off screen for West. Their representations are stereotypical. As Donald Bogle describes them: 'The domestics were always overweight, middle-aged, and made up as jolly aunt jemimas ... they had the usual names: Pearl, Beulah, and Jasmine. Their naive blackness generally was used as a contrast to Mae West's sophisticated whiteness' (60). West employs racist language with her maids, calling them Eightball and Shadow, for instance, or accusing them of being slow and lazy, but the maids are also pictured as confidantes and trusted good friends, in a manner similar to movies like Jean Harlow's *Bombshell*, *Imitation of Life*, Shirley Temple movies, and others in the 30s, a decade Bogle tags 'the Age of the Negro Servant'.

Bogle claims that because West's barely concealed status as a prostitute places her at the bottom of the social scale, she enjoys a livelier camaraderie with her black maids than with white women. Bogle is correct that West's friendly interactions with her maids can be read as a class affiliation but the camaraderie West enjoys with her black maids differs not only from her interactions with upper class white women(who are often failed rivals) but also from her interactions with other subordinate women, with whom she also shares her low social status.

In her films, West's interactions with other female characters are mediated by both class and race. As James Snead suggests, 'insofar as all of West's films are about consolidating women's power in spite of a limited social context' (68), she achieves a greater rapport with lower class women of all races than with upper class women. West's character frequently functions as counsellor to subordinate women, like the fallen white Sally in *She Done Him Wrong* whom she counsels on men ('Men's all alike ... it's their game. I happen to be smart enough to play it their way') and whose shame she ameliorates with the worldly wisdom that 'When women go wrong, men go right after 'em'. Similarly, in *Belle of the Nineties*, when her African American maid, Libby (Taylor), asks 'What kind of husband do you think I should get?', West advises her, 'Why don't you take a single man, and leave the husbands alone?' In *Klondike Annie*, West helps her Chinese maid, Fah Wong, played by Soo Yong, escape to her lover, and even speaks Chinese with her. In West's interactions with Fah Wong, however, there is none of the joking and play West enjoys with her black maids. This is true also of her interactions with her French maid in *The Heat's On* and Native American servants in *Goin' to Town*. In contrast to these relationships, West's connection with her African American maids signals not only a class affiliation but also West's identification with, and privileging of, tropes of blackness.

One scene in *I'm No Angel* shows West bantering and singing 'I Found a New Way to Go to Town' with four maids. The five women discuss West's character Tira's whirlwind romance with Kirk Lawrence, the gifts he's given her, Tira's sexual attractiveness to men, and the kind of men the maids like. The maids serve, as Bogle says, as 'foils', straight men and yes men, 'paying homage to the supreme power of their white mistress'. The scene thematizes the class affiliation Bogle describes. From her position as a cooch dancer in the circus who imitates the Harlem shimmy, as West herself did, Tira, 'the girl who discovered you don't have to have feet to be a dancer', has risen to become a lion tamer in a high class high-hat circus. In her new penthouse apartment, she first mistakenly assumes that the doorbell signals a house detective, then must be reminded by her maid Beulah to call Kirk's gift of diamonds a 'necklace' rather than 'beads'.

Still, barking orders to the four maids as she talks with them (famously, 'Beulah, peel me a grape'), West is clearly the boss and center of attention. The maids frame her and set off her whiteness as well as the whiteness of the room. West's glowing whiteness is carefully constructed here and throughout her career. In a TV documentary about West (*Mae West and The Men Who Knew Her*, dir. Gene Feldman, 1993), Herbert Kenwith claims that white women in

West's stage shows were required to have dark hair, to wear darker make-up and clothes than West, and even to put a grey gel on their teeth, so that West's whiteness would make her stand out as the star and center of attention.

West's conversation with her black maids, however, masks racial difference by focusing on gender. West talks about men, sex, and clothing, and treats Libby Taylor's comment that she likes 'dark men' not as a given, but much like her own quip that she likes two kind of men, 'domestic and foreign'. Snead describes a similar moment later in the film:

> So when West looks over her shoulder and says, referring to Cary Grant, 'My man's got rhythm', and the giggling black maids say 'Yes'm, I knows what you mean', West commits a certain breech of racial taboos in order to share both the terminology and presumably the content of sexual secrets of white and black male 'rhythm'. (69)

West thus simultaneously foregrounds her racial difference from the maids and her gendered identification with them in what Stuart Hall describes as a double move of 'othering' and identification typical of racist discourse – a complex play of repulsion and attraction combining racial insult with racial envy, and marked by the 'surreptitious return of desire' (28–9). In his analysis of the racial politics of blackface, Eric Lott describes this 'complex dialectic' as 'a pattern at times amounting to no more than two faces of our particular mode of racism, at others gesturing toward a specific kind of political or sexual danger; and all of it comprising a peculiarly American structure of racial feeling'.[2] *I'm No Angel*, like other camp uses of blackness, relies on this double move of othering and identification to position a porous and mobile queer identity.

QUEEN B

West's homosocial bonding with her maids might be readable as homosexual, if we consider Linda Nochlin's point that in painting 'the conjunction of black and white, or dark and light female bodies, whether naked or in the guise of mistress or maidservant traditionally signified lesbianism' (49). This potential homosexuality is raised obliquely when one of the maids (whose face we never see and who isn't identified in the credits) says, 'Well, men don't mean a thing to me'. The homosexual connotations feed off the contrast between the women, but also depends on the way the scene portrays the maids as West's back-up singers. McDaniel and Taylor not only sing along to 'I Found a New Way to Go to Town' with West, but also dance across the room following West's lead.

In his analysis of the mythology of the back-up singer, John Corbett claims that, while the role of the back-up singer has historically been filled by male and female performers of all races and ethnicities, the unspoken adjectives that precede the mythologized stereotype of the 'back-up singer' are always 'black' and 'female' and that the unspoken adjectives preceding 'lead singer' in stereotypical configurations of 'lead' and 'back-up' are 'white male'. Kaja Silverman argues that West's voice is coded masculine, an assertion in line with those who

see West's persona as masculine (61). West's presumed masculinity is, however, mediated by her imitation of female impersonators and is a self-conscious
feminine masquerade that plays masculine and feminine codes off each other.
And, similarly, her whiteness is mediated through and constituted by her
imitation of black female musical styles.

Ramona Curry, in line with Kobal, notes that as a stage performer, West
adopted a style of singing characteristic of 'dirty blues', similar to that of Ma
Rainey and Bessie Smith, and maintained this style in a somewhat modified,
censored, form in her films. West's performance of 'dirty blues', according to
Curry, associates West in the public mind with 'the unbound sexual behavior
that the dominant US society frequently attributes to lower class African
Americans' (1995: 220). Once established, West's association with working
class black female sexuality carries over, regardless of what she sings.

In appropriating a black female blues style, West takes on the persona of
what Hazel Carby refers to as the 'mythologized' blues singer, and 'an oral and
musical woman's culture that explicitly addresses the contradictions of feminism, sexuality, and power'. Carby describes women's blues of the 1920s and
30s as 'a discourse that articulates a cultural and political struggle over sexual
relations':

> a struggle that is directed against the objectification of female sexuality
> within a patriarchal order but which also tries to reclaim women's bodies
> as the sexual and sensuous subjects of women's song. (231)

West's performance of blues inflected songs across her films, then, not only
aligns her with black female working class sexuality, but also enables her to
address her position as a sexual subject and object in much the same way that
the direct sexuality of female burlesque does.

Not coincidentally, as Carby points out, the figure of the black female blues
singer whose style West appropriates was historically transplanted into the
figure of the black maid, as many female blues singers, including Hattie
McDaniel and Ethel Waters, moved from making race records into film careers
and maid roles. Rather than a white male lead, West, coded as simultaneously a
female impersonator and a black woman, backed-up and fawned over by the
maids, plays the Queen B or Bulldagger, a figure SDiane Bogus claims is
common in and peculiar to African American lesbian fiction and culture, a
'female blues singer who bonds with other women', 'a central figure in the
community at large' whose sway over her followers relates both to her singing
and her unorthodox sexuality.

Crucially, the Queen B requires an adoring audience. And in West's films,
her sexuality is typically not just theatricalized but performed for an audience
whose attention, approval and admiration she explicitly seeks when she says,
'Here goes my big moment' and 'How'm I doin?'. In *I'm No Angel*, West's
encounter with Cary Grant requires the presence of her maids who 1) stand in
for the film audience, 2) underscore West's sexuality as a form of masquerade,

and 3) offer an alternative site for West's desire as she diverts our attention, and Grant's, to the maids, whom she proclaims to be 'great gals'.

I am not suggesting that the Mae West character be read as a closet lesbian. Rather, I would emphasize that West's lively homosociality with her maids, in conjunction with her affinity for African American music and her association with female impersonation, marks her sexuality as particularly fluid and deeply transgressive, and not merely ironic. As Snead claims, 'If some white actresses derive their aura of purity and chasteness by their opposition to the dark and earthly maids who surround them, then West's image benefits by her kinship with, rather than her difference from, the same kinds of figures' (69). While West masks racial difference through a seemingly race-neutral gendered discourse, she simultaneously reinscribes racial difference using the maids' presence to support her camp performance and authenticate her racial impersonation.

West's sexual and racial identifications are fluid (she is white and black, male and female, gay and straight), but the maids necessarily remain static markers (black and female) of her transcendence (they set off her whiteness and potential masculinity, authenticate her blackness, foreground her sexuality). West uses camp to theatricalize sex and gender roles to point up their constructedness, yet she depends on her maids' identities being stable to do so, underlining Hortense Spillers' suggestion that there are at least two female genders, one white and one black. Because the racial difference ultimately remains in place, the viewer is reminded that although West is like a black woman, she is not one. Her transracial mobility merely reaffirms her whiteness. This whiteness, constituted through its appropriation of and difference from blackness, is neither a color nor the absence of color, both impervious to racial markers and able to absorb them.

THE REAL WEST

At the same time, West's identification with blackness sometimes goes against the grain of camp, to suggest the possibility of West having an 'authentic' self beneath or behind the discourses of camp and masquerade. As trusted good friends, the maids are pictured as knowing the real West better than anybody else. West, in effect, lets her hair down with them, and tells them her true feelings. In *I'm No Angel*, West's Tira never tells Cary Grant that she loves him. Instead, he finds out from Gertrude Howard's Beulah, who testifies in a breach of promise suit that Tira said 'she never knew she could love a man like she loves him'. West also uses the connotations of authenticity attached to African American music to portray her true feelings.

When West performs African American styles of music, she updates the burlesque tradition of minstrelsy. Performing blackness, but without blackface, West, in John Szwed's terms, 'marks the detachment of culture from race and the almost full absorption of a black tradition into white culture' (27). Almost. Because what's crucial is that the black tradition still be marked as 'other'. While commodifying African American community life and culture, minstrelization requires that the commodity still signifies blackness to the consumer. In West's films, this is signified and authenticated by the presence of African American performers.

As is common in the musical, the numbers West performs are often keyed to her characters' moods and situations. In *Belle of the Nineties*, for instance, she plays a woman, Ruby Carter, who moves from St. Louis to New Orleans to forget an old lover. She sings 'Memphis Blues' and 'My Old Flame' with the Duke Ellington band. More striking, and unusual for West, is her rendition of 'Troubled Waters' in the same film. This number is the only time West sings a song without a diegetic audience in her films. Prior to the number, Ruby explains to her maid Jasmine (Libby Taylor) why she has an unfair reputation as a bad woman: 'You know, people get reputations from people talking about people when they don't even know the people'. Giving Jasmine the rest of the night off to attend a prayer meeting, Ruby gives her money for the collection and tells her to pray for her. Then, after Jasmine leaves, Ruby is drawn to the balcony to listen to the revivalists at the prayer meeting sing 'Pray Chill-en and You'll Be Saved'.

Karl Struss films the revivalist meeting in an expressionistic style reminiscent of Vidor's *Hallelujah* (1929). After a verse of 'Pray Chill-en', the scene cuts back to West who sings a verse of 'Troubled Waters'. The lyrics of 'Troubled Waters' repeat the sentiments West expresses to her maid before she sings:

> They say that I'm one of those devil's daughters.
> They look at me with scorn. I'll never hear that horn.
> I'll be underneath the water judgement morn-ing.
> Oh Lord, am I to blame? Must I bow my head in shame?
> If people go round scandalising my name?

Rather than simply present West singing 'Troubled Waters' to reflect her state of mind, this scene links her song with the revival meeting through intercutting and dissolves. Jon Tuska describes the scene:

> The beat of the spiritual is merged with hers in a fused counterpoint. By means of complex process shots, double exposures, and superimposed images, Karl Struss pictorially integrates for McCarey the sequences of Ruby's song with the Negro chant. As it becomes increasingly wild, there are sudden closeups on faces, feverish dancing, the torchlit scene back-lighted from reflections from the river. Struss brings off a split-screen effect with the revellers, one half their dancing, one half the reflection of their dancing. Ruby's image is superimposed over this. Her song rises and blends with the jazz spiritual, only to drown it out on the soundtrack, hitting a single pitch as the camera pans a succession of grotesque faces. (93)

At the very end, one male revivalist in closeup drowns out the two songs with his chant of 'My soul's on fire, my soul's on fire'.

While the song is private and reflects Ruby's interiority, it depends on the external presence of the black revivalists. Her song is called forth by and functions as a call and response with the revivalists' song. This marks West as authentic in a double sense. First, the revival meeting serves as a back-up for West, who is visually and sonically inserted into the meeting, as her song fuses with the 'jazz spiritual'. This lends her song the presumed authenticity and spirituality of African American religion and music, despite the fact that the song 'Troubled Waters', though explicitly coded as an African American spiritual, was written for West by the Hollywood songwriting team of Johnston and Coslow. Second, the intercutting suggests that the expressionistic out of control reactions (souls on fire) are reactions to her. It sets up a contrast between her individual controlled whiteness and the familiar stereotype of the frenzied emotions and spirituality of the African Americans, and thus sets West's character off as an individual, a white angel, authentic in the sense of belonging to oneself.

IMAGINING THE AUDIENCE

West's affiliation with African American culture serves in part to underscore her identification with the marginal and her status as a transgressive woman within mainstream representations of sexuality. It also serves to authenticate her identity – an identity that is particularly porous, fluid, and mobile, but nonetheless whole. As I have suggested, within camp representation (and, of course, in other arenas as well), her use of blackness as an authenticating discourse is quite typical. As critics' frequent analogies between blackness and camp indicate, tropes of authenticity and 'realness' operate both within camp discourse and within academic identity politics. Representations of queer white subjectivity are constituted, in large part, by their constant coupling with, and contrast to, images and sounds of blackness.

Lott views the double move of othering and identification in blackface minstrelsy as a 'peculiarly American structure of racial feeling' but the use of blackness as an authenticating discourse has become part of a transnational camp aesthetic. To cite a few brief examples, Madonna, clearly, foregrounds her affinity with African American culture as much as gay male culture. Consider her video for 'Like a Prayer', where images of black religion authenticate her passion, or 'Vogue' where she sings 'It doesn't matter if you're black or white, a boy or a girl', all the while obscuring vogueing's racial and homosexual specificity. In a different vein, Joan Crawford's status as a grotesque is reaffirmed by her performance in blackface in *Torch Song*. Similarly, as Patricia Juliana Smith (1993) argues, Dusty Springfield's camp masquerade transforms her into simultaneously a black woman and a femme gay man; and Ronald Firbank's novels, according to William Lane Clark (1993), tie their camp effect to representations of transracial desire and the employment of black jazz tropes in much the same manner as Fassbinder does in *The Bitter Tears of Petra Von Kant, Ali: Fear Eats the Soul*, and other films. Elsewhere, I have described how the Australian film *The Adventures of Priscilla, Queen of the Desert* privileges its scenes with Aboriginal people – in stark contrast to its scenes with the Filipino bride or butch white woman – employing a transnational camp discourse reliant on Black Atlantic imagery and stereotypes (see Robertson).

Often, in these examples, by no means meant to be exhaustive, an appreciative black diegetic audience is inscribed in the text as both spectator and back-up for the white performers. I've described how this audience supports West and stands in for the film audience in its appreciation of West's camp masquerade in *I'm No Angel*. Similarly, in *The Adventures of Priscilla, Queen of the Desert*, Aboriginal people not only perform African American blues for (and, in the case of one man, lipsynch with) the white men, but also form the most enthusiastically appreciative audience for the white drag act. They thus authenticate the group's act and their gayness which, in turn, lends the aura of cool to the Aboriginal people, an aura denied to various groups of white rednecks elsewhere in the film. The African American gospel singers in Madonna's 'Like a Prayer' video perform a similar function, backing up and seeming to respond to Madonna's performed identification with blackness while also authenticating her passion through their contribution to the song.

Although, in a certain sense, these black diegetic audiences stand in for the film audience, the use of blackness as an authenticating discourse in white camp seems to be textually addressed primarily to a white film audience. Rather than provide points of identification for the audience, these supportive audiences primarily function to produce a spectacle of spectatorship that situates the white performer within a black context and authenticates the white performer's performance as not only imitative of but also appreciated by a black audience. But what difference would it make to our conception of camp to imagine the external audience for these various texts as black instead of white?

To begin to address this question, my discussion will take a short detour through *Without You I'm Nothing*, the 1990 film version of Sandra Bernhard's 1988 one-woman off-Broadway stage show. The film operates on the premise that Bernhard has gotten away from her 'roots' and that she has returned with her show to Los Angeles to perform in a mostly black nightclub. Rather than an authenticating back-up and appreciative audience for Bernhard's camp appropriations of blackness, the film represents the mostly black audience as singularly bored by Bernhard's performance. By placing the show in a black nightclub, the film, for Jean Walton, shifts the 'emphasis from issues of gender and sexuality to issues of race' (1994: 248). But, as I have suggested, camp is always already about race, and the film *Without You I'm Nothing* exposes this, using the black audience's unenthusiastic reaction to create feelings of discomfort in the film viewer by relaying our view of Bernhard through that of the diegetic black audience.

In various segments of the film, Bernhard performs a minstrelization of blackness without blackface. In her first number, for instance, she imitates and appropriates the music of Nina Simone. Wearing an African costume, she sings 'Four Women', the first line of which is 'my skin is black'. She also parodies Diana Ross, Dionne Warwick, and Prince as well as various unspecified images of blackness (a 'pretty' lesbian nightclub singer who sings 'Me and Mrs. Jones', a 'funked up' version of white Patti Smith). The film viewer, seeing these appropriations in the context of the black nightclub, feels embarrassed and uncomfortable and cannot respond with camp pleasure.

The film also includes scenes of a character, named Roxanne in the credits, played by African American model Cynthia Bailey, 'who enigmatically haunts the margins of the film until she enters the space of the performance as the last and only member of the audience at the end' (Nataf 1995: 76) and who, as Lauren Berlant and Elizabeth Freeman point out, 'personifies authenticity' (1992: 150). Roxanne serves as a potential object of desire and double for Bernhard throughout the film. In Berlant and Freeman's account, she 'perpetuates the historic burden black women in cinema have borne to represent embodiment, desire, and the dignity of suffering on behalf of white women' (1992: 173–4). At the end, Bernhard looks to Roxanne for approval after performing a striptease to 'Little Red Corvette', and Roxanne rejects her, writing 'Fuck Sandra Bernhard' in lipstick on her tablecloth before exiting into blinding white light.

Bernhard's show is also about being Jewish and female and includes monologues that fantasize about a WASP existence – as an attractive preppy named Babe on Christmas Eve and a Mary Tyler Moore-ish existence as an executive secretary who marries her boss. These monologues, like the use of pop music from the 1970s in the show, depend on the viewer's recognition of and identification with the fantasies. But the 'me too' of identification is blocked by the viewer's recognition that the 'me too' is not taking place among members of the nightclub audience.

The film creates a distance between our imagination of Bernhard's 'successful' stage show and her 'failure' here by 'othering' the diegetic audience who are presumed to be racially different from both the New York audience and the film audience. It enacts the split hooks describes between white camp pleasure and a 'more serious narrative' about race. The film viewer's experience, then, is distracted and divided. The film viewer senses the difference between Bernhard's 'summer of success' playing to a presumably mostly white hip New York audience (filled with white stars like Liza Minnelli) and her failure to engage this diegetic black audience. Thus, while recognizing how Bernhard's camp performance might have worked for a white audience, the viewer also guiltily recognizes how it can't work for a black audience.

Ironically, but not surprisingly, the film's deconstruction of whiteness could be seen as authenticating the 'real' Bernhard for black and white audiences by showing her as self-reflective and attuned to the racial dynamic of her character 'Sandra's' appropriations of blackness. In Z. Isiling Nataf's opinion, the film does just that. She writes:

The film speaks to black audiences about an ending of the fraud of white supremacist myths and degrading black stereotypes. It speaks to white audiences, the new generation of whom have grown up in a miscegenated and multicultural world, through the media if not in their own neighbourhoods, and a hope for resolving the 'racial gap which they don't feel responsible for'. And it does so by crossing over, by loving instead of fearing blackness, by having black heroes, by refusing racism, and ultimately by embracing African-American culture which is all Americans' culture. (1995: 77)

Given the unidirectional crossover she describes and its similarity to minstrelsy and other appropriations of blackness in American culture (including the hero worship of African American sports stars), Nataf's view seems utopian at best. To me, the film's deconstruction of whiteness still seems to be geared toward a white audience. The film creates the shock of displeasure by forcing a critical recognition of the use of blackness as an authenticating discourse in camp. But this shock is still mediated through an authenticating black presence – the on-screen diegetic audience and the figure of Roxanne.

On the surface, by encoding a critical African American response to the white star's appropriation of blackness *Without You I'm Nothing* may seem to be more subversive than *I'm No Angel* which encodes the African American response to West's similar appropriations as affirmative and supportive. But *Without You I'm Nothing* still seemingly locates camp pleasure strictly in the persona of the white star, reenacting hooks' split between white camp pleasure and a 'more serious' race narrative. *I'm No Angel*, however, suggests the possibility of an alternate mode of camp pleasure available to an African American audience insofar as the maids' performances might also be readable as a form of camp.

Reading the maids' performances as camp requires shifting the viewer's emphasis from the film's presumed center (West) to the film's presumed margins (McDaniel, Beavers, Taylor, and the unnamed African American actress). Arthur Knight's work on African American constructions of stardom between 1925 and 1945 is helpful here. Drawing on the writings of James Baldwin, Richard Wright, bell hooks, and Ralph Ellison, as well as contemporary responses to Hollywood in the African American press, Knight suggests that black 'audiences' relationships with stars overlapped with but were also voluntarily and necessarily more multi-valent than white audiences' relationship with stars' and describes how African Americans might have defined stardom 'from within a different set of values (and constraints)'. Asking 'what were Black movie-goers' relationships with Hollywood stars (and their films)', Knight describes the polar options I have identified with the diegetic black audiences in *I'm No Angel* and *Without You I'm Nothing*: 1) black identification with and desire for white stars and 2) critical distraction or interrogative resistance on the part of black viewers. But he also points to mechanisms used within African American communities to create African American stars working through and against the constraints of Hollywood, where black players were largely isolated in white diegetic worlds or segregated in wholly black worlds. In addition to creating independent 'race' films and 'race' stars (like Lorenzo Tucker, 'the Black Valentino'), Knight notes how African American publicity and live touring operated to elevate even minor black performers to the status of stars for African American audiences 'to keep the performer before the Black audience as a Black star, now overlaid with his or her position as a Hollywood performer'. These mechanisms could effectively transpose center and margin, foreground and background, lead and back-up.

Hattie McDaniel's performance, in particular, seems available to be foregrounded and doubly encoded (or double entendre) for black audiences. Billed early in her career as the 'colored Sophie Tucker' and the 'female Bert Williams', McDaniel began her career as a band vocalist and became the first African American woman to sing on American radio. She appeared on 'Amos 'n' Andy' and the 'Eddie Cantor Show', and starred in 'Beulah' on radio and TV. As Bogle notes, in films, her comments and reactions 'often can be read as a cover-up for deep hostility. Indeed, she seemed to time her lines to give her black audience that impression' (120). When West responds to Libby Taylor's comment that she likes 'dark men' by saying she 'ought to have a big time in Africa', McDaniel's facial expression – eyes widening and rolling in a kind of mock horror as she laughs – could be seen both as a stereotypical eye-popping response to the white woman's outrageous behavior and comments (à la Stepin Fetchit) and as McDaniel's own campy theatricalization of that stereotype. McDaniel makes a spectacle of herself, drawing our attention to her response and to the stereotype she embodies, offering critical commentary on West's joke and on 'the historic burden' she and the other actresses playing maids have borne as authenticating back-up for white female stars.

Thus, at the same time that West's maids offer support for her camp performance and direct attention to her as star, they could also be seen as camping it up – overplaying their delight in the white star to point to the constructedness and inauthenticity of their supportive role. Where West uses race as support and back-up for her camp sex and gender masquerade, the maids play off West's performance and campily highlight the element of masquerade in their presumably 'authentic' personae. Instead of an appreciative audience, they might be seen as a critical chorus, momentarily foregrounded to comment on the white star's actions.

The double nature of African American performances in white Hollywood films has been noted before, but such performances are generally described in relation to practices of 'signifying' rather than camp. By viewing them as camp, however, we can broaden our conception of camp to acknowledge the degree to which camp is always already about race as well as sex and gender and, conversely, to acknowledge that signifying is a sexed and gendered practice as well. We can also consider how camp can be used as a strategy from within

African American communities as well as gay communities to create a distance from oppressive stereotypes. By viewing the maids' performances as camp, we can perhaps escape the polarity of imagining the black audience's response as either affirmative or critical of the white star and instead consider the possibility of a two-sided camp response, involving both identification and irony, recognition and misrecognition, affirmation and critique. Perhaps, too, by recognizing the maids' performances as masquerade, we can begin to rethink the relationship between camp and race discourse as an exchange between two modes of masquerade rather than simply a white appropriation of black authenticity.

CONCLUSION

Authenticity seems antithetical to camp which is so doggedly committed to artifice. 'Realness', as *Paris is Burning* demonstrates, is precisely a subversive category meant to dissolve difference and any notion of authenticity. We need, though, to reconsider how 'realness' operates in camp and in queer academic discourse as a racial fantasy for both white and non-white queers and the degree to which camp and queer performativity reinscribes racial difference. We need further to acknowledge the degree to which we use essentialising tropes of authenticity to position a more authentic, because less fixed, queer identity. Acknowledging the links between camp's sexual politics and race discourse may enable us to consider non-queer forms of racial masquerade – such as the over the top sensationalist stereotyping of Blaxploitation, or the Auntie Tom performances of Mae West's maids – as forms of camp; to rethink what it means for camp to be a 'Stepin Fetchit' or 'Auntie Tom' and whether Stepin Fetchit and Auntie Tom were camp all along. It should also remind us to bring pressure to bear on our camp icons, and on our own camp readings and practices, to ensure that we do not naively assume that camp has a consistently progressive politics but may be, after all, a kind of blackface.

NOTES

1. The links between Jewish and African American cultures are too complex to delve into here. It is, however, worth considering the contrast Susan Sontag sets out between homosexual camp and Jewish 'moral seriousness' in her 'Notes on "Camp"' and how the mutual appropriation of African American culture in camp and in Jewish entertainment traditions might complicate that model, especially since the references to blackness found in most other theorists of camp are absent from Sontag's model.
2. Lott, 'The Seeming Counterfeit', 227. See also Lott, 'Love and Theft'.

REFERENCES

Bogle, Donald, *Toms, Coons, Mulattoes, Mammies, and Bucks: An Interpretive History of Blacks in American Films* (1973), New York: Bantam, 1974.

Bogus, SDiane, 'The Queen "B" Figure in Black Literature', in Karla Jay & Joanne Glasgow (ed.), *Lesbian Texts and Contexts: Radical Revisions*, New York: New York UP, 1990, 275–90.

Carby, Hazel, 'It Jus Be's Dat Way Sometime: The Sexual Politics of Women's Blues', in Todd & Fisher (eds.), *Gender and Discourse: The Power of Talk*, New York: Ablex, 1988.

Corbett, John, 'Siren Song to Banshee Wail: On the Status of the Background Vocalist', in *Extended Play: Sounding Off from John Cage to Dr. Funkenstein*, Durham: Duke UP, 1994, 56–67.

Dyer, Richard, 'White', in *The Matter of Images: Essays on Representation*, New York: Routledge, 1993.

Hall, Stuart, 'New Ethnicities', in Kobena Mercer et al., *Black Film/British Cinema*, London: ICA, 1988.

hooks, bell, 'Is Paris Burning?' in *Black Looks: Race and Representation*, Boston: South End, 1992.

Knight, Arthur, 'Star Dances: African American Constructions of Stardom, 1925–1945', paper presented at Society for Cinema Studies, Dallas, 1996.

Kobal, John, 'Mae West', in *People Will Talk*, New York: Knopf, 1986.

LaMae, Lawrence F., 'Writers Fear Hazel Scott Has Become "Hollywood", One Writes', *Chicago Defender*, 31 July 1943.

Lott, Eric, "The Seeming Counterfeit': Racial Politics and Early Blackface Minstrelsy', *American Quarterly* 43:2, June 1991.

——, 'Love and Theft: The Racial Unconscious of Blackface Minstrelsy', *Representations* 39, Summer 1992, 23–50.

Nochlin, Linda, 'The Imaginary Orient', in *The Politics of Vision: Essays in Nineteenth-Century Art and Society*, New York: Harper & Row, 1989.

Robertson, Pamela, 'Home and Away: Friends of Dorothy on the Road in Oz', in Steven Cohan & Ina Rae Hark (eds.), *The Road Movie Book*, New York: Routledge, 1997, 271–86.

Silverman, Kaja, *The Acoustic Mirror: The Female Voice in Psychoanalysis and Cinema*, Bloomington: Indiana UP, 1988.

Snead, James, 'Angel, Venus, Jezebel: Race and the Female Star in Three Thirties Films', in Colin MacCabe & Cornel West (eds.), *White Screen/Black Images: Hollywood From the Dark Side*, New York: Routledge, 1994.

Sochen, June, 'Fanny Brice and Sophie Tucker: Blending the Particular with the Universal', in Sarah Blacker Cohen (ed.) *From Hester Street to Hollywood: The Jewish American Stage and Screen*, Bloomington: Indiana UP, 1983.

Spillers, Hortense J., 'Mama's Baby, Papa's Maybe: An American Grammar Book', *diacritics* 17:2, Summer 1987, 65–81.

Szwed, John F., 'Race and the Embodiment of Culture', *Ethnicity* 2, 1975.

Tuska, Jon, *The Films of Mae West*, Secaucus: Citadel, 1973.

25

CAMPING IN THE ART CLOSET: THE POLITICS OF CAMP AND NATION IN GERMAN FILM

Johannes von Moltke

The Hit Parade of the ZDF, that is the coolest thing I know. Because until now, there has been nothing more tasteless on the television screen, and whenever something is so wildly tasteless, then it ends up having great qualities again. (Rainer Werner Fassbinder)

It's also a problem to laugh out loud at something only you may find funny (especially if it's a German film – Germany is not ever funny to these audiences). These cinema buffs are very touchy about humor ... (John Waters)

I

In a piece entitled 'Guilty Pleasures', John Waters engages in a pseudo-solemn moment of what he calls 'cinema confession' (1987: 108–15). As a Catholic, he admits that guilt comes naturally, and so it happens that, overpowered by the divine urge to 'come out of the art closet', John Waters shamefully confesses: 'I'm also secretly a fan of what is unfortunately known as the "art film"'. If there were such a thing as transgression for Waters, this would have to be it – sneaking into arty films 'in the same way business men rush in to see *Pussy Talk* on their lunch hour'.

But while Waters's confessional discourse of guilt and contrition separates the licit from the illicit – that is, trash film enthusiasm from the sins of the arthouse cinema – his irreverent readings of the cinematic high-brow also productively blur the boundaries that keep it apart from the low-brow.[1] His comments on individual art films and filmmakers strip the 'good film snob of

Originally published in *New German Critique*, 63, Fall 1994.

her/his monopoly on the category of refined taste. Hardly a VIP from the Euro-Pantheon of great directors is spared an appearance in Waters's top ten list of his secret sins, which runs from Woody Allen's *Interiors* – 'Yes, *Interiors* ..., even though my face turns scarlet as I write' – to the films of Marguerite Duras – 'If Warhol did it for the Empire State Building, why can't Marguerite Duras do it for French trucks?' Under Waters's scrutiny the entire gamut of sacred cows from the European arthouse cinema becomes fair game for the kinds of spectatorial pleasures that, at least for the purposes of this paper, I want to group under the label of 'camp'.[2]

At the close of the 'cinema confession's' (unranked!) charts we find an entire oeuvre: 'Anything by Fassbinder'. Awed, just like Warhol was, by Fassbinder's sheer productivity – but also because 'anybody who idolizes Douglas Sirk is A-OK in my book' – Waters confesses to the ultimate sin of taking pleasure in the tortured scenarios of Fassbinder's films.[3] And, judging from his own films, as well as from these confessions, it seems more than likely that in terms of cinematic pleasure Waters's thumbs up for Fassbinder translates into more than just the knowing chuckle of the average cinephile who needs to signal to her/himself and those around her/him that s/he has successfully deciphered the deeper artistic meanings of one of Fassbinder's framing devices. Rather, if this kind of chuckle can stand for the limits to the enjoyment of Fassbinder imposed by the 'legitimate' arthouse audience, then John Waters's delight is subversively camp to the extent that he lets us imagine him letting out a peal of laughter in the arthouses where 'Germany is not ever funny'. The particular quality of such laughter (which I am tempted here to read also as laughter *with* Fassbinder *at* his arthouse audience) can be traced back to one of the earliest formulations of a camp sensibility by a character from a novel by Christopher Isherwood, who famously suggests that camp is a way of 'expressing what's basically serious to you in terms of fun and artifice and elegance' (1954: 125). Or, as Susan Sontag puts it in her problematic, but still seminal piece on camp,

> the whole point of Camp is to dethrone the serious. Camp is playful, anti-serious. More precisely, Camp involves a new, more complex relation to 'the serious'. One can be serious about the frivolous, frivolous about the serious. (1964b, rpt. 1966: 288)

Where such campy fun begins in relation to Fassbinder's films, and what kinds of revisions it might imply – these are questions which the following remarks are meant to indulge. For that purpose, I want to focus especially on cinematic spectatorship as a particularly privileged site for the kinds of playfulness and incongruities that make up camp as an *'operation of taste'* (Ross 1988, rpt. 1989: 136). Considering its function in relation to the critical discourses of, and around, Fassbinder and the New German Cinema, I want to draw out the function of camp within the spectatorial pleasures and dispositions that constitute its very possibility. In this respect, I am enlisting John Waters as an exemplary spectator not only because of the way in which his unorthodox –

read: queer – taste undoes the high seriousness of American arthouse appreciation of Fassbinder; in addition, the nationally inflected laughter of a Baltimore
trash-aesthete camping in the culturally legitimized discourses of Fassbinder
reception also deterritorializes those discourses, putting their ostensibly inherent European or German affiliations up for grabs.

Before going on to trace some of these effects, I should perhaps point out that
Waters has hardly been the only sinner to frequent this particular 'art closet'; in
America especially, a number of critics have appreciated and read Fassbinder's
films for the ways in which the proximity of trash and 'art', pop and 'culture',
and other incongruities in his work yield specifically campy pleasures. Warhol's
own reaction to Fassbinder's last film, which is related by one of Fassbinder's
numerous biographers as 'it made me hot for the whole day', provides only one
example of how to camp in the art closet (but leaving the door open for everyone to see what's inside): for Warhol, the film is not the heady reflection on the
dialectics of social power and sexual desire, for which it has been criticized, but
first and foremost a turn-on.[4] And in the more institutionalized forms of
Fassbinder criticism, critics have taken sporadic recourse to a catalog of stylistic
elements which identify the films of Fassbinder as camp. The discursivization of
a campy constituency of Fassbinder spectators can be traced back to the early to
mid-1970s, when Manny Farber and Patricia Patterson eulogized Fassbinder,
the 'snarling camp-elion', as one of the 'true inheritors of early Warhol'.
Emphasizing the ritualized syntax of Fassbinder's style, Farber and Patterson
(1975: 5–7) point to his

> appetites for the outlandish, vulgar, and banal in matters of taste, the use
> of old movie conventions, a no-sweat approach to making movies,
> moving easily from one medium to another, the element of facetiousness
> and play in terms of style. The point – *to dethrone the serious, to make
> artifice and theatricality an ideal* – is evident in an amazing vivacity, re-
> introducing Fable into a Hollywood genre, while suggesting a tough
> facile guy manipulating a deck of cards. (my italics)

To be sure, such enumerations are helpful not only in concretizing the campy
elements of a given cultural product, but also in pinning down the 'fugitive
sensibility' (Sontag) of camp itself as a phenomenon. Yet, they remain slightly
at odds with the project I want to pursue here. By focusing exclusively on the
aesthetics of Fassbinder's prolific production, and on the self-fashioned 'tough
facile guy' as its author, this kind of approach to Fassbinder's particular camp
brackets what is perhaps one of the most salient prerequisites to camp itself: the
audience, or, in more specifically cinematic terms – spectatorship.

II

In Judith Mayne's book (1993) on the by now already historical role of spectatorship in film theory, it is again Fassbinder who makes a brief appearance in
the final chapter, where Mayne illustrates the 'paradoxes of spectatorship' by

rewriting the spectator-position from the point of view of homosexual (dis)-identifications. Her assumption that 'gay/lesbian audiences function as a limit-case, as an ideal testing ground for the notion of critical spectatorship' (1993: 165) leads her to reconsider a piece which she herself had written in 1977 on one of Fassbinder's earlier films, *Ali: Fear Eats the Soul* (1973) (see Mayne, in References). That re-vision is occasioned among other things by the perceived necessity to account for the way in which camp inflects notions of spectatorship in Fassbinder's work:

> what is challenging about Fassbinder's films is, precisely, the collision of different modes of spectatorship. The collision is only superficially described as Hollywood escapism versus political analysis. For two radically different notions of what constitutes spectatorship collide in *Ali*, one playing on distinctly gay styles like camp, and the other playing on Hollywood melodrama. (Mayne 1993: 170)

Why does the collision of spectatorial difference(s) constitute a challenge to the viewer or critic, if not to film theory itself? And how does it unsettle or render superficial the grounding binary of Mayne's earlier analysis which still drew a distinction between Hollywood and politics? Although Mayne's answer here seems at first to lie simply in the displacement of the earlier and now apparently outdated opposition onto a new one – namely of camp and melodrama – I would argue that the discovery of camp spectatorship operates a more profound displacement, in which the binary itself becomes a rather messy affair. I would therefore disagree with Mayne that this is a site for collision, if by collision she means that a camp viewing of the film and a generic viewing in terms of melodrama remain fundamentally at odds with one another, i.e., 'distinct'. In fact, as I hope to show, when it comes to understanding cinematic spectatorship in terms of camp, the very concept of distinction becomes the object of camp's frivolity.

Melodrama, it turns out, provides a particularly rich playground for this kind of queer deconstruction, which is why I focus mainly on those films of Fassbinder's which can be considered melodramatic in a broad sense. For although camp may be distinctly gay as a style,[5] it is hardly distinct from Hollywood melodrama; it therefore doesn't lend itself to a rigidly oppositional pairing with melodrama any more than it allows for the Hollywood vs. political analysis dichotomy. On the contrary, it seems reasonable to posit a fairly close affinity between the generic excesses of the melodramatic mode and the excessive readings performed along the lines of camp.[6] This is especially true of Fassbinder, whose own experience as a melodramatic spectator has fortunately survived in the form of a beautiful text that Jane Shattuc has rightly described as 'an elaborate defense of a camp aesthetic'.[7] Furthermore, if we look at Sirk after Fassbinder's appropriations of his work, where does camp end and melodrama begin? Once spectatorship latches onto the 'too-muchness' of the troubled plots that unfold between Rock Hudson and Jane Wyman, their melodramatic staging of 'heterosexuality' turns out to be not the opposite of camp, but its prerequisite; and it is precisely this view(ing) of Sirk's plots that Fassbinder exploits in appropriating them for his own ends. From the point of view of a camp reading, the challenge they pose to the spectator, then, is not so much one of the collision between two 'radically different' forms of spectatorship, but rather the way in which camp feeds on the melodramatic excesses of Fassbinder's films. But if it is in this sense parasitical, camp as an 'operation of taste' is necessarily also transformative: by taking up the signs of melodrama, it creates its own meanings, infusing representations of sexuality in particular with queer resonances that remain unrecognized in the knowing chuckles of the arthouse audience.

As commentators never fail to reiterate, camp *cuts across* distinctions;[8] most notably across those which demarcate boundaries of gender and sexuality. I will show further on how this movement becomes articulated in the encounter with Fassbinder's films and the images of his 'superstars' in particular. For now, I simply want to suggest that whatever forms of camp we may discover by reading one particular set of films or cinematic signifiers for their different modes of address, the way in which camp produces and procures its own meanings in a given text can provide a useful model for cinematic spectatorship more generally. This is, in fact, how I read Mayne's invocation of camp at the close of her book on that subject: her project of foregrounding the unresolvable tensions between various textual, psychoanalytic, and ethnographic attempts at pinning down the spectator can be seen to culminate in camp both as a spectatorial practice and as a trope through which to envision spectatorship per se. Thus, it should be pointed out that Mayne does *not* position gay/lesbian audiences as the 'limit-case' of simple resistance to some hegemonic account of the spectator sutured into monolithic positions by the cinematic apparatus – indeed, both resistance and hegemony are notions which Mayne is at pains to evict from studies of spectatorship. Instead, the queer spectator becomes emblematic precisely of this undoing, which in turn produces the kinds of collisions and incongruities that define spectatorship more generally, and the case of Fassbinder in particular. Camp, which Esther Newton has aptly described as a 'strategy for a situation' (1972: 105), takes up the situation of spectatorship by toying with the multiple identifications that Fassbinder's texts produce – without, however, resolving that multiplicity into a unified subject position that would stabilize the sexual signifier.

I will therefore be describing camp spectatorship as an active negotiation of gendered performances, which explores identification in terms of a number of different sexual scenarios. I am aware of the fact that my focus on Fassbinder then begs the loaded question of whether this spectatorial activity depends in any way on more than the most abstract notion of textual address: can/should camp spectatorship be theorized in terms of directorial intention or in terms of a given author's (homo)sexuality? To the degree that camp always implies a reading 'against the grain', as the example of John Waters illustrates, the relevance of intentionality is negative at best; and yet I would not want to disengage Fassbinder's sexuality or the imputed intentional direction of any of his films from a spectator-oriented approach in order to constitute camp spectatorship as a wholly autonomous and abstract activity. In the complex field of textuality, sexuality, author-functions, and intentionality, spectatorship can be said to become queer or camp when it shuttles back and forth between the various poles of that field, negotiating spectatorship and reception 'across' various modes of address. To return to Judith Mayne's initial example, I would suggest that *Ali: Fear Eats the Soul* does indeed offer a particularly complex instance of this kind of deconstruction: articulating Ali's race with Emmi's age, in a relationship which Fassbinder interestingly describes as 'childlike' (11), not only produces the kinds of incongruous sexual tensions upon which camp thrives; the melodramatic exaggeration of these roles, the isolation of the central couple through insistent framing devices which function as a kind of cinematic imprisonment for their socially sanctioned sexual transgression – these and other boundaries are created in *Ali* only to be deconstructed by the spectator who is put in a position of disarticulating stereotypes of race and age from their allegedly natural forms of sexuality.

III

Mayne's overall argument foregrounds the constitutive gap that exists between the ways in which a cinematic text addresses its spectators, and the way in which it is actually received by its different audiences. Her insistence that we resist the lure of reducing our understanding of spectatorship to either one of these impossible alternatives is highly suggestive not only for the issue of sexuality, but also for the gap that separates nationally specific modes of spectatorship and address. This is where the distance between a German audience and a 'deterritorialized' American camp spectatorship becomes operative. The transversal, or queer,[9] movement of camp that I have been attempting to describe, serves to highlight not only the tensions between address and reception which form the object of Mayne's argument; in addition, it is characteristic that camp should also draw attention to the very boundaries it violates, turning the surreptitious tactics of poaching into an 'open secret', exuberantly performed.

In the case of the New German Cinema, the spectator's authorized terrain seems at first to be clearly mapped onto the nation itself; but a number of border crossings have enlarged its constituency, leading critics to return again and again to the unique relationship between spectatorship and nation that has characterized the history of West German film since Oberhausen. I am referring here to what has been theorized repeatedly as the incongruous coincidence of a nationally determined 'search for the spectator', and the international successes of a highly subsidized mode of production. Both through their aesthetic strategies and by way of their institutional struggles, New German films inscribe, it would seem, a specifically German viewer, and yet, this cinema has garnered not only a number of prestigious prizes in the festival circuit, but also a particular constituency of 'American Friends'. This is an incongruity which figures in much Anglo-American writing on German film in terms of loss: New German Cinema, it is said, loses its historical and political specificity as it loses 'its' German audience to the range of American spectators who see nothing but 'pure' aesthetics (the arthouse audience) or the various pleasures 'poached' by the camp audience. In his history of the New German Cinema, Thomas Elsaesser similarly addresses the loss of complexity of meaning in the crossing of the national border: having listed three different *national* determinations (ideological, institutional, and spectatorial) which shape the meanings of the New German Cinema, Elsaesser goes on to note:

> 'The author-auteurs' and their international productions mesh with these national determinations in complex but demonstrable ways, making the meaning most readily available to their art cinema audiences outside Germany often a mere abstraction of the specific historical inscriptions present in the films.[10]

What gets lost, in a distinction that Elsaesser draws from an essay by Michael Rutschky, is the film's content as opposed to its sensibility; and this opposition between 'contentist' and 'sensibilist' factions within Germany can consequently be remapped as the opposition between a domestic audience, which somehow 'gets' the content, and an international audience which somehow 'goes with the flow' of a film's sensibility. Hence, as 'sensibilists', Americans and other for-eigners would be unlikely, according to Elsaesser, 'to mistake Fassbinder's camp revamping of Hollywood melodramas for an 'Open University lecture' (though *Effi Briest* might just qualify)' (Elsaesser 1989: 57). The operation performed by the often-invoked American Friends thus turns out to consist of the uprooting of a body of films 'so distinctly grounded in national experience', as Eric Rentschler puts it (1981: 25). Citing camp and the alleged influence of Douglas Sirk as the two major misapprehensions as far as Fassbinder is concerned, Rentschler demonstrates how Fassbinder reception epitomizes the tension between a nationally coded mode of reception and the 'inherently romantic terms of American appropriations'.[11]

This tension has since been recuperated by the critical discourse which reads the incongruity of American and German responses to Fassbinder in particular in terms of a 'productive misunderstanding', emphasizing, for example, how American reception can be credited with revitalizing Fassbinder exhibition in Germany (see Elsaesser, 'Primary Identification'; Uhrmeister). This view is best expressed, perhaps, in Elsaesser's pointed remark that 'for German cinema to exist, it first had to be seen by non-Germans' ('Primary Identification', 98). Thus, when spectatorship crosses the Atlantic, one thing that apparently happens is that the 'other's view', while usefully estranging the very concept of an inscribed audience, somehow legitimizes the reception by an authenticat-ing German public.

The camp instances of American reception suggest, however, that the legitimizing detour may not lead back to its original point of departure. Instead of producing some sort of closure by reintroducing a kind of national suture between a body of films and their audience,[12] camp throws a wrench into the circular relation of spectatorship and address, and thus it functions as the (humorous) *refusal* of closure. Of course it is possible to insist, as many have, that to 'fully understand' the politics of *The Third Generation*, of Fassbinder's contribution to *Germany in Autumn* (1977), or of a film like *The Marriage of Maria Braun* (1978), the viewer should be acquainted with the political, historical, and historiographical situations invoked by these films. But while this normative approach certainly furthers a philological and historical exegesis of the New German Cinema and its individual films, it does not get us very far in understanding the role of spectatorship in this context. To make such claims for a historical reading is inevitably to prioritize a certain kind of referential understanding over readings which actively appropriate the signifier on other levels, replacing referentiality by a form of spectatorship that seeks its pleasures elsewhere in the filmic text. Camp, I would argue, is only one of these ways of insisting on the autonomy and availability of cinematic signifiers, and on the appropriation of New German Cinema in terms of discourses that are no longer securely anchored in the 'reality' and 'topicality' of German national history. Such alternate readings will dislocate the ontological status of that history, turning it instead into a discursive effect of the films themselves. The supposedly immediate obviousness of the films' politics, their ostensibly transparent status as 'Open University lectures' to a German audience is constructively displaced by forms of reception which route the films either through discourses on high or avant-garde 'art' and 'artistry' (as in American arthouse appreciation), on pedagogy (as in the German departments of American colleges), or through the camp of underground cinema and its emphasis not on art, but on artificiality. Reading German film as camp therefore forces us to reconsider the ways in which the inscribed 'German' audience – which is produced at least in equal measure by the critical discourse surrounding the films as by the films themselves – is a fictional construct. This is not to suggest that we simply reverse the equation and look to camp reception for some 'authentic' spectator, who would somehow be more in tune with a given film's true intentions; on the contrary, what I find appealing about the notion of camping in German films is precisely the fact that they dislodge any certainty about intentionality and address.

To illustrate one way in which this open-ended detour through camp might function, I would now like to turn to the way in which the specifically *historical* forms of address attributed to New German Film become articulated in Fassbinder's films with a performative notion of sexuality and gender. My claim here is that by staging not only gender, but (German) history itself as a kind of drag performance – specifically in the various constructions of Hanna Schygulla's star image until Fassbinder's death – Fassbinder manages to break out of the spectatorial constraints suggested above and reproduced in the critical literature.

IV

Hair put up, lips pursed, petticoat swinging, and woman tempts eternally. (Hanna Schygulla)

She was my star from the very first rehearsal. (R. W. Fassbinder)

When he's not sneaking surreptitiously into arthouse showings of the latest European productions, John Waters is apparently given to hopping on a plane for tours of Los Angeles ('I can't think of a better place to vacation – next to Baltimore, of course'). For Waters, Los Angeles is 'everything a great American city should be: rich, hilarious, of questionable taste, and throbbing with fake glamour' (1987: 3). Before we can pause to muse what kind of glamour *isn't* fake, Waters has led us through all his favorite sites up to, and including, the Russ Meyer Museum;[13] but the epitome of the kind of glamour we were promised turns out to be Angelyne, a '1950s-glamour-girl' look-alike, whose career is built on giant billboards of herself in Hollywood, New York, and London, displaying nothing but her likeness and a phone number: 'Although she's making a record, she's currently famous for absolutely nothing. Angelyne has everything it takes to become a star'. (After all, Zsa Zsa Gabor made it, too.)

As Waters's descriptions of stardom and celebrity show, postmodern notions of simulacra and pastiche are hardly lost on him;[14] yet, what makes Angelyne camp in his account is the way in which Waters's discovery of her 'act' allows him to rewrite pastiche in terms of (the performance of) gender: as she drives around Hollywood in a hot-pink Corvette, wearing a matching, revealing outfit, blowing kisses to anyone who looks her way, Angelyne is not exactly embodying any specific role; rather, she acts out femininity as such. In the movie version of *John Waters's Tour of L.A.*, Angelyne would star as what Waters calls a 'female female-impersonator' (1987: 8).

Female impersonation by men has always been central to camp, its *pièce de résistance*, as it were.[15] Angelyne's/John Waters's particular version of camp, however, thrives on the fact that she wears her 'own' gender as drag, rather than parading/parodying that other gender that we still so thoughtlessly call the 'opposite'. Angelyne's radicalized form of drag, as the redundancy of Waters's term plainly suggests, consists in the parodic performance of excess: rather than *cross-dressing*, here is an impersonator who literally *dresses up*, as it were. The point is, obviously, that we are not going to find a biological male slipping back out of the role and the 'revealing' outfit, reassuring us that the oppositions are still there under the costumes and the make-up. Consequently, the 'troublesome' effect of Angelyne's drag – for she is indeed making precisely the kind of 'trouble' analyzed not only by Judith Butler in *Gender Trouble* but also staged hysterically by John Waters himself in *Female Trouble* – consists in robbing gender itself of its epistemological and phenomenological anchoring in any kind of substantive or expressive mode. Or, to invoke Butler's often-cited opposition: Angelyne personifies a performative understanding of gender as something we *do*, rather than as something we *are* (see Butler 1990a and 1990b).

Although Butler's invocation of the performative has multiple references in theater acting, phenomenological 'acts', and speech act theory, I am interested here primarily in the first area. But when we look at the actors in Waters's own work, it turns out that Angelyne isn't Divine: female impersonation (or: *Trouble*) in John Waters's films – as opposed to his tour of Los Angeles – is performed not by a woman, but by a biologically male transvestite diva, a 'three-hundred-pound man not trapped in but scandalously and luxuriously corporeally cohabiting with the voluptuous body of a fantasy Mae West or Jayne Mansfield' (Moon & Sedgwick 1990: 218f). Rather than looking to Waters's films, therefore, I want to return to the films of Fassbinder and to Schygulla's starring performances of femininity in order to recover the kind of performative camp that Waters found on his tour of Los Angeles.

Fassbinder said that he preferred working with women, because of the way that social role-playing figures in constructions of femininity:

> Men in this society are under a lot more pressure than women to play their roles. Of course women also have their roles, but they can break out a lot easier, or step out of line ... Men are expected to conform. To that extent they're more boring, on the whole. When women venture outside of society, they don't immediately fit into that nineteenth-century stereotype of the woman of the night.[16]

This is the kind of claim that is better followed up in Fassbinder's films than in his interviews. For whereas his essentializing distinction between male and female roles and performances is problematic, the way in which his films stage femininity *as role-playing* turns his professed 'interest' in women ('I take women more seriously than most directors do') (Fassbinder, 20) towards a broader notion of gender as performance; there are, to be sure, enough female roles in Fassbinder's *oeuvre* which foreground the impersonation of femininity as one of the defining features of the respective performances. What I want to suggest, then, is that these performances provide the occasion for the kind of camp laughter that sets Waters apart from the serious cinema-buffs in the theater.

The laugh that 'emerges in the realization that all along the original was derived' (Butler 1990a: 139) singles out not the artistry of the auteur, but the artificiality of the performer. Thus, in Fassbinder's *Lola* we find Barbara Sukowa pulling up not in a hot-pink Corvette, but in an immaculate white Porsche – from which she emerges as a latter-day Blue Angel(yne) to collect a kiss from a hapless and surprised Armin Müller-Stahl right in front of an admiring audience. Or Rosel Zech, the German version of Gloria Swanson in *Sunset Boulevard*, trying desperately to impersonate her idea of glamorous femininity (a kind of anachronistic UFA-femininity) at what turns out to be her last public performance in *Veronika Voss*. But above all, there is Hanna Schygulla. With the exception, perhaps, of Irm Herrmann whom Fassbinder called 'the only actress-in-spite-of-herself [*Schauspielerin wider Willen*] I've ever known' (210), Schygulla remains the most enigmatic of the women in Fassbinder's 'factory'. In fact, unlike Irm, whose sado-masochistic infatuation with Fassbinder kept her persistently in his vicinity, Schygulla insisted on keeping certain forms of distance, earning her some degree of scorn from the other members in the troupe; but it is presumably *because* of this carefully calculated distance that it was she, rather than, say, Irm or Ingrid Caven (his one-time wife), who got stuck with the reputation of being the Marlene Dietrich to Fassbinder's Sternberg.[17]

From the outset, Schygulla was acknowledged or branded, depending on how you look at it, as Fassbinder's 'muse', his superstar diva – not only by Fassbinder himself, but also by the critics of the time.[18] But little was or has been said about the character of Schygulla's star image, and of her performances, in particular: apart from the Dietrich-comparisons invoked by reviewers both in Germany and the United States, there are only sporadic attempts to describe the lure of Schygulla's screen presence in terms of her 'naïveté', her enigmatic self-involvement, or her 'backyard-glamour'.[19] Instead, Fassbinder criticism tends to place her squarely within an auteurist appreciation of Fassbinder's films as so many different expressions of a director's (rather than a star's) performance.[20]

Yet, in a tradition that has almost single-handedly shaped the posthumous careers of stars like Judy Garland or Zarah Leander, gay audiences have formed the core of a camp constituency that insists on pushing the star persona to the forefront, latching onto the way in which her very theatricality rewrites 'natural' gender roles, and capitalizing on what Eve Sedgwick has begun to theorize as 'queer performativity'. It is with these forms of spectatorship in mind that I want to approach the starring performances of Hanna Schygulla and to ask how she enacts a mode of address that might allow the kinds of pleasurable appropriations that characterize fan-constituencies such as Leander's or Garland's (or Garbo's or Jayne Mansfield's, for that matter). To be sure, Schygulla has never garnered quite the following that Richard Dyer (1982, 1986), for example, has found to constitute Garland's star image; but I want to suggest that her *mise-en-scène* in Fassbinder's films taps a similar tradition of camp spectatorship which it thereby also addresses. Viewed from within this tradition, Schygulla consistently delivers a performance of gender that accounts for much of the campy pleasures that can be found in these films.

Like that of any star, Schygulla's star image in Fassbinder's films plays on a double movement between continuity and rupture; in other words, while on the one hand that image is necessarily cumulative, a composite picture of her different roles in almost twenty films, there are crucial breaks which mark its development from the early films through her last role as Lale Andersen/Willie/ Lili Marleen. This development is structured by a central hiatus of four years between 1974 when, after a falling out of sorts over her performance in *Fontane Effi Briest* she 'defected' to work with Wenders in *Wrong Move*, and 1978, when she returned for three more films with Fassbinder, starring in *The Marriage of Maria Braun* (1978) and *Lili Marleen* (1981).

It is in her early roles that Hanna Schygulla's image becomes most clearly infused with the kind of low-life but glamorous femininity that she herself describes as that of a '*Vorstadt-Marilyn*' ['Marilyn of the Suburbs']. From her very first role in Fassbinder's very first film, which carefully delays and times her appearance so as to build up the spectator's anticipation (and her position as superstar), Schygulla's performance is marked by an emphasis on a highly stylized type rather than a realistically motivated individual.[21] Unlike the later films, notoriously influenced by Sirk's melodramatic explicitness, the early films such as *Love is Colder Than Death* generally hold back expository information concerning the backgrounds and biographies of their characters, situating them only in relation to a vaguely defined mobster 'Syndikat' and in a noirish ambiance of crime and toughness that is borrowed directly from the corresponding genre of American B-movies. Schygulla's role in these films turns on the image of the *femme fatale*, borrowed from the film noir tradition, and enriched with the urge to impersonate her own idols: Marilyn Monroe, Brigitte Bardot, and Marlene Dietrich, who is invoked in a number of filmic citations in *Gods of the Plague* (1969), where Hanna is introduced as a nightclub singer taken straight from the *Blue Angel*, and Marlene's portrait adorns the wall of her dressing room.[22]

'Hanna's the key to everything', Fassbinder says of her role in *Love is Colder than Death* (6). But of course, these early films and their 'tough guy' narratives don't revolve exclusively around the *femme fatale*, and there is a distinct sense in which the toughness of the male roles rubs off on the woman: in the triangulation of Franz (Fassbinder), Bruno (Uli Lommel), and Joanna in the first film, the 'feminine' position circulates rather freely; and although Schygulla clearly performs an excess of femininity at times, there are moments when the affair between Franz and Bruno (which is decidedly *not* homosocial, i.e., routed exclusively through their mutual but different relationships to Hanna) relieves her of that role, making her 'one of the guys'. There are inklings in this film of a tomboy identity for Hanna Schygulla to which I want to return when I consider her predominantly *femme* roles of the later films.

If the love triangles of these early films can be read in any way as an indication of Fassbinder's and Schygulla's positions within the Munich group, the filming of *Fontane Effi Briest* marks a definite rupture in Hanna and Rainer's relationship. The two of them simply disagreed on the conception of the role of Effi, and Schygulla has commented repeatedly on the way in which Fassbinder's direction in this film proved to be the straw that broke this camel's back[23] – whereas Fassbinder predictably blames Schygulla (Fassbinder, 156). However, my point about the significance of this rift is not the way in which the director and his star haggle about the interpretation of a role; rather, it is a question of how the role sits with Schygulla's star image itself. Hanna, as Fassbinder knew quite well, would only take starring roles, and so in *Effi Briest*, she had to be Effi. But given the intimate relation of her early superstar image to a particular *type* of femininity, I would argue that much of the problem surrounding this performance can be found in the mere fact that this was her first role in a period film (Fassbinder's first), full of constricting costume and a historicizing *mise-en-scène*. To be sure, the film's overall style (the artificiality of its language, its use of veils, mirrors, and other framing devices) marks a certain authorial continuity with the earlier films; but for Hanna Schygulla to play a nineteenth-century *girl* – who at one point gets pregnant, no less – and to turn the artificiality of her earlier performances into the rather more constricting artificiality of a highly *literary* language: all these changes must have contributed a fair deal to her decision to leave Fassbinder and hitchhike across the United States for a while.

Fontane Effi Briest uses one particularly striking and highly effective stylistic device, which consists in the repeated refusal to fade to black. Instead, in a technique that Fassbinder will take up again in his very last film, *Querelle* (1982), individual sequences which often last for only a single shot are separated by fades to a glaring white. At times, Fassbinder will use these cinematic markers to insert snippets of text from Fontane's novel; but there is one striking instance in which we are offered a photograph instead: framed in an oval with soft contours, Hanna Schygulla's portrait emerges from the blank screen, arrested in a mode of representation which remains undecided between nineteenth-century portrait photography and a Hollywood glamour portrait. This sudden image, bringing the filmic narration to a momentary halt, beautifully captures the incongruities of the transitional moment in Hanna Schygulla's star image as it gets lodged between a heady costume-film character and a glamorous subcultural persona.[24] For on the one hand, the photograph fits perfectly into the film's period style, where Schygulla's face reads as that of a helpless, almost still pre-adolescent bourgeois child; on the other hand, the glamorous star quality invoked by the photograph lets the parodic *femme fatale* of Fassbinder's earlier films erupt into the narrative frame, signifying, as it were, the incongruity of the underground superstar body in her aristocratic costume. At the time of the filming of *Fontane Effi Briest*, this incongruity is difficult for Schygulla to accept; she draws her own conclusions, packs her bags, and leaves. By the time of her return to Fassbinder, however, the double charge of a historicizing costume-film performance and the performance of her oversexed superstar status turns out to have become the defining trait of her star image. Both *The Marriage of Maria Braun* and *Lili Marleen* turn on Schygulla's performance as a peculiarly historicized Angelyne of the German art cinema.

The renewal of Schygulla's and Fassbinder's collaborative relationship in *Maria Braun* marks not only their rise to international fame (particularly in America), but also the distinct 'nationalization' of Schygulla's (super)star image. Significantly, the film's subject matter gets scripted directly onto the star's body, leading critics to speak of Schygulla's national roles as '*eine* "*deutsche Frau*" (Penkert, 6).[25] (Indeed, Schygulla herself recounts how, in a grotesque kind of Freudian screen memory, this identification has even led to comments such as 'You were wonderful in your role as *Eva* Braun'.) (Schygulla, 34) It is hardly surprising, therefore, that Hanna Schygulla's performances as Willie in *Lili Marleen* and as Maria Braun have often been read for the way in which she represents German history itself. Not only, it is argued, is she a quintessential woman of the 1940s or 1950s, respectively (which would amount to saying simply that she plays her role well in the sense of realistically); but she is seen to literally *embody* Germany, becoming a '*Germania*' of the New German Cinema.

A *Germania* among others, to be sure. However much the New German Cinema may have attempted to counteract hegemonic discourses of the nation, it has never been able nor, it seems, overly concerned to rule out certain traces of that very hegemony *within* its own representations. The recurrent inscription of Germany in terms of a violated or vulnerable female body constitutes one of those traces.[26] As Eric Rentschler has pointed out, female roles like that of Maria in Edgar Reitz's *Heimat*, the protagonist who becomes the victim of rape in *Germany Pale Mother*, or the lackadaisical but cunning Lili Marleen all function as stand-ins for a hapless Germany; the nation itself thereby is written as a nation of victims and martyrs, placing the allegedly subversive potential of the New German Cinema in the service of a revisionist discourse (Rentschler, 38). Among the Lenes and Marias of that cinema, Hanna Schygulla, too, functions as such an allegory; and yet, I want to insist that there is an additional aspect to her filmic presence, an excess which cannot be fully integrated into the national meanings represented by her role as allegorical image, but which lies instead in the more intractable histrionics of her performance. For clearly it is not simply the character of the 'average German woman of the 1950s' (Maria Braun) or the 'privileged German woman under Fascism' (Willie) which operates the actress's identification with the nation itself. Nor is this just an effect of the elaborate metaphorics of the films' respective stylistic and narrative systems (the way in which Maria Braun's rise to affluence parallels and mirrors the German economic miracle [*Wirtschaftswunder*], for example). Instead, what links the star's body so intimately to the national body and at the same time cuts across that identification is as much an effect of her particular performance as it is of her role or her narrative status as a signifier.

This is where I would want to return to a notion of drag as one way of describing this kind of embodiment which, like drag, turns literally on an act of *impersonation*. Just as Hanna Schygulla exemplifies the way gender is a matter of doing rather than of being, so are the nationalizing and historicizing dimensions of her performances characterized by an emphasis on construction, theatricality, and artifice which represent the nation and its history as a drag performance, put on by a particular body. What the link of the star of a film to a national history suggests is that, like Judith Butler's performative notion of gender, history too operates somewhere on the level of 'corporeal styles'. If history itself can be seen as a 'bodily sense', as Leslie Adelson suggests in her recent *Making Bodies, Making History*, then cinematic representation can only articulate this bodily sense through its presentation as performance (Adelson, 11).[27] In the case of Schygulla, this embodiment is marked, like the parodies of the drag performer, by excess: she is not simply a woman of the 1950s, but one who is constantly playing at playing a woman of the 1950s (in *The Marriage of Maria Braun*, this is elaborated most clearly perhaps in her vampish cat-and-mouse play with Ivan Desny). The constant emphasis on the staging devices throughout *Lili Marleen* generates a similar effect, especially the way in which the ubiquitous lighting picks out Schygulla in glamorous contrast to the other actors, even when she is not 'on stage' (although it is difficult to say whether this is ever the case). In both cases, Schygulla's performance seems both somnambulistic and keenly playful, toying with the meanings she is producing. If it is possible to read a performance in terms of its address, then Schygulla quite systematically confuses her addressee by sending mixed signals that originate not only from a role or from an extra-filmic star persona, but also from a role-playing character in the filmic narrative. I would define this kind of excessive performance as campy because rather than estranging the actor's screen presence in the Brechtian sense, it *reinforces* the theatricality of performance as well as the continuity of plot, insisting on playing the game rather than arresting it with a song or the kind of Brechtian cinematic signposts still used in *Fontane Effi Briest*.

To do so, of course, is to unsettle the stability of the historical referent by rewriting it through the individual body. It is an unsettling effect which characterizes Schygulla's performances throughout her career, but which only begins to work upon the convergence of history, gender, and sexuality with her last two films. Where the female female-impersonator erases the substantiality of the feminine, the impersonator of national history radically shifts the status of the historical subject, suggesting that it is only by 'doing' the historical moment that we can access its meanings. Schygulla's enigmatic performances as a vamp in 1950s clothing refuse the certainty that 'we already know how it ends'; indeed, even after the explosive end has come at the close of *Maria Braun*, we are still not quite sure that we know. Such uncertainty raises the question, in other words, of realism. Anton Kaes has argued that *The Marriage of Maria Braun* is characterized not so much by the constructivist mode of historical performance that I have been trying to outline here, but rather by a particular historical realism which emerges from the alleged absence of an enunciating subject:

> The realistic effect also results from the fact that the historical fiction of *Maria Braun* seems to unfold as a story without a narrating subject; until the final scene, it is not clear who is telling the story. The elimination of an enunciating subject is one of the conventional devices to achieve the effect of 'historical realism'. (Kaes, 87)

Now, apart from the fact that, as Jane Shattuc convincingly argues, all art-cinema narration does have an enunciative subject in the author function, I would argue that this realism is an effect of criticism, rather than of the highly stylized filmic narration. Where a viewer such as Kaes sees history reflected, I want to emphasize the way spectatorship might negotiate the incongruities which make up the convergence of sexuality and history in the identifications of Hanna Schygulla/Maria Braun. As Kaes rightly points out, 'the realistic historical effect ... also depends on the visual memory of the audience' (Kaes, 88). This bow to the multiplicity of spectatorship, which, after all, would only seem to be the logical corollary to what Kaes himself describes as the 'heteroglossia' of Fassbinder's filmic narration, remains unexplored in Kaes's own reading of *The Marriage of Maria Braun*.

But if we do assume the performative (as opposed to realistic) motivation of Schygulla's embodiment of national history, does this imply a voluntaristic conception of history as something we do and something we can therefore change at will? Hardly. These films clearly demonstrate that, just as in the case of gender where the sociocultural and historical limits to the 'subversion' of identity are maintained through the injunction to 'do your gender right', there always exist frameworks within which you had better 'get your history right': in the end, Maria Braun doesn't, and the consequences – no matter whether they are accidental or self-inflicted – are mortal. On the level of historiography, too, there are limits to the degree in which we stage history as a matter of individual performance, individual suffering, and play. In conclusion, I want to sketch the historiographic dimensions of a camp aesthetic, to ask where its sentimental and in a sense revisionist operations with history might take us in the context of the New German Cinema.

V

In describing the split between an inscribed German spectator and camp's play with forms of address, I treated the camp appreciation of Fassbinder as a more or less distinctly American phenomenon. And while I would not want to generalize to the point of saying that camp itself is inevitably American, there is a strong sense in which camp always involves the signs of America – its consumer culture and its fabrications, its star system, its glamour, as well as its own camp culture.[28] Consequently, as Andrew Ross points out, Hollywood nostalgia – or, in his terms, a 'cult of Hollywoodiana' – undoubtedly numbers among the constitutive 'common conditions' of all camp. Thus, Fassbinder's 'pocket version of the star system' (Elsaesser, 'Vicious Circles', 34), his self-fashioned star image, the cultivation of a number of superstars, and his incongruous mode of studio production at a kind of 'Munich Factory' make him available to the deterritorializing readings of a camp sensibility. Yet, that same nostalgia for bygone glamour and spectacle which drives camp cinephilia also accounts for the charged historicity of camp more generally. Camp, in this sense, is a form of engaging with history that works on the level of cultural memory, and this is precisely where I see the (by no means unproblematic) relevance of camp in the broader context of the New German Cinema.

Susan Sontag has remarked that 'camp sees everything in quotation marks: It's not a lamp, but a "lamp", not a woman, but a "woman"' (Sontag 1964b, rpt. 1966: 280). In Sontag's 'Notes', these examples are meant to underscore the way in which camp understands 'Being-as-Playing-a-Role', as a form of overidentifying with objects or identities by way of the theatricality that inheres in all camp. But the figurative use of quotation marks also functions to emphasize what Sontag and others have described as camp's profoundly 'sentimental' relation to the past. For camp's operation with/in history, too, can be described as a form of 'poaching' along a temporal axis, combing through historical epochs for signifiers which can be appropriated in quotation marks. One of the favorite uses to which this operation is put in camp is surely that of collecting – the way Warhol collected famous people, Fox and his lover collect the furniture of the decadent bourgeoisie in Fassbinder's *Fox and his Friends*, or the way in which Charlotte von Mahlsdorf, the hero of Rosa von Praunheim's latest film, collects furniture and ornaments from the time of rapid industrial expansion around 1871 [*Gründerzeit*].[29] Ross has described this 'collector mode' of camp in terms of 'a rediscovery of history's waste'. Much in the vein of Warhol's professed love for 'leftovers', camp treats history's waste matter

> as a 'ragbag', not drenched with tawdriness by the mock-heroism of Waste Land irony, but irradiated, this time around, with the glamour of resurrection. In liberating objects of the past from disdain and neglect, camp generates its own kind of economy. Camp, in this respect is the *re-creation of surplus value from forgotten forms of labor*.[30]

While I would disagree with Ross's overall argument, insofar as he takes up this notion of surplus value in order to suggest camp inevitably involves a mode of exploitation, I am nonetheless intrigued by Ross's use of that notion for the way in which it also suggests the existence of an otherwise hidden site of cultural memory. Thus, in the case of the New German Cinema, one of the forgotten forms of labor whose surplus value remains to be tapped is clearly the labor of remembering and forgetting itself. From the very start that cinema is engaged, aptly phrased by Eric Rentschler, in the enterprise of 'remembering not to forget': already in a 1960 film by Kluge, we find 'a ragpicker's zeal in sifting through the garbage pile of history, sorting out and recovering discarded chunks of reality lest they be forgotten and disavowed by the present'.[31] In other words, the Young German filmmakers and the New German Cinema return almost obsessively not only to fascism itself, but also the dynamics by which it recedes into the ragbag of history, to be picked over in a Nazi retro mode (see Reimer & Reimer). The task of these filmmakers would then be precisely to stem the tide of time, rescuing history and memory for the spectator. Thus, Eric Santner reads the New German Cinema in terms of a 'national elegiac art', describing its films as 'works that make use of the procedures and resources of mourning to reconstitute something like a German self-identity in the wake of the catastrophic turns of recent German history' (Santner, xiii). A similar view is suggested by Anton Kaes in his survey *From Hitler to Heimat*, where the works of Syberberg, Kluge, Sanders-Brahms, Reitz, and Fassbinder are read against the backdrop of a postmodern 'society of spectacle' whose images merely 'recycle' history on celluloid. The films analyzed by Kaes in his book, however, 'want to provide a historical memory that runs counter to Hollywood notions of German history at the risk of appearing, or indeed becoming, revisionist' (Kaes, 197).

If these views adequately describe the New German Cinema in terms of the histories it produces within the ongoing debate about German national identity, the example of Waters serves as a reminder that different modes of spectatorship will complicate this matter. For if camp, too, functions as 'cultural memory, resurrected for subversive ends', as Constance Penley has noted (1988, rpt. 1993: 135), *its* mnemonics put not only the 'cult of Hollywoodiana', but an abiding sense of spectacle and of performativity back into the representation of German history. This is why, in a discourse on German Film which would situate Fassbinder in terms of the forgotten labor of remembering, recreating the surplus value of fascism would have to constitute the objectionable point, the 'risk of appearing, or indeed becoming, revisionist'. It is a risk that camp is always willing to take, a risk that is inherent in camp's function as 'a solvent of morality' – not to be confused, as in Sontag's case, with a solvent of politics (290). But the possible functions of camp within the dynamics of spectatorship also present a risk that cannot be wished away by consigning it to the dustbin of romantic misapprehensions of the German Cinema; nor was Fassbinder one who would have opted, given the choice, to avoid such a risk in favor of clear-cut lessons for his spectators.[32] In a statement that recalls Mayne's sense of a challenging collision of different modes of spectatorship in Fassbinder's films, Hanna Schygulla also marks the unsettling effect that her performances have on the spectator – suggesting that the source of this unsettlement was shared by her and Fassbinder:

> to be sure, that was something that connected us, one reason why we got along so well: because I continued something he had, in my own way. So that people were never quite sure: is what she's doing good or is it dreadful? Is she beautiful or is she ugly? Is that banal or is it deep? (Penkert, 6; my translation)

Thus, it seems to me that the irreverent spectatorial play with different historical, national, and sexual meanings remains constitutive even where the New German Cinema and its critics seem to be at pains to reinstate the moral imperatives of memory and coming to terms with the past [*Vergangenheitsbewältigung*]. Fassbinder insists on *staging* the lure of the Third Reich – a lure which he envisions quite explicitly as the lure of the staged spectacle in the first place. And in that sense, he operates within the parameters of the kind of revisionist discourse that is also at work in statements such as the following:

> I think it's possible to say something about National Socialism, which is specifically German, simply by showing what was appealing about it ... In its self-portrayal the Third Reich did have a lot to do with spectacle ... [I]ts impact has a lot to do with the aesthetics of staging. Yet the moment you say there were also concepts like solidarity, like *Volk* (without 'one Reich, one Führer' this time), you have to say that all this can also result in something positive. (66)

But by insisting on the way in which this part of German history turns on a matter of *performance,* and by carefully evoking and constructing the 'aesthetics of staging' through the histrionics of Hanna Schygulla's performance on the screen, Fassbinder's 'historical' films clearly gesture toward a radicalized notion of history and its 'truths': 'There aren't any true happenings', he says when asked whether his television plays are based on true happenings: 'The true is the artificial' (198). This artificiality of the historical referent simply gets passed on by Fassbinder to the spectator, for whom the distinction between truth and falsehood becomes as moot an issue in terms of history as it does in terms of gender and sexuality. And it is the inscription of this ambivalence in spectatorship that remains provocative and (according to my own definition) campy in Fassbinder's films.

In a sense I want to argue, then, not only for a fresh look at Fassbinder through the spectacle(s) of camp, but for a certain historicization of his particular aesthetics and their 'revisionist' impulses. For the concept of revisionism, which still had fairly distinct and politically important contours during the years of the historians' debate [*Historikerstreit*], is becoming increasingly messy as Germany continues to struggle with its unification. Take only Fassbinder's admittedly problematic recuperation of the alleged solidarity contained in the notion of a *Volk,* surely an unmistakable and highly questionable revisionist impulse at the time *Lili Marleen* was made. But now, just over a decade later, such a recuperation has shifted from being fodder for highly politicized debates among historians, to a different discursive register altogether after it was put to the test in the streets: the slogan 'We are the people' ['*Wir sind das Volk*'] as well as its apparently inevitable permutation into 'We are one people' ['*Wir sind ein Volk*'] have given new meaning to Fassbinder's contention that 'concepts like solidarity, like *Volk* ... can also result in something positive'. This is not to suggest that the process of unification, riddled as it is with inequalities, hasty policies, and social unrest, is itself simply something positive; rather, it suggests the deep historicity of the concept of revisionism itself. As the contours of the historical moment change, Fassbinder's films, as well as the performances of his superstars, will encounter (collide with) different forms of spectatorship at every turn.[33]

Perhaps this is also a generational question: by the time I had understood who Fassbinder was, and what it was about this literally obscure series called *Berlin Alexanderplatz* that made my grandmother return almost religiously to her television every Monday night or so, Fassbinder was already dead, and his often-cited and controversial topicality had less and less to do with the Germany in which I was growing up; in other words, my pleasure in Fassbinder's films themselves has always been that of picking over a ragbag of historical images which are inflected with particularly striking performances of sexuality. Especially in his most explicitly 'historical' films, i.e. his 'BRD' Trilogy centered around Maria Braun, Lola, and Veronika Voss, as well as the spectacle that is *Lili Marleen*, I continue to be struck by the collision between the carefully researched costume-film quality of the historical images, and what could be described as their surplus value, their cinematic excess.[34] The complex role for spectatorship in these films, then, consists precisely in camping up Hanna Schygulla's highly ambivalent superstar image while simultaneously combing through the dregs of fascist history and its make-over into the Federal Republic of Germany. The inherent tensions between subversion and revision inscribed into the excess of femininity remain unresolved as well on the level of spectatorship, for which I have taken camp as a model. Or, to quote Andy Warhol:

> B: 'Is that a female impersonator?'
> A: 'Of what?' (41)

NOTES

1. The transgression-by-laughing suggested in the epigram is only one site where the trash and art aesthetics begin to merge; another such moment occurs when Waters suggests that 'arty theaters' need 'a little hype' in the trailers they offer to their public: 'Wouldn't it interest moviegoers more to stick to the tried-and-true formula here? How about "See Bibi Andersson slit her wrists" or "At last! A film that is black and white, four hours long and with subtitles – *The Mother and the Whore* – coming soon to a theater near you!"' (109).

2. It has been pointed out again and again that camp draws much of its energy from exploiting strong incongruities. Esther Newton notes, for instance, that while 'masculine-feminine juxtapositions are, of course, the most characteristic kind of camp . . ., any very incongruous contrast can be campy', listing areas such as status, age, profanity, and price as possible sites of incongruity. (1972: 107). See also Babuscio 1977, directly indebted to Newton's pioneering work. More recent commentators have pointed to a generalized incongruity which results from the play between high and low culture, and this is obviously what accounts for many of John Waters's particular 'obsessions'. See especially Ross 1988.

3. 'Anyone who made as many films as his years on earth (especially if they're all good) deserves the privilege of being a true monster'. (Waters 1987: 115). Upon being informed of Fassbinder's death, Warhol concludes in the usual deadpan tone of the *Diaries*, but not without a hint of awe, that 'He was thirty-seven and did forty movies' (Warhol & Hackett, 446). The fact that Warhol, the obsessive worker that he was, should be particularly impressed by Fassbinder's work ethic comes as no surprise.

4. See Katz, 8. In this text, Katz relates Fassbinder's reaction to Warhol's compliment as instinctively utilitarian: 'We have to remember that', Fassbinder supposedly told his producer, 'What a slogan!'

5. There is some debate about this; for the pro argument, see Babuscio 1977. For a more historiographical account arguing the opposite position, see Booth 1983.

6. On the interrelations between camp and the melodramatic mode in film and television, see Butler 1990b; Finch & Kwietniowski 1988; and Finch 1986: 24–42.

7. Shattuc 1993: 48. For a translation of Fassbinder's text on six films by Douglas Sirk, see Fassbinder.

8. This cutting across also operates, quite specifically, on the distinctions of *taste* analyzed by Pierre Bourdieu, along with all their cultural baggage of high vs. low, legitimacy vs. illegitimacy, and bourgeois vs. proletarian. See Bourdieu; one of Fassbinder's films which most clearly thematizes and confounds the parallel distinctions of bourgeois vs. proletarian and 'good taste' vs. 'tastelessness' is, of course, *Fox and his Friends* (1974) [*Faustrecht der Freiheit*] where Fox (R. W. F.) suddenly finds himself on the side of the rich after winning the lottery, but lacks the cultural capital to go with it: the gap that exists within the naturalizing equation of money with cultural 'competency' (to use Bourdieu's term) becomes readily apparent.

9. Eve Sedgwick points out that 'the word "queer" itself means *across* – it comes from the Indo-European root – *twerkw*, which also yields the German *quer* (transverse)' (Sedgwick, *Tendencies*, xii).

10. Elsaesser 1989: 41. Miriam Hansen strikes the same key: 'The manifestation of an individual style, the artist's signature, in the work of a Fassbinder, for instance, has encouraged a primarily aesthetic reception abroad – at its best in terms of avant-garde film theory, at its worst in the American blend of auteur criticism or celebration [i.e., *camp*? – J. v. M.]. Such approaches tend to occlude the more specifically political dimensions of Fassbinder's films which – his fascination with American genre film notwithstanding – address problematic continuities of German history on a more complex level than merely that of subject matter' (Hansen, 14).

11. Rentschler 1981: 34. The underlying theme of 'depoliticization' in the transatlantic exchange was already sounded in Germany in a 1977 review of Fassbinder's sudden success on Broadway and in the Village after the New York Film Festival of that year. Norbert Muhlen takes up the Warhol comparison, insisting on the political relevance of Fassbinder's Warholian lack of respect. But, he concludes, 'The American audience, mind you, hardly heard his political signals'.

12. The impossibility of such a restitution of balance between the film and its (national) spectator is aptly captured, I believe, in the notion of 'defective suture' which Elsaesser ('Afterword', 49) finds in Fassbinder's *Despair* (1977).

13. Here we learn that 'Russ is now at work on his $1.5 million ten-hour swan song, *The Breast of Russ Meyer*' – an autobiographical project with condensed versions of all his twenty-three films, three ex-wives, five close girlfriends, and army buddies, which Waters (1987: 6) thinks should be more appropriately renamed *Berlin Alexandertits*.

14. Indeed, the structure of the simulacrum and the way it complicates the very notions of an original and its copy become explicit when Waters asks Angelyne whether she identifies with the great Jayne Mansfield – whereupon she 'blasphemes: "Jayne went into the fourth dimension and copied me and did a lousy job"' (Waters 1987: 7).

15. Terminology has shifted somewhat since Esther Newton's 1972 field study, but it is significant that she can describe certain female impersonators as *personified* 'camps', noting that 'the camp is concerned with what might be called a philosophy of transformations and incongruity'; as one of the 'role models' for professional female impersonators, the camp represents 'the central role figure in the subcultural ideology of camp' (105).

16. Fassbinder, 67. Rosa von Praunheim – a both embittered and astute critic of Fassbinder's life and work – traces his interest in the distribution of social and sexual roles to the director's own transvestite identity, suggesting that 'his female

characters were always a part of his transvestite soul as well'. This reading is shared, with undue psychoanalytical essentialism concerning the role of bisexuality in artistic creation, by Hayman.

17. Schygulla suggests as much when she notes that after *Fontane Effi Briest* 'I thwarted my career. That saved it, I think . . .' (31).

18. Heinrichs explicitly links the new stardom of Schygulla to Warhol's example and goes on to note: 'There is no stopping them any more, the stars of the underground . . . Thereby, one of the most amazing movements in the film and theater subcultures of the last few years: the rediscovery of stars, has its entry into the official, subsidized culture . . . and Hanna Schygulla was Germany's first superstar . . . Because Schygulla always brought a little glamour to the dull and resigned *antiteater* scenes'.

19. '*Hinterhof-Glamour*' – the term is Schygulla's own. See Koch, 93.

20. It is hardly surprising, therefore, that she herself should suggest that especially in Germany (but no doubt in America, too) she still bears the 'invisible mark' [*unsichtbare Stempel*] of Fassbinder. See her interview in *Berliner Morgenpost*, 27 April 1990.

21. *Love is Colder Than Death* (1969); Fassbinder has told Uli Lommel that he has this girlfriend whom he loves and invites Uli to visit. We then follow Lommel on a long nocturnal search for 'Joanna' which functions in part as a characterization of the milieu in which she apparently moves: pimps, hookers, and landlords full of disdain constitute the guides in Lommel's quest, which ends with his arrival in Schygulla's and Fassbinder's small apartment, where we find Schygulla in a state of undress that will almost become her trademark – she is undoing the hooks of her garter belt.

22. See Schygulla. In a recent interview, Schygulla significantly (if laboriously) refers to Marlene Dietrich as 'one who makes a *Zeitgeist*-constituting phenomena of herself'. See *Tagesspiegel*, 19 December 1993.

23. 'The estrangement between Fassbinder and me began during the shooting of *Fontane Effi Briest* . . . [I]n my head, it should have become a completely different film. Much more engaged on my part. The way the film then turned out, it seems like death from suffocation in a more charming environment', *Filmfaust* 11.44, 1985, 8.

24. On the distinction between character, person, image, and persona, see King.

25. For better or for worse, this nationalization of Schygulla's body has stuck with her even or precisely whenever she has left Germany to work in other countries (as has generally been the case since Fassbinder's death).

26. Another version of this dialectic of complicity and resistance has recently been traced by John Davidson, who describes the way in which the metaphorically 'colonized' Young German Filmmakers went on to create a number of colonizing representations of their own, often in the service of Germany's diplomatic efforts to regain its status among the nations of the world.

27. Although Adelson is concerned, as she says, with 'the bodies of history as constructed in literary texts', as opposed to my interest here in the cinematic body, she makes a periodizing observation that connects directly with my reading of Hanna Schygulla in Fassbinder's films: 'In the West German context of the last twenty years one could argue that the body in literature functions no longer as the mere object (victim) of history or as an allegorical emblem for the nation (or its moral conscience) but rather as the heterogeneous site of contested identities' (36).

28. Indeed, America plays a fundamental role in Fassbinder's camp about his own star-director-persona. See the first chapter of Katz. Rosa von Praunheim's admiration for Tally Brown, on the other hand, provides a good example of a kind of German camp which picks up on figures and iconographies that have already been made over into camp in the United States (Praunheim 1991).

29. It is precisely her collector's activity that incidentally brought Charlotte (a.k.a. Lothar Berfelde) the Federal Cross of Merit [*Bundesverdienstkreuz*] for her conservational efforts. See Mahlsdorf.

30. Ross 1988, rpt. 1989: 151–52. Steven Shaviro also notes, 'A camp object is enjoyed in the decadent splendor of its having already vanished' (1993: 224).

31. Rentschler is referring to Alexander Kluge's and Peter Schamoni's 1960 short, *Brutalität in Stein*, which he reads as 'Young German Film's earliest sign of life'. See Rentschler, 29.

32. Indeed, in an interview with Hans Günther Pflaum, Fassbinder describes the risks he is taking with his then current project, *Lili Marleen*, as the reason, even the inspiration, for getting involved in that undertaking in the first place: 'I stand behind whatever comes of *Lili Marleen*, or the work, among other reasons because it entails a degree of risk that I find very exciting, because it could really turn into a disaster'. See Fassbinder, 59.

33. Among these new forms of spectatorship are certainly those audiences which encountered many of his films for the first time after November, 1989: in the GDR, only *The Marriage of Maria Braun* had been released for theatrical showings; for accounts of the significance of such encounters see Klauß, and Richter.

34. Jack Babuscio links this notion of filmic excess directly to the function of camp, suggesting that the latter can be described as 'an emphasis on sensuous surfaces, textures, imagery, and the evocation of mood as stylistic devices – not simply because they are appropriate to the plot, but as fascinating in themselves' (1977, rpt. 1993: 43). Historically, that excess may simply be an effect of the passage of time. Noting that in a film like *Lili Marleen*, 'the filmic status of fascism – as signifier, referent, or both – is ... extremely difficult to locate', Thomas Elsaesser recognizes that for Fassbinder, 'the cinema can deal with history only when and where history itself has acquired an imaginary dimension, where the disjunction between sign and referent is so radical that history turns on a problem of representation, and fascism emerges as a question of subjectivity within image and discourse ... rather than one of causality and determinants for a period, a subject, a nation'. Elsaesser, '*Lili Marleen*', 122.

REFERENCES

Adelson, Leslie A., *Making Bodies, Making History: Feminism and German Identity*, Lincoln: U of Nebraska P, 1993.

Bourdieu, Pierre, *Distinction: A Social Critique of the Judgement of Taste*, trans. R. Nice, Cambridge: Harvard UP, 1984.

Davidson, John, 'As Others Put Plays Upon the Stage: *Aguirre*, Neocolonialism, and New German Cinema', *New German Critique* 60, Fall 1993.

Elsaesser, Thomas, 'Afterword: Murder, Merger, Suicide – The Politics of *Despair*', in Tony Rayns (ed.), *Fassbinder*, London: BFI, 1980.

——, 'Primary Identification and the Historical Subject: Fassbinder and Germany', in Ron Burnett (ed.), *Explorations in Film Theory*, Bloomington: Indiana UP, 1991, 86–99.

——, 'A Cinema of Vicious Circles', in Tony Rayns (ed.), *Fassbinder*, London: BFI, 1980.

——, '*Lili Marleen*: Fascism and the Film Industry', *October* 21, Summer 1982.

Fassbinder, R. W., 'Imitation of Life: On the Films of Douglas Sirk', in Michael Töteberg & Leo A Lensing (eds.), *The Anarchy of the Imagination*, Baltimore: Johns Hopkins UP, 1992, 77–89.

Hansen, Miriam, 'Cooperative Auteur Cinema and Oppositional Public Sphere: Alexander Kluge's contribution to *Germany in Autumn*', *New German Critique* 24–5, Fall-Winter 1981.

Hayman, Ronald, *Fassbinder: Film Maker*, London: Weidenfeld and Nicholson, 1984.

Heinrichs, Benjamin, 'Hanna Schygulla – oder die naive Diva', *Theater heute*, Jahressonderheft 1972, 109–11.

Kaes, Anton, *From Hitler to Heimat: The Return of History as Film*, Cambridge: Harvard UP, 1989.

Katz, Robert, *Love Is Colder Than Death: The Life and Times of Rainer Werner Fassbinder*, New York: Random House, 1987.

King, Barry, 'Articulating Stardom', in Gledhill 1991.

Klauß, Cornelia, 'Zeichen auseiner anderen Welt oder: Geboren in Deutschland', and Rolf Richter, 'Fassbinder in der DDR', in *Rainer Werner Fassbinder Werkschau: Programm*, Berlin: Rainer Werner Fassbinder Foundation, 1992.

Koch, Gertrud, 'Die Frau vor der Kamera: Zur Rolle der Schauspielerin im Autorenfilm. Frauen bei Fassbinder', *Frauen und Film* 35, October 1983.

Mahlsdorf, Charlotte von, *Ich bin meine eigene Frau: Ein Leben*, St. Gallen: Edition Dia, 1992.

Mayne, Judith, 'Fassbinder and Spectatorship', *New German Critique* 12, Fall 1977, 61–74.

Mühlen, Norbert, 'Mutter Küsters Wandlung über dem Atlantik', *Die Welt*, 1 July 1977.

Praunheim, Rosa von, 'Schwul, pervers, kontrovers', *Berliner Zeitung*, 10 June 1992, 9.

Reimer, Robert & Carol Reimer, *Nazi-Retro Film: How German Narrative Cinema Remembers the Past*, Boston: Twayne, 1992.

Rentschler, Eric, 'Remembering Not to Forget: A Retrospective Reading of Kluge's *Brutality in Stone*', *New German Critique* 49, Winter 1990.

Santner, Eric, *Stranded Objects: Mourning, Memory, and Film in Postwar Germany*, Ithaca: Cornell UP, 1989.

Schygulla, Hanna, *Bilder aus Filmen von Rainer Werner Fassbinder*, Munchen: Schirmer/Mosel, 1981.

Sedgwick, Eve Kosofsky, 'Queer Performativity: Henry James' *The Art of the Novel*', *GLQ* 1.1, November 1993.

——, *Tendencies*, Durham: Duke UP, 1993.

Shattuc, Jane, 'R.W. Fassbinder's Confessional Melodrama: Towards Historicizing Melodrama within the Art Cinema', *Wide Angle* 12:1, January 1990, 44–59.

Uhrmeister, Beate, '"It was indeed a German Hollywood Film": Fassbinder-Rezeption in den USA. Notizen zu einem produktiven Mißverständnis', *Text und Kritik* 103, July 1989, 80–85.

Warhol, Andy, *The Philosophy of Andy Warhol*, New York: Harcourt Brace Jovanovich, 1975.

Warhol, Andy & Pat Hackett, *The Warhol Diaries*, New York: Warner, 1989.

26

THE DEATHS OF CAMP

Caryl Flinn

This piece was written in loving memory of Jim McLaughlin, who was supposed to have debated these issues with me in New York.

On a recent book promotion tour, Fran Leibowitz announced that camp was dead. Sontag's famous definitions, she said, worked well until the late 1970s, but since then, camp as we have known it, that is primarily as a gay male phenomenon, has become mainstreamed enough for Leibowitz to pronounce it 'decamp'. TV shows, for instance, have turned camp into what Leibowitz called a 'smugness with no edges'. She added that AIDS also furthered the demise. Leibowitz is not alone with these claims; debates are going strong as to whether camp is 'possible' any more, after AIDS, after postmodernism, even after Stonewall. The ostensible birth of gay activism at Stonewall was, after all, precipitated by the death of camp icon Judy Garland. For Mark Finch (1986) and David Román (1992), camp exists only as a pre-Stonewall phenomenon, an important but dead, if you will, moment of gay history, and, as early as 1983, Mark Booth suggested that camp's active place in dominant culture reduced the term from camp *per se* to the mere 'exaltation of mediocrity' – as opposed to exaltation of trash, which he liked (1983: 181). And, in his introduction to Philip Core's *Camp: The Lie That Tells The Truth*, George Melly wrote that the work 'may well turn out to be an elegy' (1984: 5).

It may seem somewhat odd that these death notices have been proliferating just as queer culture, scholarship, and activism have hit great stride. At the

Originally published in *Camera Obscura*, 35, May 1995.

same time it is being declared dead, new publications on camp are emerging with some regularity (Moe Meyer's *The Politics and Poetics of Camp*; David Bergman's *Camp Grounds*) and earlier studies (Esther Newton's *Mother Camp*, Roger Baker's *Drag*) are being brought back into print. But whether prematurely announced or not, the death of camp raises the issue of aspects of death in camp – for the two have been longtime associates. As Booth observes, 'There is an element of camp that shrinks from the heat of life' (1983: 67); Andrew Ross, for his part, spends a significant portion of his influential 'Uses of Camp' on camp's necrophilic tendencies; and, years after her 'Notes on Camp' was written, Susan Sontag told an interviewer 'How "to name a sensibility" . . . that was the problem I started from, and then looked for a model . . . Morbidity was my first choice', producing, "Notes on Camp" instead of "Notes on Death"' (Boyers & Bernstein 1975, rpt. 1982: 338–9).

My own essay traces this preoccupation with decay and death as it has been critically constructed by camp and as it has been applied to human bodies in particular – and to feminized ones more particularly still. For the human icons that 'body camp' brings into its fold are often deeply involved with death – a fleshy, grotesque, decaying death that, as I will show, is imposed onto some bodies with more fervor than others. Because certain deaths and decays have been much more in evidence than others (just as camp practices and definitions vary widely – see below), the assertion of 'camp's death' can never be the categorical claim that it might seem. Our look into camp's preoccupation with death and decay should lead us not only into a better understanding of camp as a critical endeavor, queer practice, and cultural phenomenon more generally, but also into questions about larger assaults on the female body under way in contemporary political and cultural arenas.

I want to stress from the outset that body camp's connection to death and decay does not emerge solely from critics' ink, nor does it reside in some notion of camp 'immanence' that would somehow precede critical inquiry. The blurred lines between camp criticism and practices can be illustrated in the frequent use of epithets in camp literature, something my own pages already make evident. What, it may he asked, is entailed in using epithets to address a style that, in effect, itself consists of epithet? Ridicule, one of the key byproducts of the critically and practitionally complicit epithet, will be a central concern of this essay, as will be the question of what displacements might be at work in engaging that ridicule, in camp's 'loving assassination', to anticipate a phrase of Leo Bersani's. We will see how very quickly camp's clever epithet becomes derisive epitaph.

One thing this essay does *not* attempt to do is to add to the considerable literature that tries to define camp. That defining camp has always posed such a quagmire for critics is not so much a result of the term's elusiveness – in spite of Sontag and others' assertions to the contrary – but of the political motivations behind these same definitions. Camp criticism from the mid-1970s and early 1980s (the 'first wave' of sustained gay scholarship) was motivated by a twofold desire to reappropriate camp specifically for gay cultures: first, to reclaim an aspect of gay culture that was often a source of opprobrium within gay communities (not to mention heterosexual ones); second, as camp became increasingly diffuse and 'popular', hitting mainstream, mass (straight) cultures, its place in gay culture and history needed to be re-secured and re-asserted. For commentators of this early period – and for others since then – camp often became an ontological construction, claimed as proceeding automatically from a uniquely 'gay sensibility'.[1] Such claims were largely made for polemical/ political purposes – hardly a bad motivation, to be sure, but troubling in terms of some of its effects and methods (psychologizing queer 'essence'; disregarding camp's non-gay impact; suggesting a purity or homogeneity of queer identity, and so forth). I make no attempt here to speak for camp *tout court*, nor for all of gay male camp; its forms are too varied, its contexts too diverse. My essay instead focuses on conventional camp icons – especially as they are put into practice with human bodies – camp forms that have historically, but not exclusively, been associated with modern gay male subculture. In one sense, my focus falls on what Christopher Isherwood described as the 'low forms' of camp. Unlike the higher forms – ballet, baroque art – that interested Isherwood, this essay addresses the body camp practices he epitomizes in the 'swishy little boy with peroxided hair ... pretending to be Marlene Dietrich' (1954: 124).

A MORBID NOSTALGIA

> One of the ways in which mankind progresses is by idealizing the past and then attempting to recreate it. Camp employs a perversion of this process in which idealized versions of the past are recreated with the intention of being retrograde rather than progressive. Camp takes styles from the past and uses them to sidestep the onward march of history. The historical is reduced to the ephemeral. (Booth 1983: 143–4)

Camp has always been fascinated with, and has fashioned itself on, the out-moded, the out of date, the artifact past its prime. Camp, as Ross points out, makes use of signs of 'power ... in decline' (1988, rpt. 1989: 140). The nuked family leaves us *Leave it to Beaver* or *The Brady Bunch*; white, middle-aged male angst churns out *Falling Down* and any other Michael Douglas movie. Mark Booth's quote above suggests a double structuring of camp as leftover that would have camp either 'sidestepping' history or being killed off by it. Writer Daniel Harris takes this point to a dizzying extreme. Arguing that after World War II, gay culture was no longer able to exert control over American and European avant-gardes, there was nothing left for it to do but to delve into camp. Harris furthers the association between gay culture and failure by arguing that camp practices likewise emerged from that subculture's inability to bring masculinity's effeminate forms into the fold (1991: 77). Camp there-fore shores up what Harris deems to be two of gay culture's shortcomings: its purported postwar loss of influence on high art and modernity, and its repudiation of effeminacy. (For the present argument, the veracity of Harris's historical reading – which is highly suspect – is less relevant than its insistence on failure and inability.) Another critic, David Román, writing as recently as 1992, argues that the only way contemporary camp can exist is nostalgically, as a fleeting retreat into what he calls a 'pre AIDS moment' (rpt. 1993: 216), a comment that might begin to explain all the ABBA soundtracks we're getting in the mid-1990s (Román's own example is Lypsinka).

Camp has been connected to a variety of other declines, lapses, and losses – with some connections more convincingly made than others. Carole-Anne Tyler, for her part, maintains that camp is a 'phallic imposture' that protects its male performer (of which the drag queen is exemplary) from the threat of loss of his virility (1991: 32). With the phrase, Tyler insists not only upon the defensive, aggressive nature of the 'posture', but the counterfeit status of the phallus itself. She makes an important point given that prevailing cultural discourses associate femininity with lack – and forcibly reinscribe both terms onto male homosexual bodies. According to her view, gay drag acknowledges the subject's ostensible fall from the benefits of full, phallic subjectivity at the same time it seems to protect him from that descent. 'The fear', she writes, 'that homosexuality means a man can be robbed of his virility, articulated as "fact" by Freud in his explanation of Leonardo Da Vinci's homosexuality, may animate homophobia outside the gay community and misogyny within it as well as without' (37).

Camp, constructed in these ways in terms of deficiency, decline, and the past, is often difficult to distinguish from nostalgia (as in the ABBA example). Consider how Samuel L. Jackson's jheri curls in *Pulp Fiction* elicit giggles from 1994 audiences wearing, in 'deadly earnest', to use Sontag's phrase, platform shoes. Camp might be said to function as a kind of *ironic* nostalgia, unlike more conventional forms of nostalgia, which mandate a much more earnest consumption of texts. But in general, as Andrew Ross explains, camp generates its effects from the 'eclipsed capacity' of artifacts (or conventions) of 'a much earlier mode of production' that 'become available, in the present, for redefinition according to contemporary codes of taste' (1988, rpt. 1989: 139–40). It is a revitalization that can only occur under certain conditions and through specific perspectives, however: ironic constructions are permissible; canonical forms are not. The artifact, in other words, cannot be *too* old, for then it might qualify as an object of 'proper' anthropological or historical inquiry. As Michael Woods writes in a piece delightfully entitled 'An Anatomy of Rubbish', 'Fads must have become *demodé* ... but they must not yet be old enough to be of interest to antiquarians or social historians' (quoted in Booth 1983: 145).

Classic icon Mae West offers a prime example of camp's reliance on the out of date for its effects. There are, of course, her intensely camped up performances in *Sextette* (1971) and *Myra Breckinridge* (1978), which feed on the already-camped image she had cultivated much earlier. But, as Pamela Robertson argues, even during her film and theater work of the 1920s and 1930s, Mae West was a 'deliberate anachronism' – one which, Robertson maintains (1993, rpt. 1993: 158), had a strong appeal for women (unlike *Myra*, which had a more conventional camp appeal to gay men). Factors that made West a throwback even in this earlier period include her burlesque comedic performance style, the late nineteenth-century settings of most of her stories, and, of course, the decidedly Victorian contours of her body.

Mae West's 1920s, along with the 1960s, might be considered the century's campiest decades, if iconic activity is any indication. The cults surrounding actors like Valentino and Novarro in the 1920s, for instance, might be partially understood as a way of bidding farewell to theatrical models of acting, self presentation, and conventions of masculinity. The logic of the campy 1960s – the time when Sontag's essay first appeared, the decade of Batman, Robin, and Andy Warhol – followed from camp's fascination with glamour, and with Hollywood glamour in particular. By this time, the classical studio system of Hollywood and its idealized conventions and icons of masculinity and femininity had been left firmly behind in its past 'glamour era', abandoned objects with the ready potential to be fetishized anew, easy camp targets. (During this same, post-classical studio period, academic film studies began to emerge, suggesting a nostalgia or necrophilia that might motivate our own work and passions as well.)[2] And to leave glamour behind, as Richard Dyer remarks, is to elicit another kind of failure: 'Not being glamorous', he writes, 'is to fail at femininity, to fail at one's sex role' (1986: 167). Many things were left by Hollywood's glamorous wayside. Ross, addressing the relationship between death, camp producers and consumers, and the post-studio period of film history, refers to 'the cult of Hollywoodiana with all of the necrophilic trappings that embellish its initiates' "sick" fascination with the link between glamour and death', joys that are exploited in necro-romps like *All About Eve*, *What Ever Happened to Baby Jane?*, *Mommy Dearest*, and in Kenneth Anger's *Hollywood Babylon* series' (1988, rpt. 1989: 138).

Camp is thus a scavenger, scrounging 'history's waste' in order to 'rediscover surplus value from forgotten forms of labor' (Ross 1988, rpt. 1989: 140). Through its investment in detritus, in used-up things, camp might be seen as a critical response to planned obsolescence, although camp's recycling hardly impedes the gears of capitalism. After all, to reuse an object and send it to back to the marketplace makes for pretty low overhead, as Andy Warhol made clear.[3] The cannibalism we encounter in camp classics like *Eating Raoul* or *Blood Diner* not only highlights camp's obsession with death, flesh, and decay, but diegetically demonstrate, like the films themselves, that money can be made by reusing, remanufacturing, death. Mark Booth has pointed out how camp in fact depends on a highly prosperous bourgeoisie, first to provide the ideological center whose 'margins' camp inhabits and secondly, to supply the economic surplus, leisure time, and wealth needed by camp for sustenance. What Booth calls the typical 'camp person' and the 'bourgeois gentilhomme' actually have a number of common features: love of possessions, concern with appearance, retreat from nature into the world of things (84). (Booth also adds that both are unconcerned with social problems, a position which would make camp's existence as a form of activism – say, in the age of AIDS – most unlikely.)[4]

WHOSE DEATH IS IT, ANYWAY?

Camp can thus be a means of undercutting rage by its derision of concentrared bitterness. Its vision of the world is comic. Laughter, rather than tears, is its chosen means of dealing with the painfully incongruous situation of gays in society. Yet it is also true that camp is something of a protopolitical phenomenon. (Babuscio 1977, rpt. 1993: 28)

In addition to the notions of historic and economic distances, camp requires semiotic distance, particularly if it is to generate its well-known effects of irony and parody. For camp demands disphasure, not just of signifier and signified, but a more general being out of step, a lagging behind, a barrier between subject and object. Such a difference exists between production and consumption; Sontag's dictum that camp is 'failed seriousness', for example, clearly assumes that that 'seriousness' be intended. Her position could never explain cherished camp artifacts like *The Rocky Horror Picture Show*, Divine, or *The Adventures of Priscilla, Queen of the Desert*, but Sontag's concern with the intentions of camp's performer or producers and her relative inattention to its target and consumer are shared by other critics, a point I will develop momentarily. Significantly, in representing camp as 'failed seriousness', Sontag acknowledges the aggression and ridicule involved in camp's effects. This aggression is frequently located in the reading, at the site of consumption, but it can also be found on the part of producers as well, as in the notion of intentional camp. In the 1990s, for instance, reruns of *The Brady Bunch* TV show are a consumer-driven camp text in which 1960s and 1970s conventions of nuclear family life get sent up; the campiness of *The Brady Bunch Movie* (1995), on the other hand, was clearly the calculation of producers from the start.[5]

Along the same lines, Thomas Hess quips that camp 'exists in the smirk of the beholder' (1965). And since smirks are always made at the expense of another, they emerge from contexts in which subject and object are at least partially differentiated in terms of power. The aggression, ridicule, and cruelty of camp practice and commentary have been issues of no small concern for critics, especially for those feminists who consider campy gay drag to be attacks on women (a typically 1970s approach but one that by no means has run its course). More recently, Leo Bersani has made the argument that gay macho camp forms – more so than less erotic, 'feminine' forms – point to an aggressive undoing of a different kind. Anticipating and developing Judith Butler's contention that drag kills off the fiction of the stable ego, Bersani's 'Is the Rectum a Grave?' maintains that gay machismo points to a sexuality that offers a full destabilization of boundaries, the dissolution of identity itself: 'Male homo-sexuality', he writes, 'advertises the risk of the sexual itself as the risk of self-dismissal, of *losing sight* of the self, and in so doing it proposes and dangerously represents *jouissance* as a mode of ascesis' (1987: 222). Although Bersani is finally more interested in locating that dissolution within a specific sexual practice (and, as the title of the article suggests, at a specific anatomical site), his comments about 'feminized' gay camp practices warrant consideration. He writes, for instance, that the 'gay male bitch . . . desublimates and desexualizes a type of femininity glamorized by movie stars, whom he thus lovingly assassi-nates with his style, even though the campy parodist may himself be quite stimulated by the hateful impulse inevitably included in his performance' (208). Bersani's provocative phrase 'loving assassination' suggests, I think, less the unintended nature of camp humor than the sheer morbidity of its aggressive-ness, an issue to which I will be returning. True, many gay and queer critics emphasize the deep affection camp has for its object, however ironically or ambivalently charged it may be, but how that affection is conveyed through 'loving assassination' remains to be seen. One might also ask the politically pertinent question of *which* stable ego and what particular fictions hear the brunt of camp's 'loving assassination?' Of whose death, in other words. are we speaking?[7]

A handful of critics have argued, Sontag perhaps most famously, for camp as a fundamentally apolitical phenomenon. Most, however, adhere to the basic belief in camp's ability to unmoor dominant ideological structures and values – not an apolitical act, to be sure. Jack Babuscio, for instance, writing in the mid-1970s, asserted that 'camp can be subversive – a means of illustrating those cultural ambiguities and contradictions that oppress us all, gay and straight, and, in particular, women' (1977, rpt. 1993: 28). Be it fully 'subversive' or not (especially for women), there is no doubt that camp troubles prevailing assump-tions about body and gender identity. For what body camp does is to take the signs of human identity and place them into a performative situation, distancing them from their 'original' sites, or indeed, the notion of an original or natural condition at all, in much the same way that Butler, Sue-Ellen Case, Marjorie Garber, and others have argued about drag and gender identity. So whether its excesses are tied to 'female impersonators' like Craig Russell or to 'women' like Mae West, body camp exaggerates gender codes, making them obvious, grot-esque. For Case and Butler, camp and drag unseat a string of binary opposi-tions: male/female; straight/queer; signifier/signified; surface/depth; self/other, and Butler (1990a: 137) emphatically spells out these claims: 'drag fully subverts the distinction between inner and outer psychic space and effectively mocks both the expressive model of gender and the notion of true gender identity . . . As much as drag creates a unified picture of 'woman' . . . it also reveals the distinctness of those aspects of gendered experience which are falsely naturalized as a unity through the regulatory fiction of heterosexual coherence. In imitating gender, drag implicitly reveals the imitative structure of gender itself – as well as its contingency'. Butler is careful not to argue that femininity or masculinity is parodied so much as the notion of an *original* normalizing fiction of gender identity.

Most criticism on camp's human icons centers on the arbitrary, constructed nature of gender and its conventions. Typically the conventions under question are heterosexual in origin – consider how many of camp's most established icons seem to wallow in the excesses of apparent heterosexual identity (Victor Mature, Marilyn Monroe). Since excess can threaten a system with its potential collapse and undoing, it is easy to see how the power of heterosexuality is undercut by such figures. Moreover, and as Moe Meyer argues, what can be pulled out of that excess is a specifically queer appropriation of queer conventions – of gender, identity, culture – which heterosexual discourse has devalued and cast out as 'moribund waste', as Ross maintained from a less queer perspective. Unlike Ross, who emphasized relations of difference in camp's brand of semiotic archaeology, Meyer stresses a relationship of likeness, in that the queer subject – frustratingly singular, ungendered, and unraced in Meyer's account – reactivates repressed queer readings of texts and icons (such as Dusty Springfield or Sal Mineo).[8]

Camp's recontextualization of signs, of making them conspicuous and self-consciously ironic, can be – and has been – compared to several modernist and postmodenist strategies or concepts (consider Russian formalism's defamiliarization, the masquerade of psychoanalysis, pastiche and the postmodern), comparisons that seem especially apt when one considers camp's treatment of human subjectivity, identity, and the body. It must be added, however, and with Meyer's comments in mind, that articulating camp in terms of these theoretical traditions potentially deracinates it from lesbian, gay, and queer contexts.[9] All things considered, though, Ross, whom Meyer eagerly revises, is probably correct in arguing that gay male camp helped set the stage for feminist formulations of masquerade and other, nonessentialist articulations of gender as a performative phenomenon underived from innate essence, soul, or anything 'in' the body.

Body camp does not merely send up or parody conventions, though. It seeks out 'deadly' obvious conventions, ones that have become so clichéd and shelfworn as to become visible, if not risible (Kathleen Turner as the murderous suburban, 1950s-styled mother who wants people to behave just a little too correctly in *Serial Mom*, knifing one woman for wearing white shoes after Labor Day). Camp adores cliché, surface, image. With its emphasis on textures, appearances, materials, and bodies, camp poses a challenge to depth models of textuality (going against, for instance, structuralism's insistence on meaning being embedded within the deep structures of a text) and models of identity (repudiating the belief that external signs of one's appearance 'express' inner truths, a stable, 'real' self). Cult artifacts – close cousins of camp – operate in much the same way, as Robin Wood has noted. Cult films, he maintains, tend to draw the audience's attention to surfaces shown in the film, specifically to the surfaces that relate to the bodies in performance (consider *Priscilla*'s fascination with fabrics and costume).[10] Indeed, not one of camp's commentators would have meaning reside 'inside' or 'underneath' its various facades – Peggy Lee wigs, George Hamilton's suntan – thus explaining the frequency with which camp has been tied to postmodernism.

Some years ago Baudrillard explained the West's wider reliance on surfaces in terms of fetishism, a term he wanted to wrest from psychoanalysis (the only place, he argued, where it was associated with lack) in order to return it to its etymological roots: to imitate by signs, to feign, fake (like *se camper*). For Baudrillard, fetishism's fakery explains the fascinating hold of the fetish object over the subject, whose passion is generated not for the object itself, but for the *code*, the abstract system to which both subject and object are in the end subordinated. Illustrated in camp's need of artifacts whose semiotic use value has declined, we see that the *passé* object is what makes it susceptible to camping, not any inherent quality of the artifact itself. Moreover, and in an appropriate selection, Baudrillard turns to the body as a prime example of a fetish-object built upon extreme artifice. 'Signs perfect the body into an object in which none of its real work (the work of the unconscious or psychic and social labor) can show through' (94). As it is positioned in discourse today, the body is unquestionably 'made up', presented as a series of perfected surfaces (even simulacra), rather than in terms of an inner truth, labor, or soul that other periods and cultures may have asserted. It is to that artificial body we now turn.

THE BODY IN EXCESS

Musicals, horror films, and Carmen Miranda: all are figured in one of Jack Babuscio's lists of camp contenders (all based, he argued, on their exaggerated style). In another, longer inventory, Babuscio (1977) cites the following: Jayne Mansfield, Bette Davis, Anita Ekberg, Cesar Romero, Jane Russell, Raquel Welch, Mamie van Doren, Jennifer Jones, Johnny Weissmuller, and Ramon Novarro, making even more transparent the issues of gender and race implied by the first list. Nearly all of the camp figures Babuscio cites are white, female, and, at least as far as their public personae are concerned, heterosexual – a point which I will develop later. Still, and in spite of the apparent 'pale' quality of the above examples, it is striking how often aspects of non-Anglo ethnicity and race are crucial to the asserted effects of body camp (Miranda, Marlon Riggs's snap queens, Mr. T, Samuel Jackson's jheri curls). At a recent conference, for instance, Pamela Robertson suggested that a troubling part of Mae West's campiness emerged not just from assertions of her combined feminine and phallic attributes, but from a flexibility of racial identity as well, namely, her ability, if not to *pass* as black, to be able to pass in and out of blackness, and to be vocally or socially identified with 'authentic' black culture through scenes in which she banters with black maids, helps out or is given assistance from nonwhite characters, and uses a blues-derived, African American singing style. Here, one wonders if it is the color or West's boundary disturbance of it that qualifies the performance as camp. (To take a different historical example, the minstrel show would suggest that it is neither.) And certainly, same-race parodies often engage considerable camp intensity, as John Waters's treatment of white trash would indicate. Robertson's study draws important attention to the power differentials involved in cross-race camp claims: that white critics can read white-to-black movement – as in the case of West – as camp, engaging its attendant notions of gaming, superficiality, the fluidity of identification, and so forth, while black-to-white movement – even in a text as campily self-aware and sympathetic as *Paris is Burning* – still tends to be framed within signifiers of tragedy and pathos, suggests that the privilege of 'gaming' identity is largely a white privilege.[11]

Class difference is another feature shamelessly sent up in camp artifacts and performance, and the potential power difference and aggressivity displayed towards the object othered is no less active than that of other forms of differences – although, here too it is often muted by a tempering fondness directed towards the icon (consider the adored and reviled Divine). Curiously, class-specific camp icons seem to move back and forth between their makers and their targets, offering even less hermeneutic fixity than notions of gender or race. Camp runs the gamut from the decaying aristocracy, often purveyed by kitschy or effete film glamour (Zsa Zsa Gabor, Dirk Bogarde); the working classes are likewise fair game (The Village People, Divine); as is the middle class (June Cleaver, The Brady Bunch). Thus it seems hard to pin a specific class as a source or object of camp, and critics who have tried come up with widely divergent claims. For Tyler and Booth, for instance, camp's tastes and choices reflect a clear middle-class bias; Sontag and Sinfield find camp the twentieth-century urban equivalent of earlier, 'aristocratic' figures of leisure like the dandy.[12] In spite of its variety of classed sources, however, camp still requires difference, distance, and disphasure – a standard 'othering' of the artifact. Sontag, whose interest in camp's ersatz aristocratic heritage is most apparent, also maintains that a sort of egalitarianism operates in camp. Its economy for her involves a pre-Baudrillardian flattening of objects – their perverse democratization, if you will – for anything, she argues, has the potential to be camped. And indeed, the array of icons of various class differences seems to support such a reading, since traits of all classes are up for grabs, with middle-class icons often read for their banality, wealthy bodies yielding luxury and decadence, and lower-class figures purveying an ostensible vulgarity.

To maintain that camp practices involve a willed, smirking control over the object being camped is not, however, to argue that this control enjoys a parallel in actual social, juridical, economic, and political forms of power, for clearly queer culture has scarcely enjoyed such privilege. Rather the point is to inquire into the dynamics of ambiguity that critics have long associated with camp, and to explore ways in which camp's capacity to ridicule offers a means of displacing the social, psychic, and historical anxiety of its subject's disempowerment onto the objects and icons othered.[13] For if, in theory, all artifacts have the capacity to be camped, camp's actual constructions and historical choices show that much less 'democracy' operates than Sontag's claim suggests. The point is made with particular clarity through the issues of vulgarity, grotesqueness, and fleshy decay – aspects of camp that do not, as popularly conceived, intersect just with icons of the 'lower' classes, but with icons of femininity as well.

DECAY AND THE DIVA

The following was written by Daniel Harris in response to a San Francisco newspaper that ran two photographs of Greta Garbo side by side soon after her death; one was taken at the pinnacle of her movie career in the 1930s, the other was taken just prior to her death by a prying journalist:

> In her youth, she is Mona Lisa, menacing, impassive, malevolent, all-powerful ... all of the terrible authority of this look ... decomposes like the painting of Dorian Gray in the bewildered face of the doddering crone beside her ... [Her] sinister mane of white hair spills girlishly around her shoulders, framing a face that looks out at us with stupefied ineffectuality, like that of an incontinent hag who passes her time reviling her nurses and complaining about her aches and pains. (414–15)

Harris's brutal and florid language spells out the repercussions of camp's fascination with death, decay, and decline when aligned with the female body, whose excesses are gauged in terms of temporal dislocation ('Greta Garbo at death's door!') as well as physical abundance, lack, and imperfection, aspects of what Mary Russo labels 'irregular bodies'. Such 'irregularities', if we may call them that, distance the performing body from culturally held somatic and behavioral norms (here, Raquel Welch in *Myra Breckinridge* is perhaps the campiest of all for attempting to approximate such impossible standards). Typically – and importantly – those somatic deviances are of abundance rather than scarcity: think of Dolly Parton, Divine, Mae West, as opposed to the thin, youthful, more 'cultish' Edie Sedgwick. Camp entails an excess of consumption, a wasted production that is literalized by/on female bodies. It operates in the 'prurient satisfaction' (416) Daniel Harris admits having experienced while regarding the two Garbo photos and in his monstrous description of having come 'face to face with the holocaust of her legendary beauty, which lies exposed for everyone to see and gasp at *like a disaster photo of a plane crash or a natural catastrophe*' (417; my emphasis). Harris's articulation of Garbo's 'fallen' iconicity raises important issues for all women and men, especially in light of its configuration within camp's larger interest in decay and morbidity. For camp doesn't just mock what is *outmoded*, but what – and who – is old.

When put in relation to the female body, camp's preoccupation with obsolescence and morbidity creates what might be called the 'aging diva' phenomenon. For what is possibly campier – and crueller – than the dead flowers sent backstage to the diva past her prime? Camp is Alexis on *Dynasty*, Gloria

Swanson in *Sunset Boulevard*, Elizabeth Taylor on the cover of *Hollywood Babylon II*.[14] There is a striking regularity with which aging and the body 'too' old, too obese, too close to death, are hurled onto middle-aged, female star-images like these.[15] Mae West, for instance, who has inspired no dearth of animated academic descriptions – as phallus, cross-dresser, as racial passer – to my knowledge has never been imaged as corpse, nor has much been said about her near-motionlessness in most production numbers, her tossing of lines from supine positions (*à la* icon Marlene Dietrich in her sofa-bound performance of 'Laziest Girl in Town' in *Stage Fright*). Even before her filmwork in the 1970s, the obvious place for such observations to be made, West's icon raises the specter of death. In *Klondike Annie*, for instance, she is doubly associated with it: in order to escape the clutches of the law, her character first feigns her own passing away and then assumes the identity of a (religious, almost saintly) female character who has, in fact, actually died.

On one level, the camped up forms of 'aging' femininity operate as the fleshy, excessive other to a more transcendent, cerebral masculinity – a fatiguingly familiar function, to be sure. At the same time, and as Elisabeth Bronfen, Kathleen Woodward, and others have demonstrated, the mortality, deterioration, and even literal deaths bestowed upon female bodies have no more to do with deathlike and other negative qualities of 'femininity' than they do with the authors, artists, and here, the campers who might effect those constructions of femininity. In this light female bodies function as ciphers for the illusions of unity, vigor, invulnerability, youthfulness, and virility that are aligned with (or withheld from) the masculine subject. She is the danger to his purity, which, it is supposed, resides outside of mortal time, history, and symbolic structuration. Significantly, the openly structuralist assumptions of this argument, which traditionally posit the opposition of heterosexual woman/heterosexual man, may in fact encourage other, non-heterosexual masculinities. Consider, for instance, the classic double structure of fetishism (adulation and abhorrence), defenses equally constructed as testimony to and denial of the subject's anxiety over imperfections, disunity, and mortality. Such psychic structuration can explain some of the ambivalence camp is purported to have regarding its object; it clearly articulates the threat of non-differentiation the camp object holds. However adored, then, the camp icon can be ridiculed or put down for its pre-sumed 'differences' from its spectator/critic/consumer.

How is age worn by or inscribed upon the female body? In the words of Daniel Harris, 'A dress is cute when it seems to allude to the sense of fashion of someone younger than the woman who wears it (although the same dress is grotesque, not cute, when the discrepancy between the age of the dress and the woman who wears it is too noticeable)' (1990: 308). Note how the final deter-mination of cuteness or grotesqueness here is made through camp's common recourse to the surface and coverings of the body. Freud, with even more unabashed flair, renders the 'older' woman grotesque, indeed moribund, in a passage from his essay 'Femininity' that ostensibly discusses woman's psyche and not her body: 'A man of about thirty strikes us as a youthful, somewhat unformed individual, whom we expect to make powerful use of the possibilities for development opened up to him by analysis. A woman of the same age, however, often frightens us by her psychical rigidity and unchangeability' (134–5). If Sontag is right about 'failed seriousness', this is perhaps Freud's campiest moment.

This is not to say that the male body has no place in camp lore: indeed, it is everywhere (Arnold Schwarzenegger, Pee Wee Herman). But its campiness is configured in very different ways. Whereas female icons are constructed as artifacts past their prime, male camp icons often highlight youthful and/or muscular excess or prowess: Marky Mark, Steve Reeves, Jean Claude Van Damme. For many students both gay and straight, for example, Rock Hudson's 1950s big cardboard body is little more than one big campfest; his body in the 1980s, on the other hand, is assuredly not. Death, perhaps, is a bit too close.

To distinguish the different treatment male and female bodies receive, consider the musical number 'Ain't There Anyone Here for Love' in *Gentlemen Prefer Blondes*. The female camp icon, hunk-crazed Jane Russell, is presented as excessive, overly mature – although it is Russell's sexual maturity rather than physical age that signals the point of excess here. While the male swimmers are every bit as campy, they are, in contrast, identified by their impossibly squeaky-clean athleticism, enthusiasm, and energetic movements throughout the number (as compared to Russell's 'apathetic and non-athletic' sequence of still poses), and their youthfulness (they go to bed at eight). The film playfully camps up the inappropriate ages of men who would be/could not be the partners of Russell and Marilyn Monroe: there is the boychild millionaire whom Monroe's character asks to be seated near at dinner, and, in the other direction, Piggy, the elderly diamond mine owner with whom Monroe cavorts. But the film's campiest endeavor is clearly its send-up of mature, female heterosexual desire: the basic goal motivating the two female protagonists, after all, is landing a man. In this regard one is reminded of Peter Wollen's influential study of Howard Hawks. Observing that his 'crazy comedies' are the flip side of the adventure, male-bonded dramas, Wollen calls the director's male characters like Cary Grant in *Bringing Up Baby* and others 'cruelly stunted' and emphasizes their 'sexual humiliation' at the hands of aggressive female predators like Katharine Hepburn, or Monroe and Russell (90, 91). Noting the homosocial contexts and pretexts of both filmgroups, one might well consider the extent to which active female heterosexual desire in comedies like *Gentlemen* as well as in action pictures like *Only Angels Have Wings* is not only depicted as inferior to the bonds between men, but as outright laughable in both kinds of films. (Recall the infantilization of the Jean Arthur character in *Angels* – insecure, uncoordinated, out of the know, and at the same time wild over the emotionally absent Grant.) In numbers like 'Ain't There Anyone Here for Love' we see the ridiculousness of Russell's over-articulation of heterosexual desire, staged as it is in a conspicuously homoerotic setting (the scene opens, for instance, with a man on an acrobatic swing in front of a mural of a Grecian soldier with erect blade poised).

Some have suggested that the male camp icon (or a female figure like Judy Garland) might be tied to the emotional, not physical, trials and excesses associated with his or her character, a result of what the icon has purportedly gone through in 'personal' life. But even on these terms, youthfulness adorns the male camped body more tenaciously than the female one. The young, anguished Sal Mineos and the James Deans far outnumber the Quentin Crisps or Liberaces, who in fact were camp icons well before they hit middle age and whose campiness as older men wasn't a consequence of emotional 'suffering' as it has been for the aging bodies of Judy Garland or Elizabeth Taylor. In these ways, youthfulness – both emotional and chronological – is fundamental to the critical discourses on male camp. Providing an interesting variation on the idea is Mark Booth, who identifies camp with what he calls, somewhat alarmingly, 'immaturity'. In a book chapter campily (and no less alarmingly) entitled 'Mummy Is the Root of All Evil', he establishes the 'beautiful boy' as an important archetype for camp practices in the 1920s and 1960s, proffering an image that even female figures like the flapper in the 1920s or Twiggy in the 1960s could inhabit. Booth's identification on the one hand of youthfulness with masculinity (whether these positions be taken up by men or women) and, on the other, of age with 'mummy, the root of evil' (women only) reproduces some of the problematic gender and age differentials discussed above. Moreover, his particular take on youthfulness effectively extinguishes the possibility of a politically-informed camp since the focus on 'immaturity' (as opposed to the signs of mere physical youth) implies that full symbolic maturity is largely unavailable to camp's practitioners. His emphasis on 'immaturity' also creates a disturbing parallel with the classic psychoanalytic view of homosexuality as a sign of 'stunted', immature, psycho-sexual development. Finally, one could challenge Booth's argument for its neglect of the fact that celebrated androgynes and 'beautiful boys' such as flappers and later, Twiggy, enjoyed privileged, mainstreamed positions in the *haute couture* of both decades. This is not to imply that *haute couture* cannot be camped (or reflexively camp itself) but it is to question the suggestion that 'beautiful boy' androgyny – youthful or not – is necessarily camp. (That said, an anonymous source from the 1930s offers a hilarious distinction between what high fashion culture and Hollywood expect from their respective feminine ideals: 'Madame Chanel wants a woman to look like a lady; Hollywood wants her to look like two ladies'.) (Core 1984: 10)

THE GROTESQUE BODY IN PIECES

As James Naremore's study of film acting tells us, comedy is often generated from a sense of the 'incoherence' of a performer's body, a prime example being Steve Martin in Carl Reiner's *All of Me* (Naremore 1988). The disunified body, the funny body that doesn't quite fit with itself, is, of course, *the* body of camp, as any drag queen will attest. It is also, through its failure to maintain boundaries – or its refusal of them – the body of grotesque realism, which Stallybrass and White describe in their assessment of Bakhtin as 'multiple, bulging, over- or undersized, protuberant and incomplete. The openings and orifices of the carnival body are emphasized, not its closure and finish' (9). 'Grotesque bodies', the kinds made visible in the work of Brueghel or of Ralph Steadman, are thus at dramatic odds with 'classical bodies' such as Michelangelo's 'David', which are organized around principles of self-sufficiency and unity. Like the disunified grotesque, camp also works to violate the standards of 'good taste', allying itself with filth, the profane, and an overall sense of disreputability. (George Melly once wrote that camp 'brought vulgarity back to popular culture') (1970: 171). Think of John Waters's classic *Pink Flamingos,* which boasts family clans fighting to be the 'filthiest people alive', Divine the 'queen of sleaze' (crowned in the film's infamous culminating shot), while her infantilized mother makes a gooey mess of the eggs she eats in her playpen and an 'evil' rival family elsewhere runs a birth farm.

In 1968, the English translation of Bakhtin's *Rabelais and His World* appeared, and it is no overestimation of its impact to say that critical discussions of 'grotesqueness' since then have all been shaped by Bakhtin's concepts. As we have seen above, the grotesque body is an important aspect of grotesque realism, a social and representational formation that Bakhtin says characterizes early modern European folk culture, and a formation that in turn plays a fundamental role in the idea of the carnivalesque. Bakhtin argues that the carnivalesque is generated by collective, non-privatized desires; it disrupts, shatters, and momentarily relaxes conventional boundaries, identities, and behaviors through parades, regional fairs, and other ritualistic but 'unofficial' fêtes and celebrations, that is, those not originating by state or religious decree. Just as Bakhtin connects the carnivalesque to the idea of collectivity and the subversive effects of the same (a connection whose romantic politics have not gone unchallenged),[16] the grotesque body is also constructed as flying in the face of the unified, singular, classical body and its subtending humanist ideology, namely, the concept of uncontradictory, autonomous, 'individual' subjectivity. In fact, the contrast between grotesque and classical is usually articulated on or by the body itself, and, as Stallybrass and White observe in regard to Bakhtin's work, tends towards a somewhat polarized account. For instance, concepts like reason, the human 'soul' and spirit, important features of the classical body, are associated with the body's actual upper regions like the head and heart. Quite opposed to that is the grotesque, which emphasizes the body 'below', a material, reproducing, and defecating body, one that generates blood, feces, semen, milk, and urine. The latter, as Stallybrass and White describe it, is an 'image of impure corporeal bulk with its orifices (mouth, flared nostrils, anus) yawning wide and its lower regions (belly, legs, feet, buttocks, and genitals) given priority over its upper regions (head, "spirit", reason)' (9). There is a sense that, as text and semiotic artifact, the grotesque body precludes closure, firmness, and security and also violates social and textual boundaries in a variety of ways. So too have the unruly bodies of camp (drag performances most spectacularly) been argued to undo myths of the unified subject and its supporting fictions of integrity, order, and stability. Both types of bodies, moreover, are associated with laughter and the sadistic, exuberant, seditious power emerging from this laughter. As Mary Russo's influential work on Bakhtin has made clear, there is the laughter emitting *from* these unbridled bodies; there is also the laughter that such 'irregular', un'whole-some' flesh actually provokes. In other words, the grotesque body in camp is a wild arid laughing body, but it is also one laughed at. Moreover, and as Russo has also maintained, that body is more often than not feminine: the hag, the pregnant woman, the cross-dressed man with balloon boobs, Divine, the egg lady in *Pink Flamingos*, the sex-starved Russell in *Gentlemen Prefer Blondes*. Clearly the excessive, grotesque body of carnivalesque and camp practices borrows its cues from physically caricatured notions of conventional femininity.[17]

Camp's exaggeration of the female form – whether worn by men or women – reproduces the familiar connection with abject excess it had in countless more traditional discourses. It is a figure that has been camped by virtue of its obesity (Divine, Liz), its ethnic voice (Miranda, Charo, the Gabor sisters), large breasts (Jayne Mansfield), or for what that body might undergo, be it substance abuse (Judy Garland) or surgical procedures (Cher). Such examples make clear that the grotesquefication of the female body occurs in mainstream culture with the same intensity as it does in camp subcultures, and illuminates the mutual interdependency and heterogeneity of these cultural arenas as well. It is useful in this regard to contrast the examples listed above with those of the trend of male cross-dressers popular in recent films: *The Crying Game*, *Farewell My Concubine*, *M Butterfly*, *Paris is Burning*. To varying degrees, all of these films attempt to denaturalize the male body through male-to-female sartorial crossings. But every one of them foregrounds the tragic, romantic dimension of its cross-dressed male figure – a connotation made even more problematic given the racial 'otherness' spectacularly gridded onto him (Dil's blackness, the Asian figures of *Concubine* and *Butterfly*, the Latinos and African-American men of *Paris*, especially Venus XTravaganza). The purported tragedy and pathos *of* the 'male-as-female' character, moreover, is achieved quite literally at the expense of the 'female-as-female' body, which is either excised from the text (Barbara Sukowa, the all but forgotten wife in *Butterfly*) or brutally assaulted for its presumed excesses and treachery (Miranda Richardson as Jude in *Crying*). Of course in *Crying*, Jude's final appearance is marked by her 'disguise': gone are the earlier, ostensibly truthful signifiers of 'Irishness' (her blonde, unkept hair, jeans, Irish fisherman's sweater), usurped by the urban apparel of a *femme fatale* (her Louise-Brooks-coiffed dark hair, power suit, etc.) – a masquerade, in short, every bit as extensive as Dil's, but deemed far more devious. The female-as-female body just doesn't cut it. Each time I saw *Crying* in theaters, audiences energetically cheered Dil on during his bloody assassination of Jude at film's end.

Formally and discursively, all of the above films anchor and fix 'maleness'; we know these cross-dressers are 'really' men through voice-over (*Paris*) or biological 'givens' established by scenes that establish the presence of a penis (*Crying*). Each of these films treats the male-to-female masquerade as something tragically ennobled because of what it might do for heterosexual white male characters and popular audiences. The woman-as-woman masquerade, on the other hand, is bracingly unsympathetic, and her character is firmly extinguished. Even the stupid *Mrs. Doubtfire*, though less violently than *Crying*, renders the nurturing female body unnecessary while appropriating its enlarged somatic signs (large breasts, padded hips, doting voice), a comic function that continues to prevail in other recent cross-dressed hits: *Priscilla*, *To Wong Foo*, and *The Bird Cage*.

A BODY IN DECLINE

Whether through the figures of Robin Williams, Doris Day, or Divine, body camp sends up certain codes of femininity. But which codes, which constructions are enlisted most frequently? What, in short, is the 'conventional femininity' to which we have been alluding? Leo Bersani offered one answer: that of 'movie stars'. The passage leading up to that point is worth repeating: 'The gay male parody of *a certain femininity* ... is both a way of giving vent to the hostility toward women that *probably afflicts every male* (and which male heterosexuals have of course expressed in infinitely nastier and *more effective* ways) *and* could also paradoxically be thought of as *helping to deconstruct that image for women themselves. A certain type* of homosexual camp speaks the *truth* of *that femininity* as mindless, asexual, and hysterically bitchy ... The gay male bitch desublimates and desexualizes *a type of femininity glamorized by movie stars*' (208; my emphases). Even though Bersani's discussion of gay camp's 'feminine' forms is framed by a larger inquiry into gay male machismo – obviously a different form of parodic send-up with, one assumes, different pathways for hostile impulses – his points seem to proceed from a couple of problematic assumptions. First is the idea that such aggression is innate in all men; second is the suggestion that there is a fixed 'truth' about that 'certain femininity' which can be articulated at all. Then there is the matter of what that 'truth' might entail: a bitchy, *asexual*, hysterical, and ultimately 'false', glamour whose wearer needs to be redundantly desexualized. (Carole-Anne Tyler [1991] has offered a cogent critique of some of these issues, suggesting, for instance, that Bersani's hostility towards homophobia is displaced onto femininity.)

In maintaining that camp's femininity is based on movie stars, Bersani demonstrates that certain codes of femininity bear the burden of camp more than others. The conventional codes of film glamour, for instance, intimate the presumption of class privilege, racial whiteness, and an 'hysterically' articulated female (hetero)sexuality. While exceptions to each of these conventions may be found in abundance, there is a very real sense in which the femininity Bersani specifies does shoulder a considerable portion of camp's inglorious 'smirk' (consider Alexis, Liz Taylor, and Norma Desmond from our previous examples).

In so far as it is perceived as a body that reproduces, that is, as an actual or potential maternal figure, the heterosexual female body is crucial to camp's death watch. Both camp and grotesque practices displace the material facts of aging onto the representation of a sexually 'productive' body that is, in turn, marked as feminine, a term made hideously overpresent, excessively corporeal, and deemed 'mature' in the sense of being overripe or rotten – like Garbo 'gone bad' for Mr. Harris.[18] Tania Modleski, in her response to *Camera Obscura's* well-known dossier on Pee Wee Herman, and more specifically to the claims made for 'Pee Wee's Playhouse' as progressive camp, focuses her attention on Mrs. Rene, 'the fat lady' who once sits on a chocolate cake, and on the andro- gynous Pee Wee, who in one episode becomes invisible. Drawing from this, Modleski writes that 'while the male, Pee-wee – always at the very least "a body without organs" – is able to disembody himself completely, it is the female who grows to "maturity", who possesses a body with organs ... and who, finally, is presented as a Rabelaisian figure of fleshly excess, dripping as excrement the very food she would greedily devour, body and organs out of control' (1991: 103). Like Mark Booth, who argues that camp's 'immature' desire is to 'escape from rather than to sex' (1983: 105), Modleski maintains that camp retreats from adult sexuality here, with the implication being that 'adult sexuality' means adult 'heterosexuality'. Mature female heterosexuality, succinctly em- bodied by Mrs. Rene, is associated with both the body's capacity to *produce* (excrement and secretions) and to *reproduce*. As David Bergman observes, 'Camp ... often depicts reproduction as one of the aspects of heterosexual society that must be inverted, as in the "sacred parody" of christening per- formed by the Mollies' (1993c: 100).[19] In this way the imperative to breed – which is culturally forced upon bodies of heterosexual women like a straight- jacket and wrenched from lesbians with equal force – is indispensable to the grotesque tradition of which camp partakes. Grotesque maternity is imposed with particular intensity on women of color, although this is arguably done with more intensity and frequency outside the realm of (intentional) camp perfor- mance than within: consider the 'welfare mother' under attack in North American political discourse who is, after all, a pejorative shorthand (especially in the US) for the idea of 'uncontrollably fertile' black women or latinas, who are treated as nothing more than beasts that breed.

Reproduction, a labor resplendent in corporeal signs – signs of exaggerated body shapes, protrusions, of temporary and uncontrollable functions – sug- gests an extreme physicality of production (recall the birth farm; the egg lady). The campiness of maternal bodies, moreover, seems to intensify as the ideo- logical imperative to bear children becomes challenged and contravened by the signs of biological aging. Perhaps that is what's so funny, the 'hysterically' sexed and reproductive bodies that 'can't'; perhaps they are the moribund 'cultural surplus', the debris with which camp toys. (This may explain the common perception of older women's pets as 'unnatural' babies – poodles, Norma Desmond's monkey, even the Queen's little pig in *Alice* in *Wonderland*.)[20] The reproductive body pointedly evokes camp's relation to debris and to what Ross calls 'wasted production': by sitting on a chocolate cake, Mrs. Rene confuses bodily consumption with the literal production of waste. Pushed to an extreme, and through its ties to debris, the reproductive body of camp cannot be said to signify birth or the generation of life, since it involves its expulsion and taking away just as well.[21] As Elisabeth Bronfen writes: 'the maternal body serves as a figure doubly inscribed by the death drive – as trope for the unity lost with the beginning of life and also as trope for loss and division always already written into life, pleasure and imaging' (35). First and foremost physical, this body (marked, moreover, by uncontrollable, 'excessive' growth, secretions, and functions) serves both as the screen on which our mortality/materiality is diverted, projected – and, of course, denied.

Although my observations here are speculative, it seems to me that camp's turning away from – or, perhaps turning *on* – the body of the presumed 'straight' woman raises important questions for camp theorists, queer theorists, and lesbian, bisexual and heterosexual feminists. Does the re-abjectification of the maternal body or the body of 'movie star' glamour in conventional camp practices essentialize heterosexual women as grotesque, as 'bad objects'? How does it articulate an anxiety of lesbian and other non-heterosexual forms of motherhood? Are right-wing fears being played out on the bodies of women of color? Why do bodies of 'lapsed', potential, but not necessarily actual mothers get sent up for 'loving assassination' in camp practices? What does it mean that male-to-female cross-dressing has been so enthusiastically received by mainstream texts? Is it that male heterosexuality is so secure, so arrogant as to allow the Terminator (the ideal *father* in *Terminator 2*) to become a *mother* in *Junior* (in contrast to the culminating horror of Ripley's birth scene in *Alien 3*)? When Patrick Swayze slums gay camp culture in a dress, we might ask what makes *him* and these other male 'movie stars' so camp?

In mocking the outmoded, body camp can give the appearance of acknowledging, even playing with death. But there is also a sense in which the 'others' that give camp its fodder might be said to be put to death – since, as Ross and others have maintained, they were semiotically moribund to begin with. In many instances, such murders are welcome: the nuclear family, corporate-sponsored models of the good life, imperatives to buy minivans, and so forth. Other deaths are less so. Still, it would be wrong to assert that camp concerns itself exclusively with death, or that it focuses a singular, aggressive deadliness directed towards its object. As most of gay male camp's own critics assert, a fundamental ambivalence is involved between camp's subject and the artifact, icon, or body it sends up (see, for instance, Bersani, Dollimore, and Sinfield). Dollimore notes that 'identification with, and desire *for*, may *coexist* with parodic subversion *of*, since a culture is not reducible to the specific desires of the individuals comprising it' (1991: 321). And many scholars stress – Bersani perhaps with greatest force – that camp's aggressivity and fascination with grotesque, disunified bodies are tied to the subject's own aphanisis, his own lacks, masochism, and *jouissance* – his 'coming' apart, in short.[22]

In spite of such qualifying remarks, a fair number of feminists today remain unswayed and wonder whether gynephobia subtends certain gay camp practices such as drag.[23] While it seems unlikely that gay male camp is either deliberately or essentially misogynist, the frequency with which the abjection of camp's ostensibly 'fading' subject gets projected onto the female body-object is cause for some concern. Much of camp's relationship to female bodies is less adulatory, or even ambivalent, than many commentators would claim. Moreover, and because campy cross-dressing and gender-instability have been considerably mainstreamed, and because we live in a time marked by increasingly vulnerable bodies, it is important to question how and why the body – especially when designated as female – still plays host to so much of the grotesque in camp and cross-dressed texts. Gay camp might well have enjoyed a 'loving brutality' towards femininity and its other targets (the phrase is Scott Long's [1989], after Bersani), but the continued use of specific female bodies/body parts is not without problems for contemporary practitioners, spectators, and scholars.

CONCLUSION

> If all gender is an act and not the direct expression of a biological essence, what counts as camp and why? (Tyler 1991: 31)

Despite the alleged 'death of camp',' Carole-Anne Tyler's question has a certain timeliness, even urgency, to it. What today constitutes camp, or the parodic, or the grotesque? It could be said that, in the less than thirty years since Bakhtin's work began to influence critical theory, our bodies inhabit a different world now, as do the critical discourses surrounding them. Perhaps it is cliché (campy?) to note that ours is an age where 'actual' bodies in industrialized and developing countries alike are under epidemiological siege, or to note the soaring incidents of breast and other cancers, treatment-resistant bacteria, AIDS, and Republican and Conservative Parties. (I don't even broach here the assaults unleashed by medical, judicial, and legal institutions.) In this climate, it is hardly surprising that we are witnessing the proliferation of both technological and discursive hardware that would enable us to deny the human body altogether: virtual reality, after all, allows us to practice safe social intercourse, and academic writing has made its own contributions as well. Anti-essentialism, for instance, a position against which few intellectuals would argue, has today gained such force as to very nearly deny the body its material – and, consequently, its historical – existence altogether. As Mary Russo argues in *The Female Grotesque*, 'The dangers of essentialism in posing the female body, whether in relation to representation or to "women's history", have been well-stated, so well-stated in fact that "antiessentialism" may well be the greatest inhibition to work in cultural theory and politics at the moment, and must be displaced' (1994: 198n20). Judith Butler acknowledges the difficulty of addressing that materiality in her title *Bodies that Matter*; Susan Bordo, for her part, identifies the trend away from bodies as belonging to a postmodern 'dream of everywhere',[24] that, like Cartesianism before it, refuses physical location. An example can be drawn from Donna Haraway's already-classic 'Cyborg Manifesto' of the mid-1980s. That the piece's more ahistorical aspects (such as the cyborg defined as without origins, 'pure ether', a 'body without organs' that is not quite human but nonetheless feminist) have enjoyed the influence they have in the last decade is quite significant, for it demonstrates the extent to which it is not just any-body that has been escaped, but the *female* body that has been prompting some of our utopian fantasies of transcendence.[25] Body camp focuses attention *on* the ways in which this particular body, with its 'certain type of femininity', can be articulated and 'assassinated' at the same time. The question remains whether the 'death of camp' changes things for female, or for any other, bodies.

My concern, then, is that camp, along with some of the activist and academic criticism that supports it, may collude unwittingly with a dominant culture that seems increasingly bent on doing damage to the female body. We hear it in diatribes against abortion and unwed mothers (woman as uncontrollable breeder), in films like *The Crying Game* (woman as deceitful bitch) or, if that body is not physically threatened, the source of big fat laughs (*Mrs. Doubtfire*). 'Grotesqueness' has become legally, medically, representationally, materiality itself. I am reminded of D.A. Miller's insightful critique of Sontag's AIDS essay for its vanishing of the homosexual body, for turning AIDS into a literary project, an exploration of style and metaphor – in short, for extracting it from the historical sphere of material, social, sexed bodies and cultures. It is a crucial challenge for gay, lesbian, and queer theorists and all feminists to reconvene discussions of the body and body practices like camp and drag, along with any attendant claims to subversion, without essentializing any of these things. Nearly two decades ago, Richard Dyer put the matter quite well, arguing for 'a culture that refuses to refuse the body anymore' (1981: 64).

There is every reason that camp can rise to the occasion.[26] For camp strenuously insists on the body and its materiality – just as it does with non-human camp artifacts (lava lamps, boas), whose surface, feel, and texture bring their campiness to life. Camp has the power to force attention onto bodies in a culture that seems increasingly interested in burying, suppressing, or transcending them, be it through right-wing legislation, or left-leaning academic work. Aging in particular need not be tied to deadly ridicule, as demonstrated by lesbian camp icons such as Agnes Moorehead's Endora in *Bewitched*, Thelma Ritter, and Eve Arden – all sidekick characters associated with playing older (that is, older than the star) sisters, aunts, various 'spinsters', mothers, and mother-in-laws who invariably are the smartest, and most smart-assed, women around.[27] Other female body camp icons like Dusty Springfield, Grace Jones,

Emma Peel, and Eartha Kitt productively rework our relationships to differ-ently gendered, raced, and sexed female bodies. A lesbian camp performance such as k.d. lang's video of 'Chatelaine', for example, offers a female-as-female drag show dripping with the clichés of heterosexual femininity (a chiffon-clad debutante, lang sings amidst swirls of Lawrence Welk-like bubbles), but the performance neither denies nor maligns the feminized body: instead the voluptuousness of 'lang's' femme body is giddily celebrated (a reading energized by the music video having come out after lang's own coming out and after her brief nude scene in Percy Adlon's *Salmonberries*). Gay men's camp practices are also embracing the challenge of political work and play, even in the disputatious realm of drag: as Philthee Ritz/Martin Worman, of the Cockettes, tells Jeffrey Hilbert, '[Political] drag is absolutely, unquestionably experiencing a comeback ... The Cockettes didn't have a dogma. Now drag has an edge and a conscience because of AIDS' (1991: 43). Drag queen Glennda Orgasm (of The Brenda and Glennda Show) puts the matter with forceful simplicity: 'People need to be educated about gay issues and gay politics ... The AIDS crisis, gay visibility, antigay violence, women's issues, reproductive issues – they're all connected. They're all about what we do with our bodies. And drag is just another choice of what we do with our bodies' (46).

There is, in the end, a stunning irony that camp's death is declared in the same era that often claims feminism to be dead or *passé*. There is an irony that, for Fran Leibowitz and many others, AIDS killed camp. There is an irony that camp, a highly theatrical form of signifying, is pronounced dead in an era when theatricality has become a central strategy of queer political activism. AIDS (and/or Stonewall, straight drag, TV shows – take your pick) have certainly *reconfigured* camp, but they have not killed it. What the 'death of camp' position perhaps finally conceals is the anxiety that camp's own death watch no longer can be projected onto the body of the purported 'others' it might mock.

NOTES

With deep thanks and appreciation to some very astute readers: Corey Creekmur, Dan Cottom, and Kay Armatage.

1. The 'sensibility' to which a number of camp critics point is not altogether clear. Most times it seems to signify an *aesthetic*, but even so there is a larger sense in which the term indicates an innate, fixed quality that perfunctorily ties camp with (usually but not exclusively) gay men. (In addition to Babuscio and Dyer, Sontag uses the term. Recently, Pamela Robertson has observed the 'female aesthetic' to which camp icon Mae West speaks and, avoiding the essentialism that might logically follow, explains how such an aesthetic is not incompatible with that of gay men's.) Kim Michasiw bluntly but accurately explains one of the problems raised by these kinds of phrasings. 'To suggest that camp was an inevitable styling of sensibility', Michasiw writes, 'is a phobic attack on gay origins and gay cultural agency' (1994: 166). A recent example of an essentializing approach which, it must be added, emerges from admirable political motivations, is Meyer 1994b. Meyer equates 'camp' with 'queer parody' and disallows camp's interaction with and infiltration of straight culture, preferring instead an improbably pure queer phenomenon. He also overlooks the fact that historically, the most frequently disseminated forms of camp

have been aligned with *male* queer culture and less involved with lesbian cultures. For examples of 1970s/1980s gay discussions of camp, see Babuscio 1977 and Dyer 1976.

2. I am reminded here of feminist theorists, working in the 1980s on TV soaps, melodrama, and the woman's film of the 1930s, 1940s, and 1950s, who openly acknowledged that we were revisiting the films of our mothers, and that shows like *I Love Lucy* furthered the occasion to speak of our mothers and our youths. Thanks also to further discussions with Janet Staiger and, originally, Tom Schatz.

3. See Ross's section, 'Warhol and the Bottom Line', 1988, rpt. 1989: 165–70.

4. Addressing the relationship between camp and capital implicitly raises the vexed question of camp's political and representational 'subversiveness'. In the considerable ink that has been spilled on the question, positions vary, with the majority of critics maintaining that camp at least *has the potential* to destabilize certain social and ideological forms and categories. Like any cultural practice (such as the cross-dressing that is such a staple of the camp repertoire), camp, in the end, is no more inherently subversive than it is submissive. Camp's ability to unseat prevailing norms needs to be approached as a tentative and ephemeral phenomenon, generating contested and contradictory effects – effects which, like the changing definitions and functions of camp, are bound to context.

5. Corey Creekmur reminds me of a point that I in turn always remind my *Nick at Nite* students regarding camp readings and audience: for many of its initial TV viewers, *The Brady Bunch* was camp from the start, and did not have to wait 20 years to be considered as such. Moreover, and as Julie D'Acci noted in conversation, its initial broadcast (1969–74) was sufficiently after 1950s and early 1960s 'classic' family shows so as to have distance already inscribed within it. These discussions raise a number of crucial issues on camp readings and receptions, and indicate that the temporal distance on which Ross and other critics insist is camp's desideratum may be reworked.

6. See, for example, Mark Booth, who writes, 'it would be easy to over-emphasize camp's misogyny, which in most cases is tempered by a great affection for women' (1983: 99).

7. Richard Dyer's remark that Judy Garland 'is not a star turned into camp, but a star who expresses camp attitudes' (1986: 179) raises a similar question: whose camp attitudes are being expressed?

8. Other aspects of Meyer's argument court a certain essentialism. His definition of camp concludes with the assertion that 'Thus there are not different kinds of Camp. There is only one. And it is queer' (1994a: 5). Non-queer camp becomes the 'camp trace'. In this regard Meyer continues from a queer perspective what gay critics were arguing about camp in the 1970s and early 1980s.

9. In Cynthia Morrill's words, 'Unfortunately, defining Camp as a type of ironic gender play through notions about mimicry and masquerade, and aligning its performance with a political critique of phallocentric ideology, often *displaces the specificity of the queer subject*, for this feminist operation requires the queer to desire phallocentrically [sic]' (1994: 111).

10. In Wood's exact words, the cult audience 'relies on film elements [that] directly relate to the human body' (1991: 157). Equally germane is Alison Graham's (1991: 111) emphasis on the fact that cult texts, like camp ones, are founded on notions of failure and disempowerment. She characterizes cult films as 'open confessions of failure' in which one sees the triumph of generic conventions (the flapping tombstones of an Ed Wood movie) over marks of individuality (of aesthetic ingenuity, for instance). In this way the author of the camp/cult text is yet again a subject constituted by loss, decline, or absence.

11. An interesting counter-example of this is offered in the recent film *Suture*, which inscribes racial difference on a set of brothers, one of whom is without memory or identity.

12. On the issue of camp's relationship to class, Wayne Koestenbaum argues, in contrast to Andrew Ross, that camp does not 'recycle discarded artifacts in order to acquire cultural capital, to convert a civilization's trash back into marketable gold' (1991b: 230). Opera, for instance, wears not merely the emblem of 'high art', but that of a cultural practice that is, according to Koestenbaum, 'malleable and attractive to marginal groups other than gay men' (he cites African-American divas like L. Price, J. Norman, and K. Battle). Opera, in the end, is not simply aligned with privilege, nor solely with the transformative potential raised through the divas above, for it was also, for Koestenbaum personally, his 'badge of shame'. What Koestenbaum demonstrates is that even cultural practices that seem rigidly in-scribed in terms of class are – like race and ethnicity in camp – less orderly and more complexly, multiply-coded than would be initially apparent. See Koestenbaum 1991b: 229–30n3.

13. Freud discusses the social and psychic function of jokes and humor as expressing positions that can't be said either because of the status of the enunciator, the transgressiveness of the enunciation, or both.

14. My colleague Dan Cottom remembers that when jokes about 'fat Liz' first became popular on late night shows, a friend of his observed, 'They're really making her pay for having been so beautiful'.

15. The aging Elvis Presley offers an important and extremely interesting exception to this trend.

16. See Stallybrass & White for a critique of Bakhtin that acknowledges his tendency to romanticize 'collectivity' and make somewhat inflated claims for its ability to undermine classical conventions.

17. Pamela Robertson makes some very pertinent remarks about Mae West's changing camp allure: 'The 1970s camp effect of *Myra Breckinridge* and *Sextette* channeled and diffused West's transgression through her construction as a grotesque figure, which disqualified her as an object of erotic desire and distanced her from a female audience. In contrast, in the 1930s, West demonstrated that camp can create an alliance, rather than further division, between women and gay men. This kind of humor was no longer a misogynist joke' (1993, rpt. 1993: 169).

18. Again, I refer the reader to Stallybrass & White, particularly to their discussion of 'displaced abjection'.

19. Scholars have rightly identified the all-male Molly houses of the late 17th and 18th centuries as an important aspect of emerging 'gay' culture.

20. This observation about pets belongs to Corey Creekmur, whom I thank for offering it.

21. Bakhtin too highlights the tension between 'negation and destruction' on the one hand and 'affirmation' on the other in his discussion of the grotesque body. Much more than Bronfen, however, or my own argument, he stresses the socially and representationally critical, disruptive function of grotesque bodies (62).

22. Kim Michasiw argues that camp enables not an identification 'with the constella-tion of male-made signs that construct the feminine, with the law of the father that puts mother in her place [and leaves the 'not castrated' status of the performer unshaken]', but an identification 'with exactly that weak point in the male heterosexist symbolic order', arguing that conventional symbolization can only be partially attained, and even then only as parodic or abject. The paternally-derived, heterosexual 'symbolic', in other words, is itself rife with lack (1994: 162).

23. Consider here the positions of feminist scholars such as bell hooks, Judith William-son, and Erika Munk.

24. See Bordo, 'Feminism', and *Unbearable Weight*.

25. Haraway, 'A Manifesto for Cyborgs'. Haraway herself has stressed her distrust of transcendentalism in terms of great significance to the present discussion on death, age, and decay. 'Any transcendentalist move', she argues, 'is deadly; it produces death, through the fear of it. These holistic, transcendentalist moves promise a way

out of history, a way of participating in the god trick. A way of denying mortality'.
See her 'Interview', 16.

26. As Carole-Anne Tyler, one of camp's most insightful commentators, puts it, 'not so long ago camp languished, theorized as the shameful sign of an unreconstructed, self-hating, and even woman-hating homosexual by gay, heterosexual feminist and lesbian feminist critics alike. Now camp has been rehabilitated with a vengeance: not only femininity but even macho masculinity is read as camp' (1991: 33).

27. For an excellent discussion of lesbian readings of such 'sidekicks', see White 1995.

REFERENCES

Bakhtin, Mikhail, *Rabelais and His World*, Bloomington: Indiana UP, 1984.

Bordo, Susan, 'Feminism, Postmodernism, and Gender-Skepticism', in Linda Nicholson (ed.), *Feminism/Postmodernism*, New York: Routledge, 1990, 133–56.

——, *Unbearable Weight: Feminism, Western Culture, and the Body*, Berkeley: U of California P, 1993.

Bronfen, Elisabeth, *Over Her Dead Body: Death, Femininity and the Aesthetic*, Manchester: Manchester UP, 1992.

Butler, Judith, *Bodies That Matter: On the Discursive Limits of 'Sex'*, New York: Routledge, 1994.

Baudrillard, Jean, *For a Critique of the Political Economy of the Sign*, St. Louis: Telos Press, 1981.

Freud, Sigmund, 'Femininity', in *The Standard Edition of the Complete Psychological Works of Sigmund Freud*, Vol. 22, trans. James Strachey, London: Hogarth, 1964.

——, *Jokes and their Relation to the Unconscious*, trans. James Strachey, New York: Norton, 1960.

Haraway, Donna, 'A Manifesto for Cyborgs: Science, Technology, and Socialist Feminism in the 1980s', in Elizabeth Weed (ed.), *Coming to Terms: Feminism, Theory, Politics,* New York: Routledge, 1989, 173–204.

——, 'Interview', in Constance Penley & Andrew Ross (eds.), *Technoculture*, Minneapolis: U of Minnesota P, 1991.

Harris, Daniel R., 'Life and Death: Some Meditations', *Antioch Review* 48, Fall 1990.

Leibowitz, Fran, 'Imprint', Toronto, Channel 19 TVO, 1 December 1994, 10 pm.

Robertson, Pamela, 'Mae West's Maids: Race and 'Authenticity' in the Discourse of Camp', Society for Cinema Studies Conference, New York City, 2 March 1995.

Stallybrass, Peter & Allon White, *The Politics and Poetics of Transgression*, London: Methuen, 1986.

Wollen, Peter, 'The Auteur Theory', in *Signs and Meaning in the Cinema*, Bloomington: Indiana UP, 1972.

DIGGING THE SCENE:
A BIBLIOGRAPHY OF SECONDARY
MATERIALS 1869–1997

Just as this volume has been as a whole, the following checklist aims at providing – rather than a mere exercise in scholarship – a means and a spur for further research, and a tool of definition of camp's vagrant history in the twentieth century, by offering a map of the circulation of the term as a condition to apprehend the discursive existence of the phenomenon, the word *camp* enacting its field of reference. I have claimed that camp as an issue needs a wider knowledge of its varying articulations in time and space, so that it might be possible to reassess what camp has been, what has been seen as camp and why, what ideological formations intervened in its construction and whose interests it served. Given the relevance of the subject position in determining these factors, the necessary step towards an understanding of the camp discourse is going back to its historical stratifications, taking into account not only 'critical' sources but also popular periodicals, newspapers, magazines, and 'primary' texts. In fact, until the mid-1970s, creative works, dictionaries, newspapers and fashionable magazines, constitute the main instrument we have for unfolding the term's historical operativeness, and I have therefore concentrated the inclusion of such sources within this time span. In accordance with this historicising suggestion, the chosen order within the following bibliography is chronological (and, for convenience, alphabetical within the single year of publication).

A note on the inclusion criteria within the following bibliography, which makes secondary materials its focus, consistently with the camp 'poetics of secondariness'. On the one hand, given the virtually infinite inclusiveness of bibliographic entries relating to camp (an inclusiveness reflecting the pervasive implications and significance of camp for a multitude of issues and critical perspectives), I have made my choice to include only those items that explicitly host the word *camp*, however *en passant*. On the other hand, primary texts are included only insofar they host our four-letter word, and not for their campiness, which may justify their 'secondary' relevance here.

EARLY REFERENCES

Park, Frederick (1869), Letter to Arthur Clinton, 21 November (cited in Bartlett 1988: 168).

Ware, J. Redding (1909), *Passing English of the Victorian Era: A Dictionary of Heterodox English, Slang, and Phrase*, London: George Routledge; New York: E. Dutton, 61.

Van Vechten, Carl (1922), 'Ronald Firbank', *Double Dealer* 3, April, 185–86. Partly rpt. in *Excavations: A Book of Advocacies*, New York: Knopf, 1926, 170–76.

McAlmon, Robert (1923), *A Companion Volume*, Paris: Contact, 214.

McAlmon, Robert (1925), 'The Lodging House', in *Distinguished Air*, Paris: privately printed; pub. as *There Was a Rustle of Black Silk Stockings*, New York: Belmont, 1963, 73–106; rpt. in *Miss Knight and Others*, Albuquerque: U of New Mexico P, 1992.

West, Mae (1928), *The Pleasure Man*, first pub. in Lillian Schlissel (ed.), *Three Plays by Mae West: Sex, The Drag, The Pleasure Man*, Nick Hern, UK; New York: Routledge, 1997, 143–202.

Anon. (1931), 'Drags, camps, flaunting hip twisters and refeer peddlers run afoul of cops on the lam', *New Broadway Brevities* (N.Y.), ii. 7/1.

West, Nathanael (1931), *The Dream Life of Balso Snell*, Paris-New York: Contact, 22; rpt. in *The Dream Life of Balso Snell/A Cool Million: Two Novels*, New York: Farrar, Straus & Giroux, 1934; in *A Cool Million/The Dream Life of Balso Snell*, New York: Avon, 1957; in *Two Novels*, New York: Noonday, 1970; in *Novels and Other Writings*, New York: Library of America, 1997.

Ford, Charles & Parker Tyler (1933), *The Young and Evil*, Paris: Obelisk; New York: Arno, 1975; London: GMP, 1989, 167, 179.

Lincoln, Maurice (1933), *Oh! Definitely*, London: Constable; New York: Laugh Club, 1934, 62.

Lambert, Constant (1934), *Music Ho! A Study of Music in Decline*, London: Faber & Faber; 2nd edn., with a new preface, New York: Scribner, 1936; London: Faber & Faber, 1937; rev. edn., London: Faber & Faber, 1941; rev. edn., London: Faber & Faber, 1945; Harmondsworth: Penguin, 1948; 3rd edn., with an introduction by Arthur Hutchings, London: Faber & Faber, 1966; New York: October House, 1967, 58, 97; new edn. with an introduction by Angus Morrison, London: Hogarth, 1985.

Myers, Leopold Hamilton (1934), *The Root and the Flower*, New York: Harcourt Brace; London: Jonathan Cape, 1935; new edn., New York: Harcourt Brace, 1947; Oxford-New York: Oxford UP, 1985; rpt. as *The Near and the Far*, London: Jonathan Cape, 1956, *passim*.

Hargan, James (1935), 'The Psychology of Prison Language', *Journal of Abnormal & Social Psychology*, 30:3, October-December, 359–65.

Pollock, Albin J. (1935), *The Underworld Speaks: An Insight to Vice-Crime-Corruption*, San Francisco: Prevent Crime Bureau, unpaginated.

Partridge, Eric Honeymoon (1937), *A Dictionary of Slang and Unconventional English: Slang – including the Language of the Underworld. Colloquialisms & Catch-phrases, Solecisms & Catachreses, Nicknames, Vulgarisms and such Americanisms as have been Naturalized.* London: G. Routledge, 122–23; 2nd edn. (enlarged), ibidem, 1938; 5th edn. (in 2 vols.), London: Routledge & Kegan Paul; New York:

Macmillan, 1961, Vol. 2, 1041. New enlarged edn., ed. by Paul Beale, London: Routledge & Kegan Paul, 1984, 164, 176–7. A later edn., reduced to one-twelfth: *Smaller Slang Dictionary*, London: Routledge & Kegan Paul; 1961; 2nd edn. with a few corrections and additions, 1964, 22.

Baker, Sidney John (1941), *A Popular Dictionary of Australian Slang*, Melbourne: Robertson & Mullens, 16; 3rd edn., exp., ibidem, 1943, 18.

Grant, William (1941) (ed.), *The Scottish National Dictionary, Designed Partly on Regional Lines and Partly on Historical Principles & Containing all the Scottish Words Known to Be in Use or to Have Been in Use Since c. 1700*, Vol. 2, Edinburgh: The Scottish National Dictionary Association, 21.

Legman, Gershon (1941), 'The Language of Homosexuality', in George W. Henry, *Sex Variants: A Study of Homosexual Patterns*, New York-London: B. Hoeber, Vol. 2, 1149–79. Excerpt in Katz 1983: 571–84.

Berrey, Lester Vincent & Melvin Van den Bark (1943), *The American Thesaurus of Slang*, London: Constable; 2nd edn., New York: Thomas Y. Crowell, 1952, 342, 472.

Williams, Tennessee (1944), 'Letter to Donald Windham, July 1944', in Donald Windham (ed.), *Tennessee Williams' Letters to Donald Windham*, Verona: Sandy Campbell, 1976; New York: Holt, Rinehart & Winston, 1977; Athens: U of Georgia P, 1996, 137–9.

Duncan, Robert (1944), 'The Homosexual in Society', *Politics* 1:7, 209–11. Rpt. in Ekbert Fass (ed.), *Young Robert Duncan: Portrait of the Poet as Homosexual in Society*, Santa Barbara: Black Sparrow, 1983, 319–22. Rpt. in Katz 1983: 591–5.

Monteleone, Vincent J. (1945), *Criminal Slang: The Vernacular of the Underworld Lingo*, Boston: Christopher; rev. edn., ibidem 1949, 42.

Burns, John Horne (1947), *The Gallery*, London-New York: Harper & Bros.; Garden City: Sun Dial, 1948; New York: Bantam, 1950, 151.

Schulberg, Budd (1947), *The Harder They Fall: A Novel*, New York: Random House, 166.

Vidal, Gore (1948), *The City and the Pillar*, New York: E. Dutton, 265 (the occurrence is deleted in *The City and the Pillar Revised*, New York: Dutton/New American Library, 1965, 189).

De Forrest, Michael Jean (1949), *The Gay Year: A Novel*, New York: Woodford, 27.

Nerf, Swarsant (pseud.) (1949), *The Gay Girl's Guide*, Boston or Cambridge: Phallus, 4–5.

Partridge, Eric Honeymoon (1949), *A Dictionary of the Underworld, British & American. Being the Vocabularies of Crooks, Criminals, Racketeers, Beggars & Tramps, Convicts, the Commercial Underworld, the Drug Traffic, the White Slave Traffic, Spivs*, London: Routledge & Kegan Paul; reissued with addenda, ivi 1961; 3rd edn., enlarged, ivi 1968, 100.

Cory, Donald Webster (pseudonym of Edward Sagarin) (1951) *The Homosexual in America: A Subjective Approach*, New York: Greenberg; Toronto: Ambassador, 112–13.

Fulford, Roger (1951), *Osbert Sitwell*, London-New York: Longmans, Green & Co., 20.

Wilson, Angus Frank Johnstone (1952), *Hemlock and After*, London: Secker & Warburg; Harmondsworth: Penguin, 1956; London: Panther, 1979, 101, 112, 191.

Beaton, Cecil (1954), *The Glass of Fashion*, London: Weidenfeld & Nicolson, 153.

Burroughs, William S. (1954), Letter to Allen Ginsberg, early October, in Oliver Harris (ed.), *The Letters of William S. Burroughs, 1945–1959*, New York-London: Viking Penguin, 1993, 234–7.

Isherwood, Christopher William Bradshaw (1954), *The World in the Evening*, London: Methuen; New York: Random House; New York: Avon, 1956; London: Landsborough, 1960; Harmondsworth: Penguin, 1966; New York: Ballantine, 1967; London: White Lion, 1973, 124–6.

Goodman, Ezra (1956), 'Rounding Up Stars in 80 Ways', *Life*, 41:17, 22 October, 87–8, 91–2.

McIntosh, Louis (1956), *Oxford Folly*, London: Christopher Johnson, 103.

Reinhardt, James Melvin (1957), 'Gay Glossary', in *Sex Perversions and Sex Crimes*, Springfield: Charles Thomas; Toronto: Ryerson; Oxford: Blackwell, 47–8.

Holmes, John Clellon (1958), *The Horn: A Novel*, New York: Random House; Greenwich: Fawcett, 1959; new edn. with a new author's introduction, Berkeley: Creative Arts, 1980; New York: Thunder's Mouths, 1988, 131.

Plagemann, Bentz (1958), *The Steel Cocoon: A Novel*, New York: Viking; Toronto: Macmillan, 113.

Brien, Alan (1959a), 'Across the Border', *Spectator*, 202, 2 January, 11–12.

—— (1959b), 'Home Sweet Home', *Spectator*, 203, 13 November, 667.

Goldin, Hyman E. (ed. in chief), Frank O'Leary (general ed.), Morris Lipsius (assistant ed.) (1959), *Dictionary of American Underworld Lingo*, New York: Twayne; New York: Citadel, 1962, 39.

Johnson, Pamela (1960), 'Proust 1900', *Encounter*, 14:2, February, 21–28.

Goff, Martyn (1961), *The Youngest Director*, London: Putnam; London: Mayflower, 1967; London: Brilliance, 1983, 53.

Hooker, Evelyn (1961), 'The Homosexual Community', in *Proceedings of the XIV International Congress of Applied Psychology*, Copenhagen: Munksgaard, 40–59. Rev. in James O. Palmer & Michael J. Goldstein (eds.), *Perspectives in Psychopathology: Readings in Abnormal Psychology*, New York-Oxford: Oxford UP, 1966, 354–64. Rpt. in John H. Gagnon & William Simon (eds.), *Sexual Deviance*, New York-Evanston-London: Harper & Row, 1967, 167–84.

Cook, Robin (1962), *The Crust on Its Uppers*, London-New York: New Authors; London: Pan, 1964, 11, 15.

Mayne, Richard (1962), 'Needlework', *New Statesman*, 64, 17 August, 207.

Mitchell, Julian (1962), 'Dot Dot Dot', *Spectator*, 209, 17 August, 222–3.

Sontag, Susan (1962), 'Happenings: An Art of Radical Juxtaposition', *The Second Coming*. Rpt. in Sontag 1966: 263–74.

Southern, Terry (1962), 'The Moon-Shot Scandal', *The Realist* 39, November, 11. Rpt. in *Red-Dirt Marijuana & Other Tastes*, New York: New American Library, 1967, 213–16.

Bassing, Eileen (1963), *Where's Annie?* New York: Random House, 291.

Connolly, Cyril Vernon (1963), 'Bond Strikes Camp', *London Magazine* ns 3:1, April, 8–23. Reissued as *Bond Strikes Camp*, London: Shenval, 1963; rpt. in *Previous Convictions*, London: Hamish Hamilton; New York: Harper & Row, 1963, 354–71.

Cory, Donald Webster (pseudonym of Edward Sagarin) & John LeRoy (1963), *The Homosexual and His Society: A View From Within*, New York: Citadel, 73, 261–6.

1964

Anon. (1964), 'Taste: "Camp"', *Time*, 84:24, 11 December, 75.

Brunvand, Jan Harold (1964), 'Camp and After', *New Statesman*, 68, 4 December, 894–5.

Fiedler, Leslie A. (1964), *Waiting for the End: The American Literary Scene from Hemingway to Baldwin*, New York: Stein & Day; London: Jonathan Cape; New York: Delta, 1965, 122–24.

Sontag, Susan (1964a), 'A Feast for Open Eyes', *Nation*, 198:16, 13 April, 374–6. Rpt. as 'Jack Smith's *Flaming Creatures*' in Sontag 1966, 263–74. Rpt. in Gregory Battock (ed.), *The New American Cinema: A Critical Anthology*, New York: Dutton, 1967.

—— (1964b), 'Notes on "Camp"', *Partisan Review* 31:4, Fall, 515–30. Rpt. in Sontag 1966: 263–74. Rpt. in Hardwick 1982a: 105–19. Rpt. in Kurzweil 1996a: 232–44.

Strait, Guy [pseud.] (1964) (ed.), *The Lavender Lexicon: Dictionary of Gay Words and Phrases*, San Francisco: Strait & Associates.

Wolfe, Tom (1964), 'The Girl of the Year', *New York* (the *New York Herald Tribune* Sunday supplement), 6 December, 8–11, 67. Rpt. in *The Kandy-Kolored Tangerine-Flake Streamline Baby*, New York: Farrar, Straus & Giroux, 1965; London: Jonathan Cape, 1966, 204–20; London-Basingstoke: Pan, 1981, 157–69. Rpt. in Wolfe 1982: 99–110. Rpt. in Gerald Howard (ed.), *The Sixties*, New York: Washington Square, 1982, 178–90.

1965

Anon. (1965a) 'Great New Camp Site: On the New Fourth!' *New York Times*, 114:39, 15 August, 25L.

—— (1965b), 'Pro Football Camps Are Camp This Week', *New York Herald Tribune*, 11 July, Sect. 4, 5.

Borowik, Ann (1965), *Lions, Three; Christians, Nothing*, New York: Pantheon, 87.

Cohen, Nathan (1965), 'In View', *Saturday Night* (Canada) 80:5, May, 9–11.

Fiedler, Leslie (1965), 'The New Mutants', *Partisan Review* 32:4, Fall, 505–25. Rpt. in Fiedler 1971: 379–400. Rpt. in *Unfinished Business*, New York: Stein & Day, 1972. Rpt. in Fiedler 1977: 189–210.

Frazier, George (1965), 'Call It Camp', *Holiday*, 38:5, November, 12, 16–17, 19, 21–3.

Glanville, Brian Lester (1965), *A Second Home*, London: Secker & Warburg, 6, 26, 44, 254.

Hancock, Marianne (1965), 'Soup's On', *Arts Magazine* 39, May-June, 16–18. Rpt. in Pratt 1997a: 12–15.

Hess, Thomas (1965), 'J'accuse Marcel Duchamp', *Art News* 63:10, 44–5, 52–54. Rpt. in Joseph Masheck (ed.), *Marcel Duchamp in Perspective*, Englewood Cliffs: Prentice-Hall, 1975, 115–20.

Meehan, Thomas (1965), 'Not Good Taste, Not Bad Taste: It's "Camp"', *New York Times Magazine*, 21 March, 30–31, 113–15.

Melly, George (1965), *Owning-Up*, London: Weidenfeld & Nicholson; Harmondsworth: Penguin, 1970, 188.

Niemoeller, A. F. (1965), 'A Glossary of Homosexual Slang', *Fact* 2:1, January-February, 24–7.

Picard, Lil (1965a), 'From ABC to Camp Art: New York Report', *Das Kunstwerk* 19:5–6, November-December, 58–9.

—— (1965b), 'Camp oder die nimmermüde Phantasie', *Die Welt*, 9 December

Sarris, Andrew (1965a), 'Do Intellectuals Really *Like* Sex? – Films', *New Statesman*, 20 August, 263–4.

—— (1965b), 'Films', *Village Voice*, 9:8, 9 December, 21.

Schickel, Richard (1965), 'Marshall McLuhan: Canada's Intellectual Comet', *Harper's Magazine*, 231, November, 62–8.

Simon, John Ivan & Susan Sontag (1965), 'Two Camps', *Partisan Review* 32:1, Winter, 154–8.

Sontag, Susan (1965), 'On Style' *Partisan Review* 32:4, Fall, 543–62. Rpt. in Sontag 1966, 15–36. Rpt. in Hardwick 1982a: 137–55.

Steinem, Gloria (1965), 'The Ins and Outs of Pop Culture', *Life*, 59:8, 20 August, 72–76, 79–86, 89.

Tillim, Sidney (1965), 'Further Observations on the Pop Phenomenon', *Artforum* 4:3, November, 17–19. Rpt. in Madoff 1997: 135–9.

Trillin, Calvin (1965), 'Barnett Frummer and Rosalie Mondle Meet Superman: A Love Story', *New Yorker*, 17 April, 40–3.

Warhol, Andy (1965), *Camp*, USA, August or September, 16mm., b/w, sound, 70', 24 FPS. Premiered by the Film-Makers' Cinematheque, 22 November 1965.

1966

Ace, Goodman (1966), 'The Second Caesarian', *Saturday Review*, 49, 12 February, 8.

Adams, Val (1966), 'Discoteque Frug Party Heralds Batman's Film and TV Premiere', *New York Times*, 115:39, 13 January, 79.

Alexander, Shana (1966), 'Don't Change a Hair for Me, Batman', *Life*, 60:5, 4 February, 21.

Andersen, Thom (1966), 'Film: *Camp*, Andy Warhol', *Artforum* 4:10, June, 58.

Anon. (1966a), 'Camp; Campy', in Philip W. Goetz & Christopher Kent (eds.), *Britannica Book of the Year 1966*, Chicago-Toronto-London etc.: Encyclopaedia Britannica, 806.

—— (1966b), '"Holy Flypaper!"', *Time*, 87:4, 28 January, 61.

—— (1966c), 'The Homosexual in America', *Time*, 87:3, 21 January, 40–1.

Atwell, Lee (1966), 'Homosexual Themes in the Cinema', *Tangents* 1:6, March 1966, 4–10; 1:7, April, 4–9.

Bart, Peter (1966), 'A Sweet Young Thing or Two', *New York Times*, 115:39, 17 July, sect. 2, 9.

Benchley, Peter (1966), 'Special Report: The Story of Pop', *Newsweek*, 25 April, 56–61. Rpt. in Madoff 1997: 148–53.

Bryden, Ronald (1966), 'Spies Who Came into Camp', *Observer Colour Supplement*, 7 August, 5–8.

Cuneo, Paul K. (1966), 'Of Many Things', *America* 114:19, 7 May, 635.

Drucker, Mort & Lou Silverstone (1966), 'Bats-Man', *Mad* 106, September, 7–12.

Gould, Jack (1966), 'Too Good to Be Camp', *New York Times*, 115:39, 23 January, sect. 2, 17.

Gornick, Vivian (1966), 'It's a Queer Hand Stoking the Campfire', *Village Voice*, 11:25, 7 Apr, 1, 20–1.

Hansen, Joseph (1966), 'The Homosexual Joke', *Tangents* 1:5, February, 26–30.

Holliday, Don (pseud. of Victor Banis) (1966), *The Man from C.A.M.P.* (paperback series), San Diego: Ember Library, 1966–1968 (issues: *The Man from C.A.M.P.*, *Color Him Gay*, *The Watercress File*, *The Son Goes Down*, *Gothic Gaye*, *Holiday Gay*, *The Gay Dogs*, *Rally Round the Fag*, *Blow the Man Down*, plus a *C.A.M.P. Cookbook* and a *C.A.M.P. Astrology File*, pub. in 1967).

Horn, John (1966), 'Wednesday Review on Satire: An Amusing, Sardonic Put-on', *New York Herald Tribune*, 7 April, 19

Isherwood, Christopher William Bradshaw (1966), 'On His Queerness', in *Exhumations: Stories, Articles, Verses*, London: Methuen; New York: Simon & Schuster; Harmondsworth: Penguin, 1969. Rpt. in Philip Larkin (ed.), *The Oxford Book of Twentieth-Century English Verse*, Oxford: Clarendon, 1973, 358.

Kauffmann, Stanley (1966), 'Homosexual Drama and Its Disguises', *New York Times*, 115:36, 23 January, sect. 2, 1. Rpt. in *Persons of the Drama: Theater Criticism and Comment*, New York: Harper & Row, 1976, 291–4.

LeShan, Eda J. (1966), 'At War With Batman', *New York Times Magazine*, 15 May, 112, 114–15, 117.

Mitchell, Bob (1966), 'The First Homosexual President', *Tangents* 1:12, September, 8–10.

'Petronius' (1966), *New York Unexpurgated: An Amoral Guide for the Jaded, Tired, Evil, Non-Conforming, Corrupt, Condemned, & the Curious – Humans & Otherwise – to Under Underground Manhattan*, New York: Matrix House, 96, 223–4.

Prideaux, Tom (1966), 'The Whole Country Goes Supermad', *Life*, 60:10, 11 March, 21–7.

Reice, Sylvie (1966), 'The Swinging Set: With the Batman at Malibu', *Detroit News*, 13 February, 5E.

Richardson, John Adkins (1966), 'Dada, Camp, and the Mode Called Pop', *Journal of Aesthetics & Art Criticism* 24:4, Summer, 549–58. Rpt. in Madoff 1997: 154–61.

Rubin, Louis D, Jr. (1966), 'The Curious Death of the Novel: Or, What to Do about Tired Literary Critics', *Kenyon Review* 28:3, June, 305–25. Rpt. in *The Curious Death of the Novel: Essays in American Literature*, Baton Rouge: Louisiana State UP, 1967, 3–23.

Sarris, Andrew (1966), 'Films: The Chelsea Girls', *Village Voice*, 12:9, 15 December, 33. Rpt. in Sarris 1971: 274–6.

Skow, John (1966), 'Has TV – Gasp! – Gone Batty?' *Saturday Evening Post*, 239:10, 7 May, 93–7.

Sontag, Susan (1966), *Against Interpretation and Other Essays*, New York: Farrar, Straus & Giroux; London: Eyre & Spottiswoode, 1967; New York: Dell, 1969 (with an author's note); New York: Octagon, 1982; New York: Anchor, 1986; London: Vintage, 1994. Reviewed in: *American Quarterly* 20, 1968:254, by John G. Cawelti; *Book Week* 30 January 1966:2, by Wylie Sypher; *Cambridge Quarterly* 2, 1966:55, by Martin Green; *Canadian Forum* 46, 1966:69, by Dennis Duffy; *Choice* 3, July 1966:419; *Choice*, 10, March 1973:40; *Christian Science Monitor*, 3 February 1966:7, by Alan Levensohn; *Commentary* 41, 1966:83, by Alicia Ostriker; *Commonweal* 84, 24 June 1966:390, by Paul Welde; *Guardian Weekly*, 96, 16 March 1967:11; *Kenyon Review* 28, November 1966:709, by Richard Freedman; *Kirkus Reviews* 33, 1 December 1965:1210; *Library Journal* 91, 1 February 1966:698, by M. Ferguson; *Listener*, 77, 16 March 1967:364; *Nation*, 202, 21 February 1966:219, by C. T. Samuels; *New Republic*, 154, 19 February 1966:24, by Elizabeth Stevens; *New Statesman*, 71, 4 March 1966:300, by Christopher Ricks; *New Statesman*, 73, 24 March 1967:408; *New York Review of Books*, 6, 9 June 1966:22, by Robert Mazzocco; *New York Times Book Review*, 23 January1966:5, by Benjamin DeMott; *Partisan Review* 33, 1966:439, by Peter Brooks; *Saturday Review*, 49, 12 February 1966:33, by Jonathan Baumbach; *Southern Review* 4, 1968:252, by James H. Justus; *Spectator*, 10 March 1967:280; *TLS*, 16 March 1967:215.

Stein, Jess (ed. in chief) & Laurence Urdang (managing ed.) (1966), *The Random House Dictionary of the English Language*, New York: Random House, 214.

Susann, Jacqueline (1966), *Valley of the Dolls: A Novel*, New York: Geis Association; New York: Grove, 1997, 393.

Stone, Judy (1966), 'Caped Crusader of Camp', *New York Times*, 115:39, 432, 9 January, sect. 2, 15.

Terwilliger, Robert E. (1966), 'The Theology of Batman', *Catholic World*, 202, November, 127.

Thompson, Howard (1966), 'TV Heroes Stay Long', *New York Times*, 115:39, 25 August, 42.

White, William (1966), '"Camp" as Adjective: 1909–1966', *American Speech* 41:1, February, 70–72.

Wolfe, Tom (1966), 'Upward with the Arts – The Success Story of Robert & Ethel Scull', *New York* (the *World Journal Tribune* Sunday magazine), 30 October, 21, 23–4, 26. Rpt. as 'Bob and Spike' in *The Pump House Gang*, New York: Farrar, Straus & Giroux, 1968; New York: Bantam, 1969, 173–203. Rpt. in Wolfe 1982: 3–26.

1967

Alloway, Laurence (1967), 'Roy Lichtenstein's Period Style', *Arts Magazine* 42:1, September-October, 24–9.

Anon. (1967), 'Checklistings: Records', *Maclean's*, 80:2, February, 84.

Brien, Alan (1967), 'Camper's Guide', *New Statesman*, 73, 23 June, 873–4.

Crafts, Stephen (1967), 'Frankenstein: Camp Curiosity or Premonition?' *Catalyst* 3, Summer, 96–103.

Croft-Cooke, Rupert (1967), *Feasting With Panthers: A New Consideration of Some Late Victorian Writers*, New York: Holt, Rinehart & Winston; London: W. H. Allen, 203–5.

Flexner, Stuart Berg (1967) (ed.), 'Supplement', in Harold Wentworth & Stuart Berg Flexner (eds.), *Dictionary of American Slang*, New York: Thomas Crowell, 670–716. 2nd, suppl. edn., ibidem 1975, 683–4. The basis for Robert L. Chapman (ed.), *New Dictionary of American Slang*, New York-London-Sydney: Harper & Row, 1986, 60, 206, 265.

Gardner, John (1967), *Madrigal*, London: Frederick Muller, 155.

Howard, Richard (1967), 'For Hephaistos,' in *The Damages: Poems*, Middletown: Wesleyan UP, 63–65. Rpt. in *Quantities/Damages: Early Poems*, Middletown: Wesleyan UP, 1984, 127–9.

Hyers, M. Conrad (1967), 'Batman and the Comic Profanation of the Sacred', *Christian Century* 85, 18 October, 1322–23.

Lawrenson, Helen (1967), 'Mirror, Mirror, on the Ceiling: How'm I Doin'?' *Esquire* 68:1, July, 72–74, 113–15.

Marine, Gene (1967), 'Who's Afraid of Little Annie Fanny?', *Ramparts* 5:8, February, 26–30.

Nairn, Tom (1967), 'The New Sensibility', *New Statesman*, 24 March, 408–09.

Rechy, John (1967), *Numbers*, New York: Grove, 40. Rev. edn., New York: Grove, 1984; new edn. with a foreword by the author, New York: Grove, 1990.

Shaw, Denis et al. (1967), 'Letters: Camp', *New Statesman*, 2 June, 759; 9 June, 796; 16 June, 833.

Simon, William & John Gagnon (1967), 'Femininity in the Lesbian Community', *Social Problems* 15:2, Fall, 212–21.

Tyler, Parker (1967), 'Dragtime and Drugtime: or, Film à la Warhol', *Evergreen Review* 11:46, April, 27–31, 87–8. Rpt. in Michael O'Pray (ed.), *Andy Warhol: Film Factory*, London: BFI, 1989, 94.

1968

Anon. (1968), 'Holy Cancellation!', *Newsweek*, 5 February, 84.

Auden, W. H. (1968), 'The Martyr as Dramatic Hero', *Listener*, 79, 4 January, 1–2.

Arbasino, Alberto (1968), *Off-off*, Milan: Feltrinelli, 139, 200, 216, 230, 257.

Baker, Roger (1968), *Drag: A History of Female Impersonation on the Stage*, London: Triton. 2nd edn., with contributions by Peter Burton & Richard Smith, published as *Drag: A History of Female Impersonation in the Performing Arts*, London: Cassell; New York: New York UP, 1994, 2, 242

Barnes, Clive (1968a), 'Theater: "The Line of Least Existence"', *New York Times*, 117:40, 25 March, 53.

—— (1968b), 'Theater: An All-Male "As You Like It"', *New York Times*, 117:40, 6 July, 9.

Bier, Jesse (1968), *The Rise and Fall of American Humor*, New York: Rinehart & Winston, 273, 291, 312.

Byrd, Scott (1968), 'A Separate War: Camp and Black Humor in Recent American Fiction', *University of South Florida Language Quarterly* 7:1–2, Fall-Winter, 7–10.

Crisp, Quentin (1968), *The Naked Civil Servant*, London: Jonathan Cape; London: Fontana, 1977; London: Duckworth, 1977, 26; London: HarperCollins, 1985.

Crowley, Mart (1968), *The Boys in the Band: A Play in Two Acts*, New York: Farrar, Straus & Giroux; Toronto: Doubleday, 1968; New York: Dell, 1969, 44–117.

Dorfles, Gillo (1968), *Il Kitsch. Antologia del cattivo gusto*, Milan: Mazzotta, 291–92. New edn., ibidem 1972. English translation: *Kitsch: The World of Bad Taste*, New York: Universe, 1969, 291–2.

Foster, Brian (1968), *The Changing English Language*, London: Macmillan; New York: St. Martin's; Harmondsworth: Penguin, 1970, 126–7.

Marc (1968), 'Life and Times in NW1: Grace and Favour', *Listener*, 79, 13 June, 770.

Michener, Wendy (1968), 'The Very Irreverent Crusade of Ti-Pop', *Saturday Night* (Canada), 83:2, February, 28–30.

Regelson, Rosalyn (1968), 'Up the Camp Staircase', *New York Times*, 117:40, 3 March, sect. 2, 1, 14.

Sarris, Andrew (1968), 'Films: The Bliss of Mrs. Blossom; The Killing of Sister George', *Village Voice*, 14:11, 26 December, 45. Rpt. in Sarris 1971, 415–17.

Schickel, Richard (1968), 'Film Review: Planet of the Apes', *Life*, 64:19, 10 May, 18. Rpt. in *Second Sight: Notes on Some Movies, 1965–1970*, New York: Simon & Schuster, 1972, 180–2.

Sheed, Wilfrid (1968), 'Fan Club in Session', *Atlantic*, 222:5, November, 142–3.

Simon, Frank (1968), *The Queen*, USA 1968, col., 70'.

Swarthout, Glendon Fred (1968), *Loveland*, Garden City: Doubleday, 14.

Toback, James (1968), 'Whatever You'd Like Susan Sontag to Think, She Doesn't', *Esquire* 70:1, July, 58–60, 114–16.

1969

Anon. (1969), 'Music in the Round', *Harper's Magazine*, 239, September, 32, 34.

Berube, Margery S. & Pamela B. DeVinne (1969) (eds.), *The American Heritage Dictionary*, Boston: Houghton Mifflin. Second College edn., ibid. 1982, 232.

Brophy, Brigid (1969), *In Transit: An Heroi-cyclic Novel*, London: Macdonald; New York: Putnam's, 1970; London: GMP, 1989.

Carroll, Paul (1969), 'What's a Warhol?' *Playboy*, 16:9, September, 132–4, 140, 278–82. Rpt. in Pratt 1997a: 42–57.

Crosby, John (1969), 'The In and Out Club', *Observer*, 16 March, 9.

Davis, Dorothy S. (1969), *Where the Dark Streets Go*, New York: Scribner; London: Hodder & Stoughton, 1970, 94.

Drabble, Margaret (1969), *The Waterfall*, New York: Knopf; London: Weidenfeld & Nicolson, 112.

Fiedler, Leslie A. (1969), 'Cross the Border – Close the Gap', *Playboy*, 16:12, December, 151, 230, 252–4, 256–8. Rpt. in Fiedler 1971: 461–85. Rpt. in *Cross the Border – Close the Gap*, New York: Stein & Day, 1972. Rpt. in Fiedler 1977, 270–94. Excerpt in Patricia Waugh (ed.), *Postmodernism: A Reader*, London-New York: Edward Arnold, 1992, 31–48.

Gransden, K. W. (1969), *Angus Wilson*, London-New York: Longmans, Green & Co., 11–12, 15, 18, 22.

Hodgart, Matthew (1969), 'Good Camper', *New York Review of Books*, 13, 11 September, 26–27.

Kael, Pauline (1969), 'Trash, Art, and the Movies', *Harper's Magazine*, 238, February, 65–83. Rpt. in *Going Steady*, Boston-Toronto: Little, Brown & Co., 1970, 85–129.

Mallett, Richard (1969), 'Criticism: At the Cinema', *Punch*, 68, 29 October, 719–20.

Marinetti, Ronald (1969), 'Cackle and Confusion', *Wall Street Journal*, 173, 29 May, 18.

Melly, George (1969), 'Active and Passive Camp Schools', *Observer Review*, 30 November, 33.

Merritt, James Douglas (1969), *Ronald Firbank*, New York: Twayne, 131.

Mitchell, Bob (1969), 'New Horizons in the Magazine Field', *Tangents* 3:8–10, May-July, 28.

Rado, Rick (1969), 'Letters: Mae West', *Life*, 66:18, 9 May, 24A.

Tyler, Parker (1969a), *Sex Psyche Etcetera in the Film*, New York: Horizon; London: Penguin, 1971, 20, 24, 25, 27, 108, 127, 148.

—— (1969b), *Underground Film: A Critical History*, New York: Grove; London: Secker & Warburg, 1971; London: Penguin, 1974; New York: Da Capo, 1995, 14, 42–59, 79–85, 91, 98, 108–9, 131, 183, 225.

1970

Anon. (1970), 'Akt in Velours', *Der Spiegel*, 1 June, 160.

Chavez, Brian (1970), 'Blatant is Beautiful' *Gay Sunshine* 1:2, October, 9.

Cocks, Jay (1970), 'Cinema: A Surplus of Capers', *Time*, 96:21, 23 November, 105.

Croce, Arlene (1970), 'The Moiseyev and Us', *Atlantic*, 226:5, November, 128–30, 132–3.

Garmonsway, G. N. & Jacqueline Simpson (1970) (eds.), *The Penguin English Dictionary* (2nd edn.), London: Allen Lane, 105.

Hyde, Harford Montgomery (1970), *The Other Love: An Historical and Contemporary Survey of Homosexuality in Britain*, London: Heinemann; London: Mayflower, 1972 (US edn.: *The Love that Dared not Speak Its Name: A Candid History of Homosexuality in Britain*, Boston: Little, Brown, 1970), 22.

Major, Clarence (1970), *Dictionary of Afro-American Slang*, New York: International, 34.

Melly, George (1970), *Revolt into Style: The Pop Arts in Britain*, London: Allen Tate; Garden City: Doubleday, 1971; London-New York: Oxford UP, 1989, 18, 147–8, 155, 177–8, 192–4, 205.

Mitchell, Julian (1970), 'Aide-de-Camp', *New Statesman*, 6 February, 191–2.

Shechner, Richard (1970), 'Collage Theater', in Henry Kariel, *The Political Order: A Reader in Political Science*, New York-London: Basic, 3–4.

Silverstein, Mike (1970), 'God Save the Queen', *Gay Sunshine* 1:3, November, 2.

Simon, John Ivan (1970), 'Dirty Movies', *New Leader*, 53:14, 6 July, 23–25. Rpt. as 'Myra Breckinridge; Freedom to Love; Censorship in Denmark; Beyond the Valley of Dolls' in Simon 1971: 151–60.

Simon, John Ivan (1970), 'Performance', *Sunday Times*, August; Rpt. in Simon 1971: 363–7.

Stanley, Julia Penelope (1970), 'Homosexual Slang', *American Speech* 45:1–2, Spring-Summer, 45–59.

Tyler, Parker (1970), 'The Prince Zoubaroff: Praise of Ronald Firbank. Part I', *Prose* 1, 135–52.

Young, Allen (1970), 'Camp Out?' *Gay Sunshine* 1:1, August-September, 9.

Zimmer, Dieter E. (1970), 'Andalusien ist natürlich weiss', *Die Zeit*, 10 April.

1971

Altman, Dennis (1971), *Homosexual: Oppression and Liberation*, New York: Outerbridge & Dienstfrey; London: Angus & Robertson, 1972. Rev. edn., London: Allen & Lane, 1974, *passim*. Reviewed in: *Best Sellers* 31, 1 January 1972, 439, by E. J. Linehan; *Choice* 9, June 1972, 582; *Harvard Educational Review* 43, August 1973, 449; *Kirkus Reviews* 39, 1 September 1971, 969; *Library Journal* 97, 1 June 1972, 2109, by J. K. Marshall; *New York Times Book Review*, 20 February 1972, 5, by Jill Johnston; *New York Times Book Review*, 10 December 1972, 28; *Nation*, 217, 2 July 1973, 25; *Publishers' Weekly*, 200, 11 October 1971, 56; *Time*, 99, 28 February 1972, 81, by A. T. Baker.

Arbasino, Alberto (1971), *Sessanta posizioni*, Milan: Feltrinelli, *passim*.

Cavell, Stanley (1971), *The World Viewed: Reflections on the Ontology of Films*, New York: Viking. Enlarged edn.: Cambridge, Mass.-London: Harvard UP, 1979, 6.

Denisoff, R. Serge (1971), *Great Day Coming: Folk Music and the American Left*, Urbana-London: U of Illinois P, 95.

Dolmetsch, Carl Richard (1971), '"Camp" and Black Humour in Recent American Fiction', in Weber & Haack 1971: 147–74. Rpt. in Alan R. Pratt (ed.), *Black Humor: Critical Essays*, New York-London: Garland, 1993, 215–47.

Fiedler, Leslie (1971), *The Collected Essays of Leslie Fiedler*, Vol. 2, New York: Stein & Day.

Gove, Philip Babcock (ed. in chief) (1971), 'Addenda', in *The Webster's Third New International Dictionary of the English Language Unabridged*, Springfield: Merriam, 59A. Expanded in Mairé Weir Kay, Frederick C. Mish & Henry Bosley Woolf (eds.), *6,000 Words: A Supplement to Webster's Third New International Dictionary Unabridged*, Springfield: Merriam, 1976, 29, and in *9,000 Words*, ibidem, 1993, 31.

Hassan, Ihab (1971), 'POSTmodernISM: A Paracritical Bibliography', *New Literary History* 3:1, Fall, 5–30. Rpt. in *Paracriticisms: Seven Speculations of the Times*, Urbana-London: U of Illinois P, 1975, 39–59. Rpt. in *The Postmodern Turn: Essays in Postmodern Theory and Culture*, Columbus: Ohio State UP, 1987, 25–45.

Jennings, Robert C. (1971), 'Mae West: A Candid Conversation With the Indestructible Queen of Vamp and Camp', *Playboy*, 18:1, January, 74–8.

Karlen, Arno (1971), 'The Erotic Disguise', in *Sexuality and Homosexuality: A New View*, New York: Norton, 352–66.

Landy, Eugene E. (1971). *The Underground Dictionary*. New York: Simon, 45–6.

Marowitz, Charles (1971), 'The Dirtiest Show in Town', *Village Voice*, May. Rpt. in *Confessions of a Counterfeit Critic: A London Theatre Notebook, 1958–1971*, London: Eyre Methuen, 1973, 181–4.

Melly, George (1971), 'Finney's Real-Life Fantasy', *Observer Review*, 12 December, 25.

Passmore, Dennis R. (1971), 'Camp Style in the Novels of Cyprian O. D. Ekwensi', *Journal of Popular Culture* 4:3, Winter, 705–16.

Rader, Dotson (1971), *Gov't Inspected Meat & Other Fun Summer Things*, New York: McKay, 36, 203, 220.

Sarris, Andrew (1971), *Confessions of a Cultist: On the Cinema, 1955–1969*, New York: Simon & Schuster.

Segura, Florencio (1971), '¿Un centenario "camp"? El genio alegre de los hermanos Quintero', *Razón y Fé* 6, 17–21.

Simon, John Ivan (1971), *Movies into Film: Film Criticism 1967–1970*, New York: Dial; New York: Dell, 1972.

Sternberg, Jacques (1971), 'Quelques mots en guise de préface', in *Les Chefs d'oeuvre du Kitsch*, Paris: Planète, 8–25. English translation: 'Introduction', in *Kitsch*, edited by Marina Henderson. London: Academy; New York: St. Martin's, 1972, 5–15.

Taylor, John Russell (1971), 'Stay at Home for Christmas', *Times*, 24 December, 5.

Wellek, René (1971), 'American Criticism of the Last Ten Years', in Weber & Haack 1971: 13–28.

Weber, Alfred & Dietmar Haack (1971) (eds.), *Amerikanische Literatur im 20. Jahrhundert/American Literature in the 20th Century*, Göttingen: Vandenhoeck & Ruprecht.

Wilde, Alan (1971), *Christopher Isherwood*, New York: Twayne.

1972

Burchfield, R. W. (1972) (ed.), *A Supplement to The Oxford English Dictionary*, Vol. 1, Oxford: Clarendon, 421–2. 2nd edn., J. A. Simpson & E. S. C. Weiner (eds.), *The Oxford English Dictionary*, ibidem, 1989, 811.

Conley, Barry (1972), 'The Garland Legend: The Stars Have Lost Their Glitter', *Gay News*, n 13, 10–11.

Farrell, Ronald A. (1972), 'The Argot of the Homosexual Subculture', *Anthropological Linguistics* 14:3, March, 97–109.

Humphreys, Laud (1972), 'Camp and Soul', in *Out of the Closets: The Sociology of Homosexual Liberation*, Englewood Cliffs: Prentice-Hall, 70–3.

Mailer, Norman (1972), 'Preface', in *Existential Errands*, Boston-Toronto: Little, Brown & Co.; New York: New American Library, 1973, ix-xi.

Newton, Esther Mary (1972), *Mother Camp: Female Impersonators in America*, Englewood Cliffs: Prentice-Hall; 2nd edn. with a new preface, Chicago-London: U of Chicago P, 1979. Based on 'The "Drag Queens": A Study in Urban Anthropology', PhD diss., University of Chicago, 1969. Partly rpt. in Bergman 1993a: 39–53. Reviewed in: *American Anthropologist* 76:6, December 1973:1961–2, by Norine Dresser; *Choice* 17, March 1980:39; *Kirkus Reviews* 40, 1 October 1972:1176; *Library Journal* 98, 15 March 1973:880, by J. J. Milholland; *Qualitative Sociology* 3:3, Fall 1980:246–48, by Mildred Daley Pagelow; *Social Forces* 52, September 1973:154; *West Coast Review of Books* 5, July 1979:61.

Rodgers, Bruce (1972), *The Queen's Vernacular: A Gay Lexicon*, San Francisco: Straight Arrow, 41–2. Rpt. as *Gay Talk: A (Sometimes Outrageous) Dictionary of Gay Slang*, New York: Paragon, 1979.

Schickel, Richard (1972), 'Savage Takeoff of a Put-On', *Life*, 72:2, 21 January, 16.

Schwartz, Barry N. (1972), 'Art Confrontation: The Sacred Against the Profane', *Arts in Society* 9:1, 150–58.

Seymour, Alan (1972), 'Wesker Undefeated', *Observer Review*, 13 August, 25.

Urdang, Laurence (1972) (ed.), *The New York Times Everyday Reader's Dictionary of Misunderstood, Misused, and Mispronounced Words*, New York: Times Books. 2nd edn., rev, 1985, 38.

Tyler, Parker (1972a), *Screening the Sexes: Homosexuality in the Movies*, New York: Holt, Rinehart & Winston; Garden City: Anchor, 1973; New York: Da Capo, 1993, 1–16, 50, 57, 158–61, 191–3, 207, 233, 337, 346.

—— (1972b), *The Shadow of an Airplane Climbs the Empire State Building: A World Theory of Film*, Garden City: Doubleday, 66, 172, 208, 222–5.

Weinberg, Martin & Alan Bell (1972) (eds.), *Homosexuality: An Annotated Bibliography*, New York: Harper & Row, 358, 390.

Zandvoort, R. W. (1972), 'A Note on "Camp"', *English Studies* 53:6, December, 544–8.

1973

Anon. (1973), 'Andy Warhol Doesn't Play Second Base for the Chicago Cubs', *Ramparts* 12:3, October, 2.

Barnhart, Robert K., Sol Steinmetz & Clarence L. Barnhart (1973) (eds.), *The Barnhart Dictionary of New English Since 1963*, New York-London: Barnhart/Harper & Row, 79–80, 206, 266. Conflated with *The Second Barnhart Dictionary of New English, 1963–1972* (New York-London: Barnhart, 1973) in *The Third Barnhart Dictionary of New English*, New York: H. W. Wilson, 1990, 75, 231, 295.

Brophy, Brigid (1973), *Prancing Novelist: A Defence of Fiction in the Form of a Critical Biography in Praise of Ronald Firbank*, London: Macmillan; New York: Barnes & Noble, 171.

Escoffier, Jeffrey (1973), 'Breaking Camp', *Gay Alternative* 1:4, 6–8.

Evans, Arthur (1973), 'How to Zap Straights', in Len Richmond & Gary Noguera (eds.), *The Gay Liberation Book: Writings and Photographs about Gay (Men's) Liberation*, San Francisco: Ramparts, 111–15.

Gagnon, John H. & William Simon (1973), *Sexual Conduct: The Social Sources of Human Sexuality*, Chicago: Aldine; London: Hutchinson, 1974, 152–3.

Gay, George R. & Charles W. Sheppard (1973), '"Sex-Crazed Dope Fiends" – Myth or Reality?' *Drug Forum* 2:2, Winter, 125–40.

Jencks, Charles (1973a), 'The Candid King Midas of New York Camp', *AAQ: Architectural Association Quarterly* 5:4, October-December, 26–42.

—— (1973b), *Modern Movements in Architecture*. Harmondsworth-Baltimore-Ringwood: Penguin, 13, 27, 50, 53, 106–8, 122, 185–237, 239. Reviewed in: *Books & Bookmen* 18, September 1973:137; *Choice* 10, January 1974:1709; *Library Journal* 98, 1 October 1973:2845, by J. Brown; *New Leader* 56, 26 November 1973:18;

New Statesman 86, 10 August 1973:190, by Malcolm MacEwen; *New York Times Book Review*, 7 July 1974:4; *Observer*, 17 June 1973:29; *TLS*, 26 October 1973:1298.

Kopkind, Andrew (1973), 'Gay Rock: The Boys in the Band', *Ramparts* 11:9, March, 49–51.

Morgan, Robin (1973), 'Lesbianism and Feminism: Synonyms or Contradiction?', *Second Wave* 2:4, 14–23. Rpt. in *Going Too Far: The Personal Chronicle of a Feminist*, New York: Random House, 1977, 170–88.

Nolan, James (1973), 'The Third Sex', *Ramparts* 12:5, December, 21–6, 56–9.

Rosenthal, Michael (1973), 'The Fixer of Modern Camp', *New York Times Book Review*, 22 July, 4.

Woolf, Henry Bosley (1973) (ed.), *Webster's New Collegiate Dictionary*, Springfield: Merriam; ivi, 1980, 158.

1974

Babuscio, Jack (1974), 'Screen Gays: Camp Women', *Gay News*, 73.

Crew Louie & Rictor Norton (1974) (eds.), 'The Homosexual Imagination in Literature, in the Classroom, in Criticism', special issue of *College English* 36:3, November.

Hodges, Andrew & David Hutter (1974), *With Downcast Gays: Aspects of Homosexual Self-Oppression*, London: Pomegranate; Toronto: Pink Triangle, 1979, 12, 24, 27–8.

Kantrowitz, Arnie (1974), 'Homosexuals and Literature', in Crew & Norton 1974: 324–30.

Kramer, Hilton (1974), 'New Art of the 70's in Chicago: Visual Bluster and Camp Sensibility', *New York Times*, 123:42, 14 July, Sect. 2, 19.

Minnelli, Vincente (with Hector Acre) (1974), *I Remember It Well*, with a foreword by Alan Jay Lerner. Garden City: Doubleday; London: Angus & Robertson, 1975; Hollywood: Samuel French, 1990, 164.

Ortleb, Chuck (1974), 'Susan Sontag: After the First Decade', *Out: The Gay Perspective* 1:2, April, 14.

Rubin, Louis D. Jr. (1974), 'Susan Sontag and the Camp Followers', *Sewanee Review* 82:3, Summer, 503–10.

Scaduto, Antony (1974), *Mick Jagger: Everybody's Lucifer*, New York: D. McKay, 2, 154, 258.

Stanley, Julia Penelope (1974), 'When We Say "Out of the Closets!"', in Crew & Norton 1974: 385–91.

Wood, Michael (1974), 'Nostalgia or Never: You Can't Go Home Again', *New Society*, 30, 7 November, 343–6. Rpt. as 'You Can't Go Home Again' in Paul Barker (ed.), *Arts in Society: A 'New Society' Collection*, London: Fontana, 1977, 21–30.

Wood, Michael (1974), 'Over the Rainbow', *New Society*, 27, 28 March, 780–1.

Young, Allen (1974), 'What is Gay Culture?' *Gay Liberator* (Detroit) 40, September-October, 1, 12–13. Rev. vers. as 'No Longer the Court Jester', in Jay & Young 1978: 23–47.

1975

Bletter, Rosemarie Haag & Cervin Robinson (1975), 'Skyscraper Style', *Progressive Architecture* 56:2, February, 68–73.

Boyers, Robert & Maxine Bernstein (1975), 'Women, The Arts and the Politics of Culture: An Interview with Susan Sontag', *Salmagundi* 31–2, Fall 1975–Winter 1976, 29–48. Rpt. as 'The *Salmagundi* Interview' in Hardwick 1982a: 327–46. Rpt. in Leland Poague (ed.), *Conversations with Susan Sontag*, Jackson: UP of Mississippi, 1995, 57–78.

Brown, Curtis F. (1975), 'Is It Kitsch or Is It Camp?' In *Star-Spangled Kitsch: An Astounding and Tastelessly Illustrated Exploration of the Bawdy, Gaudy, Shoddy Mass-Art Culture in This Grand Land of Ours*, New York: Universe, 14–16.

Farber, Manny & Patricia Patterson (1975), 'Fassbinder', *Film Comment* 11:6, November-December, 5–7.

Fein, Sara Beck & Elane M. Nuehring (1975), 'Perspectives on the Gender-Integrated Gay Community: Its Formal Structure and Social Function', *Homosexual Counseling Journal* 2:4, October, 150–63.

Greenspun, Roger (1975), 'Phantom of Liberty: Thoughts on Fassbinder's Fist-Right of Freedom', *Film Comment* 11:6, November-December, 8–10.

Johnston, Jill (1975), 'Are Lesbians "Gay"?' *Ms.* 3:12, June, 85–6.

Legman, Gershon (1975), *Rationale of the Dirty Joke: An Analysis of Sexual Humor, Second Series*, New York: Breaking Point, 120. 2nd edn.: *No Laughing Matter: An Analysis of Sexual Humor, Vol. 2*, Bloomington: Indiana UP, 1982.

Morris, William & Mary Morris (1975) (eds.), *Harper's Dictionary of Contemporary Usage*, New York-London: Harper & Row, 105.

Sarris, Andrew (1975), 'Enduring Summer Camp', *Village Voice* 20:29, 21 July, 67–9.

Sontag, Susan (1975), 'Fascinating Fascism', *New York Review of Books*, 22:1, 6 February Rpt. in *Under the Sign of Saturn*, New York: Farrar, Straus & Giroux; Toronto: McGraw Hill Ryerson, 1980, 73–105; rpt. in Hardwick 1982a: 305–25.

Steiner, George (1975), 'Eros and Idiom', rpt. in *On Difficulty and Other Essays*, Oxford: Oxford UP, 1978, 95–136. Rpt. in *George Steiner: A Reader*, London: Penguin, 1984, 314–44.

Suares, Jean-Claude (1975), 'Designer's Guide to Schlock, Camp & Kitsch – and the Taste of Things to Come', *Print* 29:1, January-February, 25–35.

Sweeney, Daniel Christopher (1975), 'The New Rhythm: Camp in the Novels of Ronald Firbank', PhD diss., Florida State University; abstract in *DAI* 36, 1975, 3738A.

Tripp, C. A. (1975), 'The Psychology of Effeminacy', in *The Homosexual Matrix*, New York: McGraw. 2nd edn.: New York-Scarborough (Ontario): New American Library, 1987, 173–87.

1976

Babuscio, Jack (1976), 'Celebrating Camp', *Gay News*, 91, 25 March-7 April, 17–18.

Buttafava, Gianni (1976), 'Il travestitismo a teatro', in Gillo Dorfles et al., *Gli uni e gli altri. Travestiti e travestimenti nell'arte, nel teatro, nel cinema, nella musica, nel cabaret e nella vita quotidiana*, Rome: Arcana, 31–5.

Dyer, Richard (1976), 'It's Being so Camp as Keeps Us Going', *Playguy*. Rpt. in *The Body Politic Review Supplement* (Toronto) 10:36, September 1977, 11–13. Rpt. in Dyer 1992: 135–46.

Hayes, Joseph J. (1976), 'Gayspeak', *Quarterly Journal of Speech* 62:3, October, 256–66. Rpt. in Chesebro 1981: 45–57.

Howes, Keith (1976a), 'Gay Sweatshop', *Gay News*, 88. Rpt. in Howes 1995: 3–4.

—— (1976b), 'Sides of Sondheim', *Gay News*, 95. Rpt. in Howes 1995: 16.

Johnston, Grahame (1976) (ed.), *The Australian Pocket Oxford Dictionary*, London-New York: Oxford UP, 113.

Lahr, John (1976), 'Introduction', in Joe Orton, *The Complete Plays*, London: Eyre Methuen, 7–28.

Purdon, Noel (1976), 'Gay Cinema', *Cinema Papers* (Australia) 10, September-October, 115–19, 179.

Robsjohn-Gibbings, T. H. (1976), 'Camp Followers', *Architectural Digest* 33:3, 22, 26.

Russo, Vito (1976), 'All About Camp', *Advocate*, 190, 19 May, 17–18. Rpt. as 'Camp' in Levine 1979a: 205–10. Partly rpt. in Mark Thompson (ed.), *Long Road to Freedom: The Advocate History of the Gay and Lesbian Movement*, New York: St. Martin's, 1994, 139.

Safire, William (1976), 'Vogue Words are Trific, Right?', *New York Times Magazine*, 21 March, 111.

Singer, June (1976), *Androgyny: The Opposites Within*, Garden City: Anchor/Doubleday; Boston: Sigo, 1989, 13.

Stanley, Julia Penelope & Susan W. Robbins (1976), 'Lesbian Humor', *Women* 5:1, 26–29.

Sykes, J. B. (1976) (ed.), *The Concise Oxford Dictionary of Current English*, Oxford: Clarendon, 142.

Thomas, Peter (1976), '*Camp* and Politics in Isherwood's Berlin Fiction', *Journal of Modern Literature* 5:1, February, 117–30.

1977

Adair, William (1977), 'Portnoy's Complaint: A Camp Version of *Notes from Underground*', *Notes on Contemporary Literature* 7:3, May, 9–10.

Babuscio, Jack (1977), 'Camp and the Gay Sensibility', in Richard Dyer (ed.), *Gays and Film*, London: BFI; rev. edn., New York: Zoetrope, 1984, 40–57 (reviewed in: *Choice* 18, June 1981, 1424; *Film Comment* 16, January 1981, 72; *TLS*, 22 July 1977, 892; *Choice* 22, May 1985, 1341). Rpt. in Bergman 1993a: 19–38. Expanded as 'The Cinema of Camp', *Gay Sunshine Journal* 35, Winter 1978, 18–22, and rpt. in Winston Leyland (ed.), *Gay Roots: Twenty Years of Gay Sunshine (An Anthology of Gay History, Sex, Politics and Culture)*, San Francisco: Gay Sunshine, 1991, 431–49.

Blau, Judith R. (with the assistance of Hilary Silver) (1977), 'Architectural Ideologies and Their Organizational Context', *Quarterly Journal of Ideology* 1:4, Summer, 16–30.

Bronski, Michael (1977), 'Eighth Row Center: Where the Boys Are', *Gay Community News* 4:48, 28 May, 10–11, 13. Expanded as 'Judy Garland and Others: Notes on Idolization and Derision', in Jay & Young 1978: 201–12.

Calinescu, Matei (1977), *Faces of Modernity: Avant-Garde, Decadence, Kitsch*, Bloomington: Indiana UP. 2nd edn.: *Five Faces of Modernity: Modernism, Avant-Garde, Decadence, Kitsch, Postmodernism*, Durham-London: Duke UP, 1987, 230–1, 312.

Carter, Angela (1977), *The Passion of New Eve*, London: Gollancz; New York: Harcourt Brace Jovanovich; London: Virago, 1982; London: Bloomsbury, 1993, 3.

Douglas, Ann (1977), *The Feminization of American Culture*, New York: Arnold A. Knopf; ibidem, 1979; New York: Anchor, 1988 (with a new preface); London-Basingstoke: Papermac, 1996, 4–5.

Dyer, Richard (1977), 'Entertainment and Utopia', *Movie* 24, Spring, 2–13. Rpt. in Rick Altman (ed.), *Genre: The Musical*, London-New York: Routledge, 1981, 175–89. Also rpt. in Dyer 1992: 17–34. Also rpt. in Simon During (ed.), *The Cultural Studies Reader*, London-New York: Routledge, 1993, 271–83.

Fiedler, Leslie (1977), *A Fiedler Reader*, New York: Stein & Day.

Howard, Philip (1977), *New Words for Old*, London: Hamish Hamilton; London: Unwin, 1980, 4–6.

Howes, Keith (1977a), 'I, Derek', *Gay News*, 117. Rpt. in Howes 1995: 43–4.

—— (1977b), 'Uncensored', *Gay News*, 133. Rpt. in Howes 1995: 51.

Showalter, Elaine (1977), *A Literature of Their Own: British Women Novelists from Brontë to Lessing*, Princeton: Princeton UP, 291. New edn., rev., London: Virago, 1982.

Smith, C. Ray (1977), 'Wit and Whimsy or Campopop', in *Supermannerism: New Attitudes in Post-Modern Architecture*, New York: E. Dutton, 160–220. Reviewed in: *Booklist*, 74, 1 December 1977, 592; *Choice*, 14, February 1978, 1637.

Sterling, M. D. (1977), 'Playing Roles', *Blueboy* (New York) 11, April-May, 10–13.

Weeks, Jeffrey (1977), *Coming Out: Homosexual Politics in Britain from the Nine-teenth Century to the Present*, London-New York: Quartet. Rev. edn.: ibidem, 1990, 42–3.

White, Edmund (1977), 'Camping', in Charles Silverstein & Edmund White, *The Joy of Gay Sex: An Intimate Guide for Gay Men to the Pleasures of a Gay Lifestyle*, New York: Crown, 36–8.

1978

Arbasino, Alberto (1978), 'Nota 1978', in *Super-Eliogabalo*, Turin: Einaudi, 350.

Baker, Rob (1978), 'New German Cinema: A Fistful of Myths', *Soho Weekly News*, 23 March, 21–3.

Brecht, Stefan (1978), *Queer Theatre*, Frankfurt am Main: Surhkamp; London-New York: Methuen, 1986, 150.

Britton, Andrew (1978), 'For Interpretation – Notes Against Camp', *Gay Left* 7, Winter 1978/79, 11–14.

Collective Editorial (1978), 'In the Balance', *Gay Left* 6, Fall, 2–4.

Howes, Keith (1978), 'Bette Midler', *Gay News*, 150, 1978. Rpt. in Howes 1995: 68.

Jay, Karla (1978), 'No Man's Land', in Jay & Young 1978: 48–65.

Jay, Karla & Allen Young (1978) (eds.), *Lavender Culture*, New York: Jove. 2nd edn., New York: New York UP, 1994. Reviewed in: *Lambda Book Report*, 4, May 1995:40; *Reference Services Review*, 12, Summer 1984:91.

Kleinberg, Seymour (1978), 'Macho Men: Or, Where Have All the Sissies Gone?', *Gay News*, 142, 16–18. Rev. as 'Where Have All the Sissies Gone?' in *Alienated Affections: Being Gay in America*, New York: St. Martin's, 1980; New York: Warner Communications, 1982, 143–56.

Lahr, John (1978), *Prick Up Your Ears: The Biography of Joe Orton*, London: Allen Lane; London: Penguin, 1980, 26, 17, 189, 248.

Lynch, Michael (1978), 'The Life Below the Life', in Louie Crew (ed.), *The Gay Academic*, Palm Springs: ETC, 178–92.

Milani, Raffaele (1978), *Il cinema underground americano*, Messina-Florence: G. D'Anna, 89–95.

Stanley, Julia & Susan Robbins (1978), 'Mother Wit: Tongue in Cheek', in Jay & Young 1978: 299–307.

1979

Ashley, Leonard R. N. (1979), '*Kinks and Queens*: Linguistic and Cultural Aspects of the Terminology for *Gays*', *Maledicta* 3:2, Winter, 215–56.

Dyer, Richard (1979), *Stars*, London: BFI, 67–8. Reviewed in: *Film Comment* 16, January 1980:71; *Journal of American Studies* 15, August 1981:312; *New States-man*, 98, 26 October 1979:642.

Edel, Leon (1979), 'The Figure Under the Carpet', in Marc Pachter (ed.), *Telling Lives: The Biographer's Art*, Washington: New Republic; Philadelphia: U of Pennsylvania P, 1981, 16–34.

Hayes, Joseph J. (1979), 'Language and Language Behavior of Lesbian Women and Gay Men: A Selected Bibliography (Part 2)', *Journal of Homosexuality* 4:3, Spring, 299–309.

Hebdige, Dick (1979), 'Glam and Glitter Rock: Albino Camp and Other Diversions', in *Subculture: The Meaning of Style*, London-New York: Methuen; London-New York: Routledge, 1988, 59–62.

Howes, Keith (1979), 'Anna Raeburn and Len Richmond', *Gay News*, 162. Rpt. in Howes 1995: 77.

Lauritsen, John (1979), 'Disruptions, Censorship, Bigotry', in Len Richmond & Gary Noguera (eds.), *The New Gay Liberation Book: Writings and Photographs about Gay (Men's) Liberation*, Palo Alto: Ramparts, 155–63.

Levine, Martin (1979a) (ed.), *Gay Men: The Sociology of Male Homosexuality*, New York-San Francisco: Harper & Row.
—— (1979b), 'Introduction', in Levine 1979a: 1–16.
Long, T. H. & Della Summers (1979) (eds.), *Longman Dictionary of English Idioms*, London: Longman, 46.
Martin, Robert K. (1979), *The Homosexual Tradition in American Poetry*, Austin-London: U of Texas P, 202–6.
Mauriès, Patrick (1979), *Second manifeste camp*, Paris: Seuil. Reviewed in: *Jardin des Modes*, October 1979; *Fiches bibliographiques* December 1979, by André-Noël Boichat; *Nouvelles littéraires*, 14 June 1979, by Patrice Delbourg; *A Suivre* July 1979; *Libération*, 24 May 1979, by Marc Voline.
Rich, Frank (1979), 'High Camp', *Time*, 114:17, 22 October, 85–6.
Weiner, Andrew (1979), 'The Apotheosis of Super-Goy', *New Society*, 47:852, 1 February, 254–5.
York, Peter (1979), 'Machomania', *Harpers & Queen*, February, 58–61.

1980

Aaron, Daniel (1980), 'Fictionalizing the Past', *Partisan Review* 47:2, Spring, 231–41. Rpt. in *American Notes: Selected Essays*, Boston: Northeastern UP, 1994, 223–34.
Arbasino, Alberto (1980), 'La *Salomé* di Wilde e Beardsley', in Oscar Wilde, *Salomé*, Milan: Rizzoli, 5–14.
Ashley, Leonard R. N. (1980), '"Lovely, Blooming, Fresh and Gay": The Onomastics of Camp', *Maledicta* 4:2, Winter, 223–48.
Camus, Renaud (1980), *Buena Vista Park*, Paris: Hachette, 19.
Cohen, Derek & Richard Dyer (1980), 'The Politics of Gay Culture', in Gay Left Collective 1980: 172–86.
Dyer, Richard (1980), 'Reading Fassbinder's Sexual Politics', in Tony Rayns (ed.), *Fassbinder*, London: BFI, 54–64.
Faris, Alexander (1980), *Jacques Offenbach*, London: Faber, 114–16.
Gay Left Collective (1980) (eds.), *Homosexuality: Power and Politics*, London-New York: Allison & Busby.
Gee, Stephen (1980), 'Gay Activism', in Gay Left Collective 1980, 198–204.
Hollinghurst, Alan J. (1980), 'The Creative Uses of Homosexuality in the Novels of E. M. Forster, Ronald Firbank and L. Hartley', M.Litt. diss., Oxford University.
Jencks, Charles (1980), 'Philip Johnson: The Candid King Midas of New York Camp', in *Late-Modern Architecture and Other Essays*, London: Academy; New York: Rizzoli, 146–50. Rpt. in *The New Moderns: From Late to Neo-Modernism*, London: Academy, 1990, 138–51.
Prawer, S. S. (1980), *Caligari's Children: The Film as Tale of Terror*, Oxford-New York: Oxford UP, 15.
Riddiough, Christine (1980), 'Culture and Politics', in Pam Mitchell (ed.), *Pink Triangles: Radical Perspectives on Gay Liberation*, Boston: Alyson, 14–33.
Schwartz, Ronald (1980), 'Cobra Meets the Spiderman: Two Examples of Cuban and Argentinian "Camp"', in Rose S. Minc & R. Marylin Frankenthaler (eds.), *Requiem for the 'Boom' – Premature? A Symposium*, Montclair: Montclair State College, 137–49.
Warhol, Andy & Pat Hackett (1980), *POPism: The Warhol Sixties*, New York: Harcourt Brace Jovanovich; London: Hutchinson, 1981; San Diego: Harvester/HBJ, 1990; London: Pimlico, 1996, 88, 127.
White, Edmund (1980a), 'The Political Vocabulary of Homosexuality', in Leonard Michaels & Christopher Ricks (ed.), *The State of the Language*, Berkeley: U of California P; London: Faber, 1990, 240. Rpt. in White 1994: 69–81.
—— (1980b), *States of Desire: Travels in Gay America*, New York: Dutton; London: Bantam, 1981, 235–6; New York: Plume, 1991.

Wood, Robin (1980), 'The Dyer's Hand: Stars and Gays', *Film Comment* 16:1, January-February, 70–2.

Zimmerman, Bonnie (1980), '*Daughters of Darkness*: Lesbian Vampires', *Jump Cut* 24:24, Fall, 23–4.

1981

Beaver, Harold (1981), 'Homosexual Signs (*In Memory of Roland Barthes*)', *Critical Inquiry* 8:1, Autumn, 99–119.

Blachford, Gregg (1981), 'Male Dominance and the Gay World', in Kenneth Plummer (ed.), *The Making of the Modern Homosexual*, London: Hutchinson; Totowa: Barnes & Noble, 184–210.

Chesebro, James W. (1981) (ed.), *Gayspeak: Gay Male and Lesbian Communication*, New York: Pilgrim. Reviewed in: *Booklist*, 78, 1 November 1981:360; *Library Journal* 106, 1 November 1981:2147, by James E. Van Buskirk; *Science Books and Films* 18, November-December 1982:62, by Victor G. Wightman.

Darsey, James (1981), '"Gayspeak": A Response', in Chesebro 1981: 58–67.

Dyer, Richard (1981), 'Getting over the Rainbow: Identity and Pleasure in Gay Cultural Politics', in George Bridges & Rosalind Brunt (eds.), *Silver Linings: Some Strategies for the Eighties (contributions to the Communist University of London)*, London: Lawrence & Wishart, 53–67. Rpt. in Dyer 1992: 159–172.

Fernbach, David (1981), *The Spiral Path: A Gay Contribution to Human Survival*, Boston: Alyson; London: GMP, 205–7.

Hayes, Joseph J. (1981), 'Lesbians, Gay Men, and Their "Languages"', in Chesebro 1981: 28–42.

Keller, Karl (1981), 'Walt Whitman Camping', *Walt Whitman Review* 26:4, December, 138–44. Rpt. in Bergman 1993a: 113–20.

Kramer, Hilton (1981), 'A Problematic Revival of A "Victorian Paragon"', *New York Times*, 29 November, 131:45, Sect. D, 31, 36. Rpt. as 'Landseer: The Victorian Paragon' in Kramer 1985: 29–32.

Marson, Ellen E. (1981), 'Mae West, Superman and the Spanish Poets of the Seventies', in Minc 1981: 191–8.

Minc, Rose S. (1981) (ed.), *Literature and Popular Culture in the Hispanic World: A Symposium*, Montclair: Montclair State College.

Nelson, Charles (1981), *The Boy who Picked the Bullets Up*, New York: Morrow; Secaucus: Meadowlands, 152.

Rentschler, Eric (1981), 'American Friends and the New German Cinema: Patterns of Reception', *New German Critique* 24–25, Fall-Winter 1981/82, 7–35.

Spears, Richard A. (1981) (ed.), *Slang and Euphemism: A Dictionary of Oaths, Curses, Insults, Sexual Slang & Metaphor, Racial Slurs, Drug Talk, Homosexual Lingo, & Related Matters*, New York: Jonathan David, 61.

Weeks, Jeffrey (1981), *Sex, Politics & Society: The Regulation of Sexuality Since 1800*, London-New York: Longman, 111, 287.

Yudice, George (1981), '*El beso de la mujer araña* y *Pubis angelical*: Entre el placer y el saber', in Minc 1981: 43–57.

1982

Adams, Charles R. (1982), 'Lexical Accession in Sharamboko: A *Camp* Language in Lesotho', *Anthropological Linguistics* 24:2, Summer, 137–82.

Altman, Dennis (1982), *The Homosexualization of America, The Americanization of the Homosexual*, New York: St. Martin's; Boston: Beacon, 1983, 152–5.

Ashley, Leonard R. N. (1982), '*Dyke* Diction: The Language of Lesbians', *Maledicta* 6:1–2, Summer-Winter, 123–62.

Blau, Herbert (1982), 'Politics and the Presentation of Self: Disseminating *Sodom*', *Salmagundi* 58–9 (1982–3), 221–51.

Boone, Bruce (1982), 'Gay Language as Political Praxis: The Poetry of Frank O'Hara', *Social Text* 1:1, Winter, 59–92.

Cawqua, Urson [pseud.] (1982), 'Two Etymons and a Query: *Gay-Fairies-Camping*', *Maledicta* 6:1–2, Summer-Winter, 224–30.

Daube, Colette (1982), 'Ronald Firbank 1886–1926. L'homme et l'oeuvre', *Doctorat d'Etat*, Université de la Sorbonne.

Dyer, Richard (1982), '*A Star is Born* and the Construction of Authenticity', in BFI Education (eds.), *Star Signs*, London: BFI, 13–22. Rpt. in Gledhill 1991: 132–40.

Eisman, Jean Ann (1982), 'Frank O'Hara and the Art of Abstract Poetry', PhD diss., University of Wisconsin-Milwaukee; abstract in *DAI* 43: 6, December 1982, 1967A.

Hardwick, Elizabeth (1982a) (ed.), *A Susan Sontag Reader*, New York: Farrar, Straus & Giroux; Toronto: McGraw-Hill Ryerson; London: Penguin, 1983. Reviewed in: *American Spectator* 16, March 1983:39; *Atlantic Monthly* 250, September 1982:88, by Hilton Kramer; *Books & Bookmen* November 1983:36; *Booklist*, 79, 15 September 1982:88; *Harper's Magazine*, 266, February 1983:62, by Marvin Mudrick; *Hudson Review* 36, Summer 1983:415; *Kirkus Reviews*, 50, 1 August 1982:931; *LA Times Book Review*, 12 December 1982:2; *New Leader*, 65, 13 December 1983:9; *New York Times Book Review*, 87, 24 October 1982:11; *Nation*, 235, 23 October 1982:404; *Observer*, 25 September 1983:31; *Publishers' Weekly*, 222, 17 September 1982:105; *Publishers' Weekly*, 12 August 1983:64; *Performing Arts Journal* 7:1, 1983:132; *Progressive* 47, March 1983:60; *Sewanee Review* 92, October 1984:649; *Village Voice Literary Supplement*, November 1982:13; *World Literature Today* 57, Spring 1983:293, by Leon S. Roudiez.

—— (1982b), 'Introduction', in Hardwick 1982a: ix-xv.

Hughes, Robert (1982), 'The Rise of Andy Warhol', *New York Review of Books*, 29:2, 18 February, 6–8, 10.

Kiernan, Robert F. (1982), 'The Breckinridge Novels', in *Gore Vidal*, New York: Frederick Ungar, 94–109.

Kohn, Michael (1982), 'Arch Connelly', *Arts Magazine* 56:10, June, 15.

Kramer, Hilton (1982), 'Postmodern: Art and Culture in the 1980s', *New Criterion* 1:1, September, 36–42. Rpt. in Kramer 1985: 1–11.

Lahr, John (1982), *Coward the Playwright*, London-New York: Methuen, 68.

Schiller, Gregory C. (1982), 'The Social Organization of Homosexual Sado-Masochism: A Brief History', *American Sociological Association*.

Wolfe, Tom (1982), *The Purple Decades: A Reader*, New York: Farrar, Straus & Giroux; London: Jonathan Cape, 1983; London-Basingstoke: Pan, 1993.

1983

Belluso, Paolo & Flavio Merkel (1983), *The Rocky Horror Picture Show*, Milan: Gammalibri, *passim*.

Booth, Mark (1983), *Camp*, London-New York: Quartet. Reviewed in: *Books & Bookmen* June 1983:33; *New Statesman*, 105, 15 April 1983:26; *Observer*, 10 April 1983:30; *Punch*, 4 May 1983:72; *Times Educational Supplement*, 1 April 1983:35.

Chambers, Iain (1983), 'Camp: A Note', *Anglistica-AION* 26:1–2, 133–4.

Corbatta, Jorgelina Fidia (1983), 'Mito personal y mitos colectivos en las novelas de Manuel Puig', PhD diss., University of Pittsburgh; abstract in *DAI* 45:4, October 1984, 1126A.

Dollimore, Jonathan (1983), 'The Challenge of Sexuality', in Alan Sinfield (ed.), *Society and Literature 1945–1970*, London: Methuen; New York: Holmes & Meier, 51–85. Partly rpt. in Dollimore 1991.

Dyer, Richard (1983), 'Seen to Be Believed: Some Problems in the Representation of Gay People as Typical', *Studies in Visual Communication* 9:2, Spring, 2–19. Rpt. in

The Matter of Images: Essays on Representations, London-New York: Routledge, 1993, 42.

Free, William J. (1983), 'Camp Elements in the Plays of Tennessee Williams', *Southern Quarterly* 21:2, Winter, 16–23.

Hansen, Sandra (1983), 'Producing Your Own – Beach Blanket Babylon', *Theatre Crafts* 17:3, March, 20–21, 56–7.

Howes, Keith (1983), 'Camp is a great *jewel*, 22 carats', *Gay News*, 261. Rpt. in Howes 1995: 92–3.

Katz, Jonathan Ned (1983) (ed.), *Gay/Lesbian Almanac: A New Documentary*, New York-London: Harper & Row.

Kramer, Hilton (1983), 'The Return of the Nativist', *New Criterion* 2:2, October, 58–63. Rpt. as 'The Return of the Nativist: Grant Wood' in Kramer 1985: 51–59.

Merlino, Giuseppe (1983), 'Camp', *Anglistica-AION* 26:1–2, 123–32.

Miller, Nory (1983), 'Hugh Hardy's Rambunctious Architecture of High Camp', *Wall Street Journal*, 201:35, 18 February, 17 (Western edn.), 29 (Eastern edn.).

Mordden, Ethan (1983), 'Dame Camp', in *Movie Star: A Look at the Women Who Made Hollywood*, New York: St. Martin's, 182–93.

Murray, Stephen (1983), 'Ritual & Personal Insults in Stigmatized Subcultures: Gay, Black, Jew', *Maledicta* 7, 189–211.

Polce, Roberto (1983), 'In morte del mostro e del *camp*', in Belluso & Merkel 1983: 111–18.

Satz, Evelyn (pseud.) (1983a), 'Camping It Up', *Films and Filming* 342, March, 20–3.

—— (1983b), 'Is There Camp After Cruising?' *Films and Filming*, 345, June, 26–9.

Waters, John (1987), *Crackpot: The Obsessions of John Waters*, New York: Random House, 40, 69.

1984

Boyd-Bowman, Susan (1984), 'Back to Camp', in Jim Cook (ed.), *Television Sitcom (BFI Dossier)*, London: BFI.

Britton, Andrew (1984), *Katharine Hepburn: The Thirties and After*, London: Tyneside Cinema, 40–1. 2nd edn., enlarged, published as *Katharine Hepburn: Star as Feminist*, New York: Continuum, 1995, 87–8.

Bronski, Michael (1984), *Culture Clash: The Making of Gay Sensibility*, Boston: South End, 12, 42–6, 97, 107, 126, 205–6. Reviewed in: *Boston Review* 10, April 1985:28; *Choice* 22, May 1985:1413, by B. Miller; *Library Journal* 109, December 1984:2291, by Jim Van Buskirk.

Core, Philip (1984), *Camp: The Lie that Tells the Truth*, London: Plexus; New York: Delilah. Reviewed in: *Punch*, 287, 22 August 1984:43; *Booklist*, 81, 1 January 1985:610; *Films in Review* 36, March 1985:183; *Village Voice*, 29, 16 October 1984:51.

Corrigan, Timothy (1984), 'On the Edge of History: The Radiant Spectacle of Werner Schroeter', *Film Quarterly* 37:4, Summer, 6–18. Rpt. as 'Schroeter's *Willow Springs* and the Excesses of History' in *New German Film: The Displaced Image*, rev. and exp. edn., Bloomington-London: Indiana UP, 1994, 169–84.

Dollimore, Jonathan (1984), '*The Revenger's Tragedy* (c. 1606): Providence, Parody and Black Camp', in *Radical Tragedy: Religion, Ideology and Power in the Drama of Shakespeare and His Contemporaries*, New York-London: Harvester Wheatsheaf; 2nd edn. with a new introduction, Harvester Wheatsheaf, 1989; London-Durham: Duke UP, 1993, 139–50.

Eco, Umberto (1984), 'Della cattiva pittura', rpt. in *Sugli specchi e altri saggi*, Milan: Bompiani, 1985, 73–7.

Grahn, Judy (1984), *Another Mother Tongue: Gay Words, Gay Worlds*, Boston: Beacon, 226–30, 305–6. 2nd edn., ibidem 1990.

Hancock, Ian (1984), 'Shelta and Polari', in Peter Trudgill (ed.), *Language in the British Isles*, Cambridge: Cambridge UP, 384–403.

Jameson, Fredric (1984), 'Postmodernism, or, the Cultural Logic of Late Capitalism', *New Left Review* 146, July-August, 53–92. Rpt. in Jameson 1991: 1–54. Rpt. in Thomas Docherty (ed.), *Postmodernism: A Reader*, New York-Oxford: Columbia UP, 1993, 62–92.

Kirk, Kris & Ed Heath (1984), *Men in Frocks*, London: GMP.

Kramer, Hilton (1984a), 'Julian Schnabel', in Prudence Carlson et al., *Art of Our Time: The Doris and Charles Saatchi Collection*, Vol 3. London: Lund Humphries; New York: Rizzoli, 1985, 25–8. Rpt. in Kramer 1985: 381–6.

—— (1984b), 'MoMA Reopened: The Museum of Modern Art in the Postmodern Era', *New Criterion* Special Issue, Summer, 1–16, 29–31, 34, 36, 41–4. Rpt. in Kramer 1985: 394–425.

Melly, George (1984), 'Preface', in Core 1984: 5–6.

Powell, L. Laurence, Jr. (1984), 'The Male Homosexual Character as Portrayed in Six Selected Plays From the American Theater, 1968–1978', PhD diss., Bowling Green State University; abstract in *DAI* 45:9, March 1985, 2696A.

Rentschler, Eric (1984), *West German Film in the Course of Time*, Bedford Hills: Redgrave, 83f.

Schiff, Stephen (1984), 'What *Dynasty* Says About America', *Vanity Fair*, 47:12, December, 64–7.

Schjeldahl, Peter (1984), 'The Oracle of Images', in Cindy Sherman, *Untitled Film Stills*, New York: Pantheon, 7–11.

Stewart, Susan (1984), *On Longing: Narratives of the Miniature, the Gigantic, the Souvenir, the Collection*, Baltimore-London: Johns Hopkins UP; 2nd edn., Durham-London: Duke UP, 1993, 167–9.

Wooten, Cecil (1984), 'Petronius and Camp', *Helios* 11:2, 133–9.

1985

Conrad, Peter (1985), 'Generalissimo's Big Parade', *Observer*, 24 February, 28.

Bell-Metereau, Rebecca (1985), *Hollywood Androgyny*, New York: Columbia UP. 2nd edn., enlarged, ibidem, 1993, 4, 5, 121, 155–66, 186, 288, 291, 315n1. Reviewed in: *Booklist*, 81, 1 May 1985:1226; *Christian Century*, 102, 14 August 1985:745; *Choice* 23, September 1985:126, by T. Cripps; *Library Journal*, 110, 1 March 1985:101, by Thomas Wiener; *New York Times Book Review*, 90, 31 March 1985:10, by Molly Haskell; *Publishers' Weekly*, 227, 1 February 1985:355; *TLS*, 24 May 1985:582, by Adam Mars-Jones; *Lambda Book Report* 4, January 1994:44; *Sight & Sound* 4:6, June 1994:38–39, by Claire Monk; *Wilson Library Bulletin* 68:7, March 1994:112–13, by Keith Snyder.

Bernheimer, Martin (1985), 'A Campy *Danae* Revived in Santa Fe', *Los Angeles Times*, 104, Sect. 6, 26 July, 1, 12.

Burton, Peter (1985), *Parallel Lives*, London: GMP.

Dynes, Wayne R. (1985), *Homolexis: A Historical and Cultural Lexicon of Homosexuality*, New York: Gay Academic Union, ii, 26–7, 119.

Escoffier, Jeffrey (1985), 'Sexual Revolution & the Politics of Gay Identity', *Socialist Review* 15:4–5, July-October, 119–53. Rpt. in Escoffier 1998: 33–64.

Humphries, Martin (1985), 'Gay Machismo', in Andy Metcalf & Martin Humphries (eds.), *The Sexuality of Men*, London-Sidney: Pluto, 70–85.

Klein, Joe (1985), 'The Real Star of "Dynasty"', *New York*, 18:34, 2 September, 32–9.

Kramer, Hilton (1985), *The Revenge of the Philistines: Art and Culture, 1972–1984*, New York: Free. Reviewed in: *American Book Review* 8, March 1986:4; *Art in America* 74, February 1986:21, by Donald B. Kuspit; *Books & Bookmen*, September 1986:14; *Book World (Washington Post)*, 15, 29 December 1985:9; *Christian Science Monitor*, 4 December 1985:33, by Tom D'Evelyn; *Encounter* 67, Summer

1986:62; *Listener*, 116, 14 August 1986:22; *Library Journal*, 111, 15 February 1986:174, by Patricia Scott; *London Review of Books*, 9, 19 March 1987:3; *Nation*, 241, 30 November 1985:590, by J. Hoberman; *National Review*, 38, 28 March 1986:58, by Terry Teachout; *New Republic*, 194, 18 April 1986:28, by Robert Hughes; *New Leader*, 68, 16 December 1985:4; *New Statesman*, 112, 15 August 1986:29, by Boyd Tonkin; *New York Times Book Review*, 90, 17 November 1985:11, by Richard Wollheim; *Observer*, 24 August 1986:20; *Spectator*, 257, 9 August 1986:23; *TLS*, 13 March 1987:273; *Village Voice Literary Supplement*, May 1986:14.

Laurie, Alison J. (1985), 'From Kamp Girls to Political Dykes', *Broadsheet* 134–5, November-December. Rpt. in Julia Penelope & Sara Valentine (eds.), *Finding the Lesbians: Personal Accounts from Around the World*, Freedom: Crossing, 1990. Rpt. in Stephan Likosky (ed.), *Coming Out: An Anthology of International Gay and Lesbian Writings*, New York: Pantheon; Toronto: Random House, 1992, 258–77.

LaValley, Al (1985), 'The Great Escape', *American Film* 10:6, April, 28–34, 70–1. Rpt. in Creekmur & Doty 1995a: 60–70.

McNaught, Brian (1985), 'Oppressing Ourselves', rpt. in *On Being Gay*, New York: St. Martin's, 1988, 21–4.

Sedgwick, Eve Kosofsky (1985), *Between Men: English Literature and Male Homosocial Desire*, New York-Chichester: Columbia UP; 2nd edn. with a new preface, ibidem, 1992, 90.

Weeks, Jeffrey (1985), *Sexuality and Its Discontents: Meanings, Myths & Modern Sexualities*, London-New York: Routledge & Kegan Paul, 190–1.

Wilson, Angus et al. (1985), 'Keeping the Camp Fires Burning', *Tatler* 281:1, December 1985/January 1986, 34, 36.

1986

Chambers, Iain (1986), *Popular Culture: The Metropolitan Experience*, London-New York: Methuen, 105–7.

Cohen, Ira (1986), 'Our Ancestor Alfred Chester', rpt. in Alfred Chester, *Head of a Sad Angel: Stories 1953–1966*, edited by Edward Field, Santa Rosa: Black Sparrow, 1990, 364–5.

Cooper, Emmanuel (1986), *The Sexual Perspective: Homosexuality and Art in the Last 100 Years in the West*, London: Routledge & Kegan Paul; 2nd edn., London-New York: Routledge, 1994, 297.

Dollimore, Jonathan (1986), 'The Dominant and the Deviant: A Violent Dialectic', *Critical Quarterly* 28:1–2, Spring-Summer, 179–92 (also pub. as Colin MacCabe (ed.). *Futures for English*, Manchester: Manchester UP, 1988). Rpt. in Wayne Dynes & Stephen Donaldson (eds.), *Homosexual Themes in Literary Studies*, New York: Garland, 1992, 87–100.

Dowling, Linda (1986), *Language and Decadence in the Victorian Fin de Siècle*, Princeton: Princeton UP, 146.

Dyer, Richard (1986), 'Judy Garland and Gay Men', in *Heavenly Bodies: Film Stars and Society*, London: Macmillan; New York: St. Martin's, 141–94.

Finch, Mark (1986), 'Sex and Address in *Dynasty*', *Screen* 27:6, November-December, 24–42. Rpt. in Manuel Alvarado & John O. Thompson (eds.), *The Media Reader*, London: BFI, 1990, 65–81.

Huyssen, Andreas (1986), *After the Great Divide: Modernism, Mass Culture and Postmodernism*, Bloomington: Indiana UP; London: Macmillan, 1988, 164, 165, 189, 194, 211. Reviewed in: *Afterimage* 15, February 1988:19; *JQ: Journalism Quarterly* 64, Winter 1987:895; *World Literature Today* 61, Autumn 1987:681; *Clio* 18, Fall 1988:94; *German Quarterly* 62, Summer 1989:446; *Poetics Today* 9:4, 1988:888; *Queen's Quarterly* 95, Autumn 1988:618.

Kiernan, Robert F. (1986), *Noel Coward*, New York: Ungar, 14, 19–20.

McRobbie, Angela (1986), 'Postmodernism and Popular Culture', in Lisa Appignanesi (ed.), *Postmodernism: ICA Documents 4*, London: Institute of Contemporary Arts, 54–8. 2nd edn., London: Free Association; New York: Columbia UP, 1989, 165–79. Rpt. in *Journal of Communication Inquiry* 10, 1986, 108–16. Partly rpt. in Paul Marris & Sue Thornham (eds.), *Media Studies: A Reader*, Edinburgh: Edinburgh UP, 1996 (2nd edn., 1999), 256–62.

Mercer, Kobena (1986), 'Monster Metaphors: Notes on Michael Jackson's "Thriller"', *Screen* 27:1, January-February, 26–43. Rpt. in Gledhill 1991: 300–16. Rpt. in Simon Frith, Andrew Goodwin & Lawrence Grossberg (eds.), *Sound and Vision: The Music Video Reader*, London-New York: Routledge, 1993, 93–108.

Newall, Venetia (1986), 'Folklore and Male Homosexuality', *Folklore* 97:2, 123–47.

Smith, Patrick S. (1986), *Andy Warhol's Art and Films*, Ann Arbor: UMI Research P, 143–6, 159, 169, 192, 197, 204, 242, 296, 321, 323, 411, 495. Based on 'Art in Extremis: Andy Warhol and His Art', PhD diss., Northwestern University, Evanston, 1981, abstract in *DAI* 43:7, January 1983, 2141A.

Taylor, John (1986a), 'John Taylor's Commentary', *Men's Wear*, 10 April, 12.

—— (1986b), 'Meanwhile Back at the Camp', *Men's Wear*, 7 August, 7.

Weeks, Jeffrey (1986), 'Masculinity and the Science of Desire', *Oxford Literary Review* 8, 22–7.

Whitam, Frederick L. & Robin M. Mathy (1986), *Male Homosexuality in Four Societies: Brazil, Guatemala, the Philippines, and the United States*, New York-Eastbourne-Toronto: Praeger, 25, 40, 109.

1987

Anon. (1987), 'Cash, Wag Club', *City Limits*, 5–12 March, 56.

Bersani, Leo (1987), 'Is the Rectum a Grave?' *October* 43, Winter, 197–222. The *October* issue reissued as Douglas Crimp (ed.), *AIDS: Cultural Analysis, Cultural Activism*, Cambridge-London: MIT P, 1988. Rev. in Jonathan Goldberg (ed.), *Reclaiming Sodom*, London-New York: Routledge, 1994, 249–64.

Degen, John A. (1987), 'Camp and Burlesque: A Study in Contrasts', *Journal of Dramatic Theory & Criticism* 1:2, Spring, 87–94.

Dynes, Wayne R. (1987), *Homosexuality: A Research Guide*, New York-London: Garland, 368–71.

Gledhill, Christine (1987), 'The Melodramatic Field: An Investigation', in Christine Gledhill (ed.), *Home Is Where the Heart Is: Studies in Melodrama and the Woman's Film*, London: BFI.

Groves, Robyn Kaye. 'Fictions of the Self: Studies in Female Modernism – Jean Rhys, Gertrude Stein, and Djuna Barnes', PhD diss, University of British Columbia (Canada), abstract in *DAI* 40:5, November 1988, 1138A.

Kratzert, Armin (1987), Afterword to *Camp*, Frankfurt: Dinu Popa, 1987, unpaginated.

La Bruce, Bruce (1987), 'Pee Wee Herman: The Homosexual Subtext', *CineAction!* 9, Summer, 3–6. Rpt. in Creekmur & Doty 1995a: 382–8.

Taylor, Elizabeth (1987), *Elizabeth Takes Off: On Weight Gain, Weight Loss, Self-Image and Self-Esteem*, New York: Putnam's, 98–9, 106.

Thompson, Mark (1987), 'Children of Paradise: A Brief History of Queens', in Mark Thompson (ed.), *Gay Spirit: Myth and Meaning*, New York: St. Martin's, 49–68. Rpt. in Creekmur & Doty 1995a: 447–63.

Walker, Tim (1987), 'High Camp and Low Church as Fans Remember Liberace', *Observer*, 13 September, 3.

Wollen, Peter (1987), 'Fashion/Orientalism/The Body', *New Formations* 1, Spring, 5–33. Rev. in *Raiding the Icebox: Reflections on Twentieth Century Culture*, London-New York: Verso, 1993, 1–35.

1988

Bartlett, Neil (1988), *Who Was That Man? A Present for Mr Oscar Wilde*, London: Serpent's Tail, 167–9.

Bolin, Anne (1988), *In Search of Eve: Transsexual Rites of Passage*, New York-London: Bergin & Garvey, 9–10. Based on the omonymous PhD diss., University of Colorado at Boulder, 1983, abstracted in *DAI* 44:4, October 1983, 1139A.

Carpenter, Humphrey (1988), *Geniuses Together: American Writers in Paris in the 1920s*, Boston: Houghton Mifflin, 71.

Case, Sue-Ellen (1988), 'Toward a Butch-Femme Aesthetic', *Discourse* 11:1, Fall-Winter 1988–9, 55–73. Rpt. in Lynda Hart (ed.), *Making a Spectacle: Feminist Essays on Contemporary Women's Theatre*, Ann Arbor: U of Michigan P, 1989, 282–99. Rpt. in Abelove, Barale & Halperin 1993: 294–306.

Cohen, Ed (1988), 'Foucauldian Necrologies: "Gay" "Politics"? Politically Gay?', *Textual Practice* 2:1, Spring, 87–101.

De Lauretis, Teresa (1988), 'Sexual Indifference and Lesbian Representation', *Theatre Journal* 40:2, May, 155–77. Rpt. in Sue-Ellen Case (ed.), *Performing Feminisms: Feminist Critical Theory and Theatre*, Baltimore: Johns Hopkins UP, 1990, 17–39. Rpt. in Abelove, Barale & Halperin 1993: 141–58.

Del Sapio, Maria (1988), *Alice nella città. Note su arte e stili metropolitani*, Pescara: Tracce, 23, 83–86.

Dolan, Jill (1988), *The Feminist Spectator as Critic*, Ann Arbor-London: UMI Research P, 112.

Finch, Mark & Richard Kwietniowski (1988), 'Melodrama and *Maurice*: Homo is Where the Het Is', *Screen* 29:3, Summer, 72–80.

Hake, Sabine (1988), '"Gold, Love, Adventure": The Postmodern Piracy of *Madame X*', *Discourse* 11:1, Fall-Winter 1988–9, 88–110.

Hollinghurst, Alan J. (1988), *The Swimming-Pool Library*, London-New York: Chatto & Windus; London: Penguin, 1989, 12, 61, 64, 160, 184, 197, 265.

Macaulay, Alastair (1988), 'The Addict of Camp: Michael Clark', *Dancing Times* 78, February, 440–41.

Moore, Suzanne (1988), 'Here's Looking at You, Kid!' In Lorraine Gamman & Margaret Marshment (eds.), *The Female Gaze: Women as Viewers of Popular Culture*, London: Women's P; Seattle: Real Comet, 1989, 44–59.

Naremore, James (1988), 'Marlene Dietrich in *Morocco* (1930)', in *Acting in the Cinema*, Berkeley-London: U of California P, 131–56.

Ortoleva, Peppino (1988), *Saggio sui movimenti del 1968 in Europa e in America*, Roma: Editori Riuniti, 1988, 140.

Pally, Marcia (1988), 'Camp Pedro', *Film Comment* 24:6, November-December, 18–19.

Penley, Constance (1988), 'The Cabinet of Dr. Pee-Wee: Consumerism and Sexual Terror', *Camera Obscura* 17, May, 133–53. Rpt. in *The Future of an Illusion: Film, Feminism, and Psychoanalysis*, London-New York: Routledge, 1989, 141–62. Rpt. in Penley & Willis 1993: 121–41.

Pine, Richard (1988), *The Dandy and the Herald: Manners, Mind and Morals from Brummell to Durrell*, London: Macmillan; New York: St. Martin's, 25–9.

Piré, Luciana (1988), 'Un transito nel moderno. L'esempio di Susan Sontag', in Vito Amoruso (ed.), *Contesti 1*, Bari: Adriatica, 179–97.

Ross, Andrew (1988), 'Uses of Camp', *Yale Journal of Criticism* 2:1, Fall, 1–24. Rpt. in Bergman 1993a: 54–77. Rev. in *No Respect: Intellectuals and Popular Culture*, New York-London: Routledge, 1989, 134–70. Reviewed in: *Afterimage* 19:6, January 1992:6–9, by Maren Stange; *American Literature* 64:1, March 1992:200–2, by Michael Bérubé; *American Quarterly* 42:4, December 1990:684–91, by David Sanjek; *Criticism* 33:4, Fall 1991:550–3, by Jerry Herron; *Journal of American Studies* 25:2, August 1991:290–2, by John Sutherland; *Journal of Popular Culture*

24:3, Winter 1990:185–6, by Ray B. Browne; *Library Journal*, 114:9, 15 May 1989:81, by Jo Cates; *Media, Culture & Society* 13:3, July 1991:415–18, by Michael Pickering; *Nation*, 249:15, 6 November 1989:538–40, by Jon Wiener; *TLS*, 8 December 1989:1364, by David Papineau; *Yale Review* 80:1–2, April 1992:197–206, by Sara Suleri.

Savage, Jon (1988), 'The Enemy Within: Sex, Rock and Identity', in Simon Frith (ed.), *Facing the Music: Essays on Pop, Rock and Culture*, New York: Pantheon; London: Mandarin, 1990, 131–73.

Wilson, Elizabeth (1988), *Hallucinations: Life in the Postmodern City*, London: Radius, 84–5, 99.

1989

Bourdon, David (1989), *Warhol*, New York: Harry N. Abrams, 68–9, 86, 196.

Bristow, Joseph (1989), 'Being Gay: Politics, Identity, Pleasure', *New Formations* 9, Winter, 61–82.

Buchloh, Benjamin H. D. (1989), 'The Andy Warhol Line', in Gary Garrels (ed.), *The Work of Andy Warhol*, DIA Art Foundation Discussions in Contemporary Art, Number 3, Seattle: Bay, 52–69.

Crysler, Greig (1989), 'Architectural Dandyism in the Age of Mass Media: The Camp Architecture of Nigel Coates', *New Art Examiner* 16:11, Summer, 32–4.

Danto, Arthur C. (1989), 'Art', *Nation*, 248, 3 April 1989, 458–61. Rpt. in Pratt 1997a: 200–7.

Elsaesser, Thomas (1989), *New German Cinema: A History*, New Brunswick: Rutgers UP; London: Macmillan, 292.

Feuer, Jane (1989), 'Reading *Dynasty*: Television and Reception Theory', *South Atlantic Quarterly* 88:2, Spring, 443–60. Rpt. in Jane Gaines (ed.), *Classical Hollywood Narrative: The Paradigm Wars*, Durham-London: Duke UP, 1992, 275–93. Rpt. as 'The Reception of Dynasty' in Feuer 1995.

Fletcher, Ian (1989), 'Inventions for the Left Hand: Beardsley in Verse and Prose', in Robert Langenfeld (ed.), *Reconsidering Aubrey Beardsley*, Ann Arbor-London: UMI Research P, 227–66.

Friedrich, Otto (1989), 'The Camping Up of Mozart', *Time*, 134:6, 7 August, 63.

Garafola, Lynn (1989), *Diaghilev's Ballets Russes*, Oxford-New York: Oxford UP, 32.

Goodwin, Joseph (1989), 'There's No Version like Perversion', in *More Man than You'll Ever Be: Gay Folklore and Acculturation in Middle America*, Bloomington: Indiana UP, 29–60. Based on the anonymous PhD diss., Indiana University, 1984, abstracted in *DAI* 46:1, July 1985, 230A.

Gough, Jamie (1989), 'Theories of Sexual Identity and the Masculinization of the Gay Man', in Simon Shepherd & Mick Wallis (eds.), *Coming On Strong: Gay Politics and Culture*, London-Boston: Unwin Hyman, 119–36.

Gross, Larry (1989), 'Out of the Mainstream: Sexual Minorities and the Mass Media', in Ellen Seiter, Hans Borchers, Gabrielle Krentzner & Eva-Maria Warth (eds.), *Remote Control: Television, Audiences and Cultural Power*, London-New York: Routledge, 130–49. Rpt. in *Journal of Homosexuality* 21:1–2, 1991, 19–46; the *Journal of Homosexuality* issue also pub. as Michelle A. Wolf & Alfred Kielwasser (eds.), *Gay People, Sex and the Media*, New York-London: Haworth, 1991. Excerpted in Dines & Humez 1995: 61–70.

Hutcheon, Linda (1989), *The Politics of Postmodernism*, London-New York: Routledge, 10.

Jacques, Damien (1989), '"Irma Vep" Succeeds with Silly Spoof', *Milwaukee Journal*, 18 September, 4B.

Jacobson, Howard (1989), 'Sex, Violence, Eloquence – and Then That Other Thing', *Sunday Correspondent*, 17 September.

Lawson, Robert (1989), 'The Lost Boy: Homosexuality in *B-Movie*', *Canadian Theatre Review* 49, Summer, 52–4.

Long, Scott (1989), 'Useful Laughter: Camp and Seriousness', *Southwest Review* 74:1, Winter, 53–70. Rpt. as 'The Loneliness of Camp' in Bergman 1993a, 78–91.

Miller, D. A. (1989), 'Sontag's Urbanity', *October* 49, Summer, 91–101. Rpt. in Abelove, Barale & Halperin 1993: 212–20.

Moon, Michael (1989), 'Flaming Closets', *October* 51, Winter, 19–54. Rpt. in Goellner & Murphy 1995: 57–78. Rpt. in Creekmur & Doty 1995a: 282–306. Rpt. in *A Small Boy and Others*, Durham-London: Duke UP, 1998, 67–94.

Norse, Harold (1989), *Memoirs of a Bastard Angel: A Fifty-Year Literary and Erotic Odyssey*, New York: Morrow, 89.

Pasti, Umberto (1989), 'Prefazione', in Violet Trefusis, *Broderie anglaise*, Milan: La Tartaruga, 6.

Perl, Jed (1989), 'Kitsch in Synch', *Vogue* 179:2, February, 326–7, 395.

Rudnick, Paul & Kurt Anderson (1989), 'The Irony Epidemic', *Spy* March, 93–8. Excerpted as 'The Irony Epidemic: The Dark Side of Fiestaware and the Flinstones', *Utne Reader* 33, May-June 1989, 34–40.

Shepherd, Simon (1989), *Because We're Queers: The Life and Crimes of Kenneth Halliwell and Joe Orton*, London: GMP, 131, 219.

Simms, Paul (1989), 'Camp Lite Goes to College', *Spy* March, 96–7.

Spears, Richard A. (1989) (ed.), *NTC's Dictionary of American Slang and Colloquial Expressions*, Lincolnwood: National Textbook, 60.

Studlar, Gaylyn (1989), 'Midnight S/Excess: Cult Configurations of "Femininity" and the Perverse', *Journal of Popular Film and Television* 17:1, Spring, 2–14. Rpt. in Telotte 1991: 138–55.

Ward, Carol (1989), *Mae West: A Bio-Bibliography*, New York-London: Greenwood, 7, 19, 34, 39, 46–9, 56, 64–7, 76.

Whissen, Thomas R. (1989), *The Devil's Advocates: Decadence in Modern Literature*, New York-London: Greenwood, 3, 59.

1990

Anderson, Walter Truett (1990), *Reality isn't What it Used to Be: Theatrical Politics, Ready-to-Wear Religion, Global Myths, Primitive Chic, & Other Wonders of the Postmodern World*, San Francisco: Harper & Row; San Francisco: HarperSan-Francisco, 1992, 99–100, 144–7.

Bacarisse, Pamela (1990), 'Chivalry and "Camp" Sensibility in Don Quijote', *Forum for Modern Language Studies* 26:2, April, 127–43.

Bérubé, Allan (1990), *Coming Out Under Fire: The History of Gay Men and Women in World War Two*, New York: Free, 72, 86–91, 97, 158, 210–13, 218, 224–5. Reviewed in: *Advocate*, 12 July 1994:74–5, by Lawrence Frascella; *American Historical Review* 96:3, June 1991:845, by Michael S. Sherry; *Armed Forces & Society* 20:4, Summer 1994:633–7, by Wilbur J. Scott; *Christianity and Crisis* 50:14–15, October 22, 1990:322 by Arthur J. Moore; *Feminist Studies* 18:3, Fall 1992:629–47 by Susan K. Cahn; *Journal of American History* 78:1, June 1991:377–8 by Clayton R. Koppes; *Journal of Homosexuality* 21:4, May 1991:107–12 by Nancy C. Unger; *Library Journal*, 115:4, 1 March 1990:102 by James E. Van Buskirk; *Oral History Review* 21:1, Spring 1993:133–37 by Loralee MacPike; *Publishers Weekly*, 237:5, 2 February 1990:74 by Genevieve Stuttaford; *Reviews in American History* 19:2 June 1991:255–59 by Elaine Tyler May; *Tikkun* 6:1, January-February 1991:86–89 by Frank Browning.

Boone, Joseph A. & Michael Cadden (1990) (eds.), *Engendering Men: The Question of Male Feminist Criticism*, London-New York: Routledge. Reviewed in: *Criticism* 34:2, Spring 1992:281–8, by Gerald MacLean; *Signs* 19:3 Spring, 1994:770–7, by Marlon B. Ross; *Studies in Women's Literature* 11:1, Spring 1992:148–9; *Victorian Studies* 35:4, Summer 1992:409–15, by Jeffrey Weeks.

Burston, Paul (1990), 'Between High Camp and High Art', *Guardian*, 15 August.

Butler, Judith (1990a), *Gender Trouble: Feminism and the Subversion of Identity*, London-New York: Routledge, 136–7.

——, (1990b), 'Lana's "Imitation": Melodramatic Repetition and the Gender Performative', *Genders* 9, Fall, 1–18.

——, (1990c), 'Performative Acts and Gender Constitution: An Essay in Phenomenology and Feminist Theory', in Sue-Ellen Case (ed.), *Performing Feminisrns: Feminist Critical Theory and Theatre*, Baltimore-London: Johns Hopkins UP, 270–82.

Cavell, Stanley (1990), 'Ugly Duckling, Funny Butterfly: Bette Davis and *Now Voyager* Followed by Postscript (1989): To Whom It May Concern', *Critical Inquiry* 16:2, Winter, 213–89.

Chambers, Ross (1990), 'Alter Ego: Intertextuality, Irony and the Politics of Reading', in Michael Worton & Judith Still (eds.), *Intertextuality: Theories and Practices*, Manchester-New York: Manchester UP, 143–58.

Craft, Christopher (1990), 'Alias Bunbury: Desire and Termination in *The Importance of Being Earnest*', *Representations* 31, Spring, 19–46. Rpt. in *Another Kind of Love: Male Homosexual Desire in English Discourse, 1850–1920*, Berkeley-London: U of California P, 1994, 125.

Crimp, Douglas & Adam Rolston (1990), 'Aids Activist Graphics: A Demonstration', in *AIDS Demo graphics*, Seattle: Bay. Rpt. in Gelder & Thornton 1997: 436–44.

Davies, Paul (1990), '"The Power to Convey the Unuttered": Style and Sexuality in the Work of Ronald Firbank', in Lilly 1990a: 199–214.

Dyer, Richard (1990), 'Underground and After', in *Now You See It: Studies on Lesbian and Gay Film*, London-New York: Routledge, 102–73. Reviewed in: *Film Quarterly* 45:4, Summer 1992:54–6, by Chris Straayer; *Library Journal*, 116:2, 1 February 1991:80, by Roy Liebman.

Dynes, Wayne R. (1990), 'Camp', in Wayne R. Dynes (chief ed.), Warren Johansson & William A. Percy (associate eds.), *Encyclopaedia of Homosexuality*, New York: Garland; London: St. James's, 189–90.

Fusso, Susanne & Priscilla Meyer (1990a) (eds.), *Essays on Gogol: Logos and the Russian Word*, Evanston: Northwestern UP. Reviewed in: *Slavic and East European Journal* 37:3, Fall 1993:383–4, by Milton Ehre; *Slavic Review* 52:1, Spring 1993:124–5, by Andrew Wachtel.

—— (1990b), 'Introduction', in Fusso & Meyer 1990a: 1–13.

Gaines, Jane (1990), 'Costume and Narrative: How Dress Tells the Woman's Story', in Jane Gaines & Charlotte Herzog (eds.), *Fabrications: Costume and the Female Body*, London-New York: Routledge, 180–211.

Hall, James (1990), 'Camp Followers?' *Apollo* (London) ns 131, April, 264–5.

Harries, Dan M. (1990), 'Camping with Lady Divine: Star Persona and Parody', *Quarterly Review of Film & Video* 12, May, 13–22.

Harris, Daniel R. (1990), 'Baby Talk', *Salmagundi* 88–9, Fall-Winter 1990–91, 303–10.

Hopkinson, Amanda (1990), 'Inspiration to the Camp Followers', *British Journal of Photography* 137, 22 March, 26.

Jeffreys, Sheila (1990), *Anticlimax: A Feminist Perspective on the Sexual Revolution*, London: Women's P, 204.

Kennedy, William G. (1990), 'Engagement and Disburdenment: The Writings of Susan Sontag', PhD diss., University of Nottingham (UK); abstract in *DAI* 52:7, January 1992, 2554A.

Kiernan, Robert F. (1990), *Frivolity Unbound. Six Masters of the Camp Novel*, New York: Continuum. Reviewed in: *Choice*, 28:3, March 1991:161, by James Hafley; *Journal of American Studies* 26:1, April 1992:115–116, by Michael Moon; *Modern*

Fiction Studies 37:2, Summer 1991:356–7, by Susan Leonardi; *Washington Post Book World* 20:50, 16 December 1990, by Michael Dirda.

Koestenbaum, Wayne (1990), 'Wilde's Hard Labor and the Birth of Gay Reading', in Boone & Cadden 1990: 176–89.

Lilly, Mark (1990a) (ed.), *Lesbian and Gay Writing: An Anthology of Critical Essays*, London: Macmillan; Philadelphia: Temple UP. Reviewed in: *Contemporary Literature* 34:2, Summer 1993:293–303 by Christopher Lane; *Feminist Review* 40, Spring 1992:96–98, by Sally Munt.

—— (1990b), 'Tennesse Williams: *The Glass Menagerie* and *A Streetcar Named Desire*', in Lilly 1990a: 153–63.

Medhurst, Andy (1990), 'Pitching Camp', *City Limits*, 10–17 May, 18–19.

Modleski, Tania (1990), 'The Incredible Shrinking He[r]man: Male Regression, the Male Body, and Film', *differences* 2:2, Summer, 55–75. Rpt. in Modleski 1991: 90–111.

Moon, Michael & Eve Kosofsky Sedgwick (1990), 'Divinity: A Dossier. A Performance Piece. A Little-Understood Emotion', *Discourse* 13:1, Fall-Winter 1990–91, 12–39. Rpt. in Eve Kosofsky Sedgwick, *Tendencies*, London-New York: Routledge, 1994, 215–51.

Paglia, Camille (1990), *Sexual Personae: Art and Decadence from Nefertiti to Emily Dickinson*, New Haven: Yale UP; London: Penguin, 1991, 209, 219, 557.

Pally, Marcia (1990), 'The Politics of Passion: Pedro Almodóvar and the Camp Esthetic', *Cinéaste* 18:1, 32–5, 38–9.

Pasti, Umberto (1990), 'L'universo fatto di "tic"', *Il Giornale* (Milan), 6 July, 3.

Pontello, Jacqueline M. (1990), 'Not a "Camp" Follower', *Southwest Art* 19:9 February, 22.

Pronger, Brian (1990), 'Camp', in *The Arena of Masculinity: Sports, Homosexuality, and the Meaning of Sex*, Toronto: U of Toronto P, 227–31.

Ross, Andrew (1990), 'Cowboys, Cadillacs, and Cosmonauts: Families, Film Genres, and Technocultures', in Boone & Cadden 1990: 87–101.

Savage, Jon (1990), 'Tainted Love: The Influence of Male Homosexuality and Sexual Divergence on Pop Music and Culture Since the War', in Alan Tomlinson (ed.), *Consumption, Identity and Style: Marketing, Meanings, and the Packaging of Pleasure*, London-New York: Routledge, 153–71.

Sayres, Sohnya (1990), *Susan Sontag: The Elegiac Modernist*, London-New York: Routledge, 3, 34, 46, 88–9, 94, 107, 116, 148. Reviewed in: *Journal of Aesthetics & Art Criticism* 49:4, Fall 1991:400–1, by Leland Poague; *World Literature Today* 65:2, Spring 1991:308–9 by Leon S. Roudiez.

Schneider, Greg (1990), 'Gay Camp', *Artweek*, 21:44, 27 December, 11.

Sedgwick, Eve Kosofsky (1990), *Epistemology of the Closet*, Berkeley: U of California P; Hertfordshire: Harvester Wheatsheaf, 1991; London: Penguin, 1994, 132, 155–6. Reviewed in: *American Literature* 64:3, September 1992:626–7, by Linnea A. Stenson; *Journal of English & Germanic Philology* 91:3, July 1992:414–18, by James R. Kincaid; *Journal of Homosexuality* 23:4, May 1992:124–8 by Martha Vicinus; *Modern Philology* 90:4, May 1993:580–4, by Sherwood Williams; *Nation*, 252:2 21 January 1991:61–3 by Mark Edmundson; *New Republic* 204:11, 18 March 1991:35–7, by Christopher Benfey; *Nineteenth-Century Literature* 46:4, March 1992:557–61 by Peter Thorslev; *Publishers Weekly*, 237:44, 2 November 1990:60, by Genevieve Stuttaford; *Raritan* 11:1, Summer 1991:115–31, by David Bergman; *Signs* 19:1, Autumn 1993:252–6, by Claudia Card; *Sociology* 31:1, February 1997:189–90, by Matthew Waites; *Victorian Studies* 35:1, Autumn 1991:114–16, by Susan Gubar; *Victorian Studies* 35:4, Summer 1992:409–15, by Jeffrey Weeks.

Segal, Lynne (1990), 'The Male Homosexual Challenge: From "Camp" to "Gay" to "Super-Macho"', in *Slow Motion: Changing Masculinities, Changing Men*, London: Virago; New Brunswick: Rutgers UP, 144–9.

Showalter, Elaine (1990), *Sexual Anarchy: Gender and Culture at the Fin de Siècle*, New York: Penguin; London: Bloomsbury, 1991; London: Virago, 1992, 163, 182.

Sinfield, Alan (1990a), 'Closet Dramas: Homosexual Representation and Class in Postwar British Theater', *Genders* 9, Fall, 112–31.

—— (1990b), 'Who Was Afraid of Joe Orton?', *Textual Practice*, 4:2, Summer, 259–77. Rpt. in Joseph Bristow (ed.), *Sexual Sameness: Textual Differences in Gay and Lesbian Writing*, London-New York: Routledge, 1992, 170–86.

Spencer, Colin (1990), *Which of Us Two? The Story of a Love Affair*, London: Viking; London: Penguin, 1991, xi, 209.

Spurr, Barry (1990), 'Camp Mandarin: The Prose Style of Lytton Strachey', *English Literature in Transition (1880–1920)*, 33:1, 31–45.

Stimpson, Catharine R. (1990), 'Reading for Love: Canons, Paracanons, and Whistling Jo March', *New Literary History* 21:4, Autumn, 957–76.

Straayer, Chris (1990), 'The She-Man: Postmodern Bi-Sexed Performance in Film and Video', *Screen* 31:3, Summer, 262–80.

Sutcliffe, Tom (1990a), 'High Heart and Low Camp', *Guardian*, 17 April.

—— (1990b), 'High on Camp', *Guardian*, 12 June.

Thorne, Tony (1990), *The Dictionary of Contemporary Slang*, New York: Pantheon, 81–2.

Timmons, Stuart (1990), *The Trouble With Harry Hay: Founder of the Modern Gay Movement*, Boston: Alyson, 61, 213.

Weinstein, Jeff et al. (1990), 'Extended Sensibilities: The Impact of Homosexual Sensibilities on Contemporary Culture', in Russell Ferguson et al. (eds.), *Discourses: Conversations in Postmodern Art and Culture*, New York: New Museum of Contemporary Art; Cambridge-London: MIT P, 130–55.

Woods, Gregory (1990), '"Absurd! Ridiculous! Disgusting!" Paradox in Poetry by Gay Men', in Lilly 1990a: 175–98.

Woodward, Chris (1990), 'Heyday Has Melted, but Wax Museums Are Making Comeback', *Los Angeles Times*, 109, 29 April, D3–4.

Yingling, Thomas E. (1990), *Hart Crane and the Homosexual Text: New Thresholds, New Anatomies*, Chicago-London: U of Chicago P, 33. Based on the omonymous PhD diss., University of Pennsylvania, 1988, abstracted in *DAI* 49:11, May 1989, 3365A.

Zholkovsky, A. K. (1990), 'Rereading Gogol's Miswritten Book: Notes on *Selected Passages from Correspondence with Friends*', in Fusso & Meyer 1990a: 172–184. Expanded version as 'Perecityvaja izbrannye opiski Gogolja', in *Bluzdajuščie sny i drugie raboty*, Moskow: Naúka, 1994, 70–86.

1991

Behrendt, Patricia Flanagan (1991), *Oscar Wilde: Eros and Aesthetics*, London: Macmillan, xii.

Bergman, David (1991), *Gaiety Transfigured: Gay Self-Representation in American Literature*, Madison-London: U of Wisconsin P, 3–4, 10, 18, 47, 103–21. Partly rpt. in Bergman 1993a: 92–109. Reviewed in: *TLS*, 25 December 1992:9, by Richard Davenport-Hines; *American Literature* 64:4, December 1992:846–7, by Hugh English; *Modern Fiction Studies* 38:2, Summer 1992:497–8, by Thomas Dukes.

Bristow, Joseph (1991), *Empire Boys: Adventures in a Man's World*, London: Harper-Collins, 84.

Case, Sue-Ellen (1991), 'Tracking the Vampire', *differences* 3:2, Summer, 1–20. Rpt. in Katie Conboy, Nadia Medina & Sarah Stanbury (eds.), *Writing on the Body: Female Embodiment and Feminist Theory*, New York-London: Columbia UP, 1997, 380–400.

Clark, Danae (1991), 'Commodity Lesbianism', in Penley & Willis 1991: 181–201. Rpt. in Abelove, Barale & Halperin 1993: 186–201. Rpt. in Creekmur & Doty 1995a: 484–500. Rpt. in Dines & Humez 1995: 142–51.

Clark, William Lane (1991), 'Subversive Aesthetics: Literary Camp in the Novels of Ronald Firbank', PhD diss., George Washington University; abstract in *DAI* 52:8, February 1992, 2929A.

De Lauretis, Teresa (1991a), 'Il fantasma del cinema. Sulla funzione spettatoriale come rapporto di produzione fantasmatico-sociale', *Cinema & cinema*, 18, September-December, 3–18. Partly translated in De Lauretis 1994: 81–148.

—— (1991b), 'Film and the Visible', in Bad Object-Choices (eds.), *How Do I Look? Queer Film and Video*, Seattle: Bay, 223–76. Partly rpt. in De Lauretis 1994: 81–148.

Devlin, B. (1991), 'Phenomenology, Homosexuality and Point of View: An Analysis of Visconti's *Morte a Venezia*', MA thesis, Warwick University (UK).

Doane, Mary Ann (1991), *Femmes Fatales: Feminism, Film Theory, Psychoanalysis*, London-New York: Routledge, 270 n16.

Dollimore, Jonathan (1991), *Sexual Dissidence: Augustine to Wilde, Freud to Foucault*, Oxford-New York: Clarendon, 55–58, 310–22. Reviewed in: *Choice* 29:9, May 1992:1434, by B.R. Burg; *Journal of British Studies* 32:2, April 1993:189–94, by Alan Bray; *Journal of Sex Research* 31:1, 1 February 1994:78–9, by Roger C. Wade; *Modern Language Quarterly* 52:3, September 1991:355–8, by Paul Giles; *Modern Language Review* 89:1, January 1994:175–7, by Jeremy Tambling; *New Statesman & Society*, 4, 30 August 1991:44, by Peter Mathews; *Signs* 19:3, Spring 1994:826–30, by Colleen Lamos; *TLS*, 25 October 1991:23, by Robin Robbins; *Victorian Studies* 36:2, Winter 1993:207–13, 223–26, by James Eli Adams & Mary Poovey; *Victorian Studies* 35:4, Summer 1992:409–15, by Jeffrey Weeks.

Doty, Alexander (1991), 'The Sissy Boy, The Fat Ladies, and the Dykes: Queerness and/ as Gender in Pee-Wee's World', in Penley & Willis 1991: 125–43. Rpt. in Doty 1993: 81–95.

Epstein, Julia & Kristina Straub (1991), 'Introduction: The Guarded Body', in Julia Epstein & Kristina Straub (eds.), *Body Guards: The Cultural Politics of Gender Ambiguity*, London-New York: Routledge, 1–28.

Fuss, Diana (1991) (ed.), *Inside/Out: Lesbian Theories, Gay Theories*, London-New York: Routledge. Reviewed in: *Canadian Literature* 134, Autumn 1992:140–42, by Philip Holden; *Choice* 29:9, May 1992:1474–5, by M. Gordon; *Feminist Review* 44, Summer 1993:117–18, by Clare Whatling; *Frontiers* 13:2, Winter 1993:168–86, by Harriet Malinowitz; *Library Journal*, 116:17, 15 October 1991:106, by James E. Van Buskirk; *Signs* 18:4, Summer 1993:984–88, by Sherri Paris.

Galef, David & Harold Galef (1991), 'What Was Camp', *Studies in Popular Culture* 13:2, 11–25.

Gledhill, Christine (1991) (ed.), *Stardom: Industry of Desire*, London-New York: Routledge. Reviewed in: *Choice* 29:6, February 1992:905, by D. Toth; *Film Quarterly* 46:2, Winter 1992:56–7, by Virginia Wright Wexman; *Journal of Communication* 44:1, Winter 1994:188–91, by Thomas Guback; *New Theatre Quarterly* 8:29, February 1992:103–4, by Paul Heritage; *Sight and Sound* 1:6, October 1991:39–40, by Graham McCann.

Graham, Allison (1991), 'Journey to the Center of the Fifties: The Cult of Banality', in Telotte 1991: 107–21.

Grant, Barry K. (1991), 'Science Fiction Double Feature: Ideology in the Cult Film', in Telotte 1991: 122–37.

Hadleigh, Boze (1991), *The Vynil Closet: Gays in the Music World*, San Diego: Los Hombres, 157.

Harris, Daniel R. (1991), 'Effeminacy', *Michigan Quarterly Review* 30:1, Winter, 72–81.

Hilbert, Jeffrey (1991), 'The Politics of Drag', *Advocate*, 23 April, 42–47. Rpt. in Creekmur & Doty 1995a: 463–9.

Hoesterey, Ingeborg (1991), 'Introduction: Postmodernism as Discursive Event', in Ingeborg Hoesterey (ed.), *Zeitgeist in Babel: The Postmodernist Controversy*, Bloomington: Indiana UP, xii, xiv.

Hollinghurst, Alan (1991), 'Introduction', in S. Moore (ed.), *The Early Firbank*, London-New York: Quartet, x-xi.

Hsu, Bill (1991), 'Spew: The Queer Punk Convention', *Postmodern Culture*, 2.1, September.

Hutchison, Beth (1991), 'Essential Fictions: Masquerade, Mimicry, and Self-Enactments in Contemporary North American Fiction', PhD diss., University of Washington; abstract in *DAI* 52:8, February 1992, 2924A.

James, Caryn (1991), 'A Sex Icon Once, Oddity Now', *New York Times*, 141, 8 November, B1 (National edn.), C1, C8 (Late edn.).

Jameson, Fredric (1991), *Postmodernism, or, The Cultural Logic of Late Capitalism*, Durham: Duke UP; London: Verso, 1–54, 90.

Jennings, Wade (1991), 'The Star as Cult Icon: Judy Garland', in Telotte 1991: 90–101.

Kawin, Bruce (1991), 'After Midnight', in Telotte 1991: 18–25.

Kirshenblatt-Gimblett, Barbara (1991), 'Who's Bad? Accounting for Taste', *Artforum* 30:3, November, 119–25.

Koestenbaum, Wayne (1991a), 'Opera and Homosexuality: Seven Arias', *Yale Journal of Criticism* 5:1, Fall, 235–54.

—— (1991b), 'The Queen's Throat: (Homo)sexuality and the Art of Singing', in Fuss 1991: 205–34.

Krauss, Rosalind E. (1991), 'Nostalgie de la boue', *October* 56, Spring, 111–20.

Landi, Paolo (1991), 'Kitsch, Camp, Snob', in *Lo snobismo di massa*. Milan: Lupetti, 35–40.

Low, Andrew Lyons (1991), 'Georg Lukacs and the Decadent Historical Novel: Objectification and Form in Flaubert, Stifter, and Pater', PhD diss., Cornell University; abstract in *DAI* 51:12, June 1991, 4111A.

Martini, Emanuela (1991), *Storia del cinema inglese 1930–1990*, Venice: Marsilio, 287.

Medhurst, Andy (1991a), 'Batman, Deviance and Camp', in Pearson & Uricchio 1991: 149–63.

—— (1991b), 'That Special Thrill: *Brief Encounter*, Homosexuality and Authorship', *Screen* 32:2, Summer, 197–208.

Meyer, Moe (1991), 'I Dream of Jeannie: Transsexual Striptease as Scientific Display', *The Drama Review* 35:1, Spring, 25–42. Rpt. as 'Unveiling the Word: Science and Narrative in Transsexual Striptease' in Senelick 1992a: 68–85.

Modleski, Tania (1991), *Feminism Without Women: Culture and Criticism in a 'Postfeminist' Age*, London-New York: Routledge, 99, 103, 155, 157, 161, 177.

Naremore, James & Patrick Brantlinger (1991), 'Introduction: Six Artistic Cultures', in James Naremore & Patrick Brantlinger (eds.), *Modernity and Mass Culture*, Bloomington-Indianapolis: Indiana UP, 1–23.

Pearson, Roberta E. & William Uricchio (1991) (eds.), *The Many Lives of the Batman: Critical Approaches to a Superhero and His Media*, New York: Routledge; London: BFI. Reviewed in: *American Studies International* 29:2, October 1991:112–13, by Kim Moreland; *Canadian Literature* 133, Summer 1992:162–3, by Jean-Paul Gabilliet; *Communication Research* 19:3, June 1992:397–8, by James Beniger; *Criticism* 33:4, Fall 1991:554–8, by David MacGregor; *ETC.* 49:2, Summer, 1992:251, by William Coleman, Jr.; *Film Quarterly* 46:4, Summer 1993:44–5, by James Hay; *Journal of Communication* 42:1, Winter 1992:141–3, by Matthew McAllister; *Library Journal*, 116:2, 1 February 1991:84–5, by Keith DeCandido; *Postmodern Culture*, 1:3, May 1991, by John Anderson; *Publishers Weekly*, 238:8, 8 February 1991:54, by Penny Kaganoff; *Sight & Sound* 1:1, May 1991:37–8, by Martin Barker.

Penley, Constance & Sharon Willis (1991) (eds.), 'Responses to "Male Trouble"', special section of *Camera Obscura* 25–26, January-May, 101–320.

Praunheim, Rosa von (1991), *Sex und Karriere*, Hamburg: Rogner & Bernhard.

Porter, Kevin & Jeffrey Weeks (1991), *Between the Acts: Lives of Homosexual Men 1885–1967*, London-New York: Routledge, 101, 105, 146.

Rodrich, Stephen (1991), 'King and Queen: Queer and Loathing in the Victory "Camps" of Queen Joan Jett Blakk and King Richard the Second', *New City*, 24 April, 9.

Ross, T. J. (1991), 'The Cult Send-Up: *Beat the Devil* or Goodbye, *Casablanca*', in Telotte 1991: 79–89.

Sinfield, Alan (1991), 'Private Lives/Public Theater: Noël Coward and the Politics of Homosexual Representation', *Representations* 36, Fall, 43–63.

Smith, Bruce R. (1991), *Homosexual Desire in Shakespeare's England: A Cultural Poetics*, Chicago-London: U of Chicago P; 2nd edn. with a new preface, ibidem 1994, 112.

Spigel, Lynn & Henry Jenkins (1991), 'Same Bat Channel, Different Bat Times: Mass Culture and Popular Memory', in Pearson & Uricchio 1991: 117–48.

Telotte, J. (1991) (ed.), *The Cult Film Experience: Beyond All Reason*, Austin: U of Texas. Reviewed in: *Film Quarterly* 45:4, Summer 1992:29–30, by Stephen Prince; *Sight & Sound* 1:7, November 1991:35, by Jonathan Rosenbaum; *Wilson Library Bulletin* 66:3, November 1991:119, by Ben Davis.

Tyler, Carole-Anne (1991), 'Boys Will Be Girls: The Politics of Gay Drag', in Fuss 1991: 32–70. Rpt. in *Female Impersonation*, New York-London: Routledge, 1999.

Viegener, Matias (1991), 'Gay Fanzines: There's Trouble in That Body', *Afterimage* 17:5, May, 12–16. Expanded as '"Kinky Escapades, Bedroom Techniques, Unbridled Passion, and Secret Sex Codes"' in Bergman 1993a: 234–56.

Waller, Gregory A. (1991), 'Midnight Movies, 1980–1985: A Market Study', in Telotte 1991: 167–86.

Watten, Barrett (1991), 'Camp Mythologies', *Artweek*, 22:41, 5 December, 13.

White, Jim (1991), 'Striking Camp', *Independent*, 28 January, 15.

Wood, Robert E. (1991), 'Don't Dream It: Performance and *The Rocky Horror Picture Show*', in Telotte 1991: 156–66.

1992

Barnes, Noreen C. (1992), 'Kate Bornstein's Gender and Genre Bending', in Senelick 1992a: 311–23.

Berlant, Lauren & Elizabeth Freeman (1992), 'Queer Nationality', *Boundary 2* 19:1, Spring, 149–180. Rpt. in Michael Warner (ed.), *Fear of a Queer Planet: Queer Politics and Social Theory*, Minneapolis: U of Minnesota P, 1993, 193–229. Rpt. in Lauren Berlant, *The Queen of America Goes to Washington City: Essays on Sex and Citizenship*, Durham-London: Duke UP, 1997, 145–73.

Blau, Herbert (1992), 'Ideology, Performance, and the Illusions of Demystification', in Reinelt & Roach 1992: 430–45.

Ceserani, Remo (1992), 'A proposito di moderno e postmoderno', *Allegoria*, 4:10, 121–31.

Cleto, Fabio (1992), 'Lo specchio ilare. La poetica dell'apparenza in Ronald Firbank', *Tesi di Laurea* (First Degree thesis), Università degli Studi di Bergamo, 1992.

Clum, John M. (1992), *Acting Gay: Male Homosexuality in Modern Drama*, New York: Columbia UP; rev. edn., 1994.

Coombe, Rosemary Jane (1992), 'The Celebrity Image and Cultural Identity: Publicity Rights and the Subaltern Politics of Gender', *Discourse* 14:3, Summer, 59–88. Rpt. as 'Author/izing the Celebrity: Publicity Rights, Postmodern Politics, and Unauthorized Genders' in Martha Woodmansee & Peter Jaszi (eds.), *The Construction of Authorship: Textual Appropriation in Law and Literature*, Durham-London: Duke

UP, 1994, 101–32. Rpt. in *Cultural Appropriations: Authorship, Alterity, and the Law*, Durham-London: Duke UP, 1998.

Curti, Lidia (1992), 'What is Real and What is Not: Female Fabulations in Cultural Analysis', in Grossberg, Nelson & Treichler 1992: 134–53.

Davy, Kate (1992), 'Fe/Male Impersonation: The Discourse of Camp', in Reinelt & Roach 1992: 231–47. Rpt. in Meyer 1994a: 130–48.

de Jongh, Nicholas (1992), *Not in Front of the Audience: Homosexuality on Stage*, London-New York: Routledge, 4, 36–37, 87, 97, 104, 126–43. Reviewed in: *American Theatre* 9:10, February 1993:44–5 by Michael Cadden; *Choice* 30:4 December 1992:628, by W. M. Tate; *Lambda Book Report* 3:6, September-October 1992:32–3 by Michael Paller; *Library Journal* 117:10, 1 June 1992:126–7 by Thomas E. Luddy; *TLS*, 15 May 1992:32 by Richard Davenport-Hines; *Theatre Journal* 45:2, May 1993:264–6 by Robert F. Gross; *Theatre Research International* 17:3, Autumn 1992:271 by Ian Lucas.

Dolan, Jill (1992), 'Practicing Cultural Disruptions: Gay and Lesbian Representation and Sexuality', in Reinelt & Roach 1992: 263–75.

Drew, Simon (1992), *Camp David: Nonsense in Art*, Woodbridge: Antique Collectors' Club.

Dyer, Richard (1992), *Only Entertainment*, London-New York: Routledge. Reviewed in: *Film Quarterly* 47:3, Spring 1994:60–1, by Jeremy G. Butler; *Sight & Sound* 3:3, March 1993:35–6, by Andy Medhurst.

Garber, Marjorie (1992), *Vested Interests: Cross-Dressing and Cultural Anxiety*. London-New York: Routledge. Partly rpt. in Gelder & Thornton 1997: 454–58.

Godfrey, John (1992), 'The New Camp', *Face*, 51, December, 109.

Grossberg, Lawrence, Gary Nelson & Paula Treichler (1992) (eds.), *Cultural Studies*, New York-London: Routledge.

Huskey, Melynda (1992), 'Pee-Wee Herman and the Postmodern Picaresque', *Postmodern Culture* 2:2, January 1992.

Isaacs, Gordon & Brian McKendrick (1992), *Male Homosexuality in South Africa: Identity Formation, Culture, and Crisis*, Oxford-New York: Oxford UP, 78–81, 101–10, 212, 247. Reviewed in *Choice* 31:2, October 1993:370, by T. A. Foor.

Jarmusch, Jim (1992), 'Jarmusch's Guilty Pleasures', *Film Comment* 28:3, May-June, 35–7.

Jeal, Nicola (1992), 'All Het Up in the Male Camp', *Observer*, 16 August, 43.

Kakutani, Michiko (1992), 'First There Was Camp, Now There's Cheese', *New York Times*, 141:49, 7 August, C1, 19.

Kalaidjian, Walter (1992), 'Mainlining Postmodernism: Jenny Holzer, Barbara Kruger, and the Art of Intervention', *Postmodern Culture* 2.3, May.

Keeps, David A. (1992), 'Packaging Camp for Fun and Profit', *New York Times*, 141, 28 June, sect. 2, 21 (Late edn.).

Kennedy, Elizabeth Lapovski & Madeline D. Davis (1992), '"There Was No One to Mess With": The Construction of the Butch Role in the Lesbian Community of the 1940s and 1950s', in Joan Nestle (ed.), *The Persistent Desire: A Femme-Butch Reader*, Boston: Alyson, 62–79.

Lane, Christopher (1992), 'Re/Orientations: Firbank's Colonial Imaginary and the Sexual Nomad', *Lit: Literature Interpretation Theory* 3:4, 271–86. Rpt. as 'Re/Orientations: Firbank's "Anglophobia" and the Sexual Nomad' in *The Ruling Passion: British Colonial Allegory and the Paradox of Homosexual Desire*, Durham-London: Duke UP, 1995, 176–92.

Lin, Catherine (1992), 'Barton & Glass: Margins of Camp', *Flash Art* (International edn.) 25:162, January-February, 115–17.

Ludlam, Charles (1992), 'Camp', rpt. in Steven Samuels (ed.), *Ridiculous Theatre – Scourge of Human Folly: The Essays and Opinions of Charles Ludlam*, New York: Theatre Communications Group, 225–7.

McHugh, Maureen F. (1992), 'A Coney Island of the Mind', in Gardner Dozois & Sheila Williams (eds.), *Isaac Asimov's Cyberdreams*, New York: Ace, 83–90.

Medhurst, Andy (1992), 'Carry On "Camp"', *Sight & Sound* ns 2:4, August, 16–19.

Mizejewski, Linda (1992), *Divine Decadence: Fascism, Female Spectacle, and the Makings of Sally Bowles*, Princeton, NJ: Princeton UP, passim. Based on 'Sally Bowles: Fascism, Female Spectacle, and the Politics of Looking', PhD diss., University of Pittsburgh, 1989, abstracted in *DAI* 50:11, May 1990, 3388A. Reviewed in: *Choice* 30:11, July-August 1993: 1777, by J. McCalla; *Historical Journal of Film, Radio & Television* 14:2, June 1994: 228–9, by Doris Bergen; *Journal of American History* 81:1, June 1994: 323–4, by Lane Fenrich; *Library Journal* 117:21, December 1992: 140, by Janice Braun; *Sight & Sound* ns 3:8, August 1993: 37–8, by Lorraine Gamman.

Ottonieri, Tommaso (1992), 'Corpo dei margini. Situarsi sull'anello che non tiene', *Allegoria* 4:11, 122–30.

Picardie, Justine (1992), 'The Grateful Fred', *Independent Magazine*, 9 May, 40–2, 44.

Probyn, Elspeth (1992), 'Technologizing the Self: A Future Anterior for Cultural Studies', in Grossberg, Nelson & Treichler 1992: 501–11.

Reich, June L. (1992), 'Genderfuck: The Law of the Dildo', *Discourse* 15:1, Fall, 112–27.

Reinelt, Janelle G. & Joseph R. Roach (1992) (eds.), *Critical Theory and Performance*, Ann Arbor: U of Michigan Reviewed in: *New Theatre Quarterly* 10:38, May 1994:202–3, by Mick Wallis; *Theatre Journal* 45:4, December 1993:557–8, by Christopher Balme; *TDR* 38:2, Summer 1994:189–91, by David J. DeRose; *Theatre Research International* 21:1, Spring 1996:89–90, by James M. Harding.

Román, David (1992), '"It's My Party and I'll Die if I Want to!": Gay Men, AIDS, and the Circulation of Camp in US Theatre', *Theatre Journal* 44:3, October, 305–27. Rpt. in Bergman 1993a: 206–33. Rpt. in Román 1998: 88–115.

Savran, David (1992), *Communists, Cowboys, and Queers: The Politics of Masculinity in the Work of Arthur Miller and Tennessee Williams*, Minneapolis-London: U of Minnesota P, 18–19, 118, 160.

Schuweiler-Daab, Suzanne (1992), 'Blowing Warhol's Cool: Decoding the Sixties Work', PhD diss., University of Illinois at Urbana-Champaign; abstract in *DAI* 53:10, April 1993, 3397A.

Senelick, Laurence (1992a) (ed.), *Gender in Performance: The Presentation of Difference in the Performing Arts*, Hanover-London: UP of New England. Reviewed in: *Choice* 30:7, March 1993: 1165, by Y. Shafer; *Lambda Book Report* 3:9, March-April 1993: 43, by Joe E. Jeffreys; *Library Journal* 117:21, December 1992: 142, by Anne Sharp; *TDR* 38:1, Spring 1994: 171–75, by Kim Marra; *Theatre Research International* 19:2, Summer 1994: 183–4, by Alasdair Cameron; *Signs* 20:3, Spring 1995: 752–56, by Anna McCarthy.

—— (1992b), 'Lady and the Tramp: Drag Differentials in the Progressive Era', in Senelick 1992a: 26–45.

Silverman, Kaja (1992), *Male Subjectivity at the Margins*, London-New York: Routledge, 221–2.

Smith, Paul Julian (1992), *Laws of Desire: Questions of Homosexuality in Spanish Writing and Film, 1960–1990*, Oxford: Clarendon, 168–71, 204–15.

Snodgrass, Chris (1992), 'Decadent Parodies: Aubrey Beardsley's Caricature of Meaning', in John Stokes (ed.), *Fin de Siècle/Fin du Globe: Fears and Fantasies of the Late Nineteenth Century*, Basingstoke-London: Macmillan, 178–209.

Staiger, Janet (1992), *Interpreting Films: Studies in the Historical Reception of American Cinema*, Princeton: Princeton UP, 159, 163, 175.

Stanley, Alessandra (1992), 'Giving an Edge to "The Nutcracker"', *New York Times*, 142, 25 December, B1–2.

Tee, Ernie et al. (1992), 'Cult & Camp', Special Section of *Skrien* (Netherlands) 187, December-January 1992/93, 3–27.

Thomas, Joe Alan (1992), 'Eroticism in American Pop Art, 1958–1968', PhD diss., University of Textas at Austin; abstract in *DAI* 53:11, May 1993, 3709A.

Twitchell, James (1992), *Carnival Culture: The Trashing of Taste in America*, New York-Chichester: Columbia UP, 54–56.

Weiss, Andrea (1992), *Vampires and Violets: Lesbians in the Cinema*, London: Cape; New York: Penguin, 1993. Based on 'A History of Lesbians in the Cinema', PhD diss., Rutgers Univ., 1991; abstract in *DAI* 52:12, June 1992, 4452A.

Wood, Lorna Elizabeth (1992), 'Structures of Dissent: Oscar Wilde's Legacy in the Works of Joe Orton and Tom Stoppard', PhD diss., Yale University; abstract in *DAI* 54:1, July 1993, 192A.

Woods, Gregory (1992), 'Notes on Queer', rpt. in *This is No Book: A Gay Reader*, Nottingham: Mushroom, 1994, 91–2.

1993

Abelove, Henry, Michèle Aina Barale & David M. Halperin (1993) (eds.), *The Lesbian and Gay Studies Reader*, New York-London: Routledge.

Anon. (1993a), 'Mystery Science Theatre 3000', *Bright Lights*, 11, Fall, 41–44.

—— (1993b), 'Viva Straight Camp', *Esquire*, 119:6, June, 92–95.

Arroyo, José (1993), 'Death, Desire and Identity: The Political Unconscious of "New Queer Cinema"', in Bristow & Wilson 1993: 70–96.

Bergman, David (1993a) (ed.), *Camp Grounds: Style and Homosexuality*, Amherst: U of Massachusetts Reviewed in: *Advocate*, 644, 14 December 1993: 76, by Steven Greenberg; *Choice* 31:11–12, July-August 1994: 1718–19, by M. J. Emery; *Lambda Book Report* 4, May 1994: 20; *Reference & Research Book News* 9, May 1994: 46; *Review of Contemporary Fiction* 14:3, Fall 1994: 234, by Steven Moore; *Village Voice Literary Supplement* 123, March 1994: 18, by Katherine Dieckmann; *Wilson Quarterly* 18:4, Autumn 1994: 95.

—— (1993b), 'Introduction', in Bergman 1993a: 3–16.

Billington, Michael (1993), 'Highs and Lows of Camp', *Guardian*, 16 January, 29.

Boym, Svetlana (1993), 'Power Shortages: The Soviet Coup and Hurricane Bob', in Marjorie Garber, Jann Matlock & Rebecca L. Walkovitz (eds.), *Media Spectacles*, London-New York: Routledge, 117–34.

Bradley, Kim (1993), 'Costus at Casa de America', *Art in America* 81:10, October, 147–8.

Bredbeck, Gregory W. (1993), 'B/O – Barthes's Text/O'Hara's Trick', *PMLA* 108:2, March, 268–82.

Bristow, Joseph & Angelia R. Wilson (1993) (eds.), *Activating Theory: Lesbian, Gay, Bisexual Politics*, London: Lawrence & Wishart.

Champagne, John (1993), 'Stabat Madonna', in Frank & Smith 1993: 111–38.

Clark, William Lane (1993), 'Degenerate Personality: Deviant Sexuality and Race in Ronald Firbank's Novels', in Bergman 1993a: 134–55.

Cleto, Fabio (1993a), 'Biografia, ideologia, autor-ità interpretativa (con un caso esemplare)', *Textus: English Studies in Italy* 6, 179–220.

—— (1993b), 'An Updated Bibliography of Firbank Criticism', *Quaderni*, University of Bergamo, 8, 37–52.

Corliss, Richard (1993), 'Madonna Goes to Camp', *Time*, 142:17, 25 October, 73.

Creech, James (1993), *Closet Writing/Gay Reading: The Case of Melville's Pierre*, Chicago: Chicago UP, 44–61, 91–180. Reviewed in: *American Literature* 67:3, September 1995:592–3, by Caleb Crain; *Choice* 31:11–12, July-August 1994:1720 by M.J. Emery; *Modern Fiction Studies* 40:4, Winter 1994: 921–23, by Thomas Dukes.

Crowder, Diane Griffin (1993), 'Lesbian and the (Re/De)Construction of the Female Body', in Catherine B. Burroughs & Jeffrey David Ehrenreich (eds), *Reading the Social Body*, Iowa City: U of Iowa P. Rpt. in Dawn Atkins (ed.), *Looking Queer:*

Body Image and Identity in Lesbian, Bisexuals, Gay and Transgender Communities, New York: Harrington Park, 1998, 47–68.

Dainotto, Roberto Maria (1993), 'The Excremental Sublime: The Postmodern Literature of Blockage and Release', *Postmodern Culture* 3:3, May.

Daniele, Daniela (1993), 'Il potere della modestia: Louisa May Alcott, *Little Women* e il romanzo domestico americano', *Quaderni del Dipartimento di Linguistica – Università della Calabria* 8, 11–26.

Davy, Kate (1993), 'From *Lady Dick* to Ladylike: The Work of Holly Hughes', in Hart & Phelan 1993: 55–84.

DelGaudio, Sybil (1993), *Dressing the Part: Sternberg, Dietrich, & Costume*, Rutherford-Madison: Farleigh UP; London-Toronto: Associated U Presses, 99–114. Based on 'Clothing Signification in the Films of Josef Von Sternberg', PhD diss., Columbia University, 1986, abstracted in *DAI* 47:10, April 1987, 3592A.

DiGangi, Mario (1993), 'Reading Homoeroticism in Early Modern England: Imaginations, Interpretations, Circulations', *Textual Practice*, 7:3, Winter, 483–97.

Dinshaw, Carolyn & David M. Halperin (1993), 'From the Editors', *GLQ: Gay and Lesbian Quarterly* 1:1, iii-iv.

Dolan, Jill (1993), *Presence and Desire: Essays on Gender, Sexuality, Performance*, Ann Arbor: U of Michigan P, 192.

Doty, Alexander (1993), *Making Things Perfectly Queer: Interpreting Mass Culture*, Minneapolis-London: U of Minnesota P, 10, 28, 83–4, 88, 95, 100, 102, 131–2 n13, 135–6 n8. Reviewed in: *American Literary History* 8:3, Fall 1996:566–81, by John Nguyet Erni; *Cineaste* 21:1–2, Winter-Spring 1995:90–2, by Michael Bronski; *Film Quarterly* 47:4, Summer 1994:46–7, by Boze Hadleigh; *Journal of Popular Film & Television* 24:4, Winter 1997:188–90, by Jeannie Ludlow; *Library Journal* 118:7, 15 April 1993:106–09, by Eric Bryant; *Publishers Weekly* 240:12, 22 March 1993:75–6; *Sight & Sound* 4:5, May 1994:34–5, by Andy Medhurst.

Drukman, Steven (1993), 'Summer Camp', *Advocate*, 636, 24 August, 60–2.

Dyer, Richard (1993), *Brief Encounter*, London: BFI, 11.

Evans, David (1993), *Sexual Citizenship: The Material Construction of Sexualities*, London-New York: Routledge, 94–100.

Finch, Mark (1993), 'George Kuchar: Half the Story', in Gever, Greyson & Parmar 1993: 76–85.

Frank, Lisa & Paul Smith (1993) (eds.), *Madonnarama: Essays on Sex and Popular Culture*, Pittsburgh: Cleis. Reviewed in: *Belles Lettres* 9:2, Winter 1993: 55–57, by Lauren Glen Dunlap; *Publishers Weekly* 240:23, 7 June 1993: 64.

Frank, Marcie (1993), 'The Critic as Performance Artist: Susan Sontag's Writing and Gay Cultures', in Bergman 1993a: 173–184.

Gever, Martha, John Greyson & Pratibha Parmar (1993) (eds.), *Queer Looks: Perspectives on Lesbian and Gay Film and Video*, London-New York: Routledge. Reviewed in: *Cineaste* 21:1–2, Winter-Spring, 1995:90–2, by Michael Bronski; *Feminist Review*, 51, Autumn 1995:113–17, by Merl Storr; *Film Quarterly* 49:4, Summer 1996:56–8, by Corey K. Creekmur; *Journal of Film & Video* 47:4, Winter 1995:48–52, by Jerry White; *Sight & Sound* 4:5, May 1994:34–5, by Andy Medhurst; *Theatre Journal* 47:2, May 1995:313–16, by Jill Dolan.

Hart, Lynda (1993), 'Identity and Seduction: Lesbians in the Mainstream', in Hart & Phelan 1993: 119–37.

Hart, Lynda & Peggy Phelan (1993) (eds.), *Acting Out: Feminist Performances*, Ann Arbor: U of Michigan. Reviewed in: *Choice* 31:5, January 1994:791, by J. Gates; *Modern Drama* 38:4, Winter 1995:530–2, by Susan Cocalis; *Signs* 20:2, Winter 1995:441–3, by Tracy Davis; *TDR* 39:4, Winter 1995:200–1, by Charlotte Canning; *Theatre Journal* 46:2, May 1994:291–2, by Jenny Spencer.

Henderson, Lisa (1993), 'Justify Our Love: Madonna & the Politics of Queer Sex', in Cathy Schwichtenberg (ed.). *The Madonna Connection: Representational Politics, Subcultural Identities, and Cultural Theory*, Boulder: Westview, 107–28.

Higgins, Patrick (1993), 'Show Business', in *A Queer Reader*, London: Fourth Estate; New York: New Press, 241–59.

Howes, Keith (1993), *Broadcasting It: An Encyclopaedia of Homosexuality on Film, Radio and TV in the UK 1923–1993*, London-New York: Cassell, 100–1.

Hutchings, Peter (1993), *Hammer and Beyond: The British Horror Film*. Manchester: Manchester UP, 114.

Innes, Chrostopher (1993), *Avant Garde Theatre 1892–1992*, London-New York: Routledge, 124.

Jeffreys, Joe E. (1993), 'Joan Jett Blakk for President: Cross-Dressing at the Democratic National Convention', *TDR-The Drama Review* 37:3, Fall, 186–95.

Jeffreys, Sheila (1993), *The Lesbian Heresy: A Feminist Perspective on the Lesbian Sexual Revolution*, North Melbourne: Spinflex; London: Women's P, 125–8.

Kennedy, Elizabeth Lapovski & Madeline D. Davis (1993), *Boots of Leather, Slippers of Gold: The History of a Lesbian Community*, London-New York: Routledge; New York: Penguin, 1994, 383–4, 424.

King, Thomas A. (1993), 'The Hermaphrodite's Erudition Occupation: Theatricality and Queerness in 17th and 18th Century London, I & II', PhD diss. Northwestern University, Illinois; abstract in *DAI* 55:1, July 1994, 14A.

Koestenbaum, Wayne (1993), *The Queen's Throat: Opera, Homosexuality, & the Mystery of Desire*, New York: Random House; London, GMP; London: Penguin, 1994, 117, 144–5.

Kopelson, Kevin (1993), 'Fake It Like a Man', in Bergman 1993a: 259–67.

Kotz, Liz (1993), 'An Unrequited Desire for the Sublime: Looking at Lesbian Representation Across the Works of Abigail Child, Cecilia Dougherty, and Su Friedrich', in Gever, Greyson & Parmar 1993: 86–102.

Lee, Josephine (1993), 'Cookbooks for Theory and Performance', *Postmodern Culture* 3.2, January.

MacFarquhar, Larissa (1993), 'Putting the Camp Back into Campus', *Lingua Franca* 3:6, September-October, 6–7.

MacIntosh, Mary (1993), 'Queer Theory and the War of the Sexes', in Bristow & Wilson 1993: 30–52.

Makris, Mary (1993), 'Reflexiones sobre "Una Ofelia sin Hamlet"', *Estreno* 19:1, Spring, 6–7.

Martin, Robert K. (1993), 'Roland Barthes: Toward an *"Ecriture Gaie"*', in Bergman 1993a, 282–98.

Mayne, Judith (1993), *Cinema and Spectatorship*, London-New York: Routledge, 169.

Merck, Mandy (1993), 'Introduction', in *Perversions: Deviant Readings*, London: Virago; New York: Routledge, 1–10.

Meyer, Moe (1993), 'The Wild(e) Body: Camp Theory, Camp Performance', PhD diss., Northwestern University; abstract in *DAI* 55:1, July 1994, 84A.

Mitchinson, Amanda (1993), 'The Happy Camper', *Independent*, Magazine, 4 December, 14–16, 18, 20.

Montefiore, Jan (1993), 'The Fourth Form Girls Go Camping: Sexual Identity and Ambivalence in Girls' School Stories', in Judith Still & Michael Worton (eds.), *Textuality and Sexuality: Reading Theories and Practices*, Manchester-New York: Manchester UP, 173–92.

Morgan, Monika (1993), 'Sternberg and Dietrich Revisited', *Bright Lights* 10, July, 16–17.

Musto, Michael (1993), 'Old Camp, New Camp', *Out Magazine* (New York), 5, April-May, 32–9.

Naremore, James (1993), *The Films of Vincente Minnelli*, Cambridge-New York: Cambridge UP, 3, 44, 127.

Newton, Esther Mary (1993), *Cherry Grove, Fire Island: Sixty Years in America's First Gay and Lesbian Town*, Boston: Beacon, 68–93, 212, 239. Reviewed in: *Advocate*, 24 August 1993:76–7, by Michael Bronski; *American Anthropologist* 96:3,

September 1994:697–700, by Elizabeth Lapovsky Kennedy; *Anthropological Quarterly* 67:3, July 1994:153–5, by William Leap; *Belles Lettres* 9:3, Spring 1994:85, by Denise Ohio; *Choice* 31:5, January 1994:877, by E. Broidy; *Lambda Book Report* 4:1, Nov-Dec, 1993:31–2, by Karen S. Wilson; *Library Journal* 118:14, 1 September 1993:209, by James Van Buskirk; *Publishers Weekly* 240:32, 9 August 1993:436; *Nation* 257:15, 8 November 1993:534–6, by Alice Echols; *Signs* 21:1 Autumn 1995:212–15, by Ann Cvetkovich; *Women's Review of Books* 11:1, October 1993:16–17, by Vera Whisman.

Niles, Richard (1993), 'Charles Busch and Theatre-in-Limbo', PhD diss., City University of New York; abstract in *DAI* 54:9, March 1994, 3268A.

Penley, Constance & Sharon Willis (1993) (eds.), *Male Trouble*, Minneapolis-London: U of Minnesota P.

Queen, Carol A. (1993), 'Talking about *Sex*', in Frank & Smith 1993: 139–52.

Riccio, Barry D. (1993), 'Popular Culture and High Culture: Dwight MacDonald, His Critics and the Ideal of Cultural Hierarchy in Modern America', *Journal of American Culture* 16:4, Winter, 7–18.

Roberts, Shari (1993), '"The Lady in the Tutti-Frutti Hat": Carmen Miranda, a Spectacle of Ethnicity', *Cinema Journal* 32:3, Spring, 3–23.

Robertson, Pamela (1993), '"The Kinda Comedy that Imitates Me": Mae West's Identification with the Feminist Camp', *Cinema Journal* 32:2, Winter, 57–72. Rpt. in Bergman 1993a: 156–72. Rpt. in Robertson 1996: 23–53.

Román, David (1993), 'Porno Afro Homos' Fierce Love: Intervening in the Cultural Politics of Race, Sexuality, and aids', *Journal of Homosexuality* 26:2–3, February-March, 195–219. Rpt. in Román 1998: 154–76.

Rosen, Charles (1993), 'The Ridiculous and Sublime', *New York Review of Books*, 22 April, 10–15.

Ross, Andrew (1993), 'This Bridge Called My Pussy', in Frank & Smith 1993: 47–64.

Roth, Marty (1993), 'Homosexual Expression and Homophobic Censorship: The Situation of the Text', in Bergman 1993a: 268–81.

Shattuc, Jane (1993), '*Contra* Brecht: R. W. Fassbinder and Pop Culture in the Sixties', *Cinema Journal* 33:1, Fall, 35–54. Rpt. as 'Shock Pop: Fassbinder and the Aesthetics of the German Counterculture' in *Television, Tabloids, and Tears: Fassbinder and Popular Culture*, London-Minneapolis: U of Minnesota P, 1995, 84–104.

Shaviro, Steven (1993), *The Cinematic Body*, Minneapolis-London: U of Minnesota.

Shingler, M. (1993), 'Bette Davis and the Ambiguities of Gender', PhD diss., University of East Anglia.

Silverman, Debra (1993), 'Playing With Clothes', *Postmodern Culture* 3.3, May.

Skal, David J. (1993), *The Monster Show: A Cultural History of Horror*, London: Plexus, 184.

Small, Ian (1993), *Oscar Wilde Revalued: An Essay on New Materials and Methods of Research*. Greensboro: ELT, 160.

Smith, Patricia Juliana (1993), '"You Don't Have to Say You Love Me": The Camp Masquerades of Dusty Springfield', in Bergman 1993a: 185–205.

Travers, Andrew (1993), 'An Essay on Self and Camp', *Theory, Culture & Society* 10:1, February, 127–43.

Viegener, Matias (1993), '"The Only Haircut that Makes Sense Anymore": Queer Subculture and Gay Resistance', in Gever, Greyson & Parmar 1993: 116–33.

Wagner, Jon Nelson (1993), 'Film Fatal: Essays on Spectatorial Decline', PhD diss., University of Southern California; abstract in *DAI* 55:3, September 1994, 402A.

Waugh, Thomas (1993), 'The Third Body: Patterns in the Construction of the Subject in Gay Male Narrative Film', in Gever, Greyson & Parmar 1993: 141–61.

Woods, Gregory (1993), 'High Culture and High Camp: The Case of Marcel Proust', in Bergman 1993a: 121–33.

1994

Ainley, Rosa & Sarah Cooper (1994), 'She Thinks I Still Care: Lesbians and Country Music', in Hamer & Budge 1994: 41–56.

Allen, Carol (1994), 'Wilde One Pitches Camp in W6', *Times*, 1 September, 35.

Andermahr, Sonya (1994), 'A Queer Love Affair? Madonna and Lesbian and Gay Culture', in Hamer & Budge 1994: 28–40.

Anon. (1994), 'Arias on Holiday', *New Yorker*, 70:26, 22 August, 46–7.

Belsey, Catherine (1994), *Desire: Love Stories in Western Culture*, Oxford-Cambridge: Blackwell, 91.

Bolin, Anne (1994), 'Transcending and Transgendering: Male-to-Female Transsexuals, Dichotomy and Diversity', in Herdt 1994a: 447–85.

Bolze, Thomas Arthur (1994), 'Female Impersonation in the United States, 1900–1970', PhD diss., State University of New York at Buffalo; abstract in *DAI* 55:11, May 1995, 3617A.

Bredbeck, Gregory W. (1994), 'Narcissus in the Wilde: Textual Cathexis and the Historical Origins of Queer Camp', in Meyer 1994a: 51–74.

Brousse, Françoise (1994), 'Sarah Schulman. Vers une esthetique gaie', *Annales du Centre de Recherches sur l'Amerique Anglophone (ACRAA)* 19:212, 119–25.

Brown, Terry (1994), 'The Butch Femme Fatale', in Doan 1994: 229–43.

Chauncey, George (1994), *Gay New York: Gender, Urban Culture, and the Making of the Gay Male World, 1890–1940*, New York: Basic; also pub. as *Gay New York: The Making of the Gay Male World, 1890–1940*, London: Flamingo, 1995, passim. Reviewed in: *American Historical Review* 100:5, December 1995:1705–6, by Mark Carnes; *American Journal of Sociology* 100:6, May 1995:1636–7, by Vern L. Bullough; *American Quarterly* 48:3, September 1996, 500–6, by Ramón A. Gutiérrez; *Contemporary Sociology* 24:3, May 1995:355–6, by Ken Plummer; *Historian* 59:2, Winter 1997:404; *Gay Community News* 20:4, Winter 1995:14–17, by Ann Holder; *GLQ* 3:2–3, November 1996:327–31, by Pieter Judson; *Progressive* 60:1, January1996:41–3, by Susan Douglas; *Quarterly Journal of Speech* 81:3, August 1995:418–19, by James Tarbox; *Radical America* 25:3, July-September 1992 (in fact, January 1995), 53–64, by Ann Holder; *Reviews in American History* 24:2, June 1996:304–9, by Clayton R. Koppes.

Coates, Paul (1994), *Film at the Intersection of High and Mass Culture*, Cambridge: Cambridge UP, 3–5, 28.

Cohen, Vlad (1994), 'Cleverness, Courage and Camp: Interventions by Gay Men in Contemporary Canadian Art', *Volute* (Canada) 6, Fall, 37–44.

Cox, L. & R. Fay (1994), 'Gayspeak, the Linguistic Fringe: Bona, Polari, Camp, Queerspeak and Beyond', in S. Whittle (ed.), *The Margins of the City: Gay Men's Urban Lives*, Aldershot: Arena.

De Lauretis, Teresa (1994), *The Practice of Love: Lesbian Sexuality and Perverse Desire*, Bloomington-Indianapolis: Indiana UP, 102–10, 135–7, 289. Reviewed in: *Artforum* 33:8, April 1995:32, by Bruce Hainley; *Feminist Review*, 54, Autumn 1996:122–4, by Noreen O'Connor; *Lambda Book Report* 4:5, July-August 1994:19, by Ellen Brinks; *Signs* 21:2, Winter 1996:478–81, by Judith Roof; *Tulsa Studies in Women's Literature* 14:2, Fall 1995:395–7, by Paula Bennett.

Dellamora, Richard (1994), *Apocalyptic Overtures: Sexual Politics and the Sense of An Ending*, New Brunswick: Rutgers UP, 39, 130, 143, 145, 176. Partly rpt. in Horne & Lewis 1996: 28–47.

Doan, Laura (1994) (ed.), *The Lesbian Postmodern*, New York: Columbia UP. Reviewed in: *Choice* 32:3, November 1994:454 by D.A. Barton; *Feminist Review* 51, Autumn 1995:123–5 by Suzanne Raitt; *TLS*, 6 January 1995:26 by David Dibosa.

Dollimore, Jonathan (1994), 'Shakespeare Understudies: The Sodomite, the Prostitute, the Transvestite and Their Critics', in Jonathan Dollimore & Alan Sinfield (eds.),

Political Shakespeare: Essays in Cultural Materialism, Manchester: Manchester UP, 129–52.

Drewal, Margaret Thompson (1994), 'The Camp Trace in Corporate America: Liberace and the Rockettes at Radio City Music Hall', in Meyer 1994a: 149–81.

Drucker, Stephen (1994), 'Summer Camp on Long Island', *Architectural Digest* 51:7, July, 140–5, 151.

Edelman, Lee (1994), *Homographesis: Essays in Gay Literary and Cultural Theory*, London-New York: Routledge.

Franklin, Nancy (1994), 'Camping Out', *New Yorker*, 70:15, 30 May, 100–1.

Gemünden, Gerd (1994a) (ed.), "Rainer Werner Fassbinder", special issue of *New German Critique* 63, Fall.

—— (1994b), 'Re-Fusing Brecht: The Cultural Politics of Fassbinder's German Hollywood', in Gemünden 1994a: 55–76.

Griggers, Cathy (1994), 'Lesbian Bodies in the Age of (Post)Mechanical Reproduction', in Doan 1994: 118–34.

Hamer, Diane & Belinda Budge (1994) (eds.), *The Good, the Bad and the Gorgeous: Popular Culture's Romance with Lesbianism*, London-San Francisco: Pandora. Reviewed in: *Feminist Review* 51, Autumn 1995, 113–17, by Kate Soper; *Lambda Book Report* 4:9, March-April 1995, 30, by Rachel Pepper.

Harding, Jenny (1994), 'Making a Drama Out of Difference: *Portrait of a Marriage*', in Hamer & Budge 1994: 119–31.

Harper, Phillip Brian (1994), 'Walk-On Parts and Speaking Subjects: Screen Representations of Black Gay Men', in Thelma Golden (ed.), *Black Male: Representations of Masculinity in Contemporary American Art*, New York: Whitney Museum of American Art, 141–8. Rpt. in *Callaloo*, 18:2, Spring 1995, 390–4.

Hekma, Gert (1994), '"A Female Soul in a Male Body": Sexual Inversion as Gender Inversion in Nineteenth-Century Sexology', in Herdt 1994a: 213–39.

Heller, Dana A. (1994), 'Almost Blue: Policing Lesbian Desire in *Internal Affairs*', in Doan 1994: 173–88.

Henke, Richard (1994), 'Imitation World of Vaudeville', *Jump Cut* 39, June, 31–9.

Herdt, Gilbert (1994a) (ed.), *Third Sex, Third Gender: Beyond Sexual Dimorphism in Culture and History*, New York: Zone.

—— (1994b), 'Introduction: Third Sexes and Third Genders', in Herdt 1994a: 21–81.

Ivanov, Andrea Jean (1994a), 'Mae West Was Not a Man: Sexual Parody and Genre in the Plays and Films of Mae West', in Gail Finney (ed.), *Look Who's Laughing: Gender and Comedy*, Langhorne: Gordon & Breach, 275–97.

—— (1994b), 'Sexual Parody in American Comedic Film and Literature, 1925–1948', PhD diss., University of Southern California; abstract in *DAI* 56:9, March 1996, 3582A.

Jeffreys, Sheila (1994), 'The Queer Disappearance of Lesbians: Sexuality in the Academy', *Women's Studies International Forum* 17:5, September-October, 459–72.

Johnson, Stephen Paul (1994), 'Mass Culture and Class Distinctions in the Novels of Nathaniel West', PhD diss., Loyola University of Chicago; abstract in *DAI* 55:1, July 1994, 87A.

Kellner, Douglas (1994), 'Madonna, Fashion, and Identity', in Shari Benstok & Suzanne Ferriss (eds.), *On Fashion*, New Brunswick: Rutgers UP, 159–82. Rpt. in *Media Culture: Cultural Studies, Identity and Politics between the Modern and the Postmodern*, London-New York: Routledge, 1995.

Kennedy, Rosanne (1994), 'The Gorgeous Lesbian in *LA Law*: The Present Absence?', in Hamer & Budge 1994: 132–41. Rpt. in Charlotte Brunsdon, Julie D'Acci, Lynn Spigel (eds.), *Feminist Television Criticism: A Reader*, Oxford: Clarendon, 1997, 318–24.

King, Thomas (1994), 'Performing "Akimbo": Queer Pride and Epistemological Prejudice', in Meyer 1994a: 23–50.

Kleinhans, Chuck (1994), 'Taking Out the Trash: Camp and the Politics of Parody', in Meyer 1994a: 182–201.

Klinger, Barbara (1994), *Melodrama and Meaning: History, Culture, & the Films of Douglas Sirk*, Bloomington: Indiana UP.

Labranca, Tommaso (1994), 'Trash, Camp & Kitsch', in *Andy Warhol era un coatto. Vivere e capire il trash*, Florence: Castelvecchi, 31–6.

Lamos, Colleen (1994), 'The Postmodern Lesbian Position: *On Our Backs*', in Doan 1994: 85–103.

Lighter, J. E. (1994) (ed.), *Random House Dictionary of American Slang*, Vol. 1, New York: Random House, 351.

Lucas, Ian (1994), *Impertinent Decorum: Gay Theatrical Manoeuvres*, London-New York: Cassell, 24–5, 111–23. Reviewed in *Library Journal* 119:13, August 1994:110 by Robert Malinowsky.

McRobbie, Angela (1994), *Postmodernism and Popular Culture*, London-New York: Routledge, 19, 20, 82, 85–7.

Manzor-Coats, Lillian (1994), 'Performative Identities: Scenes Between Two Cubas', *Michigan Quarterly Review* 33:4, Fall, 748–61.

Meyer, Moe (1994a) (ed.), *The Politics and Poetics of Camp*, London-New York: Routledge. Reviewed in: *Advocate*, 27 December 1994: 64–5, by John Weir; *Comparative Drama* 29:4, Winter 1995–6: 534–37, by David Bass; *TDR* 40:2, Summer 1996: 135–8, by Steven Drukman; *Lambda Book Report* 4, January 1995: 44.

—— (1994b), 'Introduction: Reclaiming the Discourse of Camp', in Meyer 1994a: 1–22.

—— (1994c), 'Under the Sign of Wilde: An Archaeology of Posing', in Meyer 1994a: 75–109.

Meyer, Richard (1994), 'Warhol's Clones', *Yale Journal of Criticism* 7:1, Spring, 79–109. Rpt. in Monica Dorenkamp & Richard Henke (eds.), *Negotiating Lesbian and Gay Subjects*, London-New York: Routledge, 1995, 93–122.

Meyerding, Jane (1994), 'Life as She is Lived: A Meditation on Gender, Power, and Change', *Social Anarchism* 19.

Michasiw, Kim (1994), 'Camp, Masculinity, Masquerade', *differences* 6:2–3, Summer-Fall, 146–73. The *differences* issue pub. as Naomi Schor & Elizabeth Weed (eds.), *Feminism Meets Queer Theory*, Bloomington: Indiana UP, 1997.

Moltke, Johannes von (1994), 'Camping in the Art Closet: The Politics of Camp and Nation in German Film', in Gemünden 1994a: 77–106.

Moore, F. Michael (1994), *Drag! Male and Female Impersonators on Stage, Screen and Television – An Illustrated History*, Jefferson: McFarland, 242.

Morawski, Stefan (1994), 'The Hopeless Game of *Flânerie*', in Keith Tester (ed.), *The Flâneur*, London-New York: Routledge, 181–97.

Morrill, Cynthia (1994), 'Revamping the Gay Sensibility: Queer Camp and *Dyke Noir*', in Meyer 1994a: 110–29.

Murray, Raymond (1994), 'Camp', in *Images in the Dark: An Encyclopedia of Gay and Lesbian Film & Video*, Philadelphia: TLA; 2nd edn., rev. and updated, New York-London: Plume, 1996, 467–78.

Musto, Michael (1994), 'Pitching Camp', *Spin*, April 1994, 50–5.

Myers, Terry R. (1994), 'Painting Camp: The Subculture of Painting, the Mainstream of Decoration', *Flash Art* (International edn.) 27:179, November-December 1994, 73–6.

Olson, Ray (1994), Review of Ronald Firbank's 'Complete Plays', *Booklist* 90, 1–15 June, 1735.

O'Connor, Patrick Jude (1994), 'Passages of Revolutionary Desire: The Writings of Julio Coltazar and Walter Benjamin', PhD diss, Yale University; abstract in *DAI* 55:6, December 1994, 1574A.

O'Sullivan, Sue (1994), 'Girls Who Kiss Girls and Who Cares?', in Hamer & Budge 1994: 78–95.

Povert, Lionel (1994), 'L'esprit camp', in *Dictionnaire Gay*, Paris: Jacques Grancher, 111–13.

Roen, Paul (1994), *High Camp: A Gay Guide to Camp & Cult Films*, Vol. 1. San Francisco: Leyland. Reviewed in: *Lambda Book Report* 4, May 94, 20.

Rosen, Charles (1994), 'Music à la Mode', *New York Review of Books*, 41:12, 23 June, 60.

Russo, Mary (1994), *The Female Grotesque: Risk, Excess and Modernity*, London-New York: Routledge, 104.

Sage, Lorna (1994), 'The Women's Camp', *Times Literary Supplement*, 15 July, 11.

Saltzman, Arthur Michael (1994), 'The Figure in the Static: *White Noise*', *Modern Fiction Studies* 40:4, Winter, 807–26.

Savran, David (1994), 'Tony Kushner Considers the Longstanding Problems of Virtue and Happiness', *American Theatre* 11:9, October, 20–7, 100–4.

Schmidgall, Gary (1994), *The Stranger Wilde: Interpreting Oscar*, New York: Dutton; London, Abacus, 459 n314.

Segal, Lynne (1994), *Straight Sex: Rethinking the Politics of Pleasure*. London: Virago; Berkeley: U of California P, 188–90.

Sieglohr, U. (1994), 'Imaginary Identities in Werner Schroeter's Cinema: An Institutional, Theoretical, and Cultural Investigation', PhD diss., University of East Anglia.

Sinfield, Alan (1994), *The Wilde Century: Effeminacy, Oscar Wilde and the Queer Moment*, London: Cassell; New York: Columbia UP, 1995, 3, 156, 194–203. Reviewed in: *Journal of the History of Sexuality* 7:1, July 1996:123–5, by Michael Lucey; *Lambda Book Report* 4:9, March-April 1995:44, by Henry Agusti; *Library Journal* 119:13, August 1994:87, by Henry Carrigan, Jr.; *Modern Fiction Studies* 42:1, Spring 1996: 178–80, by Ellis Hanson; *Mosaic* 30:3. September 1997: 185–96, by Barbara Charlesworth Gelpi; *New Statesman & Society*, 7, 17 June 1994:38, by Richard Canning; *TLS*, 20 January1995:24–5, by Will Eaves.

Tasker, Yvonne (1994), 'Pussy Galore: Lesbian Images and Lesbian Desire in the Popular Cinema', in Hamer & Budge 1994: 172–83.

Ulmer, Gregory L. (1994), 'The Miranda Warnings: An Experiment in Hyperrhetoric', in George Landow (ed.), *Hyper/text/theory*, Baltimore-London: Johns Hopkins UP, 345–77.

Vincent, Sally (1994), 'Mein Camp', *Sunday Times*, 1 May, 30–6, 38.

Walton, Jean (1994), 'Sandra Bernhard: Lesbian Postmodern or Modern Postlesbian?', in Doan 1994: 244–62.

Weinberg, Jonathan (1994), 'Boy Crazy: Carl Van Vechten's Queer Collection', *Yale Journal of Criticism* 7:2, Fall, 25–49.

White, Edmund (1994a), *The Burning Library: Writings on Art, Politics, Sexuality 1969–93*, edited by David Bergman, London: Chatto & Windus; New York: Knopf; London: Picador, 1995.

—— (1994b), 'The Gay Philosopher', in White 1994a: 3–19.

Yarza, Alejandro (1994a), 'El reciclaje de la historia: Camp, monstruos y travestis en el cine de Pedro Almodóvar', PhD diss., University of California, Irvine; abstract in *DAI* 55:3, September 1994, 588A–9A.

—— (1994b), 'Un caníbal en Madrid: El altar y la estética *Kitsch/Camp* en *Entre tinieblas* de Pedro Almodóvar', *RLA: Romance Languages Annual* 6, 624–32.

1995

Abel, Sam (1995), 'The Rabbit in Drag: Camp and Gender Construction in American Animated Cartoon', *Journal of Popular Culture* 29:3, Winter, 183–202.

Allen, Louise (1995), '*Salmonberries*: Consuming k.d. lang', in Wilton 1995a: 70–84.

Barrett, Eileen (1995), 'Response: Decamping Sally Potter's *Orlando*', in Eileen Barrett & Patricia Cramer (eds.), *Re-Reading, Re-Writing, Re-Teaching Virginia Woolf*, New York: Pace UP, 197–9.

Bergman, David (1995), 'Camp', in Summers 1995: 130–5.

Berlant, Lauren & Michael Warner (1995), 'What Does Queer Theory Teach Us About X', *PMLA* 110:3, May, 343–9.

Blackmer, Corinne (1995), 'Ronald Firbank', in Summers 1995, 274–6.

Boym, Svetlana (1995), 'Kitsch i Sozialisticeskij Realizm', *NLO* 15, 54–65.

Branagh, Kenneth (1995), *In the Bleak Midwinter*, GB, 1995, b&w, 95'.

Brandes, Wendy (1995), 'Low Prices, High Camp Help Win Cult Following for Shopping Show', *Wall Street Journal*, 225:70, 11 April, B1.

Brandhorst, Henny (1995), 'Das Leben als Theater. Camp als Performanz von queer Identitäten', *Forum Homosexualität und Literatur* 24, 75–85.

Brasell, R. Bruce (1995), 'Bullets, Ballots and Bibles: Documenting the History of the Gay and Lesbian Struggle in America', *Cineaste* 21:4, Fall, 17–21.

Bristow, Joseph (1995), *Effeminate England: Homoerotic Writing After 1885*, Buckingham: Open UP; New York: Columbia UP, 109–10.

Burston, Paul & Colin Richardson (1995) (eds.), *A Queer Romance: Lesbians, Gay Men and Popular Culture*, London-New York: Routledge.

Burt, Ramsay (1995), *The Male Dancer: Bodies, Spectacle, Sexualities*, London-New York: Routledge, 181–87, 207 n14.

Cagle, Van M. (1995), *Reconstructing Pop/Subculture: Art, Rock, and Andy Warhol*, Thousand Oaks-London, Sage, 142.

Champagne, John [Gerard] (1995), *The Ethics of Marginality: A New Approach to Gay Studies*, Minneapolis-London: U of Minnesota P, 119, 206 n47. Based on 'The Ethics of Transgression: Criticism and Cultural Marginality', PhD diss., University of Pittsburgh, 1993, abstracted in *DAI* 54:9, March 1994, 3244A.

Ciment, Michel (1995), 'Entretien avec Tim Burton: Un optimisme étrange et perverti', *Positif* 412, June, 17–22.

Cook, Gareth (1995), 'The Dark Side of Camp', *Washington Monthly* 27:9, September, 10–14.

Collins, Jim (1995), 'After the End of Early Postmodernism: The Pragmatics of Excess', in *Architectures of Excess: Cultural life in the Age of Information*, London-New York: Routledge, 1–29.

Collins, Scott (1995), 'Ghoul Crazy', *Los Angeles Times*, 114, 31 October, D1, 6.

Creekmur, Corey K. (1995), 'Dossier on Popular Music: Introduction', in Creekmur & Doty 1995a: 403–6.

Creekmur, Corey K. & Alexander Doty (1995a) (eds.), *Out in Culture: Gay, Lesbian and Queer Essays on Popular Culture*, London: Cassell; Durham: Duke UP. Reviewed in: *Choice* 33:5, January1996:831, by J. A. Brown; *Advocate*, 30 May 1995:63–4, by John Weir.

—— (1995b), 'Introduction', in Creekmur & Doty 1995a: 1–11.

Cruz-Malavé, Arnaldo (1995), 'Toward and Art of Transvestism: Colonialism and Homosexuality in Puerto Rican Literature', in Emilie L. Bergmann & Julian Paul Smith (eds.), *¿Entiendes? Queer Readings, Hispanic Writings*, Durham-London: Duke UP, 137–67. Shorter vers. in Duberman 1997a: 226–44.

Curry, Ramona (1995), '*Goin' to Town* and Beyond: Mae West, Film Censorship and the Comedy of U*n*marriage', in Karnick & Jenkins 1995: 211–37.

Dickinson, Peter (1995), '"Go-go Dancing on the Brink of the Apocalypse": Representing AIDS (An Essay in Seven Epigraphs)', in Richard Dellamora (ed.), *Postmodern Apocalypse: Theory and Cultural Practice at the End*, Philadelphia: U of Pennsylvania P, 219–40.

Dines, Gail & Jean M. Humez (1995) (eds.), *Gender, Race and Class in Media: A Text-Reader*, London: Sage. Reviewed in: *Journal of Communication* 47:3, Summer 1997:117–19, by John Miller; *Women's Studies in Communication* 19:1, Spring 1996:95–6, by Anne Johnston.

Doty, Alexander (1995), 'Queerness, Comedy and *The Women*', in Karnick & Jenkins 1995: 332–47.

Drukman, Steven C. (1995), 'The Gay Gaze, or Why I Want My MTV', in Burston & Richardson 1995: 81–95.

Edgards, Geoff (1995), 'Anti-Hip', *Boston Phoenix*, 10 April.

Ellis, Robert Richmond (1995), 'Camping it Up in the Francoist Camp: Reflections on and in *Ante El Espejo* of Louis Antonio de Villena', *MLN-Modern Language Notes* 110:2, March, 320–34.

Escoffier, Jeffrey (1995), 'Intellectuals, Identity Politics, and the Contest for Cultural Authority', in Marci Danowski, Barbara Epstein & Richard Flacks (eds.), *Social Movements and Cultural Authority*, Philadelphia: Temple UP. Rpt. in Escoffier 1998: 142–57.

Evans, Caroline & Lorraine Gamman (1995), 'The Gaze Revisited, or Reviewing Queer Viewing', in Burston & Richardson 1995: 13–56.

Feil, Kenneth Jonathan (1995), 'From Queer to Hybridity: Questions of Cultural Difference in Contemporary Queer Film and Video', PhD diss., University of Texas at Austin; abstract in *DAI* 56:10, April 1996, 3776A.

Feuer, Jane (1995), *Seeing Through the Eighties: Television and Reaganism*, Durham: Duke UP, 10, 51, 118–21, 129–47.

Flinn, Caryl (1995), 'The Deaths of Camp', *Camera Obscura* 35, May, 53–84.

Fox, Lorna Scott (1995), 'Barbie Gets a Life', *London Review of Books*, 17:15, 20 July, 13.

Gaitet, Pascale (1995), 'The Politics of Camp in Jean Genet's *Our Lady of Flowers*', *Esprit Créateur* 35:1, Spring, 40–9.

Galbraith, Stuart (1995), 'Vamp, Camp and Comedy', *Filmfax* 51, July-August, 69–72.

Garber, Marjorie (1995), *Vice Versa: Bisexuality and the Eroticism of Everyday Life*, New York: Simon & Schuster; London: Hamish Hamilton, 219, 491.

Garelick, Rhonda (1995), 'Outrageous Dieting: The Camp Performance of Richard Simmons', *Postmodern Culture* 6:1, September.

Goellner, Ellen W. & Jacqueline Shea Murphy (1995) (eds.), *Bodies of the Text: Dance as Theory, Literature as Dance*, New Brunswick: Rutgers UP. Reviewed in: *Choice* 33:2, October 1995:304, by C. W. Sherman; *Dance Research Journal* 28:2, Fall 1996:83–6, by Karen Woods; *Signs* 22:4, Summer 1997:1034–7, by Jane Desmond; *TDR* 40:4, Winter 1996:158–60, by Amy Konitz.

Gordinier, Jeff (1995), 'Camping Out', *Entertainment Weekly*, 281–2, 30 June-7 July, 73.

Graham, Paula (1995), 'Girl's Camp? The Politics of Parody', in Wilton 1995a: 163–81.

Gripsrud, Jostein (1995), *The Dynasty Years: Hollywood Television and Critical Media Studies*, London-New York: Routledge, 129, 193, 201.

Halperin, David M. (1995), *Saint Foucault: Towards a Gay Hagiography*, New York-Oxford: Oxford UP, 29, 196 n, 211n.

Hamilton, Marybeth (1995), *When I'm Bad, I'm Better: Mae West, Sex and Popular Culture*, New York: HarperCollins; also published as *The Queen of Camp: Mae West, Sex and Popular Culture*, London: HarperCollins, 1996; and as *When I'm Bad, I'm Better: Mae West, Sex, and American Entertainment*, Berkeley: U of California P, 1997. Reviewed in: *American Theatre* 13:1, January 1996:60–62 by Rachel Shteir; *New Statesman & Society*, 9, 15 March 1996:35 by Susan Jeffreys; *Sight & Sound* 6:5, May 1996: 44, by Ian Christie; *Theatre History Studies* 17, June 1997:157–9 by Daniel-Raymond Nadon; *TLS*, 31 May 1996:36, by Aisling Foster.

Harris, Daniel R. (1995), 'The Aesthetic of Drag', *Salmagundi* 108, Fall, 62–74. Rpt. in Harris 1997: 203–18.

Healy, Murray (1995), 'Were We Being Served? Homosexual Representation in Popular British Comedy', *Screen* 36:3, Autumn, 243–56.

Hermes, Joke (1995), *Reading Women's Magazines: An Analysis of Everyday Media Usage*, Oxford-Cambridge: Polity, 1, 121–2, 133–41, 160.

Howes, Keith (1995), *OutSpoken: Keith Howes' Gay News Interviews 1976–1983*, London-New York: Cassell.

Hubbard, Tom (1995), *Seeking Mr Hyde*, Frankfurt-a-M: Peter Lang, 39–40.

Indiana, Gary (1995), 'Queen of Queens', *Voice Literary Supplement*, 135, May, 9.

Jackson, Earl, Jr. (1995), *Strategies of Deviance: Studies in Gay Male Representation*, London-Minneapolis: Indiana UP, 49, 93, 243–5, 251, 261, 263.

Jenkins, Henry & Kristine Brunovska Karnick (1995a), 'Acting Funny', in Karnick & Jenkins 1995: 149–67.

—— (1995b), 'Comedy and the Social World', in Karnick & Jenkins 1995: 265–81.

Johnson, Patrick (1995), 'SNAP! Culture: A Different Kind of "Reading"', *Text & Performance Quarterly* 15:2, 122–42.

Johnson, Freya (1995), 'Holy Homosexuality Batman!: Camp and Corporate Capitalism in *Batman Forever*', *Bad Subjects* 23, December.

Johnstone, Rosemarie (1995), 'The Alcoholism of the Text', PhD diss., University of Minnesota; abstract in *DAI* 56:10, April 1996, 3959A.

Karlen, Neal (1995), 'Terminal Kitsch', *New York Times Magazine*, 12 February, 27.

Karnick Kristine Brunovska & Henry Jenkins (1995) (eds.), *Classical Hollywood Comedy*, New York-London: Routledge. Reviewed in: *Canadian Literature* 152–3, Spring-Summer, 1997:221–2, by Stephen Guy-Bray; *Choice* 33:6 February 1996:956–7, by T. Lindvall; *TLS*, 3 March 1995:18, by Graham McCann.

Katz, Jonathan David (1995), 'Opposition, Inc.: The Homosexualization of Postwar American Art', PhD diss, Northwestern University; abstract in *DAI* 56:7, January 1996, 2453A.

Kennedy, Liam (1995), *Susan Sontag: Mind as Passion*, Manchester-New York: Manchester UP.

Lo, Mun-Hou (1995), 'David Leavitt and the Etiological Maternal Body', in Roof 1995: 439–65.

Morrow, Bruce (1995), 'An Interview with Isaac Julien', *Callaloo* 18:2, Spring, 406–15.

Medhurst, Andy (1995), 'Foreword', in Smith 1995: xv-xvii.

Muñoz, José (1995), 'Disidentifications', PhD diss., Duke University, 1995, abstract in *DAI* 56:9, March 1996, 3584A.

Murphy, Jacqueline Shea (1995), 'Unrest and Uncle Tom: Bill T. Jones/Arnie Zane Dance Company's *Last Supper at Uncle Tom's Cabin/The Promised Land*', in Goellner & Murphy 1995: 81–105.

Murphy, Michael Christian (1995), 'Camp Happens: Modernity, Post-Modernity, and Recycled Culture', PhD diss., Syracuse University; abstract in *DAI* 57:2, August 1996, 677A.

Nataf, Z. Isiling (1995), 'Black Lesbian Spectatorship and Pleasure in Popular Cinema', in Burston & Richardson 1995: 57–80.

O'Donnell, Patrick (1995a) (ed.), 'Postmodern Narratives', special issue of *Modern Fiction Studies* 41:1, Spring.

—— (1995b), 'Editor's Preface', in O'Donnell 1995a: 1–4.

Olster, Stacey Michelle (1995), 'Remakes, Outtakes, and Updates in Susan Sontag's *The Volcano Lover*', in O'Donnell 1995a: 117–39.

Ortoleva, Peppino (1995), *Mediastoria: Comunicazione e cambiamento sociale nel mondo contemporaneo*, Parma: Nuove Pratiche, 19 n9.

Raven, Charlotte (1995), ' Culture: Future Sex', *Observer*, 29 October, Life Section, 32–4.

Raymond, Leigh (1995), 'Boys and Girls: Pierre et Gilles' Sydney Mardi Gras Poster', *Artlink* (Australia) 15: 14, Summer, 55–6.

Razzini, Vieri (1995), 'Qualcosa sul Camp', in Marina Ganzerli, Loredana Leconte & Giovanni Minerba (eds.), *Da Sodoma a Hollywood. Fotogrammi sovversivi attraverso cento anni di cinema*, Turin: L'altra comunicazione, 61–5.

Richardson, Colin (1995), 'Tvod: The Never-Bending Story', in Burston & Richardson 1995: 216–48.

Robertson, Pamela (1995), 'Camping Under Western Stars: Joan Crawford in *Johnny*

Guitar', *Journal of Film & Video* 47:1–3, Spring-Fall, 33–49. Rev. vers. in Robertson 1996, 85–114.

Robson, Jocelyn & Beverley Zalcock (1995), 'Looking at *Pumping Iron II: The Women*', in Wilton 1995a: 182–92.

Roemer, Richard Dean (1995), 'The Thief of Bad Gags: Charles Ludlam and the Ridiculous Theatrical Company – A Serious Look at a "Ridiculosity"', PhD diss, UCLA; abstract in *DAI* 56:10, April 1996, 3796A-97A.

Roof, Judith (1995) (ed.), 'Sexuality and Narrative', double issue of *Modern Fiction Studies* 41:3–4, Fall-Winter.

Ross, Andrew (1995), 'Taking the Tennis Count Oath', in Susan M. Schultz (ed.), *The Tribe of John: Ashbery and Contemporary Poetry*, Tuscaloosa: U of Alabama P, 193–210.

Rowe, Kathleen (1995), *The Unruly Woman: Gender and the Genres of Laughter*, Austin: U of Texas P, 63, 67, 123, 182. Based on the anonymous PhD diss., University of Oregon, 1992, abstracted in *DAI* 53:10, April 1993, 3397A.

Sanderson, Heather Gail (1995), 'Love, War and Fascism: Troubled Genders in Timothy Findley's Fiction', PhD diss., Queen's University at Kingston (Canada); abstract in *DAI* 57:1, July 1996, 238A.

Sedgwick, Eve Kosofsky (1995), 'Shame and Performativity: Henry James's New York Edition Prefaces', in David McWhirter (ed.), *Henry James's New York Edition: The Construction of Authorship*, Stanford: Stanford UP, 206–39.

Smigiel, Frank (1995), 'Shop-Talk: Exchanging Narrative, Sex, and Value', in Roof 1995: 635–55.

Smith, Richard (1995), *Seduced and Abandoned: Essays on Gay Men and Popular Music*, London-New York: Cassell, passim.

Snodgrass, Chris (1995), *Aubrey Beardsley: Dandy of the Grotesque*, New York-Oxford: Oxford UP, 283.

Stachey, Jackie (1995), '"If You Don't Play, You Can't Win": *Desert Hearts* and the Lesbian Romance Films', in Wilton 1995a: 92–114.

Stewart, William (1995), *Cassell's Queer Companion*, London-New York: Cassell, 41–3.

Summers, Claude J. (1995) (ed.), *The Gay and Lesbian Literary Heritage: A Reader's Companion to the Writers and Their Works, From Antiquity to the Present*, New York: Henry Holt.

Thornton, Sara (1995), *Club Cultures: Music, Media and Subcultural Capital*, Cambridge: Polity/Wesleyan UP. Excerpted in Gelder & Thornton 1997: 200–9.

Tinkcom, Matthew John (1995), 'Camp and the Question of Value', PhD diss., University of Pittsburgh; abstract in *DAI* 56:9, March 1996, 3353A.

Van Leer, David (1995), *The Queening of America: Gay Culture in Straight Society*, London-New York: Routledge, 3, 20–56, 60–8, 112–13, 169–70, 195.

Westmoreland, Maurice (1995), 'Camp in the Works of Luis Zapata', *Modern Language Studies* 25:2, Spring, 45–59.

Wheale, Nigel (1995), 'Postmodernism: From Elite to Mass Culture?', in Nigel Wheale (ed.), *The Postmodern Arts: An Introductory Reader*, London-New York: Routledge, 33–56.

White, Patricia (1995), 'Supporting Character: The Queer Career of Agnes Moorehead', in Creekmur & Doty 1995a: 91–114.

Wilton, Tamsin (1995a) (ed.), *Immortal, Invisible: Lesbians and the Moving Image*, London-New York: Routledge. Reviewed in: *Journal of the History of Sexuality* 7:3, January1997:458–60, by A. A. Markley; *Library Journal* 120:5, 15 March 1995:72, by Lisa N. Johnston; *Sight & Sound* 5:5, May 1995:37, by Yvonne Tasker.

—— (1995b), 'Introduction: On Invisibility and Mortality', in Wilton 1995a: 1–19.

—— (1995c), 'On Not Being Lady Macbeth: Some (Troubled) Thoughts on Lesbian Spectatorship', in Wilton 1995a: 143–62.

Wolcott, James (1995), 'Gods and Demons', *New Yorker*, 71:3, 13 March, 32.

Woods, Gregory (1995), 'We're Here, We're Queer and We're Not Going Catalogue Shopping', in Burston & Richardson 1995: 147–63.

1996

Abel, Sam (1996), *Opera in the Flesh: Sexuality in Operatic Performances*, Boulder-Oxford: Westview, 18, 194 n12.

Andrae, Thomas (1996), 'Television's First Feminist: *The Avengers* and Female Spectatorship', *Discourse* 18:3, Spring, 112–36.

Anon. (1996), 'Camp and Commerce', *Time*, 148:5, 22 July, 62.

Atkins, Robert (1996), 'Goodbye Lesbian/Gay History; Hello *Queer Sensibility*: Meditating on Curatorial Practice', in Rando & Weinberg 1996: 80–5.

Beemyn, Brett & Mickey Eliason (1996) (eds.), *Queer Studies: A Lesbian, Gay, Bisexual and Transgender Anthology*, New York-London: New York UP. Reviewed in: *Lambda Book Report* 5:7, January1997:13–14, by Bill McCauley.

Berger, Arion (1996a), 'Atlas Shrugged: Xena, Hercules, Barbie and Ken', *Los Angeles Weekly*, 18, 31 May-6 June, 41.

—— (1996b), 'Plan B from Outer Space: Camping Out with *Reel Wild Cinema*', *Los Angeles Weekly*, 28 June-4 July, 38.

Bergman, David (1996), 'Introduction: Native Innocence, Alien Knowledge', *Review of Contemporary Fiction* 16:3, Fall, 7–12.

Bignami, Marialuisa & Caroline Patey (1996) (eds.), *Moving the Borders*, Milan: Unicopli.

Birringer, Johannes H. (1996), 'La Melancolía de la Jaula', *Performing Arts Journal* 18:1, January, 103–28.

Boney, Bradley (1996), 'The Lavender Brick Road: Paul Bonin-Rodriguez and the Sissy Bo(d)y', *Theatre Journal* 48:1, March, 35–57.

Bottoms, Stephen (1996), 'Restaging Roy: Citizen Cohn and the Search for Xanadu', *Theatre Journal* 48:2, May, 157–84.

Brantley, Ben (1996), 'Into Camp Season, Not Necessarily With Kayaks', *New York Times*, 150:50, 16 April, B1, 4.

Case, Sue-Ellen (1996), 'The Apparitional Community', *American Quarterly* 48:1, March, 161–6.

Christiansen, Adrienne E. & Jeremy J. Hanson. 'Comedy as Cure for Tragedy: Act Up and the Rhetoric of AIDS', *Quarterly Journal of Speech* 82:2, May, 157–70.

Cleto, Fabio (1996a), '"Camp": l'estetismo nella cultura di massa', in Franco Marenco (ed.), *Storia della civiltà letteraria inglese*, Turin: UTET, 1996, vol. 3, 529–69.

—— (1996b), 'Foreign-language Criticism', in Moore 1996: 113–42.

—— (1996c), '"Oscar Wilde" e i materialisti. Appunti sulla scena critica radicale in Gran Bretagna', *Nuova Corrente* 43:117, 19–72.

—— (1996d), 'Theoretical Issues in Camp Aesthetics', in Bignami & Patey 1996: 120–49.

Collins, Bradford R. & David Cowart (1996), 'Through the Looking-Glass: Reading Warhol's *Superman*', *American Imago* 53:2, Summer, 107–37.

Conover, Kirsten (1996), 'Dust Off Your Albums, Campy ABBA Classics Have Made a Return', *Christian Science Monitor*, 88:100, 18 April, 18.

Curry, Ramona (1996), *Too Much of a Good Thing: Mae West as Cultural Icon*, Minneapolis-London: U of Minnesota P, xvii, xviii, xxii, 12, 107, 113–24, 186–7, 192. Based on 'Power and Allure: The Mediation of Sexual Difference in the Star Image of Mae West', PhD diss., Northwestern University, 1990, abstracted in *DAI* 52:8, February 1992, 2736A.

Damon, Maria (1996), 'Gertrude Stein's Jewishness, Jewish Social Scientists, and the "Jewish Question"', *Modern Fiction Studies* 42:3, Fall, 489–506.

DeCecco, John P. (1996), 'Gays, Lesbians, and Consumer Behavior: Theory, Practice, and Research Issues in Marketing', special issue of *Journal of Homosexuality* 31: 1–2; simultaneously pub. under the same title, edited by Daniel L. Wardlow, New York: Harrington Park.

Doyle, Jennifer, Jonathan Flatley & José Esteban Muñoz (1996a) (eds.), *Pop Out: Queer Warhol*, Durham-London: Duke UP. Reviewed in: *Artforum* 34:10, Summer 1996:16, 18–19, 22, by Bruce Hainley; *Art History* 20:1, March 1997:164–8, by Gavin Butt; *Lambda Book Report* 5:2, September-October 1996:30, by Douglas A. Mendini; *Sight & Sound* 6:5, May 1996:44; *Screen* 38:2, Summer 1997:200–4, by Michael O'Pray.

—— (1996b), 'Introduction', in Doyle, Flatley & Muñoz 1996a: 1–19.

Farwell, Marylin R (1996), *Heterosexual Plots and Lesbian Narratives*, New York-London: New York UP, 12, 105.

Finnegan, B.A. (1996), *Camp as Knickers!*, Dublin: NFK.

Freitas, Anthony, Susan Kaiser & Tania Hammidi (1996), 'Communities, Commodities, Cultural Space, and Style', in DeCecco 1996: 83–108.

Frith, Simon (1996), *Performing Rites: On the Value of Popular Music*, Cambridge: Harvard UP; Oxford: Oxford UP.

Gabriel, Trip (1996), '*Showgirls* Crawls Back as High Camp at Midnight', *New York Times*, 145, sect. 1, 31 March, 43, 46.

Geyrhalter, Thomas (1996), 'Effeminacy, Camp and Sexual Subversion in Rock: The Cure and Suede', *Popular Music*, 15:2, May, 217–24.

Goldstein, Lynda (1996), 'Revamping MTV: Passing for Queer Culture in the Video Closet', in Beemyn & Eliason 1996: 262–79.

Grantley, Darryll (1996), '"What meanes this shew?" Theatricalism, Camp and Subversion in *Doctor Faustus* and *The Jew of Malta*', in Darryll Grantley & Peter Roberts (eds.), *Christopher Marlowe and English Renaissance Culture*, Aldershot: Scolar, 224–38.

Green, James Naylor (1996), 'Beyond Carnival: Homosexuality in Twentieth-Century Brazil', PhD diss., UCLA; abstract in *DAI* 57:7, January 1997, 3706A.

Hall, Donald E. & Maria Pramaggiore (1996) (eds.), *RePresenting BiSexualities: Subjecs and Cultures of Fluid Desire*, New York-London: New York UP.

Harris, Daniel R. (1996a), 'A Psychohistory of the Homosexual Body', *Salmagundi* 109–10, Winter-Spring, 105–26. Rpt. in Harris 1997: 86–110.

—— (1996b), 'From *After Dark* to *Out*: The Invention of the Teflon Magazine', *Antioch Review* 54:2, Spring, 174–93. Rpt. in Harris 1997: 64–85.

—— (1996c), 'The Death of Camp: Gay Men and Hollywood Diva Worship, From Reverence to Ridicule', *Salmagundi* 112, Fall, 166–91. Rpt. in Harris: 1997, 8–39. Excerpted in *Harper's Magazine* 294:1, January 1997, 25–8.

Hess-Luttich, Ernest W. B. (1996), 'Dandy, Camp und fin du globe: Wildes Inversion viktorianischer Werte', *Forum Homosexualität und Literatur* 26, 43–68.

Horne, Peter (1996), 'Sodomy to Salome: Camp Revisions of Modernism, Modernity and Masquerade', in Mica Nava & Alan O'Shea (eds.), *Modern Times: Reflections on a Century of English Modernity*, London-New York: Routledge, 129–60.

Horne, Peter & Reina Lewis (1996a) (eds.), *Outlooks: Lesbian and Gay Sexualities and Visual Cultures*, London-New York: Routledge. Reviewed in *Observer*, 3 November 1996, 16.

—— (1996b), 'Introduction: Re-framed – Inscribing Lesbian, Gay and Queer Presences in Visual Culture', in Horne & Lewis 1996a: 1–10.

Hsu, Melinda L. (1996), 'Celibate Cries: Queer Readings of Morrissey's Sexual Persona', MA Thesis, California State University, Fresno; abstract in *MAI*, 35:1, February 1997, 69.

Humberstone, Nicola (1996), 'Lesbians Framed', in Lynne Harne & Elaine Miller (eds.), *All the Rage: Reasserting Radical Lesbian Feminism*, London: Women's P; New York: Teachers College, 159–73.

Inness, Sherrie A. & Michele E. Lloyd (1996), 'G.I. Joes in Barbie Land: Recontextualizing Butch in Twentieth-Century Lesbian Culture', in Beemyn & Eliason 1996: 9–34.

Kaye, Richard A. (1996), 'Losing His Religion: Saint Sebastian as Contemporary Gay Martyr', in Horne & Lewis 1996a: 86–106.

Kidd, Kenneth (1996), 'Men Who Run with Wolves, and the Women Who Love Them: Child Study and Compulsory Heterosexuality in Feral Child Films', *The Lion and the Unicorn* 20:1, June, 90–112.

Kurzweil, Edith (1996a) (ed.), *A Partisan Century: Political Writings from Partisan Review*, New York: Columbia UP.

—— (1996b), 'Introduction', in Kurzweil 1996a: xiii-xxiv.

Leitch, Vincent B. (1996), 'Costly Compensations: Postmodern Fashion, Politics, Identity', *Modern Fiction Studies* 42:1, Spring, 111–28.

Loftus, Brian (1996), 'Biopia: Bisexuality and the Crisis of Visibility in a Queer Symbolic', in Hall & Pramaggiore 1996: 207–33.

Lyttle, John (1996), 'You Say Camp is Everywhere', *Independent*, 13 December, 3.

Martell, Cecilia (1996), 'Unpacking the Baggage: "Camp" Humour in Timothy Findley's *Not Wanted on the Voyage*', *Canadian Literature* 148, Spring, 96–111.

McCarthy, Todd (1996), 'A Narrow "Escape" from B-pic Camp', *Variety*, 364:2, 12 August, 32.

McKee, Stuart (1996), 'Rainbows, Closets, and Drag: Appropriation of Gay and Lesbian Imagery', *AIGA: Journal of Graphic Design* 14: 1, January, 22–3.

Merck, Mandy (1996), 'Figuring Out Andy Warhol', in Doyle, Flatley & Muñoz 1996a: 224–37.

Michel, Frann (1996), 'Do Bats Eat Cats? Reading What Bisexuality Does', in Hall & Pramaggiore 1996: 55–69.

Moore, Steven (1996), *Ronald Firbank: An Annotated Bibliography of Secondary Materials, 1905–1995*, Normal: Dalkey Archive, passim.

Mort, Frank (1996), *Cultures of Consumption: Masculinities and Social Space in Late Twentieth-Century Britain*, London-New York: Routledge.

Murphy, Michael (1996), '"One Hundred Per Cent Bohemia": Pop Decadence and the Aestheticization of Commodity in the Rise of the Slicks', in Kevin J. H. Dettmar & Stephen Watt (eds.), *Marketing Modernisms: Self-Promotion, Canonization, Rereading*, Ann Arbor: U of Michigan P, 61–91.

Namaste, Ki (1996), '"Tragic Misreadings": Queer Theory's Erasure of Transgender Subjectivity', in Beemyn & Eliason 1996: 183–203.

Newton, Esther (1996), 'Dick(less) Tracy and the Homecoming Queen: Lesbian Power and Representation in Gay Male Cherry Grove', in Ellen Lewin (ed.), *Inventing Lesbian Cultures in America*, Boston: Beacon, 161–93.

Phillips, Glasgow (1996), 'Shiny Adidas Track-Suits and the Death of Camp', *Might* 13, November-December.

Pribisic, Milan (1996), 'Camp as a Signifying System in American Theatre, 1964 to 1995', PhD diss., Kent State University; abstract in *DAI* 58:2, August 1997, 342A.

Pustianaz, Marco (1996), 'Teoria gay e lesbica', in Donatella Izzo (ed.), *Teoria della letteratura. Prospettive dagli Stati Uniti*, Rome: NIS, 1996, 109–29.

Qualls, Larry (1996), 'Five Video Artists', *Performing Arts Journal* 18:3, September, 1–13.

Rando, Flavia & Jonathan Weinberg (1996) (eds.), 'We're Here: Gay and Lesbian Presence in Art', special issue of *Art Journal* 55:4, Winter.

Reed, Christopher (1996), 'Imminent Domain: Queer Space in the Built Environment', in Rando & Weinberg 1996: 64–70.

Robertson, Pamela (1996), *Guilty Pleasures: Feminist Camp from Mae West to Madonna*, Durham-London: Duke UP. Based on 'Guilty Pleasures: Feminist Camp and the Female Spectator', PhD diss., University of Chicago, 1993. Reviewed in: *Artforum* 34:10, Summer 1996:14, by Deb Schwartz; *Choice* 34, December

1996:622; *Journal of American History* 84:3, December 1997:1136–7, by Ann Douglas; *Publishers Weekly*, 243:15, 8 April 1996:64–5.

Rucker, Margaret, Anthony Freitas & Oscar Huidor (1996), 'Gift-Giving Among Gay Men: The Reification of Social Relations', in DeCecco 1996: 43–56.

Ruesga, G. Albert (1996), 'Singing and Dancing in the Baser Manner: A Plea for the Democratization of Taste', *Journal of Popular Culture* 29:4, Spring, 117–35.

Runzo, Sandra (1996), 'Dickinson, Performance, and the Homoerotic Lyric', *American Literature* 68:2, June, 347–63.

Sands, Kathleen M. (1996), 'Ifs, Ands, and Butts: Theological Reflections on Humor', *Journal of the American Academy of Religion* 64:3, Fall, 499–523.

Santos, Lidia (1996), 'La narrativa del Caribe hispanico (años 70–80) como recuperacion de la marginalidad', *Alba de América* 14:26–27, July, 313–19.

Shiller, Romy (1996), 'Drag King Invasion: Taking Back the Throne', *Canadian Theatre Review* 86, Spring, 24–8.

Sedgwick, Eve Kosofsky (1996), 'Introduction: Queerer than Fiction', *Studies in the Novel* 28:3, Fall, 277–80.

Simpson, Mark (1996), *It's a Queer World*, London: Vintage, 173, 175.

Sinfield, Alan (1996a), 'Diaspora and Hybridity: Queer Identities and the Ethnicity Model', *Textual Practice* 10:2, Summer, 271–93. Rpt. in Sinfield 1998: 18–43.

—— (1996b), 'Oscar Wilde and the Scope for Minority Reading', in Bignami & Patey 1996: 275–83.

Smigiel, Frank A. (1996), 'Metaphors of the Market: Postmodern Commerce, Postmodern Art', PhD diss., University of Delaware; abstract in *DAI* 58:1, July 1997, 176A.

Spindler, Amy M. (1996), 'Esoteric, Asymmetrical and Coolly Campy', *New York Times*, 145, 2 November, Metro Section, 11 (National edn.), 31 (Late edn.).

Steele, Robert (1996), 'Camp, Liberation, and the (Straight) Male Gaze: *Les Amitiés particulières*', *Annual of Foreign Films and Literature* 2, 129–42.

Stevenson, Jack (1996), *Desperate Visions: Camp America (John Waters, George & Mike Kuchar)*, London: Creation.

Stewart, Steve (comp.) (1996), *Campy, Vampy, Trampy Movie Quotes*, Laguna Hills: Companion.

Stokes, John (1996), *Oscar Wilde: Myths, Miracles, and Imitations*, Cambridge-New York: Cambridge UP, 14, 17.

Stradling, Matthew (1996), 'The Aura of Timelessness', in Horne & Lewis 1996a: 139–44.

Stringer, Julian (1996), 'Problems with Treatment of Hong Kong Cinema as Camp', *Asian Cinema* 8:2, Winter 1996–97, 44–65.

Suárez, Juan (1996), *Bike Boys, Drag Queens, and Superstars: Avant-Garde, Mass Culture, and Gay Identities in the 1960s Underground Cinema*, Bloomington-Buckingham: Indiana UP, xviii, 44, 232. Based on 'Avant-Garde Cinema and Mass Culture: The 1960s American Underground', PhD diss, Indiana University, 1993, abstracted in *DAI* 54:11, May 1994, 3910A.

Tinkcom, Matthew John (1996), 'Working Like a Homosexual: Camp Visual Codes and the Labor of Gay Subjects in the MGM Freed Unit', *Cinema Journal* 35:2, Winter, 24–42.

Torres, Sasha (1996), 'The Caped Crusader of Camp: Pop, Camp, and the *Batman* Television Series', in Doyle, Flatley & Muñoz 1996a: 238–56.

Vilanch, Bruce (1996), 'Camp Versus Kitsch', *Advocate*, 717, 1 October, 55.

Walters, Suzanna Danuta (1996), 'From Here to Queer: Radical Feminism, Postmodernism, and the Lesbian Menace (Or, Why Can't a Woman Be More Like a Fag?)', *Signs* 21:4, Summer, 830–69.

Watney, Simon (1996), 'Queer Andy', in Doyle, Flatley & Muñoz 1996a: 20–30.

Watson, Wallace Steadman (1996), *Understanding Rainer Werner Fassbinder: Film as Private and Public Art*, Columbia: U of South Carolina P, 137, 144, 150.

Waugh, Thomas (1996), 'Cockteaser', in Doyle, Flatley & Muñoz 1996a: 51–77.
Wollen, Peter (1996), 'The Same Old Solotaire', *London Review of Books*, 18:13, 4 July, 22–3.

1997

Ammer, Christine (1997) (ed.), *The American Heritage Dictionary of Idioms*, Boston: Houghton Mifflin, 99–100.
Arroyo, José (1997), 'Kiss Kiss Bang Bang', *Sight & Sound* ns 7:3, March, 6–9.
Avins, Mimi (1997), 'Generation Next: Men's Fashion, the Gay Influence", *Los Angeles Times*, 22 May.
Bazzana, Kevin (1997), '"Hot With Chutzpah"', *Philosophy and Literature* 21:2, October, 381–91.
Benshoff, Harry Morgan (1997), *Monsters in the Closet: Homosexuality and the Horror Film*, New York-Manchester: Manchester UP. Based on the anonymous PhD diss, University of Southern California, 1996, abstracted in *DAI* 57:9, March 1997, 3722A.
Bergengren, Charles (1997), 'Febrile Fiber Phantom: Ken Jacobs at the C.I.A', *TDR* 41:1, Spring, 72–85.
Bergman, David (1997), Review of 'The Complete Prose Works of W.H. Auden: Vol. 1, 1926–1938', *Lambda Book Report* 6:2, September, 10–12.
Betsky, Aaron (1997), *Queer Space: Architecture and Same-Sex Desire*, New York: Morrow, 81–2.
Boyd, Nan Alamilla (1997), 'Bodies in Motion: Lesbian and Transsexual Histories', in Duberman 1997b: 134–52.
Bruzzi, Stella (1997), 'Mannish Girl: k.d. lang – From Cowgirl to Androgyny', in Whiteley 1997a: 191–206.
Bryant, Wayne M. (1997), 'Bi Camp', in *Bisexual Characters in Film: From Anaïs to Zee*, New York: Haworth, 99–108.
Cain, James (1997), 'Putting on the Girls: Cross-Dressing as a Performative Strategy in the Twelfth-Century Latin Comedy *Alda*', *Theatre Survey* 38:1, May, 43–71.
Califia, Pat (1997), *Sex Changes: The Politics of Transgenderism*, San Francisco: Cleis, 227–29, 273.
Caserio, Robert L. (1997a), 'Artifice and Empire in Ronald Firbank's Novels', *Western Humanities Review*, 51:2, Summer, 227–35.
—— (1997b), 'Queer Passions, Queer Citizenship: Some Novels about the State of the American Nation 1946 – 1954', *Modern Fiction Studies* 43:1, Spring, 170–205.
Ceserani, Remo (1997a), 'Questioni di stile. Bellezza e fascino sul fascino del tramonto', *Il Manifesto*, 16 May, 22–3.
—— (1997b), *Raccontare il postmoderno*, Turin: Bollati Boringhieri.
Cleto, Fabio (1997), 'Il sapere travestito. Per una definizione del discorso camp', *Tesi di Dottorato* (PhD diss.), Università di Genova, Italy.
Connelly, Stacey J. (1997), 'Playing for Time: Nelson Jewell and the HIV Ensemble', *Theatre Topics* 7:1, March, 59–76.
Connor, J. D. (1997), 'Disappearing, Inc.: Hollywood Melodrama and the Perils of Criticism', *MLN-Modern Language Notes* 112:5, December, 958–70.
Corber, Robert J. (1997), *Homosexuality in Cold War America: Resistance and the Crisis of Masculinity*, Durham-London: Duke UP, 14–15, 18, 59, 66, 100–3, 141–6, 204, 213, 219–22.
Cubitt, Sean (1997), 'Rolling and Tumbling: Digital Erotics and the Culture of Narcissism', in Whiteley 1997a: 295–316.
David, Hugh (1997), *On Queer Street: A Social History of British Homosexuality, 1895–1995*, London: HarperCollins, 78, 79, 82, 84.
De Gaetano, Alessandro (1997), *Butch Camp*, USA, 103', col. Premiered at the Sydney Gay and Lesbian Mardi Gras Film Festival, 19 February.

Duberman, Martin (1997a) (ed.), *Queer Representations: Reading Lives, Reading Cultures*, New York-London: New York UP. Reviewed in: *Lambda Book Report* 6:3, October 1997:12–13, by Jim Van Buskirk.

—— (1997b) (ed.), *A Queer World: The Center for Lesbian and Gay Studies Reader*, New York-London: New York UP. Reviewed in: *Lambda Book Report* 6:3, October 1997:12–13; *Nation*, 265:16, 17 November 1997:28–30, by Steven Drukman.

Escoffier, Jeffrey (1997), 'Homosexuality and the Sociological Imagination: The 1950s and 1960s', in Duberman 1997b: 248–61. Rpt. in Escoffier 1998: 79–97.

Fernihough, Anne (1997), '"Is she fact or is she fiction?": Angela Carter and the Enigma of Woman', *Textual Practice* 11:1, Spring, 89–107.

Fessler, Jeff & Karen Rauch (1997), *When Drag is Not a Car Race: An Irreverent Dictionary of Over 400 Gay and Lesbian Words and Phrases*, New York: Simon & Schuster, 61, 79–80.

Foster, Thomas C. (1997), '"Trapped by the Body"? Telepresence Technologies and Transgendered Performance in Feminist and Lesbian Rewritings of Cyberpunk Fiction', *Modern Fiction Studies* 43:3, Fall, 708–42.

Frankel, David (1997), 'John Kelly', *Artforum* 35:5, January, 78.

Fusillo, Massimo (1997), 'Petronio e il lettore', *La Rivista dei Libri*, November, 19–21.

Gehring, Verna V. (1997), 'Tedium Vitae: Or, My Life as a "Net Serf"', *Ratio* ns 10:2, September, 124–90.

Gelder, Ken & Sarah Thornton (1997) (eds.), *The Subcultures Reader*, New York-London: Routledge.

Gerstner, David Anthony (1997), 'Queer Modernism: Vincente Minnelli, American Creativity, American Masculinity', PhD diss., UCLA, 1997; abstract in *DAI* 58:6, December, 1966A.

Glenn, Joshua (1997) (ed.), 'Camp'. Special Double Issue of *Hermenaut* 11–12, Winter.

Graver, David (1997), 'Performance Review', *Theatre Journal* 49:1, March, 56–9.

Gross, Robert F. (1997), 'O'Neill's Queer Interlude: Epicene Excess and Camp Pleasures', *Journal of Dramatic Theory & Criticism* 30:3, September, 3–22.

Halberstam, Judith (1997), 'Mackdaddy, Superfly, Rapper: Gender, Race, and Masculinity in the Drag King Scene', *Social Text* 52–3, 15:3–4, Fall-Winter 1997–8, 105–31. Rpt. as 'Drag Kings: Masculinity and Performance', in *Female Masculinity*, Durham-London: Duke UP, 1998, 231–66.

Harris, Daniel R. (1997), *The Rise and Fall of Gay Culture*, New York: Hyperion, 8–39, 239, 251–2, 269, 271. Reviewed in: *Advocate*, 29 April 1997:71–2, by Robert L. Pela; *Antioch Review* 55:4, Fall 1997:498, by Melinda Kanner; *Lambda Book Report* 6:1, August 1997:32–3, by Ira Elliott; *Publishers Weekly* 244:15, 14 April 1997:67–8, by Paul Nathan; *San Francisco Bay Guardian*, 25 June 1997, by Johnny Ray Huston.

Hawkins, Stan (1997), 'The Pet Shop Boys: Musicology, Masculinity and Banality', in Whiteley 1997a: 118–33.

Hinz, Evelyn J. (1997) (ed.), 'The Lure of the Androgyne', special issue of *Mosaic* 30:3, September

Hunter, I. Q. & Heidi Kaye (1997), 'Introduction', in Deborah Cartmell, I. Q. Hunter, Heidi Kaye & Imelda Whelehan (eds.), *Trash Aesthetics: Popular Culture and Its Audience*, London-Chicago: Pluto, 1–13.

Jarraway, David R. (1997), '"Creatures of the Rainbow": Wallace Stevens, Mark Doty, and the Poetics of Androgyny', in Hinz 1997: 169–83.

Jivani, Alkarim (1997), *It's Not Unusual: A History of Lesbian and Gay Britain in the Twentieth Century*, Bloomington: Indiana UP; London: O'Mara, 13, 15.

Johnson, Heather (1997), 'Unexpected Geometries: Transgressive Symbolism and the Transsexual Subject in Angela Carter's *The Passion of New Eve*', in Joseph Bristow & Trev Lynn Broughton (eds.), *The Infernal Desires of Angela Carter: Fiction, Femininity, Feminism*, London-New York: Longman, 166–83.

Kaplan, Deborah (1997), 'Learning "to Speak the English Language": *The Way of the World* on the Twentieth-Century American Stage', *Theatre Journal* 49:3, October, 301–21.

Keesey, Pam (1997), *Vamps: An Illustrated History of the Femme Fatale*, San Francisco: Cleis, 106.

Kennedy, Elizabeth Lapovsky (1997), 'Telling Tales: Oral History and the Construction of Pre-Stonewall Lesbian History', in Duberman 1997b: 181–97.

Lane, Christopher (1997), 'The Voided Role: On Genet', *MLN-Modern Language Notes* 112:5, December, 876–908.

Limon, John (1997), 'Nectarines', *Yale Journal of Criticism* 10:1, Spring, 121–43.

Lingiardi, Vittorio (1997), *Compagni d'amore: Da Ganimede a Batman. Identità e mito nelle omosessualità maschili*, Milan: Raffaelo Cortina, 32, 200n17.

McCully, Susan (1997), 'Out on the Edge: 1996 Festival of Lesbian & Gay Theater', *Theatre Journal* 49:3, October, 367–8.

Madoff, Steven Henry (1997) (ed.), *Pop Art: A Critical History*, Berkeley-London: California UP. Reviewed in: *ArtNews* 97:1, January 1998:80–1, by Rex Weil; *Library Journal* 122:16, 1 October 1997:80, by Mary Hamel-Schwulst.

Montero, Oscar (1997), 'Notes for a Queer Reading of Latin American Literature', in Duberman 1997a: 216–25.

Nesbet, Anne (1997), 'Inanimations: *Snow White* and *Ivan the Terrible*', *Film Quarterly* 50:4, Summer, 20–31.

Piggford, George (1997a), 'Camp Sites: Forster and the Biographies of Queer Bloomsbury', in Robert K. Martin & George Piggford (eds.), *Queer Forster*, Chicago: U of Chicago P, 89–112.

—— (1997b), 'Who's that Girl?: Annie Lennox, Woolf's *Orlando*, and Female Camp Androgyny', in Hinz 1997: 39–58.

Pratt, Alan R. (1997a) (ed.), *The Critical Response to Andy Warhol*, Westport-London: Greenwood.

—— (1997b), 'Introduction: The Warhol Legacy', in Pratt 1997a: xvii-xxviii.

Roen, Paul (1997), *High Camp: A Gay Guide to Camp and Cult Films. Vol. 2*, San Francisco: Leyland.

Sedgwick, Eve Kosofsky (1997), 'Paranoid Reading and Reparative Reading; or, You're So Paranoid, You Probably Think This Introduction is About You', in Eve Kosofsky Sedgwick (ed.), *Novel Gazing: Queer Readings in Fiction*, Durham-London: Duke UP, 1–39.

Skeggs, Beverley (1997), *Formations of Class and Gender: Becoming Respectable*, Thousand Oaks-London: Sage, 137.

Tinkcom, Matthew John (1997), 'Warhol's Camp', in Colin MacCabe, Mark Francis & Peter Wollen (eds.), *Who Is Andy Warhol?* London: BFI; Pittsburgh: The Andy Warhol's Museum, 107–16.

Tomc, Sandra (1997), 'An Idle Industry: Nathaniel Parker Willis and the Workings of Literary Leisure', *American Quarterly* 49:4, December, 780–805.

Waszink, Paul M. (1997), 'Artist or Scoundrel? Some Notes on Camp, Pasternak and Gogol's "Dead Souls"', *Essays in Poetics* 22, Autumn, 43–88.

Waugh, Thomas (1997), 'Walking on Tippy Toes: Lesbian and Gay Liberation Documentary of the Post-Stonewall Period 1969–1984', in Chris Holmlund & Cynthia Fuchs (eds.), *Between the Sheets, in the Streets: Queer, Lesbian, Gay Documentary*, Minneapolis-London: U of Minnesota P, 107–24.

Whiteley, Sheila (1997a) (ed.), *Sexing the Groove: Popular Music and Gender*, London-New York: Routledge.

—— (1997b), 'Little Red Rooster *v.* The Honky Tonk Woman: Mick Jagger, Sexuality, Style and Image', in Whiteley 1997a: 67–99.

Williamson, Catherine (1997), '"Draped Crusaders": Disrobing Gender in *The Mark of Zorro*', *Cinema Journal* 36:2, Winter, 3–16.

Woods, Mark (1997), 'Film Review: Butch Camp', *Variety*, 366:10, 7–13 April, 47.

Wolf, Stacy (1997), '"Never Gonna Be a Man/Catch Me if You Can/I Won't Grow Up": A Lesbian Account of Mary Martin as Peter Pan', *Theatre Journal* 49:4, December, 493–509.

Yarza, Alejandro (1997), 'Iconografia religiosa y estetica camp en *Atame*, de Pedro Almodóvar', *Revista Canadiense de Estudios Hispanicos* 22:1, Fall, 109–24.

Young, Stuart (1997), "Performance Review: *The Gay Detective/Mojo*', *Theatre Journal* 49:3, October, 368–71.

ADDENDA 1998

Boxwell, D.A. (1998), '(Dis)orienting Spectacle: The Politics of *Orlando*'s Sapphic Camp', *Twentieth-Century Literature* 44:3, Fall, 306–27.

Denisoff, Dennis (1998), 'Camp, Aestheticism, and Cultural Inclusiveness in Isherwood's Berlin Stories', in Shannon Hengen (ed.), *Performing Gender and Comedy: Theories, Texts and Contexts*, Amsterdam: Gordon & Breach, 81–94.

D'Erasmo, Stacey (1998), 'Never Too Old to ...: Septuagenarian Stripper Makes the Scene', *New York* 31, 5 October, 14.

Escoffier, Jeffrey (1998), *American Homo: Community and Perversity*, Berkeley-London: California UP, 55–6, 58, 88, 89, 114, 147–9. Reviewed in: *Lambda Book Report* 7:2, Sept 1998, 13–14, by Michael Bronski; *Library Journal* 123:12 July 1998, 116, by Jeffrey Ingram.

Garelick, Rhonda K. (1998), *Rising Star: Dandyism, Gender, and Performance in the Fin de Siècle*, Princeton: Princeton UP, 3, 16, 48, 64, 80, 125–7, 128–153, 161. Reviewed in: *Choice* 36:2, Oct 1998: 322, by M. Winkler; *Library Journal* 123:1, January 1998: 102, by Jeffery Ingram.

Gordy, Douglas (1998), 'Joseph Cino and the First Off-Off Broadway Theater', in Schanke & Marra 1998a: 303–23.

Harbin, Billy J. (1998), 'Monty Woolley: The Public and Private Man from Saratoga Springs', in Schanke & Marra 1998a: 262–79.

Harvey, Dennis (1998), 'Celebration of Camp', *Variety* 371:10, 20 July, 37.

Harvey, Keith (1998), 'Translating Camp Talk: Gay Identities and Cultural Transfer', *Translator* 4:2, November, 295–320.

Hillman, Melissa (1998), 'The Camp-Drag-Disco Musical Extravaganza: Camp, Drag, and Intertextuality in the Theatre of "Generation X"', PhD diss., University of California at Berkeley.

Kushner, Tony (1998), 'Afterword', in Moisés Kaufman, *Gross Indecency: The Three Trials of Oscar Wilde*, New York: Vintage; Toronto: Random House, 135–43.

Levine, Martin P. (1998), *Gay Macho: The Life and Death of the Homosexual Clone*, ed. Michael S. Kimmel, New York-London: New York UP, 21–3, 26–7, 58–9.

Matthews, Lydia (1998), 'Camp Out: DIWA Arts and the Bayanihan Spirit', *The Drama Review* 42:4, Winter, 115–35.

Miklitsch, Robert (1998), *From Hegel to Madonna: Toward a General Economy of 'Commodity Fetishism'*, Albany: SUNY, 131, 138, 182–3.

Olalquiaga, Celeste (1998), *The Artificial Kingdom: A Treasury of the Kitsch Experience*, New York: Pantheon.

Román, David (1998), *Acts of Intervention: Performance, Gay Culture, and aids*, Bloomington: Indiana UP, 89–114, 165, 168, 242, 247, 256, 265.

Roth, Moira (1998), *Difference/Indifference: Musings on Postmodernism, Marcel Duchamp and John Cage*, commentary by Jonathan D. Katz, Amsterdam: G+B Arts International, 171.

Schanke, Robert A. & Kim Marra (1998a) (eds.), *Passing Performances: Queer Readings of Leading Players in American Theater History*, Ann Arbor: U of Michigan P.

—— (1998b), 'Introduction', in Schanke & Marra 1998a: 1–15.

Sinfield, Alan (1998), *Gay and After*, London-New York: Serpent's Tail, 2–3, 29, 33, 34, 119, 149–50, 165, 169, 192.

Stevens, Hugh (1998), *Henry James and Sexuality*, Cambridge: Cambridge UP, 73, 100, 162–3, 166–73.

Walker, Pierre A. & Greg W. Zacharias (1998), 'James's Hand and Gosse's Tail: Henry James's Letters and the Status of Evidence', *Henry James Review*, 19:1, Winter, 72–9.

Woods, Gregory (1998), *A History of Gay Literature: The Male Tradition*, New Haven-London: Yale UP, passim.

INDEX OF NAMES

Note: For reasons of space, this index does not include the chronological bibliography on camp (pp. 458–512). It includes, though, all names (art names, pseudonyms, organisations and pop groups' names) appearing not only in the text, but also in the notes (referred to with an extra 'n') and in the references sections (referred to with an 'r') of each essay.